AUTOCOURSE™

THE WORLD'S LEADING GRAND PRIX ANNUAL

icon
PUBLISHING LIMITED

Legendary.

Chronoris Grand Prix '70
Limited Edition

www.oris.ch

CONTENTS

AUTOCOURSE
2009-2010

is published by:
Icon Publishing Limited
Regent Lodge
4 Hanley Road
Malvern
Worcestershire
WR14 4PQ

Tel: +44 (0)1684 564611

Website: www.autocourse.com

Printed in the United Kingdom by
Butler Tanner & Dennis Ltd,
Caxton Road, Frome, Somerset,
BA11 1NF

ISBN: 978-1-905334-52-0

DISTRIBUTORS

Gardners Books
1 Whittle Drive, Eastbourne,
East Sussex, BN23 6QH
Tel: +44 (0)1323 521555
email: sales@gardners.com

Menoshire Ltd
Unit 13
21 Wadsworth Road
Perivale
Middlesex UB6 7LQ
Telephone: +44 (0)20 8566 7344
Fax: +44 (0)20 8991 2439

NORTH AMERICA
Motorbooks International
PO Box 1
729 Prospect Avenue
Osceola
Wisconsin 54020, USA
Telephone: 1 715 294 3345
Fax: 1 715 294 4448

Dust jacket: Jenson Button took
the world driver's championship for
Brawn GP in their first season of
competition.

Title page: The Red Bull Racing pair
of Sebastian Vettell and Mark
Webber won six races between
them in 2009.

Photos: Peter J Fox/www.crash.net

Acknowledgements

The Editor of *AUTOCOURSE* wishes to thank the following for their assistance in compiling the 2009-2010 edition.
France: ACO; Fédération Française du Sport Automobile; FIA (Richard Woods, Alan Donnelly, Alexandra Scherin, Charlie
Whiting, Herbie Blash and Pat Behar); Renault F1 (Flavio Briatore, Bob Bell, Pat Symonds, Patrizia Spinelli, Clarisse
Hoffmann and Will HIngs); World Series by Renault; **Germany:** Formula 3 Vereinigung; Mercedes-Benz (Norbert Haug,
Wolfgang Schattling and Frank Reichert); Sabine Kehm; Michael Schmidt; **Great Britain:** Ann Bradshaw; *Autocar;* Mark
Blundell; Brawn GP (Ross Brawn, Nick Fry, Nicola Armstrong); Martin Brundle; Bob Constanduros; Maurice Hamilton;
Jules Kulpinski; McLaren (Ron Dennis, Martin Whitmarsh, Jonathan Neale, Matt Bishop, Steve Cooper, Justine Bowen,
Clare Robertson, Lyndy Redding, Simon Points, Paddy Lowe and Neil Oatley); Red Bull Racing (Helmut Marko, Christian
Horner, Adrian Newey, Katie Tweedle and Britta Roeske); Force India (Ian Phillips and Lucy Genon); Nigel Roebuck;
Sir Jackie Stewart; Williams F1 (Sir Frank Williams, Patrick Head, Sam Michael, Jonathan Williams, Claire Williams, Silvia
Hoffer Fragipane and Liam Clogger); **Italy:** Commissione Sportiva Automobilistica Italiana; Scuderia Ferrari (Stefano
Domenicali, Luca Colajanni and Stefania Bocci); Scuderia Toro Rosso (Franz Tost, Giorgio Ascanelli, Eric Silbermann,
Fabiana Valenti and Marieluise Mammitsch); **Japan:** Bridgestone (Rachel Ingham and Andy Stobart); Toyota (John
Howett, Alastair Moffat, Fernanda Villas); **Switzerland:** BMW Sauber (Mario Theissen, Peter Sauber, Hanspeter Brack,
Heikke Hinnitsch and Jorg Kottmeier). **USA:** ALMS Media Services; Speed TV; Indy Racing League; Indianapolis Motor
Speedway; Daytona International Speedway, NASCAR, Roger Penske, *SportsCar.*

Photographs published in AUTOCOURSE 2009-2010 have been contributed by:

Chief photographer: Peter J Fox. **Chief contributing photographers:** Bernard Asset; Paul-Henri Cahier; GP Photo (Peter
Nygaard); Lucas Gorys; WRi2 (Jad Sherif, Jean François-Galeron, Frits van Eldik).
Other photographs contributed by: LAT Photographic/LAT South USA (Phil Abbott, Autostock, Tyler Barrick,
Jeff Bloxham, Dan R. Boyd, Brian Czobat, Jakob Ebrey, R. D. Ethan, Andrew Ferraro, Drew Gibson, Nigel Kinrade, Michael
Levitt, F-Pierce Williams, Kevin Wood); BMW Motorsport; Force India F1 Team; ING Renault F1 Team; Shell Motorsport;
Red Bull Racing; Scuderia Toro Rosso; Vodafone McLaren Mercedes; Formula 3 Euroseries; GP2 Media Services;
Indy Racing League; Simon Arron; Chris Walker/www.kartpix.net; KSP; Luca Bassini, Malcolm Bryan, Dieter Mathis and
Studio Colombo for WRi2.

publisher
STEVE SMALL
steve.small@iconpublishinglimited.com

commercial director
BRYN WILLIAMS
bryn.williams@iconpublishinglimited.com

editor
ALAN HENRY

f1 correspondent
SIMON ARRON

f1 technical editor
MARK HUGHES

text editor
IAN PENBERTHY

results and statistics
DAVID HAYHOE

chief photographer
PETER J FOX

chief contributing photographers
BERNARD ASSET

PAUL-HENRI CAHIER

JEAN-FRANÇOIS GALERON

LUKAS GORYS

PETER NYGAARD

JAD SHERIF

f1 illustrations
ADRIAN DEAN
f1artwork@blueyonder.co.uk

www.autocourse.com

FOREWORD by JENSON BUTTON

"2009 has been a fantastic year for myself and Brawn GP. Just 23 days before the start of the season, we didn't know if we would be at the first race in Melbourne and now, just nine months later, I am the Formula One World Champion with the team winning the Constructors' Championship.

Motor racing has been a part of my life since my Dad bought my first go-kart at the age of eight and achieving my lifelong dream of becoming World Champion is the result of hard work, self-belief and the unstinting support of my family, friends and team.

You have to give your full commitment to this sport to succeed and never ever give up. I am incredibly proud of what we have achieved at Brawn GP this year and we are going to really enjoy the honour of being World Champions!"

The Home of Business

The Bahrain International Circuit is setting new standards in the world of business. Set against a stunning desert landscape, BIC provides a unique and exclusive setting to host conferences, stage seminars, hold media events and organise private functions.

and Motorsport

What's more, you can even hire the world-famous Formula One track at the circuit to cater to your business needs. All this comes with the best of 5-star catering. Simply put, welcome to the home of business and motorsport in the Middle East.

For more information: +973 17 45 0000/www.bahraingp.com

F1 ON FANTASY ISLAND?

Above: It ain't Silverstone! The super rich enjoy the comforts on their yachts moored behind the pit complex of Yas Marina circuit at the Abu Dhabi. An indication of the escalating glamourization of modern-day F1.

Centre right: Bernie Ecclestone's relentless determination and unerring eye for a deal continued to shape the future of the F1 business.
Photos: Paul-Henri Cahier

Bottom right: Jenson Button's Brawn shows a clean pair of heels to the pack at Melbourne, chapter one of a remarkable and unexpected story.
Photo: Peter J. Fox

JENSON Button's glorious triumph in succeeding Lewis Hamilton as the 2009 world champion driver was not only a fine achievement that *AUTOCOURSE* is delighted to celebrate, but also the first time that two British drivers had claimed successive title crowns since Jackie Stewart became champion in 1969, the Scot having taken over from Graham Hill, who had successfully achieved that accolade the previous year.

Moreover, while Hamilton had gone into 2008 confident that he was likely to be a contender for the title, after narrowly losing out on the crown in his debut season, Button had not even been sure that he would have a drive only a few weeks before the first race of the new campaign in Australia.

Yet in a year book-ended by the departure of Honda and Toyota respectively, the former's team successfully completed a Cinderella-like transformation and duly went to the F1 ball, reincarnated as Brawn GP. The rebranded Honda squad, now powered by Mercedes V8s, hit the ground running, and Button surged to an extraordinary six wins out of the first seven races. It looked as though he would have an easy run to the title crown, but the early perform-

ance edge conferred by his Brawn-Mercedes – even though not as big as some perceived – faded slightly mid-season.

That meant the British driver had to face a reinvigorated challenge from not only his veteran team-mate, Rubens Barrichello, but also the Red Bull Renaults of Sebastian Vettel and Mark Webber, who won six races between them. Lewis Hamilton also won two races beautifully for McLaren and Mercedes, and with one win to Kimi Räikkönen, there were six drivers who took their turns at the top of the podium.

Vettel confirmed his reputation as a huge star in the making, but Webber, who had broken a leg during the winter in a charity cycle event, exceeded even his greatest fans' expectations by emerging as one of the sensations of the year. Only the Brawn team's early pace and its gamble to adopt the controversial 'double diffuser' configuration for its cars from the outset enabled Button to build the cushion he needed to ensure he was not too seriously troubled by their late sprint in the closing races.

As usual, Formula One never lost its capacity to surprise or spring unexpected developments on its participants. The season began on a tense note, with

McLaren under the spotlight again after Melbourne, where, it was established, Lewis Hamilton and the team's sporting director, Dave Ryan, had lied to the stewards over the issue of whether or not the British driver had deliberately encouraged Toyota driver Jarno Trulli to overtake him in an effort to trick the Italian into incurring a penalty. The matter ended with Hamilton losing his third place, and Ryan, one of the most popular personalities in the business, losing his job.

At the other end of the season, we had the colourful Flavio Briatore, together with the Renault team's executive director of engineering, Pat Symonds, resigning their posts after it emerged that Nelson Piquet Junior had followed their suggestion to deliberately crash out in the 2008 Singapore Grand Prix, a race won by his team-mate, Fernando Alonso. By any standards, this was a bizarre episode, and many insiders believe that there are too many unanswered questions swirling around this scandal, not least why it took the governing body the best part of a year to initiate a serious investigation into the circumstances

of the whole affair. Certainly, the FIA concluded that Alonso knew nothing about it, a view that was far from unanimous in the pit lane.

One man who expressed his doubts was the popular Felipe Massa, although the Brazilian had more to worry about from mid-summer onwards. Having missed out on the 2008 World Championship to Lewis Hamilton in the closing moments of the season, his bid to try again was thwarted by serious head injuries sustained in qualifying at the Hungaroring. Happily, by the end of the year, Massa was back on the pit wall and was expected to be back racing in 2010. That can't come quickly enough for Maranello, which won just a single race in the 2009 season, thanks to Kimi Räikkönen's efforts in Belgium. There was a flurry of excitement when it briefly seemed that Michael Schumacher might guest as Felipe's stand-in, but the job eventually devolved to Luca Badoer and Giancarlo Fisichella. Both proved hopelessly uncompetitive.

F1 budgets and how to keep them under control were ever-present issues. In the end, it was

FLY FREE
Music/ Lyrics by Paul Stewart

FLY FREE, BE STRONG...

IT may have been the year in which he celebrated the 40th anniversary of winning the first of his three F1 world championships as well as his 70th birthday, but it was absolutely typical of the Scot's determined character that he should see this not only as an opportunity to celebrate, but also to leverage the two events for charitable purposes.

Jackie has been one of the driving forces behind the The Grand Prix Mechanics' Charitable Trust which was formally created in 1987 since which time it has accumulated a fund of over £1m while supporting current and former mechanics in times of hardship and need. Over the years the fund has offered an invaluable lifeline to that group of men who Jackie has described as "the real unsung heroes of the F1 business."

Thus when his two sons recorded a tribute song for their father's surprise 70th birthday party and recorded it with family friend Eric Clapton on the guitar, it set Jackie thinking about making it available to a wider audience – in support of the charity.

Paul Stewart sang the composition to him while Jackie's younger son Mark produced an accompanying film, which was also played to Sir Jackie on the night.

Paul, who dedicated the song to both his mother and father says: "The words are really close to our hearts ¬ when we were growing up our father always said to us if you fly with crows you'll be shot at... Fly free, be strong. It's a simple message but one that my brother Mark and I live by".

The song and its sentiments touched Jackie so deeply that he felt that he should share it. The decision was taken to release the song and DVD on download with all proceeds going to F1's chosen charity The Grand Prix Mechanics' Charitable Trust.

It's downloadable from iTunes, Amazon, or, direct from: www.sirjackiestewart.com

Right: Jean Todt successfully saw off a challenge from Ari Vatanen to succeed Max Mosley in the role of FIA president.
Photo: Jean-François Galeron/WRi2

Top right: Juan Pablo Montoya enjoys the cut and thrust of NASCAR racing as he drafts his no 42 Chevy on the Talledega bankng.
Photo: Robert Laberge/LAT USA

Right: Peugeot finally beat Audi for the holy grail in sports cars at the Le Mans 24 hour race.
Photo: Jeff Bloxham/LAT Photographic

supremely disappointing that BMW and Toyota decided to follow Honda out of the business, but one of the lessons history teaches us is that the sport has a Teflon-coated ability to regenerate and reinvent itself in times of apparent trouble. In 2010, there could be four new teams competing, all established by canny businessmen with a shrewd understanding of the motor racing industry.

Certainly there seemed to be no trouble in finding new promoters ready to pay the ever-increasing sanctioning fees demanded by F1's entrepreneur-in-chief, Bernie Ecclestone, the sport's commercial rights holder. A decade ago, the United Arab Emirates had hardly any motorsport to mention; in 2009, they had two F1 races, Bahrain being joined by the stupendous Yas Marina track in Abu Dhabi. In 2010, it could be South Korea. Then possibly India, or even Russia.

On the political front, Max Mosley kept his promise to stand down from the FIA presidency, a role that he had occupied since 1991, in the process giving his persuasive support to former Ferrari team principal Jean Todt in the battle to succeed him. Todt eventually saw off a challenge from former World Rally champion Ari Vatanen, after quite a tetchy campaign. It is to be hoped that this will be followed by a period of relative tranquillity.

British fans will have watched with mounting alarm as Donington Park's plans to hold the British Grand Prix from 2010 gradually evaporated against the backdrop of the same economic problems that drove Honda, BMW and Toyota out of the sport. Despite Ecclestone repeatedly extending the deadline for the circuit promoter Simon Gillett to prove that he had the necessary funding in place, time eventually ran out in mid-October, when the track looked more like a building site than an F1 circuit. Down the road at Silverstone, nobody at the British Racing Drivers' Club was surprised at its rival's failure, so its officials braced themselves to reopen negotiations with Ecclestone with a view to ensuring that the race remained at the Northamptonshire circuit.

Silverstone represented the old guard, part of the F1 bedrock on which the success of the World Championship has been built. Not that Ecclestone took a sentimental view of the situation, of course. He spelled it out in words of one syllable. There would be no cut-price deal for Silverstone, as he had plenty of new venues crying out for races. Clearly, the negotiating process would be demanding, painful even.

Outside the F1 firmament, there was huge diversity, with German rising star Nico Hulkenberg taking the GP2 crown to put himself on a fast track to the Williams F1 squad in 2010, as team-mate to Rubens Barrichello. Elsewhere on the international motorsport stage, Peugeot finally toppled Audi when it won the prestigious Le Mans 24-hour race; Dario Franchitti returned from an unhappy sojourn in NASCAR to win his second Indy Racing League crown; while Juan Pablo Montoya continued to relish the challenge of racing stock cars on the banked ovals, proving yet again that there *is* life after F1. As the over-ambitious A1GP Series appeared to have finally floundered hit the rocks in the autumn, Andy Soucek emerged the first champion to be produced by the newly introduced Formula 2 Championship, a programme that was sadly marred by the tragic death of the popular Henry Surtees at Brands Hatch.

Despite, all in all, the sport survived well against a taxing economic backdrop, although the demise of three high-spending F1 teams will certainly leave a worrying level of unemployment within the business in the short-to-medium term. More crucially, from a wider perspective, is how F1 will be perceived in the post-manufacturers' era and how long it will take the new teams to establish the credibility they require, from the viewpoint of attracting fresh investment and in terms of what can be expected from them on the track.

Alan Henry
Tillingham, Essex, UK
November 2009

FIA FORMULA 1 WORLD CHAMPIONSHIP 2009

TOP TEN DRIVERS

Chosen by the Editor, taking into account their racing performances
and the equipment at their disposal

Photographs by Peter J. Fox

1 | JENSON BUTTON

GIVE him the equipment and he will get the job done. Observers from the sidelines had been saying this about Button for years, but apart from a brief period with Honda in 2005–06, until 2009 the British driver seldom had the machinery to showcase his potential. Eight years ago, Flavio Briatore waspishly inquired of Button whether he was thinking about buying property in Monaco: why else would he be driving so slowly through the streets of the principality?

It was uncharitable, yet somehow cruelly to the point – and frankly a question that not only Briatore posed. But Button has grown immeasurably in stature. Not simply in terms of his track performance, but in the way that he conducts himself personally. Few drivers are more professional, measured and even-tempered than the 29-year-old from Frome. And it was those qualities, every bit as much as his pure driving ability, that enabled him to get the best out of the situation in which he found himself at the start of the season.

There were two distinctive parts to Button's year – and that's not simply stating the obvious. There was that amazing opening run, which yielded six wins out of the first seven races, where Button capitalised on squeezing every ounce of potential from the Brawn BGP001. Early in the year, Ross Brawn told a highly impressed Jackie Stewart that he had never worked with a driver as good as Button in terms of getting everything out of a car. And the British engineer included Michael Schumacher in that list.

"That was a big statement," said Sir Jackie, himself a three-time champion. "Looking at the in-car camera, he was like Prost. I would have liked to look that good. He was driving so perfectly."

The test for Button, of course, was in the second half of the season. When the Brawn team lost its way in terms of the fine edge of chassis set-up, Rubens Barrichello seemed to grasp the initiative. A better improviser when the car was not completely *au point*, in this respect Barrichello displayed the qualities that had enabled him to outpace Schumacher on occasion during their days at Ferrari.

Yet look closely at Button's race performances when the car was off-pitch, and his capacity to recover the situation was impressive, particularly taking account of the fact that he needed to retain a tactical dimension. And his championship clinching drive at Interlagos, highlighted by bold overtaking moves and crisp, decisive driving, had the hallmark of a champion every bit as much as the races he dominated from the front earlier in the year.

2 | LEWIS HAMILTON

IN terms of pure skill, the best driver out there perhaps? Splitting hairs is a straightforward task alongside that of quantifying the performance differential between Lewis Hamilton, Jenson Button and Sebastian Vettel. As has so often proved to be the case throughout F1 history, handling the year in which a driver has to mount a defence of his title as reigning world champion can be the most difficult of all.

It was not an easy season for Hamilton, starting as it did on that much discussed and very unfortunate note when he was disqualified from the Australian Grand Prix at Melbourne, after it had been determined that he and the McLaren sporting director, Dave Ryan, had lied to the stewards when questioned about the facts surrounding Lewis's late-race battle with Jarno Trulli.

In the short-term, it was a bruising experience for Hamilton. There was even fleeting talk that he might give up Formula One and seek a career racing in the USA. Happily, that was all said amid the pressure of the moment, and happily the prospect of the contemporary F1 scene being deprived of one of its most gifted new performers faded.

The other problem facing Hamilton was the McLaren-Mercedes MP4-24, which was definitely not up to scratch for the first half of the season. The new car displayed a serious aerodynamic imbalance from the start of the year, and not until the German Grand Prix at Nürburgring – round nine of the 17-race series – did it begin to hit the sweet spot. Lewis now had a machine that would allow him to remind everybody of his star quality, and he won the Hungarian and Singapore GPs in fine style. A high-speed crash on the last lap at Monza deprived him of a strong third place behind a Brawn 1-2, while a shunt in qualifying ruined his prospects at Monaco, but generally Lewis made few driving errors in 2009.

Assessing a driver from the touchlines is always difficult, but the dynamics of Lewis's relationship with the McLaren team changed materially in the wake of the departure of Ron Dennis, the man who had given him his chance as a teenage kartist, from the role of team principal. Hamilton seemed to become more mature as a result, although the rights and wrongs of how McLaren's chairman was marginalised are another story, although happily he was back in the paddock at Abu Dhabi, the first race after Max Mosley had stood down as FIA president.

SCHUMACHER with a smile. That was how young Vettel was described perceptively by one of his countrymen. Correct as far as it went, perhaps, but there was so much more to the most exciting new young talent produced by Formula One in recent years than contained in a glib one-liner that raised inevitable comparisons with the seven-time world champion. And if smiley means soft, then forget it.

It was more of the same from Vettel in 2009. The poise and maturity deployed by the German driver to brilliant effect in winning the rain-soaked '08 Italian Grand Prix at the wheel of a Toro Rosso translated seamlessly into sustained front-line excellence when he stepped up to take on the role of David Coulthard's successor alongside Mark Webber at Red Bull Racing. Yet none of this should have come as a surprise to anybody who had been watching attentively.

Between them, Vettel and Webber won six races in 2009. There were still a few rough edges to be smoothed down in the 22-year-old's racing repertoire, but he was a contender for the World Championship almost to the very end. His win in torrential conditions at Shanghai served as further endorsement of his wet-weather genius, but anybody who thought that he was a fluffy, good natured, overgrown schoolboy should have been watching his body language closely when things went wrong.

After a mid-race adjustment in strategy contributed to dropping him from second to third, behind his team-mate, he was seriously unamused. The same was true after he qualified 16th at Interlagos, where he hurled his steering wheel away as his exasperation boiled over.

Red Bull had not been one of the teams who took the double-diffuser route from the start of the season, and technically it took some time to catch up after the FIA ruling on this somewhat vexed issue. Obviously, that had an impact on Vettel's ability to demonstrate his flair from the front. True enough, Monaco saw him throw away any chance of scoring points with a spin at Ste Dévote, but his dominant run to victory at Silverstone, the manner in which he mastered the high-speed challenge of Suzuka on his first F1 outing at the Japanese track, and his victory in the inaugural Abu Dhabi Grand Prix confirmed that Vettel was indeed someone very special.

4 | MARK WEBBER

SOMETHING deep in the pit of my stomach – not to mention Formula One correspondent Simon Aron's resonant tones in my ear – suggests that I may have undervalued Mark Webber's place in the F1 community by placing him only fourth. But it's at moments like this that we really need a dozen places in the Top Ten! Indeed, in my 20 years of editing AUTOCOURSE, I can never recall such intensively conducted debate among the contributors than that concerning the relative positions of the two Red Bull-Renault drivers.

Webber's drives to victory in the German and Brazilian GPs were masterly. By half-distance in the championship battle, he was wheel to wheel with team-mate Vettel in the points standings. He may have been 12 years older than his colleague, and he had started the season with a steel splint in one leg after fracturing it in an off-season charity cycle event in Tasmania, but Webber was tough. By that, I don't just mean physically tough in the sense that he is fit – which he is – but mentally tough as well, he seemed able to handle everything that was thrown at him.

That accident meant that Webber was only able to take part in very limited pre-race testing, yet frequently he was able to out-race Vettel. He won at the Nürburgring after being obliged to take a drive-through penalty, having been held to blame for a harmless brush with Rubens Barrichello's Brawn going away from the start, and his pass on Button in torrential rain at Shanghai was possibly the best single overtaking move of the year.

Later in the season, the collective euphoria surrounding Button's title clinching efforts at Interlagos overshadowed the fact that Webber had dominated the race completely from start to finish to wrap up his second career F1 victory.

Then he rounded off the year with a spirited defence of second place in the closing stages at Abu Dhabi, expertly fending off a very precise and seemingly relentless challenge for second place from Jenson Button's Brawn-Mercedes over the final few laps. Even though Webber was grappling with deteriorating rear grip, which caused problems under high-speed braking, he did not allow himself to be flustered unduly and held on to stay ahead until the chequered flag.

MANY respected Formula One insiders regard Fernando Alonso as the best all-rounder in the business – quick enough to get the job done, consistent and never ragged under pressure on the circuit. Yet for all that, third place in the Singapore Grand Prix was the best he could manage all year, a bitter-sweet achievement considering the unpalatable legacy left by the race he had won through the same flood-lit streets 12 months before.

Officially, Alonso had been absolved of any involvement in the race fixing scandal that emerged after it became clear that Nelson Piquet Junior had been instructed to crash deliberately in a tactical bid to help the Spaniard in the 2008 event. Felipe Massa, for one, did not believe that Alonso could not have been involved in the deception. And many people in the F1 pit lane shared the view of the Brazilian driver, who, assuming he continues his steady recovery from the head injuries he sustained in qualifying at Hungaroring, will line up as Alonso's Ferrari team-mate in 2010.

Alonso had always been 'in transit' since he left McLaren under a mutual cloud of distrust at the end of 2007. Although he had won both the 2005 and 2006 World Championships during his previous stint with the French team, for the subsequent seasons it was conspicuously unable to provide him with consistently competitive equipment. But Alonso was always going to Ferrari, even though the apparent road block caused by the terms of Kimi Räikkönen's contract with the Prancing Horse made it seem as though that move might have to be deferred until the 2011 season.

Although Alonso only scored championship points in nine of the season's 17 races, there was never any doubting his class. He opened the season with a respectable fifth in Melbourne, but the Renault R29 was never the package to match the similarly powered Red Bull, for example, while Adrian Newey's excellent rival machine also highlighted the fact that the French V8 engine was not in the same league as the Mercedes product.

Yet Alonso's talent should not be judged in terms of hard results alone. Talk to any of the Renault crew, and they would tell you that Fernando is an inspirational figure and a valuable yardstick in the sense that if he cannot produce the results, then in all likelihood the car is at fault. Such qualities will be welcomed by Ferrari in 2010.

6 | RUBENS BARRICHELLO

HAVING reinvented himself as a grand prix winning force in 2009, Rubens Barrichello reminded his many fans of the pivotal role he had played at Ferrari as Michael Schumacher's team-mate throughout the early years of the decade. In a sense, the Brazilian had been something of an overlooked talent – or at least slightly forgotten – although his third place in the 2008 British Grand Prix at Silverstone was the Honda team's best result of the season and its only podium placing that year.

Like Button, Barrichello had opted to take a significant pay cut to stay with the newly rebranded Brawn squad and, again like the British driver, was extremely impressed at the power and driveability of the Mercedes V8, which took the place of the original Honda power unit quite late in the day.

Yet Rubens looked like a man who somehow had been wrong-footed by the sheer speed that Button seemed able to deploy from the start of the year. By the fifth race of the season, the Spanish Grand Prix at Barcelona, Barrichello was openly questioning the team's even-handedness when it came to strategy. He even threatened to hang up his helmet and retire immediately if he actually found evidence of the team favouring Button.

It was a tense moment, but one that Ross Brawn diplomatically – and sensitively – defused. When the same problem arose again after the German Grand prix, Brawn was on hand again with soothing reassurance. Yet this sensitive streak was definitely an Achilles heel for the Brazilian, even though it was more a reflection of his pleasant nature than any deliberately perverse attitude.

In the second half of the season, Barrichello was more convincing. His victories at Valencia and Monza were top-drawer performances, meticulously executed and dominantly delivered. How will this sensitive soul fare at Williams in 2010?

7 | ROBERT KUBICA

AFTER winning his maiden grand prix in Canada in 2008, the popular Pole and the BMW Sauber squad looked ready to sustain possibly an even more formidable winning momentum into the new season. Sadly, a succession of derailments – none of which could be laid at Robert Kubica's door – conspired to undermine their efforts.

To start with, the team lined up on the wrong side of the double-diffuser controversy, with the result that its car needed a comprehensive redesign, a task that was not completed until the Singapore Grand Prix. Then the senior BMW management decided that, given the seriousness of the global economic downturn, it would be appropriate to follow Honda's example in calling time on the company's F1 involvement. This was a bitter blow, particularly as the team's failure to sign the Concorde agreement seriously jeopardised the possibility of selling the outfit as a going concern.

Against this uncertain backdrop, Kubica was probably as well suited as anybody to deal with such setbacks. Racing is all that matters to this man; the rest is detail. He's never been one for paddock politics, and consistently performs with determination and grit. He started the year by qualifying a promising fourth at Melbourne, only to be eliminated in a collision, but even so he could hardly have imagined that it would take him until the Turkish Grand Prix before he finally got his points tally off the ground with a seventh-place finish.

Later in the season, he drove the heavily revised car predictably well at Spa-Francorchamps to finish fourth from fifth on the grid. Eighth at Singapore was respectable, but then a storming second at Interlagos, behind Mark Webber's Red Bull, was hailed by some as possibly the best single performance by any driver all year.

Make no mistake, Kubica remains a champion in waiting. On the strength of Renault's 2009 performance with Alonso, one could argue that he faces something of an uphill struggle in 2010, but by comparison with 2009's BMW Sauber, driving for the French team should be a breeze in terms of relative competitiveness. Kubica is tough enough and sufficiently philosophical to ride out the short-term turbulence that may be ahead.

8 | NICO ROSBERG

THE burning question surrounding Nico Rosberg's departure from Williams, after driving for the Grove squad for four years, was did he jump or was he pushed? Consistency has been his stock-in-trade, precision even. But does he lack the ultimate racer's edge, which makes the difference between a genuine front-runner and a member of the supporting cast? Certainly in 2009, Rosberg looked more consistent than hitherto, scoring championship points in ten of the season's 17 races. He could qualify quite consistently, too, but there was something almost intangible about the way in which his relationship with the Williams team progressed that suggested, from quite early on, that it might be the end of the road for what had seemed a gilded partnership.

Rosberg always seemed calm and collected. Anybody listening in to his radio conversations with his engineer on the pit wall would have been impressed by his methodical approach to his craft. Yet, if paddock gossip is to be believed, Frank Williams got wind of the fact that the young German driver was planning to leave the team at the end of the year and decided to pre-empt that decision by telling him that there would not be a place for him in the squad in 2010. "Nobody walks out on us," seemed to be the team's credo.

Yet to be fair to Williams, it gave Rosberg pretty much bulletproof machinery. Only once did his FW31 fail to make it to the chequered flag, and that was in Brazil, where it succumbed to gearbox problems. In Singapore, scene of his great run to second place in 2008, Rosberg dropped the ball most spectacularly when he lurched across the white line delineating the pit-lane exit from the edge of the track proper, incurring a drive-through penalty that dropped him to 11th at the finish. Since he had qualified third, this was a huge disappointment.

Wherever Rosberg goes in 2010, the chances are he will face a much more formidable team-mate than the pleasant, if erratic, Kazuki Nakajima. The 2009 season suggested that there was probably more to come from Rosberg, but precisely how much remains open to debate.

9 | KIMI RÄIKKÖNEN

THROUGHOUT what turned out to be his final season with Ferrari, Kimi Räikkönen remained one of the sport's most enigmatic of characters. He was woefully inconsistent for much of the time, yet the controlled and disciplined manner in which he first outfumbled, and then outpaced Giancarlo Fisichella's Force India to take and keep the lead of the Belgian Grand Prix at Spa-Francorchamps served as a reminder that he still had what it takes to be a world-class driver.

Not until Monaco did he manage his first podium of the season, with a third-place finish behind the two Brawns. Then he buoyed the Maranello squad in the wake of Massa's dreadful qualifying accident by driving a strong race to second place in Hungary, followed by third at Valencia and then the only Ferrari victory of the year at Spa-Francorchamps. A potentially good showing at Interlagos was thwarted by a first-lap collision, after which his car was enveloped momentarily in flame as he accelerated down the pit lane behind Heikki Kovalainen's McLaren, which was dragging its refuelling hose behind it. Räikkönen's eyelids were scorched by the searing heat, but he shrugged it aside as an unimportant incident with his customary insouciance.

Of course, as far as the 2009 season is concerned, Räikkönen will be best remembered for the manner in which his management team negotiated healthy severance terms from his binding 2010 contract with the Ferrari team, which involved a retainer of £27m – the highest in the pit lane. Quite what proportion of this amount was paid to persuade Räikkönen to walk away from his contract will remain in the realm of speculation, but it was certainly a testimony to the astute negotiating flair of his management team, David and Steve Robertson, that the Finn was able to benefit substantially from the remarkable deal.

10 | JARNO TRULLI

IT is the tradition that inclusion in the *AUTOCOURSE* Top Ten has been the exclusive preserve of drivers who have competed in the entire season under review. For 2009, one might argue, it might have been quite acceptable to suspend those terms of reference to include the dogged Felipe Massa and the simply remarkable Japanese new boy, Kamui Kobayashi, who left everybody transfixed as stand-in for the injured Timo Glock at both Interlagos and Abu Dhabi.

Instead, however, we have stuck to our self-imposed terms of reference and have awarded Jarno Trulli tenth place in the rankings for his efforts with Toyota. In a sense, it was more of the same from the Italian driver, who tends to blow hot and cold for no discernible reason. A third-place start to the season in Melbourne was more noteworthy for the controversy it caused with the McLaren squad, but Trulli delivered a good fourth in Malaysia, a third in Bahrain and a fourth in Turkey. Later in the year, he qualified second on the front row of the grid at Spa-Francorchamps, only to squander the team's best chance of a maiden victory with a slow getaway and a minor collision at the first corner.

Trulli then sought to make amends with a great drive to second place at Suzuka, following on from Glock's fine second at Singapore. But the Toyota management, at that stage still looking nervously at its proposed Formula One budget for 2010, made it clear that when it said it was really looking for wins, that didn't mean second places, no matter how worthy they might be. It was possible that Trulli could have hung on to his drive in 2010, partnered by Kobayashi, although there were some within the Toyota organisation who thought that his best days were behind him and that the team needed to aim higher.

Certainly his very public spat with Adrian Sutil on the trackside at Interlagos, after their collision on the opening lap of the Brazilian Grand Prix, served as a reminder that he can be every bit as volatile as he can be charismatic.

ON THE BUTTON
WORLD CHAMPION PROFILE by MAURICE HAMILTON

CONSIDER Jenson Button when the 2008 Australian Grand Prix had finished, and then take a look at him at the end of the same race in 2009. It was night and day, loser and winner.

In 2008, Button had left the circuit by the time Lewis Hamilton stepped on to the winner's podium to start an ultimately successful championship campaign. At least a first-corner collision had spared him the misery of a difficult race in the Honda and the embarrassment that had engulfed him post-race 12 months before.

Button had been considered a reasonable hope for the 2007 championship, but not only did he start 14th and finish 15th in Melbourne that year, he also had to watch helplessly as the British media rushed past the Honda garage in search of the new star, Hamilton having finished third at the end of a very impressive Formula One debut. Few gave Button the time of day, and it would have been a supreme optimist who suggested that a world championship would come his way.

Fast forward two years and return to that same delightful paddock, with its trees and manicured lawns at the back of the garages. Now it was Hamilton's turn to retreat to his hospitality unit and accept second best as the British national anthem rang out, this time for Jenson Alexander Lyons Button, not long turned 29, originally from Frome in Somerset, but now living quietly in Monaco.

This was only Button's second grand prix win, the first having come in Hungary in 2006, when a wet track allowed his exceptional touch to overcome the shortcomings of his car. There was no doubt that he had the skill, but his career thus far had been blighted, some thought permanently, by a succession of decisions and moves that would consign the Brit to the role of likeable nearly-man. Despite the quality of his pole-to-flag victory in Melbourne, the feeling persisted at this early stage of 2009 that Button would never make it stick. A superficial glance at his Formula One history tended to back that up.

Button had come from virtual obscurity. He had won a Formula Ford championship in 1998, but precious little else. The key to his candidature for an F1 seat had been instant and remarkable speed during an F1 test for Prost, followed by more of the same with Williams that would win him a race seat in 2000. He was far from the finished article, however, and it was no surprise when he crashed during qualifying for his first race in Melbourne. The pressure was on from the start. Williams was beginning an important relationship with BMW, and the precious Ralf Schumacher was Button's team-mate. The team was keen to employ Juan Pablo Montoya in 2001 and had no hesitation in lending Button to Renault for two years, a typically pragmatic move that said little for his prospects and ignored an important hint of his latent natural ability: he qualified strongly at Spa and Suzuka, two very difficult circuits.

However, Button had achieved little other than the wrong sort of headlines in the national newspapers. His profile was notable for the trappings of the trade as parties and glamour found prominence in print over decent results. Indeed, one of the few references to speed had been a booking when clocked by French police at 144mph in a BMW 330d, arguably the best mileage the Williams engine supplier would have from Button all season.

The move to Renault came at a bad time as the former Benetton team regrouped, and Flavio Briatore eventually shoved Button towards the exit, in favour of Fernando Alonso for 2003. By now, the gushing headlines ('Boy Wonder': front cover, *Autosport*, 20th January, 2000) had been tempered by the harsh reality of F1.

"I definitely wasn't ready for F1 when I arrived in 2000," said Button. "I could see that after the first 12 months. Going well in pre-season testing was one thing, but I couldn't believe how everything rose to a completely different level at the first grand prix. It was a big shock. I found the media attention one of the hardest things to come to terms with. It was okay at first. My father kept all the magazines and, looking at them at the end of the first year, I was amazed at the coverage; pictures of me on the front of magazines even before I had raced an F1 car. At the time, I thought that was the way it was in F1. I didn't realise that coverage was very unusual. I didn't have a clue."

With his career appearing to have stalled at the

ripe old age of 22, Button was taken on by BAR-Honda, thanks largely to David Richards and his eye for the promise that lurked beneath what had once been a flash exterior. Button had begun to abandon the excesses of stardom, although a dubious choice of managers led to strange decisions, not least a farcical series of contractual wrangles and nearly-moves to Williams that damaged a reputation made vulnerable by the absence of lasting success on the track.

There would be significant progress as BAR finished second in the 2004 Constructors' Championship. Button had scored his first podium with third in Malaysia, and taken his first pole at Imola; third place in the championship suggested that his moment had come. But it would be a false dawn and the prelude to a long slide to the back of the grid. He finished ninth, sixth, 15th and 18th in the points standings as BAR became Honda in 2006 and then seriously lost its way.

The nadir was the beginning of 2007, when Button drove the car for the first time and instantly knew that it was no good. Aged 27, he faced a year of going nowhere just when he should have been approaching his peak. It was a disaster on several counts, not least because the car was hopelessly uncompetitive,

but also because it looked a complete joke, even when standing still. On the advice of Simon Fuller and his 19 Entertainment agency, Honda had gone for the so-called 'Earth Dreams' car, a concept aimed at riding an environmentally friendly bandwagon, but its wheels fell off from the outset. Fuller vanished as quickly as he had arrived, leaving Button to face the prospect of a reputation being crushed by the rise and rise of Hamilton at the opposite end of the field.

It wasn't much better 12 months later, although there was promise on the horizon thanks to the arrival of Ross Brawn, fresh from a year's sabbatical and five world championships with Ferrari. But that would not have any effect until 2009.

When Button climbed from his Honda after the last race of 2008, the car caught fire.

No one would have blamed Button if he had left one of the most difficult cars he had ever driven to its miserable fate. After 18 races, all he had to show was a mere six points and relentless effort expended going nowhere. Still, there was the 2009 car to look forward to; all the signs were excellent.

Those hopes were dashed without warning in December 2008, however, when Honda, faced with plummeting sales and a worldwide recession, pulled the plug on its F1 team without further ado. Over 700

Above: Jenson's victory at Monaco was just one example of his delicate touch behind the wheel, which prompted observers to liken his style to that of Alain Prost and Michael Schumacher.

Left: Who could have expected it? Only weeks after it seemed as though Jenson might be out of a drive in 2009, he embraces an elated Ross Brawn after winning in Melbourne.

Photos: Peter J. Fox

people faced redundancy, among them the highest paid employee.

"I had just landed from a week's training in Lanzarote, and I was thinking, 'Shit, I'm fit!'" said Button. "And then I got the call from Richard [Goddard], my manager. The phone just dropped out of my hand. Everyone was staring at me thinking, 'What's the matter with him? He's just got off a Ryanair flight!'

"I couldn't do anything about the decision. I just had to train as I would coming into a new season, thinking I was racing. For sure, I wasn't as smiley as I usually would be. The family noticed that over Christmas. And it wasn't like I knew [about the various take-over attempts] before the rest of the world did. I was up one day, down the next. It was very tough mentally.

"I would have been a horrible person to live with over the winter. Luckily enough, I started dating Jessica [Michibata, a Japanese lingerie model], so she looked after me. My friends and family, particularly the Ol' Boy [Button's father, John], were very supportive."

Despite the terrible uncertainty hanging over them, the workforce at Brackley continued building the car while the management pursued the alternative of a buy-out. With just one test session in Barcelona remaining before the start of the season, the 2009 Brawn-Mercedes appeared for the first time on 9th March. No one gave it much hope.

When Button was fastest that day, just under three weeks before the first race in Australia, F1 insiders felt sure that the car was running below the weight limit in an attempt to record an encouraging time and attract desperately needed sponsorship. But Button knew better. His past experiences in bad cars qualified him to appreciate a good one. He could barely contain his excitement when telling his father. He knew that moment had come.

The story of Button's roller-coaster season is told in the pages that follow. Five wins in the first six races, and the talk was of winning the championship by the Belgian Grand Prix at the end of August. Ironically, that particular race would prove to be a low point and the only retirement, after a mid-field start in rough

company led to the almost inevitable punt into the gravel trap on the first lap. But, throughout, Button kept his cool, made the fewest mistakes and used his beautifully smooth style to score more points than anyone else.

"It's quite weird how quickly you can get used to being at the front after two pretty poor seasons," said Button. "When you get on the podium, it's not like, 'Oh my God, this is the most amazing experience ever.' It's more a case of, 'Okay, we've done that one. Let's move on to the next race.' In a way, that was good. If I didn't win, it would be a slight disappointment, but you have to remember it's a 17-race championship. If you go out to win every race and you end up being disappointed to finish second, third or a little bit worse, I don't think you have the right mentality. It's not a one- or a two-race season; it's a big event that goes on for a long time, and I think you have to be a little bit clever in the way you work, grabbing points when you can. Scoring in every race is the key in F1 and always has been."

After taking the championship at the penultimate round in Brazil, Button was able to sit down for the first time and assess the might of his achievement a month before signing for the 2010 'dream team' alongside Lewis Hamilton at McLaren.

"When we were kids starting out in karts, you don't think 'whoa, I want to be a F1 driver because I'm going to earn shed-loads of money.' You just think about the racing. You don't take your eye off the ball, which is to be out there, racing against the best drivers in the world and hopefully winning races. So long as you don't forget that, the rest doesn't matter.

"At the beginning of 2009, it was a case of everyone having to sacrifice certain things as we tried to save the team. I wanted to go racing. That was always the most important thing for me. I always believed, from what I had seen of the car, that this team would give me the best chance of that this year. Sure, there were times before Australia when I wondered if I had done the right thing, but I knew that we had a car that was going to be competitive, and I wanted to be in it. It was worth all the risk. And now I'm world champion!"

Right: After years of adversity, the 2009 season saw a more mature and rounded Jenson Button with the confidence to complement his experience.

Below left: Button has enjoyed his taste of championship glory and will be out to repeat it in 2010, although he knows that the opposition is likely to be even more formidable.

Below right: Button and Brawn were literally a blur to their rivals, at least for the first half of the season, during which they built up an unassailable lead iin the points standing.

Photos: Peter J. Fox

INTERVIEW
THE QUIET MAN

ALAN HENRY meets Red Bull Racing design supremo ADRIAN NEWEY

THERE is a quiet confidence about Adrian Newey, Red Bull Racing's chief technical officer, which almost never seems to be ruffled by events going on around him. He retains a clarity of focus that, in the past, has helped him direct a razor-sharp confidence in whichever direction his design instincts may take him. Think Williams FW14B, a succession of McLaren-Mercedes MP4s and now the Red Bull Renault RB5. In all those cases, there is persuasive evidence to suggest that they were the best Formula One cars of their respective eras...

Newey smiles when confronted with such a contention. Scratch the surface and he is self-effacing, although that modest nature is overlaid with a veneer of strong self-confidence. He admits to not reading the motor racing Press. Not because it particularly annoys him, you understand, but because he doesn't feel that doing so contributes anything to the number-one priority in his professional life, namely making his F1 car go faster than the next.

To an extent, this is false modesty. His services have been much fought over in the past. Some Williams insiders believe that the texture of recent F1 history would have been very different if Sir Frank and Patrick Head had offered Newey a shareholding in their company as an inducement to stay when he was romanced by McLaren in the mid-1990s.

Later, with an ironic twist, Newey was made an offer he very nearly couldn't refuse by the then team principal of Jaguar, Bobby Rahal. Ron Dennis got to hear about it and successfully goaded him into a change of mind. Then, in 2005, Newey finally left McLaren and agreed to oversee the development of Red Bull Racing, the former Jaguar team.

Above: Adrian Newey consolidated his reputation as one of the great design exponents of contemporary F1 by overseeing the design of a car that challenged hotly for the World Championship.
Photo: Red Bull Racing/Clive Mason-Getty Images

Main photograph: The Red Bull Renault RB5 showcased Newey's attention to detail and tight packaging, which has always been his technical hallmark. The car won six of the season's 17 races.
Photo: Red Bull Racing

In short, every team that has employed Newey considers him to have been worth every penny of his substantial salary. His perceived technical pre-eminence inevitably gave rise to the phrase "Who needs Schuey if you've got Newey?"

Newey confessed to remembering that quotation: "It rather took me back to my days at Leyton House in 1988, when I was praised for doing what people considered to be a really good car. Then in 1989, we had a more difficult season and the Press wrote me off. Hero to zero in a single stroke!"

He paused, before adding with a self-deprecating smile, "I think from that point onwards, I stopped worrying too much what the Press wrote about me. Not that I have anything against the Press, of course."

Newey obviously feels comfortable at Red Bull Racing, even though it's a long drive from his Surrey home to the team's base at Milton Keynes. When free from the race-to-race intensive schedule of the season, he works from an office at home a couple of days a week, then stays for a night or two at a hotel that is close to the factory. The arrangement seems to work well.

In an era when the architectural grandeur of an F1 team's headquarters seems to have become as important a calling card as its success on the circuit, Newey seems reassured by the unobtrusive normality of the RBR headquarters, believing it to be an "old-fashioned racing team" located in what he calls "a plain and conventional building".

That's certainly not to be taken as any criticism of Ron Dennis, of course. Although he describes Red Bull as "quite simply a place populated by people who want to do well", he still retains high regard for the team that he helped steer Mika Häkkinen to the 1998 and '99 World Championships.

"The upside of McLaren was the huge drive generated by Ron," he said. "As they diversified, they have perhaps got slightly less of a feel as a racing team. I came into the business not to design road cars, but to design racing cars; that was my motivation. But McLaren, in my mind, remain a great team."

Mention of his relationship with McLaren also serves as a reminder that Newey is not a pushover. Don't be fooled by his outwardly gentle demeanour. In many ways, his strong character was defined when, on joining McLaren in 1996, he immediately had his drawing office repainted in duck egg blue, a dramatic counterpoint to the muted grey décor that dominated the building.

Dennis strode in unannounced, took a good long look at his technical director's revisionist taste of colour, and walked out without making a comment. The matter was never raised again.

Newey prefers to conceptualise his designs on a drawing board rather than on a computer screen. He explained, "I have a team of people who take my drawings and put them on to a cad-cam system. I would rather have the whole thing laid out in large scale in front of me. I can draw it without thinking.

Above: Sebastian Vettel and Mark Webber cruise into the Silverstone pit lane after a crushing 1-2 victory in the British Grand Prix.

Photo: Paul-Henri Cahier

Right: Sebastian Vettel confirmed himself as one of the sport's dynamic young driving talents with a brilliant future ahead of him.

Photo: Jean-Francois Galeron/WRi2

I think I can get the initial ideas down on paper quicker this way than if I used a cad-cam system."

The 2009 season saw Newey's design philosophy finally bear fruit for his third team in two decades. The RB5's keynote is typical of him: ultra-tight packaging – some might say almost marginal – and with detail touches that emphasise his desire to push limits, thinking out of the box as often as he can do so within the constraints of the regulations.

With that in mind, you might think it surprising that he did not see the furore over the so-called 'double diffuser' coming over the horizon. But he is sufficiently honest and open to confess that he didn't.

"No, I have to confess that I really did not see that dispute coming," he admitted. "We'd looked at it briefly around June-time last year [2008], but came to the conclusion that it probably wasn't legal. So we did not initially pursue it."

Following along from that logic, he confessed that he would not have opted for pull-rod suspension on the rear of the RB5 had he reached the conclusion that the double diffuser would be decreed legal.

"I thought it was an elegant solution to a single-diffuser car, but given the rule changes, it is much more difficult to make the pull-rod layout work satisfactorily in conjunction with a double diffuser," he said.

"We took the decision to use the pull-rods because the start of the diffuser had moved from the front of the rear wheel to the rear axle centre-line. What the double diffuser does is, in effect, to completely circumvent that rule. So certainly the shape of the double diffuser we had latterly on the RB5 was compromised slightly by the pull-rod layout."

With six wins to the RB5's credit during the course of the 2009 season, Newey is obviously pretty satisfied with the way things unfolded, particularly in the latter part of the season, when the revised RB5 really hit its stride. Understandably, he has a high opinion of both Sebastian Vettel and Mark Webber who, arguably, were the strongest driver line-up of the year.

Yet Newey was reluctant to point to one specific aspect of the Red Bull RB5 as its strongest competitive aspect. He was also unwilling to 'rate' the car in a pecking order among the designs he had conceived over the years.

"I would like to think that it was a pretty homogenous design from front to back," he said reflectively.

"That's in contrast, perhaps, to some cars on the grid, where you wonder if the suspension designer had ever talked to the aerodynamicist. So I would not really be able to name any single feature which gives

the car a performance edge, but it hopefully works pretty well as a complete package."

For all his quiet demeanour, Newey has very strong views about the way in which F1 should evolve. He would welcome technical rule changes every year, even though he understands the economic imperative of rule stability. From a purely personal viewpoint, he would like rule changes to be imposed at relatively short notice to stretch and tax engineering ingenuity.

He also holds strong views on the issue of improving overtaking, pointing out that it has been obvious for many years that for this to be achieved, there should be a wholesale change in the approach to circuit design.

"I also think you have to accept that if you want to have cars which generate downforce, then you have to accept that the car behind won't often be able to run close enough," he added.

"To change that state of affairs, we would have to go back to cars like we had in the 1970s, which did not have much downforce, but created a sufficiently large hole in the air to permit slipstreaming. But that would be a completely different sort of challenge."

And one that Adrian Newey would doubtless embrace with enthusiasm. And success.

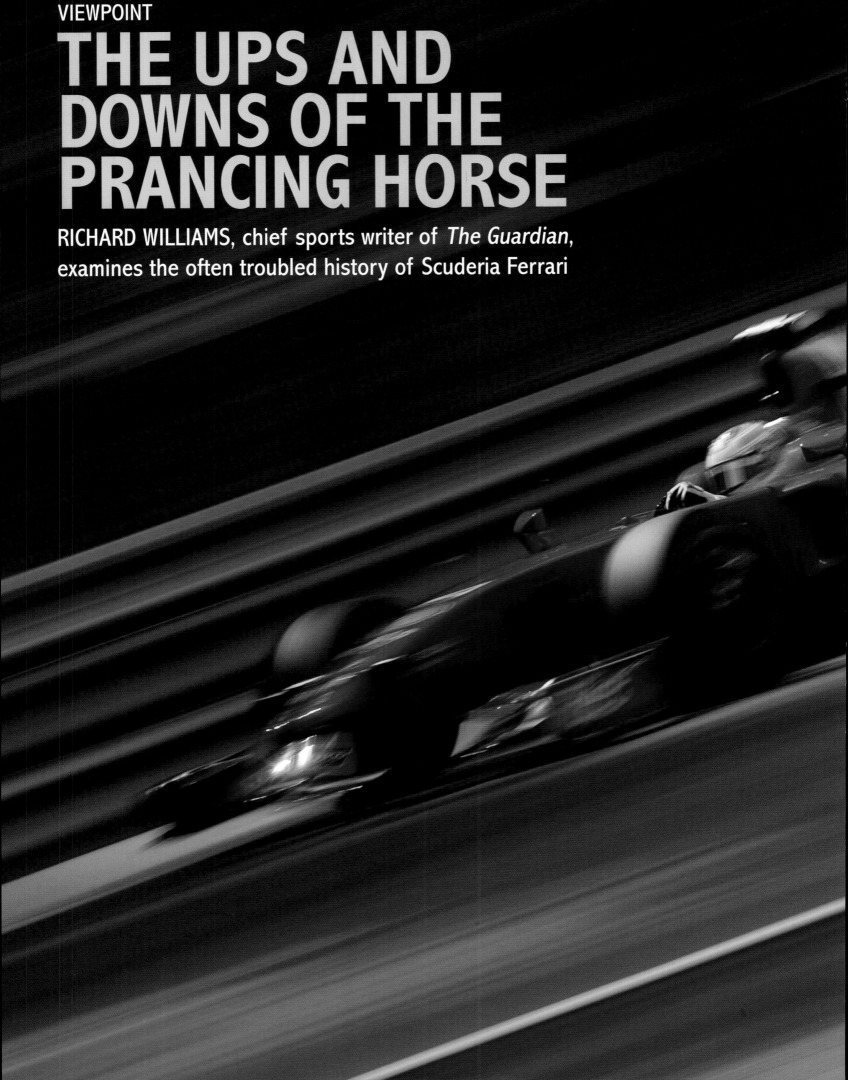

THE UPS AND DOWNS OF THE PRANCING HORSE

RICHARD WILLIAMS, chief sports writer of *The Guardian*, examines the often troubled history of Scuderia Ferrari

The red of the Ferrari sets the pulse racing of any Formula One fan, regardless of their allegiance.

Photo: Peter J. Fox

WHEN Giancarlo Fisichella traipsed across the line in 17th place, the last of the finishers, under the floodlights in Abu Dhabi, it marked the end of Scuderia Ferrari's most ignominious season in three-and-a-half decades. Not that this was the only time a Ferrari F60 had finished a grand prix in 2009 as the *lanterne rouge*, or tail-end charlie, without the excuse of mechanical problems. It had happened to Luca Badoer, too, in Belgium three months earlier, in the second of his two races as a stand-in for the injured Felipe Massa.

On that day, Badoer's embarrassment was largely obscured by a streaky victory for Kimi Räikkönen, the team's sole win in a season during which it managed only five other podium finishes and, for the first time since 1993, not a single pole position.

In fact, Ferrari's drivers had only one start from the front row during the whole year, and their average position on the grid was a humble tenth. This was a dismal showing by a team that only two years earlier had said goodbye to a driver, Michael Schumacher, who had started their cars from pole position on 58 occasions. Following Räikkönen's championship in 2007 and Massa's near-miss 12 months later, these

statistics seemed to illustrate the vertiginous decline from the heights to which Ferrari and its supporters had become accustomed. But with Ferrari, of course, the periodic opportunity to watch the team toiling to extricate itself from the slough of despond has always been half the fun.

A regular occurrence while the mercurial, volcanic, scheming and self-willed Enzo Ferrari was still alive, the phenomenon of the Scuderia's zenith-to-nadir fortunes may be less familiar to the younger generation of Formula One fans. They have grown up watching the run of almost unbroken success – 96 grand prix victories, six drivers' titles and seven constructors' championships – that began with Jean Todt's appointment as sporting director in 1993 and ended with the Frenchman's departure in 2007.

Ended? That may be a little premature. But Räikkönen's championship victory, the last under Todt's aegis, coincided with the beginning of the team's biggest internal convulsion since the winter of 1961/62, when a large number of top engineers stormed out of the Maranello factory, along with their newly crowned world champion driver, Phil Hill, in revolt against the constant interventions of Laura

Ferrari, the *Commendatore*'s wife. On that occasion, it took a reconstituted team three seasons to pull itself together and win another title, with John Surtees at the wheel. Arriving three decades later, Todt took eight seasons to achieve a reconstruction, which was not completed until Schumacher's first championship in 2000. So effectively was the work carried out, however, that the German driver's five consecutive titles made Ferrari's total dominance of F1 seem natural.

In fact, turmoil and underachievement had just as often marked the team's efforts, and frequently the Scuderia's earlier crises had played out in the public eye. When the 'Old Man' accepted a state sponsored gift of the entire Lancia grand prix team in the middle of a disastrous 1955 season, or an infuriated Jean Behra socked Romolo Tavoni, one of Todt's many predecessors, on the jaw after his engine failed at Rheims in 1959, there was no disguising the internal trauma. In 1973, a disastrous car, the original 312B3, was publicly condemned when Ferrari sent only one machine to Silverstone for the British Grand Prix and then let Jacky Ickx, his number-one driver, leave the team in mid-season, before missing the next two races altogether.

That particular period of depression, however, was relieved by the appointment of Luca di Montezemolo to the job of sporting director. In partnership with designer Mauro Forghieri and driver Niki Lauda, the young Montezemolo had Ferrari winning again within a couple of seasons. Returning to the colours as company president 20 years later, it was he who hired Todt and encouraged the creation of an all-conquering, multinational team that included Schumacher, technical director Ross Brawn, designer Rory Byrne, software expert Tad Czapski, and engine men Paolo Martinelli and Gilles Simon.

After the team climbed back to the top, however, the group began to break up. Czapski was the first to leave, returning to Renault in time for Fernando Alonso's two championship seasons in 2005 and 2006. Martinelli moved up to an executive role within Fiat, the parent company, in 2006, and at the end of the year, Brawn took a sabbatical, returning to Formula One 12 months later as technical head of the Honda team. Midway through the 2007 season, Nigel Stepney, the team's English chief mechanic during Schumacher's championship years, was dismissed for passing technical information to a McLaren designer.

While Byrne was retained as a consultant, the role of chief designer was given to Nick Tombazis, a Greek born aerodynamicist.

But it was when Todt resigned from the company early in 2008, 18 months after being promoted to chief executive, that a major change of culture within Ferrari became apparent. Todt appeared to have fallen out with Montezemolo, who had signed a £27m-a-year deal with Räikkönen and was intent on pairing the Finnish driver with Massa. The president was not interested in his chief executive officer's desire to retain Schumacher for another season. The Frenchman's unexpected departure strengthened the position of Stefano Domenicali, who stepped up from the role of sporting director to take the title of team principal.

Domenicali, an engaging and widely liked man in his forties, was welcomed into Formula One's inner councils as a more open and emollient presence than the confrontational and intransigent Todt. And before long, the new man appeared to have embarked on a process of what could be called 're-Italianisation' of the team: he was now flanked by race strategist Luca Baldisseri, engineering chief Aldo Costa and opera-

Above: Rob Smedley *(left),* in conversation with Rory Byrne, one of the few surviving members of the team recruited by Jean Todt.
Photo: WRi2/Jean-François Galeron

Above left: In the stormy political waters of Formula One in 2009, the vastly experienced Luca di Montezemolo is once again masterminding the Scuderia's racing future.
Photo: WRi2/Studio Colombo

Top: Team manager Stefano Domenicali has the unenviable task of returning Ferrari to the top of the podium on a regular basis.
Photo: Peter J. Fox

tions director Mario Almondo, as well as Simon, who had taken over from Martinelli, and Tombazis.

All seemed to be going well when the team won the constructors' title during Domenicali's first year in sole charge. Over the winter of 2008/9, however, the team committed itself to developing the new KERS energy recycling system and missed a more important trick when designing a car to meet the new technical regulations. Ross Brawn, Ferrari's old technical boss, had spotted the opportunity to create the now-notorious double diffuser, forcing the rest of the field to catch up while his KERS-less cars won six of the first seven races. Some of Brawn's rivals, notably Red Bull and McLaren, eventually managed to match the new team's pace. Despite Räikkönen's KERS assisted win at Spa, however, Ferrari never came close to achieving consistent competitiveness.

Internal problems were revealed by the mid-season decisions to relieve Baldisseri of his strategic responsibilities and move him back to a role at the factory, and to dismiss John Iley, the team's chief aerodynamicist. Simon also left the company, to be replaced as head of engine development by Luca Marmorini, a Ferrari man throughout the 1990s, who had returned to Maranello after a ten-year spell with the Toyota Formula One team. Soon after the win in Belgium, Domenicali signalled the virtual abandonment of the 2009 effort by announcing a halt to further development of the F60. Taking a leaf from Brawn's successful approach to the task of reviving the Honda project, all available resources would be thrown into the creation of a car for the following season.

Some wondered if these were the actions of a management taking a bold approach to intractable problems, or the sort of panicky decision making that had characterised the team in the years before Todt's arrival, and during many earlier periods in its 60-year history. Had the process of re-Italianisation merely reintroduced Ferrari to the sort of pit-lane soap opera that Todt had witnessed at first hand during his debut as sporting director at Kyalami in 1993, when the mechanics had sweated to change Jean Alesi's failed engine in record time to get his car on to the grid?

The loss of Massa with six races to go was a piece of dreadful luck for both team and driver. The Brazilian was expected to return for 2010, however, partnered by Alonso, Montezemolo apparently willing to pay off the last year of Räikkönen's vastly remunerative contract to secure the services of the latter-day prince of Asturias. The chemistry between the two Latin drivers could be combustible, given that Massa almost won the title in his last complete season with the team, and that Alonso, who moved from Renault to regain his title, has already proved, during his troubled year with McLaren in 2007, that he is only interested in being a team's number-one driver.

Then there is the question of any possible effect on the team of Todt's new role as president of the FIA, in succession to Max Mosley. Allegations of favourable treatment have often arisen as a result of the historic closeness between the governing body and Formula One's oldest entrant, but the failure of the expensive KERS system, Mosley's pet project, and what appears to be a new coolness between Todt and Montezemolo may have changed the balance of the relationship. Ferrari may now be even more closely aligned with the other members of the Formula One Teams Association, in which Montezemolo played a leading role throughout the early months of 2009, when a stand-off in negotiations with the FIA led to the threat of a breakaway series. At the end of the 2009 season, a posting on the team's official website likened the FIA's attitude to the major manufacturers, and the disappearance of Honda, BMW and Toyota to an Agatha Christie murder mystery, in which the characters are bumped off one by one.

Ferrari's history, which includes six decades of continuous involvement in the FIA World Championship, is both the team's greatest strength and, sometimes, its greatest handicap. Over the last few seasons, for instance, a series of changes to the sporting regulations, aimed at cutting costs, have deprived the team of the ability to make unimpeded use of the facilities so carefully and expensively constructed over the decades, notably the Fiorano test track and the two wind tunnels housed in a spectacular Renzo Piano designed building.

Politics and handicaps aside, however, its imperative for 2010 is clear. Now that the last vestiges of the *ancien regime* have disappeared, Stefano Domenicali must use his team's resources to produce a car that is capable of challenging for race wins from the moment the teams arrive at Bahrain's Sakhir circuit in March. Ferrari will be measured by the spectacular performance, 12 months earlier, of the team masterminded by Ross Brawn, who, had the cards fallen differently, would have been doing Domenicali's job. Anything less simply will not do.

Left: Out with the old. Kimi Räikkönen's three-year tenure with the team began with a world championship, but the relationship ended with a massive pay-off to the Finn.
Photo: Peter J. Fox

Right: In with the new. The season is over, and Montezemolo presents Fernando Alonso at a Ferrari demonstration run at Valencia's Ricardo Tormo Circuit.
Photo: WRi2/Studio Colombo

Below: Felipe Massa must find his way back to form following his enforced absence, as well as meeting the challenge of Alonso.
Photo: Paul-Henri Cahier

OUT OF THE STORM

ALAN HENRY discusses the birth of Brawn GP with ROSS BRAWN

THERE had been no obvious signs of the seismic events that were about to take place. Ross Brawn, the Honda F1 team principal, and Nick Fry, the team's chief executive officer, continued with their intensive preparations for the 2009 World Championship season. Although the chill winds of the global recession had started to blow, there had been nothing to suggest that Honda would not be competing. Then, towards the end of November 2008, came the bolt from the blue...

Inset above: Ross Brawn drew on all his F1 expertise, accumulated from time with Williams, Haas, Arrows, Benetton and Ferrari, to help shape the fortunes of the team that now carried his name to brilliant effect.
Photo: Paul Henri Cahier

Main photo: The clouds at Interlagos during practice may look intimidating, but Jenson Button never put a wheel wrong in the Brazilian Grand Prix, surging through the pack to clinch his world championship with a fifth-place finish.
Photo: Peter Nygaard/Grand Prix Photo

It was a devastating blow for the sport as a whole, not just the motorsport industry in the Brackley area, that close-knit community of sub-contractors in the Northamptonshire countryside, just north of Oxford. It seemed unimaginable that a major Formula One competitor was about to be driven out of business by the commercial realities of a wider world, from which optimists had misguidedly believed their high-octane business was immune.

Yet out of this disappointment and uncertainty would rise a new, lean F1 operation, which would stun its rivals by winning the World Championship at its first attempt. That unlikely event seemed no more than a dream, however, as Brawn and his colleagues tried to take in Honda's decision.

"I'd been to Honda only a few weeks before, discussing our plans and what we were doing, and the economic crisis had hit then. They had indicated that there would have to be some belt tightening, and we were in the process of doing that," Brawn recalled.

"Then one day we were invited to what we thought would be a routine meeting to discuss how we went forward into 2010. It was due to take place at one of the hotels near Heathrow airport and, when we arrived, we inquired as to whether it would be possible to get a room where we could have a meeting.

"Then a porter said, 'There's a room down there with a lot of Japanese people in it,' and that's when we began to wonder what was happening. We were invited in, told the decision that Honda had taken, that they would be pulling out, and then invited to begin discussing the mechanism by which we would implement the closure. It was a pretty devastating

moment, as you can well imagine. So we then moved into meetings with Honda senior legal personnel to start the process of closure."

Ross admitted that he was absolutely stunned, but both he and Nick Fry gathered their thoughts and began to think of an alternative. Mid-way through the meeting, they surprised the Honda executives by suggesting that they try to find a buyer.

"They had given no thought to finding a buyer, as it was the view that, in the current economic crisis, nobody would be interested," said Brawn. "It was only during the meeting that Nick and myself asked them whether they would mind if we tried to find a buyer for the team. They were clearly surprised at this because their view was that the team was unsaleable.

"The path developed over several months and was still evolving after Christmas. After the announcement [that the team was for sale], we were deluged with expressions of interest, but we quickly whittled those down to a few... Bernie [Ecclestone] was always there in the background, saying, 'I will always help out, but for the moment I'll leave you alone to try and sort it out. But if it gets critical, then come and see me.'

"One of the more serious buyers had their proposal provisionally accepted by Honda, but that eventually did not proceed." There seemed only one way out: Brawn and Fry would have to buy the company to save it.

Brawn added, "I suggested that it made sense for us to take over, but we didn't have clarity of what it would cost for Honda to close down the operation. But when it became clear that cost would be substantial, that enabled us to go back to Honda with the

suggestion of a buy-out, saying, in effect, 'Look, this might be a better route for you.'

"A management buy-out is unheard of in Japan, so trying to negotiate it with our Japanese colleagues was very difficult, because they are not very familiar with it over there. When it came down to negotiating the numbers, we had to present a case which was more economic for Honda than simply closing it down." Eventually, that was managed successfully, although it would turn out to be a very close call to get the cars built, tested and ready for the opening race in Melbourne.

Once the decision had been taken, Brawn had to split his time between managing the take-over and keeping an eye on the re-engineering of the car, which, of course, had lost its original Honda V8 engine.

"I'd say I was probably spending three or four days of the working week on the business side, with technical progress meetings and reviews squeezed in between," he said. "I was there for any crisis, so if problems needed to be resolved, then the engineering staff could find me somewhere or other at some time of the day."

Issues such as who would drive the cars and which engines would be used seemed pretty straightforward compared with what had gone into setting up the newly branded Brawn GP operation.

"Mercedes were more relaxed about progressing without a contract," Brawn said, "while Ferrari were becoming anxious about their capacity to service the necessary number of engines. If we chose the Ferrari engine, they needed reasonable notice, so I think it was more difficult for Ferrari to hang on, whereas

Mercedes were happy." The team went with Mercedes and never regretted it.

Brawn grinned momentarily as he acknowledged that both Jenson Button and Rubens Barrichello hadn't much choice but to accept the austerity deal that was offered to them. If the team were going to have a sporting chance of getting to the first race, it was a case of sorry boys, but this is how it is.

"We just had to tell both the drivers that we just hadn't seen this coming, to the point where we talked to Honda's senior management after the decision had been taken [to disband the team], asking if it was reversible, and they told us, no, it wasn't," said Brawn thoughtfully.

"So that's where we were. We were out of contract with Rubens, but there was a contract in place with Jenson, which needed to be resolved. Fortunately, I suppose you could say, this all happened at a point where it was unlikely that they were going to be able to find another good team. For them, it became Hobson's choice, which rather worked in our favour."

So when did they begin to realise how good the car really was? "I think it was almost immediately they drove it for the first time," said Brawn. "Jenson drove the car at the Silverstone shake-down, but said that he didn't really want to comment until he'd driven it at Barcelona, although he did admit that the car felt pretty solid.

"Then we got down to Barcelona and he did his first run, then came in and said it felt good, even though the track surface was in pretty bad shape with lots of rubber and diesel on it. So we knew straight away that we'd got a good car here, although there was all the usual speculation that we were running underweight at these tests in order to clinch a sponsor. That's the thing in F1, nobody ever gives you the benefit of the doubt."

By the time the cars arrived in Melbourne, the team almost felt that it had already won the World Championship. That was an achievement in itself, because there were definitely more than a few days over the winter when Brawn and Fry couldn't actually see that this would happen.

"I've said many times, the thing that I'm very proud of was the capacity of the workforce to knuckle down so single-mindedly over the winter, not really knowing what the future might hold and suspecting that there was a good chance of being made redundant," said Brawn, with genuine admiration. "They kept working away and never stinted. I was hugely proud of that."

Inevitably, it was necessary to trim the head count – by more than 200 – and this unpleasant axe fell when the team was celebrating its 1-2 in Melbourne. "It was a big disappointment to have to do this," said Brawn, "but we were able to give them the same terms as those planned under the proposed Honda closure. It was a very unpleasant experience, but it was essential to make everything work."

What did Brawn feel was the team's great moment of the year? He had no doubts. "That 1-2 in Melbourne," he said, "even though it was a slightly fortuitous 1-2, but being up there on the rostrum, thinking about everything that had taken place, was a very special moment. The Monza 1-2 was also very good, and Jenson's great drive in Brazil was another highlight of a season which really had a lot of highlights.

"It really was a season of two halves. We were fairly dominant in the first half, although the margins were not as big as they were perceived by some people. In the second half, we scored 60 points, Red Bull scored 61 and McLaren 57. We built the lead in the first half and maintained it in the second."

Understandably, Brawn finished the year with his admiration for the team's two drivers at an all-time high: "Rubens was rejuvenated, absolutely outstanding. Jenson, what can you say? He did pretty much the perfect job for most of the time. All credit to him for getting the job done. Both of them maximised their opportunities pretty well."

So will the second year be more difficult for Brawn GP? "It is and isn't. Watching next year's car being put together, I don't see anything we're chronically short of. People are having to work harder and more efficiently, the wind tunnel is working pretty well up to its operational capacity. I think we've still got the ability to surprise a few people in 2010."

The Brawn team gather to celebrate Rubens Barrichello's win at Monza.
Photo: Peter J. Fox

APPRECIATIONS 2009

BY ALAN HENRY

PETER ARUNDELL

The first of a host of South African drivers who competed in Formula One during the 1960s, **TONY MAGGS** blazed a trail that was followed by his compatriot Jody Scheckter, who went on to win the 1979 World Championship. Maggs succumbed to cancer at the beginning of June, aged 72.

Born into a military family, Antony Francis O'Connell Maggs drove in 25 world championship grands prix between 1961 and 1965, finishing second at the wheel of a factory Cooper-Climax in the French Grand Prix of 1962 and 1963. He shot to prominence originally while competing with Ken Tyrrell's Formula Junior Cooper-Austin team in 1961, when he shared the European championship with Jo Siffert.

Maggs had arrived in Europe in 1959, at the age of 22, and soon made contact with Essex farmer John Ogier, whose Tojeiro-Jaguar sports car he raced in the 1960 Formula Libre South African Grand Prix. That same year, he drove a Formula Two Cooper for Ogier with some success in European events. Later he had a few outings in the Chequered Flag's Formula Junior, during which he caught the eye of Ken Tyrrell, who signed him to drive alongside John Love the following year.

In 1961, Maggs also dipped his toe into the F1 water, driving in the British and German grands prix at the wheel of a Lotus 18 entered by Louise Bryden-Brown. Although he only managed to finish 13th and 11th respectively, his prowess attracted the attention of John Cooper, who signed him to run alongside Bruce McLaren for the next two seasons.

After spending two years with Cooper, he was dropped at the end of 1963 in favour of former world champion Phil Hill. He drove in three races the following year, however, at the wheel of a Scuderia Centro-Sud BRM, and completed his F1 swansong in the 1965 South African Grand Prix with a Parnell Lotus-BRM. He also won the Kyalami nine-hour endurance event on two occasions, sharing a Ferrari with legendary Maranello privateer David Piper.

Later in 1965, Maggs took part in some F2 races with a Midland Racing Partnership Lola until an accident involving his Brabham BT10 at the Roy Hesketh circuit in Natal resulted in the death of a child. That prompted him to retire from racing for good, and he concentrated on farming in the Zontspanberg area of Northern Transvaal. He had a lucky escape some years later, when he survived a light aircraft crash in which his farm manager was killed.

Photo: LAT Photographic

Partner to Jim Clark in the Lotus F1 team during the opening races of 1964, and then again throughout the 1966 season, **PETER ARUNDELL** died in June at the age of 75. Inevitably, he suffered from being cast in the role of number-two driver to the great Scottish ace, but Arundell is remembered as having a breezy confidence that sent the firm message that he believed he could beat Jimmy, given the chance.

One of the brightest rising stars to emerge from the British Formula Junior scene in the early 1960s, Arundell had started his racing career in an MG TC, followed by a Lotus Eleven and then a Lola sports car. Colin Chapman spotted his potential, and signed him up to drive alongside Clark and Trevor Taylor in the Lotus Formula Junior squad. In 1961, he added to his reputation by winning the Monaco Formula Junior race, going on to take 18 wins from 25 starts in 1962 and winning the Monaco event once again.

Arundell won the 1962 British Formula Junior championship so decisively that the respected German journalist Richard von Frankenberg unwisely accused Lotus of running an illegal engine in Peter's Lotus 22. He challenged the Lotus boss to take the car to Monza, have the engine checked and then see if Arundell could match the speed he had previously demonstrated when winning the Monza Lottery race earlier in the year. Arundell achieved the goal easily, winning $3,000 for his delighted boss.

For the 1963 season, Arundell piloted the Ron Harris Team Lotus monocoque type 27, but failed to make it a hat trick at Monaco, although he did take six consecutive victories after the car had been redesigned. He also drove a works Lotus 25 in the non-championship F1 races at the highly demanding circuits of Solitude and Enna-Pergusa, finishing second in both events.

Eventually, in 1964, Arundell took over from Taylor as the Lotus number two, having waited patiently for the opportunity to present itself; he got his F1 career off to a great start by finishing third in the Monaco and Dutch grands prix. Tragically, he only ran in four rounds of the title chase that season before being seriously injured in a huge F2 accident at Reims.

Colin Chapman very loyally kept open Arundell's seat in the team, even though he was not fully fit until the beginning of 1966. When he returned to the cockpit that year, it appeared that the magic had gone, however, and he struggled to make any sort of a mark. Having scored a sixth place in the US Grand Prix at Watkins Glen, he retired at the end of the season and did not race seriously again. He lived in Florida for some years, but returned to Suffolk with Rikky, his wife of 50 years, where he died in sadly reduced circumstances after a long battle with illness.

Photo: LAT Photographic

TONY MAGGS

FRANK GARDNER

Photo: LAT Photographic

TONY MARSH

Photo: Autocourse

JACKIE PRETORIUS

Photo: Autocourse

Despite only starting four grands prix during his career as a privateer, **TONY MARSH**, who died in May, aged 77, gained a well-earned reputation as one of the most versatile all-rounders on the UK motorsport scene.

Born into wealthy circumstances – "with a silver spanner in my hand," as he put it – Marsh began his career driving a Dellow sports car in off-track events. Subsequently, he switched to circuit racing with a succession of 500cc Coopers, which he also used for hillclimbing, winning the British hillclimb championship in 1955, 1956 and 1957. Then, at the wheel of a Cooper-Climax T43, he went on to win the British Formula Two championship in 1957.

Marsh drove the Cooper in the F2 class at the 1957 and 1958 German grands prix, but in 1960 switched to a Lotus 18, which he ran in various non-championship races. In 1961, he was persuaded by BRM boss Raymond Mays to take on a BRM P48 Mk II, at the wheel of which he scored the marque's only win that season in the Lewis-Evans Trophy race at Brands Hatch. The relationship with BRM came to a sticky end early in 1962, however, when Marsh returned his V8-engined type 57 to the factory, complaining that it was substandard. Thankfully, their disagreement stopped short of legal action.

Throughout much of the 1960s, Marsh concentrated again on hillclimbing, taking a second hat-trick of British championship crowns between 1965 and 1967 with his own potent Buick-engined Marsh Special. From 1967 to 1989, he retired from the sport, but then returned to compete in hillclimbs once more with various Cosworth-propelled machinery through to the start of the 21st century. By any standards, his was an amazing career.

One of the most popular and charismatic personalities on the UK motor racing scene in the 1960s and 1970s, **FRANK GARDNER**, the laconic Australian racing driver, died at the end of August after a long illness. He was 78.

Although never in the front line of international drivers, Gardner gained a respected reputation as a tough and uncompromising competitor. He raced a wide variety of cars and usually had a pithy, ironic assessment of those whose performance he considered below par.

Memorably, in the 1969 Nürburgring 1,000km race, he was hired to drive the prototype Porsche 917 sports car with British co-driver David Piper. It was a luridly powerful car that was unpredictable to drive in the most benign conditions, let alone the tortuous 14-mile track through the Eifel mountains. Gardner did not remember the experience with affection.

"The computer said that the 917 would handle fine on nine-inch wheel rims, but then the computer was not strapped in the cockpit," he recalled. "If you'd stopped concentrating for a second, you would have needed a map to find your way back to the circuit." Later he added, "I never wanted to be the fastest racing driver, just the oldest."

A tough all-round sportsman who had excelled at boxing, swimming and motorcycle racing in his youth, Sydney-born Gardner bought a Jaguar C-type sports racing car with which he won the New South Wales sports car championship in 1956. Like compatriot Jack Brabham before him, he soon realised that to expand his racing horizons, he would have to leave his native shores for England, where he could immerse himself in his chosen profession.

He arrived in the UK in 1958 and began working as a mechanic with the Aston Martin sports car racing team, which was followed by a stint with the legendary Jim Russell racing drivers' school at Snetterton, before moving to the Brabham factory in Surrey. There he built and raced cars in the thriving Formula Junior category, which was the most important class for aspiring grand prix stars.

In 1963, he drove sports cars and Formula Junior machinery for the North London based Ian Walker racing team, before switching to the team run by the huge John Willment Ford dealership in Twickenham, which was one of the most important planks of the US car maker's onslaught on international motorsport throughout the mid-1960s.

Frank raced Willment Ford Cortinas in the British saloon car championship and made his Formula One debut in the 1964 British Grand Prix at Brands Hatch, where Willment fielded a Brabham Formula Two car fitted with a production-based Ford twin-cam engine. He collided with another competitor on the grid and never got away from the start.

Willment bought a Brabham-BRM F1 car the following year, but Gardner never scored any championship points, contenting himself with a third-place best in the 1965 Mediterranean Grand Prix at Enna-Pergusa, a flat-out sprint around a broiling snake-infested lake in central Sicily, following home Jo Siffert's Brabham and Jim Clark's Lotus.

Yet it was in touring cars that Gardner would find his true métier. In 1967, driving for the Byfleet based Alan Mann racing organisation, he won the British touring car championship at the wheel of a Ford Falcon V8, then repeated the achievement the following year in one of the newly unveiled Ford Escorts. In 1973, he won the title for a third time with a fearsomely powerful 7-litre Chevrolet Camaro.

He retired from driving in the early 1980s and returned to live in Australia. Subsequently, he had two stints running the BMW team in the Australian touring car championship. Gardner also supported many road safety initiatives, and for many years he drove the safety car at the Australian Grand Prix, with an aplomb and control that reflected his vast experience behind the wheel.

One of the most experienced and versatile members of South Africa's motor racing community, **JACKIE PRETORIUS** died in hospital in March, just three weeks after being attacked and beaten in his home in Johannesburg. His wife, Shirley, had been killed in almost identical circumstances some seven years before, a bizarre coincidence that heightened the sense of tragedy surrounding his death.

Pretorius had just three outings in Formula One world championship qualifying events. He made an unsuccessful attempt to qualify one of Doug Serrurier's LDS-Alfa Romeos for the 1965 South African Grand Prix, then drove a Brabham BT11-Climax in the 1968 race at Kyalami.

In 1971, at the wheel of a Brabham BT26-Cosworth, he competed in his home grand prix again, during what proved to be his most successful season in his national F1 series. Pretorius had his final F1 outing at Kyalami in 1973, at the wheel of one of the Frank Williams Iso-Marlboros, deputising for the injured Nanni Galli.

TOM WHEATCROFT

That towering, jovial and very astute motor racing entrepreneur, **TOM WHEATCROFT**, who had revived the Donington Park circuit, where the mighty Mercedes and Auto Union battles had been enacted in the 1930s, died on the eve of the Abu Dhabi Grand Prix at the end of October.

A millionaire building contractor and shrewd dealer over the years in some of the world's rarest and most desirable racing cars, Wheatcroft was a passionate fan of the sport, which had shaped his life ever since, as a teenage schoolboy, he had cycled to Donington Park to watch the battling Silver Arrows.

Just over 30 years later, Wheatcroft, who never lived more than a few dozen miles from Castle Donington and by now had become a successful businessman, paid a reputed £100,000 to purchase part of the 1,100-acre Donington Hall estate, including the old racetrack. The first task was to clear the site of debris. During the war, the track had been used as one of the country's biggest military vehicle storage depots, and it would not be until 1977 that it reopened, albeit much shortened from its original configuration.

Even before the track was revived, Wheatcroft's Donington Collection had been opened, becoming one of the most remarkable motor racing museums in the world, home for many years to Bernie Ecclestone's collection of Brabham F1 cars. Wheatcroft and Ecclestone became close friends, dealing in historic racing cars over the years.

Eventually, on Easter Sunday 1993, Wheatcroft realised his life's ambition when Ayrton Senna's McLaren won the rain soaked European Grand Prix. It had been 55 years since the teenager had stood in the spectator area at the track, watching his great hero Tazio Nuvolari winning the Donington Grand Prix in an Auto Union. He acknowledged that the race had cost him £3m, but that it had been "worth every penny!"

Although Wheatcroft had achieved his ambition, what he really wanted to do was to persuade Ecclestone to switch the British Grand Prix to his circuit. But the general view within F1 was that Donington Park was too small and lacked the necessary room for expansion.

Only after Wheatcroft had granted a long-term lease on his circuit to a company called Donington Ventures Leisure Ltd, headed by Simon Gillett and, initially, Lee Gill, did the leaseholders sign a 17-year contract with Ecclestone to run Britain's round of the title chase at the circuit from 2010. Wheatcroft lived just long enough to witness the costly failure of their well-intentioned efforts.

One of the most pleasant and popular personalities in recent Formula One history, **JEAN SAGE**, the former Renault sporting director, died at Annecy following a short illness in October. He was 68.

Sage presided over Renault's F1 efforts from the moment its first 1.5-litre turbo spluttered and crackled into tentative action at the 1977 British Grand Prix. At the time, most of the F1 community thought it was a very bad joke that would never work properly. Two years later, Sage, who had competed in Formula Three during the 1960s, had the last laugh at Dijon-Prenois as Jean-Pierre Jabouile stormed past the chequered flag to score the turbo's first grand prix victory.

In 1983, Sage presided over Alain Prost's close call for the World Championship, when the Frenchman was pipped at the post for the title by Nelson Piquet in Bernie Ecclestone's Brabham-BMW. Prost left the team at that point, but I well remember Sage's enthusiasm when it came to recruiting Britain's Derek Warwick the following year to partner Patrick Tambay. They didn't win any races, but were nice blokes, and I always felt that counted for a lot with the good-natured Sage.

After the works Renault team closed its doors at the end of 1985, Sage continued with the operation for another couple of years until the company briefly ceased its supply of customer engines. Subsequently, he ran a team of Ferrari F40s in sports car events, and remained involved in the classic car movement for the remainder of his life.

JEAN SAGE

HENRY SURTEES

It is both poignant and ironic that **HENRY SURTEES**, son of 1964 world champion John Surtees, should have lost his life as the result of freak accident during an international F2 race at Brands Hatch on 19th July. His legendary father had raced both motorcycles and cars during an era when the prospect of death or serious injury lurked around every corner, yet his son's accident served as a reminder that motorsport will always be a hazardous pastime, no matter how much effort is expended on active and passive safety measures.

Surtees suffered fatal head injuries after a wheel shed by another crashing car bounced across the track and hit his helmet a glancing blow. The 18-year-old had only just scored his first podium finish in the first race at Brands Hatch the previous day. This achievement, following on from an excellent pole position at Brno, offered genuine momentum to a fledgling career that looked as though it promised a great deal.

Henry Surtees began his racing career in karting, moving on to Ginetta juniors, Formula BMW and then Formula Renault. He was roundly regarded as a charming, warm-hearted young man with genuine competitive promise and was a huge loss to his close-knit family.

TEDDY MAYER

One of the driving forces behind the early success of the McLaren F1 team, **TEDDY MAYER**, who died in January, aged 73, played a vital management role in not only establishing the company, but also winning its first two world championship titles, with Emerson Fittipaldi in 1974 and James Hunt two years later.

Mayer ran the team for ten years after Bruce McLaren's death in a testing accident at Goodwood in June 1970, until the organisation's dwindling form caused so much anxiety to its main sponsor, the Philip Morris tobacco group, that the backer insisted Mayer amalgamate the team with Ron Dennis's emergent Project 4 operation as a condition of retaining the lucrative backing. He finally left McLaren in 1982, after selling his shareholding to Dennis and the team's then technical director, John Barnard.

Edward Everett Mayer was born into a wealthy Pennsylvanian family. His father was a stockbroker, and an uncle, Will Scranton, had been a state governor. He gained a law degree at Cornell University, but when he and his younger brother, Tim, acquired an Austin Healey 100-6 sports car in 1958, the die was cast when their thoughts turned towards a future in motorsport.

A combative and feisty personality, Mayer became involved in racing mainly to look after the career of his dazzlingly talented brother. In 1961, he ran a team of Formula Three Coopers in the USA, the drivers being his brother, the cosmetics heir Peter Revson – who would later score two grand prix victories for McLaren in 1973, during the Mayer regime – and an old friend, Bill Smith. Of the 16 races it contested, the so-called Rev-Em racing team won 15, and took 14 second places and 14 thirds.

Tim had been due to join Bruce McLaren in the Cooper F1 works team in 1964, but he was killed practising for a race in Longford, Tasmania, at the start of that year, driving a Cooper-Climax Tasman series car fielded by the newly formed Bruce McLaren Motor Racing Team. Teddy, perhaps as a way of dealing with his grief, abandoned his career as a lawyer and threw in his lot with McLaren, bringing some much-needed finance as well as mental acuity to the management of the business.

McLaren and Mayer worked well together. The former's laid-back charm and sunny disposition, his outward tolerance and reservoir of goodwill acted as a foil to the latter's somewhat abrupt business style. They were an unlikely team, but a successful one.

After McLaren's death, Mayer steadily built the team into a leading Formula One force, which reached its zenith in the mid-1970s, when he lured Emerson Fittipaldi away from Lotus, for whom the Brazilian had won his first world championship in 1972, and gave the driver the equipment to win his second title two years later.

When Fittipaldi decided to move on, to join his elder brother Wilson's fledgling Copersucar team at the end of 1975, Mayer pulled a masterstroke by signing James Hunt to replace him. Hunt went on to take the championship in 1976 by a single point from Niki Lauda. The photograph of the furious and distracted Englishman erupting from the cockpit of his McLaren M23 at the Mount Fuji circuit – with Mayer in front of him, holding three fingers aloft to signify he had achieved the third place necessary to win the championship – is one of the defining F1 images of that decade.

After leaving McLaren, Mayer ran his own Indy car team, Mayer Motor Racing, in partnership with his long-time collaborator and fellow American, Tyler Alexander, who had been a mechanic for the Rev-Em team and one of the handful of staff who were with McLaren from the very beginning.

In 1985, he switched to a management role with the short-lived, Ford-backed Beatrice Lola F1 team, after which he ran the UK manufacturing base for the famed Penske Indy car team in Poole, Dorset. He remained a consultant with Penske until 2007.

B.R.M

R-50-TN-AR

www.brm-manufacture.com

For stockist enquiries please telephone +33 (0)1 61 02 00 25

BRM America : (+1) 214 235 91 27
BRM Belgium : (+32) 2 344 48 57
BRM Dubaï : (+971) 4 3526204
BRM Eastern Europe : (+33) 6 85 14 56 57
BRM England : (+33) 1 61 02 00 25

BRM France : (+33) 1 61 02 00 25
BRM Indonesia : (+62) 21 3983 8810
BRM Italy : (+39) 02 308 57 05
BRM Japan : (+81) 3 5295 0411
BRM Luxembourg : (+32) 2 344 48 57

BRM Malaysia : (+60) 32141 3131
BRM Singapore : (+65) 6333 6663
BRM Switzerland : (+33) 1 61 02 00 25
BRM Thailand : (+66) 2 610 9883

FORMULA 1 REVIEW

Team Reviews: MARK HUGHES

Technical Specifications: ALAN HENRY

F1 Illustrations: ADRIAN DEAN

Photo: Bernard Asset

VODAFONE McLAREN MERCEDES

A THIRD place in the constructors' championship, even if it was a distant third, was an achievement of sorts for the 2008 World Championship winning team, given the horrific start to its season. Not only did it begin with a car that was dramatically lacking in performance, but also it became embroiled in yet another controversy with the governing body, following an innocuous incident for Lewis Hamilton behind the safety car in Australia.

The fall-out of the false account given to the stewards about the incident was catastrophic and cost McLaren's long-serving sporting director, Davey Ryan, his job, and it was no coincidence that team chief Ron Dennis renounced any role in the F1 team henceforth. For a brief moment, the team appeared to be in a nose dive to oblivion, but under Martin Whitmarsh's stewardship, calm resolve brought things back on course and, in the second half of the season, the irrepressible Hamilton was gunning for race victories once more.

The team got a terrible surprise when it tested its new car in earnest for the first time and discovered that it was three seconds off the pace of the best of the 2009 cars! There had been a catastrophic miscalculation of the downforce levels that would be achievable under the new aerodynamic regulations, as engineering chief Paddy Lowe explained: "The original overtaking working group target had been to halve the downforce of the 2006 cars. Last year, a good car had a coefficient of lift of about 3.5–3.6, and when we first put our '09 car in the tunnel, it was 1.5. We then set ourselves a target of 2.5. There was a bit of concern when Ross Brawn warned the group back in February that he was already seeing figures well in excess of 2.5, but everyone was sort of thinking he must've got his calibration wrong. Later in the car's gestation, we discovered a bit more and so we raised the figure to 2.8, and that's pretty much what we had when we went to that first test. It was incredibly difficult setting a target, we put a stake in the ground, came up with a number, and it was the wrong number."

The car, the MP4-24, looked elegant enough, if slightly bulky in the sidepods courtesy of the KERS battery and electrical unit sited there. McLaren, along with seven other teams, had gone along with the spirit of the new aero regs in using a plain, single diffuser, but the car's performance shortfall was about much more than just the concept of its diffuser. It retained the team's traditional front wing endplate philosophy of directing much of the air between the wheels, in contrast to most other designs where the endplates directed as much flow as possible around the outside of the wheels, thereby ensuring a cleaner airflow to the floor and diffuser. The new aero regs specified a full-width front wing with a standardised central

LEWIS HAMILTON

McLAREN-MERCEDES MP4-24

SPONSORS	Vodafone • Mobil1 • Santander • Johnny Walker • Schuco • Aigo • SAP • Boss • Hilton • Kenwood • Nescafe • Fedex • Bridgestone TAG Heuer • Sonax • Olympus • Sparco • Kangaroo • Steinmetz • Enkei • Mazak
ENGINE	*Type:* Mercedes-Benz FO108W *No. of cylinders:* V8 2.4-litre *Spark plugs:* NGK *Electronics:* McLaren Electronics ECU *Fuel:* Mobil unleaded *Oil:* Mobil1
KERS	Electronic E-motor (60kw) with lithium battery (400kj)
TRANSMISSION	*Gearbox:* McLaren Racing 7-speed, semi-automatic, 'e-shift' *Clutch:* AP Racing carbon-carbon multi-plate
CHASSIS	*Front and rear suspension:* Double wishbone/pushrod operating inboard mounted torsion-bar/damper units *Dampers:* Koni *Wheel diameter:* 13in front and rear *Wheels:* Enkei, magnesium forged *Tyres:* Bridgestone Potenza *Brake discs and pads:* Carbone Industry *Brake callipers:* Akebono 6-piston *Steering:* McLaren power-assisted *Instruments:* McLaren Electronic Systems *Battery:* GS Yuasa *Radio systems:* Kenwood
DIMENSIONS	*Wheelbase:* Not given *Overall length:* Not given *Overall height:* 950mm *Overall width:* 1800mm
	Formula weight: 605kg, including driver and camera

HEIKKI KOVALAINEN 2

Below: Heikki Kovalainen often struggled for pace in his second year at McLaren.
Photo: Peter J. Fox

Photo: Vodafone McLaren Mercedes

Norbert Haug

Martin Whitmarsh

VODAFONE McLAREN MERCEDES: PERSONNEL

Team Principal: Martin Whitmarsh

Vice President M-B Motorsport: Norbert Haug

Managing Director, (McLaren Racing): Jonathan Neale

Managing Director, (M-B HPE): Thomas Fuhr

Engineering Director, (McLaren): Paddy Lowe

Engineering Director, (M-B HPE): Andy Cowell

Design & Development Director: Neil Oatley

Team Manager: Dave Redding

Chief Engineer, MP4-24A: Pat Fry

Chief Aerodynamicist: Doug McKiernan

Chief Mechanic: Pete Vale

Race Engineer, Hamilton: Phil Prew

Race Engineer, Kovalainen: Mark Slade

Jonathan Neale

Paddy Lowe

Pat Fry

Photos: Vodafone McLaren Mercedes

ured double-diffuser floor became the endeavour of the team over the following few weeks. The McLaren's gearbox wasn't as badly situated or shaped as, say, Ferrari's or BMW's when it came to converting the car to a twin-diffuser layout, so a twin diffuser of sorts was on the car as early as Spain, the first European race. It did not transform the car's competitiveness, however, and it wasn't until a much more extreme twin diffuser was combined with a final switch to the 'around the wheels' type of endplate that the car finally became respectable, from Germany onwards. Immediately prior to that, during the Turkish and British grands prix, the McLaren was unquestionably the slowest car of all, having briefly risen from that status between the winter tests and the beginning of the season.

"Yes, it was a matter of face saving not turning up at the start of the season with the slowest car," said Lowe, "and we pulled through a lot of developments we had in the wind tunnel in extra-quick time. We turned things around from tunnel to production way quicker than we'd ever done before. It meant we were harvesting the gains we were finding in the tunnel earlier, whereas our competitors would bring the same stuff in one lump later on, which was why we looked relatively good at Bahrain. We'd gone from the back to half-way, then we went back down to Q1 level by Spain."

For a time, it was the worst car, but powered by the best engine and best KERS package. The engineers at the Mercedes Performance Engines base in Brixworth had benefited from a massive investment in the KERS programme and put it to good use. The initial prototype system weighed in at almost 100kg. The first unit installed in a car was down to 37kg, and for much of the season it was running at 25kg. It was reliable, could be used for the full 6.7 seconds per lap in one hit without overheating the battery and harvested the energy very efficiently.

The system played a key part in the team's breakthrough race victory in Hungary, where Hamilton used it to power past Mark Webber's Red Bull to take the lead. In general, however, the system was papering over the cracks of the chassis' lack of downforce, even in its much improved post-Silverstone guise, allowing more wing to be used than otherwise would have been feasible.

Even though the Mercedes KERS was probably the lightest of all the systems, that 25kg still meant that at the start of the season there was no ballast with which to vary the car's weight distribution from track to track. Eventually, weight saving in other parts of the car enabled the use of some ballast, but mostly the car was stymied by not being able to get as much weight up front as was needed by the new front slick tyres.

For this reason, a 7cm-shorter-wheelbase version of the car was produced and was raced to second by Hamilton at Valencia. He didn't like the feel of it, though, and it wasn't used again. Hamilton was even more the team leader than in 2008, as Heikki Kovalainen proved unable to match his pace. The combination of Lewis's skills and some good tactical calls by the team – notably in Brazil, where he finished third from 18th on the grid – produced a steady stream of good results in the latter half of the season, including a dominant performance from pole in Singapore. Even within the team, however, the feeling was very much that, much improved though the car was, it was being flattered by a genius of a driver.

For 2010, McLaren aimed to give him something more worthy of that ability.

Above: Once the car was radically overhauled, Lewis Hamilton scored two wins for the team – and it could have been more.
Photo: Peter J. Fox

Right: The Mercedes-Benz powerplant was indisputably the most powerful force on the grid.

Above right: Mechanics work on the MP4-24. The KERS battery unit can be seen amidships.

Far right: The McLaren Mercedes crew wait for their moment to go into action in Abu Dhabi.
Photos: Jad Sherif/WRi2

section, and it seemed surprising that McLaren had retained this philosophy.

"Eventually, we were in a minority of one on that," admitted Lowe, "and we did look at what everyone else had done when the other cars launched. But the fact we didn't go that direction on endplate initially doesn't mean we didn't give it a go. It's one thing to try it, another to make it work for you. You cannot just blindly copy."

Obtaining an understanding of how more conventional endplates could work in unison with a reconfig-

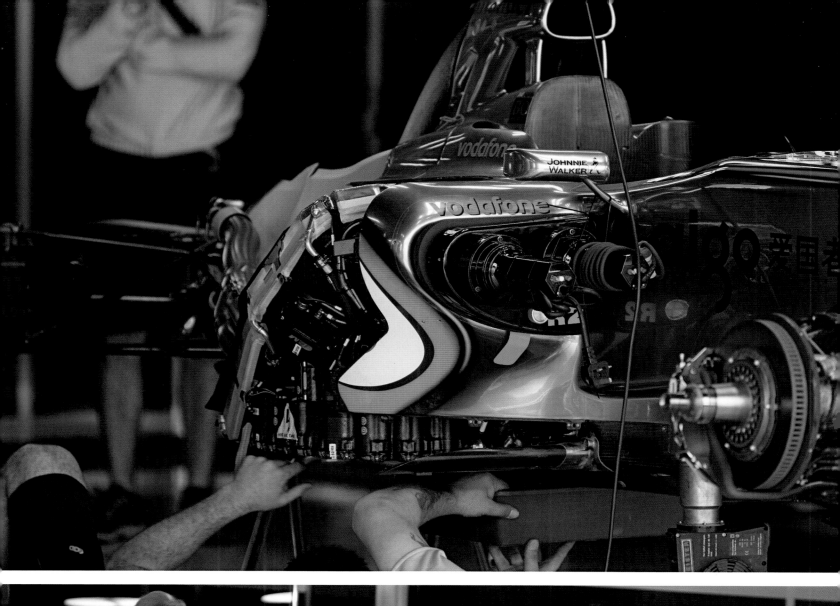

SCUDERIA MARLBORO FERRARI

LIKE McLaren, its title rival of the previous season, Ferrari took a stumble into 2009, thwarted from the start by a car that was configured around a single diffuser, and it never quite caught up, despite adapting to the twin-diffuser concept as best it could. Once again, the Italian team found itself in a fight with McLaren in the constructors' championship, but this time only for third place, a struggle that eventually it lost. Kimi Räikkönen scored the team's solitary victory at his happy hunting ground of Spa, but this wasn't enough to prevent the team from buying out the remaining year of his contract to make room for Fernando Alonso in 2010.

The F60 was a conventional design with many of the team's signature features, such as the single-flap front wing, the long wheelbase and tightly-waisted rear. Indeed, this car led the way on the packaging of the rear mechanical components until the appearance of the Red Bull with its pull-rod rear suspension. The RB5 instantly dated the Ferrari – and most of the other cars on the grid, too. Chief aerodynamicist John Iley, with the team since 2004, was released in July, and this was believed to be related to the team's disappointment in the F60.

A conventional single diffuser projected beyond a new gearbox casing that was wider and lower than before, chasing a lower centre of gravity (cg). Quite large radiator outlets suggested that the Ferrari en-

gine had greater heat rejection than some of its rivals. A KERS system, developed in association with Magneti Marelli, was used, the battery being located beneath the fuel tank. This actually lowered the cg with empty tanks, but increased it significantly with full tanks. The weight of the system was believed to be in the high-20kg region, something that militated against reaching the optimum forward-biased weight distribution. It was for this reason that the wheelbase was shortened from Silverstone onwards. Occasionally, in the early part of the season, the KERS was not used while a few technical bugs were ironed out, but thereafter it was a regular feature.

A double diffuser of sorts was on the car by Barcelona, and Felipe Massa drove a great race there, running third until a faulty fuel-level display forced him to back off in the closing laps. He was even more impressive at Monaco, with a fantastically fast and consistent middle stint, and but for traffic at crucial times, he might have pushed Barrichello's Brawn for second rather than taking fourth. This period of the season, when the team had put a lot of performance on the car, saw it at its most competitive. Thereafter, it was a gentle downward drift away from the front – with peaks and troughs according to the circumstances of any given weekend – as the decision was taken quite early not to pursue a major development programme. In particular, a plan to make a new gear-

3

Photo: Peter J. Fox

FELIPE MASSA

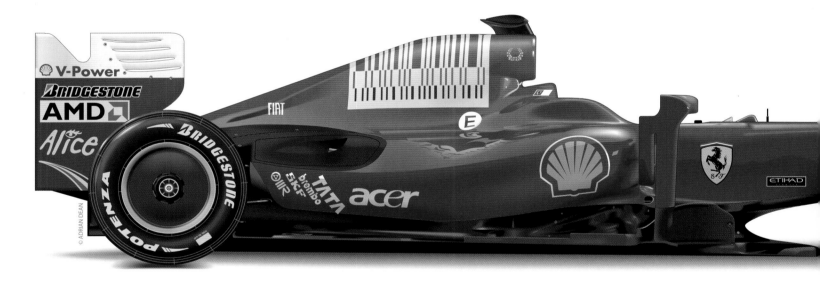

© ADRIAN DEAN

FERRARI F60

TITLE SPONSOR	Philip Morris
MAJOR SPONSORS	Fiat • Shell • Etihad • Alice • Bridgestone • AMD • Acer • Mubadala

ENGINE	*Type:* Ferrari 056 *No of cylinders (vee angle):* V8 (90-deg) *Electronics:* Magneti Marelli *Fuel:* Shell V-power ULG 64 *Oil:* Shell SL-1098
TRANSMISSION	*Gearbox:* Ferrari longitudinal gearbox, limited-slip differential; semi-automatic, sequential electronically controlled quick-shift mechanism *Number of gears:* 7, plus reverse
CHASSIS	*Suspension:* Front and rear: Independent suspension, pushrod activated torsion bars *Wheel diameter:* 13in front and rear *Wheels:* BBS *Tyres:* Bridgestone Potenza *Brake discs:* Brembo ventilated carbon-fibre *Brake pads:* Brembo *Brake callipers:* Brembo
DIMENSIONS:	As regulations
	Formula weight: 605kg, including driver and camera

LUCA BADOER

Photo: Peter J. Fox

Photo: Studio Colombo/WRi2

GIANCARLO FISICHELLA

4   **KIMI RÄIKKÖNEN**

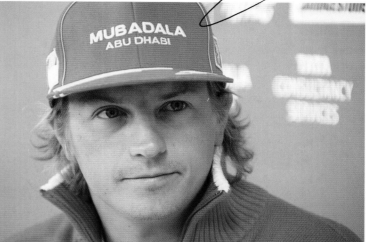

Photo: Studio Colombo/WRi2

Photo: Peter J. Fox

Stefano Domenicali

Photo: Lukas Gorys

Aldo Costa

SCUDERIA MARLBORO FERRARI: PERSONNEL

General Director: Stefano Domenicali

Technical Director: Aldo Costa

Sporting Director: Chris Dyer

Engine and Electronics: Gilles Simon/Luca Marmorini

Chief Designer: Nicolas Tombazis

Race Engineer, Räikkönen: Andrea Stella

Race Engineer, Massa/Badoer/ Fisichella: Rob Smedley

Race Engine Manager: Martino Binotto

Right: Even Michael Schumacher could not help Giancarlo Fisichella unlock the secrets of the Ferrari after the Italian's late-season switch to the Scuderia from Force India.

Photo: Studio Colombo/WRi2

box casing that was more suitable for a twin-diffuser layout was shelved.

"If we'd designed a twin-diffuser car from scratch, it would have had a different gearbox, rear suspension, rear crash structure, and so the whole back half of the car would have been different," said Chris Dyer, the team's chief track engineer, "and not just in terms of bodywork, but of mechanical layout as well. We brought the first version of the double diffuser to Barcelona, and it was a really huge change for us, not just in terms of floor and bodywork, but on the mechanical side. Certainly in my history at Ferrari, we have never brought such a huge mechanical update to the track so quickly. There was an awful lot of resource involved in designing and making the pieces, and then they went to the track untested and ran for a race. We're also talking about hydraulic systems, electrical systems, and they are not always easy things to get right straight out of the box. They are the kind of things that give us problems in winter testing, so for us it was a pretty huge achievement to get all those pieces on the car and get it running reliably. I think if the season had been panning out differently, we would have to have been considering even bigger steps later in the year.

"A new gearbox was evaluated, but at end of the day we chose not to. With no testing and a four-race limit on the box, to homologate a gearbox for four races, you need to test for eight Fridays, so it makes it extremely difficult."

Operationally, the team was caught out a couple of times in the early season by the closeness of the times, and one of its cars was stuck in Q1 after it erroneously believed it had done enough not to need to go out late in the session. This happened with Massa in Malaysia and Räikkönen in Barcelona. Reliability was poor in the first half of the season, too, and there were several key personnel reshuffles, notably Luca Baldisserri who, post-China, was switched from the pit wall to a factory based job.

Generally, the car followed the pattern of all Ferraris of recent years, in that it struggled to bring its front tyres up to temperature quickly enough, making qualifying difficult and particularly blunting the challenge of Räikkönen, whose driving style was much less suited than Massa's to the car's understeering trait. It struggled particularly badly if the tyre compounds were too hard, but the other side of that coin was that frequently it would be in good shape if the softer of the tyres was especially marginal for the track and conditions. It was in such circumstances that Räikkönen gave the car its only place on the front row – at Monaco.

"I think this was a more critical factor than any aerodynamic trait actually," said Dyer. "At circuits where tyres are working well for us, the car is competitive, and at the tracks where we are struggling to get the best out of the tyres, we are less competitive. We've seen generally that we can survive on the soft tyre a bit better than other people, and in some circuits that gives us an advantage." But by "advantage", he meant less of a disadvantage than usual, because in general the car lacked downforce, essentially because of the serious compromises in the diffuser's design brought about by the wide gearbox casing. Even though the diffuser design was revised regularly during the second half of the season, the basic shortfall remained. The downforce the car did produce, however, appeared to cost less in drag than, say, the McLaren. At Spa, it was vastly quicker down the long straights of sectors one and three for a similarly slow pace in the twisting middle sector. In combination with the tactical advantage of KERS and the panache of Räikkönen, this was enough to win Ferrari the race on a day when the McLarens failed to figure.

The team's potential to score points with both cars was severely blunted by the absence of Massa after his accident during qualifying in Hungary. Tester Luca Badoer was hopelessly out of his depth after a decade away, and his replacement, Giancarlo Fisichella, had KERS-related problems in adapting to the car's behaviour under braking.

5

ROBERT KUBICA

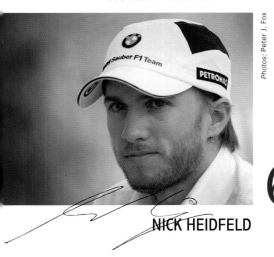

Photos: Peter J. Fox

6

NICK HEIDFELD

BMW SAUBER F1 TEAM

IN 2009, BMW's methodical timetable of success came spectacularly off the rails. After the first grand prix victory achieved in 2008, the plan was to fight for the championship in '09. Instead it finished a distant sixth with a scant 36 points. Worse than that, BMW announced its pull-out from Formula One, effective from the end of the season.

The BMW F1.09 was an intrinsically uncompetitive car, born in an unsettled environment with changes to senior technical management during its gestation. Long-time technical director Willi Rampf went on sabbatical at the end of 2008 and was replaced by Walter Riedl, who oversaw the programme for only three months before Rampf returned in his former role.

According to insiders, this team had become wracked by internal politics, one of the triggers of which was the Munich based parent company insisting that it pursue a KERS programme, much against the general wishes of the Sauber part of the operation in Hinwil. With team principal Mario Theissen spending much of his time in Munich, rivalry among the personnel at the factory impacted upon the effectiveness of the team.

It was only BMW's insistence that it run a KERS programme that prevented all the other teams from turning their backs on the newly allowed technology to save costs. The F1.09 was conceived around a KERS that relied on air cooling for the batteries. Consequently, they had to be sited in the airflow and were positioned in recesses in the inboard ends of the sidepods, significantly increasing the height of the car's centre of gravity. This arrangement also prevented the sidepods from being as deeply undercut as necessary to obtain good upper-body airflow to the rear of the car.

A single diffuser further limited the car's initial potential. "We were first alerted to the double diffuser when we saw the Williams," said Rampf. "We didn't think this would be allowed and so we didn't immediately jump on it. This was a wrong conclusion. We should have put a lot of resource on it immediately, but instead we started in the tunnel with the idea four weeks later. What you don't have on a car for Melbourne, you can't put it on a car for the next few races, and so we were stuck with it. I underestimated it."

Although the weight of the KERS was competitive with that of the Mercedes and Ferrari systems, it was much less effective. It couldn't always be used for the full allowable duration in one hit without risking overheating of the batteries, and it had an adverse effect on the car's braking stability, something that was never fully cured. The 59kg Nick Heidfeld could still get the required weight distribution with KERS fitted, but the 72kg Robert Kubica could not. After the first

BMW SAUBER F1.09

SPONSORS	Petronas • TSystems • Intel • FxPro • Go-GP.ORG • Certina • Syntium • Puma •
TECHNICAL PARTNER	Bridgestone
ENGINE	*Type:* BMW P86/9 *No of cylinders:* V8 *Sparking plugs:* NGK *Electronics:* SECU *Fuel:* Petronas *Oil:* Petronas
	Cooling system: BMW Sauber F1 Team
	Materials: Engine block: Aluminium, cast in BMW's foundry *Crankshaft:* steel *Pistons:* aluminium *Connecting rods:* titanium
	Engine dimensions: Length: 518mm Width: 555mm Height: 595mm (overall) Weight: 95kg
TRANSMISSION	*Gearbox:* 7-speed quick-shift gearbox, longitudinally mounted, titanium (as of Singapore GP, aluminium) *Clutch:* AP Racing
CHASSIS	*Suspension:* Upper and lower wishbones (front and rear) Inboard springs and dampers, actuated by pushrods
	Dampers: Sachs Race Engineering *Wheel diameter:* 330mm front and rear *Wheels:* OZ *Tyres:* Bridgestone Potenza
	Brake pads and discs: Brembo/Carbone Industrie *Brake callipers:* Brembo *Steering:* BMW Sauber F1 Team power steering
	Chassis electronics: SECU, MES
DIMENSIONS	*Length:* 4690mm *Width:* 1800mm *Wheelbase:* not given *Track width, front:* 1470mm *Track width, rear:* 1410mm
	Formula weight: 605kg, including driver and camera

Willy Rampf   Walter Riedl   Markus Duesmann

Peter Sauber   Mario Theissen

BMW SAUBER F1 TEAM: PERSONNEL

BMW Motorsport Director: Mario Theissen

Head of Engineering: Willy Rampf

Director, Powertrain: Markus Duesmann

Head of Aerodynamics: Willem Toet

Team Manager: Beat Zehnder

Chief Race Engineer: Giampaolo Dall'Ara

Chief Mechanic: Amiel Lindesay

Race Engineer, Kubica: Antonio Cuquerella

Race Engineer, Heidfeld: Paul Russell

Head of Sponsorship and Business Relations:
Guido Stalmann

Head of BMW Sport Communications:
Jörg Kottmeier

Top: Kubica on the grid in Melbourne, where hopes where high for a successful year.
Photo: Paul-Henri Cahier

Right: Race engineer Paul Russell confers with his driver Nick Heidfeld in Japan.
Photo: BMW Motorsport

Photos: BMW Motorsport

Above: Robert Kubica gives the much-revised BMW F1.109 its final race outing in Abu Dhabi.

Top right: Sitting impassively in his car, Kubica listens to his engineer, Antonio Cuquerella.

Centre right: The BMW mechanics busy themselves in readiness for another run for Nick Heidfeld.

Right: BMW Sauber personnel celebrate the team's last tangible success – Robert Kubica's second place in Brazil.

Photos: BMW Motorsport

three races, however, even Heidfeld discarded the system. Time spent on trying to develop it seemed to have been at the expense of the car's aerodynamic development; uniquely among all the cars, no new development parts were fitted for the first four flyaway races.

"The KERS always gave an issue with brake stability, because you have to cut it after recharge, and we could never sort it 100 per cent," admitted Rampf. "Then with no track testing in the season, you can't really use the Friday to sort out a brake stability problem. This is why we said we cannot concentrate on three things, let's concentrate on aero because it has more potential, especially after we have seen what is possible with the double diffuser."

Kubica flattered the car in qualifying in Australia, using an unusual tyre sequence to put himself in contention for a second place or even a win in the closing stages of the race. Only Sebastian Vettel's Red Bull stood in the way of him trying to pounce on Jenson Button's lead with four laps to go, but Vettel's defence against Kubica's passing attempt led to a big collision between them. Such opportunities would be rare with the car, although Heidfeld coaxed a halfpoints second place from the rain-shortened Malaysian Grand Prix by making fewer stops than the others for different tyres.

An update package for Barcelona brought a slight improvement in competitiveness, but the introduction of a double diffuser for Turkey succeeded only in maintaining the previous deficit to the front, as everyone else was fitting them by then, too.

A modified KERS system with a smaller battery, and therefore less capacity, was made, but was never raced, while at Valencia a version of the car appeared with no room for KERS. The sidepods had been made slimmer and the tub lightened significantly, which improved the car's competitiveness substantially. At Spa for the following race, Heidfeld qualified a solid third, by far the car's best showing of the season.

The slimmer sidepods finally opened the way for development of the car's brutally square-edged front wing endplates, as Rampf explained: "We tried various endplates before this, but they never worked. It only really started to work when we went to much tighter sidepods, to get air around the side of the sidepods to the upper surface of the diffuser. Before that, we were locked into these square bulky endplates."

The new, much more svelte endplates appeared on the car at Singapore as part of a total reconfiguration based on a new, narrower gearbox, which allowed much greater advantage to be taken of the twin-diffuser concept. In Brazil, Kubica drove a storming race to second, beating Barrichello's Brawn on merit, despite an overheating engine. But it was too little, too late.

ING RENAULT F1 TEAM

FERNANDO ALONSO

FAR from taking off from where it had left off at the end of 2008, the Renault team reverted to the indifferent form it had shown in the first half of that year. Even the talent of Fernando Alonso could do little with a car that simply lacked downforce – for a variety of reasons. Then when the spectre of Singapore 2008 came back to haunt the team late in the year, after the sacked Nelson Piquet Jr had confessed to the governing body that he had crashed there deliberately, and that it had been a plan orchestrated by the team, the fall-out was catastrophic. Team principal Flavio Briatore and director of engineering Pat Symonds left the team in the aftermath. With Alonso due to leave at the end of the year, it was the final break-up of the double title-winning partnership.

The first setback in the team's troubled season came when it questioned the governing body about the legality of introducing slots for the diffuser between the floor's step plane and reference plane – the same ruse that allowed Brawn, Williams and Toyota to come up with their twin diffusers – and was told by the FIA's technical delegate, Charlie Whiting, that such an arrangement would not be legal. Whiting is obliged not to inform teams of the enquiries other teams have made, but the difference between Renault's query and what was allowed on the other cars was that Renault had asked about a specific method of concealing the slots with radiused edges. That was

what Whiting had said no to, not the general idea of having such slots.

So the Renault design team assumed that a twin diffuser would not be legal and set about configuring a car around a conventional single diffuser. The R29 was an unusual-looking device with an ugly wide nose, the idea being to create a low-pressure area over the full width of the new standardised central section of the front wing, thereby creating an artificial aerofoil effect, despite the section being neutral in profile. "It was an idea someone had in the design team," said former technical director and later team principal Bob Bell. "We looked at it in CFD and it seemed to give better numbers, so fairly early on in the programme we adopted it because the nose is one of the things you fix early, so that you can go and do your nose impact tests and get them out of the way. Then everything else develops around it. We just locked ourselves into it."

The car was designed to incorporate the team's version of the Magneti Marelli-based KERS system. As in the Ferrari, the batteries were installed under the fuel tank. Unlike the Ferrari, however, there was a facility to lower the tank when the KERS was not in use. As it happened, this was most of the time, because the drivers found the car very unstable whenever the KERS was fitted, particularly under braking.

In the previous season, Briatore had dispensed

RENAULT R29

SPONSORS	ING • Renault • Mutua Madrilena • Pepe Jeans • MEGAFON • T.W. Steel
ENGINE	*Type:* RS27-2009 18,000rpm mandatory rev limit *No of cylinders (vee angle):* V8 (90-deg)
	Electronics: Magneti Marelli *Fuel:* Total *Oil:* Total
TRANSMISSION	*Gearbox:* Renault 7-speed quick-shift activated longitudinal titanium gearbox with reverse *Clutch:* AP Racing
CHASSIS	*Front suspension:* Carbon-fibre double wishbone with pushrod and rocker operated inboard torsion bar/damper units
	Rear suspension: Carbon-fibre double wishbone with gearbox mounted vertical torsion bars and horizontally mounted damper units
	on top of the gearbox casing *Wheels:* OZ *Tyres:* Bridgestone Potenza *Brake pads and discs:* Hitco *Brake callipers:* AP Racing
	Radiators: Marston *Fuel tanks:* ATL *Steering:* Renault F1 hydro-mechanical servo system (power assisted)
	Instruments: Renault F1 team
DIMENSIONS	*Length:* 4580mm *Width:* 1800mm *Height:* 1000mm *Wheelbase:* 3110mm
	Formula weight: 605kg, including driver and camera

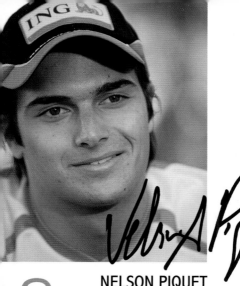

Jean-François Caubet

8 NELSON PIQUET

ROMAIN GROSJEAN

Bob Bell

Rob White

Flavio Briatore

Bernard Rey

Pat Symonds

ING RENAULT F1 TEAM: PERSONNEL

President: Bernard Rey

Managing Director: Jean-François Caubet/
Flavio Briatore *(until September 2009)*

Deputy Managing Director, Engine: Rob White

Technical Director: Bob Bell

Deputy Technical Director: James Allison

Executive Director of Engineering: Pat Symonds
(until September 2009)

Chief Race Engineer: Alan Permane

Chief Designer: Tim Densham

Engine Project Manager: Malcolm Stewart

Head of Aerodynamics: Dirk de Beer

Sporting Manager: Steve Nielson

Chief Mechanic: Gavin Hudson

Race Engineer, Alonso: Simon Rennie

Race Engineer, Piquet/Grosjean: Phil Charles

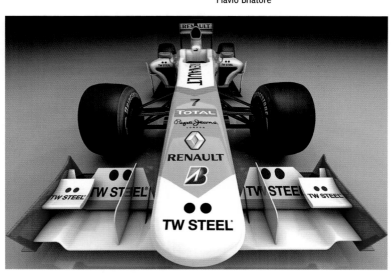

with significant numbers of technical personnel, particularly in the aerodynamic department, anticipating the future resource limit. By the time it became clear that he'd been somewhat over-zealous in his trimming, the new car's gestation was already suffering. Basically, the R29 was under-developed. "It had no particular vices," reported Bell. "It's not hard on its tyres, it's not difficult to get a balance. We can warm the tyres up if they're too cold; if they're too hot, we can put things in place to cool them down. We can do all the things we want to do; it just lacks aero performance."

Briatore's misplaced certainty that the teams would decide not to go ahead with KERS because of the costs involved meant that Renault's programme was started too late. "That's been an enormous frustration," said Bell. "I think by the start of the season, we'd spent about £10m on the project. But Flavio was so strong in his conviction that we only did lip service to its early development. It meant that we had to do it in quite a condensed period in the end. Of all the things I've seen us do in recent years to be proud of, that project is one of them, because although we haven't exploited it very much on the car, the effort that went into getting it on the car, making it as good as anyone else's and to have a system that was completely reliable was a heck of an achievement for the four-person team that did it." Bell left unsaid how much aero development could have been bought for £15m...

Although the system worked well enough, the negative effect it had on the car's dynamics was felt to be roughly the lap time equivalent of the positive benefit of the extra power. With so much else to concentrate on, and the drivers' general dislike of the way the car drove with KERS fitted, it was discarded after Bahrain and only used once more, at Monza.

On average, the car was just over 0.4 second off the ultimate pace, although the trend was definitely in the right direction: it was closer to the pace by the end of the season than at the beginning. Ironically,

the highlight was Alonso's third place in Singapore, but it was a distant third. There was a fastest lap at the Nürburgring as he chased down the tyre-troubled Brawns on a combination of a light fuel load and new rubber late in the race, and there was a fuel weight assisted pole position in Hungary, courtesy of an optimistic three-stop strategy. In general, however, even Alonso hovered on the outer edges of the Q3 cut-off point. Piquet struggled to keep pace and was dismissed after Hungary, triggering the Singapore '08 controversy. His replacement, Romain Grosjean – without the benefit of testing – showed promising speed at times, although he was involved in quite a few car damaging incidents.

As the 2009 season came to an end, Renault faced a new era. Some of the redundant aerodynamicists had been rehired, while Robert Kubica – a driver much in the mould of Alonso – had also been recruited. Everyone concerned was ready to forget the nightmare of 2009.

Above: Fernando Alonso celebrates his only podium appearance of the season at Singapore.

Right: Alonso leads team-mate Romain Grosjean at the season's finale under the lights of the Yas Marina circuit in Abu Dhabi.
Photos: Renault F1 Team

Below right: Night shift. A chassis is prepared for action by Renault mechanics at the Chinese Grand Prix.
Photo: Lukas Gorys

Below: Nelson Piquet emerges from the Melbourne shadows in his Renault. The young Brazlian's unhappy time with the team came to an abrupt end when he was replaced by Romain Grosjean in mid-season.
Photo: Renault F1 Team

PANASONIC TOYOTA TEAM

JARNO TRULL

I N the end, fifth place in the constructors' championship was nowhere near enough to save Panasonic Toyota. Even after storming second places at Singapore and Suzuka, you could sense the disappointment in the attitude of the senior Toyota management, which no longer wanted second places, but wins.

Only three days after the final race in Abu Dhabi, the axe fell. Team principal Tadashi Yamashina sobbed at a press conference in Tokyo as he announced that Toyota was quitting F1. After 139 grands grix, the dream was over.

The basic concept of the TF109 was right: it was equipped with a double diffuser and a front wing that was perfectly configured to give the floor the best airflow possible. This combination of the two crucial 'must-have' features was shared initially only with the Brawn, but the development path followed thereafter was not particularly fruitful. A lock-out of the front row of the grid in Bahrain produced only a 3-7 finish, while the big Barcelona update was removed after inconclusive Friday testing. Subsequently, the team seemed to lose its way somewhat, not re-emerging from the midfield until quite late in the season.

Although its Bahrain qualifying form had been flattered by low fuel loads, the Toyota was genuinely the second fastest car there, and much of the disappointing race result could be put down to the team's choice of tyres for the middle stints of both Jarno Trulli and Timo Glock. Another lost opportunity occurred at Spa, where Trulli qualified on the front row with a heavier fuel load than the pole man and looked to be in a perfect position to win. That prospect died within a few seconds of the start, however, when an electrical malfunction saw him swamped as the gantry lights went out. Between such peaks, the car was an inconsistent performer, seemingly unable to capitalise on a concept that was essentially right for the new regulations from the start.

"We still don't really fully understand the variance in performance," said the team's chassis technical director, Pascal Vasselon. "In Bahrain, we were just not quite fast enough; Button was always that little bit faster. We were scratching our heads on Saturday, trying to work out how we could beat them, and we gambled on the tyre choice, but the reason we didn't win there was our basic performance. After that, we had races where if we'd qualified on the front row, our race pace was such that we would have won: for example, at Budapest and Valencia. But we didn't get the best out of the car in qualifying at those races, and it was so tight this year that if you made a mistake, you were down five or seven places, not one or two."

It seems likely that the variance in performance,

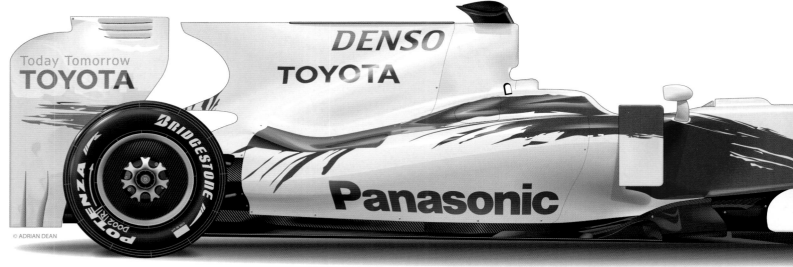

© ADRIAN DEAN

TOYOTA TF109

TITLE SPONSOR	Panasonic
MAJOR SPONSORS	Denso • Bridgestone • EMC² • KDDI • Fill The Cup • Alpinestars • Chiemsee • Dassault Systemes • Deutsche Post DHL Magneti Marelli • MAN • REMAX • Würth • Takata
ENGINE	*Type:* RVX-09 *No of cylinders (vee angle):* V8 (90-deg) *Electronics:* Toyota, Magneti Marelli plus McLaren Electronic Systems ECU (as required by FIA rules) *Valve actuation:* Pneumatic *Throttle actuation:* Hydraulic *Spark Plugs:* DENSO *Fuel:* Esso *Lubricants:* Esso
TRANSMISSION	*Gearbox:* Semi-automatic, sequential electronically controlled quick-shift mechanism *Number of gears:* 7, plus reverse
CHASSIS	*Suspension:* Carbon-fibre double wishbone arrangement, with carbon-fibre trackrod and pushrod *Wheel diameter:* 13in front and rear *Wheels:* BBS *Tyres:* Bridgestone Potenza *Brakes:* Toyota/Brembo callipers, Brembo master cylinders, Hitco material (carbon/carbon)
DIMENSIONS	*Overall length:* 4636mm *Overall height:* 950mm *Overall width:* 1800mm
	Formula weight: 605kg, including driver and camera

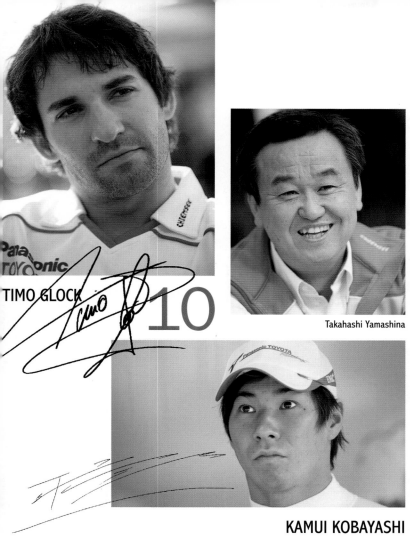

TIMO GLOCK 10

Takahashi Yamashina

KAMUI KOBAYASHI

John Howett

Pascal Vasselon

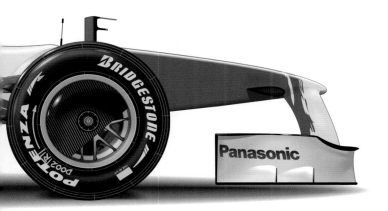

PANASONIC TOYOTA TEAM: PERSONNEL

Chairman and Team Principal: Takahashi Yamashina

General Director: John Howett

Senior General Manager, Chassis: Pascal Vasselon

Senior General Manager, Engine: Kazuo Takeuchi

Director Technical Co-ordination: Noritoshi Arai

Team Manager: Jens Marquardt

Chief Engineer: Dieter Gass

Race Engineer, Trulli: Francesco Nenci/
Juan Pablo Ramirez

Race Engineer, Glock: Gianluca Pisanello

like that suffered by almost every other car in the field, was connected to the sensitivity of the Bridgestone control tyres. Get them working, and they switched on as if by magic. Fail to put enough initial load in them, and they wouldn't reach their working temperature. In this, the Toyota was not unlike the Brawn and Ferrari, but with the added complication that the car seemed ill-suited to slow-speed corners. Like all Toyotas of recent seasons, it retained a very high mounting point for the lower front wishbone. While this was aerodynamically advantageous, the suspension geometry it imposed could cause problems at low speeds.

The car did appear to carry a lot of raw downforce, although the last of it appeared to be less efficient in its cost in drag than on the Brawn or Red Bull. At its best, it was probably the third fastest car after those two, but its narrower operating parameters may have made it less usable than the McLaren and Ferrari.

It was a very peaky car, a condition that did not suit Trulli particularly, since he needed consistency to deliver his best. The fast sweeps of Suzuka suited car and driver well, however, and Trulli emerged on top of a close fight for second with Hamilton, although both were left behind by Vettel's victorious Red Bull. It was in qualifying for this race that Timo Glock was injured after an off at the final corner, which put him out of the final two races. As usual, Glock proved to be more adaptive to the car's inconsistencies, but when it was at its best, he seemed to struggle to get the final couple of tenths from it in qualifying.

Operationally, the team seemed to make some odd decisions, exemplified at Barcelona, where almost everyone had aero update packages on the cars. Toyota tried its new design on Friday, but seemed to be thrown when the results did not tally with what the simulation had suggested. In response, the team removed the update and reverted to the earlier spec, something that left it struggling somewhat on a track that might have been expected to suit it. Some members of the team were adamant that the inconclusive results from that Friday were caused by nothing other than variation in the state of the track, and that the original plan should have been followed.

In general, the team still seemed to be too formally structured in its decision making, hampered by overtones of its corporate background. For Turkey, a further modified upgrade was fitted and this time remained on the car. Essentially, it comprised a modified diffuser, which had a larger central section to give more consistent grip through a wider range of ride heights and a better interaction with the rear beam wing. A series of minor updates followed throughout the year, but none appeared to address the car's basic inconsistency.

Team boss John Howett was convinced that not all of the inconsistency was down to the car, but that the drivers were also to blame. He was openly critical of their performance, and as the season concluded, he was trying to finalise a different driver line-up.

Sadly, decisions taken at a much higher level rendered his deliberations superfluous.

SCUDERIA TORO ROSSO

11

JAIME ALGUERSUARI

SÉBASTIEN BOURDAIS

THE little Toro Rosso team – it numbers little more than 200 people – came back down to earth in 2009 after its giant-killing performances with Sebastian Vettel in 2008. It inherited a very good basic car, the STR 04 being effectively a Ferrari powered Red Bull RB5, but without a driver of Vettel's calibre, and with a combination of no testing and rookie drivers, it was a fairly low-key season. The ban on testing also increased the importance of in-factory development, an area in which the team was ill equipped to compete. That said, Sébastien Buemi was beginning to show the car's potential by the end of the year.

As in previous years, significant work was required to adapt the basic car from Red Bull Technologies to the Ferrari engine. A different fuel system, fuel tank, hydraulic system, clutch and radiators were required, and all this was done at the team's Faenza base. Technical director Giorgio Ascanelli was rightly proud of the speed by which this was accomplished. "We did it in 22 days, from delivery to shipping the cars to Melbourne," he said. "We also this time had differences between the planned KERS installation of the two cars, and even though we never used the KERS, it still impacted on other systems. We were able to keep the same wheelbase as the Red Bull, but we could not match the weight distribution."

It was not possible to place as much weight forward on the Toro Rosso, something that was particularly important in 2009, as the move to slick tyres had more than proportionally increased the front rubber contact path compared to the rear. This had implications on the aerodynamic performance, too, as a forward bias is generally favourable on tracks with high-speed bends, such as Barcelona, Silverstone, Spa and Suzuka.

"We did the first four races with the aero spec that Red Bull launched with, so without the pre-Australia updates," explained Ascanelli. Buemi got in as much mileage as possible pre-season, most of it with the 2008 car, but he impressed on his debut in Australia by comprehensively out-qualifying his more experienced team-mate, Sébastien Bourdais. In the race, the team benefited from the late crash between Kubica and Vettel, which put both cars in the points, Buemi ahead of Bourdais.

In fact, it became something of a pattern that the young Swiss rookie outperformed the experienced Frenchman. In the first nine races, Buemi qualified faster six times, and impressively he got through to Q3 in China, faster than assorted cars from much bigger teams. The more normal early-season situation, however, was both cars failing to graduate from Q1.

Red Bull's initial twin-diffuser floor was not fitted to the Toro Rosso. "It would have involved a major redesign because of the different ancillaries," said

© ADRIAN DEAN

TORO ROSSO STR4

TITLE SPONSOR	Red Bull
MAJOR SPONSORS	Hangar-7 • Bridgestone • Volkswagen • Puma • Advanti • USAG • Magneti Marelli
ENGINE	*Type:* Ferrari V8 Type 056 *No of cylinders (vee angle):* V8 (90-deg) *Electronics:* Magneti Marelli plus McLaren Electronic Systems ECU (as required by FIA rules) *Spark Plugs:* Champion *Fuel:* Shell *Lubricants:* Shell
TRANSMISSION	*Gearbox:* Longitudinally mounted with hydraulic system for power shift and clutch operation *Clutch:* Sachs triple-plate pull type *Number of gears:* 7, plus reverse
CHASSIS	*Suspension:* Upper and lower carbon wishbones, torsion bar springs and anti-roll bars *Dampers:* Sachs *Wheel diameter:* 13in front and rear *Wheels:* Advanti Racing *Tyres:* Bridgestone Potenza *Brakes:* Brembo callipers, Brembo master cylinders
DIMENSIONS	*Overall length:* As regulated *Overall height:* As regulated *Overall width:* As regulated
	Formula weight: 605kg, including driver and camera

12

SÉBASTIEN BUEMI

Below: Untried Spanish youngster Jaime Alguersuari replaced Sébastien Bourdais in mid-season, and did all that was expected of him.
Photo: Peter J. Fox

Giorgio Ascanelli

Gianfranco Fantuzzi

Laurent Mekies

Franz Tost

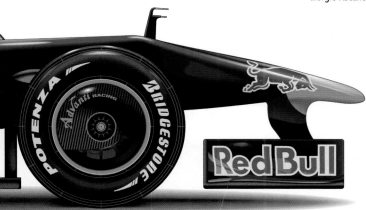

TORO ROSSO: PERSONNEL

Owner: Dietrich Mateschitz

Team Principal: Franz Tost

Technical Director: Giorgio Ascanelli

Chief Engineer: Laurent Mekies

Team Manager: Gianfranco Fantuzzi

Race Engineer, Bourdais/Alguersuari: Claudio Balestri/ Andrea Landi

Race Engineer, Buemi: Riccardo Adami

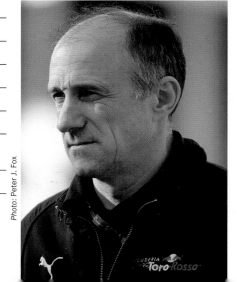

Ascanelli. However, the more highly evolved version, which appeared on the RB5 at Silverstone, together with re-sited axles, was used by Toro Rosso from Hungary onwards. "The Hungary package meant redoing a large part of the hydraulics," explained Ascanelli, "because there was something in the way. Why? Because of the electronics for the KERS." Such programmes robbed the team of the little factory development time it had.

Buemi rewarded the effort of getting the new car ready by qualifying it in a solid 11th place, although he spun away his chances on the first lap of the race. This was the debut of another rookie from the Red Bull roster, Jaime Alguersuari, who had been taken on in place of the dismissed Bourdais, who subsequently would announce a legal action against the team for allegedly breaking the terms of his contract. Bourdais never did gel with the oversteering characteristics of a Formula One car in his season-and-a-half in the category, and his constant attempts at dialling these out with set-up tweaks, rather than simply driving it harder, induced a lot of frustration among the team. Alguersuari acquitted himself reasonably well, given his lack of preparation, but generally was no threat to Buemi, who impressed with his lead-footed enthusiasm.

The car's characteristics were well suited to the fast sweeps of Suzuka, and Buemi was impressively quick on his first visit to the track. But also a little wild. After hitting the Degner barriers hard early in Q2, he proceeded to take the patched-up car around fast enough to qualify for Q3 – but then went off again and earned a grid penalty for causing a hazard by driving the heavily damaged car back to the pits. Two weeks later, he qualified on the third row in Brazil and drove a perfectly mature race to sixth place.

For Ascanelli and the little team in Faenza, the difficulty steps up another gear in 2010, when the rules will no longer permit one team to share a car design with another. "I'm thankful to the ownership that they've done a big investment in computing capacity in terms of CFD," he said. "The whole philosophy of the company has to be changed, because it has to be independent now of Red Bull. You can't use any more the tools that are familiar to you, and we are having to recruit more people, and commissioning and calibrating a wind tunnel. We are doing this while trying to do a new car."

So the struggle continues, but at least in 2009 it was a struggle that had its bright moments.

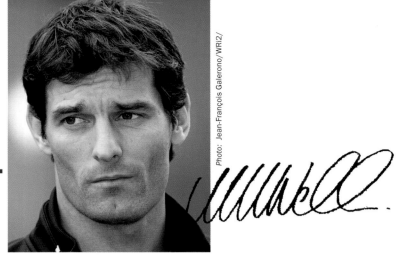

14

MARK WEBBER

15

SEBASTIAN VETTEL

Photo: Jean-François Galerono/WRi2/

Photo: Peter J. Fox

RED BULL RACING

THE new aerodynamic regulations offered a great opportunity for the Red Bull team to make the transition from occasional podium challenger to race winner and ultimately title contender. It was a challenge that was met head-on, with six grand prix victories and a comfortable second place in the constructors' championship.

The team's resident design genius, Adrian Newey, saw the new regs as the ideal opportunity to break the trend of the team always trailing one step behind the bigger teams in the accepted process of constantly modifying a well-honed basic theme. It was an opportunity to beat those teams by out-thinking them on the new aero regs, rather than allowing them to win simply by spending more.

As such, the RB5 was the most radical of all the 2009 cars. Central to its philosophy was the re-introduction of a concept not seen in Formula One for 22 years – pull-rod rear suspension. The new diffuser dimensions specified in the rules created the space to move the suspension rockers from the top to the bottom. This cleared a huge amount of space in the upper bodywork at the rear, creating a vastly wider path for the airflow to the rear beam wing and the top of the diffuser. As a result, there was a greater pressure differential with the air flowing through the diffuser, which effectively drew it out faster, increasing downforce. The benefits of the layout snowballed.

© ADRIAN DEAN

RED BULL RB5

TEAM PARTNERS	Rauch • Trust • Casio • Logwin
INNOVATION PARTNERS	Siemens • Platform Computing • MSC Software • DMG • Hexagon Metrology • USI Italia • Oz Racing •Agie Charmilles
TEAM SUPPLIERS	Renault • Bridgestone • Total • Puma • Sabelt • Nautilus
SUPPLIERS	Magnetti Marelli • P&O Ferries • Singha Beer • VW Commercial Vehicles
ENGINE	*Type:* Renault RS27 – 2009 *No of cylinders:* V8 *Sparking plugs:* Champion *Electronics:* MES, McLaren Electronic Systems
	Fuel: Total *Oil:* Total
TRANSMISSION	*Gearbox:* 7-speed, longitudinally mounted, with hydraulic system for shift and clutch operation
	Clutch: AP Racing
CHASSIS	*Suspension:* Front, aluminium alloy uprights, upper and lower carbon wishbones, pushrods, springs and anti-roll bar
	Rear, aluminium alloy uprights, upper and lower carbon wishbones, pull-rods, springs and anti-roll bar
	Dampers: Multimatic *Wheel diameter:* 13in front and rear *Wheels:* OZ *Tyres:* Bridgestone Potenza.
	Brake pads and discs: Brembo *Brake callipers:* Brembo *Steering:* Red Bull *Radiators:* Marston/Red Bull *Fuel tank:* Red Bull/ATL
DIMENSIONS	*Length:* As regulated by front and rear overhang *Width:* 1800mm
	Formula weight: 605kg, including driver and camera

Above: Sebastian Vettel was dominant at Silverstone, one of four victories for the young German driver in 2009.
Photo: Peter J. Fox

RED BULL RACING: PERSONNEL

Team Owner: Dietrich Mateschitz

Team Principal: Christian Horner

Chief Technical Officer: Adrian Newey

Chief Designer: Rob Marshall

Team Manager: Jonathan Wheatley

Racing Director: Mark Smith

Chief Engineer, Vehicle Performance: Mark Ellis

Head of Engines, Renault: Fabrice Lom

Head of Aerodynamics: Peter Podromou

Chief Test Engineer: Ian Morgan

Race Engineer, Webber: Ciaran Pilbeam

Race Engineer, Vettel: Guillame Rocquelin

Christian Horner

Adrian Newey

Photo: Red Bull Racing

Photo: Red Bull Racing

Fabrice Lom
Photo: Red Bull Racing

Helmut Marko
Photo: Red Bull Racing

As well as a lower centre of gravity (cg), derived from the lower position of the rockers, it enabled the gearbox to be lowered by 15cm compared to the RB4, thus further lowering the cg. The tract of open space formerly occupied by the rockers allowed an aerodynamically profiled upper wishbone to be fully exposed, further increasing downforce.

Up front, the nose was U-shaped in section at the top, inverse U-shaped at the bottom. This got around the regulation that defined the height of the nose's corners while still allowing a smaller surface area. In all, it was an imaginatively conceived design that made all the others look out of date. But it missed one vital trick – the twin diffuser. The fact that the RB5 was the Brawn's closest rival, even in original conventional-diffuser form, says everything about the high quality of the basic aerodynamic design. It was stunningly effective through high-speed corners, even in this form, but less well suited to slow turns. It also had a tendency to overwork its rear tyres on slow-corner tracks; Sebastian Vettel's super-soft tyres were destroyed within just five laps at Monaco.

Once the double-diffuser concept had been ruled legal, there was an ongoing development of the floor and diffuser, together with accompanying changes to the very intricate front wing. The team manufactured a total of 74 front wings during the season, 52 of which were different from each other!

Jonathan Wheatley
Photo: Peter J. Fox

However, there was a basic problem in adopting a twin-diffuser layout for this car – the gearbox and those low-mounted suspension rockers were smack in the way! "It took a while to understand, within the hardware constraints we had, how best to fit the double diffuser on," said Newey. "One of the things we said from the start, once it became apparent that it was legal, was we didn't really have the time or the resources to change the gearbox or the rear suspension." The car's first double diffuser appeared at Monaco, but brought very little benefit because of the mechanical components that were in the way of the revised airflow.

The solution was to move the axle line further back, thereby creating the space for a more effective twin-diffuser airflow. The wheelbase had to remain the same, however, to maintain the forward-biased weight distribution that Newey sought. Consequently, the front axle line was moved back to match. This required a major retuning of the aerodynamics around the new mechanical layout, making it essentially a redesign. The revised car was finally revealed at Silverstone, and so different was the layout that it really merited an 'RB5B' tag. The tunnel figures suggested that it was a full 0.7 second faster than the original.

Around the Northamptonshire track's fast sweeps, the new car was devastatingly effective, and Red Bull trounced the opposition every bit as convincingly as Brawn had done earlier in the season. Vettel took an-

other victory to add to that gained in the wet of China and again was followed home by team-mate Mark Webber. The only difference between the two drivers on this occasion was that Webber had encountered a dawdling Kimi Räikkönen when on his final lap of qualifying, allowing Vettel to take the pole, while Webber started from third.

But those expecting the young German to overshadow the veteran Aussie had plenty of cause to rethink. Despite the latter having broken a leg during the off-season, he frequently raced better – notably in Spain, Monaco and Turkey – but had yet to make the breakthrough to victory. This was corrected with a totally dominant performance at the Nürburgring. Thereafter, he went through a barren patch that did for his championship aspirations.

In part, this was due to the succession of slow-corner tracks that followed the German race, the car showing an unhealthy appetite for rubber again in Hungary, and being just plain ill-suited to Valencia's street circuit. A new front wing for Singapore transformed this aspect of its performance, giving it a more consistent aerodynamic platform that supplied the rear with a more regular airflow. This reduced the sudden spike loadings on the tyres that used up their energy so quickly. "The improvement in tyre use wasn't all aerodynamic though," stressed Newey. "Some of the changes we made then were mechanical as well. The intention of those was to help that aspect, and I think they bore fruit."

Playing a part in the team's lack of form between Webber's Nürburgring victory and Vettel's in Suzuka six races later was engine performance. The Renault unit seemed to lack the mid-range torque of the Mercedes. "Bear in mind that one per cent power, 7bhp, is worth somewhere around 0.13 second per lap," said Newey. "There's lots of conjecture on engine power, and a fair bit of evidence that one manufacturer is significantly ahead of the rest of us, but having said all of that, we were very happy with Renault in terms of the service and relationship."

In the RB5 at least, the Renault was also far less reliable than the Mercedes. Vettel had used up his full season's allocation of eight engines by the Belgian Grand Prix at Spa, and thereafter the team had to mix and match motors that hadn't quite done their full mileage for practice sessions. Their track time was limited for the same reason. By Brazil, Webber was also on his final engine, but that didn't stop him from delivering a convincing victory; the car was clearly the fastest around the sort of bumpy track that might have presented problems in its previous incarnation.

Red Bull succeeded in making the transition from minor-league team to established regular winner in 2009; at its peak, the RB5 was the fastest car in the field, despite not being ideally configured to take advantage of the twin-diffuser concept. As the season came to an end, the challenge was to maintain that momentum for 2010.

WILLIAMS F1 TEAM

16

OR Williams, the 2009 technical regulations did not prove to be the big opportunity the team had hoped for to get back into a winning position. Seventh in the constructors' championship reflected a generally upper midfield performance from the FW31 and its lead driver, Nico Rosberg. There was less variation in performance than with many other cars, and in contrast to recent seasons, the short-fall was not particularly derived from a lack of performance through quick, aerodynamically-demanding corners. It was more a case of lacking a little just about everywhere.

Overall, the Williams team's performance must register as something of a disappointment, given that it was one of only three competitors that had de-signed its car from the start around the twin-diffuser concept. Right from the beginning of the season, the single-diffuser Red Bull was significantly faster, as were the twin-diffuser Brawn and Toyota. That situ-ation never really changed throughout the season, and Williams was further demoted during the second half as McLaren began to come on strong. Only in Malaysia and Singapore were there truly competitive performances. Rosberg led the early stages of the former race, but lost huge amounts of time in the wet to Button's Brawn and others, while at Singapore a good upgrade in combination with Rosberg's dramatic kerb-hopping style put him in a strong second,

until he was thwarted by a drive-through penalty for crossing the pit-lane exit line.

The deficit from the front did not change signifi-cantly through the year, indicating that the team's development programme was competitive, and that, at least, was a source of satisfaction for technical director Sam Michael in a season during which test-ing was banned. "Every single aero part we put on the car worked on the track," he said, "and gave the lap time gains it should have done. In Singapore, we had 2.5 tenths. You can measure the downforce with data and diffuser pressure tappings, and it translated exactly from what the tunnel said."

A major upgrade at Silverstone gained 0.5 second, so the team was somewhat dismayed to find Red Bull a further 0.2 second ahead than before, giving some indication of the effectiveness of the RB5's update. New front and rear wings for Singapore, and a front brake duct that produced more downforce, helped move the car forward on the grid there.

The team pursued two parallel KERS development programmes, one a flywheel type, the other a more conventional battery-based system, although nei-ther was raced. "We got them to a pretty good stage of development," said Michael. "Both of them would be something that if we wanted to we could probably bring to the car, but by the time we'd got them that far it wasn't worth the expense. We

NICO ROSBERG

WILLIAMS-TOYOTA F31

SPONSORS	AT&T • Philips • RBS • Randstad • Accenture • Oris • Thomson Reuters • Air Asia • McGregor • Ridge Solutions • Hell Energy Drinks Allianz • Rays Wheels • MAN • PPG • Sparco
ENGINE	*Type:* Toyota 2.4L *No of cylinders (vee angle):* V8 (90-deg) *Valve train:* Pneumatic *Fuel management and ignition systems:* Toyota Engine materials include block and pistons in aluminium, crankshaft in steel billet, connecting rods in titanium
TRANSMISSION	*Gearbox:* Williams F1 7-speed seamless sequential semi-automatic shift, plus reverse gear, in an aluminium maincase *Gear selection:* Electro-hydraulically actuated *Clutch:* AP Carbon, multi-plate
CHASSIS	*Front suspension:* Carbon-fibre double wishbone arrangement, with composite toelink and pushrod activated springs and anti-roll bar *Rear suspension:* Double wishbone and pushrod activated springs and anti-roll bar *Dampers:* Williams F1 *Wheel diameter:* 350mm front, 375mm rear *Wheels:* RAYS forged magnesium *Tyres:* Bridgestone Potenza *Brakes:* 6-piston AP calipers all round *Discs and pads:* Carbon Industrie *Steering:* Williams F1 power assisted rack and pinion *Chassis electronics:* McLaren MES FIA standard electronic control unit *Cooling:* Marston/Williams F1 oil, water and gearbox
DIMENSIONS	*Length:* 4800mm *Width:* 1800mm *Height:* 950mm *Wheelbase:* 3100mm *Formula weight:* 605kg, including driver and camera

KAZUKI NAKAJIMA

17

Sir Frank Williams

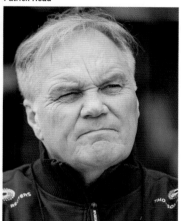

Patrick Head

Above: Lead driver Nico Rosberg spearheaded the team's hopes – and scored all its points.
Photos: Peter J. Fox

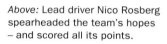

Sam Michael

Tim Newton

WILLIAMS F1 TEAM: PERSONNEL

Team Principal: Sir Frank Williams

Director of Engineering: Patrick Head

Chief Executive: Adam Parr

Technical Director: Sam Michael

Chief Operating Officer: Alex Burns

Chief Designer: Ed Wood

Head of Aerodynamics: Jon Tomlinson

Chief Operations Engineer: Rod Nelson

Team Manager: Tim Newton

Race Engineer, Rosberg: Tony Ross

Race Engineer, Nakajima: Xevi Pujolar

Photos: Peter J. Fox

Above: The Williams team poses for a mid-season photograph at the Hungaroring.
Photo: Jad Sherif/WRi2

Top right: The Williams F31 had a double diffuser from the start of the season.
Photo: Jean-François Galeron/WRi2

Above centre right: The suspension and gearbox assembly.
Photo: Jad Sherif/WRi2

Right: Mechanics busy themselves around Kazuki Nakajima's car.
Photo: Peter J. Fox

were limited by resource, and we could either do that or pursue the aero programme."

This was a reflection of the general level of staff trimming that had been going on throughout Formula One as the recession hit and the teams planned for the obligatory resource restriction from 2010. From approaching 700 people at its peak, Williams was down to around 490.

In the main, the reasonable haul of points was derived from excellent mechanical reliability and sufficient pace to get into the lower points paying positions, which Rosberg did consistently. "Back in 2006, we had horrific reliability," said Michael, "with 20 DNFs, 11 of them mechanical. That hurt so much that it forced us to look at our quality control and engineering systems, and we've put a lot into place on that over the last three years. We're a bit smarter now and don't tend to design ourselves into corners. We've made sure the designers leave enough room for things that are hot, etc." Reliability from the Toyota engines was also excellent, although there was a general feeling throughout the paddock that almost everyone's engines were down on the performance of the Mercedes in the Brawns, McLarens and Force Indias.

Second driver Kazuki Nakajima – part of the Toyota engine supply deal – failed to score points, despite generally closing the deficit to Rosberg compared to 2008, when he was an occasional scorer. "I think that's just a reflection of how much tighter it all was this year," said Michael, "because in his delta to Nico and his general contribution, he was definitely better than last year."

The two low-downforce tracks of Spa and Monza proved particularly poorly suited to the car and gave the team its two least competitive outings of the season. At Monza, it failed even to get out of Q1. "We didn't put a lot of development into our low-downforce wing," explained Michael. "If you go back three [or] four years ago, there were 16 races, four of them low-drag: Monza, Spa, Indy and Montreal. Now there are 17 with only two low-drag, so the percentage shifts massively. Every race is important, but we had the choice of doing another iteration on the Spa and Monza package or doing something for Singapore that we thought would work for all the last four races. So we took the decision to put everything into that package.

"In the last few seasons, we have been pretty poor on high-speed tracks, whereas this year we've been relatively good on them, and still stayed good on street circuits. When you analyse things like that, it's extremely difficult internally to work out why other people are strong and weak. I remember in 2003 when Williams and Ferrari were fighting, and you'd go to some tracks knowing Ferrari were going to be better, and we'd go to others and you'd know you were going to be stronger than them. We've had people come from Ferrari to Williams, and we'd say to them, 'How would you do this?', and they'd do exactly the opposite to us. And they'll pull themselves to bits trying to work out why they were so bad on these tracks, in the same way as we were doing on the others. It's still like that. On a street track, we could expect to beat Red Bull, but they would thrash us at Silverstone."

Giving some indication of just how tight the performance spread was in 2009, the Williams averaged just over 0.3 second off the ultimate pace through the season. Given such small margins, it is not surprising that the team was looking for a change of engine and driver line-up to close that gap.

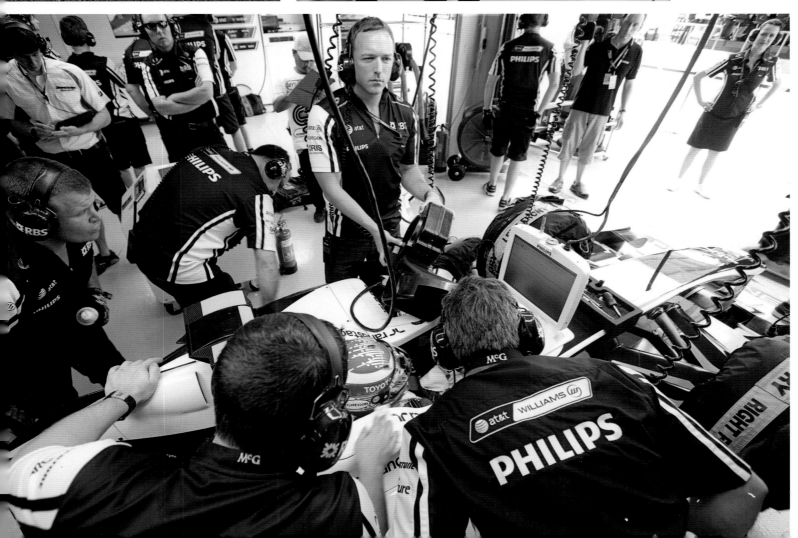

FORCE INDIA F1 TEAM

ALTHOUGH the little team scored only 13 points, Force India's impact upon the latter half of the season was out of all proportion to that standing. The team had emerged re-energised from a new association with Mercedes and McLaren, and with the regulations moving towards the limited-resource manner in which the team has always worked, the VJM 02 became a serious contender, setting pole and finishing second at Spa, and starting from the front row at Monza. Even away from the specialised demands of these two low-downforce tracks, it showed a good turn of speed.

This was all the more remarkable, given the lateness of the Mercedes/McLaren deal. The team would receive a supply of Mercedes engines in place of the previously used Ferraris (making Mercedes the ninth engine supplier to the team in all its incarnations, going right back to Jordan's entry in 1991), and with the motors came McLaren gearboxes. A senior McLaren engineer, Simon Roberts, was also part of the package, being seconded as chief operating officer of the team. This deal came in the wake of the dismissal of former technical chief Mike Gascoyne.

James Key remained as technical director, with Mark Smith as design director and Simon Philips as chief of aerodynamics. They oversaw a frantic adaptation of a car that had been designed for the Ferrari engine and KERS system. "The architecture of the Mercedes engine was totally different, and that impacted on the whole rear end of the car, as did the different KERS and the McLaren box," said Key. "We retained the tub, but the changes impacted on the body surfaces of the whole car. The whole rear of the car had to be raised to fit the gearbox and accommodate the KERS. The team did a fantastic job to have it ready in such a short space of time, but it meant we were always basically one development step behind, which was why we didn't see the real performance potential of the car until later in the season."

This came in the wake of redundancies as the test team was disbanded, reducing the staff level to around 260. With the gearbox and associated hydraulics coming as a complete package from an outside supplier, staff from that department were reallocated, too, but generally the no-testing regulations and the tighter budgets being set at the bigger teams moved the general environment towards the way in which this small team has always worked. Therefore, Force India was quite well placed to thrive in the new, more-cost-conscious Formula One.

The car was characterised by a high nose with under-chassis barge boards to guide the airflow from the front wing to the sidepods. The rear-view mirrors doubled as flow conditioners, directing the airflow to the tops of the sidepods in a way that reduced the lift generated in that region. There was a neat, McLaren-

ADRIAN SUTIL

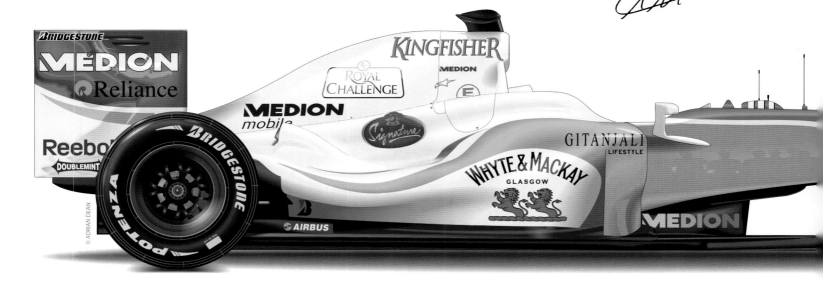

© ADRIAN DEAN

FORCE INDIA VJM02

MAJOR SPONSORS	Kingfisher • Medion • Alpinestars • Whyte & Mackay • Royal Challenge • Reliance • EADS • Airbus • Fly Kingfisher • Signature Doublemint
ENGINE	*Type:* Mercedes-Benz FO108W *No of cylinders (vee angle):* V8 (90-deg) *Electronics:* McLaren Electronic Systems ECU (as required by FIA rules) *Spark Plugs:* NGK *Fuel:* Mobil1 *Lubricants:* Mobil1
TRANSMISSION	Gearbox: McLaren Racing 7-speed, semi-automatic, 'e-shift' *Clutch:* AP Racing carbon-carbon multi-plate *Number of gears:* 7, plus reverse
CHASSIS	*Front suspension:* Aluminium MMC uprights with carbon-fibre composite wishbones, trackrod and pushrod Inboard chassis mounted torsion springs, dampers and anti-roll bar assembly *Rear suspension:* Aluminium MMC uprights with carbon-fibre composite wishbones, trackrod and pushrod; Inboard gearbox mounted torsion springs, dampers and anti-roll bar assembly *Dampers:* Penske *Wheel diameter:* 13in front and rear *Wheels:* Forged to Force India specification *Tyres:* Bridgestone Potenza *Brakes:* Brembo callipers, Brembo master cylinders
DIMENSIONS	*Overall length:* 4900mm *Overall width:* 1800mm *Overall height:* 950mm *Wheelbase:* 3200mm Track: front 1480mm, rear 1420mm *Formula weight:* 605kg, including driver and camera

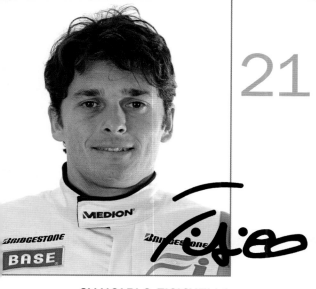

GIANCARLO FISICHELLA

TONIO LIUZZI

FORCE INDIA F1 TEAM: PERSONNEL

Chairman and Team Principal: Dr Vijay Mallya

Co-owner: Michiel Mol

Team Director and Deputy Team Principal: Bob Fernley

Chief Operating Officer: Otmar Szafnauer

Project Leader: Akio Haga

Technical Director: James Key

Design Director: Mark Smith

Head of Aerodynamics: Simon Phillips

Team Manager: Andy Stevenson

Chief Race Engineer: Dominic Harlow

Race Engineer, Sutil: Jody Egginton

Race Engineer, Fisichella/Liuzzi: Bradley Joyce

Vijay Mallya

James Key

Mark Smith

All portrait photos: Force India F1 Team

Otmar Szafnauer (left) succeeded Simon Roberts as CEO

Top: Adrian Sutil was very close to securing a podium at Monza for the team, narrowly losing out to Räikkönen's Ferrari.
Photo: Peter J. Fox

like, undercut engine airbox, which reduced the spillage of air to the benefit of the rear wing. Key had targeted a much lower drag number than the previous car, and the highly impressive speed-trap figures through the season tended to confirm that this had been achieved.

There was general admiration for the job done at such short notice by such a small group of people in just getting the cars to the grid in Melbourne, and when Giancarlo Fisichella and Adrian Sutil qualified 18th and 19th, around 1.5 seconds off the pace of the Brawns, it seemed that the team was set for another season at or near the back. But actually, it had barely begun to scratch at the car's potential, having lost around a month's development work while the car had been adapted.

The first signs of improvement came in Bahrain, two races later, when Force India was the first single-diffuser team to respond to the double-diffuser ruling with both cars. "We'd looked at it before," said Key, "but weren't convinced it would be allowed. But we had done a bit of a study and so that gave us a bit of a head start, and we didn't wait for the ruling. As soon as we saw the Williams and Toyota, we got to work on it." This briefly moved the cars closer to Q2 before they sank back down again at Barcelona as the other teams installed their first major upgrade packages. Tellingly, although Force India lined up on the back row for that race, the deficit to the fastest car in Q1 was just one second. Therefore, it was not going to take that much of an improvement to move it up significantly.

That improvement came at Silverstone, but it was disguised when Sutil crashed heavily with a brake problem just as he was about to complete a lap that would have put him comfortably through to Q2. Red flags for his incident also spoiled a sure-fire Q2 lap from Fisichella. The update comprised a much more complex, Brawn-like front wing and associated changes to the floor. "Actually, the double diffuser did us a favour on two fronts. As well as the extra downforce it gave in itself, it also energised the front end of the car. We'd been struggling getting the front end of the car to respond to changes we were trying in the tunnel, but as soon as we got the double diffuser working, suddenly the front began to really work."

Sutil's noted wet-weather skills were the major factor in placing the car seventh on the grid at the Nürburgring, but two races later, at Valencia, a further aero upgrade put the car in genuinely interesting territory. "The tunnel was telling us that was worth in the order of 0.7 second, so we were starting to get quite excited by this point," related Key. Sutil got the car comfortably through to Q2. The big aero jump came largely from an earlier decision that the team would not run KERS, so the space in the sidepods reserved for the components could be saved. Much tighter sidepods allowed more of the airflow to find its way over the diffuser, thereby giving it a more powerful scavenging effect.

As the circus moved to the low-downforce demands of Spa and Monza, the revised car – already very good in the low-drag part of its aero map – truly came alive. The first-lap safety car probably denied Fisichella a victory there, but second was a terrific achievement. At Monza, Sutil only narrowly missed making it two consecutive Force India poles, while at conventional tracks, the car was still quick, Sutil making it to fourth and third on the grid in Suzuka and Interlagos.

"The performance improvement has come from the aero group," said Key. "Simon Roberts has done a fantastic job in co-ordinating the Mercedes and McLaren side of things, and has helped get the whole place running very efficiently. The Mercedes is clearly a good engine, too. But the thing that has found us the extra performance through the season has been Force India's own aero group, and we're immensely proud of that."

Above: The team celebrates Giancarlo Fisichella's second-place finish at Spa-Francorchamps.

Above left: Tonio Liuzzi replaced the Ferrari-bound Fisichella at Monza and seemed well placed for a points finish before a gearbox failure caused his retirement.

Left: A great moment for the team as 'Fisi' convincingly leads the Belgian Grand Prix on the opening lap of the race.
Photos: Force India F1 Team

22

JENSON BUTTON

23

RUBENS BARRICHELLO

BRAWN GP

FOR Brawn GP to achieve the world constructors' and drivers' championships in its first season of existence was a unique feat in the sport's history. There were more aspects than just that to the fairytale, however, as the team was only formed at the 11th hour from the ashes of Honda F1 in the wake of the Japanese manufacturer's shock withdrawal in late November 2008. For a time, it looked like the team would go under, but with some help from Honda, team principal Ross Brawn led a management buy-out. Honda's help did not extend to a continuing supply of engines, and it took the assistance of the team body FOTA, and particularly that of McLaren, to source a supply of Mercedes engines. This was only concluded in February, by which time all the other teams were well into their test programmes. It was against this background that the team showed up for the last week of testing in Barcelona and stunned everyone by immediately moving the goalposts of performance by almost a second per lap.

For Brawn, this wasn't quite as much of a shock as for its rivals. When Honda had taken over Super Aguri in late 2007, it had inherited a small aero group headed by Ben Wood. Ross Brawn gave this group the task of configuring a car for the all-new 2009 aero regulations, and shortly after there were indications that it was on a very fruitful path, as the team principal recalled: "It quickly became clear from our

studies with this car that the target downforce levels the overtaking working group were setting were going to be exceeded. So during 2008, I said that we should revise the rules again, and maybe simplify a few things, particularly the underbody. The numbers I was seeing already, with some anticipation of where we were going to get to, made me think that we were going to exceed those targets." It's now a matter of ironic record that two of the other teams – Renault and BMW – blocked this suggestion, thereby opening the door to the twin-diffuser concept.

This was a central part of the car's aerodynamic philosophy. Like its counterparts at Williams and Toyota, the Honda aero group realised that with the diffuser moving forward under the new regs, and its exit being lowered, there was a lot more potential in a previously unfruitful interpretation of the reference plane/step plane wording in place since the mid-1990s. The regs said no holes in either floor surface, but if you considered them as two separate surfaces, there was nothing to stop you having a gap in the transition between them. That gap could be used to direct the airflow above the nominal diffuser tunnel and out the back, which would give significant downforce if the underside of the rear crash structure was formed into a diffuser-like ramp with a higher angle than the 'official' one. The linking of the slots to the underside of the crash structure rendered the 'official' diffuser sup-

BRAWN GP001

MAJOR SPONSORS	Bridgestone • MIG • Virgin • Henri Lloyd • Graham • Perkin Elmer
ENGINE	*Type:* Mercedes-Benz FO108W *No of cylinders (vee angle):* V8 (90-deg) *Electronics:* McLaren Electronic Systems ECU (as required by FIA rules) *Spark Plugs:* NGK *Fuel:* Mobil1 High Performance Unleaded *Lubricants:* Mobil1
TRANSMISSION	*Gearbox:* McLaren Racing 7-speed, semi-automatic, 'e-shift' *Clutch:* Sachs, carbon multi-plate *Number of gears:* 7, plus reverse
CHASSIS	*Front and rear suspension:* Wishbone & pushrod activated torsion springs & rockers *Dampers:* Sachs *Wheel diameter:* 360mm front and rear *Wheels:* BBS forged magnesium *Tyres:* Bridgestone Potenza *Radiators:* Marston *Fuel tank:* ATL *Instruments:* Carbon-fibre construction
DIMENSIONS	*Overall length:* 4700mm *Overall width:* 1800mm *Overall height:* 950mm
	Formula weight: 605kg, including driver and camera

Above: Button finished the season on a high note with a podium place in Abu Dhabi.

Below: Barrichello is chaired by his crew following his victory in Valencia.

Photos: Peter J. Fox

Ross Brawn

Nick Fry

Photo portraits: Peter J. Fox

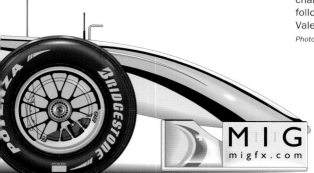

BRAWN GP: PERSONNEL

Team Principal: Ross Brawn

Chief Executive Officer: Nick Fry

Sporting Director: Ron Meadows

Head of Aerodynamics: Loic Bigois

Head of Vehicle Engineering & Dynamics: Craig Wilson

Operations Director: Gary Savage

Design Manager: Russell Cooley

Chief Race Engineer: Simon Cole

Senior Race Engineer, Button: Andrew Shovlin

Senior Race Engineer, Barrichello: Jock Clear

plementary to this one. It went way beyond the intent of the regulations, but Brawn and others believed it was made legal by the wording – wording that Ross himself had suggested needed tidying up.

But the effectiveness of the Brawn BGP001 was due to much more than just the twin diffuser. Under the 2009 regs, which standardised the front wing's central section, the endplate treatment was crucial in feeding the floor with the necessary airflow to make the twin diffuser work properly. In this, the car was the beneficiary of huge resource spread over a longer gestation period than any other 2009 car, given that it was initiated in 2007 and benefited from the very early cessation of development of the hopeless 2008 Honda. A vast amount of attention had been given to compliances in mechanical components, particularly the suspension at the hubs and tub attachment points; the whole structure was much stiffer than the overly-flexible 2008 car.

All of which made the sudden pull-out even more frustrating. The team knew from the numbers that it had a great car, and also from the pace its rivals were setting during winter testing. "They weren't going as fast as we believed they should have been if they had the figures we were seeing from our car in the tunnel," said Ross Brawn.

Ironically, Honda's pull-out ended up gifting what was the best car with the best engine. The Honda unit was generally acknowledged as the weakest of the 2008 engines, the Mercedes as the best. However, adapting the car to the German engine was not without its problems. "It was a bit crude," said Ross. "We

cut the back of the chassis off and bonded on a new rear bulkhead with different engine mounts. We went the Mercedes route because it was very close to the Honda's architecture. The Ferrari, for example, had a very low front top engine mount, which would really have been in the middle of nowhere on our car. Probably the biggest deficiency was the fact that we had to lift up the rear suspension and gearbox by about 6mm because the output shaft of the engine and input shaft of the gearbox were different heights. The Honda crankshaft was lower, so we've been living with an assembly that's about 6mm too high all year and had to do various mods to deal with that." These ad-hoc solutions added around 8kg of weight to the car and, in the process, made the decision not to pursue a KERS programme yet easier.

Although it was all hands to the pump to ready two cars for the start of the season, the harsh financial reality was that the team could not continue with a staff level in excess of 650 at the Brackley factory, so once the team was up and running, and the cars had been built, 250 were made redundant. The desperate need to avoid the disruption of damaged cars also made it an easy decision for Ross Brawn not to go ahead with the Honda plan of employing a rookie, so the Jenson Button/Rubens Barrichello line-up was retained. This was vindicated with a 1-3 in the drivers' championship, achieved with a total of just three chassis all year.

The other teams were already catching up by the time the season kicked off in Melbourne, where the Brawns were 'only' around 0.7 second faster than the

opposition, still enough to give the team a historic 1-2 on its debut – and race winner Button put himself in a championship lead that he would retain for the rest of the season to win the title in his tenth year in Formula One. In fact, of the first seven races, it was only in the pouring rain of China that he was beaten – by the two Red Bulls that were much more suited to the conditions. Having never tested in the rain because of its late start, the team had no knowledge of the aero balance the car needed in the wet, and subsequently it was found that the front wing was very ineffective when running a low flap angle. Accordingly, this was corrected.

Button's most resounding victory came in Turkey, although ironically it was his last, as through the second half of the season, the Brawn's Achilles heel was revealed: it had a dislike of cool track temperatures. This was the other side of the coin that had allowed it to look after its tyres so fantastically well in the hot races. In the cool of Silverstone and Hockenheim – and even the relative warmth of Hungary – the tyres were around 20°C shy of their minimum working temperature of 80°C, and suddenly the car was nowhere.

Barrichello's more aggressive style was able to overcome this drawback slightly better than Button's silky smoothness. This, coupled with some errors in qualifying from the Brit due to pressure, saw the Brazilian launch a counterattack, with victories in Valencia and Monza. It wasn't enough though, and with an aggressive drive from another pressure-compromised qualifying place in Brazil, Button sealed the title.

Left: Fry's Brazilian delight! Nick Fry embraces Norbert Haug of Mercedes-Benz after Button's championship is finally achieved at Interlagos.
Photo: Studio Colombo/WRi2

Far left: Rubens Barrichello overcame early-season uncertainty to become a formidable challenger to his Brawn GP team-mate.

Below: Button celebrates his victory in Malaysia – just one of his six wins in a momentous year.

Bottom: Brawn's double diffuser gave the team a crucial early-season advantage
Photos: Peter J. Fox

CHASSIS LOGBOOK 2009

COMPILED BY DAVID HAYHOE

1 AUSTRALIA

McLAREN-MERCEDES		
1	Lewis Hamilton	MP4-24/04
2	Heikki Kovalainen	MP4-24/03
FERRARI		
3	Felipe Massa	F60/275
4	Kimi Räikkönen	F60/276
BMW SAUBER-BMW		
5	Robert Kubica	F1.09/03
6	Nick Heidfeld	F1.09/04
RENAULT		
7	Fernando Alonso	R29/03
8	Nelsinho Piquet	R29/01
TOYOTA		
9	Jarno Trulli	TF109/04
10	Timo Glock	TF109/03
TORO ROSSO-FERRARI		
11	Sébastien Bourdais	STR04/02
12	Sébastien Buemi	STR04/01
RED BULL-RENAULT		
14	Mark Webber	RB5/2
15	Sebastian Vettel	RB5/3
WILLIAMS-TOYOTA		
16	Nico Rosberg	FW31/03
17	Kazuki Nakajima	FW31/04
FORCE INDIA-MERCEDES		
20	Adrian Sutil	VJM02/03
21	Giancarlo Fisichella	VJM02/01
BRAWN-MERCEDES		
22	Jenson Button	BGP 001/02
23	Rubens Barrichello	BGP 001/01

2 MALAYSIA

McLAREN-MERCEDES		
1	Lewis Hamilton	MP4-24/04
2	Heikki Kovalainen	MP4-24/03
FERRARI		
3	Felipe Massa	F60/275
4	Kimi Räikkönen	F60/276
BMW SAUBER-BMW		
5	Robert Kubica	F1.09/05
6	Nick Heidfeld	F1.09/04
RENAULT		
7	Fernando Alonso	R29/03
8	Nelsinho Piquet	R29/01
TOYOTA		
9	Jarno Trulli	TF109/04
10	Timo Glock	TF109/05
TORO ROSSO-FERRARI		
11	Sébastien Bourdais	STR04/02
12	Sébastien Buemi	STR04/01
RED BULL-RENAULT		
14	Mark Webber	RB5/2
15	Sebastian Vettel	RB5/1
WILLIAMS-TOYOTA		
16	Nico Rosberg	FW31/03
17	Kazuki Nakajima	FW31/04
FORCE INDIA-MERCEDES		
20	Adrian Sutil	VJM02/03
21	Giancarlo Fisichella	VJM02/01
BRAWN-MERCEDES		
22	Jenson Button	BGP 001/02
23	Rubens Barrichello	BGP 001/01

3 CHINA

McLAREN-MERCEDES		
1	Lewis Hamilton	MP4-24/04
2	Heikki Kovalainen	MP4-24/03
FERRARI		
3	Felipe Massa	F60/275
4	Kimi Räikkönen	F60/276
BMW SAUBER-BMW		
5	Robert Kubica	F1.09/05
6	Nick Heidfeld	F1.09/04
RENAULT		
7	Fernando Alonso	R29/03
8	Nelsinho Piquet	R29/01
TOYOTA		
9	Jarno Trulli	TF109/04
10	Timo Glock	TF109/05
TORO ROSSO-FERRARI		
11	Sébastien Bourdais	STR04/02
12	Sébastien Buemi	STR04/01
RED BULL-RENAULT		
14	Mark Webber	RB5/2
15	Sebastian Vettel	RB5/1
WILLIAMS-TOYOTA		
16	Nico Rosberg	FW31/03
17	Kazuki Nakajima	FW31/04
FORCE INDIA-MERCEDES		
20	Adrian Sutil	VJM02/03
21	Giancarlo Fisichella	VJM02/01
BRAWN-MERCEDES		
22	Jenson Button	BGP 001/02
23	Rubens Barrichello	BGP 001/01

4 BAHRAIN

McLAREN-MERCEDES		
1	Lewis Hamilton	MP4-24/04
2	Heikki Kovalainen	MP4-24/03
FERRARI		
3	Felipe Massa	F60/275
4	Kimi Räikkönen	F60/276
BMW SAUBER-BMW		
5	Robert Kubica	F1.09/05
6	Nick Heidfeld	F1.09/04
RENAULT		
7	Fernando Alonso	R29/03
8	Nelsinho Piquet	R29/01
TOYOTA		
9	Jarno Trulli	TF109/06
10	Timo Glock	TF109/05
TORO ROSSO-FERRARI		
11	Sébastien Bourdais	STR04/02
12	Sébastien Buemi	STR04/01
RED BULL-RENAULT		
14	Mark Webber	RB5/2
15	Sebastian Vettel	RB5/1
WILLIAMS-TOYOTA		
16	Nico Rosberg	FW31/03
17	Kazuki Nakajima	FW31/04
FORCE INDIA-MERCEDES		
20	Adrian Sutil	VJM02/03
21	Giancarlo Fisichella	VJM02/01
BRAWN-MERCEDES		
22	Jenson Button	BGP 001/02
23	Rubens Barrichello	BGP 001/01

RED BULL RB5

Photo: Red Bull Racing

McLAREN MP4-24

Photos: Vodafone McLaren Mercedes

5 SPAIN

McLAREN-MERCEDES

1	Lewis Hamilton	MP4-24/05
2	Heikki Kovalainen	MP4-24/02

FERRARI

3	Felipe Massa	F60/275
4	Kimi Räikkönen	F60/279

BMW SAUBER-BMW

5	Robert Kubica	F1.09/03
6	Nick Heidfeld	F1.09/06

RENAULT

7	Fernando Alonso	R29/04
8	Nelsinho Piquet	R29/01

TOYOTA

9	Jarno Trulli	TF109/06
10	Timo Glock	TF109/05

TORO ROSSO-FERRARI

11	Sébastien Bourdais	STR04/02
12	Sébastien Buemi	STR04/01

RED BULL-RENAULT

14	Mark Webber	RB5/2
15	Sebastian Vettel	RB5/1

WILLIAMS-TOYOTA

16	Nico Rosberg	FW31/03
17	Kazuki Nakajima	FW31/02

FORCE INDIA-MERCEDES

20	Adrian Sutil	VJM02/03
21	Giancarlo Fisichella	VJM02/04

BRAWN-MERCEDES

22	Jenson Button	BGP 001/02
23	Rubens Barrichello	BGP 001/01

6 MONACO

McLAREN-MERCEDES

1	Lewis Hamilton	MP4-24/04
2	Heikki Kovalainen	MP4-24/02

FERRARI

3	Felipe Massa	F60/276
4	Kimi Räikkönen	F60/279

BMW SAUBER-BMW

5	Robert Kubica	F1.09/03
6	Nick Heidfeld	F1.09/06

RENAULT

7	Fernando Alonso	R29/04
8	Nelsinho Piquet	R29/01

TOYOTA

9	Jarno Trulli	TF109/06
10	Timo Glock	TF109/05

TORO ROSSO-FERRARI

11	Sébastien Bourdais	STR04/01
12	Sébastien Buemi	STR04/03

RED BULL-RENAULT

14	Mark Webber	RB5/2
15	Sebastian Vettel	RB5/1

WILLIAMS-TOYOTA

16	Nico Rosberg	FW31/03
17	Kazuki Nakajima	FW31/04

FORCE INDIA-MERCEDES

20	Adrian Sutil	VJM02/01
21	Giancarlo Fisichella	VJM02/04

BRAWN-MERCEDES

22	Jenson Button	BGP 001/02
23	Rubens Barrichello	BGP 001/01

7 TURKEY

McLAREN-MERCEDES

1	Lewis Hamilton	MP4-24/04
2	Heikki Kovalainen	MP4-24/03

FERRARI

3	Felipe Massa	F60/276
4	Kimi Räikkönen	F60/279

BMW SAUBER-BMW

5	Robert Kubica	F1.09/03
6	Nick Heidfeld	F1.09/06

RENAULT

7	Fernando Alonso	R29/04
8	Nelsinho Piquet	R29/01

TOYOTA

9	Jarno Trulli	TF109/06
10	Timo Glock	TF109/05

TORO ROSSO-FERRARI

11	Sébastien Bourdais	STR04/01
12	Sébastien Buemi	STR04/03

RED BULL-RENAULT

14	Mark Webber	RB5/2
15	Sebastian Vettel	RB5/1

WILLIAMS-TOYOTA

16	Nico Rosberg	FW31/03
17	Kazuki Nakajima	FW31/04

FORCE INDIA-MERCEDES

20	Adrian Sutil	VJM02/01
21	Giancarlo Fisichella	VJM02/04

BRAWN-MERCEDES

22	Jenson Button	BGP 001/02
23	Rubens Barrichello	BGP 001/01

8 GREAT BRITAIN

McLAREN-MERCEDES

1	Lewis Hamilton	MP4-24/04
2	Heikki Kovalainen	MP4-24/02

FERRARI

3	Felipe Massa	F60/277
4	Kimi Räikkönen	F60/279

BMW SAUBER-BMW

5	Robert Kubica	F1.09/03
6	Nick Heidfeld	F1.09/06

RENAULT

7	Fernando Alonso	R29/04
8	Nelsinho Piquet	R29/01

TOYOTA

9	Jarno Trulli	TF109/06
10	Timo Glock	TF109/05

TORO ROSSO-FERRARI

11	Sébastien Bourdais	STR04/01
12	Sébastien Buemi	STR04/03

RED BULL-RENAULT

14	Mark Webber	RB5/2
15	Sebastian Vettel	RB5/4

WILLIAMS-TOYOTA

16	Nico Rosberg	FW31/03
17	Kazuki Nakajima	FW31/04

FORCE INDIA-MERCEDES

20	Adrian Sutil	VJM02/01
		(VJM02/03 – Fri/Sat)
21	Giancarlo Fisichella	VJM02/04

BRAWN-MERCEDES

22	Jenson Button	BGP 001/02
23	Rubens Barrichello	BGP 001/01

9 GERMANY

	McLAREN-MERCEDES	
1	Lewis Hamilton	MP4-24/04
2	Heikki Kovalainen	MP4-24/03
	FERRARI	
3	Felipe Massa	F60/277
4	Kimi Räikkönen	F60/279
	BMW SAUBER-BMW	
5	Robert Kubica	F1.09/03
6	Nick Heidfeld	F1.09/06
	RENAULT	
7	Fernando Alonso	R29/04
8	Nelsinho Piquet	R29/03
	TOYOTA	
9	Jarno Trulli	TF109/06
10	Timo Glock	TF109/05
	TORO ROSSO-FERRARI	
11	Sébastien Bourdais	STR04/01
12	Sébastien Buemi	STR04/03
	RED BULL-RENAULT	
14	Mark Webber	RB5/2
15	Sebastian Vettel	RB5/4
	WILLIAMS-TOYOTA	
16	Nico Rosberg	FW31/03
17	Kazuki Nakajima	FW31/04
	FORCE INDIA-MERCEDES	
20	Adrian Sutil	VJM02/01
21	Giancarlo Fisichella	VJM02/04
	BRAWN-MERCEDES	
22	Jenson Button	BGP 001/02
23	Rubens Barrichello	BGP 001/01

10 HUNGARY

	McLAREN-MERCEDES	
1	Lewis Hamilton	MP4-24/04
2	Heikki Kovalainen	MP4-24/03
	FERRARI	
3	Felipe Massa	F60/277
4	Kimi Räikkönen	F60/279
	BMW SAUBER-BMW	
5	Robert Kubica	F1.09/04
6	Nick Heidfeld	F1.09/06
	RENAULT	
7	Fernando Alonso	R29/04
8	Nelsinho Piquet	R29/03
	TOYOTA	
9	Jarno Trulli	TF109/06
10	Timo Glock	TF109/05
	TORO ROSSO-FERRARI	
11	Jaime Alguersuari	STR04/02
12	Sébastien Buemi	STR04/03
	RED BULL-RENAULT	
14	Mark Webber	RB5/2
15	Sebastian Vettel	RB5/4
	WILLIAMS-TOYOTA	
16	Nico Rosberg	FW31/03
17	Kazuki Nakajima	FW31/04
	FORCE INDIA-MERCEDES	
20	Adrian Sutil	VJM02/01
21	Giancarlo Fisichella	VJM02/04
	BRAWN-MERCEDES	
22	Jenson Button	BGP 001/02
23	Rubens Barrichello	BGP 001/01

11 EUROPE

	McLAREN-MERCEDES	
1	Lewis Hamilton	MP4-24/05
2	Heikki Kovalainen	MP4-24/03
	FERRARI	
3	Luca Badoer	F60/280
4	Kimi Räikkönen	F60/279
	BMW SAUBER-BMW	
5	Robert Kubica	F1.09/08
6	Nick Heidfeld	F1.09/07
	RENAULT	
7	Fernando Alonso	R29/04
8	Romain Grosjean	R29/03
	TOYOTA	
9	Jarno Trulli	TF109/06
10	Timo Glock	TF109/05
	TORO ROSSO-FERRARI	
11	Jaime Alguersuari	STR04/02
12	Sébastien Buemi	STR04/03
	RED BULL-RENAULT	
14	Mark Webber	RB5/3
15	Sebastian Vettel	RB5/1
	WILLIAMS-TOYOTA	
16	Nico Rosberg	FW31/03
17	Kazuki Nakajima	FW31/04
	FORCE INDIA-MERCEDES	
20	Adrian Sutil	VJM02/01
21	Giancarlo Fisichella	VJM02/04
	BRAWN-MERCEDES	
22	Jenson Button	BGP 001/02
23	Rubens Barrichello	BGP 001/01

12 BELGIUM

	McLAREN-MERCEDES	
1	Lewis Hamilton	MP4-24/05
2	Heikki Kovalainen	MP4-24/03
	FERRARI	
3	Luca Badoer	F60/280
4	Kimi Räikkönen	F60/279
	BMW SAUBER-BMW	
5	Robert Kubica	F1.09/08
6	Nick Heidfeld	F1.09/07
	RENAULT	
7	Fernando Alonso	R29/04
8	Romain Grosjean	R29/03
	TOYOTA	
9	Jarno Trulli	TF109/06
10	Timo Glock	TF109/05
	TORO ROSSO-FERRARI	
11	Jaime Alguersuari	STR04/02
12	Sébastien Buemi	STR04/03
	RED BULL-RENAULT	
14	Mark Webber	RB5/3
15	Sebastian Vettel	RB5/1
	WILLIAMS-TOYOTA	
16	Nico Rosberg	FW31/03
17	Kazuki Nakajima	FW31/04
	FORCE INDIA-MERCEDES	
20	Adrian Sutil	VJM02/01
21	Giancarlo Fisichella	VJM02/04
	BRAWN-MERCEDES	
22	Jenson Button	BGP 001/02
23	Rubens Barrichello	BGP 001/03

13 ITALY

	McLAREN-MERCEDES	
1	Lewis Hamilton	MP4-24/04
2	Heikki Kovalainen	MP4-24/03
	FERRARI	
3	Giancarlo Fisichella	F60/280
4	Kimi Räikkönen	F60/279
	BMW SAUBER-BMW	
5	Robert Kubica	F1.09/08
6	Nick Heidfeld	F1.09/07
	RENAULT	
7	Fernando Alonso	R29/04
8	Romain Grosjean	R29/03
	TOYOTA	
9	Jarno Trulli	TF109/06
10	Timo Glock	TF109/05
	TORO ROSSO-FERRARI	
11	Jaime Alguersuari	STR04/02
12	Sébastien Buemi	STR04/03
	RED BULL-RENAULT	
14	Mark Webber	RB5/2
15	Sebastian Vettel	RB5/1
	WILLIAMS-TOYOTA	
16	Nico Rosberg	FW31/03
17	Kazuki Nakajima	FW31/04
	FORCE INDIA-MERCEDES	
20	Adrian Sutil	VJM02/01
21	Vitantonio Liuzzi	VJM02/04
	BRAWN-MERCEDES	
22	Jenson Button	BGP 001/02
23	Rubens Barrichello	BGP 001/03

14 SINGAPORE

	McLAREN-MERCEDES	
1	Lewis Hamilton	MP4-24/02
	(MP4-24/04 – Friday)	
2	Heikki Kovalainen	MP4-24/03
	FERRARI	
3	Giancarlo Fisichella	F60/280
4	Kimi Räikkönen	F60/279
	BMW SAUBER-BMW	
5	Robert Kubica	F1.09/08
6	Nick Heidfeld	F1.09/07
	RENAULT	
7	Fernando Alonso	R29/04
8	Romain Grosjean	R29/03
	TOYOTA	
9	Jarno Trulli	TF109/06
10	Timo Glock	TF109/05
	TORO ROSSO-FERRARI	
11	Jaime Alguersuari	STR04/02
12	Sébastien Buemi	STR04/03
	RED BULL-RENAULT	
14	Mark Webber	RB5/2
15	Sebastian Vettel	RB5/1
	WILLIAMS-TOYOTA	
16	Nico Rosberg	FW31/03
17	Kazuki Nakajima	FW31/04
	FORCE INDIA-MERCEDES	
20	Adrian Sutil	VJM02/01
21	Vitantonio Liuzzi	VJM02/04
	BRAWN-MERCEDES	
22	Jenson Button	BGP 001/02
23	Rubens Barrichello	BGP 001/03

15 JAPAN

	McLAREN-MERCEDES	
1	Lewis Hamilton	MP4-24/02
2	Heikki Kovalainen	MP4-24/03
	FERRARI	
3	Giancarlo Fisichella	F60/280
4	Kimi Räikkönen	F60/279
	BMW SAUBER-BMW	
5	Robert Kubica	F1.09/08
6	Nick Heidfeld	F1.09/07
	RENAULT	
7	Fernando Alonso	R29/04
8	Romain Grosjean	R29/03
	TOYOTA	
9	Jarno Trulli	TF109/06
10	Timo Glock	TF109/05
10	Kamui Kobayashi	TF109/05
	TORO ROSSO-FERRARI	
11	Jaime Alguersuari	STR04/02
12	Sébastien Buemi	STR04/03
	RED BULL-RENAULT	
14	Mark Webber	RB5/4
	(RB5/2 – Fri/Sat)	
15	Sebastian Vettel	RB5/1
	WILLIAMS-TOYOTA	
16	Nico Rosberg	FW31/03
17	Kazuki Nakajima	FW31/04
	FORCE INDIA-MERCEDES	
20	Adrian Sutil	VJM02/01
21	Vitantonio Liuzzi	VJM02/04
	BRAWN-MERCEDES	
22	Jenson Button	BGP 001/02
23	Rubens Barrichello	BGP 001/03

16 BRAZIL

	McLAREN-MERCEDES	
1	Lewis Hamilton	MP4-24/02
2	Heikki Kovalainen	MP4-24/03
	FERRARI	
3	Giancarlo Fisichella	F60/280
4	Kimi Räikkönen	F60/279
	BMW SAUBER-BMW	
5	Robert Kubica	F1.09/08
6	Nick Heidfeld	F1.09/07
	RENAULT	
7	Fernando Alonso	R29/04
8	Romain Grosjean	R29/03
	TOYOTA	
9	Jarno Trulli	TF109/06
10	Kamui Kobayashi	TF109/04
	TORO ROSSO-FERRARI	
11	Jaime Alguersuari	STR04/01
12	Sébastien Buemi	STR04/03
	RED BULL-RENAULT	
14	Mark Webber	RB5/4
15	Sebastian Vettel	RB5/1
	WILLIAMS-TOYOTA	
16	Nico Rosberg	FW31/03
17	Kazuki Nakajima	FW31/04
	FORCE INDIA-MERCEDES	
20	Adrian Sutil	VJM02/01
21	Vitantonio Liuzzi	VJM02/04
	BRAWN-MERCEDES	
22	Jenson Button	BGP 001/02
23	Rubens Barrichello	BGP 001/03

TORO ROSSO STR04

RENAULT R29

FORCE INDIA VJM02

17 ABU DHABI

	McLAREN-MERCEDES	
1	Lewis Hamilton	MP4-24/02
2	Heikki Kovalainen	MP4-24/03
	FERRARI	
3	Giancarlo Fisichella	F60/280
4	Kimi Räikkönen	F60/279
	BMW SAUBER-BMW	
5	Robert Kubica	F1.09/08
6	Nick Heidfeld	F1.09/07
	RENAULT	
7	Fernando Alonso	R29/01
8	Romain Grosjean	R29/03
	TOYOTA	
9	Jarno Trulli	TF109/06
10	Kamui Kobayashi	TF109/04
	TORO ROSSO-FERRARI	
11	Jaime Alguersuari	STR04/01
12	Sébastien Buemi	STR04/03
	RED BULL-RENAULT	
14	Mark Webber	RB5/4
15	Sebastian Vettel	RB5/1
	WILLIAMS-TOYOTA	
16	Nico Rosberg	FW31/03
17	Kazuki Nakajima	FW31/04
	FORCE INDIA-MERCEDES	
20	Adrian Sutil	VJM02/01
21	Vitantonio Liuzzi	VJM02/04
	BRAWN-MERCEDES	
22	Jenson Button	BGP 001/02
23	Rubens Barrichello	BGP 001/03

GRANDS PRIX 2009

FIA FORMULA 1 WORLD CHAMPIONSHIP • ROUND 1

AUSTRALIAN
GRAND PRIX

MELBOURNE CIRCUIT

MELBOURNE QUALIFYING

NEW rules, new hierarchy, new reasons to carp to stewards about rivals' potential ineligibility… Formula One's intended shift to a greener, cleaner future got to an unconvincing start as swathes of forestation were sacrificed to prime the Melbourne officials' overworked printer.

The cars of Brawn, Toyota and Williams were protested almost as soon as they had passed scrutineering on Thursday. Red Bull, Renault and Ferrari were the plaintiffs (BMW Sauber attempted to join them, but submitted its paperwork too late), but stewards ruled in favour of the accused and the matter went to appeal. The prosecution implied that the renegade trio had holes in their diffusers where none should exist. The defence maintained that these weren't holes, but gaps between independent surfaces.

Meanwhile, Williams countered with a protest against the bodywork detailing of Renault and Red Bull, although this was withdrawn shortly before midnight on Saturday.

On the surface this was manna for Max Mosley and Bernie Ecclestone, whose tried, trusted, divide-and-conquer methods were being challenged by the perceived unity of the Formula One Teams' Association (FOTA). In reality, it was little more than healthy, competitive bickering as teams established exactly where the goalposts now stood.

Diffuser aside, the other question about the Brawn BGP001 was its true pace. Late to the track, following weeks of prolonged talks to rescue and reconstitute the team formerly known as Honda, it had been instantly fast in testing. Was this genuine pace or the oldest trick in the winter book, a little ballast-free running to set eyecatching times that might lure a few sponsors?

It was sand-bagging of a sort, but not the kind rivals had in mind. "We've not been pulling any stunts," said team manager Ron Meadows. "We've had sensible levels of fuel in the car for most of what little running we've done. During one of our last tests in Barcelona, Rubens Barrichello completed a 22-lap race simulation… and 18 of those laps were quicker than anybody else managed all day. If anything, we've been running quite conservatively."

On Saturday, the hitherto stickerless, virgin-white car morphed into a white car embellished with Virgin stickers as Richard Branson flew in to confirm an embryonic sponsorship deal, and watch Jenson Button and Barrichello qualify first and second – the first time a world championship newcomer had done such a thing since Juan Manuel Fangio and Karl Kling spearheaded Mercedes-Benz's challenge ahead of the 1954 French GP. Button was 2kg lighter and 0.303 second brisker than his team-mate – and both Brawns were significantly heavier than their closest adversaries, Sebastian Vettel (Red Bull) and Robert Kubica (BMW Sauber).

"The last few months have been incredibly tough," Button said. "Rubens and I have gone from not knowing whether we had a drive, or any future in racing, to qualifying on the front row. It is just amazing, it really is, and I have to credit the whole team for making it happen."

Defending world champion Lewis Hamilton had taken a trip in the opposite direction. The McLaren MP4-24 wasn't quite as far off the pace as it had been during testing, but that still translated only to 15th place. Transmission failure during Q1 prompted an unscheduled gearbox change and a five-position grid penalty, although he didn't start quite last because the Toyotas of Timo Glock and Jarno Trulli – originally sixth and eighth – were ordered to start from the pit lane after their rear wings were adjudged to be illegally flexible.

CLUTCHING a flute of champagne, Sir Richard Branson beamed his best PR smile and proclaimed, "I've always been a lucky bastard."

Barely 36 hours had passed since the Virgin entrepreneur jetted in to Melbourne for a whistle-stop visit. He confirmed a last-gasp sponsorship deal with Brawn Grand Prix shortly before Jenson Button and Rubens Barrichello qualified the reconstituted team's cars on the front row – and the following evening he became one of the TV cameras' focal points, in a manner usually reserved for racing drivers' fathers and fiancées, as Button and Barrichello swept to a memorable one-two. It was by no means as straightforward, however, as such bland statistics suggest.

The 2009 Australian Grand Prix was advertised as the sport's first twilight race – a late-afternoon start having been engineered at Bernie Ecclestone's whim to make life easier for European TV audiences (presumably because Bernie doesn't appreciate the relish with which some people rise in the middle of the night to watch live from Melbourne – a detail that always set the race apart from others). It didn't much

help the locals, though, because the schedule made it impossible to catch Sunday flights home to Sydney and elsewhere in the race's immediate aftermath. The atmosphere was good, as is unfailingly the case in Albert Park (the only Formula One venue with a pelican-rich lake in its midst), but spectator numbers were down and some of the traditional corporate hospitality villages were conspicuous by their credit crunch-enforced absence.

For the drivers, too, the timetable caused complications. "It was really difficult in the fading light," said Button. "This is an open circuit, but you could not see the corner exits at all. I used a slightly tinted visor, which was the correct thing to do, but it was so tricky because of the sun's glare and the light changing through the trees. The bad light always seemed to affect the most difficult corners and it would have been very easy to put a wheel wrong."

But he didn't. The Brawn BGP001 was clearly beautifully balanced – neither driver had spun during what little pre-season testing they had accumulated – and Button controlled the pace from the off. He made

a clean start to lead into Turn One, but Barrichello floundered. "My initial start seemed okay," he said, "but then the car went into anti-stall mode, which selects neutral if you don't have the right revs."

He recovered smartly, but then dived inside Mark Webber's Red Bull – eighth on the grid – and triggered a chain-reaction shunt. Webber was punted into Nick Heidfeld, causing both to spin, and the Australian's wayward car then took out Heikki Kovalainen, too. Adrian Sutil – a traditional magnet for first-lap trouble – did nothing particularly wrong on this occasion, but struck some of the gathering debris and dislodged his Force India's front wing. Barrichello insisted that Kovalainen had been the catalyst for the whole thing – "One of the McLarens hit me really hard," he said, and damage to the rear of his car confirmed as much – but by that point, he was already committed to a distinctly slender gap.

By the lap's end, Button was 3.995 seconds clear of Sebastian Vettel, who had to repel the KERS-embellished advances of Felipe Massa and Robert Kubica, while Kimi Räikkönen, Nico Rosberg,

Above: Sebastian Vettel was right on the front-running pace on his debut outing in the Red Bull-Renault, but a late tangle with Robert Kubica's BMW Sauber wrote the German out of the equation.
Photo: Bernard Asset

Aerodynamic key to the speed of the Brawn *(bottom left)* was the team's interpretation of the 'double diffuser' regulations, contrasting with the single-diffuser configuration of the Renault *(centre left)* and the McLaren *(centre right)*.
Photos: Lukas Gorys and Peter J. Fox

Opening spread: Only a month earlier, neither of them had been certain they even had a drive for the 2009 season. Small wonder that Jenson Button and Rubens Barrichello looked so utterly ecstatic after pulling off a commanding 1-2 debut grand slam for the Brawn team in Melbourne.
Photo: Peter J. Fox

Barrichello, Kazuki Nakajima, Nelson Piquet, Sébastien Buemi, Giancarlo Fisichella, Sébastien Bourdais, Lewis Hamilton, Fernando Alonso, Jarno Trulli and Timo Glock completed the list of healthy runners. Heidfeld, Sutil and Webber rejoined at the back after pitting for repairs, but Kovalainen's front left suspension was too badly damaged for him to continue.

Having been gifted as much of a cushion as he would ever need during the first 3.295 miles, Button settled into a comfortable rhythm and was able to keep the gap to Vettel pegged at about four seconds. Tyre stops began in earnest between laps ten and 12, when the minority who started on the super-soft Bridgestone (including both Ferrari drivers, Kubica, Trulli and Hamilton) came in earlier than planned because the tyres were beginning to grain quite badly on a track that had still to rubber in.

Vettel was still more than four seconds adrift when he peeled in for his first scheduled stop, on lap 16, and he was followed two laps later by Barrichello, Buemi and Glock. Button might have come in, too,

at this point, because Nakajima's crumpled Williams was parked precariously at Turn Four after the Japanese driver had slithered into the wall. The threat of a safety car is rarely far away in Melbourne and, had it been dispatched immediately, Button's race might have been compromised seriously. It was not scrambled until lap 19, however, just after Button had refuelled on schedule. His lead was diminished, but remained intact.

The race resumed at the start of lap 25, with Button leading Vettel, Massa (his race now effectively ruined, because he was fuelled short for an aggressive second stint, but had been hamstrung by the race's neutralisation), Kubica, Räikkönen, Rosberg, Piquet, Trulli, Buemi, Barrichello, Glock, Hamilton, Alonso, Fisichella, Bourdais, Heidfeld, Sutil and Webber, although Piquet only made it as far as Turn One before he spun into the gravel – the Brazilian claimed his brakes had been troubling him from the start and that the pedal had gone soft (an accusation that some in the paddock also levelled at the driver).

Button struggled to generate tyre heat at the second stint's dawn – and also flat-spotted his front left just before the restart, triggering a vibration that made life rather harder than it should have been. Even so, he managed to ease more than five seconds clear of Vettel by the time the German pitted again – for the mandatory set of super-softs – on lap 45. Two laps later, Button did likewise: it wasn't a good stop, however. He entered the pit lane in second gear, rather than first, which delayed the engagement of neutral, and he also slightly overshot his pit, which complicated attachment of the fuel hose. About five seconds were wasted, but he was still more than a second ahead of Vettel when he rejoined, with Barrichello (still to make his final stop, on lap 51) and Kubica fairly close behind. And the Pole was running on the more durable medium Bridgestone: his decision to start on the super-soft had initially looked flawed, but circumstance now made him a factor.

Button began lapping consistently in the 1m 29s range – and for a short time Vettel matched him. The

Left: Rubens Barrichello certainly had his hands full battling to second place after a busy first corner.
Photo: Paul-Henri Cahier

Right: Ross Brawn could rightly permit himself a smile of satisfaction after his team's maiden success straight out of the box.
Photo: Peter J. Fox

Right: Nelson Piquet's season got off to the worst possible start – setting the tone for subsequent events, perhaps?
Photo: Peter Nygaard

Below right: McLaren chairman Ron Dennis, was at the race. Henceforth he would concentrate his energies on developing the road-car side of the McLaren business.
Photo: Peter J. Fox

Below far right: F1 in Melbourne does not always attract unanimous and unqualified approval.
Photo: Peter Nygaard/GP Photo

Bottom right: Jarno Trulli leads Lewis Hamilton during what would turn out to be a highly-controversial safety-car period.
Photo: Peter J. Fox

been able to contain Kubica, had the Pole passed Vettel. That we will never know: Vettel's super-softs had grained and Button's hadn't – he might have had a couple of 1m 27s laps in reserve, but it wasn't a question his tyres had to be asked. "Kubica was clearly a big danger," Ross Brawn said, "but Sebastian solved that potential problem."

Only a few weeks after facing the serious risk of unemployment – and, perhaps, the prospect that he would never again compete in a grand prix – Button now led the World Championship standings for the first time in his F1 career. He'd also just scored more points in one afternoon than he'd managed in the previous two seasons...

"That's pretty rubbish, isn't it?" he said. "The last

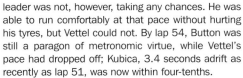

leader was not, however, taking any chances. He was able to run comfortably at that pace without hurting his tyres, but Vettel could not. By lap 54, Button was still a paragon of metronomic virtue, while Vettel's pace had dropped off; Kubica, 3.4 seconds adrift as recently as lap 51, was now within four-tenths.

Their evolving duel played into Button's hands, particularly on lap 56, when Kubica got alongside Vettel through Turn Three. The German's robust defence led the two cars to become momentarily entwined, and both suffered damage that caused them to fly off the road, independently, when they tried to negotiate Turn Four. Kubica's car was particularly badly mangled and the safety car was summoned once more. The incident cost both drivers a podium finish, and Vettel was also penalised ten grid positions in Malaysia, for causing an avoidable accident.

The race remained neutralised until the end of the 58th lap, whereupon Button simply had to accelerate across the finishing line to cement a merited victory. The unanswered question was whether he would have

two years have been very tough. The car Rubens and I had last season was a handful – we didn't really know what it would do from corner to corner. It was a beast. We knew there were some very talented people in the team, though, and this car reflects as much. After a tough few months, I have to give all credit to Ross and everybody for making this happen. It's just amazing."

Despite his efforts to make contact with almost everybody else on the racetrack (there was a significant brush with Räikkönen on lap ten, as well as the opening-lap skirmish), Barrichello inherited second to complete Brawn's one-two. Later in the evening, Bernie Ecclestone would call Richard Branson on his mobile phone. "He wanted to know if I'd fly home and accompany him to a casino," Branson said. "He wanted to stick a million pounds on whatever number I chose."

Barrichello's result owed a lot to speed, even more to his car's tank-like durability ("I don't think our diffuser made that much difference," said Ross Brawn, "because Rubens didn't have much of his left by the end.") and a little to luck. The Vettel/Kubica incident aside, he was aided by problems that befell both Ferrari drivers. The first safety car partially hindered Massa, and a broken front nose support eventually put him out. Räikkönen had to make an extra stop for a new nose, after spinning into the wall on lap 43,

and differential failure obliged him to pull up shortly before the finish.

Jarno Trulli was initially classified third – a fine drive after starting from the pits, to which both Toyotas had been condemned in the wake of a successful protest by Ferrari *(see Qualifying)* – but was excluded later in the wake of an incident during the second safety-car period.

Running at reduced pace on cold tyres, the Italian slithered across the grass on lap 56 and lost a place to Hamilton. The Toyota driver reclaimed it next time around – because he thought Hamilton was letting him through – and had 25 seconds added to his race time by way of retribution. With the field tightly bunched up, that dropped him to 12th. McLaren team manager David Ryan told stewards that Hamilton had not voluntarily ceded a place to Trulli, but radio transmissions subsequently proved otherwise. It was a week later, in Malaysia, that Trulli was reinstated and Hamilton expelled because he and the team had misled the stewards. A pity that one of the most mature and accomplished performances of the defending champion's still-fledgling career should end in such controversy. Immediately after the race, he'd admitted that third place felt at least as good as a victory. As it did, while it lasted. "I thought I might

be able to finish eighth if I kept my nose clean and one or two people dropped out," he said, "but this is just unbelievable."

Like Trulli, Glock recovered well from a pit-lane start to take fourth, although he was frustrated to spend much of the race bottled up behind Alonso. The Spaniard dropped right down the field at the start, after taking to the grass to avoid Webber, Heidfeld and co, but the safety-car interruptions shuffled the hierarchy sufficiently to permit him the artifice of fifth, ahead of Rosberg (who had been fifth, ahead of Trulli, until lap 53, at which point his super-softs melted because he had been heeding his team's instructions to push hard), Buemi (a thoroughly sensible debut, well rewarded) and Bourdais, who drove a 36-lap final stint – "At first it felt as though I was towing a caravan, with all that fuel on board."

Sutil benefited from a short second stint on the super-softs to recover to ninth, while Heidfeld, Fisichella and Webber were the only other drivers still running at the end. The Italian lost almost 20 seconds during his first stop because he overshot his pit box by a considerable margin. "Last year I was accustomed to stopping at the first garage and I simply became confused," he said.

Simon Arron

EDITOR'S VIEW
BUTTON and BRAWN TAKE FAIRYTALE WIN

NINE years had passed since Jenson Button had made his F1 debut in the Australian Grand Prix at Melbourne, the 20-year-old having delivered an unquestionably capable display at the wheel of a Williams-BMW. He had been Britain's latest golden boy and tipped for the big time. Yet there were times during the decade that followed when many outsiders came to suspect that the amenable youngster from Frome was nothing more than a likeable also-ran who would never break into the big time on a consistent basis.

Thus the events in Melbourne at the start of 2009 not only served as a total vindication of Button's confidence and self-belief, which had endured much buffeting from the storms of pit-lane punditry over the years, but also reminded the cynics that, just sometimes, the most unlikely of outsiders can come home and deliver the goods.

By the start of December 2008, the situation was looking dire for Button. He had an ongoing, highly lucrative contract to drive for the Honda squad, but suddenly the news that the pit lane had been fearing for so long was translated into stark reality. The Japanese car maker had decided to quit the F1 business and put its team up for sale.

Team principal Ross Brawn, who had been recruited to weave for Honda the magic spell he had so successfully cast across Ferrari fortunes for more than a decade, appeared to have been stopped abruptly in his tracks.

The team had taken a gamble in 2008. Rather than straining every sinew to achieve top results with a below-par racing car, Honda had invested hugely in ensuring that the 2009 car would be an outstanding machine. Informed rumour had it that the team's 2008 aerodynamic development budget was twice that of McLaren's. And this supposed excellence of the forthcoming new machine provided a major selling point from which Brawn and CEO Nick Fry pitched their bids for support in an effort to save the team.

Perhaps inevitably, the image of a team with no future beating the drum about how good its next car was going to be – assuming that it could just get to the first race of the new season – looked like the last gasps of drowning men. Surely Honda was going to fail to find a buyer and the first, high-profile failure of F1's credit-crunch era would be the best part of 1,000 employees being thrown out of work, along with the company and its suppliers in the Brackley area. The commercial, emotional and personal consequences of such a development were just too ghastly to contemplate.

After the initial announcement that the team was going to be put up for sale, Brawn and Fry flew to Tokyo to confer with Honda's senior management. It quickly became clear to them that the car maker's disastrous drop in global sales meant that there was no choice but to sell the company. For Brawn and Fry, it was now a question of seeing whether it was possible to keep things running as an independent entity, effectively taking over Honda's commercial rights and benefits and, with some help from Bernie Ecclestone and a generous contribution from Honda in terms of what would otherwise be severance costs, keep the show on the road.

Initially it was suggested that Honda's board of management had told Brawn and Fry that the team would only be funded for another three months before the factory's doors would be closed for good unless a buyer could be found.

Salvation came as much through force of circumstance as business acumen. The F1 community desperately did not want to lose another competitor, credit crunch or no credit crunch. Honda wanted to get out as tidily and promptly as possible, and Mercedes-Benz's willingness to supply engines was part welcome commercial bottom line, part driven by McLaren's wish to keep FOTA thriving as a political power base.

Yet one would have to say that the absolute master stroke was to keep the driver line-up of Jenson Button and Rubens Barrichello. There were plenty of commentators offering the view that there was no chance of achieving any serious results with those two battle-worn warhorses still in harness.

At the end of the day, their combination of mature and self-assured equilibrium would prove the bedrock on which Brawn's remarkable season would be constructed. And the canvas on which Jenson Button would prove to his most enduring critics that they had been so wrong.

Alan Henry

Above: Sébastien Buemi drove with great restraint and composure to score a couple of points with seventh place on his championship debut.
Photo: Bernard Asset

Right: Job well done. The entire Brawn team, together with Virgin boss Sir Richard Branson, celebrate a remarkable debut victory.
Photo: Peter J. Fox

ALBERT PARK, MELBOURNE
Circuit: 3.295 miles/5.303 km
58 laps

Hill 280/175 — 6
Ascari 138/86 — 3
Waite 233/145 — 5
Senna 84/52 — 2
Turn 9 140/226 — 6
Stewart 205/128 — 5
Clark chicane 115/71 — 3
Prost 180/112 — 4
Lauda 255/159 — 6
188/300 — 7
Marina 134/84 — 3
Brabham 200/124 — 4
Hellas corner 145/90 — 3
Jones 145/90 — 3
Whiteford 239/149 —
Sports Centre 92/57 — 2
100/62 kmh/mph
4 Gear

Photos: Peter J. Fox

BRAWN GP

FIA F1 WORLD CHAMPIONSHIP ROUND 1
ING
AUSTRALIAN
GRAND PRIX
MELBOURNE 27-29 MARCH 2009

RACE DISTANCE: 58 laps, 191.118 miles/307.574km • RACE WEATHER: Sunny (track 25-32°C, air 21-22°C)

Pos.	Driver	Nat.	No.	Entrant	Car/Engine	Tyres	Laps	Time/Retirement	Speed (mph/km/h)	Gap to leader	Fastest race lap
1	Jenson Button	GB	22	Brawn GP Formula 1 Team	Brawn BGP 001-Mercedes FO108W V8	B	58	1h 34m 15.784s	121.650/195.775		1m 28.020s 17
2	Rubens Barrichello	BR	23	Brawn GP Formula 1 Team	Brawn BGP 001-Mercedes FO108W V8	B	58	1h 34m 16.591s	121.632/195.747	+ 0.807s	1m 29.066s 43
3	Jarno Trulli	I	9	Panasonic Toyota Racing	Toyota TF109-RVX-09 V8	B	58	1h 34m 17.388s	121.615/195.720	+ 1.604s	1m 28.916s 50
DQ*	*Lewis Hamilton*	GB	1	*Vodafone McLaren Mercedes*	*McLaren MP4-24-Mercedes FO108W V8*	*B*	*58*	*1h 34m 18.698s*	*121.587/195.675*	*+ 2.914s*	*1m 29.020s 39*
4	Timo Glock	D	10	Panasonic Toyota Racing	Toyota TF109-RVX-09 V8	B	58	1h 34m 20.219s	121.554/195.622	+ 4.435s	1m 28.416s 53
5	Fernando Alonso	E	7	ING Renault F1 Team	Renault R29-RS27 V8	B	58	1h 34m 20.663s	121.545/195.607	+ 4.879s	1m 28.712s 53
6	Nico Rosberg	D	16	AT&T Williams	Williams FW31-Toyota RVX-09 V8	B	58	1h 34m 21.506s	121.527/195.578	+ 5.722s	1m 27.706s 48
7	Sébastien Buemi	CH	12	Scuderia Toro Rosso	Toro Rosso STR04-Ferrari 056 V8	B	58	1h 34m 21.788s	121.520/195.568	+ 6.004s	1m 29.230s 34
8	Sébastien Bourdais	F	11	Scuderia Toro Rosso	Toro Rosso STR04-Ferrari 056 V8	B	58	1h 34m 22.082s	121.514/195.558	+ 6.298s	1m 29.823s 50
9	Adrian Sutil	D	20	Force India Formula One Team	Force India VJM02-Mercedes FO108W V8	B	58	1h 34m 22.119s	121.513/195.556	+ 6.335s	1m 28.943s 43
10	Nick Heidfeld	D	6	BMW Sauber F1 Team	BMW Sauber F1.09-BMW P86/9 V8	B	58	1h 34m 22.869s	121.497/195.530	+ 7.085s	1m 28.283s 48
11	Giancarlo Fisichella	I	21	Force India Formula One Team	Force India VJM02-Mercedes FO108W V8	B	58	1h 34m 23.158s	121.491/195.521	+ 7.374s	1m 29.005s 51
12	Mark Webber	AUS	14	Red Bull Racing	Red Bull RB5-Renault RS27 V8	B	57			+ 1 lap	1m 28.508s 38
13	Sebastian Vettel	D	15	Red Bull Racing	Red Bull RB5-Renault RS27 V8	B	56	accident		+ 2 laps	1m 28.140s 8
14	Robert Kubica	PL	5	BMW Sauber F1 Team	BMW Sauber F1.09-BMW P86/9 V8	B	55	accident		+ 3 laps	1m 27.988s 36
15	Kimi Räikkönen	FIN	4	Scuderia Ferrari Marlboro	Ferrari F60-056 V8	B	55	differential		+ 3 laps	1m 28.488s 35
	Felipe Massa	BR	3	Scuderia Ferrari Marlboro	Ferrari F60-056 V8	B	45	front suspension			1m 29.141s 30
	Nelsinho Piquet	BR	8	ING Renault F1 Team	Renault R29-RS27 V8	B	24	spin			1m 30.502s 17
	Kazuki Nakajima	J	17	AT&T Williams	Williams FW31-Toyota RVX-09 V8	B	17	accident			1m 29.923s 6
	Heikki Kovalainen	FIN	2	Vodafone McLaren Mercedes	McLaren MP4-24-Mercedes FO108W V8	B	0	accident			no time

* finished 4th but disqualified for misleading the race stewards after the race.

Jarno Trulli was originally awarded a 25-second penalty for overtaking behind the safety car, but this was later removed.

Fastest race lap: Nico Rosberg on lap 48, 1m 27.706s, 135.253mph/217.668km/h.

Lap record: Michael Schumacher (Ferrari F2004 V10), 1m 24.125s, 141.010mph/226.933km/h (2004).

| 20 | TRULLI · Toyota *illegal rear wing/started from pits* | 11 | BOURDAIS · Toro Rosso | 21 | FISICHELLA · Force India | 12 | BUEMI · Toro Rosso | 17 | NAKAJIMA · Williams | 6 | HEIDFELD · BMW Sauber |
| 10 | GLOCK · Toyota *illegal rear wing/started from pits* | 1 | HAMILTON · McLaren *penalty for gearbox change* | 20 | SUTIL · Force India | 8 | PIQUET · Renault | 2 | KOVALAINEN · McLaren | 7 | ALONSO · Renault |

Grid order		1	2	3	4	5	6	7	8	9	10	11	12	13	14	15	16	17	18	19	20	21	22	23	24	25	26	27	28	29	30	31	32	33	34	35	36	37	38	39	40	41	42	43	44
22	BUTTON	22	22	22	22	22	22	22	22	22	22	22	22	22	22	22	22	22	22	22	22	22	22	22	22	22	22	22	22	22	22	22	22	22	22	22	22	22	22	22	22	22	22	22	22
23	BARRICHELLO	15	15	15	15	15	15	15	15	15	15	15	15	15	15	15	15	15	15	15	15	15	15	15	15	15	15	15	15	15	15	15	15	15	15	15	15	15	15	15	15	15	15	15	15
15	VETTEL	3	3	3	3	3	3	3	3	3	3	5	16	16	16	16	23	8	3	3	3	3	3	3	3	3	3	3	3	5	5	5	5	5	5	5	23	23	23	23	23				
5	KUBICA	5	5	5	5	5	5	5	5	5	5	16	23	23	23	23	17	17	21	5	5	5	5	5	5	5	5	5	5	4	4	4	4	4	4	4	5	12	16	16	16	5			
16	ROSBERG	4	4	4	4	4	4	4	4	4	16	23	17	17	17	17	8	8	7	8	4	4	4	4	4	4	4	4	4	9	9	23	23	23	23	23	12	16	1	1	5	7			
3	MASSA	16	16	16	16	16	16	16	16	16	23	17	8	8	8	8	12	12	3	4	16	16	16	16	16	9	9	9	9	9	9	23	23	12	12	12	12	12	16	1	5	5	7	10	
4	RÄIKKÖNEN	23	23	23	23	23	23	23	23	23	17	8	12	12	12	12	21	21	5	16	8	8	8	23	23	23	23	23	23	12	12	16	16	16	16	16	1	5	7	7	7	10	16		
14	WEBBER	17	17	17	17	17	17	17	17	1	12	21	21	21	21	7	7	9	9	9	9	9	9	12	12	12	12	12	16	16	1	1	1	1	1	1	4	7	4	4	4	1			
6	HEIDFELD	8	8	8	8	8	1	1	1	1	8	21	7	7	7	7	10	10	3	9	23	23	23	23	23	16	16	16	16	1	7	7	7	7	7	7	4	10	10	21	3				
7	ALONSO	12	12	12	1	1	8	8	8	8	12	7	10	10	10	10	3	9	23	23	23	23	23	1	1	1	1	1	7	7	10	10	10	10	10	10	10	21	9	1					
17	NAKAJIMA	21	21	1	12	12	12	12	12	12	21	3	5	3	3	3	5	12	10	10	10	10	10	7	7	7	7	7	10	10	20	21	21	21	21	21	21	9	3						
2	KOVALAINEN	11	1	21	21	21	21	21	21	7	10	3	5	16	4	23	7	1	1	1	1	1	10	10	10	10	10	20	20	9	9	9	9	9	9	9	3	12	12						
12	BUEMI	1	11	11	9	9	9	9	9	9	10	4	4	4	4	4	16	10	1	7	7	7	7	21	21	21	21	20	20	3	21	21	3	3	3	3	3	3	12	6	11				
8	PIQUET	7	9	9	11	7	7	7	7	4	1	9	9	9	9	9	1	21	21	21	20	20	20	20	20	3	3	11	11	6	6	6	6	6	6	11	20								
21	FISICHELLA	9	7	7	7	11	10	10	10	10	9	1	1	1	1	1	11	11	11	11	11	11	11	11	11	11	11	6	6	6	6	11	11	11	11	20	6								
20	SUTIL	10	10	10	10	10	11	11	11	11	11	11	11	11	11	20	20	20	6	6	6	6	6	6	6	20	20	20	20	20	20	20	20	20	20	20	20	20	20	4	4				
11	BOURDAIS	6	6	6	6	6	6	6	6	6	6	6	6	6	6	6	6	20	20	14	14	14	14	14	14	14	14	14	14	14	14	14	14	B	14	20	14	14	14	14	14	14	14	14	14
1	HAMILTON	20	20	20	20	20	20	20	20	20	20	20	20	20	20	20	20	14	14	14	14	14	14																						
9	TRULLI	14	14	14	14	14	14	14	14	14	14	14	14	14	14	14	14																												
10	GLOCK																																												

TIME SHEETS

PRACTICE 1 (FRIDAY)
Partly cloudy/sunny
(track 21-28°C, air 17-18°C)

Pos.	Driver	Laps	Time
1	Nico Rosberg	19	1m 26.687s
2	Kazuki Nakajima	21	1m 26.736s
3	Kimi Räikkönen	24	1m 26.750s
4	Rubens Barrichello	21	1m 27.226s
5	Heikki Kovalainen	15	1m 27.453s
6	Jenson Button	12	1m 27.467s
7	Felipe Massa	24	1m 27.642s
8	Timo Glock	24	1m 27.710s
9	Adrian Sutil	20	1m 27.993s
10	Fernando Alonso	16	1m 28.123s
11	Nick Heidfeld	20	1m 28.137s
12	Jarno Trulli	21	1m 28.142s
13	Robert Kubica	22	1m 28.511s
14	Giancarlo Fisichella	16	1m 28.603s
15	Sébastien Buemi	27	1m 28.785s
16	Lewis Hamilton	18	1m 29.042s
17	Mark Webber	7	1m 29.081s
18	Nelsinho Piquet	25	1m 29.461s
19	Sébastien Bourdais	21	1m 29.499s
20	Sebastian Vettel	4	1m 32.784s

PRACTICE 2 (FRIDAY)
Sunny
(track 26-28°C, air 18-19°C)

Pos.	Driver	Laps	Time
1	Nico Rosberg	36	1m 26.053s
2	Rubens Barrichello	38	1m 26.157s
3	Jarno Trulli	42	1m 26.350s
4	Mark Webber	30	1m 26.370s
5	Jenson Button	38	1m 26.374s
6	Timo Glock	42	1m 26.443s
7	Kazuki Nakajima	33	1m 26.560s
8	Sebastian Vettel	19	1m 26.740s
9	Adrian Sutil	29	1m 27.040s
10	Felipe Massa	35	1m 27.064s
11	Kimi Räikkönen	32	1m 27.204s
12	Fernando Alonso	28	1m 27.232s
13	Giancarlo Fisichella	32	1m 27.282s
14	Nick Heidfeld	34	1m 27.317s
15	Robert Kubica	36	1m 27.398s
16	Sébastien Bourdais	36	1m 27.479s
17	Heikki Kovalainen	35	1m 27.802s
18	Lewis Hamilton	31	1m 27.813s
19	Nelsinho Piquet	35	1m 27.828s
20	Sébastien Buemi	33	1m 28.076s

PRACTICE 3 (SATURDAY)
Sunny
(track 29-31°C, air 19-20°C)

Pos.	Driver	Laps	Time
1	Nico Rosberg	21	1m 25.808s
2	Jarno Trulli	19	1m 25.811s
3	Jenson Button	20	1m 25.981s
4	Felipe Massa	17	1m 26.020s
5	Kazuki Nakajima	18	1m 26.078s
6	Rubens Barrichello	19	1m 26.348s
7	Mark Webber	16	1m 26.355s
8	Timo Glock	25	1m 26.410s
9	Robert Kubica	18	1m 26.514s
10	Nick Heidfeld	19	1m 26.555s
11	Heikki Kovalainen	13	1m 26.652s
12	Lewis Hamilton	18	1m 26.714s
13	Sebastian Vettel	12	1m 27.009s
14	Adrian Sutil	12	1m 27.062s
15	Sébastien Bourdais	16	1m 27.152s
16	Sébastien Buemi	19	1m 27.192s
17	Fernando Alonso	18	1m 27.357s
18	Giancarlo Fisichella	20	1m 27.492s
19	Nelsinho Piquet	22	1m 27.739s
20	Kimi Räikkönen	5	1m 28.801s

QUALIFYING (SATURDAY)
Sunny (track 29-31°C, air 21°C)

Pos.	Driver	First	Second	Third	Weight
1	Jenson Button	1m 25.211s	1m 24.855s	**1m 26.202s**	664.5kg
2	Rubens Barrichello	**1m 25.006s**	**1m 24.783s**	1m 26.505s	666.5kg
3	Sebastian Vettel	1m 25.938s	1m 25.121s	1m 26.830s	657kg
4	Robert Kubica	1m 25.922s	1m 25.152s	1m 26.914s	650kg
5	Nico Rosberg	1m 25.846s	1m 25.123s	1m 26.973s	657kg
6	Timo Glock	1m 25.499s	1m 25.281s	1m 26.975s	670kg
7	Felipe Massa	1m 25.844s	1m 25.319s	1m 27.033s	654kg
8	Jarno Trulli	1m 26.194s	1m 25.265s	1m 27.127s	660kg
9	Kimi Räikkönen	1m 25.899s	1m 25.380s	1m 27.163s	655.5kg
10	Mark Webber	1m 25.427s	1m 25.241s	1m 27.246s	662kg
11	Nick Heidfeld	1m 25.827s	1m 25.504s		691.5kg
12	Fernando Alonso	1m 26.026s	1m 25.605s		680.7kg
13	Kazuki Nakajima	1m 26.074s	1m 25.607s		685.3kg
14	Heikki Kovalainen	1m 26.184s	1m 25.726s		690.6kg
15	Lewis Hamilton	1m 26.454s	no time		655kg
16	Sébastien Buemi	1m 26.503s			675.5kg
17	Nelsinho Piquet	1m 26.598s			694.1kg
18	Giancarlo Fisichella	1m 26.677s			689kg
19	Adrian Sutil	1m 26.742s			684.5kg
20	Sébastien Bourdais	1m 26.964s			662.5kg

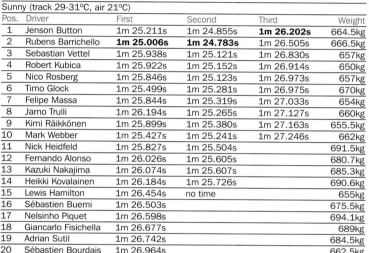

4 RÄIKKÖNEN · Ferrari

16 ROSBERG · Williams

15 VETTEL · Red Bull

22 BUTTON · Brawn

14 WEBBER · Red Bull

3 MASSA · Ferrari

5 KUBICA · BMW Sauber

23 BARRICHELLO · Brawn

FOR THE RECORD

1st GRAND PRIX START/POLE/WIN: **Brawn GP**

1st GRAND PRIX START/POINT: **Sébastien Buemi**

200th GRAND PRIX START: **Jarno Trulli**

50th GRAND PRIX POINT: **Toro Rosso**

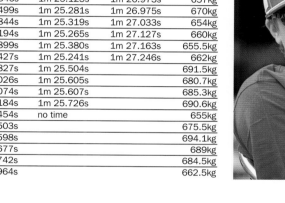

DID YOU KNOW?

This was the first time since Wolf in Argentina 1977 (Jody Scheckter) that a constructor had achieved a win in its debut race.

The last time that a constructor's first win coincided with a 1-2 in the same race was Netherlands 1968, where Stewart and Beltoise scored a 1-2 for Matra. (previously Alfa Romeo in 1950, Mercedes-Benz in 1954).

The last time that a constructor's first pole was also a 1-2 on the grid was South Africa 1970, when Stewart and Amon lined up on the front row for March.

POINTS

DRIVERS

1	Jenson Button	10
2	Rubens Barrichello	8
3	Jarno Trulli	6
4	Timo Glock	5
5	Fernando Alonso	4
6	Nico Rosberg	3
7	Sébastien Buemi	2
8	Sébastien Bourdais	1

CONSTRUCTORS

1	Brawn	18
2	Toyota	11
3	Renault	4
4	Williams	3
5	Toro Rosso	3

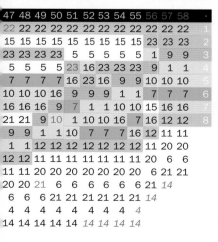

47	48	49	50	51	52	53	54	55	56	57	58	
22	22	22	22	22	22	22	22	22	22	22	22	1
15	15	15	15	15	15	15	15	15	23	23	23	2
23	23	23	23	5	5	5	5	5	1	9	9	3
5	5	5	5	23	16	23	23	23	9	1	1	4
7	7	7	16	23	16	9	9	10	10	10	10	5
10	10	10	16	9	9	1	1	7	7	7	7	6
16	16	16	9	7	1	1	10	10	15	16	16	7
21	21	9	10	1	10	10	16	7	16	12	12	8
9	9	1	1	10	7	7	7	16	12	11	11	
1	1	12	12	12	12	12	12	11	20	20		
12	12	11	11	11	11	11	11	20	6	6		
11	11	20	20	20	20	20	20	6	21	21		
20	20	21	6	6	6	6	6	21	14			
6	6	6	21	21	21	21	21	14				
4	4	4	4	4	4	4	4	4				
14	14	14	14	14	14	14	14	14				

14 One lap or more behind
21 Pit stop
■ Safety car deployed on laps shown

RACE TYRE STRATEGIES

The tyre regulations stipulate that two dry tyre specifications must be used during the race.

The Super-Soft compound Bridgestone Potenza tyre is marked with a green stripe on the sidewall of the tyre.

	Driver	Race Stint 1	Race Stint 2	Race Stint 3	Race Stint 4
1	Jenson Button	Medium: 1-19	Medium: 20-47	Super-Soft: 48-58	
2	Rubens Barrichello	Medium: 1-18	Medium: 19-51	Super-Soft: 52-58	
3	Jarno Trulli	Super-Soft: 1-10	Medium: 11-33	Medium: 34-58	
4	Timo Glock	Medium: 1-18	Medium: 19-50	Super-Soft: 51-58	
5	Fernando Alonso	Medium: 1-19	Medium: 20-51	Super-Soft: 52-58	
6	Nico Rosberg	Medium: 1-16	Medium: 17-44	Super-Soft: 45-58	
7	Sébastien Buemi	Medium: 1-12	Medium: 13-41	Super-Soft: 42-58	
8	Sébastien Bourdais	Super-Soft: 1-9	Medium: 10-21	Medium: 22-58	
	Adrian Sutil	Medium: 0-1	Medium: 2-22	Super-Soft: 23-34	Medium: 35-58
	Nick Heidfeld	Medium: 0-1	Medium: 2-18	Medium: 19-44	Super-Soft: 45-58
	Giancarlo Fisichella	Medium: 1-19	Medium: 20-34	Super-Soft: 35-58	
	Mark Webber	Medium: 0-1	Medium: 2-34	Super-Soft: 35-57	
	Sebastian Vettel	Medium: 1-15	Medium: 16-45	Super-Soft: 46-56	
	Robert Kubica	Super-Soft: 1-12	Medium: 13-39	Medium: 40-55	
	Kimi Räikkönen	Super-Soft: 1-10	Medium: 11-39	Medium: 40-43	Super-Soft: 44-55
	Felipe Massa	Super-Soft: 1-11	Medium: 12-31	Medium: 32-45 (dnf)	
	Nelson Piquet	Medium: 1-19	Medium: 20-24 (dnf)		
	Kazuki Nakajima	Medium: 1-17 (dnf)			
	Heikki Kovalainen	Medium: 0 (dnf)			
	Lewis Hamilton (dsq)	Super-Soft: 1-11	Medium: 12-43	Medium: 44-58	

MALAYSIAN GRAND PRIX

SEPANG CIRCUIT

Adrian Sutil's Force India sits at the end of the pit lane in atrocious conditions, which eventually led to the race being halted early.
Photo: Bernard Asset

SEPANG QUALIFYING

THE Sepang paddock is a spacious domain, but there was barely room to manoeuvre amid Thursday afternoon's fug of hyperbole. It became particularly crowded outside the McLaren pit, not because of anything the team was about to do on the track, but because of what had happened post-Melbourne, in the stewards' haven.

Fresh evidence indicated that Lewis Hamilton and McLaren team manager Dave Ryan had misled officials in the immediate aftermath of the season's opening race – a detail that had led to Jarno Trulli being penalised for an alleged breach of safety-car protocol and allowed Hamilton to claim third place. Pit-to-car radio transmissions – and a *parc fermé* media interview – revealed, however, that Hamilton had let the Italian through and had not been passed illegally. The upshot? Trulli was reinstated, Hamilton excluded and McLaren summoned to appear before the World Motor Sport Council. That was the perplexing bit. Every time two drivers appear before race stewards, in any formula, they tend to come up with significantly different versions of the same event, so by definition one must be attempting to mislead. The situation is usually dealt with on the spot and the sport moves on, but the Hamilton/Trulli incident morphed into headline news as though no team or driver had ever attempted to hoodwink officials in the past.

McLaren suspended Ryan on Friday morning, a move that soon became permanent, while Hamilton apologised for his conduct during a melancholy conference, and an initially trivial incident threatened to overwhelm the real story, the superlative form of a team that had faced extinction only a matter of weeks beforehand.

Jenson Button captured Brawn's second straight pole position, just 0.092 second faster than Jarno Trulli's 3.5kg lighter Toyota. The championship leader hadn't been entirely happy with his balance on Friday – the car kept locking up at the rear – but subtle overnight tweaks had brought their reward. "That's the nice thing about this car," Button said. "It responds to change in a way that last year's didn't. In fact, it's probably faster in reverse than the 2008 car was going forwards."

There were clouds on the horizon – quite literally – for the BGP001 had yet to run in the wet,

and rain was a forecast certainty on Sunday afternoon. A lack of testing also meant that potential reliability flaws had yet to be uncovered, as Button's team-mate, Rubens Barrichello, discovered when an unscheduled gearbox change and consequent five-slot grid penalty dropped him from third down to eighth.

On pace, Sebastian Vettel, fuelled very light, ought to have been third, but had to take a ten-position penalty for causing a collision with Robert Kubica in Melbourne. He dropped to 13th, one place behind pantomime villain Hamilton. Felipe Massa, meanwhile, was stranded in 16th after Ferrari assumed, incorrectly, that a single run would be enough to get him through Q1.

The diffuser police weren't quite as busy as they had been in Australia. BMW Sauber lodged a protest (on time, this weekend) against Brawn, Toyota and Williams, but, as in Melbourne, the race stewards rejected it. Nine days after the race, the FIA appeal court would meet in Paris and rule definitively in favour of twin-deck diffusers: those without would have to commit to various degrees of re-engineering – hardly a cost cut of the kind the FIA was keen to implement, but a

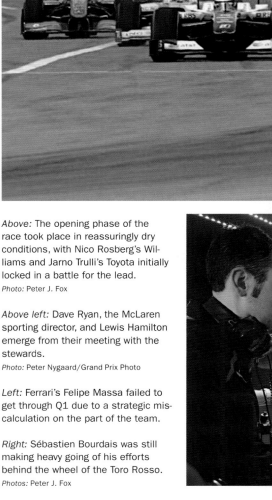

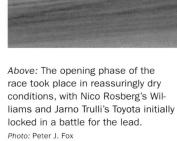

Above: The opening phase of the race took place in reassuringly dry conditions, with Nico Rosberg's Williams and Jarno Trulli's Toyota initially locked in a battle for the lead.
Photo: Peter J. Fox

Above left: Dave Ryan, the McLaren sporting director, and Lewis Hamilton emerge from their meeting with the stewards.
Photo: Peter Nygaard/Grand Prix Photo

Left: Ferrari's Felipe Massa failed to get through Q1 due to a strategic miscalculation on the part of the team.

Right: Sébastien Bourdais was still making heavy going of his efforts behind the wheel of the Toro Rosso.
Photos: Peter J. Fox

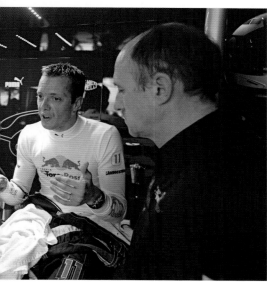

FOR an industry that's reputed to employ some of the sharpest brains on the planet, motorsport remains prone to fundamental folly. The notion of a twilight race in Melbourne might have been thought of as mildly eccentric, because of lengthening shadows that compromised drivers' vision, but the teatime start in Kuala Lumpur nudged Formula One into gloomier territory – and straight into the path of a monsoon-strength storm.

Predictable, really, given their late-afternoon frequency in this part of the world. By tampering with schedules to suit European TV, the authorities had left time for only half a race. Jenson Button had cause to smile, though. His deft touch and Brawn GP's calm approach had laid the foundations for a second straight success, but such solid essentials were embellished by a little luck...

There had been a foretaste of what might happen when a fierce cloudburst delayed the start of the GP2 Asia sprint race by half an hour. That was at 13.30, though, when watery impediments could be

accommodated; there would be no such guarantees at 17.00.

Although the circuit was dry by the time Nico Rosberg nipped through from fourth on the grid to lead the field into Turn One, the first time he'd done such a thing through merit rather than strategic artifice, the sky was a rich shade of slate. Button made a fairly average start from pole, but Rosberg's was simply sensational. The Englishman's quest for immediate retribution carried him wide into Turn One, whereupon Jarno Trulli and Fernando Alonso – up from ninth, with a helping finger on his KERS trigger – helped themselves to second and third. Button repassed the Spaniard before the lap's end, but by then he trailed Trulli by 2.7 seconds and Rosberg by almost four.

Behind Alonso, Rubens Barrichello ran fifth from Kimi Räikkönen, Mark Webber, Timo Glock (down from third after a poor getaway), Nick Heidfeld, Lewis Hamilton, Sebastian Vettel, Felipe Massa, Nelson Piquet, Kazuki Nakajima, Sébastien Bourdais, Giancarlo Fisichella, Adrian Sutil, Sébastien Buemi

(who damaged his nose by running wide at the final turn and had to pit on lap two for a replacement) and Robert Kubica, who limped away from sixth on the grid because his engine had all but died. "It was producing strange noises on the warm-up and there was very little power," he said. "Starting in those circumstances was not easy, but I continued to drive and asked the team what I should do. The car caught fire on lap two, though, before I got an answer…" He lasted fractionally longer than Heikki Kovalainen, who spun off at Turn Five on the opening lap: driver error, pure and simple.

The race remained reasonably tranquil for the first 15 laps, while the sky became ever more menacing. Rosberg edged away from Trulli by increasing fractions and Button was wedged in the Toyota's slipstream. Barrichello passed Alonso on the fourth lap, by which stage he was 6.5 seconds adrift of his team-mate, a margin that didn't alter significantly during the opening stint.

Rosberg ceded his advantage when he made his first scheduled stop, on lap 15. Trulli stayed out two laps longer and handed the lead to Button, who immediately posted a 1m 36.641s, the fastest lap of the afternoon so far, by a whopping 0.843 seconds. The sky was almost carbon black by the time Button peeled in, on schedule, on lap 19, but despite appearances it wasn't yet raining. Those extra low-

fuel laps put him comfortably ahead of Rosberg and Trulli when he rejoined, still on slicks – a tactic that wasn't adopted by all. Having helped himself to fifth place on lap 11, when Alonso lost momentum with a brief sideways moment, Räikkönen pitted on lap 18 and was sent back out on wets. "At the time," said Ferrari sporting director Stefano Domenicali, "our information indicated that the storm was imminent." You didn't need a team of crack meteorologists to tell you that, but the fact remained that the circuit stayed dry. Räikkönen was condemned to losing almost 20 seconds per lap while waiting for the rain to arrive, and in the process he was ripping his Bridgestones to shreds, so they would be past their best when it did.

Inevitability finally morphed into reality on lap 22, whereupon Alonso skated into the nearest gravel trap and dropped from fifth to tenth. Six seconds clear of the rest, Button headed a mad dash for the pits, being followed in by Rosberg, Trulli, Barrichello, Hamilton (making his first stop after starting with a sizeable fuel load), Heidfeld (ditto), Piquet, Massa, Webber, Alonso, Glock and Vettel. Glock gambled on intermediates, but everybody else plumped for wets. "When it rains at Sepang, it usually chucks it down," Button said, "but this was unusual because at first it was only spitting."

Manna for Glock, in other words. "I had seen the rain coming," he said, "but it seemed to take an age

to arrive. I thought, 'Okay, if it is taking so long I'll take a risk and go for intermediates'. Everybody else was on full wets and I could see they were struggling. I was overtaking car after car, but my tyres were going off as well. Even so, my engineer was telling me I was still the quickest guy on the track."

The German rejoined in tenth position, 54.8 seconds behind Button, but that soon dwindled dramatically. Between laps 24 and 28, the leader's times ranged from 2m 00.345s to 2m 03.779s, which looked mighty alongside anything Rosberg or Trulli could conjure, but paled against Glock's five-lap sequence: 1m 53.903s, 1m 52.996s, 1m 56.699s, 1m 57.992s and 1m 57.011s. The Toyota was now second – and only 16.4 seconds adrift of Button when the latter pitted for intermediates on lap 29. Glock took the lead while the Brawn was stationary, but the Englishman's fresh rubber enabled him to reclaim first place during lap 30, by which stage it had started to rain torrentially, a detail that persuaded Glock to peel in for full wets.

Button opted to do likewise at the end of the following lap – his fourth stop, in case you've lost count – but he was far enough in front to resume just ahead of Heidfeld, who was plodding along on his original set of full wets, after coaxing them through the drizzle, and Glock. The two Germans traded places at the start of the 32nd lap, when Glock dived down the

Left: Under pressure. For Martin Whitmarsh, it was not the ideal note on which to start his tenure as McLaren's team principal, being grilled by the media in the wake of Lewis Hamilton and the team's sporting director Dave Ryan having been found guilty of misleading the stewards the previous weekend at Melbourne.

Far left: Nick Heidfeld kept his composure admirably in the difficult conditions at Sepang, his BMW Sauber ending up in second place by the time the race was stopped.
Photos: Peter J. Fox

Left: "No, I'm not thinking about coming back! Not yet, anyway." Michael Schumacher isn't listening to any outside speculation.
Photo: Paul-Henri Cahier

Below: Ferrari's decision to put Kimi Räikkönen on full wet tyres was disastrously mistimed from a tactical viewpoint.
Photo: Peter Nygaard/GP Photo

was flying behind us on the intermediate, so we put that on, then as I came back out I could see his tyres were bald, and it was raining quite hard at the back of the circuit... I managed one lap on the inter at a reasonable pace and was able to come in again, switch back to wets and still keep the lead."

The final couple of laps were particularly confusing for Glock, who climbed the podium steps thinking he was second and arrived at the top to discover that, actually, he wasn't. "I was hoping they wouldn't dock me any more positions when I came back down," he said.

Brawn mostly made the right calls at the right time, albeit not quite as spectacularly as Glock, but the result might have had a very different complexion. Almost unnoticed in all the spray, Webber had driven a sensational second stint: on badly worn wets, he posted a sequence of 1m 58.909s, 1m 59.627s and 1m 58.268s between laps 26 and 28, when Button was just the other side of the 2m 00s touchstone. To put that into context, Barrichello, an acclaimed master in the wet, was lumbering around in the 2m 02s–2m 03s range...

Webber had risen to third, ahead of Heidfeld, when he came in for intermediates on lap 29. The German was intending to pit at that stage, too, but BMW came on the radio and advised him to stay out because the rain was increasing. By that stage, Webber was preparing to rejoin on what was now the wrong rubber, so he was obliged to return for full wets one lap later. Had Red Bull sent him out on those in the first instance, he'd have won. As it was, he had to settle for sixth. Such are the details that tend to be overlooked at times of pandemonium.

"It would have been nice to do a few more laps, to have a crack at getting on the podium," Webber said, "but stopping the race was the right call, so I have mixed emotions."

Hamilton, who customarily also thrives in the wet, drove another mature race to score his first permanent point of the campaign, in seventh. "I love it when it rains," he said, "but this was just too much – it had become too dangerous. It was just a matter of trying to keep the car on the track." To underline as much, he had a quick spin during the subsequently discounted 32nd lap.

With Rosberg claiming the final half-point, Ferrari had still to trouble the scorers in 2009. Massa was classified ninth, but Räikkönen's initially promising

inside at Turn One, and moments later Heidfeld spun as the rain became even more intense. The safety car was dispatched, but wasn't really much use in the conditions. "It was pulling away from me," said Button, "and that's when you know it's too wet for an F1 car."

At that point, the red flag came out and the race was suspended – an opportunity for TV viewers to switch on the kettle, but a catalyst for 50 minutes of soggy uncertainty in the grandstands. The 2009 regulations might have allowed for the recovery and storage of kinetic energy, but they mentioned nothing about headlights or windscreen wipers, both of which would have been useful by the time the rain eased sufficiently for the track to be driveable. The race was called off and the result declared at the end of lap 31, at which point Button had led Heidfeld, Glock, Trulli and Barrichello. For only the fifth time in the World Championship's history – after Spain and Austria in 1975, Monaco in 1984 and Australia in 1991 – half-points were awarded.

"That was a really crazy race," Button said. "My start was pretty bad and the car oversteered a lot early on – I don't think I got enough heat into the rear tyres. My pace was good once I got back to the front, but then the rain started and tyre choice was difficult. The full wet just destroyed itself because, at first, it didn't rain as heavily as usual. I knew Timo

EDITOR'S VIEW
OBJECTIVE JUSTICE OR THE RULE OF THE MOB?

ANYBODY who had been involved for any time in an opportunistic and cut-throat business like F1 could have been forgiven for thinking, "There but for the grace of God go I," as the interlocking sequence of catastrophic events conspired to wreck one man's career after 35 years in the sport and tarnish the image of the world champion so seriously that there are those within the racing community who believe he will never quite shed the ignominy throughout his career.

Yet, objectively, the spontaneous collaboration between Davey Ryan, McLaren's long serving sporting director, and Lewis Hamilton, which resulted in Ryan being fired and Hamilton being forced to offer up a humiliating apology, after they conspired to stitch up Jarno Trulli during the safety-car period in the closing stages of the Melbourne race, attracted penalties that were completely disproportionate to the offences involved.

Hamilton and Ryan may have lied to the stewards, but this was no hanging offence by any stretch of the imagination. It was an example of competitive urge and an aching passion to beat a rival, which pushed them over the edge into making a silly mistake. But it was certainly not unforgiveable. You could say that the McLaren corporate entity overreacted in concluding that this was the right time to don a hair shirt and offer a grovelling apology to the FIA's World Motor Sport Council, but with more than a thousand family mortgages back in Woking depending on the top brass making the right call, it was absolutely understandable that a symbolic gesture was made. So Ryan had to go, while Ron Dennis, having relinquished the role of team principal to Martin Whitmarsh only a few weeks beforehand, graciously opted to withdraw completely from McLaren's F1 front-line operation.

Obviously, because the whole episode involved newly crowned world champion Lewis Hamilton, it attracted a firestorm of media interest, the whole affair being whipped up out of all proportion by the tabloids. Suggestions were voiced that Hamilton and McLaren might be kicked out of the World Championship, as they were sure to be found guilty of bringing the sport into disrepute less than two years after being hauled up in front of the governing body for allegedly taking advantage of illegally obtained Ferrari F1 technology.

From the touchlines, of course, it was difficult to conclude that this would reduce the level of mutual antipathy that had existed between Dennis and the FIA president, Max Mosley, for some considerable time. After the so-called 'Ferrarigate' fiasco, McLaren had taken care to tread cautiously through the F1 political minefield, concentrating on never putting a foot out of line as the team sought to rebuild its rather tarnished reputation.

At the end of the day, of course, there would always be a number of unanswered questions. To start with, did Anthony Hamilton, the world champion's father and manager, really pick up the telephone and call Max Mosley in the aftermath of the Melbourne affair in a bid to insulate his son from the more extreme consequences of his own unfortunate actions?

If he did, then it was an unfortunate tactical error, as it sent a firm message that the Hamiltons were going to be the first in the lifeboats if the McLaren team really was preparing itself for what might well have been described as a 'Titanic, iceberg interface scenario'. In reality, the situation was a little more complicated than that, but from Lewis's perspective, it certainly looked like a clumsily managed episode and one from which he would take some time to recover.

Alan Henry

Right: A sodden Jenson Button waits beneath an umbrella for a restart that never came.

Below left: Lewis gives his version of events to the assembled media.
Photos: Peter J. Fox

Below: F1 components do not always finish the day looking as immaculate and superbly engineered as they start out.
Photos: Paul-Henri Cahier

2009 FORMULA 1™ PETRONAS MALAYSIAN GRAND PRIX

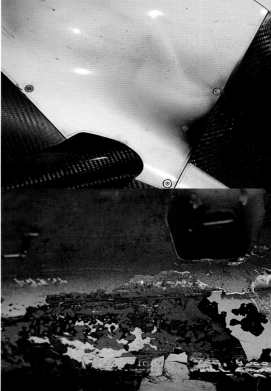

afternoon fell apart in the slipstream of that disastrous tyre call. He was officially 14th, but would not have been in any position to restart due to a KERS malfunction. While rivals loitered on the grid, wondering whether their task was over for the day, he returned to the Ferrari motorhome to change into civvies and tuck into an ice cream.

Despite his bright start, Alonso admitted he could do little more than defend against the cars around him "because we were just too slow". His subsequent adventures dropped him to 11th, between Bourdais and Nakajima, while Piquet and Räikkönen were the only others to complete 31 laps. Vettel, Buemi and Fisichella spun off just before the race was stopped, while Sutil was classified 17th, a lap down.

Vettel might still have been a few months short of his 22nd birthday, but his post-race reaction was revealing. "I was on badly-worn intermediates just before the final downpour," he said. "I was being very cautious, but there was just too much water approaching Turn Seven and my tyres were not designed for those conditions. A simple spin shouldn't have been a problem, but the anti-stall didn't work. In the past, drivers had a throttle, a brake and a clutch, and if you spun you knew exactly what to do. It's not in our hands any more, and it's a shame to retire for that stupid reason."

Atypical, perhaps, but a perspective that complements his fondness for trawling second-hand record shops in a quest to find old Beatles vinyl.
Simon Arron

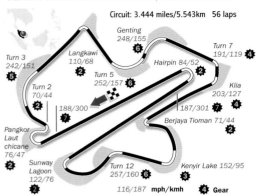

SEPANG INTERNATIONAL CIRCUIT, KUALA LUMPUR

Circuit: 3.444 miles/5.543km 56 laps

Genting 248/155
Langkawi 110/68
Turn 7 191/119
Turn 3 242/151
Hairpin 84/52
Turn 5 252/157
Turn 2 70/44
Klia 203/127
188/300
187/301
Berjaya Tioman 71/44
Pangkor Laut chicane 76/47
Sunway Lagoon 122/76
Turn 12 257/160
Kenyir Lake 152/95
116/187 mph/kmh   Gear

FIA F1 WORLD CHAMPIONSHIP ROUND 2

PETRONAS
MALAYSIAN
GRAND PRIX

KUALA LUMPUR 3-5 APRIL 2009

Photos: Peter J. Fox

RACE DISTANCE: 31 laps, 106.772 miles/171.833km • RACE WEATHER: Cloudy/wet/very wet/drizzle (track 27-37°C, air 24-31°C)

Pos.	Driver	Nat.	No.	Entrant	Car/Engine	Tyres	Laps	Time/Retirement	Speed (mph/km/h)	Gap to leader	Fastest race lap	
1	Jenson Button	GB	22	Brawn GP Formula 1 Team	Brawn BGP 001-Mercedes FO108W V8	B	31	55m 30.622s	115.408/185.730		1m 36.641s	18
2	Nick Heidfeld	D	6	BMW Sauber F1 Team	BMW Sauber F1.09-BMW P86/9 V8	B	31	55m 53.344s	114.626/184.472	+ 22.722s	1m 39.084s	17
3	Timo Glock	D	10	Panasonic Toyota Racing	Toyota TF109-RVX-09 V8	B	31	55m 54.135s	114.598/184.428	+ 23.513s	1m 39.406s	18
4	Jarno Trulli	I	9	Panasonic Toyota Racing	Toyota TF109-RVX-09 V8	B	31	56m 16.795s	113.830/183.191	+ 46.173s	1m 37.591s	12
5	Rubens Barrichello	BR	23	Brawn GP Formula 1 Team	Brawn BGP 001-Mercedes FO108W V8	B	31	56m 17.982s	113.789/183.126	+ 47.360s	1m 37.484s	17
6	Mark Webber	AUS	14	Red Bull Racing	Red Bull RB5-Renault RS27 V8	B	31	56m 22.955s	113.622/182.857	+ 52.333s	1m 37.672s	14
7	Lewis Hamilton	GB	1	Vodafone McLaren Mercedes	McLaren MP4-24-Mercedes FO108W V8	B	31	56m 31.355s	113.341/182.404	+ 1m 00.733s	1m 39.141s	17
8	Nico Rosberg	D	16	AT&T Williams	Williams FW31-Toyota RVX-09 V8	B	31	56m 42.198s	112.980/181.823	+ 1m 11.576s	1m 37.598s	13
9	Felipe Massa	BR	3	Scuderia Ferrari Marlboro	Ferrari F60-056 V8	B	31	56m 47.554s	112.802/181.537	+ 1m 16.932s	1m 39.250s	17
10	Sébastien Bourdais	F	11	Scuderia Toro Rosso	Toro Rosso STR04-Ferrari 056 V8	B	31	57m 12.786s	111.973/180.203	+ 1m 42.164s	1m 39.242s	17
11	Fernando Alonso	E	7	ING Renault F1 Team	Renault R29-RS27 V8	B	31	57m 20.044s	111.736/179.822	+ 1m 49.422s	1m 39.006s	17
12	Kazuki Nakajima	J	17	AT&T Williams	Williams FW31-Toyota RVX-09 V8	B	31	57m 26.752s	111.519/179.472	+ 1m 56.130s	1m 39.387s	17
13	Nelsinho Piquet	BR	8	ING Renault F1 Team	Renault R29-RS27 V8	B	31	57m 27.335s	111.500/179.442	+ 1m 56.713s	1m 39.268s	18
14	Kimi Räikkönen	FIN	4	Scuderia Ferrari Marlboro	Ferrari F60-056 V8	B	31	57m 53.463s	110.661/178.092	+ 2m 22.841s	1m 38.453s	17
15	Sebastian Vettel	D	15	Red Bull Racing	Red Bull RB5-Renault RS27 V8	B	30	accident		+ 1 lap	1m 38.427s	10
16	Sébastien Buemi	CH	12	Scuderia Toro Rosso	Toro Rosso STR04-Ferrari 056 V8	B	30	accident		+ 1 lap	1m 38.938s	16
17	Adrian Sutil	D	20	Force India F1 Team	Force India VJM02-Mercedes FO108W V8	B	30			+ 1 lap	1m 39.464s	17
18	Giancarlo Fisichella	I	21	Force India F1 Team	Force India VJM02-Mercedes FO108W V8	B	29	spin		+ 2 laps	1m 39.407s	16
	Robert Kubica	PL	5	BMW Sauber F1 Team	BMW Sauber F1.09-BMW P86/9 V8	B	1	engine/fire			no time	
	Heikki Kovalainen	FIN	2	Vodafone McLaren Mercedes	McLaren MP4-24-Mercedes FO108W V8	B	0	spin			no time	

Race scheduled for 56 laps, but stopped prematurely due to heavy rain.

Fastest race lap: Jenson Button on lap 18, 1m 36.641s, 128.303mph/206.483km/h.

Lap record: Juan Pablo Montoya (Williams FW26-BMW V10), 1m 34.223s, 131.596mph/211.782km/h (2004).

All results and data © FOM 2009

20	SUTIL · Force India
8	PIQUET · Renault
11	BOURDAIS · Toro Rosso
15	VETTEL · Red Bull penalty for accident in Rd 1
17	NAKAJIMA · Williams
7	ALONSO · Renault
12	BUEMI · Toro Rosso
21	FISICHELLA · Force India
3	MASSA · Ferrari
2	KOVALAINEN · McLaren
1	HAMILTON · McLaren
6	HEIDFELD · BMW Sauber

Grid order	1	2	3	4	5	6	7	8	9	10	11	12	13	14	15	16	17	18	19	20	21	22	23	24	25	26	27	28	29	30	31
22 BUTTON	16	16	16	16	16	16	16	16	16	16	16	16	16	16	16	9	22	22	22	23	22	22	22	22	22	22	22	22	22	22	
9 TRULLI	9	9	9	9	9	9	9	9	9	9	9	9	9	9	9	22	9	23	23	22	16	16	16	16	16	16	23	10	10	10	6
10 GLOCK	22	22	22	22	22	22	22	22	22	22	22	22	22	22	22	23	23	16	16	16	9	9	9	9	9	9	14	14	6	10	3
16 ROSBERG	7	7	7	23	23	23	23	23	23	23	23	23	23	23	23	16	16	9	9	9	23	23	23	23	23	14	6	6	14	9	
14 WEBBER	23	23	23	7	7	7	7	7	7	7	7	4	4	4	4	4	4	4	7	7	7	1	6	6	14	14	10	23	3	23	23
5 KUBICA	4	4	4	4	4	4	4	4	4	4	7	14	14	14	14	14	7	7	1	1	1	6	14	14	6	10	16	9	16	9	14	6
4 RÄIKKÖNEN	14	14	14	14	14	14	14	14	14	14	14	7	7	7	7	7	1	1	6	6	6	3	1	1	1	6	3	23	16	1	
23 BARRICHELLO	10	10	10	10	10	10	10	10	10	10	10	10	10	10	1	6	6	3	3	3	3	10	1	3	16	9	15	16			
7 ALONSO	6	6	6	6	6	6	6	15	15	15	15	1	1	10	6	3	3	8	14	8	10	3	3	1	8	1					
6 HEIDFELD	1	1	1	15	15	15	15	15	1	1	1	15	6	6	3	8	17	17	14	7	10	8	8	8	8	1	15	3	11		
17 NAKAJIMA	15	15	15	1	1	1	1	6	6	6	6	6	3	3	8	17	17	11	14	17	10	17	17	15	15	7	15	8	12	7	
1 HAMILTON	3	3	3	3	3	3	3	3	3	3	3	8	17	17	11	11	14	10	10	15	15	15	17	7	17	7	12	7	17		
15 VETTEL	8	8	8	8	8	8	8	8	8	8	8	8	8	17	17	11	21	14	10	15	15	17	7	7	7	17	15	17	4	11	9
2 KOVALAINEN	17	17	17	17	17	17	17	17	17	17	17	17	11	11	21	14	21	15	4	12	4	4	4	4	4	4	4	7	17	4	
11 BOURDAIS	11	11	11	11	11	11	11	11	11	11	11	11	20	21	10	10	10	4	12	4	11	11	11	11	11	12	12	11	8		
3 MASSA	21	21	21	21	20	20	20	20	20	20	20	20	21	20	15	15	15	12	11	11	12	12	12	12	12	11	11	17	4		
8 PIQUET	20	20	20	20	21	21	21	21	21	21	21	21	15	15	20	20	20	21	21	21	21	21	21	21	21	21	21	20			
21 FISICHELLA	12	12	12	12	12	12	12	12	12	12	12	12	12	12	20	20	20	20	20	20	20	20	20	20	20	20					
20 SUTIL	5																														
12 BUEMI																															

12 Pit stop   14 One lap or more behind

Race stopped on lap 32 under safety car – Final classification after 31 laps

TIME SHEETS

PRACTICE 1 (FRIDAY)
Sunny
(track 33-41°C, air 29-33°C)

Pos.	Driver	Laps	Time
1	Nico Rosberg	27	1m 36.260s
2	Kazuki Nakajima	25	1m 36.305s
3	Jenson Button	20	1m 36.430s
4	Rubens Barrichello	22	1m 36.487s
5	Felipe Massa	21	1m 36.561s
6	Kimi Räikkönen	18	1m 36.646s
7	Lewis Hamilton	16	1m 36.699s
8	Mark Webber	23	1m 36.703s
9	Sebastian Vettel	25	1m 36.747s
10	Timo Glock	27	1m 36.980s
11	Jarno Trulli	26	1m 36.982s
12	Giancarlo Fisichella	20	1m 37.025s
13	Robert Kubica	18	1m 37.039s
14	Nelsinho Piquet	20	1m 37.199s
15	Adrian Sutil	18	1m 37.241s
16	Fernando Alonso	12	1m 37.395s
17	Sébastien Buemi	22	1m 37.634s
18	Nick Heidfeld	17	1m 37.640s
19	Sébastien Bourdais	19	1m 38.022s
20	Heikki Kovalainen	7	1m 38.483s

PRACTICE 2 (FRIDAY)
Sunny
(track 34-41°C, air 29-35°C)

Pos.	Driver	Laps	Time
1	Kimi Räikkönen	40	1m 35.707s
2	Felipe Massa	38	1m 35.832s
3	Sebastian Vettel	40	1m 35.954s
4	Nico Rosberg	39	1m 36.015s
5	Mark Webber	36	1m 36.026s
6	Rubens Barrichello	37	1m 36.161s
7	Jenson Button	31	1m 36.254s
8	Kazuki Nakajima	35	1m 36.290s
9	Heikki Kovalainen	40	1m 36.397s
10	Nelsinho Piquet	35	1m 36.401s
11	Lewis Hamilton	30	1m 36.515s
12	Jarno Trulli	34	1m 36.516s
13	Sébastien Buemi	32	1m 36.628s
14	Timo Glock	29	1m 36.639s
15	Fernando Alonso	20	1m 36.640s
16	Adrian Sutil	36	1m 36.875s
17	Robert Kubica	38	1m 37.267s
18	Sébastien Bourdais	30	1m 37.278s
19	Giancarlo Fisichella	27	1m 37.432s
20	Nick Heidfeld	37	1m 37.930s

PRACTICE 3 (SATURDAY)
Sunny/partly cloudy
(track 37-43°C, air 32-33°C)

Pos.	Driver	Laps	Time
1	Nico Rosberg	19	1m 35.940s
2	Mark Webber	13	1m 36.048s
3	Felipe Massa	13	1m 36.089s
4	Jarno Trulli	21	1m 36.132s
5	Timo Glock	22	1m 36.189s
6	Sebastian Vettel	14	1m 36.194s
7	Kimi Räikkönen	14	1m 36.322s
8	Kazuki Nakajima	18	1m 36.325s
9	Rubens Barrichello	19	1m 36.519s
10	Jenson Button	17	1m 36.541s
11	Robert Kubica	18	1m 36.563s
12	Lewis Hamilton	15	1m 36.657s
13	Heikki Kovalainen	13	1m 36.742s
14	Fernando Alonso	16	1m 37.004s
15	Nick Heidfeld	18	1m 37.026s
16	Nelsinho Piquet	18	1m 37.032s
17	Adrian Sutil	18	1m 37.118s
18	Sébastien Buemi	17	1m 37.282s
19	Sébastien Bourdais	16	1m 37.322s
20	Giancarlo Fisichella	19	1m 37.398s

QUALIFYING (SATURDAY)
Sunny/partly cloudy (track 35-39°C, air 30-31°C)

Pos.	Driver	First	Second	Third	Weight
1	Jenson Button	1m 35.058s	**1m 33.784s**	**1m 35.181s**	660kg
2	Jarno Trulli	1m 34.745s	1m 33.990s	1m 35.273s	656.5kg
3	Sebastian Vettel	1m 34.935s	1m 34.276s	1m 35.518s	647kg
4	Rubens Barrichello	**1m 34.681s**	1m 34.387s	1m 35.651s	664.5kg
5	Timo Glock	1m 34.907s	1m 34.258s	1m 35.690s	656.5kg
6	Nico Rosberg	1m 35.083s	1m 34.547s	1m 35.750s	656kg
7	Mark Webber	1m 35.027s	1m 34.222s	1m 35.797s	656kg
8	Robert Kubica	1m 35.166s	1m 34.562s	1m 36.106s	663kg
9	Kimi Räikkönen	1m 35.476s	1m 34.456s	1m 36.170s	662.5kg
10	Fernando Alonso	1m 35.260s	1m 34.706s	1m 37.659s	680.5kg
11	Nick Heidfeld	1m 35.110s	1m 34.769s		692kg
12	Kazuki Nakajima	1m 35.341s	1m 34.788s		683.4kg
13	Lewis Hamilton	1m 35.280s	1m 34.905s		688kg
14	Heikki Kovalainen	1m 35.023s	1m 34.924s		688.9kg
15	Sébastien Bourdais	1m 35.507s	1m 35.431s		670.5kg
16	Felipe Massa	1m 35.642s			689.5kg
17	Nelsinho Piquet	1m 35.708s			681.9kg
18	Giancarlo Fisichella	1m 35.908s			680.5kg
19	Adrian Sutil	1m 35.951s			655.5kg
20	Sébastien Buemi	1m 36.107s			686.5kg

DID YOU KNOW?

This was the shortest grand prix since Australia 1991, which ran for just over 24 minutes (14 laps) due to rain. Apart from that race, there have been three other occasions when half-points were awarded: Spain '75, Austria '75 and Monaco '84.

POINTS

DRIVERS

1	Jenson Button	15
2	Rubens Barrichello	10
3	Jarno Trulli	8.5
4	Timo Glock	8
5	Nick Heidfeld	4
6	Fernando Alonso	4
7	Nico Rosberg	3.5
8	Sébastien Buemi	2
9	Mark Webber	1.5
10	Lewis Hamilton	1
11	Sébastien Bourdais	1

CONSTRUCTORS

1	Brawn	25
2	Toyota	16.5
3	BMW Sauber	4
4	Renault	4
5	Williams	3.5
6	Toro Rosso	3
7	Red Bull	1.5
8	McLaren	1

4 RÄIKKÖNEN · Ferrari

14 WEBBER · Red Bull

10 GLOCK · Toyota

22 BUTTON · Brawn

23 BARRICHELLO · Brawn
penalty for gearbox change

5 KUBICA · BMW Sauber

16 ROSBERG · Williams

9 TRULLI · Toyota

RACE TYRE STRATEGIES

The tyre regulations stipulate that the two dry tyre specifications must be used during the race.

The Soft compound Bridgestone Potenza tyre is marked with a green stripe on the sidewall of the tyre.

	Driver	Race Stint 1	Race Stint 2	Race Stint 3	Race Stint 4	Race Stint 5
1	Jenson Button	Soft: 1-19	Soft: 20-22	Wet: 23-29	Inter: 30	Wet: 31
2	Nick Heidfeld	Soft: 1-22	Wet: 23-31			
3	Timo Glock	Soft: 1-15	Soft: 16-22	Inter: 23-30	Wet: 31	
4	Jarno Trulli	Soft: 1-17	Soft: 18-22	Wet: 23-28	Inter: 29-30	Wet: 31
5	Rubens Barrichello	Soft: 1-20	Soft: 21-22	Wet: 23-28	Inter: 29-30	Wet: 31
6	Mark Webber	Soft: 1-16	Soft: 17-22	Wet: 23-28	Inter: 29	Wet: 30-31
7	Lewis Hamilton	Soft: 1-22	Wet: 23-26	Inter: 27-29	Wet: 30-31	
8	Nico Rosberg	Soft: 1-15	Soft: 16-22	Wet: 23-27	Inter: 28-29	Wet: 30-31
	Felipe Massa	Soft: 1-22	Wet: 23-29	Inter: 30	Wet: 31	
	Sébastien Bourdais	Soft: 1-19	Wet: 20-26	Inter: 27-30	Wet: 31	
	Fernando Alonso	Soft: 1-22	Wet: 23-28	Inter: 29-30	Wet: 31	
	Kazuki Nakajima	Soft: 1-21	Wet: 22-26	Inter: 27-30	Wet: 31	
	Nelson Piquet	Soft: 1-22	Wet: 23-29	Inter: 30	Wet: 31	
	Kimi Räikkönen	Soft: 1-18	Wet: 19-29	Inter: 30	Wet: 31	
	Sebastian Vettel	Soft: 1-13	Soft: 14-22	Wet: 23-26	Inter: 27-30 (dnf)	
	Sébastien Buemi	Soft: 1-2	Soft: 3-21	Wet: 22-28 (dnf)		
	Adrian Sutil	Soft: 1-15	Soft: 16-18	Wet: 19-30		
	Giancarlo Fisichella	Soft: 1-18	Wet: 19-29 (dnf)			
	Robert Kubica	Soft: 0-1 (dnf)				
	Heikki Kovalainen	Soft: 0 (dnf)				

FIA FORMULA 1 WORLD CHAMPIONSHIP • ROUND 3

CHINESE GRAND PRIX

SHANGHAI CIRCUIT

SHANGHAI QUALIFYING

FREE practice sessions tend to be fragmented affairs, and it isn't always obvious when a car or two goes missing for technical – rather than strategic – reasons, but brows in the Red Bull garage were deeply furrowed.

On Saturday morning, Sebastian Vettel and Mark Webber stopped with driveshaft boot failures after seven and eight laps respectively, and for Vettel the problem recurred during Q1. After more than 3,500 miles of trouble-free testing, this was a fresh development of uncertain, unwelcome provenance.

The German's first flying lap had been just fast enough to squeak into Q2, but the car's ultimate pace looked promising and the team didn't want to waste an opportunity, so it took a gamble. With his car dripping grease and its durability looking questionable, Vettel remained in his garage until the final moments of Q2, whereupon he popped out and banged in a 1m 35.130s, 0.043 second quicker than Webber. From nowhere, he was suddenly fastest.

Circumstance obliged him to use the same tactic in Q3, but the result was no different. Fernando Alonso's flyweight Renault split the Red Bulls, and Webber – who would have another split driveshaft boot by the session's end – was fractionally compromised by an extra 2.5kg of fuel, but Vettel's 1m 36.184s illustrated perfectly how pressure should be absorbed and swatted aside.

"Not knowing whether the car would last made things difficult," he said, "and in Q3 I had no chance to adapt to the heavier fuel load because I didn't have a first run. I knew the car was quick, though, from Mark's pace in Q1 and Q2, so basically I had no concerns. But if you only have one lap and make a mistake by going wide or whatever, there is no second chance. It wasn't so easy, but I am very, very happy. It's unbelievable that I made it to pole." Quite so – and then you factored in his age and relative inexperience.

Alonso hadn't done much morning running, either, because Renault was busy fettling its freshly delivered twin diffuser, which initially ran too close to the exhaust. The team's reparatory methods were refreshingly redolent of a Formula Ford paddock from the mid-1970s, gaffer tape being used to hold various bits together. They were effective, too, even though subsequent performance was flattered by a wispy fuel load – the Spaniard's car was seven kilos nimbler than Vettel's and would start 60kg lighter than Heikki Kovalainen's McLaren, which was brimmed with almost enough fuel to last until Bahrain.

Rubens Barrichello and Jenson Button were fourth and fifth for Brawn, both complaining about a touch too much understeer when fuel levels were topped up in Q3, while defending champion Lewis Hamilton could see light on the horizon after he qualified ninth courtesy of an uprated diffuser. "There's a long way to go," he said, "but this feels like the start of the road to recovery."

Could the Red Bulls last a race distance? One theory was that the team's driveshaft grease, which had been freighted by sea, might have become contaminated in transit and caused the boots to expand through overheating, but culpability was finally apportioned to a rogue batch. A simple fix lay in the adjacent pit garage, where sister team Toro Rosso used an identical component, albeit turned inside out. These were duly appropriated and fitted, whereupon the earlier problems vanished.

Above: Magic carpet ride. Kazuki Nakajima's Williams and Giancarlo Fisichella's Force India give their drivers moments of tension as they slither over the trackside Astroturf in the dreadful conditions.
Photo: Jean-Francois Galeron/WRi2

Left: That winning smile: Vettel celebrates pole position, another display of youthful virtuosity.
Photo: Peter J. Fox

IT was almost as if somebody had stumbled upon a new, unwritten regulation that forbade convention. Australia had been a cocktail of twilight and mild anarchy, Malaysia the curtailment of a misguided plan to blend Formula One cars with monsoon conditions and the onset of darkness. For all that the timetable looked relatively straightforward in China, however, the weather was anything but.

Sunday morning's light drizzle eventually morphed into heavy, incessant rain, and the Shanghai International Circuit was thoroughly soaked by the time of the start. In the expectation of dry conditions, the Red Bulls had been fuelled for three stops, Mark Webber notionally being able to convert to two, and the Brawns for two. "A three-stopper is potentially quicker around here," said Ross Brawn, "but only if the race runs absolutely smoothly." He expected his cars' heavier fuel loads to give them a tactical edge over 56 laps since with weights taken into account,

both they and Jarno Trulli's Toyota had qualified fractionally quicker than the Red Bulls. The change in conditions, however, trashed strategies drawn up 24 hours earlier, and Sebastian Vettel's pole position guaranteed him an early lead when a safety-car start was decreed.

The German duly trickled away from Fernando Alonso, Mark Webber, Rubens Barrichello, Jenson Button, Trulli, Nico Rosberg, Kimi Räikkönen, Lewis Hamilton Sébastien Buemi, Nick Heidfeld, Heikki Kovalainen, Felipe Massa, Kazuki Nakajima, Sébastien Bourdais, Nelson Piquet, Adrian Sutil, Giancarlo Fisichella, Robert Kubica and Timo Glock, the last two of whom opted to start from the pits. Glock had originally qualified 14th, but lost five positions in the wake of an unscheduled gearbox change on Saturday morning.

The safety car stayed out for eight laps, during which time the order shuffled slightly: both Ferrari drivers ran very wide at Turn 16, without losing a place, but the Force Indias swapped positions when Sutil did likewise. The German subsequently pitted and dropped to the back of the field. Williams refuelled Rosberg on lap six, in the belief that it wouldn't cost much time because the race was likely to be neutralised for quite a while, but that condemned him to struggle with a heavy car when the field was unleashed shortly afterwards. Renault brought in Alonso one lap later, mainly because he hadn't started with much fuel in the first place.

With the only clear view in the house, Vettel was able to put 2.4 seconds between himself and Webber on that opening lap. Just as crucially, he had caressed his throttle behind the safety car and now was able to stay out as long as his team-mate during the opening stint. Instead of running one lap longer, therefore, as had been planned originally, the Australian was now tactically disadvantaged because he would have to

refuel one lap earlier than Vettel, to avoid the two of them queuing in the pits. Webber was 6.014 seconds adrift when he peeled in on lap 14 and 8.606 seconds in arrears by the time Vettel had refuelled one lap later. And now they were separated by Buemi and Massa, who had yet to stop.

Button inherited the lead when the Red Bulls dropped momentarily from the radar – he'd passed Barrichello on lap 11, when the Brazilian became the latest of many to explore Turn 16's greener extremes – and he was still ahead when the safety car made its second appearance of the afternoon. The catalyst was Jarno Trulli, who was as poor in the wet as he had been marvellous in the dry. He had been tumbling down the order for a while and, when he slowed for the final corner on lap 16, he caught the following Kubica, unsighted in the spray, by surprise. "I braked very hard," the Pole said, "but I hit standing water and my car simply accelerated." The BMW was only lightly

Right: For the third successive race in 2009, the safety car had to be deployed to slow the field while accident debris were cleared from the circuit.

Below: Heavy rain failed to dampen the spirits of the fans, who watched Vettel take a commanding victory.

Photos: Peter J. Fox

Above: The outstanding overtaking move of the day was Mark Webber's decisive lunge on Jenson Button, which rounded off a Red Bull 1-2 finish, breaking the Brawn team's early run of success.

Photo: Jad Sherif/WRi2

Left: Robert Kubica and Jarno Trulli scatter shards of carbon fibre across the already treacherously slippery track as they make unscheduled contact. Kubica's BMW Sauber continued, but Trulli's Toyota went out.

Photo: Lukas Gorys

damaged, given the force of the subsequent impact and the height the car reached, and Kubica was able to continue after pitting for repairs. Trulli's rear wing was torn off, though, and the circuit was littered with carbon debris. The Italian dawdled around for another lap before retiring, and the safety car was scrambled.

Indirectly, the incident almost ruined Vettel's afternoon. Aware of the impending appearance of the safety car, the German had eased up, but was still catching the trundling Trulli, whom he spotted very late. He jinked to avoid the Toyota and strayed directly into the path of the pit-bound Buemi, whose long first stint had carried him up to fifth. The Swiss sustained a broken front wing, but Vettel emerged unscathed. "I was happy that nothing happened to the car," he said, "because it was already difficult enough in those conditions."

Button and Barrichello pitted at the end of lap 19, with the race neutralised, and the championship leader split the Red Bulls when he rejoined. The race resumed at the start of the 23rd lap, when Vettel was immediately able to capitalise on his car's ability to conjure tyre heat more swiftly than the Brawn: within a lap, he was 4.3 seconds clear.

"I felt like I was really slow," Button said, "because I was trying to miss every river, but the problem with that is that the circuit conditions are changing every lap and the position of the rivers is constantly moving. When I saw that Mark and I were pulling away from the people behind, I was reasonably happy and just sort of settled into a pace."

Button then appeared to have thrown second away by running wide at Turn 14, on lap 29, but two laps later Webber goofed, too, and went bounding beyond the kerbs at Turn 16. That laid the foundations for the race's finest move, one that Webber felt was the best of his career. As they came into Turn Seven for the 32nd time, the Australian started to have a peep at the outside line. "I didn't have a clue where he was," Button said. "It came as a bit of a shock because you couldn't see anything. He suddenly appeared around the outside, cut across the front and made the move stick. It was impossible to do anything about it."

In the Red Bull garage, the car-to-pit radio suddenly fizzed into life. "Now that's what you call a ****ing pass," said the Australian voice at the other end. His crew didn't hear him properly the first time and wondered what he meant. Had he taken a short cut? Did he think he might have to let Jenson Button back ahead? "No," he replied. "I said, 'That's what you call…'"

It was a glorious moment, but the last of significance between the top three. The final stops went without a hitch and Vettel ran home more than ten seconds clear of Webber to record his second grand prix victory – and Red Bull's first.

"It was the right decision to start behind the safety car," he said. "The circuit was okay at some points, but at others there was a lot of aquaplaning every lap. Conditions were very, very difficult, especially at the last corner. It is slightly uphill, so the water gathers and there was one place where basically you had no control, so I just tried not to unsettle the car – don't downshift, don't brake too much…every lap you had to be cautious."

For the second time in his F1 career, he'd been handed a winning opportunity, and for the second time, he'd taken it, without making a mistake worth the name. And conditions had been just as testing as they had been at Monza six months before, if not more so.

"During the first few laps, it was impossible to stay close to Seb," Webber said. "I could hardly see anything. I was on and off the throttle over some of the blind crests and having lots of moments. It was a question of playing with the rivers, seeing how aggressive you could be and how much you could get away with. Sometimes I won, sometimes I lost – it was a fantastic challenge."

Off the podium's top step for the first time in 2009, Button wasn't too disheartened. "I didn't expect so much aquaplaning," he said. "If it's wet, it's wet.

Above: The ultra-slick McLaren crew services Lewis Hamilton's car during his climb from ninth on the starting grid to sixth at the chequered flag.

Photo: Fritz Van Eldik/WRi2

Right: Winners at last. Four years after Red Bull acquired the team, a 1-2 success made a first grand prix victory even sweeter.

Photo: Peter J. Fox

You can normally master the line and try to find an area on the circuit where it's dry or where you're not aquaplaning, but here it was very difficult. You were aquaplaning as you came on to the main straight and as you went down the dip across the start/finish line. In that situation, there's nothing you can do, and just getting to the end of the race was a relief."

Barrichello took fourth, despite struggling early on to generate sufficient brake heat – only three discs worked properly during his first stint – while Kovalainen drove faultlessly to take fifth for McLaren, largely because team-mate Hamilton spent almost as much time off the circuit as he did on it.

The Englishman spun early in the race and later ran very wide on a couple of occasions, the second such incident, on lap 47, gifting a place to Kovalainen. Two laps later, Hamilton spun again, allowing Sutil to take sixth, albeit briefly. The German had been fuelled to run to the end as early as lap 19, and that long final stint allowed him to make stealthy progress, but also took a toll on his tyres. He was obliged to push hard, due to pressure from the recovering Hamilton, and on lap 51, with just five to go, he slithered irretrievably into the tyres at Turn Six.

"I was short of downforce," Hamilton said, "and I don't know whether it's me or the car, but I kept destroying my tyres."

Glock, ever dependable in the rain, survived an early brush with Heidfeld and went on to maintain his 100-per-cent scoring record, in seventh, with Buemi claiming the final point after another spirited drive.

Qualifying might have flattered the Renault R29, but Alonso believed genuine improvements had been made. His early stop dictated an afternoon in traffic, however, which masked the true extent of the team's progress, and he recovered only to ninth. After a long, 27-lap first stint, Räikkönen, tenth, felt that his car subsequently had lost grip. He was also probably sick of the sight of Hamilton, who passed him on three separate occasions between assorted incidents.

Massa started with enough fuel to stop only once, but hopes that he might have been able to translate that into a podium challenge fizzled out along with his electrical system.

Bourdais headed the remaining finishers, from Heidfeld, Kubica, Fisichella, Rosberg (whose team-mate Nakajima had dropped out with transmission trouble) and Piquet, but uniquely the Frenchman was insistent that the race ought not to have started. "I don't think we should have raced," he said, "because there was so much aquaplaning. The situation is aggravated because cars have a lot less downforce this year. I had a couple of spins, but might have had 15 or 20. The one positive thing is that it was probably a good show for the fans."

One thing they missed was his comedic parting shot. In the race's immediate aftermath, he picked up a wheel gun and – for reasons the team was powerless to explain – attempted to blow-dry his helmet visor. As soon as he pulled the trigger, however, it recoiled in his hand, hit him on the head and inflicted a sizeable bruise.

Simon Arron

EDITOR'S VIEW
RED BULL ON THE RAMPAGE

I F the Brawn-Mercedes displayed an early-season performance edge, it was always going to take a few races before an accurate comparative balance emerged between the former Hondas and their most obvious and consistent challengers.

Even in Australia, we had seen the first signs that Adrian Newey's attention to the smallest detail on the Red Bull RB5 had the potential to make it the obvious challenger to the Brawn, which had enjoyed as much as an extra nine months' engineering largesse courtesy of Honda. This, reputedly, had included the services of up to four separate wind tunnels.

So by the time we arrived in Shanghai, we were all still finding our feet as far as calibrating the relative technical merits of the two teams. And the third round of the World Championship really did not tell us a great deal more than we knew at the start of the year about Sebastian Vettel's raw speed in torrential rain. We'd known that ever since Monza '08, where he'd started the Ferrari-engined Toro Rosso from pole position and never looked back, beating a tentative, and indeed tense looking, Heikki Kovalainen convincingly back into second place.

In this business, a series of tiny plus-points, seemingly insignificant when viewed in isolation, can be amassed to harvest a decisive performance edge. So it was in the streaming wet conditions in Shanghai. Due to the torrential rain, the race was started under the safety car, thereby eliminating any possibility of pole-sitter Vettel risking his prospects with a first-corner tangle. When the safety car was withdrawn, he had a clean run away from the pack and a blank canvas on which to draw a victory that was every bit as dominant and decisive as his success at Monza six months earlier.

An off-season switch to Brembo brakes had been driven strongly by Vettel with Webber's support. Both drivers liked the progressive feel that they gave to the pedal and the progressive, sensitive manner in which they responded to the drivers' demands. All in all, it was a perfect day for the Red Bulls, and while this was Vet-

tel's second win, Webber duly delivered the best result of his entire career with a strong second place. Over the previous year or so, we had seen the rugged Australian trim and tidy his act, adding consistency and predictability to the mix, which already included out-and-out speed.

Granted, Mark had a mud-kicking ride on the wild side when he shaved the grass in a particularly lurid moment during the course of the race, but there was no repeat of the embarrassing episode at Silverstone in '08, where he had qualified on the front row of the grid, only to spin in the rain on the opening lap and end up facing the pursuing pack as they went out on to the Hangar Straight for the first time. If Shanghai was a race where Vettel consolidated his already glittering – indeed glistening – reputation, then it was also the race where Webber proved beyond doubt that he was made of the Right Stuff.

Granted Webber had carried a lap or so more fuel in qualifying, which suggested that he would stay out the longest, but when it came to the race itself, the Red Bull squad showed it had sufficient tactical flexibility to do pretty much as it pleased. To cement Vettel's position in the lead, the team pitted Webber first and ran Sebastian right up to the outer edge of his potential fuel range.

That was enough to deprive Jenson Button, who by then only had a four-lap fuel advantage on which to capitalise before making his first stop, of any chance of out-fumbling the Red Bulls to take the lead at the first round of stops.

The story might have been different in dry and hot conditions, but such theorising does not alter the fact that Red Bull had thrown its hat into the ring as Brawn's most consistently formidable challenger. In that respect, it had been a significant race indeed. Many wondered what the team might achieve with a double diffuser, the legality of which had been confirmed by the FIA only the previous week.

Alan Henry

SHANGHAI INTERNATIONAL CIRCUIT
Circuit: 3.387 miles/5.451 km
56 laps

116/187 mph/kmh

4 Gear

Turn 1 117/188 **5**
2 53/85 **2**
3 53/85 **2**
5 177/285 **6**
4 123/196 **3**
7 **6** 270/168
2 6 76/47
16 159/99 **4**
8 **4** 94/152
3 12 102/164
108/67 9 **3**
15 120/192 **3**
11 85/53 **2**
10 115/185 **3**
14 73/45 **2** 317/197 **7**
13 250/155 **6**

FIA F1 WORLD CHAMPIONSHIP ROUND 3
CHINESE
GRAND PRIX
SHANGHAI 17-19 APRIL 2009

Photos: Peter J. Fox

RACE DISTANCE: 56 laps, 198.559 miles/305.066km • RACE WEATHER: Rain (track 21°C, air 20°C)

All results and data © FOM 2009

Pos.	Driver	Nat.	No.	Entrant	Car/Engine	Tyres	Laps	Time/Retirement	Speed (mph/km/h)	Gap to leader	Fastest race lap	
1	Sebastian Vettel	D	15	Red Bull Racing	Red Bull RB5-Renault RS27 V8	B	56	1h 57m 43.485s	96.611/155.480		1m 52.627s	42
2	Mark Webber	AUS	14	Red Bull Racing	Red Bull RB5-Renault RS27 V8	B	56	1h 57m 54.455s	96.461/155.239	+ 10.970s	1m 52.980s	42
3	Jenson Button	GB	22	Brawn GP Formula 1 Team	Brawn BGP 001-Mercedes FO108W V8	B	56	1h 58m 28.460s	96.000/154.497	+ 44.975s	1m 53.546s	44
4	Rubens Barrichello	BR	23	Brawn GP Formula 1 Team	Brawn BGP 001-Mercedes FO108W V8	B	56	1h 58m 47.189s	95.748/154.091	+ 1m 03.704s	1m 52.592s	42
5	Heikki Kovalainen	FIN	2	Vodafone McLaren Mercedes	McLaren MP4-24-Mercedes FO108W V8	B	56	1h 58m 48.587s	95.729/154.061	+ 1m 05.102s	1m 54.516s	41
6	Lewis Hamilton	GB	1	Vodafone McLaren Mercedes	McLaren MP4-24-Mercedes FO108W V8	B	56	1h 58m 55.351s	95.638/153.915	+ 1m 11.866s	1m 54.665s	39
7	Timo Glock	D	10	Panasonic Toyota Racing	Toyota TF109-RVX-09 V8	B	56	1h 58m 57.961s	95.603/153.858	+ 1m 14.476s	1m 52.703s	42
8	Sébastien Buemi	CH	12	Scuderia Toro Rosso	Toro Rosso STR04-Ferrari 056 V8	B	56	1h 58m 59.924s	95.577/153.816	+ 1m 16.439s	1m 54.590s	42
9	Fernando Alonso	E	7	ING Renault F1 Team	Renault R29-RS27 V8	B	56	1h 59m 07.794s	95.472/153.647	+ 1m 24.309s	1m 54.481s	38
10	Kimi Räikkönen	FIN	4	Scuderia Ferrari Marlboro	Ferrari F60-056 V8	B	56	1h 59m 15.235s	95.372/153.487	+ 1m 31.750s	1m 55.396s	38
11	Sébastien Bourdais	F	11	Scuderia Toro Rosso	Toro Rosso STR04-Ferrari 056 V8	B	56	1h 59m 17.641s	95.340/153.435	+ 1m 34.156s	1m 53.474s	43
12	Nick Heidfeld	D	6	BMW Sauber F1 Team	BMW Sauber F1.09-BMW P86/9 V8	B	56	1h 59m 19.319s	95.318/153.399	+ 1m 35.834s	1m 54.158s	40
13	Robert Kubica	PL	5	BMW Sauber F1 Team	BMW Sauber F1.09-BMW P86/9 V8	B	56	1h 59m 30.338s	95.171/153.163	+ 1m 46.853s	1m 55.350s	44
14	Giancarlo Fisichella	I	21	Force India F1 Team	Force India VJM02-Mercedes FO108W V8	B	55			+ 1 lap	1m 56.239s	37
15	Nico Rosberg	D	16	AT&T Williams	Williams FW31-Toyota RVX-09 V8	B	55			+ 1 lap	1m 54.243s	55
16	Nelsinho Piquet	BR	8	ING Renault F1 Team	Renault R29-RS27 V8	B	54			+ 2 laps	1m 55.535s	42
17	Adrian Sutil	D	20	Force India F1 Team	Force India VJM02-Mercedes FO108W V8	B	50	accident		+ 6 laps	1m 54.777s	41
	Kazuki Nakajima	J	17	AT&T Williams	Williams FW31-Toyota RVX-09 V8	B	43	transmission			1m 56.167s	38
	Felipe Massa	BR	3	Scuderia Ferrari Marlboro	Ferrari F60-056 V8	B	20	electrics			1m 56.484s	16
	Jarno Trulli	I	9	Panasonic Toyota Racing	Toyota TF109-RVX-09 V8	B	18	accident damage			2m 00.330s	14

Fastest race lap: Rubens Barrichello on lap 42, 1m 52.592s, 108.298mph/174.289km/h.

Lap record: Michael Schumacher (Ferrari F2004 V10), 1m 32.238s, 132.196mph/212.749km/h (2004).

10	GLOCK · Toyota penalty for gearbox change started from pit lane
5	KUBICA · BMW Sauber started from pitlane
11	BOURDAIS · Toro Rosso
3	MASSA · Ferrari
6	HEIDFELD · BMW Sauber
1	HAMILTON · McLaren
21	FISICHELLA · Force India
20	SUTIL · Force India
8	PIQUET · Renault
17	NAKAJIMA · Williams
2	KOVALAINEN · McLaren
12	BUEMI · Toro Rosso

Grid order	1	2	3	4	5	6	7	8	9	10	11	12	13	14	15	16	17	18	19	20	21	22	23	24	25	26	27	28	29	30	31	32	33	34	35	36	37	38	39	40	41	42	43	44
15 VETTEL	15	15	15	15	15	15	15	15	15	15	15	15	15	15	15	22	22	22	22	15	15	15	15	15	15	15	15	15	15	15	15	15	15	15	15	15	14	14	22	15	15	15	15	44
7 ALONSO	7	7	7	7	7	7	14	14	14	14	14	14	14	14	14	23	23	23	23	22	22	22	22	22	22	22	14	14	22	14	14	14	14	14	14	14	22	22	15	22	22	14	14	
14 WEBBER	14	14	14	14	14	14	23	23	23	23	22	22	22	22	15	15	15	15	3	14	14	14	14	14	14	14	22	22	14	22	22	22	22	22	15	15	14	14	14	23	22			
23 BARRICHELLO	23	23	23	23	23	23	22	22	22	22	23	23	23	23	12	12	12	3	14	4	4	1	1	1	1	1	1	1	1	1	1	1	1	1	23	23	23	23	23	23	23	12		
22 BUTTON	22	22	22	22	22	22	7	9	9	9	1	9	12	12	3	3	3	3	12	4	1	1	4	4	4	2	2	2	2	2	2	2	7	7	12	12	12	12	12	12	12	23		
9 TRULLI	9	9	9	9	9	9	4	1	1	9	12	9	3	14	14	14	14	14	1	23	23	2	2	2	23	23	23	23	23	23	2	12	1	1	1	1	1	1	1	1				
16 ROSBERG	16	16	16	16	4	4	4	1	4	4	4	3	9	1	4	4	4	4	23	2	2	23	23	23	4	12	12	12	7	7	7	12	1	20	20	20	20	20	2	2				
4 RÄIKKÖNEN	4	4	4	4	1	1	1	12	12	12	12	4	4	4	4	1	1	1	2	11	12	12	12	12	7	7	7	12	12	12	1	20	2	2	2	2	2	20	20	20				
1 HAMILTON	1	1	1	1	12	12	12	6	6	6	3	2	1	1	9	12	12	12	11	12	10	10	7	7	7	7	11	11	11	20	20	20	20	2	7	6	6	6	6	6	6	6		
12 BUEMI	12	12	12	12	16	6	6	3	2	3	2	1	2	2	11	11	11	12	10	17	17	7	17	20	5	5	5	5	6	6	16	16	16	10	10	10	10	10	10	10				
6 HEIDFELD	6	6	6	6	3	3	3	11	11	11	11	11	11	11	11	12	10	10	7	7	7	11	11	11	11	5	20	21	6	16	16	6	4	4	7	7	7							
2 KOVALAINEN	2	2	2	2	3	3	17	11	11	6	6	10	10	10	10	17	17	17	7	11	11	10	21	20	20	21	21	6	16	16	4	4	10	10	4	7	4	4	4	4				
3 MASSA	3	3	3	3	3	17	17	11	10	10	17	17	17	7	7	7	7	21	21	21	20	5	6	6	6	16	16	4	4	10	10	7	7	7	16	11	11	11	11					
17 NAKAJIMA	17	17	17	17	17	11	8	8	8	17	21	21	21	21	16	16	5	21	16	16	16	4	4	10	10	5	11	11	11	11	11	16	11	16										
11 BOURDAIS	11	11	11	11	8	8	21	21	8	21	20	20	20	5	5	5	20	16	16	6	4	4	4	17	10	21	11	11	21	21	21	11	5	5	5									
8 PIQUET	8	8	8	8	21	5	10	10	21	8	5	5	5	20	16	6	16	6	6	10	10	17	10	17	11	21	11	17	17	17	5	21	21	21										
5 KUBICA	20	20	21	21	21	5	5	5	5	20	7	7	20	5	16	20	6	8	20	8	8	8	17	17	10	11	17	17	17	5	5	17	17	17	8	8								
20 SUTIL	21	21	20	20	5	10	10	20	20	20	5	8	8	6	6	6	8	10	10	10	8	8	8	8	8	8	8	8	8	8	8	8	8	8	8	17								
10 GLOCK	5	5	5	5	10	20	20	16	16	16	16	7	6	6	6	9	9	5	20																									
21 FISICHELLA	10	10	10	10	20	16	16	7	7	7	7	16	16	16	16	16	9																											

■ Safety car deployed on laps shown

124 CHINESE GRAND PRIX

TIME SHEETS

PRACTICE 1 (FRIDAY)
Sunny
(track 27-33°C, air 18-20°C)

Pos.	Driver	Laps	Time
1	Lewis Hamilton	22	1m 37.334s
2	Jenson Button	18	1m 37.450s
3	Rubens Barrichello	19	1m 37.566s
4	Heikki Kovalainen	23	1m 37.672s
5	Mark Webber	20	1m 37.752s
6	Jarno Trulli	19	1m 37.764s
7	Nico Rosberg	24	1m 37.860s
8	Timo Glock	21	1m 37.894s
9	Fernando Alonso	19	1m 38.089s
10	Sébastien Bourdais	24	1m 38.195s
11	Kimi Räikkönen	23	1m 38.223s
12	Sebastian Vettel	20	1m 38.274s
13	Sébastien Buemi	26	1m 38.307s
14	Adrian Sutil	18	1m 38.319s
15	Felipe Massa	20	1m 38.418s
16	Nick Heidfeld	21	1m 38.456s
17	Giancarlo Fisichella	19	1m 38.460s
18	Robert Kubica	18	1m 38.463s
19	Kazuki Nakajima	25	1m 38.730s
20	Nelsinho Piquet	20	1m 38.825s

PRACTICE 2 (FRIDAY)
Sunny
(track 33-36°C, air 21-22°C)

Pos.	Driver	Laps	Time
1	Jenson Button	35	1m 35.679s
2	Nico Rosberg	36	1m 35.704s
3	Rubens Barrichello	35	1m 35.881s
4	Mark Webber	32	1m 36.105s
5	Sebastian Vettel	22	1m 36.167s
6	Jarno Trulli	42	1m 36.217s
7	Kazuki Nakajima	32	1m 36.377s
8	Timo Glock	40	1m 36.548s
9	Heikki Kovalainen	34	1m 36.674s
10	Sébastien Bourdais	34	1m 36.800s
11	Adrian Sutil	30	1m 36.829s
12	Felipe Massa	34	1m 36.847s
13	Lewis Hamilton	28	1m 36.941s
14	Kimi Räikkönen	33	1m 37.054s
15	Sébastien Buemi	34	1m 37.219s
16	Nelsinho Piquet	36	1m 37.273s
17	Robert Kubica	34	1m 37.491s
18	Nick Heidfeld	28	1m 37.544s
19	Fernando Alonso	28	1m 37.638s
20	Giancarlo Fisichella	31	1m 37.750s

PRACTICE 3 (SATURDAY)
Sunny/partly cloudy
(track 35-37°C, air 22°C)

Pos.	Driver	Laps	Time
1	Nico Rosberg	17	1m 36.133s
2	Jarno Trulli	22	1m 36.272s
3	Lewis Hamilton	17	1m 36.330s
4	Jenson Button	16	1m 36.463s
5	Nelsinho Piquet	16	1m 36.464s
6	Felipe Massa	18	1m 36.528s
7	Heikki Kovalainen	13	1m 36.547s
8	Kazuki Nakajima	17	1m 36.560s
9	Kimi Räikkönen	17	1m 36.568s
10	Rubens Barrichello	17	1m 36.642s
11	Nick Heidfeld	14	1m 36.702s
12	Robert Kubica	14	1m 36.742s
13	Sébastien Buemi	16	1m 36.742s
14	Sébastien Bourdais	17	1m 36.834s
15	Mark Webber	8	1m 37.330s
16	Sebastian Vettel	7	1m 37.349s
17	Adrian Sutil	17	1m 37.534s
18	Giancarlo Fisichella	18	1m 37.732s
19	Fernando Alonso	6	1m 38.003s
20	Timo Glock	6	1m 39.110s

QUALIFYING (SATURDAY)
Sunny (track 40-41°C, air 23°C)

Pos.	Driver	First	Second	Third	Weight
1	Sebastian Vettel	1m 36.565s	**1m 35.130s**	**1m 36.184s**	644kg
2	Fernando Alonso	1m 36.443s	1m 35.803s	1m 36.381s	637kg
3	Mark Webber	1m 35.751s	1m 35.173s	1m 36.466s	646.5kg
4	Rubens Barrichello	1m 35.701s	1m 35.503s	1m 36.493s	661kg
5	Jenson Button	**1m 35.533s**	1m 35.556s	1m 36.532s	659kg
6	Jarno Trulli	1m 36.308s	1m 35.645s	1m 36.835s	664.5kg
7	Nico Rosberg	1m 35.941s	1m 35.809s	1m 37.397s	650.5kg
8	Kimi Räikkönen	1m 36.137s	1m 35.856s	1m 38.089s	673.5kg
9	Lewis Hamilton	1m 35.776s	1m 35.740s	1m 38.595s	679kg
10	Sébastien Buemi	1m 36.284s	1m 35.965s	1m 39.321s	673kg
11	Nick Heidfeld	1m 36.525s	1m 35.975s		679kg
12	Heikki Kovalainen	1m 36.646s	1m 36.032s		697kg
13	Felipe Massa	1m 36.178s	1m 36.033s		690kg
14	Timo Glock	1m 36.364s	1m 36.066s		648kg
15	Kazuki Nakajima	1m 36.673s	1m 36.193s		682.7kg
16	Sébastien Bourdais	1m 36.906s			690kg
17	Nelsinho Piquet	1m 36.908s			697.9kg
18	Robert Kubica	1m 36.966s			659kg
19	Adrian Sutil	1m 37.669s			648kg
20	Giancarlo Fisichella	1m 37.672s			679.5kg

POINTS

DRIVERS

1	Jenson Button	21
2	Rubens Barrichello	15
3	Sebastian Vettel	10
4	Timo Glock	10
5	Mark Webber	9.5
6	Jarno Trulli	8.5
7	Nick Heidfeld	4
8	Fernando Alonso	4
9	Heikki Kovalainen	4
10	Lewis Hamilton	4
11	Nico Rosberg	3.5
12	Sébastien Buemi	3
13	Sébastien Bourdais	1

CONSTRUCTORS

1	Brawn	36
2	Red Bull	19.5
3	Toyota	18.5
4	McLaren	8
5	BMW Sauber	4
6	Renault	4
7	Toro Rosso	4
8	Williams	3.5

16 ROSBERG · Williams

22 BUTTON · Brawn

14 WEBBER · Red Bull

15 VETTEL · Red Bull

4 RÄIKKÖNEN · Ferrari

9 TRULLI · Toyota

23 BARRICHELLO · Brawn

7 ALONSO · Renault

45	46	47	48	49	50	51	52	53	54	55	56	
15	15	15	15	15	15	15	15	15	15	15	15	1
14	14	14	14	14	14	14	14	14	14	14	14	2
22	22	22	22	22	22	22	22	22	22	22	22	3
12	23	23	23	23	23	23	23	23	23	23	23	4
23	1	2	2	2	2	2	2	2	2	2	2	5
1	2	1	1	20	20	1	1	1	1	1	1	6
2	20	20	20	1	1	10	10	10	10	10	10	7
20	6	6	6	6	6	12	12	12	12	12	12	8
6	10	10	10	10	10	6	6	6	7	7	7	
10	12	12	12	12	12	7	7	7	6	6	4	
7	7	7	7	7	7	11	11	11	11	4	11	
4	4	11	11	11	11	4	4	4	4	11	6	
11	11	4	4	4	5	5	5	5	5	5	5	
16	5	5	5	5	5	*21*	*21*	*21*	*21*	*21*		
5	16	16	*21*	*21*	*21*	16	16	16	16			
21	*21*	*21*	16	16	16	8	8	8	8			
8	8	8	8	8	8							

21 Pit stop
14 One lap or more behind

RACE TYRE STRATEGIES

Wet and Intermediate Bridgestone Potenza tyres were used in the Chinese Grand Prix

	Driver	Race Stint 1	Race Stint 2	Race Stint 3	Race Stint 4
1	Sebastian Vettel	Wet: 1-15	Wet: 16-37	Wet: 38-56	
2	Mark Webber	Wet: 1-14	Wet: 15-39	Wet: 40-56	
3	Jenson Button	Wet: 1-19	Wet: 20-42	Wet: 43-56	
4	Rubens Barrichello	Wet: 1-19	Wet: 20-43	Wet: 44-56	
5	Heikki Kovalainen	Wet: 1-34	Wet: 35-56		
6	Lewis Hamilton	Wet: 1-33	Wet: 34-56		
7	Timo Glock	Wet: 1-24	Wet: 25-56		
8	Sébastien Buemi	Wet: 1-12	Wet: 13-45	Wet: 46-56	
	Fernando Alonso	Wet: 1-7	Wet: 8-35	Wet: 36-56	
	Kimi Räikkönen	Wet: 1-27	Wet: 28-56		
	Sébastien Bourdais	Wet: 1-30	Wet: 31-56		
	Nick Heidfeld	Wet: 1-18	Wet: 19-56		
	Robert Kubica	Wet: 1-17	Wet: 18-35	Wet: 36-56	
	Giancarlo Fisichella	Wet: 1-33	Wet: 34-55		
	Nico Rosberg	Wet: 1-5	Wet: 6-40	Intermediate: 41-48	Wet: 49-55
	Nelson Piquet	Wet: 1-21	Wet: 22-28	Wet: 29-45	Wet: 46-54
	Adrian Sutil	Wet: 1-4	Wet: 5-19	Wet: 20-50 (dnf)	
	Kazuki Nakajima	Wet: 1-32	Wet: 33-40	Wet: 41-43 (dnf)	
	Felipe Massa	Wet: 1-20 (dnf)			
	Jarno Trulli	Wet: 1-18 (dnf)			

FIA FORMULA 1 WORLD CHAMPIONSHIP • ROUND 4

BAHRAIN
GRAND PRIX

SAKHIR CIRCUIT

In torrid conditions at Sakhir, Jenson Button and his Brawn-Mercedes performed without a slip, making it three wins out of the first four grands prix of the 2009 season.
Photo: Peter J. Fox

SAKHIR QUALIFYING

RARELY anything other than a paragon of commitment during qualifying, Jarno Trulli was in his element at Sakhir. The Toyota TF109 suited Bahrain well – a pre-season test campaign on the desert's fringe was a partial catalyst – but in the immediate aftermath of a stirring 1m 33.431s lap, the Italian's mind was elsewhere.

"I'd like to dedicate this pole to my team, who have worked so hard," he said, "and, most of all, to the people of my home region Abruzzo, who suffered a disastrous earthquake this month. Recently, my thoughts have always been with them." He had set up a charitable trust to help those suffering and had coaxed many of his rivals to become involved, too. Racing drivers constantly complain about minor handling imperfections as though they are in some way cataclysmic, but Trulli's world view is better adjusted than most.

This was his, and the team's, first pole position since Indianapolis 2005, but the circumstances could hardly have been more different. Back then, Toyota hit upon a simple PR ruse: it was one of seven Michelin teams that knew they were unlikely to be racing the following day, because of tyre-wear concerns, so it fuelled its car ultra-light to capture the overnight headlines. This time, Trulli had to work a little harder.

Fuel pick-up concerns obliged the team to run with a little more Esso than it might ordinarily have done in Q1 and Q2, and the Italian was also troubled by a brake pedal that became ever softer as the session wore on. "It wasn't easy," he said, "but I knew the car was good, even if I couldn't brake the way I wanted."

And how did he feel his performance would be perceived at home? "Unfortunately," he said, "Formula One in Italy is represented by Ferrari, not by me or Giancarlo Fisichella. You just have to deal with it."

Timo Glock embellished Toyota's euphoria by lining up second, but he was quick to acknowledge his team-mate's exquisite touch – not that he had much choice, given that he was lighter as well as 0.281 seconds slower. "I made one small mistake," he said, "but even without that, I wouldn't have done enough for pole. Jarno is really, really good when it comes to getting everything out of the car in qualifying."

Sebastian Vettel, third, had the heaviest fuel load in the top six, but there was a real risk that such promising mathematics might be compromised by those around him. It wasn't so much Jenson Button's fourth-placed Brawn, which had lacked grip and suffered persistently locking brakes, but Lewis Hamilton's KERS-equipped McLaren immediately behind.

"Lewis could be a bit of a worry for all of us on the run to the first corner," Glock said, "because the KERS cars have shown that they are very, very strong at the start."

But did Vettel have any particular fears for the race? "Yes," he said. "A sandstorm."

Right: Timo Glock accelerates his Toyota TF109 straight into the lead at the start of the Bahrain GP, outgunning his pole-sitting team-mate, Jarno Trulli.

Below: Trulli and Glock raised Toyota's hopes of a sea change in race fortune, but failed to deliver on their front-row promise.

Below right: BMW Sauber personnel monitor the progress of Robert Kubica and Nick Heidfeld from this high-tech command post rigged up on the pit wall.
Photos: Peter J. Fox

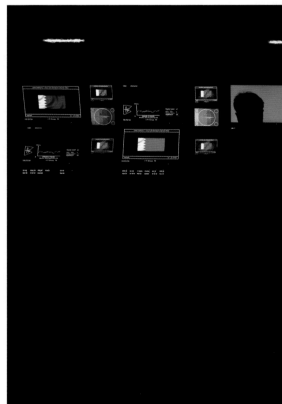

THE attention is in the detail. It wasn't so much what happened over 57 laps that conditioned the outcome of the sixth Bahrain Grand Prix, but what Jenson Button accomplished during the first lap and a bit. All week there had been talk of fierce winds disrupting the event's smooth passage – and such a thing would have been no surprise, in light of the sport's recent meteorological turmoil – but rivals felt only the force of Button's astute racecraft.

Uniquely among the front-runners, the Brawn BGP001 hadn't been updated since its appearance in Australia, and it was by no means the quickest car in Bahrain. The Toyotas on the front row had qualified lighter than Button, but Sebastian Vettel's third-placed Red Bull had an extra 6.5kg of fuel on board. If the championship leader didn't succeed in passing him straight away, the race might be lost almost before it started.

Timo Glock made the brightest getaway to lead team-mate Jarno Trulli into Turn One, while Button aimed for the outside line and – despite initial clutch-slip hesitancy – succeeded in engineering enough space to ease past Vettel, not least because the German was squeezed between the Brawn and the KERS-trigger-happy Lewis Hamilton, who sliced up the inside to vault from fifth to third. For Button, the resolution of one problem coincided with another's

creation: now he needed to dislodge Hamilton as a matter of some urgency, or the balance of power would soon tilt Toyota's way.

Hamilton's brisk start briefly carried him past Trulli, too, but he ran wide at Turn Four and dropped back behind the Italian to spend the balance of the opening lap repelling Button's advances.

"Lewis is very difficult to overtake at the best of times," Button said, "but he made a few mistakes on the first lap and I dived inside him several times. He made a small error at the final corner and I thought I'd be able to get alongside on the main straight, but he used his KERS button and I had to tuck in behind. I picked up a tow, though, and was able to get him into Turn One. That really made the race for us."

Later Button was moved to describe the opening lap as the finest of his career, but things did not go quite so smoothly for others. Rubens Barrichello slotted into sixth initially, ahead of Kimi Räikkönen, Fernando Alonso, Felipe Massa, Nico Rosberg, Nelson Piquet, Nick Heidfeld, Giancarlo Fisichella, Mark Webber (who'd started 18th after Adrian Sutil blocked him during Q1, an indiscretion that cost the German a three-position grid penalty), Robert Kubica, Kazuki Nakajima. Heikki Kovalainen (who started on the prime tyre, a decision he described as "disastrously bad"), Sutil, Sébastien Bourdais and Sebastien Bue-

Right: Lewis Hamilton drove strongly to fourth for McLaren, but by this stage of the season, the MP4-24 was not yet sufficiently developed aerodynamically to challenge seriously at the front of the field.
Photo: Paul-Henri Cahier

Clockwise from above left: Fernando Alonso shares his thoughts on a season that remains difficult; Felipe Massa, wonders when he will score his first points of the year; Jean Alesi, reflects on times past; Flavio Briatore enjoys a joke.
Photos: Peter J. Fox

Below: Fixed concentration. Kimi watches and waits.
Photo: Paul-Henri Cahier

mi, who dropped to the back while leaving the line in a fug of tyre smoke.

The opening corner was particularly costly for Massa, who clattered into team-mate Räikkönen, and both BMW drivers, who had an equally incestuous collision at the same point. Kubica got on the radio to signal his intention to pit, but the message was lost in translation and the Pole came in for repairs on lap two. Nakajima stopped at the same point: he, too, needed a fresh front wing. The Japanese driver claimed that he'd made contact with another car at the start of lap two, and he'd certainly been close to Kubica going into Turn One, but later Sutil reported that Nakajima had run into him during the opening lap. Massa and Heidfeld peeled in on lap three: the German feared his collision with Kubica had caused suspension damage, but both parties were able to continue with replacement nose wings.

In a parallel universe, meanwhile, Glock and Trulli remained at the front until they made their first scheduled stops on laps 11 and 12 respectively, whereupon Button breezed into the lead. His cause was helped by Toyota's decision to send both drivers out on medium-spec Bridgestones, rather than the more effective super-softs, for their second stints – and team principal John Howett acknowledged that this had been a simple error of judgment. Button emerged more than three seconds clear of Trulli after pitting on lap 15 and, better still from his perspective, Vettel's long first run (19 laps) was not enough to catapult him beyond the Italian.

The German had lost ample time behind Hamilton during his first stint and now was about to fritter away some more, because he was trapped behind a smartly driven Toyota fitted with the wrong rubber. "You only have to follow a car for a couple of laps before your tyres go off, front and rear," Vettel said. "I had that

problem in both stints on the super-soft tyres, so was never able to use them properly."

Vettel finally cleared Trulli after both had made their second and final stops, but by then Button had more than 13 seconds in hand, not that the Englishman was having a completely straightforward afternoon. Brawn had been concerned about the fierce heat's potentially detrimental effect on its Mercedes V8s and had consciously avoided using its full allocation of free practice mileage, but the extreme conditions were taking their toll elsewhere in the BGP001: an electrical transformer was becoming uncomfortably hot, and its proximity to Button's seat gave him a toasted left buttock by the race's end. He was sore only about the conduct of a few backmarkers, though.

"The final part of the race might not have been so exciting," he said, "but the start was very good for me. The Toyotas seemed very quick on the option tyre and I was a bit surprised by their pace, so I wasn't sure how things would work out, but it helped that Sebastian got stuck behind Lewis. The biggest problem for me, though, was the traffic, which was terrible. I am sorry if any of my radio conversations were played live, because I might have said a few words that weren't good for TV.

"On Friday and Saturday, we struggled a little bit with engine temperatures and thought we might have to race with reduced revs, which would have been a disaster, but luckily enough I was in clean air for most of the afternoon and the engine remained reasonably cool."

Backside apart, so had he. "I don't think I put a foot wrong," he said. "Our car is still competitive, but that doesn't make it easy to drive, and I ran slightly wide once or twice after locking a rear wheel. That's something we need to work on."

Red Bull sporting director Christian Horner admit-

ted he had mixed feelings about the circumstances that stifled what might have been a second straight success. "It's quite good when you feel slightly disappointed about finishing second," he said, "because it shows how far we've come."

Trulli raced with a fresh set of brake discs – a precaution that fixed the problems he'd encountered during qualifying – but admitted to feeling a sense of disappointment at not being able to convert pole into a serious victory tilt.

"I think I dropped a bit of oil at the start," he said, "so I spun my wheels and that cost me the lead. I struggled on the harder tyres during the second stint, but was then much quicker than Sebastian when I switched back to the super-softs at the end. There was no way to pass him though, so that was that."

Hamilton's early brio translated into a safe fourth place on a largely incident-free afternoon, and he was happy enough with that. "We lacked downforce compared with the other guys around us," he said. "We're not yet fighting at the front, but I think we've done a better job than quite a few people."

Barrichello executed the race's only planned three-stop strategy, but its effectiveness required co-operational traffic, and his first stop dropped him behind Piquet, where he remained stuck – losing time – for the next nine laps. He ended up fifth, ahead of Kimi Räikkönen, who survived his early clash with Massa unscathed to notch up Ferrari's first points of the year. The Finn acknowledged that the result was a touch circuit-specific, because Bahrain was missing a few of the things that least suited the F60 – proper corners, mainly. "I've been around long enough not to get excited about finishing sixth," he said.

Early leader Glock's short first stint dropped him into the thick of time-consuming traffic, and such

were his struggles on the medium tyres that he curtailed his second stint prematurely to switch back to the super-softs. He was visibly quicker than Räikkönen during the final stages, but couldn't find a way past and was happy to score points for the fourth time in as many races.

Fernando Alonso showed his customary spirit and passed Trulli on the 14th lap, when the Renault was light and the two were running out of sequence, but he had to cope without fluid for most of the race because his drinks bottle pump had failed. Bahrain might not be a particularly physical circuit, but the heat is still a catalyst for significant dehydration. The Spaniard finished eighth, but then almost collapsed when he was ushered to the TV compound to conduct the mandatory post-race interviews. He wasn't in a position to comment, although he recovered swiftly enough, but Webber – who had converted from three stops to two and wound up 11th, behind Rosberg and Piquet – had a few forthright opinions on the subject.

"Teams regard driver weight loss as low-hanging fruit," he said. "It's an easy way to shed a couple of kilos to compensate for the extra bulk of a KERS system. In reality, we need to increase the minimum weight limit of the car or else do away with

EDITOR'S VIEW
McLAREN AIMING FOR PEACE WITH FIA

THE McLaren team's management must have come away from the Bahrain Grand Prix wondering whether their conciliatory efforts behind the scenes to build bridges with the sport's governing body had paid off. They were due to appear before the FIA's World Motor Sport Council in Paris the following week to answer charges that they had brought the sport into disrepute as a result of the so-called 'Liar-gate' scandal.

The allegations stemmed from the events that had taken place in the closing stages of the Australian Grand Prix at Melbourne, where Lewis Hamilton, apparently encouraged by the team's former sporting director, Dave Ryan, had tricked Jarno Trulli into illegally repassing the British driver's McLaren during a period when the safety car had been deployed in the closing stages of the race.

Subsequently, both men denied this at two consecutive stewards' meetings, despite having been played recordings of their conversation over the McLaren pit-to-car radio.

Hamilton and McLaren faced the horrifying possibility of being excluded from the World Championship, or at least suspended from a number of races, but the team had been working hard behind the scenes to demonstrate that its approach towards the FIA had become less confrontational.

The first signs of this strategy appeared in the paddock at Bahrain, when Richard Lapthorne, the McLaren Group's recently appointed non-executive chairman, lunched with Bernie Ecclestone, the F1 rights holder, and Alan Donnelly, right-hand man of FIA president Max Mosley.

Ryan had been sacked, and the former McLaren team principal, Ron Dennis, who had had a tense and testy relationship with Mosley, had withdrawn from F1 to concentrate on developing a new range of road cars. The symbolism signalled by this staffing 'realignment' was almost more significant than the actual items on the council's agenda.

McLaren's team principal, Martin Whitmarsh, had opted to put the McLaren case on his own without the help of a QC. Rather than subject the meeting to a barrage of paperwork, he decided simply to read a prepared statement, take questions from the council and effectively submit the team to its verdict without further debate. He was accompanied by McLaren's lawyer, Tim Murnane.

Whitmarsh gambled that coming clean and effectively throwing the team on the mercy of the council would go some way towards mitigating the harshness of any penalty. For his part, Hamilton, who was not present, just wanted to put the whole sorry episode behind him and get on with the defence of his World Championship title.

Whitmarsh's strategy was completely vindicated. McLaren was given a three-race suspended ban for lying to officials in an attempt to influence the outcome of the Australian Grand Prix, and the new team principal attracted complimentary remarks for his conciliatory and open approach to the proceedings. It is to be hoped that this drew a line under the matter for good.

Alan Henry

KERS altogether. It's a crazy situation. Fernando is usually in incredibly good shape, but today he was on the edge."

The same was true initially of Kovalainen, although for different reasons. His medium Bridgestones deteriorated badly almost immediately and the Finn struggled with a severe vibration throughout his 12-lap first stint, even though the tyres hadn't flat-spotted. He wound up 12th, ahead of Bourdais (happy with his race pace, after setting the day's fastest Ferrari-powered lap), the delayed Massa, Fisichella, Sutil, Buemi, Kubica and Heidfeld. Nakajima was the only driver not to be classified, although he was within ten laps of the chequered flag when the team called him in as a safeguard because his Toyota V8's oil pressure was fluctuating.

It had been a particularly appalling weekend for BMW Sauber, which had taken pole position here, as well as third and fourth places, just 12 months earlier. Its drivers' first-lap clash hadn't helped, but the cars were more or less undriveable long before that. Afterwards, Kubica was asked what needed to be done differently. "Ask the team," he replied. "I don't think I need to change anything I'm doing."

He had a point.

Simon Arron

Above: Jenson Button is already pulling away strongly in the opening stages of the race, with Sebastian Vettel's Red Bull leading the pursuit of Trulli's second-placed Toyota.
Photo: Dieter Mathis/WRi2

Left: Victorious Button shares his trophies with race engineer Andy Shovlin *(right)* and assistant race engineer Peter Bonnington.
Photo: Jean-François Galeron/WRi2

Right: The new McLaren group CEO, Richard Lapthorne *(left)*, in conversation with team principal Martin Whitmarsh.
Photo: Peter J. Fox

BAHRAIN INTERNATIONAL
CIRCUIT, SAKHIR
Circuit: 3.363 miles/5.412km 57 laps

4
111/69
11 126/78
5 190/118
116/187 mph/kmh
Gear
300/187
10 225/140
300/188
7a 205/128
7 79/49
9 149/93
3 221/138
12 128/80
8 63/39
2 158/98
Turn 1 63/39
300/188

FIA F1 WORLD CHAMPIONSHIP ROUND 4

GULF AIR
BAHRAIN
GRAND PRIX
SAKHIR 24-26 APRIL 2009

Photo: Peter J. Fox

RACE DISTANCE: 57 laps, 191.530 miles/308.238km • RACE WEATHER: Sunny (track 44-51°C, air 36-38°C)

Pos.	Driver	Nat.	No.	Entrant	Car/Engine	Tyres	Laps	Time/Retirement	Speed (mph/km/h)	Gap to leader	Fastest race lap	
1	Jenson Button	GB	22	Brawn GP Formula 1 Team	Brawn BGP 001-Mercedes FO108W V8	B	57	1h 34m 15.784s	125.179/201.456		1m 34.588s	11
2	Sebastian Vettel	D	15	Red Bull Racing	Red Bull RB5-Renault RS27 V8	B	57	1h 31m 55.369s	125.016/201.193	+ 7.187s	1m 34.756s	16
3	Jarno Trulli	I	9	Panasonic Toyota Racing	Toyota TF109-RVX-09 V8	B	57	1h 31m 57.352s	124.971/201.121	+ 9.170s	1m 34.556s	10
4	Lewis Hamilton	GB	1	Vodafone McLaren Mercedes	McLaren MP4-24-Mercedes FO108W V8	B	57	1h 32m 10.278s	124.679/200.651	+ 22.096s	1m 34.915s	13
5	Rubens Barrichello	BR	23	Brawn GP Formula 1 Team	Brawn BGP 001-Mercedes FO108W V8	B	57	1h 32m 25.961s	124.326/200.083	+ 37.779s	1m 34.901s	25
6	Kimi Räikkönen	FIN	4	Scuderia Ferrari Marlboro	Ferrari F60-056 V8	B	57	1h 32m 30.239s	124.230/199.929	+ 42.057s	1m 35.498s	42
7	Timo Glock	D	10	Panasonic Toyota Racing	Toyota TF109-RVX-09 V8	B	57	1h 32m 31.062s	124.211/199.899	+ 42.880s	1m 34.574s	6
8	Fernando Alonso	E	7	ING Renault F1 Team	Renault R29-RS27 V8	B	57	1h 32m 40.957s	123.991/199.544	+ 52.775s	1m 35.722s	29
9	Nico Rosberg	D	16	AT&T Williams	Williams FW31-Toyota RVX-09 V8	B	57	1h 32m 46.380s	123.870/199.349	+ 58.198s	1m 35.816s	37
10	Nelsinho Piquet	BR	8	ING Renault F1 Team	Renault R29-RS27 V8	B	57	1h 32m 53.331s	123.716/199.101	+ 1m 05.149s	1m 35.441s	37
11	Mark Webber	AUS	14	Red Bull Racing	Red Bull RB5-Renault RS27 V8	B	57	1h 32m 55.823s	123.660/199.012	+ 1m 07.641s	1m 35.165s	50
12	Heikki Kovalainen	FIN	2	Vodafone McLaren Mercedes	McLaren MP4-24-Mercedes FO108W V8	B	57	1h 33m 06.006s	123.435/198.649	+ 1m 17.824s	1m 35.520s	54
13	Sébastien Bourdais	F	11	Scuderia Toro Rosso	Toro Rosso STR04-Ferrari 056 V8	B	57	1h 33m 06.987s	123.413/198.614	+ 1m 18.805s	1m 35.410s	30
14	Felipe Massa	BR	3	Scuderia Ferrari Marlboro	Ferrari F60-056 V8	B	56			+ 1 lap	1m 35.065s	41
15	Giancarlo Fisichella	I	21	Force India F1 Team	Force India VJM02-Mercedes FO108W V8	B	56			+ 1 lap	1m 36.376s	9
16	Adrian Sutil	D	20	Force India F1 Team	Force India VJM02-Mercedes FO108W V8	B	56			+ 1 lap	1m 36.219s	28
17	Sébastien Buemi	CH	12	Scuderia Toro Rosso	Toro Rosso STR04-Ferrari 056 V8	B	56			+ 1 lap	1m 36.473s	38
18	Robert Kubica	PL	5	BMW Sauber F1 Team	BMW Sauber F1.09-BMW P86/9 V8	B	56			+ 1 lap	1m 35.706s	50
19	Nick Heidfeld	D	6	BMW Sauber F1 Team	BMW Sauber F1.09-BMW P86/9 V8	B	56			+ 1 lap	1m 35.924s	52
	Kazuki Nakajima	J	17	AT&T Williams	Williams FW31-Toyota RVX-09 V8	B	48	oil pressure			1m 36.153s	39

Fastest race lap: Jarno Trulli on lap 10, 1m 34.556s, 128.033mph/206.049km/h.

Lap record: Michael Schumacher (Ferrari F2004 V10), 1m 30.252s, 134.263mph/216.074km/h (2004) (3.366-mile/5.417km circuit).

All results and data © FOM 2009

		20	SUTIL · Force India — penalty for impeding	21	FISICHELLA · Force India	8	PIQUET · Renault	5	KUBICA · BMW Sauber	2	KOVALAINEN · McLaren	16	ROSBERG · Williams

	11	BOURDAIS · Toro Rosso	14	WEBBER · Red Bull	12	BUEMI · Toro Rosso	6	HEIDFELD · BMW Sauber	17	NAKAJIMA · Williams	4	RÄIKKÖNEN · Ferrari

Grid order	1	2	3	4	5	6	7	8	9	10	11	12	13	14	15	16	17	18	19	20	21	22	23	24	25	26	27	28	29	30	31	32	33	34	35	36	37	38	39	40	41	42	43	44
9 TRULLI	10	10	10	10	10	10	10	10	10	10	9	9	22	22	22	15	15	15	15	4	4	22	22	22	22	22	22	22	22	22	22	22	22	22	22	22	22	15	15	15	22	22	22	22
10 GLOCK	9	9	9	9	9	9	9	9	9	9	10	22	1	1	15	4	4	4	22	22	9	9	9	9	9	9	9	9	9	9	9	9	9	9	9	9	15	22	22	22	4	4	4	4
15 VETTEL	1	22	22	22	22	22	22	22	22	22	1	15	15	1	22	22	22	22	9	9	15	15	15	15	15	15	15	15	15	15	15	15	15	9	4	4	4	15	15	15				
22 BUTTON	22	1	1	1	1	1	1	1	1	1	15	23	23	4	7	9	9	9	15	15	1	1	1	1	1	1	1	1	1	1	1	1	1	1	9	9	9	9	9	9	9			
1 HAMILTON	15	15	15	15	15	15	15	15	15	15	23	4	4	7	9	16	16	16	16	1	23	23	23	23	10	10	10	10	10	10	4	4	4	4	23	23	23	23	23	23				
23 BARRICHELLO	23	23	23	23	23	23	23	23	23	23	4	9	7	9	1	1	1	1	16	10	10	10	10	10	4	4	4	4	4	7	7	7	7	23	1	1	1	1	1	1				
7 ALONSO	4	4	4	4	4	4	4	4	4	4	7	7	9	16	1	10	10	10	23	23	8	4	4	4	4	7	7	7	7	7	10	23	23	7	16	16	16	16	16	16				
3 MASSA	7	7	7	7	7	7	7	7	7	7	16	16	16	8	23	10	10	4	8	7	7	23	23	23	23	23	23	16	16	8	8	8	8	8	10	10								
16 ROSBERG	3	16	16	16	16	16	16	16	16	16	10	10	8	23	8	7	16	16	16	16	16	16	16	16	8	10	10	10	10	7	7													
4 RÄIKKÖNEN	16	3	3	8	8	8	8	8	8	8	8	8	23	23	7	7	7	7	16	16	21	21	21	21	21	21	8	8	10	10	10	10	7	7	7	7	8	8						
2 KOVALAINEN	8	8	8	14	14	14	14	14	14	14	14	14	21	21	20	20	20	20	20	20	20	8	8	8	8	8	8	8	21	21	21	21	21	20	20	20	20	3	3					
17 NAKAJIMA	6	14	14	21	21	21	21	21	21	21	14	20	20	14	14	14	14	14	14	14	14	14	14	2	12	12	3	3	14	14	14													
5 KUBICA	21	21	21	2	2	2	2	2	2	2	20	20	12	11	11	21	21	21	14	14	3	3	3	3	2	2	2	2	14	3	3	14	14	2	2	2								
6 HEIDFELD	14	6	2	20	20	20	20	20	20	20	12	12	11	11	14	14	3	3	2	2	3	11	11	11	11	11	20	21	21	2	2	11	11	11										
8 PIQUET	5	2	20	12	12	12	12	12	12	12	2	11	11	14	14	14	3	3	2	11	11	20	20	20	20	20	12	2	14	11	11	21	21	21										
12 BUEMI	17	20	12	11	11	11	11	11	11	11	11	3	3	3	3	2	11	20	20	20	20	12	12	12	12	3	14	2	21	21	20	20	20											
21 FISICHELLA	2	12	11	3	3	3	3	3	3	3	3	2	2	20	20	11	11	11	11	12	12	12	12	5	5	5	5	5	3	11	11	12	12	12	12	12								
14 WEBBER	20	11	6	5	5	5	5	5	5	5	5	5	5	5	5	5	5	5	5	5	5	5	3	3	3	5	6	6	17	17	17	17	17	17	17									
20 SUTIL	11	5	5	6	17	17	17	17	17	17	17	17	17	17	17	17	17	17	17	17	17	17	17	17	6	6	6	17	17	5	5	5	5	5	5	5								
11 BOURDAIS	12	17	17	17	6	6	6	6	6	6	6	6	6	6	6	6	6	6	6	6	6	6	6	6	17	17	17	17	5	5	5	5	6	6	6	6								

TIME SHEETS

FOR THE RECORD

1st ALL FRONT ROW:	Toyota
1st FASTEST LAP:	Jarno Trulli
1st FRONT ROW:	Timo Glock
10th FRONT ROW:	Jarno Trulli

PRACTICE 1 (FRIDAY)
Sunny
(track 42-47ºC, air 33-35ºC)

Pos.	Driver	Laps	Time
1	Lewis Hamilton	19	1m 33.647s
2	Nick Heidfeld	17	1m 33.907s
3	Robert Kubica	17	1m 33.938s
4	Nico Rosberg	24	1m 34.227s
5	Jenson Button	15	1m 34.434s
6	Heikki Kovalainen	24	1m 34.502s
7	Rubens Barrichello	18	1m 34.531s
8	Felipe Massa	17	1m 34.589s
9	Mark Webber	21	1m 34.827s
10	Kimi Räikkönen	19	1m 34.827s
11	Kazuki Nakajima	24	1m 34.880s
12	Sebastian Vettel	21	1m 34.938s
13	Nelsinho Piquet	21	1m 34.974s
14	Adrian Sutil	18	1m 35.021s
15	Jarno Trulli	22	1m 35.036s
16	Giancarlo Fisichella	16	1m 35.042s
17	Timo Glock	20	1m 35.333s
18	Fernando Alonso	24	1m 35.348s
19	Sébastien Bourdais	22	1m 35.353s
20	Sébastien Buemi	15	1m 35.369s

PRACTICE 2 (FRIDAY)
Sunny
(track 47-51ºC, air 37-39ºC)

Pos.	Driver	Laps	Time
1	Nico Rosberg	36	1m 33.339s
2	Fernando Alonso	25	1m 33.530s
3	Jarno Trulli	37	1m 33.616s
4	Sebastian Vettel	29	1m 33.661s
5	Mark Webber	32	1m 33.676s
6	Jenson Button	35	1m 33.694s
7	Adrian Sutil	30	1m 33.763s
8	Timo Glock	37	1m 33.764s
9	Rubens Barrichello	30	1m 33.885s
10	Kazuki Nakajima	36	1m 33.899s
11	Lewis Hamilton	30	1m 33.994s
12	Giancarlo Fisichella	23	1m 34.025s
13	Sébastien Buemi	37	1m 34.127s
14	Sébastien Bourdais	26	1m 34.366s
15	Nelsinho Piquet	29	1m 34.411s
16	Felipe Massa	34	1m 34.564s
17	Robert Kubica	31	1m 34.605s
18	Kimi Räikkönen	28	1m 34.670s
19	Heikki Kovalainen	35	1m 34.764s
20	Nick Heidfeld	33	1m 34.790s

PRACTICE 3 (SATURDAY)
Sunny
(track 48-51ºC, air 36-39ºC)

Pos.	Driver	Laps	Time
1	Timo Glock	16	1m 32.605s
2	Felipe Massa	20	1m 32.728s
3	Nico Rosberg	18	1m 32.906s
4	Lewis Hamilton	16	1m 32.975s
5	Kimi Räikkönen	18	1m 32.986s
6	Nelsinho Piquet	19	1m 33.176s
7	Robert Kubica	13	1m 33.195s
8	Kazuki Nakajima	17	1m 33.302s
9	Jarno Trulli	19	1m 33.397s
10	Nick Heidfeld	14	1m 33.415s
11	Sebastian Vettel	16	1m 33.443s
12	Heikki Kovalainen	12	1m 33.478s
13	Fernando Alonso	13	1m 33.482s
14	Adrian Sutil	17	1m 33.534s
15	Jenson Button	17	1m 33.586s
16	Rubens Barrichello	17	1m 33.686s
17	Sébastien Buemi	15	1m 33.720s
18	Mark Webber	14	1m 33.726s
19	Giancarlo Fisichella	15	1m 33.962s
20	Sébastien Bourdais	7	1m 34.990s

Photo: Peter Nygaard/GP Photo

QUALIFYING (SATURDAY)
Sunny (track 51-53ºC, air 40-41ºC)

Pos.	Driver	First	Second	Third	Weight
1	Jarno Trulli	1m 32.779s	1m 32.671s	**1m 33.431s**	648.5kg
2	Timo Glock	1m 33.165s	1m 32.613s	1m 33.712s	643kg
3	Sebastian Vettel	**1m 32.680s**	**1m 32.474s**	1m 34.015s	659kg
4	Jenson Button	1m 32.978s	1m 32.842s	1m 34.044s	652.5kg
5	Lewis Hamilton	1m 32.851s	1m 32.877s	1m 34.196s	652.2kg
6	Rubens Barrichello	1m 33.116s	1m 32.842s	1m 34.239s	649kg
7	Fernando Alonso	1m 33.627s	1m 32.860s	1m 34.578s	650.5kg
8	Felipe Massa	1m 33.297s	1m 33.014s	1m 34.818s	664.5kg
9	Nico Rosberg	1m 33.672s	1m 33.166s	1m 35.134s	670.5kg
10	Kimi Räikkönen	1m 33.117s	1m 32.827s	1m 35.380s	671.5kg
11	Heikki Kovalainen	1m 33.479s	1m 33.242s		678.5kg
12	Kazuki Nakajima	1m 33.221s	1m 33.348s		680.9kg
13	Robert Kubica	1m 33.495s	1m 33.487s		698.6kg
14	Nick Heidfeld	1m 33.377s	1m 33.562s		696.3kg
15	Nelsinho Piquet	1m 33.608s	1m 33.941s		677.6kg
16	Adrian Sutil	1m 33.722s			678.5kg
17	Sébastien Buemi	1m 33.753s			652kg
18	Giancarlo Fisichella	1m 33.910s			656kg
19	Mark Webber	1m 34.038s			679kg
20	Sébastien Bourdais	1m 34.159s			667.5kg

Photo: Peter J. Fox

POINTS

DRIVERS

1	Jenson Button	31
2	Rubens Barrichello	19
3	Sebastian Vettel	18
4	Jarno Trulli	14.5
5	Timo Glock	12
6	Mark Webber	9.5
7	Lewis Hamilton	9
8	Fernando Alonso	5
9	Nick Heidfeld	4
10	Heikki Kovalainen	4
11	Nico Rosberg	3.5
12	Kimi Räikkönen	3
13	Sébastien Buemi	3
14	Sébastien Bourdais	1

CONSTRUCTORS

1	Brawn	50
2	Red Bull	27.5
3	Toyota	26.5
4	McLaren	13
5	Renault	5
6	BMW Sauber	4
7	Toro Rosso	4
8	Williams	3.5
9	Ferrari	3

7	ALONSO · Renault	
1	HAMILTON · McLaren	
15	VETTEL · Red Bull	
9	TRULLI · Toyota	
3	MASSA · Ferrari	
23	BARRICHELLO · Brawn	
22	BUTTON · Brawn	
10	GLOCK · Toyota	

46	47	48	49	50	51	52	53	54	55	56	57	·	
22	22	22	22	22	22	22	22	22	22	22	22		1
15	15	15	15	15	15	15	15	15	15	15	15		2
9	9	9	9	9	9	9	9	9	9	9	9		3
23	23	1	1	1	1	1	1	1	1	1	1		4
1	1	23	23	23	23	23	23	23	23	23	23		5
4	4	4	4	4	4	4	4	4	4	4	4		6
10	10	10	10	10	10	10	10	10	10	10	10		7
7	7	7	7	7	7	7	7	7	7	7	7		8
16	16	16	16	16	16	16	16	16	16	16	16		
8	8	8	8	8	8	8	8	8	8	8	8		
3	14	14	14	14	14	14	14	14	14	14	14		
14	2	2	2	2	2	2	2	2	2	2	2		
2	11	11	11	11	11	11	11	11	11	11	11		
11	21	21	21	3	3	3	3	3	3	3	3		
21	3	3	3	21	21	21	21	21	21	21	21		
20	20	20	20	20	20	20	20	20	20	20	20		
12	12	12	12	12	12	12	12	12	12	12	12		
17	17	17	5	5	5	5	5	5	5	5	5		
5	5	5	6	6	6	6	6	6	6	6	6		
6	6	6											

21 Pit stop   14 One lap or more behind

RACE TYRE STRATEGIES

The tyre regulations stipulate that the two dry tyre specifications must be used during the race.

The Super-Soft compound Bridgestone Potenza tyre is marked with a green stripe on the sidewall of the tyre.

	Driver	Race Stint 1	Race Stint 2	Race Stint 3	Race Stint 4
1	Jenson Button	Super-Soft: 1-15	Super-Soft: 16-37	Medium: 38-57	
2	Sebastian Vettel	Super-Soft: 1-19	Super-Soft: 20-40	Medium: 41-57	
3	Jarno Trulli	Super-Soft: 1-12	Medium: 13-37	Super-Soft: 38-57	
4	Lewis Hamilton	Super-Soft: 1-15	Super-Soft: 16-37	Medium: 38-57	
5	Rubens Barrichello	Super-Soft: 1-14	Super-Soft: 15-26	Super-Soft: 27-47	Medium: 48-57
6	Kimi Räikkönen	Super-Soft: 1-21	Super-Soft: 22-44	Medium: 45-57	
7	Timo Glock	Super-Soft: 1-11	Medium: 12-33	Super-Soft: 34-57	
8	Fernando Alonso	Super-Soft: 1-16	Super-Soft: 17-37	Medium: 38-57	
	Nico Rosberg	Super-Soft: 1-21	Super-Soft: 22-45	Medium: 46-57	
	Nelson Piquet	Super-Soft: 1-23	Super-Soft: 24-42	Medium: 43-57	
	Mark Webber	Super-Soft: 1-14	Medium: 15-37	Super-Soft: 38-57	
	Heikki Kovalainen	Medium: 1-12	Super-Soft: 13-37	Super-Soft: 38-57	
	Sébastien Bourdais	Medium: 1-18	Super-Soft: 19-36	Super-Soft: 37-57	
	Felipe Massa	Super-Soft: 1-3	Super-Soft: 4-29	Super-Soft: 30-46	Medium: 47-56
	Giancarlo Fisichella	Super-Soft: 1-15	Super-Soft: 16-37	Medium: 38-56	
	Adrian Sutil	Super-Soft: 1-23	Super-Soft: 24-41	Medium: 42-56	
	Sébastien Buemi	Super-Soft: 1-21	Super-Soft: 22-39	Medium: 40-56	
	Robert Kubica	Medium: 1-2	Medium: 3-34	Super-Soft: 35-56	
	Nick Heidfeld	Medium: 1-3	Medium: 4-36	Super-Soft: 37-56	
	Kazuki Nakajima	Super-Soft: 1-2	Super-Soft: 3-30	Super-Soft: 31-48 (dnf)	

Previously a winner in front of his home crowd, Fernando Alonso and his Renault lacked for sheer pace at the Circuit de Catalunya. Here the French team services the double world champion's car during his climb from eighth on the grid to fifth at the chequered flag.
Photo: Bernard Asset

SPANISH GRAND PRIX

CATALUNYA CIRCUIT

CATALUNYA QUALIFYING

FOR all Formula One's fiendish complexity and reliance on split-second timing, moments like this owe more to luck than judgment.

Jenson Button hadn't been particularly happy with the balance of his Brawn since the fitting of an aero upgrade package, but on Friday evening he studied the set-up adopted by team-mate Rubens Barrichello – who had been quicker so far – and borrowed a few ideas.

On Saturday morning, with a reasonable fuel load, things were definitely much improved, although the car felt a little edgy when running light in Q2. A minor front-wing adjustment and a top-up of fuel restored a little decorum for Q3, but the championship leader still felt certain that pole would be beyond him.

He left his final run as late as he dared, to capitalise on every last streak of rubber laid down by his rivals, but then came a misunderstanding: via the radio, the team ordered him to let Robert Kubica through, in the mistaken belief that the Pole was on a flying lap. Kubica, though, was already done – and Button let him through before the mistake was realised. He was now stuck behind the BMW and had to complete the track's final sector within four seconds of the norm if he were to begin his lap before the session ended. He managed it with 1.6 seconds to spare.

"That was unexpected," he said, "but very pleasing, and probably my most satisfying pole of the season. My final lap in Q3 was by far the best I've done this weekend."

The vanquished Barrichello, third, was swift to acknowledge the quality of Button's performance. "Q3 came as a little bit of a surprise," he said. "My lap was good, but I might have been on the track too early. Jenson is doing a really fine job, though, and deserves to be where he is. I'll just have to try harder and harder to get him."

The biggest threat was perceived to come from the Red Bulls, with Sebastian Vettel splitting the Brawns and Mark Webber fifth. Their cars were fuelled identically, but the Australian had used some Bridgestone softs to get through Q1 and had one set fewer left at the end.

"I'm happy with our performance," Button said, "but I think things are very close and obviously don't know when Sebastian will be stopping."

The response from his right was instant, and accompanied by an impish grin: "Lap 27."

Button, too, smiled. "That's okay then," he said, "because we are running until lap 32…"

By far the weightiest of the front-running cars, though, was Felipe Massa's fourth-placed Ferrari, a symbol of the significant progress the team had made courtesy of its latest aero upgrade. Hitherto, the F60 had had all the grace of a panel van whenever a corner was laid before it, but the team had recovered much of the poise that had been its trademark since the late 1990s.

This didn't extend to its off-track performance, however. In a repeat of the error made with Massa in Malaysia, Kimi Räikkönen remained in his pit garage during the final moments of Q1, because it was assumed that he had already done a time that would be quick enough to see him through. For the sake of 0.102 seconds, it wasn't.

Above: Toro Rosso team-mates Sébastien Bourdais and Sébastien Buemi obviously won't hear a word against each other.
Photo: Bernard Asset

Left: That winning smile: Jenson appeared relaxed and fully in control all weekend.
Photo: Peter J. Fox

Right: Lewis Hamilton bounces his McLaren over Barcelona's high kerbs. He could only qualify 14th, and finished the race in ninth place.
Photo: Simon Arron

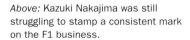

Above: Kazuki Nakajima was still struggling to stamp a consistent mark on the F1 business.

Left: Lewis's girlfriend, Nicole Scherzeger, tries the McLaren for size.

Right: Routine business of the weekend: Heidfeld, Fisichella, Hamilton and Alonso under scrutiny at one of the official FIA press conferences.
Photos: Peter J. Fox

DURING the season's staccato opening burst of four races in five weekends, it had been a matter of course to see team personnel standing in airport immigration queues with bubble-wrapped new parts that had been hurriedly exported for last-minute installation. The people carrying them, though, never wore Brawn apparel.

That the team was on the grid at all was a result, that it should have been ultra-competitive, a serious bonus. It didn't have endless resources to throw at incessant upgrades – the sight of Ross Brawn and his cohorts flying to Barcelona on EasyJet confirmed as much – but in Spain it finally gave its car a facelift, in a bid to claw back some of the performance advantage it appeared to have lost, despite what the championship tables might have said. The changes included revised rear bodywork to improve airflow to the rear wing, plus an uprated diffuser and sidepods.

The upshot? The BGP001 still wasn't quite as quick over a lap as the Red Bull RB5 – still in interim spec while awaiting Adrian Newey's definitive twin-diffuser update – but it was swift enough for astute team strategy to make a difference. And Jenson Button's mesmerising consistency would be equally crucial.

Button and Rubens Barrichello were planning three-stop races – quicker according to the team's simulation software, so long as your race ran without

a hitch – but the Englishman's afternoon was potentially compromised within moments of the red lights going out. He got away smartly enough, but Barrichello's start from third, in the slightly heavier of the two Brawns, was sensational. He grabbed the lead into Turn One while Button settled for second and Sebastian Vettel was overcome by a horrible sense of déjà vu. In Bahrain, his first stint had been undone by Lewis Hamilton's KERS button; this time, he saw only a flash of red as Felipe Massa capitalised on a squirt of extra power on the long run to the opening right-hander.

Mark Webber slotted into fifth, ahead of Fernando Alonso, but they were pursued by a cloud of carbon shrapnel. Jarno Trulli hadn't made a particularly good start from seventh on the grid – he claimed his engine hadn't responded with its usual sharpness – and lost places to both Alonso and Nico Rosberg. Then the latter ran slightly wide through Turn Two, and the adjacent Trulli had little option but to plant a wheel on the right-hand grass verge at the exit of the corner, whereupon he looped around and began to slide back across the track.

Blissfully unaware, because he had bypassed the first corner altogether, Adrian Sutil emerged from the escape road just in time to smash into Trulli's stricken Toyota and, by way of change, had his regular first-

corner accident at Turn Two instead. Just behind, Sébastien Buemi braked fiercely to avoid the disintegrating cars ahead and was struck squarely by team-mate Sébastien Bourdais, whose car teetered briefly on its left-side wheels before landing the right way up.

All four cars were eliminated on the spot and the safety car was deployed, with Barrichello leading Button, Massa, Vettel, Webber, Alonso, Rosberg, Timo Glock, Nick Heidfeld, Kimi Räikkönen, Heikki Kovalainen, Kazuki Nakajima, Robert Kubica (who had lost several positions off the line because of a clutch problem), Nelson Piquet (both Renaults now running with the twin diffuser that had been introduced on Alonso's car in China), Lewis Hamilton and Giancarlo Fisichella, who made a tactical stop to switch from hard to soft Bridgestones.

Nakajima pitted on the second lap, to replace a front wing that had been damaged by flying debris, but didn't lose much time as the race remained neutralised until lap six.

Upon its resumption, Barrichello immediately pulled almost a full second clear, but Brawn's strategists were working at least as quickly. As the opening stint evolved, the team calculated that a three-stopper would hurt Button badly in terms of track position. "As we approached the pit window," said Ross Brawn, "it became apparent that Jenson would come out

Far left: Button and Barrichello embrace to celebrate yet another Brawn 1-2 as the championship battle begins its European leg.
Photo: Paul-Henri Cahier

Left: Some Alonso fans were already confidently anticipating their great hero's switch to Ferrari for 2010.
Photo: Lukas Gorys

Below: The Toro Rossos of Buemi and Bourdais managed to eliminate each other on the opening lap. Also a victim was Adrian Sutil's Force India.
Photo: Lukas Gorys

directly behind Rosberg if we stuck with his planned strategy, so we took the decision to switch him to a two-stopper."

The Englishman came in on lap 18, for more Bridgestone softs and a 30-lap fuel top-up, which put him several seconds behind Rosberg – but in clean air – and altered the race's complexion. "I wasn't sure about the tactical switch," Button said, "but the team realised I was far enough ahead of Massa to take on the extra fuel. The car felt heavy, but I just had to put my head down and concentrate on putting the laps in."

Barrichello came in on lap 19, remained on his three-stopper and predictably sped away from Button during their second stints. On the surface, the Brazilian appeared to be doing a decent job, but Button's performance was sensational: he should have been about 1.3–1.4 seconds per lap slower than his team-mate at this stage, but he kept the deficit down to eight- or nine-tenths.

Barrichello sacrificed yet more vital time during his third stint. "I just didn't have the pace I had previously," he said, "and was locking wheels all over the place." From lap 34 to 48, when he made his final stop, Button was equal parts speed and consistency, setting a string of 1m 24.3s/1m 24.4s laps, while Barrichello's times fluctuated erratically, from just south of Button to somewhere at least half a second adrift. When the Brazilian peeled in for the final time, 16 laps from home, he was only 14.907 seconds clear of his team-mate – about half the margin he required. The race was lost.

"It was difficult during the second stint," Button said, "because I had to be very aggressive. That's the good thing about this car, though. You can drive like that and it doesn't seem to eat up the tyres. It's not usually my style, but it's something I had to adopt."

Barrichello wasn't best pleased in the race's immediate aftermath – and rumours about conspiratorial team orders were zapping around the media room long before the race had finished. Questioned on the subject, Button was admirably concise. "According to our strategy," he said, "a three-stop race was faster, full stop." The simple truth was that Barrichello hadn't

driven quickly enough at critical moments of the race, a detail the Brazilian eventually came to accept.

Button's stellar second stint was mirrored, almost to the hundredth, by Webber. Beaten by Vettel in qualifying, when the cars were fuelled identically, the Australian endured the twin pains of following his team-mate throughout the opening stint and, as least favourably placed Red Bull, having to make the first scheduled stop.

The Australian made a crucial move just after the restart, on lap six, when Alonso used the grass and a bit of KERS assistance to pass him on the approach to Turn One. Webber hit back immediately, though, to stave off the threat of further compromise.

When he made his first stop, on lap 19, he rejoined with a 31-lap fuel load, and proceeded to drive with wonderful speed and consistency. "The car was horribly lethargic when I came out of the pits with all that fuel on board," he said. "It felt like they'd stuck a caravan on the back." His lap times didn't reflect as much, though.

Team-mate Vettel pitted on lap 20, but failed to clear Massa, who had refuelled at the same time. Subsequently, the pair ran until lap 43, again rejoining in the same order. It was during the following seven laps that Webber's relentless precision carried him past both, although the effort took its toll on his tyres, which were through to the canvas by the time he finally came in. Button's effort had been a masterclass in racecraft, but Webber's was no less so – a fitting

accomplishment on the 50th anniversary of compatriot Jack Brabham's maiden F1 world championship success in Monaco.

Vettel spent 62 laps staring at the Etihad advertisement on Massa's rear wing, but his frustration finally ended when circumstance obliged the Brazilian to back off. He had not been given sufficient fuel during the final stop – a problem with the car rather than the rig – and he had to more or less cruise the final four laps, which allowed both Vettel and Alonso to slip ahead, the latter's pass, predictably, raising the day's loudest cheer.

Heidfeld took seventh, describing the race as "one of my toughest, but also one of my best", after vaulting Rosberg during the final stops. The Williams driver ran steadily during the first stint, but then his car began to fluctuate between neutrality and oversteer, self-correcting without warning in the interim. "It was hard to commit in that situation," he said, "but without such problems, I really believe fifth place was possible."

McLaren knew beforehand that the MP4-24's absence of appetite for quick corners would make Spain a weekend to endure. The pain was relatively short-lived for Kovalainen, whose gearbox packed up on lap seven, but there was no such relief for Hamilton. He did engage in a brief, spirited dice with Alonso, however, largely because the McLaren was running on little more than fumes at that stage, while the Renault was freshly fuelled.

"The car was sliding so much in high-speed corners that my rear tyres went off very quickly," Hamilton said. "If we had Fernando's pace in the high-speed corners, we'd be up there with the Brawns, because we're fine in the slower stuff. It would have been nice to have a bit more of a battle, but we can't do that at the moment. We're just not fast enough to switch the tyres on. The rear of car was all over the place, like driving on ice."

A flawless afternoon's work ultimately proved fruitless, and he wound up ninth. The defending champion also had to face the unpleasant realities of life as an also-ran. At 1h 37m 18s, the FIA timing screens flashed up a message: "Waved blue flag for car 1". Hamilton was being ordered to move aside for Button, an irrelevant detail in the race's evolution, but symbolic nonetheless.

Glock, Kubica, Piquet, Nakajima and Fisichella completed the finishers, the last having to make his final scheduled stop twice, because precious little fuel went in at the first time of asking, while Räikkönen's low-key weekend concluded as early as lap 18, when hydraulic problems deprived him of throttle control.

And with that, the winning team prepared to renew acquaintance with EasyJet. "I didn't have enough legroom on the way out," said Ross Brawn, "because I forgot to pay for Speedy Boarding. I know we have to be careful with our money, but I think we can probably stretch to an extra £8."

Simon Arron

EDITOR'S VIEW
MANUFACTURER TEAMS FLEX THEIR MUSCLES

ALTHOUGH political spats in Formula One don't come along every day, like London buses, when they do, they seem to be queued at the kerb all around the FIA's lavish headquarters fronting the Place de la Concorde in Paris. In 2007, we had the 'Ferrari-gate' row, which spilled over into the following season, and in 2009, we were treated to the Melbourne 'Liar-gate' controversy involving Lewis Hamilton and Jarno Trulli.

By the time the '09 F1 World Championship had wended its way back to Europe to begin its metronomic fortnightly schedule, controversy had settled into a familiar area: the FIA versus the rest of the world, which in this case meant all the competing teams.

The debate over whether or not it was legitimate for a sporting body to interfere with and dictate the rules of engagement and business *modus operandi* of independent commercial organisations had ground on relentlessly for years. Even in the wake of Honda's seismic withdrawal at the start of the season, there was an impression that some of the teams were paying polite lip service to the arguments concerning economic sustainability that were being peddled by the governing body.

Some offered the rationale that teams had come and gone from F1 almost cyclically over the years, arguing that their failure or survival had been linked directly to how they had performed on the track, to changes in ownership, or to the quality of management and engineering. Lotus had faded into oblivion once the lingering afterglow of Colin Chapman's brilliance had finally burned out. Brabham had thrived under Bernie Ecclestone's entrepreneurial genius, but had run out of steam in the hands of a succession of less enlightened owners. However, these were individual cases whose destiny had been sealed by a tightly focused sequence of events that had affected each in a specific manner.

What was different about the crisis that emerged in 2009 was that the chill wind of economic reality was blowing right across the board, with scant regard for the financial reserves of the companies concerned. In Barcelona, the latest bout of displeasure was centred on the downright refusal of both Ferrari and Toyota to accept what they regarded as the unacceptably draconian implications of the FIA-ordained £40m budget cap proposed for those intending to compete in the 2010 World Championship.

Toyota laid it on the line in no uncertain terms, making it clear that there was no possibility of it submitting an entry for the 2010 title chase by the 29th May closing date unless there was a substantial revision of the governing body's plans. Some cynics in the paddock concluded that this was a ruse, designed to lay a smokescreen over the fact that Toyota wanted to get out of the F1 business as quickly as possible, given the disastrous global sales figures it had published in the previous week. In truth, however, all it wanted was the sport's cost reductions to be introduced on a more gradual basis.

Ferrari's robust line was underpinned by the political impossibility of slashing its workforce from around 650 to just over the 200 that it reckoned would be needed if the planned rules were adopted in their entirety. The Italian team also enjoyed a commercial deal that guaranteed it five per cent of the estimated $1bn annual commercial rights purse before it was sliced up and distributed to the various competing teams. In other words, it benefited from two bites of the cherry, plus the right to veto technical regulations until 2012.

Unfortunately, the FIA had delivered the new rules package as a *fait accompli* at the previous meeting of the World Motor Sport Council, so they were effectively set in stone before Ferrari could consider lodging its veto. There was much tension in the Barcelona paddock on Sunday, with suggestions that some of the manufacturers were thinking in terms of creating a breakaway championship.

Would it happen? No, not a chance. The business of compromise, which has long been elevated to the status of an art form in this high-octane game, would prevail as it always does. Self-preservation tends to focus people's minds quite dramatically – even in F1.

Alan Henry

Above: Mark Webber drove strongly for Red Bull, claiming third place on the podium next to the Brawn drivers.

Right: Indisputably, Ferrari remains the most powerful brand in the F1 business.

Photos: Peter J. Fox

CIRCUIT DE CATALUNYA, BARCELONA

Renault 150/240 [5]
Repsol 142/88 [3]
Seat 102/64 [2]
Campsa 230/143 [5]
Europcar 128/79 [3]
188/117 [4]
185/115 [4]
Banc Sabadell 125/78 [3]
Elf 141/88 [3]
Würth 145/90 [3]
187/116 [3]
190/304 [7]
La Caixa 74/46 [2]
171/107 [3]
New Holland 212/132 [4]
95/59 [2]

Circuit:
2.892 miles/4.655km
66 laps

187/116 kmh/mph [4] Gear

FIA F1 WORLD CHAMPIONSHIP ROUND 5

GRAN PREMIO DE
ESPAÑA
TELEFÓNICA

CATALUNYA 8-10 MAY 2009

RACE DISTANCE: 66 laps, 190.826 miles/307.104km • RACE WEATHER: Sunny/cloudy (track 37-40°C, air 24-25°C)

Pos.	Driver	Nat.	No.	Entrant	Car/Engine	Tyres	Laps	Time/Retirement	Speed (mph/km/h)	Gap to leader	Fastest race lap	
1	Jenson Button	GB	22	Brawn GP Formula 1 Team	Brawn BGP 001-Mercedes FO108W V8	B	66	1h 37m 19.202s	117.648/189.336		1m 22.899s	17
2	Rubens Barrichello	BR	23	Brawn GP Formula 1 Team	Brawn BGP 001-Mercedes FO108W V8	B	66	1h 37m 32.258s	117.386/188.914	+ 13.056s	1m 22.762s	28
3	Mark Webber	AUS	14	Red Bull Racing	Red Bull RB5-Renault RS27 V8	B	66	1h 37m 33.126s	117.368/188.886	+ 13.924s	1m 23.112s	18
4	Sebastian Vettel	D	15	Red Bull Racing	Red Bull RB5-Renault RS27 V8	B	66	1h 37m 38.143s	117.268/188.724	+ 18.941s	1m 23.090s	41
5	Fernando Alonso	E	7	ING Renault F1 Team	Renault R29-RS27 V8	B	66	1h 38m 02.368s	116.785/187.947	+ 43.166s	1m 23.420s	14
6	Felipe Massa	BR	3	Scuderia Ferrari Marlboro	Ferrari F60-056 V8	B	66	1h 38m 10.029s	116.633/187.702	+ 50.827s	1m 23.089s	14
7	Nick Heidfeld	D	6	BMW Sauber F1 Team	BMW Sauber F1.09-BMW P86/9 V8	B	66	1h 38m 11.514s	116.603/187.655	+ 52.312s	1m 23.878s	29
8	Nico Rosberg	D	16	AT&T Williams	Williams FW31-Toyota RVX-09 V8	B	66	1h 38m 24.413s	116.349/187.245	+ 1m 05.211s	1m 23.621s	24
9	Lewis Hamilton	GB	1	Vodafone McLaren Mercedes	McLaren MP4-24-Mercedes FO108W V8	B	65			+ 1 lap	1m 23.839s	29
10	Timo Glock	D	10	Panasonic Toyota Racing	Toyota TF109-RVX-09 V8	B	65			+ 1 lap	1m 24.134s	44
11	Robert Kubica	PL	5	BMW Sauber F1 Team	BMW Sauber F1.09-BMW P86/9 V8	B	65			+ 1 lap	1m 24.078s	26
12	Nelsinho Piquet	BR	8	ING Renault F1 Team	Renault R29-RS27 V8	B	65			+ 1 lap	1m 24.286s	41
13	Kazuki Nakajima	J	17	AT&T Williams	Williams FW31-Toyota RVX-09 V8	B	65			+ 1 lap	1m 24.155s	38
14	Giancarlo Fisichella	I	21	Force India F1 Team	Force India VJM02-Mercedes FO108W V8	B	65			+ 1 lap	1m 23.796s	63
	Kimi Räikkönen	FIN	4	Scuderia Ferrari Marlboro	Ferrari F60-056 V8	B	17	hydraulics			1m 24.490s	16
	Heikki Kovalainen	FIN	2	Vodafone McLaren Mercedes	McLaren MP4-24-Mercedes FO108W V8	B	7	gearbox			1m 28.719s	6
	Jarno Trulli	I	9	Panasonic Toyota Racing	Toyota TF109-RVX-09 V8	B	0	accident			no time	
	Sébastien Buemi	CH	12	Scuderia Toro Rosso	Toro Rosso STR04-Ferrari 056 V8	B	0	accident			no time	
	Sébastien Bourdais	F	11	Scuderia Toro Rosso	Toro Rosso STR04-Ferrari 056 V8	B	0	accident			no time	
	Adrian Sutil	D	20	Force India F1 Team	Force India VJM02-Mercedes FO108W V8	B	0	accident			no time	

Fastest race lap: Rubens Barrichello on lap 28, 1m 22.762s, 125.818mph/202.484km/h.

Lap record: Giancarlo Fisichella (Renault R25 V10), 1m 15.641s, 136.835mph/220.213km/h (2005) (2.875 mile/4.627km circuit).

Lap record (current configuration): Kimi Räikkönen (Ferrari F2008 V8), 1m 21.670s, 127.500mph/205.192km/h (2008)

All results and data © FOM 2009

| 20 | SUTIL · Force India | 11 | BOURDAIS · Toro Rosso | 12 | BUEMI · Toro Rosso | 6 | HEIDFELD · BMW Sauber | 17 | NAKAJIMA · Williams | 16 | ROSBERG · Williams |
| 21 | FISICHELLA · Force India | 2 | KOVALAINEN · McLaren | 4 | RÄIKKÖNEN · Ferrari | 1 | HAMILTON · McLaren | 8 | PIQUET · Renault | 5 | KUBICA · BMW Sauber |

Grid order / lap chart (laps 1–53 shown):

Grid order	Laps 1 → 53
22 BUTTON	23 23 23 23 23 23 23 23 23 23 23 23 23 23 23 23 23 23 · 3 23 23 23 23 23 23 23 23 23 23 · 22 22 22 22 22 22 22 22 22 22 22 22 22 22 22 22 22 22 22 22 · 23 23 22
15 VETTEL	22 22 22 22 22 22 22 22 22 22 22 22 22 22 22 22 22 22 · 3 15 16 16 16 16 16 22 22 22 22 22 22 · 3 3 3 3 3 3 3 3 3 3 3 · 23 23 23 23 23 14 14 23
23 BARRICHELLO	3 3 3 3 3 3 3 3 3 3 3 3 3 3 3 3 3 3 · 15 23 22 22 22 22 22 · 3 3 3 3 3 · 15 15 15 15 15 15 15 15 15 15 15 · 14 14 14 14 14 22 22 14
3 MASSA	15 15 15 15 15 15 15 15 15 15 15 15 15 15 15 15 15 15 · 14 16 3 3 3 3 3 · 15 15 15 15 23 23 23 23 23 23 23 23 23 23 · 7 3 3 3 3 3 3 3
14 WEBBER	14 14 14 14 14 14 14 14 14 14 14 14 14 14 14 14 14 14 · 16 22 15 15 15 15 15 · 6 6 6 6 6 · 14 14 14 14 14 14 14 14 14 14 · 3 15 15 15 15 15 15 15 1
10 GLOCK	7 7 7 7 7 7 7 7 7 7 7 7 7 7 7 7 7 7 · 22 6 6 6 6 6 6 · 1 1 1 1 1 · 7 7 7 7 7 7 7 7 7 7 · 15 16 16 16 16 16 16 16
9 TRULLI	16 16 16 16 16 16 16 16 16 16 16 16 16 16 16 16 16 16 · 6 5 5 5 1 1 1 · 14 14 14 14 14 · 1 16 16 16 16 16 16 16 16 16 · 6 6 6 6 6 6 6 6
7 ALONSO	10 10 10 10 10 10 10 10 10 10 10 10 10 10 10 10 10 10 · 6 5 1 1 1 1 14 14 · 7 7 7 7 7 · 6 6 6 6 6 6 6 6 7 · 7 7 7 7 16 16 16
16 ROSBERG	6 6 6 6 6 6 6 6 6 6 6 6 6 6 6 6 6 6 · 5 1 14 14 14 14 7 · 16 16 16 16 16 · 16 17 17 17 17 1 1 1 1 1 · 1 1 1 1 1 17 17 17
5 KUBICA	4 17 4 4 4 4 4 4 4 4 4 4 4 4 4 4 4 1 · 8 7 7 21 21 21 21 21 21 17 17 · 1 1 1 1 10 10 10 10 10 10 10 10 10 · 17 1 1 1 1
17 NAKAJIMA	2 4 2 2 2 5 5 5 5 5 5 5 5 5 5 5 5 8 · 7 7 8 21 21 17 17 17 17 17 21 · 10 10 10 10 5 5 5 5 5 5 5 · 17 10 10 10 10
8 PIQUET	17 2 5 5 5 2 1 1 1 1 1 1 1 1 1 1 1 21 · 21 21 17 17 10 10 10 10 10 10 5 · 5 5 5 8 8 8 8 8 8 8 8 · 5 5 5 5 5
6 HEIDFELD	5 5 8 8 8 8 8 8 8 8 8 8 8 8 8 8 17 17 · 17 10 10 5 5 5 5 5 5 8 8 · 8 17 17 17 17 17 17 17 17 · 21 21 21 21 2
1 HAMILTON	8 8 1 1 1 1 21 21 21 21 21 21 21 10 10 10 10 8 · 8 8 8 8 8 8 21 21 21 21 21 · 21 21 21 21 21 21 8 8 8 8 · 1
12 BUEMI	1 1 21 21 21 21 17 17 17 17 17 17 17 17 17
4 RÄIKKÖNEN	21 21 17 17 17 17 2
11 BOURDAIS	
2 KOVALAINEN	
20 SUTIL	
21 FISICHELLA	

Safety car deployed on laps shown

TIME SHEETS

PRACTICE 1 (FRIDAY)
Partly cloudy/sunny
(track 24-33°C, air 19-24°C)

Pos.	Driver	Laps	Time
1	Jenson Button	21	1m 21.799s
2	Jarno Trulli	30	1m 22.154s
3	Robert Kubica	24	1m 22.221s
4	Nick Heidfeld	14	1m 22.658s
5	Kazuki Nakajima	24	1m 22.659s
6	Nico Rosberg	26	1m 22.667s
7	Nelsinho Piquet	24	1m 22.753s
8	Timo Glock	29	1m 22.828s
9	Felipe Massa	15	1m 22.855s
10	Rubens Barrichello	24	1m 22.859s
11	Kimi Räikkönen	20	1m 22.873s
12	Mark Webber	25	1m 22.934s
13	Sebastian Vettel	24	1m 22.959s
14	Lewis Hamilton	21	1m 23.077s
15	Sébastien Bourdais	30	1m 23.088s
16	Giancarlo Fisichella	25	1m 23.089s
17	Fernando Alonso	18	1m 23.157s
18	Sébastien Buemi	31	1m 23.185s
19	Heikki Kovalainen	17	1m 23.522s
20	Adrian Sutil	19	1m 23.536s

PRACTICE 2 (FRIDAY)
Sunny/partly cloudy
(track 35-38°C, air 25°C)

Pos.	Driver	Laps	Time
1	Nico Rosberg	43	1m 21.588s
2	Kazuki Nakajima	40	1m 21.740s
3	Fernando Alonso	36	1m 21.781s
4	Rubens Barrichello	39	1m 21.843s
5	Mark Webber	37	1m 22.027s
6	Jenson Button	35	1m 22.052s
7	Sebastian Vettel	45	1m 22.082s
8	Nelsinho Piquet	26	1m 22.349s
9	Sébastien Buemi	17	1m 22.571s
10	Kimi Räikkönen	40	1m 22.599s
11	Sébastien Bourdais	30	1m 22.615s
12	Giancarlo Fisichella	32	1m 22.670s
13	Lewis Hamilton	31	1m 22.809s
14	Heikki Kovalainen	29	1m 22.876s
15	Felipe Massa	35	1m 22.878s
16	Robert Kubica	40	1m 22.948s
17	Nick Heidfeld	39	1m 23.173s
18	Timo Glock	46	1m 23.360s
19	Jarno Trulli	47	1m 23.623s
20	Adrian Sutil		no time

PRACTICE 3 (SATURDAY)
Sunny/cloudy
(track 26-32°C, air 20-22°C)

Pos.	Driver	Laps	Time
1	Felipe Massa	18	1m 20.553s
2	Kimi Räikkönen	22	1m 20.635s
3	Jenson Button	19	1m 21.050s
4	Rubens Barrichello	17	1m 21.163s
5	Robert Kubica	21	1m 21.239s
6	Jarno Trulli	23	1m 21.256s
7	Lewis Hamilton	16	1m 21.346s
8	Timo Glock	26	1m 21.377s
9	Sébastien Buemi	19	1m 21.424s
10	Fernando Alonso	17	1m 21.499s
11	Heikki Kovalainen	15	1m 21.519s
12	Nico Rosberg	20	1m 21.594s
13	Mark Webber	19	1m 21.629s
14	Sébastien Bourdais	19	1m 21.649s
15	Nelsinho Piquet	18	1m 21.685s
16	Sebastian Vettel	18	1m 21.689s
17	Giancarlo Fisichella	19	1m 21.909s
18	Kazuki Nakajima	19	1m 22.043s
19	Adrian Sutil	19	1m 22.232s
20	Nick Heidfeld	8	1m 23.457s

QUALIFYING (SATURDAY)
Sunny/cloudy (track 36-39°C, air 24-26°C)

Pos.	Driver	First	Second	Third	Weight
1	Jenson Button	1m 20.707s	1m 20.192s	**1m 20.527s**	646kg
2	Sebastian Vettel	1m 20.715s	1m 20.220s	1m 20.660s	651.5kg
3	Rubens Barrichello	1m 20.808s	**1m 19.954s**	1m 20.762s	649.5kg
4	Felipe Massa	**1m 20.484s**	1m 20.149s	1m 20.934s	655kg
5	Mark Webber	1m 20.689s	1m 20.007s	1m 21.049s	651.5kg
6	Timo Glock	1m 20.877s	1m 20.107s	1m 21.247s	646.5kg
7	Jarno Trulli	1m 21.189s	1m 20.420s	1m 21.254s	655.5kg
8	Fernando Alonso	1m 21.186s	1m 20.509s	1m 21.392s	645kg
9	Nico Rosberg	1m 20.745s	1m 20.256s	1m 22.558s	668kg
10	Robert Kubica	1m 20.931s	1m 20.408s	1m 22.685s	660kg
11	Kazuki Nakajima	1m 20.818s	1m 20.531s		676.6kg
12	Nelsinho Piquet	1m 21.128s	1m 20.604s		677.4kg
13	Nick Heidfeld	1m 21.095s	1m 20.676s		676.3kg
14	Lewis Hamilton	1m 20.991s	1m 20.805s		683kg
15	Sébastien Buemi	1m 21.033s	1m 21.067s		678kg
16	Kimi Räikkönen	1m 21.291s			673kg
17	Sébastien Bourdais	1m 21.300s			669kg
18	Heikki Kovalainen	1m 21.675s			657kg
19	Adrian Sutil	1m 21.742s			675kg
20	Giancarlo Fisichella	1m 22.204s			656kg

9 — TRULLI · Toyota

14 — WEBBER · Red Bull

23 — BARRICHELLO · Brawn

22 — BUTTON · Brawn

7 — ALONSO · Renault

10 — GLOCK · Toyota

3 — MASSA · Ferrari

15 — VETTEL · Red Bull

FOR THE RECORD

20th PODIUM: **Jenson Button**

250th GRAND PRIX START: **Renault**

300th POINT: **Felipe Massa**

Photos: Peter J. Fox

POINTS

DRIVERS
1	Jenson Button	41
2	Rubens Barrichello	27
3	Sebastian Vettel	23
4	Mark Webber	15.5
5	Jarno Trulli	14.5
6	Timo Glock	12
7	Lewis Hamilton	9
8	Fernando Alonso	9
9	Nick Heidfeld	6
10	Nico Rosberg	4.5
11	Heikki Kovalainen	4
12	Felipe Massa	3
13	Kimi Räikkönen	3
14	Sébastien Buemi	3
15	Sébastien Bourdais	1

CONSTRUCTORS
1	Brawn	68
2	Red Bull	38.5
3	Toyota	26.5
4	McLaren	13
5	Renault	9
6	BMW Sauber	6
7	Ferrari	6
8	Williams	4.5
9	Toro Rosso	4

Lap chart (laps 54-66)

	54	55	56	57	58	59	60	61	62	63	64	65	66	·
1	22	22	22	22	22	22	22	22	22	22	22	22	22	
2	23	23	23	23	23	23	23	23	23	23	23	23	23	
3	14	14	14	14	14	14	14	14	14	14	14	14	14	
4	3	3	3	3	3	3	3	3	3	15	15	15	15	
5	15	15	15	15	15	15	15	15	15	3	3	3	7	
6	7	7	7	7	7	7	7	7	7	7	7	7	3	
7	6	6	6	6	6	6	6	6	6	6	6	6	6	
8	16	16	16	16	16	16	16	16	16	16	16	16	16	
	1	1	1	1	1	1	1	1	1	1	1	1	1	
	10	10	10	10	10	10	10	10	10	10	10	10	10	
	5	5	5	5	5	5	5	5	5	5	5	5	5	
	8	8	8	8	8	8	8	8	8	8	8	8	8	
	17	17	17	17	17	17	17	17	17	17	17	17	17	
	21	21	21	21	21	21	21	21	21	21	21	21	21	

Pit stop

One lap or more behind

RACE TYRE STRATEGIES

The tyre regulations stipulate that two dry tyre specifications must be used during the race.

The Super-Soft compound Bridgestone Potenza tyre is marked with a green stripe on the sidewall of the tyre.

	Driver	Race Stint 1	Race Stint 2	Race Stint 3	Race Stint 4
1	Jenson Button	Super-Soft: 1-15	Super-Soft: 16-37	Medium: 38-57	
2	Sebastian Vettel	Super-Soft: 1-19	Super-Soft: 20-40	Medium: 41-57	
3	Jarno Trulli	Super-Soft: 1-12	Medium: 13-37	Super-Soft: 38-57	
4	Lewis Hamilton	Super-Soft: 1-15	Super-Soft: 16-37	Medium: 38-57	
5	Rubens Barrichello	Super-Soft: 1-14	Super-Soft: 15-26	Super-Soft: 27-47	Medium: 48-57
6	Kimi Räikkönen	Super-Soft: 1-21	Super-Soft: 22-44	Medium: 45-57	
7	Timo Glock	Super-Soft: 1-11	Medium: 12-33	Super-Soft: 34-57	
8	Fernando Alonso	Super-Soft: 1-16	Super-Soft: 17-37	Medium: 38-57	
	Nico Rosberg	Super-Soft: 1-21	Super-Soft: 22-45	Medium: 46-57	
	Nelson Piquet	Super-Soft: 1-23	Super-Soft: 24-42	Medium: 43-57	
	Mark Webber	Super-Soft: 1-14	Medium: 15-37	Super-Soft: 38-57	
	Heikki Kovalainen	Medium: 1-12	Super-Soft: 13-37	Super-Soft: 38-57	
	Sébastien Bourdais	Medium: 1-18	Super-Soft: 19-36	Super-Soft: 37-57	
	Felipe Massa	Super-Soft: 1-3	Super-Soft: 4-29	Super-Soft: 30-46	Medium: 47-56
	Giancarlo Fisichella	Super-Soft: 1-15	Super-Soft: 16-37	Medium: 38-56	
	Adrian Sutil	Super-Soft: 1-23	Super-Soft: 24-41	Medium: 42-56	
	Sébastien Buemi	Super-Soft: 1-21	Super-Soft: 22-39	Medium: 40-56	
	Robert Kubica	Medium: 1-2	Medium: 3-34	Super-Soft: 35-56	
	Nick Heidfeld	Medium: 1-3	Medium: 4-36	Super-Soft: 37-56	
	Kazuki Nakajima	Super-Soft: 1-2	Super-Soft: 3-30	Super-Soft: 31-48 (dnf)	

FIA FORMULA 1 WORLD CHAMPIONSHIP • ROUND 6

MONACO GRAND PRIX

MONTE CARLO CIRCUIT

The magical vista offered by the Hôtel de Paris, overlooking Casino Square, never fails to impress and overwhelm with its sheer presence.

Photo: Bernard Asset

MONTE CARLO QUALIFYING

AS bolts from the blue go, this was less of a thunderclap than most. Brawn always looked a likely contender for pole position in Monaco, but only on one side of the pit garage. While Rubens Barrichello thrived in one of his favourite racing environments, Jenson Button struggled to get anywhere close and initially was almost a second shy of his team-mate.

"I was a long way off in first free practice on Thursday," Button said, "and really didn't know where we were. I had very low grip, but worked with the balance and just improved little by little. That's the great thing with this car. If I'd started Thursday like that in last year's chassis, I'd have struggled massively. But this car listens to changes."

Button admitted that he'd started his weekend by trying to adopt an aggressive approach, tailoring his driving to the track rather than fine-tuning the chassis to suit his customarily smooth, unhurried style, but that led to a locked-wheel epidemic and a feeling of deep unease. Reverting to square one, he began focusing on the car and ended up going faster in Q3 than he had with less fuel on board in Q2. For the first time all weekend, he was the quickest man in the principality, and his timing could not have been better.

"Rubens has been bloody fast all weekend," Button said, "but that's been good because it has spurred me on. I'd been nowhere near as fast as him through the swimming-pool complex, but in the end I drove through there as quickly as I could and thought I might end up on Flavio Briatore's boat." A very large target, that, with a huge, gold "FB" monogram adorning its funnel.

Barrichello had hoped to annex pole as a 37th birthday treat, but he was sanguine in defeat and there was no trace of the post-race histrionics we'd seen in Barcelona.

"I've had a great Saturday," he said. "My fastest lap of the weekend was on used rubber, which is unusual, and we need to see why new tyres are not working so well for me. I did a 1m 14.8s in Q2, and with fuel in the car, I did a 1m 15.0s, so I've got to be extremely happy with that. I never thought Jenson could do a 14.9s with fuel on board, so his was a pretty amazing lap. As soon as I got out of my car, I asked him how he did it…"

Running slightly lighter, and with his Ferrari's handling improving by the lap as more rubber went down, Kimi Räikkönen managed to split the Brawns. How much satisfaction did he derive from that, given his patchy start to the campaign? "Not much," he said. "I'd rather be in front. We're not really in the championship, and I'm only interested in winning."

He was in a much better place, though, than Lewis Hamilton. The defending champion's affinity for Monaco had been expected to combine well with his McLaren MP4-24's appetite for slow corners, but after looking like a genuine podium contender, he locked up at Mirabeau in Q1 and reversed into the tyre wall. He did enough damage to require a replacement gearbox, an unscheduled change that carried a five-position grid penalty, obliging him to start right at the back.

Right: Jenson Button guides his Brawn out on to the waterfront at Portier and aims it towards the tunnel.
Photo: Paul-Henri Cahier

Below: Max Mosley, the FIA president, is also a resident in the principality.

Bottom: There really is no other racetrack like it.
Photos: Peter J. Fox

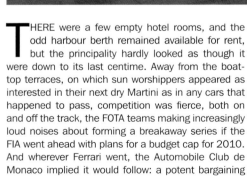

THERE were a few empty hotel rooms, and the odd harbour berth remained available for rent, but the principality hardly looked as though it were down to its last centime. Away from the boat-top terraces, on which sun worshippers appeared as interested in their next dry Martini as in any cars that happened to pass, competition was fierce, both on and off the track, the FOTA teams making increasingly loud noises about forming a breakaway series if the FIA went ahead with plans for a budget cap for 2010. And wherever Ferrari went, the Automobile Club de Monaco implied it would follow: a potent bargaining tool, that.

Ferrari wasn't going anywhere on Sunday afternoon – or at least it wasn't doing so quite quickly enough. The Monaco pit straight isn't long enough for KERS to be a significant benefit, but it might have given Kimi Räikkönen half a chance of deposing Jenson Button on the drag to the portside chicane. For that, though, he needed to be right behind the Englishman, but he was immediately beaten down to third at the start when Rubens Barrichello got away particularly smartly.

"The track seemed to be very slippery on my side,"

Räikkönen said, "and both Brawns were on the softer tyre, which definitely helped off the line."

Thus the race's complexion was settled. Button was almost a second clear of his team-mate by the end of the opening lap, with Räikkönen third, ahead of Sebastian Vettel, Felipe Massa, Nico Rosberg, Heikki Kovalainen, Mark Webber, Fernando Alonso, Kazuki Nakajima, Nelson Piquet, Sébastien Buemi, Sébastien Bourdais, Adrian Sutil, Giancarlo Fisichella, Nick Heidfeld, Robert Kubica, Lewis Hamilton, Jarno Trulli and Timo Glock. Hamilton gained a place at Kubica's expense on the second lap, but the Pole was bound for the pits after sustaining a rear puncture.

The super-soft Bridgestones were thought to be marginal in terms of wear, but the Brawn was kinder to its rubber than most, and Button's ever-improving lap times confirmed as much. Red Bull was running its new twin diffuser for the first time, but the potential benefits were wholly concealed because fourth-fastest qualifier Vettel had aped the Brawns' tyre strategy and within a few minutes his Bridgestones were shot: it took only seven laps for him to drop more than three seconds off the pace, and most of the field were soon queuing behind while the first three broke away.

"We had no hesitation about starting on the super-soft," said Button. Barrichello, running in his partner's turbulence, however, felt his rear tyres begin to grain after ten laps and was in for replacements after 16. Button came in slightly early for his first stop, too, on lap 17, a couple ahead of schedule, but by then he had stretched his advantage to more than 18 seconds and was free to spend the balance of his afternoon on the more dependable prime.

There had been little doubt about the probable outcome by the time he came out of Ste Dévote on the opening lap, and certainly there was none now. He made his final stop on lap 51 and was sufficiently far ahead that he had time to let his mind drift as the race drew towards its inevitable conclusion. "I claimed beforehand that victory here wouldn't mean more than it did anywhere else," he said, "but that was a lie really because I was just trying to remove any pressure. The problem with Monaco is that it is mentally very tough. You are focusing so much that the track feels narrower and narrower as the race wears on. To win here feels very special, and I think the final two laps were the most enjoyable of my career. I could just savour winning Monaco, something

I've been dreaming about since I was a kid. It's the first time I've ever looked around during a race here, even though somebody claimed I was doing that in 2001…"

A barbed reference, that, to Flavio Briatore, who had recently described Button as a *"paracarro"*, an unflattering accusation of slothfulness: it's the Italian word for a roadside marker post. The Renault F1 chief apparently considered Button and Barrichello – "a nice bloke, but half-way to retirement" – unworthy title contenders, which amused Button more than anything. "Flavio needs to remember that he tried to hire me this year," he said.

The Englishman made his only significant error after the flag. He forgot that Monaco protocol requires the first three finishers to park their cars on the pit straight, in front of the royal box, and left his Brawn in the commoners' car park, by the pit entrance. After 1h 40m 44.282s of racing, he was obliged to run the length of the pit straight, in overalls and crash helmet, to collect his champagne.

Pit fluctuations apart, the top three remained unaltered from Ste Dévote on the opening lap to the Virage Anthony Noghès on the 78th – and Barrichello

felt that the opening laps had been decisive. "Before the start, we thought the option might be the tyre to use for three-quarters of the race," he said, "and it definitely worked for us at the start. I was running comfortably behind Jenson, but being so close affected my tyres a little bit more because you lose a bit of aero balance and start to slide. It felt to me as though the tyre pressures had risen, but the team could see on TV that graining had started, and that cost me four seconds. Jenson and I had a very similar pace, but that's basically when the race was lost."

It was the Brazilian's fourth second place in the principality. "I wish I had won some races here," he said, "but I'm looking at things differently this time. Jenson is a long way ahead, and I have to score as many points as possible while I'm not winning. It's the championship that matters right now, and Jenson is on a flier. He's not making any mistakes."

The sense of frustration was more tangible at Ferrari. Räikkönen had tried to use KERS during the short burst at the start, but pointed out, "It's not much use if you start spinning your wheels straight away. I was faster than Rubens when he had his tyre problems, but after that it all played out at a very similar pace. Without dropping to third at the start, I could probably have taken second place, but overall we're not yet really fast enough to fight for wins."

Massa had more than enough pace to finish second, but spent the first six laps of the race bottled up behind the hobbling Vettel. On the seventh, he passed the German at the chicane, but left his brak-

ing so late that he completely failed to take the corner and was obliged to hand the place back on the following straight. When he did so, however, Rosberg – on Vettel's tail – opportunistically nipped through, too, leaving Massa to follow the Williams until it made its first scheduled stop on lap 18. The Brazilian felt he might have beaten Kimi: he ran three laps longer during his second stint, but spent them behind the heavily fuelled Button, who had just rejoined the race. The key, though, was losing more than 20 seconds following Vettel during the opening stages. Massa's quick, consistent second stint, during which he set fastest lap, was the finest barometer of Ferrari's improving form and earned him fourth place. He did receive a warning, shortly after half-distance, however, for persistent chicane cutting.

Vettel struggled so much on his super-softs that Rosberg, Massa and Kovalainen all passed him on the track during lap ten, before he reached the pits, but then he managed only five laps on the superior soft before piling into the tyre wall at Ste Dévote: "I just locked the rears and lost it."

Mark Webber lasted long enough to demonstrate the benefit of Red Bull's new floor, however. From eighth on the grid, he had to rely on a longish 22-lap first stint to vault Rosberg and Kovalainen after the opening stops, but he matched, and often exceeded, the Ferraris' pace during the race's middle sector, although he was still 2.6 seconds shy of Massa when they came in together on lap 56, and thus had to settle for fifth, ahead of Rosberg.

Kovalainen ran seventh until lap 52, when he crashed heavily at the swimming-pool complex. "I hit a kerb and the car's rear end stepped out," he said. "It was my fault and I'd like to apologise to the team." He'd just demolished McLaren's only hope of a points finish, for Hamilton, trapped at the back, had precious little hope of making serious progress – and none at all after he damaged his front wing when, moments after his first stop, he clipped Heidfeld at Ste Dévote. He was plagued with understeer until he received a new nose during his second stop, on lap 53, and finished only 12th, not quite on a par with 2008.

Kovalainen's lapse promoted Alonso to seventh and allowed Bourdais – faultless throughout – to score a point as best of the one-stoppers. "I didn't do a particularly good job in qualifying," he said, "so I'm happy with eighth, given that there weren't many incidents among the leaders. The car performed consistently, especially on the soft tyre, and I tried to look after the super-softs because I'd had trouble with them during practice on Thursday. I just settled into a rhythm and concentrated on bringing the car home."

His capable efforts were matched by those of Fisichella and Glock, who drove opening stints of 52 and 57 laps respectively en route to ninth and tenth. It was one of Fisichella's finest drives since drilled throttle pedals were the height of fashion and carried him to within a couple of seconds of Force India's maiden point. Glock's result was partial compensation for what had hitherto been a dreadful weekend. Both Toyotas had been hopelessly short of mechani-

Left: Nico Rosberg just manages to squeeze his Williams inside Felipe Massa's Ferrari, on the way into Tabac, as the Brazilian is wrong-footed by Sebastian Vettel's Red Bull.
Photo: Studio Colombo/WRi2

Right: Second best. Once again, Rubens Barrichello had to follow in the wake of his dominant team-mate, Jenson Button.
Photo: Peter J. Fox

Below: The Renault of hapless Nelson Piquet is punted off the road at Ste Dévote by an over-anxious Sébastien Buemi in the Toro Rosso.
Photo: Studio Colombo/WRi2

cal grip up to and during qualifying, but Glock's car was extracted from *parc fermé* for suspension alterations – a detail that obliged him to start from the pits – and performed better in race trim. Two-stopping team-mate Jarno Trulli – "I always seemed to be in the wrong place at the wrong time in terms of traffic." – was 13th, behind Heidfeld, who was condemned to a 36-lap second stint on the super-soft tyres, and Hamilton.

For many drivers, post-Monaco custom dictates that they slink away to their apartments. Glock, refreshingly, repaired to a modest roadside pizzeria with his girlfriend and a couple of mates, sitting there unmolested and enjoying a quiet meal. There's a lot to be said for combining a front-line grand prix career with a balanced lifestyle, but it is a privilege denied to some.

Adrian Sutil planned a one-stop race, but started on super-softs and had to pit after 11 laps because they were shot: the switch to a two-stopper left him 14th, classified only ahead of Nakajima, who was on course to finish tenth until he crashed at Rascasse on the penultimate lap.

Kubica pulled into the pits after 28 laps with brake trouble, while Buemi and Piquet retired after a collision on the 11th lap. The Swiss had lost out to the Brazilian at the start and, in his impatience to repass, had created an eight-wheeled Toro Rosso/Renault hybrid by ramming his rival and shoving him all the way down the escape road. Buemi's car finished up in the tyre wall, while Piquet's hobbled back to the pits with crumpled rear suspension.

Later Buemi went to find Piquet to offer a fulsome apology, although he also pointed out that he felt his rival had hit the brake pedal a touch early.

Simon Arron

Above: Prince Albert leads the applause in the Royal Box as an ecstatic Button celebrates another job well done.
Photo: Paul-Henri Cahier

Left: Sébastien Bourdais sweeps by as Lewis Hamilton walks away from his wrecked McLaren during qualifying.
Photo: Luca Bassani/WRi2

Right: The devil wears Prada? Robert Kubica seems unimpressed by the shopping opportunities on offer.
Photo: Studio Colombo/WRi2

Far right: Walking the plank. Flavio Briatore leads his fellow team principals down the gangway of his luxury yacht.
Photo: Jean-François Galeron/WRi2

EDITOR'S VIEW
LIFE'S RICH, FOR SOME...

I N the early months of 2009, Formula One people frequently talked about the impossibility of the sport continuing without Ferrari, of a political split leading to a breakaway series or a wholesale withdrawal by the remaining major car companies. Yet it became clear in the run-up to the Monaco Grand Prix just how much the sport might be risking, and the massive own goal it might be poised to score, if it continued along the path of waging such a potentially dangerous public war, one that even Prince Albert of Monaco felt he needed to enter with a few well-chosen words of caution.

The prince talked about "the need for a level playing field" and "the difficulties of going against the governing body". One could easily interpret his view as a belief that Monaco could, if necessary, promote its own stand-alone event. In many ways, just as few give a brass farthing about any oval race other than the Indy 500, so Monaco stands as the absolute pinnacle of F1 races. So much so that it gets its race for free, mute testimony to its unique attraction. It could survive without the grand prix, although undoubtedly it would be damaged economically. Yet without Monaco, F1, as a business and a sport, would be diminished to a much greater extent.

"The grand prix is the biggest event of the year in Monaco," said the prince. "Its economic impact and importance for tourism cannot be overestimated. For us, it is of vital importance. As I grow older, I expect the novelty to wear off, but each year I find I'm as excited as ever. The whole event is very enticing."

Successive generations of the Grimaldi dynasty have shown themselves to be no fools, transforming what was once a rather seedy and run-down bolt hole for wealthy Somerset Maugham look-alikes into a fizzing playground for the super-rich and wannabe celebrities. And only Monaco, let's not forget, has a long-established deal to have a 'free day' without any F1 track activity on the Friday of each grand prix weekend, the more to encourage the public's frenetic levels of spending. Alan Whicker, the legendary globe-trotting travel journalist, once wrote that the Monégasques are so greedy that even the rest of the Riviera French have noticed. Makes you think, doesn't it?

Even so, in some peoples' minds, there was huge irony in FIA president Max Mosley being canvassed for his lofty views on the subject of the proposed £40m F1 budget cap in such a lavish environment as this Mediterranean tax haven, where he has lived for some years after inheriting many millions of pounds on the death of his mother in 2003. Nothing wrong in that, of course. Most peoples' objections to inherited wealth stem from not having enough of it in their own bank accounts. Nonetheless, it still made one smile.

Alan Henry

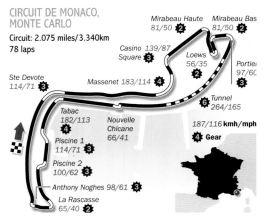

CIRCUIT DE MONACO, MONTE CARLO

Circuit: 2.075 miles/3.340km
78 laps

Mirabeau Haute 81/50
Mirabeau Bas 81/50
Casino 139/87
Square
Loews 56/35
Portiel 97/60
Ste Devote 114/71
Massenet 183/114
Tunnel 264/165
Tabac 182/113
Nouvelle Chicane 66/41
187/116 kmh/mph
Piscine 1 114/71
Gear
Piscine 2 100/62
Anthony Noghes 98/61
La Rascasse 65/40

FIA F1 WORLD CHAMPIONSHIP ROUND 6

GRAND PRIX DE
MONACO
MONTE CARLO 21-24 MAY 2009

RACE DISTANCE: 78 laps, 161.880 miles/260.520km • **RACE WEATHER: Sunny (track 34-38°C, air 25°C)**

Pos.	Driver	Nat.	No.	Entrant	Car/Engine	Tyres	Laps	Time/Retirement	Speed (mph/km/h)	Gap to leader	Fastest race lap	
1	Jenson Button	GB	22	Brawn GP Formula 1 Team	Brawn BGP 001-Mercedes FO108W V8	B	78	1h 40m 44.282s	96.416/155.166		1m 15.190s	49
2	Rubens Barrichello	BR	23	Brawn GP Formula 1 Team	Brawn BGP 001-Mercedes FO108W V8	B	78	1h 40m 51.948s	96.294/154.970	+ 7.666s	1m 15.685s	46
3	Kimi Räikkönen	FIN	4	Scuderia Ferrari Marlboro	Ferrari F60-056 V8	B	78	1h 40m 57.724s	96.202/154.822	+ 13.442s	1m 15.382s	47
4	Felipe Massa	BR	3	Scuderia Ferrari Marlboro	Ferrari F60-056 V8	B	78	1h 40m 59.392s	96.175/154.779	+ 15.110s	1m 15.154s	50
5	Mark Webber	AUS	14	Red Bull Racing	Red Bull RB5-Renault RS27 V8	B	78	1h 41m 00.012s	96.166/154.764	+ 15.730s	1m 15.321s	45
6	Nico Rosberg	D	16	AT&T Williams	Williams FW31-Toyota RVX-09 V8	B	78	1h 41m 17.868s	95.883/154.309	+ 33.586s	1m 15.772s	48
7	Fernando Alonso	E	7	ING Renault F1 Team	Renault R29-RS27 V8	B	78	1h 41m 22.121s	95.816/154.201	+ 37.839s	1m 15.371s	64
8	Sébastien Bourdais	F	11	Scuderia Toro Rosso	Toro Rosso STR04-Ferrari 056 V8	B	78	1h 41m 47.424s	95.419/153.562	+ 1m 03.142s	1m 16.178s	47
9	Giancarlo Fisichella	I	21	Force India F1 Team	Force India VJM02-Mercedes FO108W V8	B	78	1h 41m 49.322s	95.389/153.514	+ 1m 05.040s	1m 16.419s	74
10	Timo Glock	D	10	Panasonic Toyota Racing	Toyota TF109-RVX-09 V8	B	77			+ 1 lap	1m 16.066s	72
11	Nick Heidfeld	D	6	BMW Sauber F1 Team	BMW Sauber F1.09-BMW P86/9 V8	B	77			+ 1 lap	1m 16.268s	49
12	Lewis Hamilton	GB	1	Vodafone McLaren Mercedes	McLaren MP4-24-Mercedes FO108W V8	B	77			+ 1 lap	1m 15.706s	65
13	Jarno Trulli	I	9	Panasonic Toyota Racing	Toyota TF109-RVX-09 V8	B	77			+ 1 lap	1m 16.011s	57
14	Adrian Sutil	D	20	Force India F1 Team	Force India VJM02-Mercedes FO108W V8	B	77			+ 1 lap	1m 16.245s	66
15	Kazuki Nakajima	J	17	AT&T Williams	Williams FW31-Toyota RVX-09 V8	B	76	accident		+ 2 laps	1m 15.792s	73
	Heikki Kovalainen	FIN	2	Vodafone McLaren Mercedes	McLaren MP4-24-Mercedes FO108W V8	B	51	accident			1m 15.672s	48
	Robert Kubica	PL	5	BMW Sauber F1 Team	BMW Sauber F1.09-BMW P86/9 V8	B	28	brakes			1m 17.558s	25
	Sebastian Vettel	D	15	Red Bull Racing	Red Bull RB5-Renault RS27 V8	B	15	accident			1m 17.634s	15
	Nelsinho Piquet	BR	8	ING Renault F1 Team	Renault R29-RS27 V8	B	10	accident			1m 18.514s	7
	Sébastien Buemi	CH	12	Scuderia Toro Rosso	Toro Rosso STR04-Ferrari 056 V8	B	10	accident			1m 18.582s	7

Fastest race lap: Felipe Massa on lap 50, 1m 15.154s, 99.414mph/159.991km/h.

Lap record: Michael Schumacher (Ferrari F2004 V10), 1m 14.439s, 100.369mph/161.528km/h (2004).

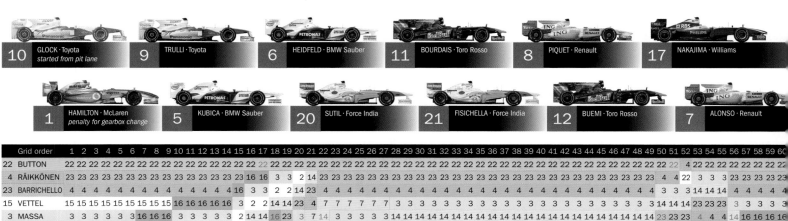

	GLOCK · Toyota started from pit lane		TRULLI · Toyota		HEIDFELD · BMW Sauber		BOURDAIS · Toro Rosso		PIQUET · Renault		NAKAJIMA · Williams
10		9		6		11		8		17	
1	HAMILTON · McLaren penalty for gearbox change	5	KUBICA · BMW Sauber	20	SUTIL · Force India	21	FISICHELLA · Force India	12	BUEMI · Toro Rosso	7	ALONSO · Renault

	Grid order	1 2 3 4 5 6 7 8 9 10 11 12 13 14 15 16 17 18 19 20 21 22 23 24 25 26 27 28 29 30 31 32 33 34 35 36 37 38 39 40 41 42 43 44 45 46 47 48 49 50 51 52 53 54 55 56 57 58 59 60
22	BUTTON	22 22 22 22 22 22 22 22 22 22 22 22 22 22 22 22 22 22 22 22 22 22 22 22 22 22 22 22 22 22 22 22 22 22 22 22 22 22 22 22 22 22 22 22 22 22 22 22 22 22 22 22 22 22 22 4 22 22 22 22 22 22 22 22
4	RÄIKKÖNEN	23 23 23 23 23 23 23 23 23 23 23 23 23 23 16 16 3 3 2 14 23 23 23 23 23 23 23 23 23 23 23 23 23 23 23 23 23 23 23 23 23 23 23 23 23 23 23 4 4 22 3 3 3 23 23 23 23
23	BARRICHELLO	4 4 4 4 4 4 4 4 4 4 4 4 4 16 3 3 2 14 23 4 4 4 4 4 4 4 4 4 4 4 4 4 4 4 4 4 4 4 4 4 4 4 4 4 4 4 4 4 4 4 3 3 14 14 14 4 4 4 4
15	VETTEL	15 15 15 15 15 15 15 15 15 16 16 16 16 16 3 2 14 14 23 4 7 7 7 7 7 3 3 3 3 3 3 3 3 3 3 3 3 3 3 3 3 3 3 3 3 3 3 3 3 14 14 14 23 23 23 3 3 3 3
3	MASSA	3 3 3 3 3 3 16 16 16 3 3 3 3 2 14 16 23 3 7 14 3 3 3 3 14 14 14 14 14 14 14 14 14 14 14 14 14 14 14 14 14 14 14 14 14 14 23 23 23 4 4 14 16 16 16 16
16	ROSBERG	16 16 16 16 16 16 3 3 2 2 2 2 14 23 23 23 4 4 3 14 14 14 14 16 16 16 16 16 16 16 16 16 16 16 16 16 16 16 16 16 16 16 16 16 16 16 16 16 16 14 14 14 14
2	KOVALAINEN	2 2 2 2 2 2 2 2 14 14 14 14 14 4 4 4 4 7 7 2 16 16 16 16 16 16 2 2 2 2 2 2 2 2 2 2 2 2 2 2 2 2 2 2 2 2 2 2 7 7 7 7 7 7 7 7
14	WEBBER	14 14 14 14 14 14 14 14 14 7 7 7 7 7 7 16 16 16 2 2 7 7 17 17 17 17 17 11 11 11 11 11 11 11 11 11 11 11 11 11 11 11 11 11 11 11 11 11 11 11 11 21 21 21 21 21
7	ALONSO	7 7 7 7 7 7 7 7 14 17 17 17 17 17 17 17 17 17 17 17 17 17 17 7 11 11 11 11 11 11 21 21 21 21 21 21 21 21 21 21 21 21 21 21 21 7 7 11 21 21 21 21 21 21 21 21
17	NAKAJIMA	17 17 17 17 17 17 17 17 8 11 11 11 11 11 11 11 11 11 11 11 11 11 11 11 11 11 11 21 21 21 21 21 7 7 7 7 7 7 7 7 7 7 7 7 7 11 11 17 17 17 17 17 17 17 17
12	BUEMI	8 8 8 8 8 8 8 8 8 12 21 21 21 21 21 21 21 21 21 21 21 21 21 21 7 7 7 7 7 7 6 6 6 6 6 6 17 17 17 17 17 17 17 17 10 10 10 10 10 6 6 6
8	PIQUET	12 12 12 12 12 12 12 12 12 11 6 6 6 6 6 6 6 6 6 6 6 6 6 6 6 6 6 6 17 17 17 17 17 9 9 9 9 9 9 10 10 6 6 6 6 9 9 9
21	FISICHELLA	11 11 11 11 11 11 11 11 11 15 15 15 15 15 9 9 9 9 9 9 9 9 9 9 9 9 9 9 9 9 9 9 9 9 6 10 10 10 10 10 10 6 6 1 9 9 9 9 10 10 10
11	BOURDAIS	20 20 20 20 20 20 20 21 6 9 9 9 9 10 10 10 10 10 10 10 10 10 10 10 10 10 10 10 10 10 6 6 6 6 6 6 1 1 1 9 1 1 1 1 1 1
20	SUTIL	21 21 21 21 21 21 20 20 15 10 10 10 10 10 5 5 5 5 5 5 5 5 5 5 1 1 1 1 1 1 1 1 1 1 1 1 1 1 1 1 9 9 20 20 20 20 20 20 20
6	HEIDFELD	6 6 6 6 6 6 6 6 6 20 5 5 5 5 1 1 1 1 1 1 1 1 1 1 1 1 20 20 20 20 20 20 20 20 20 20 20 20 20 20 20 20 20 20 20
5	KUBICA	5 1 1 1 1 1 1 1 1 9 20 1 1 1 1 20 20 20 20 20 20 20 20 20 20 20
9	TRULLI	1 9 9 9 9 9 9 9 9 10 1 20 20 20 20
1	HAMILTON	9 10 10 10 10 10 10 10 10 5
10	GLOCK	10 5 5 5 5 5 5 5 5 1

21 Pit stop
20 One lap or more behind

TIME SHEETS

PRACTICE 1 (THURSDAY)
Sunny
(track 32-36ºC, air 25ºC)

Pos.	Driver	Laps	Time
1	Rubens Barrichello	26	1m 17.189s
2	Felipe Massa	31	1m 17.499s
3	Lewis Hamilton	26	1m 17.578s
4	Heikki Kovalainen	30	1m 17.686s
5	Kimi Räikkönen	30	1m 17.839s
6	Kazuki Nakajima	29	1m 18.000s
7	Nico Rosberg	27	1m 18.024s
8	Jenson Button	28	1m 18.080s
9	Fernando Alonso	31	1m 18.283s
10	Mark Webber	22	1m 18.348s
11	Sébastien Buemi	37	1m 18.695s
12	Nelsinho Piquet	36	1m 19.204s
13	Sebastian Vettel	16	1m 19.233s
14	Sébastien Bourdais	31	1m 19.255s
15	Giancarlo Fisichella	28	1m 19.534s
16	Robert Kubica	20	1m 19.560s
17	Nick Heidfeld	23	1m 19.579s
18	Adrian Sutil	24	1m 19.600s
19	Timo Glock	24	1m 19.698s
20	Jarno Trulli	28	1m 19.831s

PRACTICE 2 (THURSDAY)
Sunny
(track 34-35ºC, air 24-25ºC)

Pos.	Driver	Laps	Time
1	Nico Rosberg	45	1m 15.243s
2	Lewis Hamilton	35	1m 15.445s
3	Rubens Barrichello	41	1m 15.590s
4	Jenson Button	36	1m 15.774s
5	Felipe Massa	42	1m 15.832s
6	Sebastian Vettel	33	1m 15.847s
7	Heikki Kovalainen	45	1m 15.984s
8	Kimi Räikkönen	43	1m 15.985s
9	Kazuki Nakajima	43	1m 16.260s
10	Nelsinho Piquet	43	1m 16.286s
11	Fernando Alonso	39	1m 16.552s
12	Mark Webber	27	1m 16.579s
13	Adrian Sutil	38	1m 16.675s
14	Jarno Trulli	43	1m 16.915s
15	Sébastien Buemi	48	1m 16.983s
16	Sébastien Bourdais	48	1m 17.052s
17	Nick Heidfeld	40	1m 17.109s
18	Timo Glock	45	1m 17.207s
19	Giancarlo Fisichella	45	1m 17.504s
20	Robert Kubica	2	no time

PRACTICE 3 (SATURDAY)
Sunny/partly cloudy
(track 33-35ºC, air 24-25ºC)

Pos.	Driver	Laps	Time
1	Fernando Alonso	24	1m 15.164s
2	Jenson Button	29	1m 15.233s
3	Heikki Kovalainen	24	1m 15.278s
4	Rubens Barrichello	26	1m 15.286s
5	Felipe Massa	23	1m 15.293s
6	Kimi Räikkönen	25	1m 15.382s
7	Lewis Hamilton	23	1m 15.389s
8	Sebastian Vettel	23	1m 15.722s
9	Nico Rosberg	23	1m 15.758s
10	Mark Webber	24	1m 15.985s
11	Kazuki Nakajima	22	1m 16.103s
12	Adrian Sutil	30	1m 16.228s
13	Sébastien Bourdais	23	1m 16.301s
14	Giancarlo Fisichella	29	1m 16.317s
15	Nelsinho Piquet	27	1m 16.382s
16	Sébastien Buemi	22	1m 16.432s
17	Timo Glock	29	1m 16.527s
18	Robert Kubica	26	1m 16.599s
19	Nick Heidfeld	22	1m 16.661s
20	Jarno Trulli	26	1m 16.810s

QUALIFYING (SATURDAY)
Sunny (track 29-31ºC, air 21ºC)

Pos.	Driver	First	Second	Third	Weight
1	Jenson Button	1m 15.210s	1m 15.016s	**1m 14.902s**	647.5kg
2	Kimi Räikkönen	1m 15.746s	**1m 14.514s**	1m 14.927s	640kg
3	Rubens Barrichello	1m 15.425s	1m 14.829s	1m 15.077s	648kg
4	Sebastian Vettel	1m 15.915s	1m 14.879s	1m 15.271s	631.5kg
5	Felipe Massa	1m 15.340s	1m 15.001s	1m 15.437s	643.5kg
6	Nico Rosberg	**1m 15.094s**	1m 14.846s	1m 15.455s	642kg
7	Heikki Kovalainen	1m 15.495s	1m 14.809s	1m 15.516s	644kg
8	Mark Webber	1m 15.260s	1m 14.825s	1m 15.653s	646.5kg
9	Fernando Alonso	1m 15.898s	1m 15.200s	1m 16.009s	654kg
10	Kazuki Nakajima	1m 15.930s	1m 15.579s	1m 17.344s	668kg
11	Sébastien Buemi	1m 15.834s	1m 15.833s		670kg
12	Nelsinho Piquet	1m 16.013s	1m 15.837s		673.1kg
13	Giancarlo Fisichella	1m 16.063s	1m 16.146s		693kg
14	Sébastien Bourdais	1m 16.120s	1m 16.281s		699.5kg
15	Adrian Sutil	1m 16.248s	1m 16.545s		670kg
16	Lewis Hamilton	1m 16.264s			680kg
17	Nick Heidfeld	1m 16.264s			696kg
18	Robert Kubica	1m 16.405s			688.3kg
19	Jarno Trulli	1m 16.548s			645.5kg
20	Timo Glock	1m 16.788s			700.8kg

14	WEBBER · Red Bull	16	ROSBERG · Williams	15	VETTEL · Red Bull	4	RÄIKKÖNEN · Ferrari
2	KOVALAINEN · McLaren	3	MASSA · Ferrari	23	BARRICHELLO · Brawn	22	BUTTON · Brawn

FOR THE RECORD

DID YOU KNOW?
Jenson Button became the seventh driver to record five wins in the first six races of a season, the previous six being: Ascari, Fangio, Clark, Stewart, Mansell and Michael Schumacher.

POINTS

DRIVERS
1	Jenson Button	51
2	Rubens Barrichello	35
3	Sebastian Vettel	23
4	Mark Webber	19.5
5	Jarno Trulli	14.5
6	Timo Glock	12
7	Fernando Alonso	11
8	Kimi Räikkönen	9
9	Lewis Hamilton	9
10	Felipe Massa	8
11	Nico Rosberg	7.5
12	Nick Heidfeld	6
13	Heikki Kovalainen	4
14	Sébastien Buemi	3
15	Sébastien Bourdais	2

CONSTRUCTORS
1	Brawn	86
2	Red Bull	42.5
3	Toyota	26.5
4	Ferrari	17
5	McLaren	13
6	Renault	11
7	Williams	7.5
8	BMW Sauber	6
9	Toro Rosso	5

	64	65	66	67	68	69	70	71	72	73	74	75	76	77	78	
2	22	22	22	22	22	22	22	22	22	22	22	22	22	22	22	1
3	23	23	23	23	23	23	23	23	23	23	23	23	23	23	23	2
4	4	4	4	4	4	4	4	4	4	4	4	4	4	4	4	3
3	3	3	3	3	3	3	3	3	3	3	3	3	3	3	3	4
6	16	14	14	14	14	14	14	14	14	14	14	14	14	14	14	5
4	14	7	16	16	16	16	16	16	16	16	16	16	16	16	16	6
7	7	16	7	7	7	7	7	7	7	7	7	7	7	7	7	7
1	11	11	11	11	11	11	11	11	11	11	11	11	11	11	11	8
1	21	21	21	21	21	21	21	21	21	21	21	21	21	21	21	
7	17	17	17	17	17	17	17	17	17	17	17	17	17	17	10	
6	6	6	6	6	6	10	10	10	10	10	10	10	6			
9	9	10	10	10	10	10	6	6	6	6	6	6	6	1		
10	10	9	9	9	9	9	1	1	1	1	1	1	9			
1	1	1	1	1	1	1	9	9	9	9	9	9	20			
10	20	20	20	20	20	20	20	20	20	20	20	20				

RACE TYRE STRATEGIES

The tyre regulations stipulate that two dry tyre specifications must be used during the race.

The Super-Soft compound Bridgestone Potenza tyre is marked with a green stripe on the sidewall of the tyre.

	Driver	Race Stint 1	Race Stint 2	Race Stint 3
1	Jenson Button	Super-Soft: 1-17	Soft: 18-51	Soft: 52-78
2	Rubens Barrichello	Super-Soft: 1-16	Soft: 17-50	Soft: 51-78
3	Kimi Räikkönen	Soft: 1-15	Soft: 16-53	Super-Soft: 54-78
4	Felipe Massa	Soft: 1-20	Soft: 21-56	Super-Soft: 57-78
5	Mark Webber	Soft: 1-22	Soft: 23-56	Super-Soft: 57-78
6	Nico Rosberg	Soft: 1-18	Soft: 19-65	Super-Soft: 66-78
7	Fernando Alonso	Soft: 1-28	Soft: 29-66	Super-Soft: 67-78
8	Sébastien Bourdais	Soft: 1-50	Super-Soft: 51-78	
9	Giancarlo Fisichella	Soft: 1-52	Super-Soft: 53-78	
10	Timo Glock	Soft: 1-57	Super-Soft: 58-77	
11	Nick Heidfeld	Soft: 1-42	Super-Soft: 43-77	
12	Lewis Hamilton	Super-Soft: 1-10	Soft: 11-53	Soft: 54-77
13	Jarno Trulli	Soft: 1-49	Soft: 50-65	Super-Soft: 66-77
14	Adrian Sutil	Super-Soft: 1-11	Soft: 12-49	Soft: 50-76
	Kazuki Nakajima	Soft: 1-35	Soft: 36-71	Super-Soft: 72-76
	Heikki Kovalainen	Soft: 1-21	Soft: 22-51 (dnf)	
	Robert Kubica	Soft: 1-2	Soft: 3-28 (dnf)	
	Sebastain Vettel	Super-Soft: 1-10	Soft: 11-15 (dnf)	
	Nelson Piquet	Soft: 1-10 (dnf)		
	Sébastien Buemi	Soft: 1-10 (dnf)		

FIA FORMULA 1 WORLD CHAMPIONSHIP • ROUND 7

TURKISH
GRAND PRIX

ISTANBUL PARK CIRCUIT

ISTANBUL QUALIFYING

YOU didn't need telemetry to relay the message – a human ear did the job just as well. If you stood close to the first of several apexes at Turn Eight, where drivers turn in at 160mph and gather momentum as the corner unravels, the faltering engine note was obvious every time a McLaren approached.

In Monaco, Lewis Hamilton had failed to progress beyond Q1 for the first time in his Formula One career, but only because he'd crashed at a critical moment. In Turkey, it happened again, and this time it was beyond his control. The sport's improvisational maverick was unable to do anything in a car that was simply too slow. "We lack rear downforce," he said. "It just switches off in fast corners and leaves you with very little grip. The airflow of an F1 car is incredibly complex, and we just aren't finding the problem. To give you some idea of the scale, we are 10–15kph slower than the Force Indias through Turn Eight."

The Force Indias, that is, with the same Mercedes V8 in the back.

The world champion's discomfort contrasted starkly with the more prosaic dilemma of those at the front: hard or soft Bridgestone?

"Their performance was quite similar," said Jenson Button. "The prime [hard] was a little too twitchy for my liking, so in Q3 I continued to run the option tyre because it had a more gradual, rolling feel."

Sebastian Vettel ploughed the same furrow and, running 6kg lighter than Button, posted a 1m 28.316s to take the pole by 0.105 seconds. He had lost useful track time on Friday, when a vibration three laps into

the afternoon session had heralded a broken Renault V8, but said, "I still had a good feeling for the car, and the team did a great job to fit some new parts at the last minute." The RB5's twin diffuser, introduced in Monaco, was already due its first update. Vettel went into the race knowing his two previous F1 pole positions had translated into victory – and that the fastest qualifier had won each of the four previous Turkish GPs.

Rubens Barrichello – 3kg lighter than Button, but 0.158 second adrift – was the only one of the top three to set his final time on the harder tyre. "It gave me a better feeling through the high-speed corners," he said. "It was the best choice for me, so I went for just one run on the primes in Q3. I lost my first two flying laps to traffic, but the third was really good."

Mark Webber was heaviest of the leading quartet, with half a kilo more fuel than Button.

Given how appalling the Toyota had been in Monaco, Jarno Trulli felt relief more than anything that he was able to qualify fifth, ahead of both Ferraris. Felipe Massa set the pace during Saturday morning's final free practice, but contrasting fuel strategies had long since rendered that virtually useless as a performance barometer.

Finally, there was a small dose of comfort for BMW Sauber, which introduced its own twin diffuser. "It is difficult to draw firm conclusions," said Robert Kubica, tenth, "because this track is so different from Monaco and, obviously, we have not been allowed to test. It feels like a step in the right direction, though."

Opening spread: Jenson Button relaxes before donning his helmet prior to taking his Brawn to its sixth victory in seven races. But it was destined to be the end of his glorious early-season run.

Right: Toro Rosso team-mates Buemi and Bourdais examine their performance data while the team's technicians check their calculations.

Below: Sebastian Vettel shone brightly in qualifying to place his Red Bull firmly on pole.
Photos: Peter J. Fox

Below right: Rubens Barrichello prepares for the start. Disappointingly, the Brazilian's race delivered the first Brawn retirement of the year.
Photo: Paul-Henri Cahier

IMAGES of the inaugural Turkish Grand Prix's chaotic appeal – cars abandoned on the local highway, spectators tramping through fields in a desperate effort to reach the circuit on time – remained fresh in the memory, but were difficult to reconcile with Istanbul Park's sense of emptiness just five seasons later. The TV helicopters were perceived to be flying a touch lower than usual throughout the weekend, probably, it was suggested, to keep camera shots tight and avoid highlighting row upon row of empty seats. The absentees missed a masterclass in racecraft.

The formation lap was painfully slow, a tactic that might have been designed to hinder the Brawns, which were less proficient than the Red Bulls at generating tyre temperature, and later pole-sitter Sebastian Vettel was hauled in by the stewards to explain himself – as, for the same reason, were Timo Glock and Adrian Sutil. Their apparent sloth went unpunished, however.

According to Red Bull's abacus, Vettel's three-stop strategy should have put him about 2.5 seconds clear of the field after the final round of stops, assuming he had a clear opening stint at the front and didn't subsequently lose time in traffic. The German made a clean enough start, as did Jenson Button, from the dustier side of the grid, but all tactical impetus was lost by Turn Ten, where Vettel simply ran wide and allowed Button to slip ahead. "I think that was the most critical part of the circuit today," the Red Bull driver said. "The wind direction changed: it was behind us today, rather than against us, and that made things very slippery. There is a kind of a dip there and I lost the rear of the car, ran over the Astroturf and scrubbed off lots of speed for the straight, so it was no problem for Jenson to pass me. I almost went off there again on the second lap, too."

Button was more than half a second clear of Vettel by the lap's end, with Mark Webber another 2.5 seconds adrift. The Australian dropped behind Jarno Trulli after making an indifferent start, but reclaimed third when the Italian skated off-line at Turn Nine. Nico Rosberg ran fifth, from Felipe Massa, Fernando Alonso, Robert Kubica, Kimi Räikkönen, Kazuki Nakajima, Heikki Kovalainen, Rubens Barrichello (who made an awful start from third after his anti-stall kicked in), Nick Heidfeld, Glock, Nelson Piquet, Lewis Hamilton, Sutil, Giancarlo Fisichella, Sébastien Buemi and Sébastien Bourdais.

Even with a slightly heavier fuel load, Button was able to pull away from Vettel and was almost six seconds to the good by the time the German made his first stop, on lap 15. Red Bull had the option of converting Vettel to a two-stopper, but in the end decided to stick with Plan A. This surprised a few people, not least the bloke in the car.

"We didn't think we had anything to lose," said Red Bull sporting director Christian Horner. "If Seb had managed to pass Jenson and pull away during his second stint, a three-stopper might still have worked. The worst-case scenario was that he'd finish second or third, which is what would have happened anyway if we'd switched him to two stops."

Button made his first stop on lap 17 and rejoined ahead of Vettel, but there was a 14-lap difference in fuel weight. Initially 4.448 seconds, the gap between them immediately shrank. By lap 25, Vettel was only

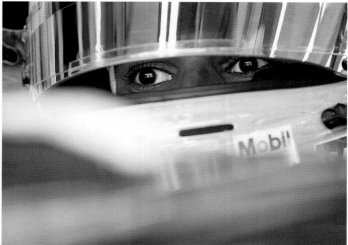

Left: Lewis Hamilton's low-key season continued in its frustratingly familiar vein. He wound up a distant 13th.
Photo: Peter J. Fox

Far left: Pit stop for a frustrated Kimi Räikkönen's Ferrari. The Finn qualified on the third row, but finished out of the points in ninth place.
Photo: Peter Nygaard/GP Photo

Below: Giancarlo Fisichella's stern expression reflected the frustration he was experiencing in getting the best out of his Force India.
Photo: Paul-Henri Cahier

0.274 seconds in arrears, but Button remained resolute. "Even if you know the other guy is lighter," he said, "it's still a strange feeling when you are leading, but losing up to one second per lap. When he caught me, I just had to cover my lines a little bit. I was on the rev limiter for about five seconds on the back straight, so was concerned about Sebastian diving up the inside, but I was able to hold him off."

Vettel felt he'd seen one sliver of a chance. "I was catching up massively and there was one opening at the final corner," he said. "I tried to pass, but he covered the inside and ran slightly wide. I didn't get the best of exits, though, so was not able to do anything on the run to Turn One. It would have been too risky."

Button was left unmolested for the balance of the afternoon. "Really," he said, "this is the first race in which the car has been absolutely perfect. I wanted the whole team on the podium with me because this was definitely a victory for all of us."

He turned down the wick for the final few laps, in the interest of engine conservation, but Red Bull had

done likewise and Button was able to cruise. "I was very surprised that they went for a three-stopper," he said. "Perhaps they thought we were going to do the same, but we filled the car up after we saw what they had done and it worked very well."

With Vettel on a different strategy, the most telling comparison was that between Button and Webber during the second stints: as in Barcelona, they were fuelled similarly, but whereas in Spain their laps had mirrored each other almost to the hundredth, here the Brawn was consistently quicker by about half a second. "We were caned fair and square," Webber said. "The track was good once it had rubbered in, but it would have been nicer if there had been one fewer cars competing. Jenson was on another planet."

His second stint might have been slower than Button's, but it was a paragon of consistency. Opting for the hard-hard-soft tyre strategy adopted by the majority – there was precious little to choose between compounds, but the hard was felt to be slightly more dependable in race conditions – he emerged ahead

of Vettel after the final stops and duly wound down his engine. The team instructed the German to do likewise – "Mark is faster" was the message relayed via radio – and he obeyed, albeit without actually slowing down. "I like driving quickly," Vettel said, "and didn't see any sense in just carrying the car home." Ever cherubic when a camera points his way, Vettel was reported to be in a fairly sour mood behind closed doors.

Trulli and Rosberg completed the 58th lap as they had the first, in fourth and fifth, although they swapped places at both pit stops. Rosberg gained by running two laps longer during his first stint, but lost out again by pitting three laps earlier than Trulli after his second.

Ferrari was expected to make a reasonable impact at Istanbul, given its recently improved form and the fact that Felipe Massa had only once been beaten in Turkey – in 2005, when he was still driving a Sauber. A new rear wing and uprated diffuser improved the F60's feel, but not its performance, and the Brazilian had a quiet afternoon en route to sixth. "The car felt

EDITOR'S VIEW
FERRARI BOSS ISSUES F1 WARNING

IT might have been turning into a long, hot summer for those teams chasing Jenson Button's Brawn-Mercedes, but Formula One's perpetually febrile political eco-system continued to provide a sizzling sub-text to the on-track activity as the season unfolded. Nothing new there, then, although the optimistic and upbeat belief among many competitors that the recently established Formula One Teams' Association (FOTA) would thrive as a credible – and enduring – power base looked like a distinctly fragile premise.

Of course, ascertaining the teams' abiding priorities was the interpretive key to this issue. As usual, it was the FIA versus the teams, with the eventual line of compromise set to be drawn in the sand somewhere between the two extreme views. The FIA wanted draconian cost cuts, largely on their own terms. The teams wanted significant changes in the sport's long-term governance. That, roughly translated, meant that they wanted assurances that Max Mosley would not submit himself as a candidate for the FIA presidential elections in October 2009.

The muscle flexing began in earnest when Luca di Montezemolo warned that unless the matter was resolved, there was a very real chance of a breakaway racing series being established by the major car makers.

The Ferrari president was speaking on a high-profile visit to the Le Mans 24-hour race, which enjoys considerable manufacturer involvement from the likes of Peugeot, Audi and Aston Martin, and was won nine times by Ferrari between 1949 and 1965. It could provide one alternative racing category for Ferrari to consider in the future. Or at least use as a bargaining chip in the teams' dispute with the FIA.

"In a couple of years, the problem with F1 will be solved, as I really hope, with a responsible FIA, as we want, or as happened in other sports, organising our own championship," said di Montezemolo ahead of another meeting between the dissenting teams and the sport's governing body, which was scheduled to take place at a Heathrow hotel the week after the French classic.

He added, "When you have engines, gearboxes, brands, technology, organisation and [the] capability to invest, it [starting another series] is not difficult."

A few days earlier, Ferrari, together with Red Bull and Toro Rosso, had been listed by the FIA as confirmed entries for the 2010 F1 World Championship, despite having only entered on the understanding that the FIA amended its controversial regulations to their liking for that season.

Di Montezemolo indicated that he was becoming frustrated at having to reiterate the Ferrari position, which, he claimed, had never changed on what he clearly regarded as a pivotal issue for the sport. He also repeated his support for FOTA, indicating that Ferrari, Red Bull and Toro Rosso were firmly aligned with the other five teams – McLaren, BMW Sauber, Renault, Toyota and Brawn – who so far had lodged only conditional entries and had been 'invited' by the FIA to lift those conditions before Friday 19th June, the first practice day for the British Grand Prix at Silverstone.

"Everyone sees what is happening in F1," said Montezemolo. "I do not understand the reason. I think our [FOTA's] conditions are constructive and are very clear: [good] governance and stable rules. People don't understand the rules anymore, as they change every six months."

The Ferrari president added that he had become depressed and frustrated by the situation that had developed in F1. Even so, he was hopeful that there would be factions within the FIA who could move to "prevent the sport being destroyed".

Max Mosley responded to the threat of Ferrari considering a move to Le Mans by saying that he was "not aware that Maranello had a diesel [engine]." Earlier, he had commented on rumoured links between Ferrari and the Indy Racing League by remarking, "Oh, so Ferrari will consider running a Dallara-Honda, then?"

It was good knock-about stuff, but with deadly serious undertones.

Alan Henry

Above left: Ferrari boss Luca di Montezemolo was not prepared to mince his words when it came to offering the F1 community a few home truths.
Photo: Peter J. Fox

Above: Lewis Hamilton and Nelson Piquet tough it out wheel to wheel.
Photo: Lukas Gorys

very well balanced," he said, "and we were respectably quick through sectors two and three. Mainly, though, I think we lost out in the first sector because we are a bit short of downforce."

Having reached an apparent plateau in his F1 career, Nakajima delivered one of his finest drives yet – "The best of my career so far," as he put it. A long, 26-lap opening stint enabled him to vault both Kubica and Räikkönen after the first stops, but his front left wheel nut jammed during his second, and 20 lost seconds relegated him from a rightful seventh to a more typical, but unrepresentative, 12th.

Kubica took seventh, the first points of the campaign for the most consistent driver of 2008, prompting BMW Motorsport figurehead Dr Mario Theissen to describe the race as "thrilling for us, all the way from the start to the chequered flag": a team's decline summarised in a moment of glaring overstatement.

Glock completed the points – an unexpected bonus, after he had been forced wide at the first

corner and dropped a couple of positions – ahead of Räikkönen, who made a poor start and then was unfailingly unexceptional all afternoon. Not for the first time, though, he stirred towards the end and set a personal best on his final lap. "We definitely expected more from this weekend," said team principal Stefano Domenicali, "especially given what we had seen up to the end of Saturday morning, when our level of competitiveness was pretty good. We have to understand why the performance of our car evolved in a negative fashion."

Renault put Alonso on soft Bridgestones at the start, a clutching-at-straws attempt to salvage something from eighth on the grid with a lightly fuelled car: that'll be tenth, then.

Heidfeld finished 11th, which failed to draw any exultations from Dr Theissen, in front of the unfortunate Nakajima and the McLarens of Hamilton and Kovalainen. In 2008, tyre-wear concerns – a by-product of his aggressive technique, particularly through the high-speed Turn Eight – had obliged Hamilton to

make three stops en route to second place. Slicks being more durable than their grooved antecedents, this time he was able to manage with just the one. "It was quite an uneventful race," he said, "but I actually enjoyed it because I think I drove to my full potential." Different days.

Kovalainen, whose race-winning pace had been stifled by a Räikkönen-induced puncture one year beforehand, described the weekend as "character-building for everybody". He was lapped by the end, as were Buemi, Piquet, Sutil and Bourdais.

Fisichella dropped out after five laps with a softening brake pedal – he'd had similar problems all weekend – and Barrichello posted the only other retirement. In the wake of his cataclysmic start, he appeared to be on course to beat the record he'd set in Australia for the number of incidents a driver can endure while still completing a race distance. He'd passed Kovalainen cleanly on the eighth lap, only for the Finn to retaliate courtesy of KERS. Next time around, Barrichello tried again, but then spun and slipped to 17th. He

swiftly dispensed with Hamilton and Piquet, shortly after which he lost seventh gear. That didn't curb his enthusiasm, however, and on lap 13 he clipped Sutil while trying to recover another position, the catalyst for an early stop for a replacement front wing. Eventually, though, it became clear that his anti-stall drama at the start had over-torqued the transmission and done significant gearbox damage, so the car was withdrawn before the problem deteriorated – the first ever race retirement for Brawn GP.

This, though, had been all about his team-mate, who had racked up six wins from seven starts without so much as scratching his car: speed, precision, consistency. The clues had been there all along, but bygone circumstance had masked them.

"I thought it would be tougher today," Button said, "but this is the best things have felt all year. I was enjoying myself so much. The car put a smile on my face every single lap and I could have carried on for another 200 miles."

Simon Arron

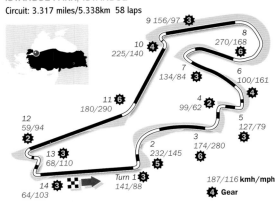

ISTANBUL PARK, ISTANBUL
Circuit: 3.317 miles/5.338km 58 laps

9 156/97
10 225/140
8 270/168
7 134/84
6 100/161
11 180/290
4 99/62
5 127/79
12 59/94
3 174/280
13 68/110
2 232/145
14 64/103
Turn 1 141/88
187/116 kmh/mph
Gear

FIA F1 WORLD CHAMPIONSHIP ROUND 7

ING
TURKISH
GRAND PRIX

ISTANBUL 5-7 JUNE 2009

Photos: Peter J. Fox

RACE DISTANCE: 58 laps, 192.250 miles/309.396km • RACE WEATHER: Sunny (track 46-52°C, air 30-31°C)

Pos.	Driver	Nat.	No.	Entrant	Car/Engine	Tyres	Laps	Time/Retirement	Speed (mph/km/h)	Gap to leader	Fastest race lap	
1	Jenson Button	GB	22	Brawn GP Formula 1 Team	Brawn BGP 001-Mercedes FO108W V8	B	58	1h 26m 24.868s	133.485/214.823		1m 27.579s	40
2	Mark Webber	AUS	14	Red Bull Racing	Red Bull RB5-Renault RS27 V8	B	58	1h 26m 31.562s	133.312/214.545	+ 6.714s	1m 27.809s	42
3	Sebastian Vettel	D	15	Red Bull Racing	Red Bull RB5-Renault RS27 V8	B	58	1h 26m 32.309s	133.293/214.514	+ 7.461s	1m 27.622s	51
4	Jarno Trulli	I	9	Panasonic Toyota Racing	Toyota TF109-RVX-09 V8	B	58	1h 26m 52.691s	132.771/213.675	+ 27.843s	1m 27.868s	40
5	Nico Rosberg	D	16	AT&T Williams	Williams FW31-Toyota RVX-09 V8	B	58	1h 26m 56.387s	132.678/213.524	+ 31.539s	1m 28.222s	36
6	Felipe Massa	BR	3	Scuderia Ferrari Marlboro	Ferrari F60-056 V8	B	58	1h 27m 04.844s	132.463/213.178	+ 39.996s	1m 28.176s	41
7	Robert Kubica	PL	5	BMW Sauber F1 Team	BMW Sauber F1.09-BMW P86/9 V8	B	58	1h 27m 11.095s	132.304/212.923	+ 46.247s	1m 28.008s	58
8	Timo Glock	D	10	Panasonic Toyota Racing	Toyota TF109-RVX-09 V8	B	58	1h 27m 11.807s	132.287/212.895	+ 46.959s	1m 27.883s	56
9	Kimi Räikkönen	FIN	4	Scuderia Ferrari Marlboro	Ferrari F60-056 V8	B	58	1h 27m 15.094s	132.204/212.761	+ 50.246s	1m 28.061s	58
10	Fernando Alonso	E	7	ING Renault F1 Team	Renault R29-RS27 V8	B	58	1h 27m 27.268s	131.897/212.267	+ 1m 02.420s	1m 28.389s	57
11	Nick Heidfeld	D	6	BMW Sauber F1 Team	BMW Sauber F1.09-BMW P86/9 V8	B	58	1h 27m 29.175s	131.849/212.190	+ 1m 04.327s	1m 28.214s	43
12	Kazuki Nakajima	J	17	AT&T Williams	Williams FW31-Toyota RVX-09 V8	B	58	1h 27m 31.224s	131.797/212.107	+ 1m 06.376s	1m 27.988s	58
13	Lewis Hamilton	GB	1	Vodafone McLaren Mercedes	McLaren MP4-24-Mercedes FO108W V8	B	58	1h 27m 45.302s	131.445/211.540	+ 1m 20.454s	1m 28.562s	53
14	Heikki Kovalainen	FIN	2	Vodafone McLaren Mercedes	McLaren MP4-24-Mercedes FO108W V8	B	57			+ 1 lap	1m 29.174s	41
15	Sébastien Buemi	CH	12	Scuderia Toro Rosso	Toro Rosso STR04-Ferrari 056 V8	B	57			+ 1 lap	1m 28.624s	57
16	Nelsinho Piquet	BR	8	ING Renault F1 Team	Renault R29-RS27 V8	B	57			+ 1 lap	1m 28.340s	45
17	Adrian Sutil	D	20	Force India F1 Team	Force India VJM02-Mercedes FO108W V8	B	57			+ 1 lap	1m 29.192s	55
18	Sébastien Bourdais	F	11	Scuderia Toro Rosso	Toro Rosso STR04-Ferrari 056 V8	B	57			+ 1 lap	1m 29.022s	53
	Rubens Barrichello	BR	23	Brawn GP Formula 1 Team	Brawn BGP 001-Mercedes FO108W V8	B	47	gearbox overheating			1m 28.526s	37
	Giancarlo Fisichella	I	21	Force India F1 Team	Force India VJM02-Mercedes FO108W V8	B	4	brakes			1m 34.070s	3

Fastest race lap: Jenson Button on lap 40, 1m 27.579s, 136.343mph/219.422km/h.

Lap record: Juan Pablo Montoya (McLaren MP4-20-Mercedes Benz V10), 1m 24.770s, 140.861mph/226.693km/h (2005)

All results and data © FOM 2009

11	BOURDAIS · Toro Rosso	12	BUEMI · Toro Rosso	1	HAMILTON · McLaren	2	KOVALAINEN · McLaren	17	NAKAJIMA · Williams	5	KUBICA · BMW Sauber
21	FISICHELLA · Force India	8	PIQUET · Renault	20	SUTIL · Force India	10	GLOCK · Toyota	6	HEIDFELD · BMW Sauber	16	ROSBERG · Williams

Grid order	1	2	3	4	5	6	7	8	9	10	11	12	13	14	15	16	17	18	19	20	21	22	23	24	25	26	27	28	29	30	31	32	33	34	35	36	37	38	39	40	41	42	43	44
15 VETTEL	22	22	22	22	22	22	22	22	22	22	22	22	22	22	22	14	22	22	22	22	22	22	22	22	22	22	22	22	22	22	22	22	22	22	22	22	22	22	22	22	22	22	22	22
22 BUTTON	15	15	15	15	15	15	15	15	15	15	15	15	15	15	15	16	15	15	15	15	15	15	15	15	15	15	15	15	14	14	14	14	14	14	14	14	14	14	14	14	14	14	14	
23 BARRICHELLO	14	14	14	14	14	14	14	14	14	14	14	14	14	14	9	16	22	5	5	14	14	14	14	14	14	14	15	15	15	15	15	15	15	15	15	15	15	15	14					
14 WEBBER	9	9	9	9	9	9	9	9	9	9	9	9	9	9	16	3	15	14	14	17	17	17	17	17	16	16	16	16	16	16	16	16	16	16	16	16	16	9	9	9	9			
9 TRULLI	16	16	16	16	16	16	16	16	16	16	16	16	16	16	3	15	5	17	17	16	16	16	16	16	10	10	10	10	9	9	9	9	9	9	9	9	3	3	17	16				
4 RÄIKKÖNEN	3	3	3	3	3	3	3	3	3	3	3	3	3	3	15	4	16	16	9	9	9	9	10	10	9	9	9	9	3	3	3	3	3	3	3	3	17	17	16	5				
3 MASSA	7	7	7	7	7	7	7	7	7	7	7	7	7	7	5	5	4	17	9	9	10	10	10	10	9	9	3	3	3	3	17	17	17	17	17	17	17	16	16	5	10			
7 ALONSO	5	5	5	5	5	5	5	5	5	5	5	5	5	4	4	17	9	2	10	3	3	3	3	3	6	6	17	17	5	5	5	5	5	5	5	5	5	5	10	4				
16 ROSBERG	4	4	4	4	4	4	4	4	4	4	4	4	4	17	17	9	2	10	3	6	6	6	6	6	17	17	5	5	7	7	7	7	7	7	7	10	10	10	4	3				
5 KUBICA	17	17	17	17	17	17	17	17	17	17	17	17	17	2	2	2	10	3	6	5	5	5	5	5	7	1	1	10	10	10	10	10	10	4	4	4	3	6						
6 HEIDFELD	2	2	2	2	2	23	2	2	2	2	2	2	10	10	10	3	6	20	7	7	7	7	7	8	8	10	4	4	4	4	4	4	4	6										
17 NAKAJIMA	23	23	23	23	23	2	10	10	10	10	10	10	6	6	6	20	7	8	8	8	8	8	1	1	10	4	6	6	6	6	6	6	7	7	7	8								
10 GLOCK	6	10	10	10	10	10	10	6	6	6	6	6	20	20	20	7	8	4	1	1	1	4	4	6	2	2	2	2	2	2	8	2	8	17										
2 KOVALAINEN	10	6	6	6	6	6	20	20	20	20	20	20	7	7	7	8	1	4	4	4	4	6	2	20	20	20	23	23	8	8	8	8	1	1										
20 SUTIL	8	20	20	20	20	20	8	8	23	23	23	23	8	8	8	4	1	12	12	12	12	2	2	2	23	23	8	8	12	12	12	12	23	23										
1 HAMILTON	1	8	8	8	8	8	1	23	8	8	8	8	1	1	1	1	2	20	20	20	20	23	8	8	12	12	1	1	2															
8 PIQUET	20	1	1	1	1	1	1	23	1	1	1	12	12	12	12	2	20	20	20	20	23	8	1	12	1	1	23	23	23	12	12													
12 BUEMI	21	21	21	12	12	12	12	12	12	12	12	11	11	11	11	11	11	11	11	11	12	12	1	20	20	20	20	20	20	20														
21 FISICHELLA	12	12	12	11	11	11	11	11	11	11	11	23	23	23	23	23	23	23	23	23	11	11	11	11	11	11	11	11	11	11														
11 BOURDAIS	11	11	11	21																																								

164 TURKISH GRAND PRIX

TIME SHEETS

PRACTICE 1 (FRIDAY)
Sunny
(track 30-35°C, air 22-23°C)

Pos.	Driver	Laps	Time
1	Nico Rosberg	24	1m 28.952s
2	Lewis Hamilton	23	1m 29.263s
3	Jarno Trulli	26	1m 29.271s
4	Sebastian Vettel	18	1m 29.337s
5	Felipe Massa	22	1m 29.342s
6	Kazuki Nakajima	21	1m 29.371s
7	Kimi Räikkönen	25	1m 29.398s
8	Fernando Alonso	24	1m 29.422s
9	Rubens Barrichello	25	1m 29.525s
10	Heikki Kovalainen	20	1m 29.590s
11	Jenson Button	20	1m 29.747s
12	Adrian Sutil	22	1m 29.864s
13	Timo Glock	26	1m 29.934s
14	Nelsinho Piquet	18	1m 30.132s
15	Mark Webber	22	1m 30.176s
16	Robert Kubica	22	1m 30.645s
17	Nick Heidfeld	20	1m 30.689s
18	Giancarlo Fisichella	22	1m 30.729s
19	Sébastien Bourdais	24	1m 30.838s
20	Sébastien Buemi	26	1m 30.944s

PRACTICE 2 (FRIDAY)
Sunny
(track 37-41°C, air 25°C)

Pos.	Driver	Laps	Time
1	Heikki Kovalainen	37	1m 28.841s
2	Fernando Alonso	35	1m 28.847s
3	Robert Kubica	35	1m 29.056s
4	Kazuki Nakajima	37	1m 29.091s
5	Sebastian Vettel	4	1m 29.202s
6	Jarno Trulli	41	1m 29.207s
7	Nico Rosberg	40	1m 29.257s
8	Rubens Barrichello	35	1m 29.305s
9	Mark Webber	39	1m 29.383s
10	Nelsinho Piquet	38	1m 29.401s
11	Felipe Massa	38	1m 29.416s
12	Jenson Button	33	1m 29.430s
13	Lewis Hamilton	31	1m 29.435s
14	Timo Glock	40	1m 29.518s
15	Kimi Räikkönen	33	1m 29.520s
16	Nick Heidfeld	40	1m 29.550s
17	Adrian Sutil	33	1m 30.081s
18	Giancarlo Fisichella	38	1m 30.091s
19	Sébastien Bourdais	39	1m 30.295s
20	Sébastien Buemi	37	1m 30.629s

PRACTICE 3 (SATURDAY)
Sunny
(track 39-41°C, air 25-28°C)

Pos.	Driver	Laps	Time
1	Felipe Massa	26	1m 27.983s
2	Jarno Trulli	21	1m 28.022s
3	Timo Glock	23	1m 28.094s
4	Kazuki Nakajima	19	1m 28.122s
5	Robert Kubica	20	1m 28.320s
6	Rubens Barrichello	21	1m 28.332s
7	Jenson Button	19	1m 28.360s
8	Nico Rosberg	19	1m 28.364s
9	Kimi Räikkönen	16	1m 28.415s
10	Sebastian Vettel	18	1m 28.451s
11	Nelsinho Piquet	15	1m 28.503s
12	Lewis Hamilton	19	1m 28.563s
13	Mark Webber	18	1m 28.678s
14	Nick Heidfeld	19	1m 28.715s
15	Heikki Kovalainen	19	1m 28.738s
16	Adrian Sutil	18	1m 29.050s
17	Sébastien Bourdais	19	1m 29.076s
18	Sébastien Buemi	21	1m 29.167s
19	Fernando Alonso	15	1m 29.261s
20	Giancarlo Fisichella	17	1m 29.421s

QUALIFYING (SATURDAY)
Sunny (track 44-45°C, air 28°C)

Pos.	Driver	First	Second	Third	Weight
1	Sebastian Vettel	**1m 27.330s**	**1m 27.016s**	**1m 28.316s**	649.5kg
2	Jenson Button	1m 27.355s	1m 27.230s	1m 28.421s	655.5kg
3	Rubens Barrichello	1m 27.371s	1m 27.418s	1m 28.579s	652.5kg
4	Mark Webber	1m 27.466s	1m 27.416s	1m 28.613s	656kg
5	Jarno Trulli	1m 27.529s	1m 27.195s	1m 28.666s	652kg
6	Kimi Räikkönen	1m 27.556s	1m 27.387s	1m 28.815s	658kg
7	Felipe Massa	1m 27.508s	1m 27.349s	1m 28.858s	654kg
8	Fernando Alonso	1m 27.988s	1m 27.473s	1m 29.075s	644.5kg
9	Nico Rosberg	1m 27.517s	1m 27.418s	1m 29.191s	660kg
10	Robert Kubica	1m 27.788s	1m 27.455s	1m 29.357s	664kg
11	Nick Heidfeld	1m 27.795s	1m 27.521s		681.5kg
12	Kazuki Nakajima	1m 27.691s	1m 27.629s		680.4kg
13	Timo Glock	1m 28.160s	1m 27.795s		689kg
14	Heikki Kovalainen	1m 28.199s	1m 28.207s		665kg
15	Adrian Sutil	1m 28.278s	1m 28.391s		668.5kg
16	Lewis Hamilton	1m 28.318s			696.5kg
17	Nelsinho Piquet	1m 28.582s			686.5kg
18	Sébastien Buemi	1m 28.708s			686.5kg
19	Giancarlo Fisichella	1m 28.717s			688.5kg
20	Sébastien Bourdais	1m 28.918s			701kg

7 ALONSO · Renault

4 RÄIKKÖNEN · Ferrari

14 WEBBER · Red Bull

22 BUTTON · Brawn

3 MASSA · Ferrari

9 TRULLI · Toyota

23 BARRICHELLO · Brawn

15 VETTEL · Red Bull

FOR THE RECORD

10th PODIUM: Brawn

50th POINT: Nico Rosberg

DID YOU KNOW?

Previously, only Ascari (1952), Fangio (1954), Clark (1965) and Michael Schumacher (1994 & 2004) had won the first six out of seven grands prix in a season.

POINTS

DRIVERS

1	Jenson Button	61
2	Rubens Barrichello	35
3	Sebastian Vettel	29
4	Mark Webber	27.5
5	Jarno Trulli	19.5
6	Timo Glock	13
7	Nico Rosberg	11.5
8	Felipe Massa	11
9	Fernando Alonso	11
10	Kimi Räikkönen	9
11	Lewis Hamilton	9
12	Nick Heidfeld	6
13	Heikki Kovalainen	4
14	Sébastien Buemi	3
15	Robert Kubica	2
16	Sébastien Bourdais	2

CONSTRUCTORS

1	Brawn	96
2	Red Bull	56.5
3	Toyota	32.5
4	Ferrari	20
5	McLaren	13
6	Williams	11.5
7	Renault	11
8	BMW Sauber	8
9	Toro Rosso	5

RACE TYRE STRATEGIES

The tyre regulations stipulate that two dry tyre specifications must be used during the race.

The Soft compound Bridgestone Potenza tyre is marked with a green stripe on the sidewall of the tyre.

	Driver	Race Stint 1	Race Stint 2	Race Stint 3	Race Stint 4
1	Jenson Button	Hard: 1-17	Hard: 18-43	Soft: 44-58	
2	Mark Webber	Hard: 1-18	Hard: 19-43	Soft: 44-58	
3	Sebastian Vettel	Hard: 1-15	Hard: 16-29	Soft: 30-49	Soft: 49-58
4	Jarno Trulli	Hard: 1-16	Hard: 17-43	Soft: 44-58	
5	Nico Rosberg	Hard: 1-18	Hard: 19-40	Soft: 41-58	
6	Felipe Massa	Hard: 1-17	Hard: 18-42	Soft: 43-58	
7	Robert Kubica	Hard: 1-20	Hard: 21-44	Soft: 45-58	
8	Timo Glock	Hard: 1-30	Hard: 31-47	Soft: 48-58	
9	Kimi Räikkönen	Hard: 1-18	Hard: 19-44	Soft: 45-58	
10	Fernando Alonso	Soft: 1-14	Hard: 15-39	Hard: 40-58	
11	Nick Heidfeld	Hard: 1-28	Hard: 29-45	Soft: 46-58	
12	Kazuki Nakajima	Hard: 1-26	Hard: 27-43	Soft: 44-58	
13	Lewis Hamilton	Hard: 1-32	Soft: 33-58		
14	Heikki Kovalainen	Soft: 1-19	Hard: 20-42	Soft: 43-57	
15	Sébastien Buemi	Hard: 1-25	Hard: 26-42	Soft: 43-57	
16	Nelson Piquet	Hard: 1-31	Hard: 32-47	Soft: 48-57	
17	Adrian Sutil	Hard: 1-20	Hard: 21-36	Soft: 37-57	
18	Sébastien Bourdais	Hard: 1-32	Soft: 33-57		
	Rubens Barrichello	Hard: 1-13	Hard: 14-38	Soft: 39-47 (dnf)	
	Giancarlo Fisichella	Hard: 1-4 (dnf)			

47	48	49	50	51	52	53	54	55	56	57	58	
22	22	22	22	22	22	22	22	22	22	22	22	1
15	15	14	14	14	14	14	14	14	14	14	14	2
14	14	15	15	15	15	15	15	15	15	15	15	3
9	9	9	9	9	9	9	9	9	9	9	9	4
16	16	16	16	16	16	16	16	16	16	16	16	5
10	3	3	3	3	3	3	3	3	3	3	3	6
3	5	5	5	5	5	5	5	5	5	5	5	7
5	10	10	10	10	10	10	10	10	10	10	10	8
4	4	4	4	4	4	4	4	4	4	4	4	9
7	7	7	7	7	7	7	7	7	7	7	7	10
8	6	6	6	6	6	6	6	6	6	6	6	11
6	17	17	17	17	17	17	17	17	17	17	17	12
17	1	1	1	1	1	1	1	1	1	1	1	13
1	2	2	2	2	2	2	2	2	2	2		14
23	12	12	12	12	12	12	12	12	12	12		15
2	8	8	8	8	8	8	8	8	8	8		16
12	20	20	20	20	20	20	20	20	20	20		17
20	11	11	11	11	11	11	11	11	11	11		18
11												19
21 Pit stop		*14 One lap or more behind*										20

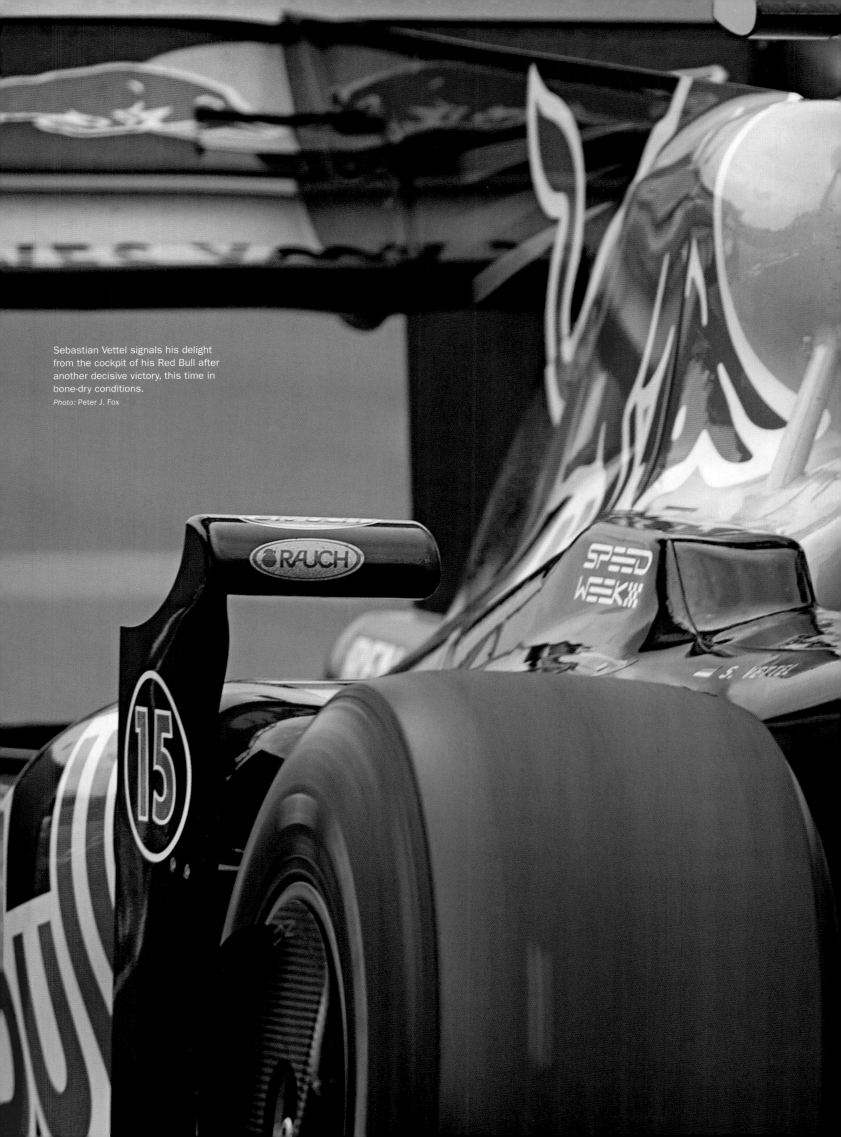

Sebastian Vettel signals his delight from the cockpit of his Red Bull after another decisive victory, this time in bone-dry conditions.
Photo: Peter J. Fox

BRITISH GRAND PRIX

SILVERSTONE CIRCUIT

SILVERSTONE QUALIFYING

I F Adrian Newey could have designed a racing circuit to complement the Red Bull RB5, it would probably have looked a lot like Silverstone. The car's appetite for quick corners was already a given, and it swatted aside Club (170mph, sixth gear) and the Becketts complex (entered at 190mph in top, dropping swiftly to 140mph in fifth) as though they were gentle kinks rather than two of the season's most thrilling obstacles. The Red Bull passed through with little more than a flick of the driver's wrist and, significantly, its sublime turn of speed wasn't limited to the quick stuff.

Teams were continuing to spend, spend, spend their way to a supposedly cheaper future and, like many, Red Bull Racing had introduced a collage of new parts – front wing, rear wing endplates, yet another diffuser upgrade – that gave the car added bite and poise through the slower corners at the lap's end. The RB5 looked simply unbeatable, although the grid's final shape owed as much to Kimi Räikkönen as it did to Newey's eye for aerodynamic detail.

Mark Webber was sent out to spearhead the Red Bull attack, with two fewer laps of fuel than Sebastian Vettel, but his final Q3 run was compromised when he encountered Räikkönen, who wasn't going for a time, on the approach to Stowe Corner. "I would have liked the lap to be slightly cleaner," he said, "but I've no idea what Kimi was doing. He was dreaming, drinking vodka or something. He was on the racing line, which wrecked my rhythm and forced me to tighten my approach to Stowe."

That translated to a 1m 19.868s, 0.359 seconds behind the jubilant Vettel – "You always think you can get a bit more from a lap, but I'm not sure that was true today" – and, potentially crucial, a fraction slower than Rubens Barrichello's Brawn.

Unlike team-mate Jenson Button, who languished – a relative term – in sixth, the Brazilian's more forceful style enabled him to coax his Bridgestones into their working temperature range in the cool, spring-like conditions that prevailed.

"I'm really happy to be starting from the front of the grid at a track I love," Barrichello said. "It feels like home to me." That much showed.

Kazuki Nakajima qualified fifth, a career best, while Nico Rosberg, 9kg heavier, was seventh – a decent turn-around given that aero tracks have been the team's bugbear in recent years. Nakajima was particularly chipper to do well at his favourite circuit, and by no means was he alone in underlining Silverstone's qualities as a racetrack as the British GP notionally prepared to switch to Donington Park, a lovely location, but still little more than a building site through the summer of 2009.

Lewis Hamilton loves Silverstone, too, and harbours fond memories of his stellar 2008 victory, when teeming rain failed to deflect his stride as he put more than a minute between himself and closest rival Nick Heidfeld. This time, for the third race in succession, he failed to progress beyond Q1 in a McLaren that remained relatively hopeless through fast sweeps of the kind that proliferate at Silverstone. He was forced to abort his final run after Adrian Sutil crashed heavily at Abbey, causing the session to be red-flagged, but it didn't make too much difference. "I really don't think I could have got any more from the car," Hamilton said.

Right: Force India produced some important technical upgrades for the team's 'local' race at Silverstone.
Photo: Jad Sherif/WRi2

Below right: The 'Prawn GP' brigade added a light-hearted touch to proceedings with their Jenson masks.
Photo: Malcolm Bryan/WRi2

Bottom right: Robert Kubica seems happy enough, despite his BMW Sauber being uncompetitive around Silverstone.
Photo: Studio Colombo/WRi2

Below: Follow the snake. Kimi Räikkönen guns his Ferrari into the far corners of the Silverstone circuit.
Photo: Peter J. Fox

MODERN protocol demands sobriety. Old-school pastimes – Ayrton Senna grabbing a Brazilian flag as a victory-lap accompaniment, that kind of thing – have long since been frowned upon. As, too, have crowd-pleasing 'dough-nuts', but on this occasion the stewards turned a blind eye to Lewis Hamilton's post-race exuberance. The 2008 British Grand Prix winner finished only 16th this time, in a gripless McLaren, but for three days the crowd had applauded almost every steering input, and Hamilton's response was both a vote of gratitude and an appropriately extravagant farewell gesture as Formula One prepared to say a possible goodbye to Silverstone.

McLaren team principal Martin Whitmarsh was more alarmed than the officials by Hamilton's gyrations. After all, that engine and gearbox had further race distances to complete.

McLaren had known all along that its continual struggle to generate downforce would be a significant handicap at Silverstone. What rivals hadn't suspected was that Red Bull would add bite and slow-corner traction, hitherto its weak spot, to an already articulate high-speed package. That the RB5 was quickest through sector three – Priory, Brooklands and Luffield, a sequence of slow turns tackled in less than 21 seconds – was highly significant and translated into wholesale dominance.

Sebastian Vettel made a brisk, clean start from pole position and, with Rubens Barrichello's Brawn as a useful barrier, was 1.501 seconds clear of the field within a lap, and virtually invisible within ten.

Mark Webber retained third place on the opening lap and was followed by Kazuki Nakajima, Kimi Räikkönen, Nico Rosberg, Jarno Trulli, Felipe Massa, Jenson Button, Timo Glock, Nick Heidfeld, Fernando Alonso, Robert Kubica, Giancarlo Fisichella, Hamil-ton, Nelson Piquet, Sébastien Bourdais, Sébastien Buemi, Heikki Kovalainen and Adrian Sutil.

Button made partial amends for a poor start – "Trulli was slow off the line in front of me and I had nowhere to go. I tried the inside, then the outside, but everyone shot past." – by demoting Massa when the Brazilian ran wide at Abbey on lap two.

The only possible threat to Vettel – from team-mate Webber – was snuffed out by Barrichello during the opening stint. Having been beaten away by the Brazilian at the start, Webber went into fuel-saving mode and managed to extend his first stint by one lap, enough to ensure he overhauled the Brawn after they stopped on laps 20 and 19 respectively. Vettel had sufficient juice to see him through to lap 22, though, and by then was 22.086 seconds to the good. Job done.

"It was disappointing to see Sebastian disappearing," Webber said, "but I don't think I could have got much more out of today. I knew beforehand that my first race was with Rubens, and if I'd passed him quickly, maybe I could have challenged Sebastian. Given how closely matched we are, though, there was never any way that I was going to make up 22 seconds in two stints."

In a parallel universe, meanwhile, life was much more straightforward at the front. "The start was very important," Vettel said, "and during the first stint, I tried to pull away to build a gap. The car was fantastic, just unbelievable. I was able to push more and more, and the tyres were very consistent.

"The second stint wasn't so easy, because lots of lapped cars were battling each other, so the team told me to be careful. From the last pit stop, though, I was in clean air and just counting down each lap. I had quite a big gap to Mark and controlled the race from that point on.

Right: Push the button. Unfortunately, Jenson's special helmet design did not bring him good luck in the race.
Photo: Peter J. Fox

Far right: Rubens Barrichello finished third at Silverstone for the second year running.
Photo: Bernard Asset

Below: Jenson Button tracks Jarno Trulli as he climbs through the field to an eventual sixth.
Photo: Paul-Henri Cahier

Bottom: A determined Lewis Hamilton takes to the dirty line in a bid to pass Fernando Alonso.
Photo: Peter Nygaard/Grand Prix Photo

"I enjoyed this race so much. Silverstone is a fantastic circuit, and when I looked in the grandstands everyone was standing up and clapping. When I took the chequered flag, the atmosphere was great, the kind of thing I dreamed about when I was younger and watched Nigel Mansell winning British grands prix. It's almost unreal to think that I'm now here and have made it. I'm slightly sorry I'm not English..."

Lapped traffic apart, Red Bull's only real concern occurred during the race's later stages, after Webber ran over debris left behind when Sébastien Bourdais rammed Heikki Kovalainen at Vale on lap 34 – both continued after pitting for repairs, but the Finn was soon obliged to retire because his rear suspension had been too badly buckled, while failing water pressure forced Bourdais out one lap later. Webber's car incurred rear bodywork damage, and the team instructed him to adapt his driving, by using different gears and rev profiles, to maintain optimum exhaust temperature.

Like Vettel, Webber was effusive about the last-grand-prix-that-might-not-be at Silverstone. "It is an amazing track and the fans are always fantastic," he

said. "I love driving F1 cars here; going through that first sector lap after lap is incredible. It is a brilliant place and destroys a lot of the other venues that have been chosen for us during the last few years."

His positive demeanour concealed deep-rooted frustration that he knew this could have been his race and, but for Räikkönen's momentary inattention during Q3, Vettel would have had a proper fight on his hands.

Barrichello's performance belied extreme personal discomfort – an army of doctors and physios had helped him suppress back pain that had threatened to ruin his weekend. He and team-mate Jenson Button qualified on 19-lap fuel loads, but the Brazilian's more abrasive driving style enabled him to coax an extra ten degrees of tyre temperature during qualifying, when Button had slithered around watching his Bridgestones grain.

"I'm very proud of the job I did," Barrichello said, "because I knew yesterday that the Red Bulls would be the class of the field, and third was the best I could hope to achieve." He also felt that his second stint, on the hard Bridgestone – soft-soft-hard was the most popular tactic – had been particularly tough. There wasn't much to choose between the different compounds, but he reckoned the soft would have been a more consistent choice over 28 laps.

Conversely, the hard tyre worked fine for Nico Rosberg during the first two stints, although he was stuck behind the temporarily hobbled Barrichello during the middle stint, which slowed him enough to allow Massa to jump ahead after the final stops.

This reflected an excellent drive on the Brazilian's part. The Ferrari F60 looked fairly hopeless during qualifying, but on a warmer track, the car worked its tyres more effectively and Massa capitalised in full. A strong start, partly thanks to KERS, which only Ferrari used in the race, although Kovalainen had experimented with it for McLaren on Friday, elevated him from 11th to eighth, although he swiftly slipped behind Button after the aforementioned lapse at Abbey. A 23-lap opening stint elevated him to fifth, and he passed Rosberg after running two laps longer prior to his second stop. "It almost feels as though I've won," he said. "I wasn't expecting such a strong result, so I'm doubly happy. We had a good strategy and I pushed to the maximum at key moments. KERS was a great help, especially at the start, but the whole car worked well, and the result speaks for itself."

Button felt he could have beaten Rosberg and Massa on pace, but he had to make his first stop one lap earlier than scheduled because he and Barrichello were identically fuelled, and the Brazilian had positional advantage. The extra lap might have carried the championship leader ahead of both Räikkönen and Trulli – and that would have made Rosberg a catchable target during the second stops. If, if, if...

He ended the afternoon sixth, but, like Hamilton, he was serenaded by a klaxon symphony everywhere he went. "Every point is important at this stage of the season," he said, "and to come away with three is okay. It has been a frustrating home race, though. I struggled to get the harder tyres into their working range during a long middle stint with heavy fuel in cool conditions, but I was easily able to close on Rosberg and Massa towards the end, when I was running on the softs. The car's pace was pretty good, but we still need to understand why it doesn't work so well at low temperatures."

ECCLESTONE v THE BRDC

S O it was the last British Grand Prix to be held at Silverstone. One more high-octane twirl and the one-time RAF base would follow Aintree and Brands Hatch into oblivion within the sepia-tinted pages of the motor racing history books. In 2010, Formula One in the UK would celebrate the start of a brave new world at Donington Park. Or maybe not.

The ongoing saga of Silverstone, the British Grand Prix and the love-hate relationship between Bernie Ecclestone and the track's owner, the British Racing Drivers' Club, makes *Gone with the Wind* look like a fleeting TV ad.

Ecclestone had stressed repeatedly that he did not believe that Silverstone's facilities were up to the level that the sport required and insisted that, despite being given many opportunities to improve things, the BRDC had never properly stepped up to the plate. For its part, the club had always contended that Ecclestone needed to take a more realistic attitude to the budget it could afford as promoter, bearing in mind the impossibility of securing the sort of government funding for the race that is seen elsewhere in the world.

In the run-up to the 2009 event, Ecclestone continued to stress that, if Donington were not ready in 2010, there was no question of the race returning to Silverstone. The British Grand Prix would simply be cancelled for one year.

Throughout all this, Damon Hill, the president of the BRDC, had worked hard to maintain a dialogue with Ecclestone. He picked his words with meticulous care as he sought to resolve the problem. Whatever might or might not happen at Donington Park in 2010, Hill, winner of the '94 British Grand Prix at Silverstone in a Williams, was determined to keep the lines of communication firmly open.

"This is one of the most profitable events on the circuit," said Hill. "We're good business; we've high ticket prices, sell-out crowds over three days, so it's a big do. But in comparison to a subsidised event, such as Australia and many others where the government recognises its value in economic terms, we're only able to afford it on our commercial model.

"We have done very well to provide the maximum we can for Formula One, and also to survive as a business. But it's not the highest payer, and the reason is simply because I am not king and this isn't my country.

"It's all too easy to throw rocks at Silverstone, but this year we will be providing one of the best and most successful grands prix we have ever had, and we're still in business, which is the key."

Yet by the end of a brilliant afternoon in the early summer sunshine, during which Sebastian Vettel had topped off a Red Bull 1-2, ahead of team-mate Mark Webber, the jungle drums were beating out a new message.

"The chance of there not being a British Grand Prix [in 2010] is very small," said Max Mosley. "I think it is highly probable that it will be at Silverstone." And with Donington boss Simon Gillett still stating confidently that the race would be at the famous circuit near Derby, Ecclestone added, "And if they can't, for sure we will come back to Silverstone."

Nice to keep people guessing, isn't it?

Alan Henry

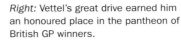

Right: Vettel's great drive earned him an honoured place in the pantheon of British GP winners.
Photo: Fritz Van Eldik/WRi2

Below: BRDC president Damon Hill continued to work tirelessly in an attempt to keep the grand prix at Silverstone.

Bottom: Quite so, but do the FIA or FOM care?
Photos: Jean-François Galeron/WRi2

Below right: Bernie is always at the epicentre of F1 matters political.
Photo: Peter J. Fox

Trulli and Räikkönen completed the scorers, the Italian complaining that his Toyota was sliding around too much, and the Finn unhappy that he was trapped behind it. Räikkönen was acutely aware that a light fuel load and ninth on the grid weren't a productive combination, and his feisty, KERS-assisted start was the afternoon's only highlight. "I was unable to push as much as I could have done because I was always in traffic," he said. "After the first round of pit stops, I found myself right behind Trulli. From then on, my race was pretty much over."

Towards the end, the second Toyota had become a thorn in his side, too, but despite a last-lap lunge at Luffield, Glock was unable to find a way through.

Fisichella took tenth place after an engaging cameo, never more so than on lap two, when he passed Kubica before overhauling Alonso and Heidfeld as they compromised each other at Becketts. A 21-lap first stint also enabled him to pass Nakajima, whose short first stint dropped him into traffic and out of contention.

Piquet finished a workmanlike 12th after stopping only once, with Kubica, Alonso and Heidfeld behind. "We decided to take a risk and start the race with a high fuel load and hard tyres," Kubica said, "but it didn't pay off because I had big problems heating them up at the start."

Alonso's race was ruined when a poor start trapped him behind the heavily fuelled Heidfeld for the first stint's duration, during which the German struggled with a mildly damaged front wing, bent during the opening-lap onslaught. It wasn't too much of a handicap, though, so he left it unchanged until his first scheduled stop.

Hamilton, Buemi and Sutil completed the finishers, the German's qualifying mishap having obliged him to start from the pits in a car built around Force India's spare chassis. He had last-minute fuel pressure concerns before the start, too, but the team was able to fix them and send him on his way.

"I really gave it my all today," Hamilton said. "I was absolutely on the limit, despite fighting for the lower positions, but the fans have been the best thing about this weekend: they cheered me throughout, which was some consolation."

Atmosphere of a kind that can be neither bought nor beaten.

Simon Arron

SILVERSTONE GRAND PRIX CIRCUIT

187/116 **kmh/mph**
🅴 **Gear**
Circuit: 3.194 miles/5.141km 60 laps

Club 226/141 🅴
Vale 🅰 95/59
Luffield 111/69 🅱
Bridge 264/165 🅰
Stowe 199/124 🅰
Abbey 133/83 🅱
Priory 212/132 🅱
Woodcote 265/165 🅴
Hangar straight 188/302 🅱
Brooklands 96/60 🅱
Maggotts 291/181 🅱
Chapel 211/131 🅱
Becketts 249/155 🅱
Copse 287/179 🅱

FIA F1 WORLD CHAMPIONSHIP ROUND 8

SANTANDER
BRITISH
GRAND PRIX

SILVERSTONE 19-21 JUNE 2009

Photos: Peter J. Fox

 RACE DISTANCE: 70 laps,191.603 miles/308.355km • RACE WEATHER: Cloudy (track 23-25°C, air 16-17°C)

Pos.	Driver	Nat.	No.	Entrant	Car/Engine	Tyres	Laps	Time/Retirement	Speed (mph/km/h)	Gap to leader	Fastest race lap	
1	Sebastian Vettel	D	15	Red Bull Racing	Red Bull RB5-Renault RS27 V8	B	60	1h 22m 49.328s	138.805/223.385		1m 20.735s	16
2	Mark Webber	AUS	14	Red Bull Racing	Red Bull RB5-Renault RS27 V8	B	60	1h 23m 04.516s	138.382/222.705	+ 15.188s	1m 20.915s	57
3	Rubens Barrichello	BR	23	Brawn GP Formula 1 Team	Brawn BGP 001-Mercedes FO108W V8	B	60	1h 23m 30.503s	137.665/221.550	+ 41.175s	1m 21.429s	18
4	Felipe Massa	BR	3	Scuderia Ferrari Marlboro	Ferrari F60-056 V8	B	60	1h 23m 34.371s	137.559/221.379	+ 45.043s	1m 21.509s	22
5	Nico Rosberg	D	16	AT&T Williams	Williams FW31-Toyota RVX-09 V8	B	60	1h 23m 35.243s	137.534/221.340	+ 45.915s	1m 21.054s	17
6	Jenson Button	GB	22	Brawn GP Formula 1 Team	Brawn BGP 001-Mercedes FO108W V8	B	60	1h 23m 35.613s	137.524/221.324	+ 46.285s	1m 21.189s	54
7	Jarno Trulli	I	9	Panasonic Toyota Racing	Toyota TF109-RVX-09 V8	B	60	1h 23m 57.635s	136.923/220.356	+ 1m 08.307s	1m 21.806s	17
8	Kimi Räikkönen	FIN	4	Scuderia Ferrari Marlboro	Ferrari F60-056 V8	B	60	1h 23m 58.950s	136.887/220.299	+ 1m 09.622s	1m 21.656s	14
9	Timo Glock	D	10	Panasonic Toyota Racing	Toyota TF109-RVX-09 V8	B	60	1h 23m 59.151s	136.882/220.290	+ 1m 09.823s	1m 21.671s	51
10	Giancarlo Fisichella	I	21	Force India F1 Team	Force India VJM02-Mercedes FO108W V8	B	60	1h 24m 00.850s	136.836/220.216	+ 1m 11.522s	1m 21.810s	20
11	Kazuki Nakajima	J	17	AT&T Williams	Williams FW31-Toyota RVX-09 V8	B	60	1h 24m 03.351s	136.768/220.107	+ 1m 14.023s	1m 21.845s	14
12	Nelsinho Piquet	BR	8	ING Renault F1 Team	Renault R29-RS27 V8	B	59			+ 1 lap	1m 22.505s	25
13	Robert Kubica	PL	5	BMW Sauber F1 Team	BMW Sauber F1.09-BMW P86/9 V8	B	59			+ 1 lap	1m 22.182s	41
14	Fernando Alonso	E	7	ING Renault F1 Team	Renault R29-RS27 V8	B	59			+ 1 lap	1m 21.852s	36
15	Nick Heidfeld	D	6	BMW Sauber F1 Team	BMW Sauber F1.09-BMW P86/9 V8	B	59			+ 1 lap	1m 21.956s	59
16	Lewis Hamilton	GB	1	Vodafone McLaren Mercedes	McLaren MP4-24-Mercedes FO108W V8	B	59			+ 1 lap	1m 22.576s	24
17	Adrian Sutil	D	20	Force India F1 Team	Force India VJM02-Mercedes FO108W V8	B	59			+ 1 lap	1m 23.475s	50
18	Sébastien Buemi	CH	12	Scuderia Toro Rosso	Toro Rosso STR04-Ferrari 056 V8	B	59			+ 1 lap	1m 22.711s	24
	Sébastien Bourdais	F	11	Scuderia Toro Rosso	Toro Rosso STR04-Ferrari 056 V8	B	37	accident damage			1m 22.466s	26
	Heikki Kovalainen	FIN	2	Vodafone McLaren Mercedes	McLaren MP4-24-Mercedes FO108W V8	B	36	accident damage			1m 22.418s	32

All results and data © FOM 2009

Fastest race lap: Sebastian Vettel on lap 16, 1m 20.735s, 142.442mph/229.238km/h.

Lap record: Nigel Mansell (Williams FW11B-Honda V6 turbo), 1m 09.832s, 153.059mph/246.324km/h (1987) (2.969-mile/4.778km circuit)

Lap record (current configuration): Michael Schumacher (Ferrari F2004 V10), 1m 18.739s, 146.053mph/235.049km/h (2004).

12	BUEMI · Toro Rosso	11	BOURDAIS · Toro Rosso	6	HEIDFELD · BMW Sauber	2	KOVALAINEN · McLaren	3	MASSA · Ferrari	4	RÄIKKÖNEN · Ferrari
20	SUTIL · Force India chassis change - started from pit lane	1	HAMILTON · McLaren	21	FISICHELLA · Force India	8	PIQUET · Renault	5	KUBICA · BMW Sauber	7	ALONSO · Renault

Grid order	1	2	3	4	5	6	7	8	9	10	11	12	13	14	15	16	17	18	19	20	21	22	23	24	25	26	27	28	29	30	31	32	33	34	35	36	37	38	39	40	41	42	43	44	45	46	4
15 VETTEL	15	15	15	15	15	15	15	15	15	15	15	15	15	15	15	15	15	15	15	15	15	15	15	15	15	15	15	15	15	15	15	15	15	15	15	15	15	15	15	15	15	15	15	15	15	14	14
23 BARRICHELLO	23	23	23	23	23	23	23	23	23	23	23	23	23	23	23	23	23	14	14	3	3	3	14	14	14	14	14	14	14	14	14	14	14	14	14	14	14	14	14	14	14	14	14	14	15	15	1
14 WEBBER	14	14	14	14	14	14	14	14	14	14	14	14	14	14	14	14	14	23	3	21	14	14	23	23	23	23	23	23	23	23	23	23	23	23	23	23	23	23	23	23	23	23	23	23	23	23	2
9 TRULLI	17	17	17	17	17	17	17	17	17	17	17	17	17	17	4	16	16	16	3	21	14	23	23	16	16	16	16	16	16	16	16	16	16	16	16	16	16	16	16	3	3	3	22	2
17 NAKAJIMA	4	4	4	4	4	4	4	4	4	4	4	4	4	4	16	9	9	9	10	23	23	16	16	3	3	3	3	3	3	3	3	3	3	3	3	3	3	3	3	16	9	9	9	1
22 BUTTON	16	16	16	16	16	16	16	16	16	16	16	16	16	16	17	4	22	3	21	16	16	9	9	9	9	9	9	9	9	9	9	9	9	9	9	9	9	9	9	22	22	10		
16 ROSBERG	9	9	9	9	9	9	9	9	9	9	9	9	9	9	22	3	22	16	9	9	4	4	4	4	4	4	4	4	4	4	4	4	4	4	4	22	22	21	10	3	1
10 GLOCK	3	22	22	22	22	22	22	22	22	22	22	22	22	22	3	10	10	9	4	4	22	22	22	22	22	22	22	22	22	22	22	22	4	21	10	21	16		
4 RÄIKKÖNEN	22	3	3	3	3	3	3	3	3	3	3	3	3	3	10	21	4	22	22	17	17	17	17	17	17	17	17	17	17	17	17	17	17	17	21	10	16	16	4		
7 ALONSO	10	10	10	10	10	10	10	10	10	10	10	10	10	10	21	4	4	22	17	17	21	21	21	21	21	21	21	21	21	21	21	21	21	10	4	4	4	21	2
3 MASSA	6	21	21	21	21	21	21	21	21	21	21	21	21	21	17	17	17	10	10	10	10	10	10	10	10	10	10	10	10	10	10	10	10	17	17	17	17	17	17
5 KUBICA	7	6	6	6	6	6	6	6	6	6	6	6	6	6	6	6	6	5	5	5	5	5	8	2	2	5	5	5	5	5	5	5	5	5	5	5	5	5	5
2 KOVALAINEN	5	7	7	7	7	7	7	7	7	7	7	7	7	7	7	7	7	5	5	6	8	8	8	8	8	5	2	5	5	7	7	7	7	7	8	8	8	8	8
8 PIQUET	21	1	5	5	5	5	5	5	5	5	5	5	5	5	1	1	8	8	11	11	11	11	11	11	2	5	20	20	20	7	8	8	8	8	1	1	6	6	7
6 HEIDFELD	1	5	1	1	1	1	1	1	1	1	1	1	1	1	7	8	11	11	12	2	2	2	20	20	8	8	7	20	1	1	1	6	6	6	6	7	7	6
21 FISICHELLA	8	8	8	8	8	8	8	8	8	8	8	8	8	8	11	12	2	20	20	20	20	7	1	1	2	6	6	6	12	12	7	1	1	1	1	
11 BOURDAIS	11	11	11	11	11	11	11	11	11	11	11	12	12	2	20	7	7	7	1	1	1	1	12	12	12	12	7	7	12	20	20	20	20	2
1 HAMILTON	12	12	12	12	12	12	12	12	12	12	12	2	2	20	7	1	1	1	11	11	11	11	11	20	20	20	20	20	12	12	12	12	1
12 BUEMI	2	2	2	2	2	2	2	2	2	2	2	20	20	7	1	6	6	6	6	6	6	6	6	20	2	11
20 SUTIL	20	20	20	20	20	20	20	20	20	20	20	20	20	20	7	7	1	6	12	12	12	12	12	12	12	12	2	11	11

TIME SHEETS

PRACTICE 1 (FRIDAY)
Cloudy
(track 20-23°C, air 15-16°C)

Pos.	Driver	Laps	Time
1	Sebastian Vettel	20	1m 19.400s
2	Mark Webber	19	1m 19.682s
3	Jenson Button	20	1m 20.227s
4	Rubens Barrichello	29	1m 20.242s
5	Fernando Alonso	26	1m 20.458s
6	Felipe Massa	23	1m 20.471s
7	Jarno Trulli	32	1m 20.585s
8	Lewis Hamilton	26	1m 20.650s
9	Nico Rosberg	32	1m 20.815s
10	Giancarlo Fisichella	25	1m 20.838s
11	Adrian Sutil	22	1m 20.913s
12	Heikki Kovalainen	22	1m 21.029s
13	Nick Heidfeld	24	1m 21.103s
14	Kimi Räikkönen	27	1m 21.179s
15	Sébastien Bourdais	23	1m 21.384s
16	Timo Glock	32	1m 21.386s
17	Kazuki Nakajima	26	1m 21.489s
18	Nelsinho Piquet	30	1m 21.525s
19	Sébastien Buemi	37	1m 21.590s
20	Robert Kubica	16	1m 21.801s

PRACTICE 2 (FRIDAY)
Partly cloudy
(track 23-28°C, air 17-19°C)

Pos.	Driver	Laps	Time
1	Sebastian Vettel	39	1m 19.456s
2	Mark Webber	35	1m 19.597s
3	Adrian Sutil	41	1m 20.141s
4	Kazuki Nakajima	36	1m 20.209s
5	Fernando Alonso	36	1m 20.237s
6	Rubens Barrichello	26	1m 20.244s
7	Lewis Hamilton	35	1m 20.417s
8	Jarno Trulli	40	1m 20.458s
9	Nico Rosberg	42	1m 20.468s
10	Nelsinho Piquet	37	1m 20.608s
11	Robert Kubica	23	1m 20.622s
12	Heikki Kovalainen	37	1m 20.733s
13	Timo Glock	37	1m 20.762s
14	Jenson Button	28	1m 20.767s
15	Nick Heidfeld	35	1m 20.932s
16	Sébastien Bourdais	36	1m 20.945s
17	Felipe Massa	37	1m 21.005s
18	Kimi Räikkönen	38	1m 21.132s
19	Giancarlo Fisichella	40	1m 21.413s
20	Sébastien Buemi	37	1m 21.668s

PRACTICE 3 (SATURDAY)
Sunny/partly cloudy
(track 17-20°C, air 15-17°C)

Pos.	Driver	Laps	Time
1	Nico Rosberg	20	1m 18.899s
2	Kazuki Nakajima	19	1m 19.102s
3	Jarno Trulli	15	1m 19.125s
4	Sebastian Vettel	15	1m 19.371s
5	Felipe Massa	19	1m 19.596s
6	Kimi Räikkönen	13	1m 19.855s
7	Timo Glock	19	1m 19.868s
8	Fernando Alonso	14	1m 19.917s
9	Mark Webber	15	1m 19.946s
10	Rubens Barrichello	14	1m 20.028s
11	Lewis Hamilton	16	1m 20.048s
12	Jenson Button	17	1m 20.157s
13	Nelsinho Piquet	18	1m 20.232s
14	Sébastien Bourdais	17	1m 20.459s
15	Adrian Sutil	15	1m 20.548s
16	Giancarlo Fisichella	17	1m 20.572s
17	Heikki Kovalainen	18	1m 20.638s
18	Nick Heidfeld	20	1m 20.696s
19	Sébastien Buemi	11	1m 21.024s
20	Robert Kubica	13	1m 21.039s

QUALIFYING (SATURDAY)
Sunny/partly cloudy (track 21-23°C, air 17-18°C)

Pos.	Driver	First	Second	Third	Weight
1	Sebastian Vettel	1m 18.685s	**1m 18.119s**	**1m 19.509s**	666.5kg
2	Rubens Barrichello	1m 19.325s	1m 18.335s	1m 19.856s	657.5kg
3	Mark Webber	1m 18.674s	1m 18.209s	1m 19.868s	659.5kg
4	Jarno Trulli	1m 18.886s	1m 18.240s	1m 20.091s	658kg
5	Kazuki Nakajima	**1m 18.530s**	1m 18.575s	1m 20.216s	652.5kg
6	Jenson Button	1m 18.957s	1m 18.663s	1m 20.289s	657.5kg
7	Nico Rosberg	1m 19.228s	1m 18.591s	1m 20.361s	661.5kg
8	Timo Glock	1m 19.198s	1m 18.791s	1m 20.490s	660kg
9	Kimi Räikkönen	1m 19.010s	1m 18.566s	1m 20.715s	654kg
10	Fernando Alonso	1m 19.167s	1m 18.761s	1m 20.741s	654kg
11	Felipe Massa	1m 19.148s	1m 18.927s		675kg
12	Robert Kubica	1m 19.730s	1m 19.308s		689.5kg
13	Heikki Kovalainen	1m 19.732s	1m 19.353s		695.5kg
14	Nelsinho Piquet	1m 19.555s	1m 19.392s		682.5kg
15	Nick Heidfeld	1m 19.559s	1m 19.448s		665.5kg
16	Giancarlo Fisichella	1m 19.802s			668kg
17	Sébastien Bourdais	1m 19.898s			687.5kg
18	Adrian Sutil	1m 19.909s			692kg
19	Lewis Hamilton	1m 19.917s			666kg
20	Sébastien Buemi	1m 20.236s			672.5kg

 **16** ROSBERG · Williams

 **17** NAKAJIMA · Williams

 **14** WEBBER · Red Bull

15 VETTEL · Red Bull

 **10** GLOCK · Toyota

 **22** BUTTON · Brawn

 **9** TRULLI · Toyota

23 BARRICHELLO · Brawn

FOR THE RECORD

1st FASTEST LAP: Sebastian Vettel/Red Bull

100th POINT: Brawn

10th PODIUM: Red Bull

DID YOU KNOW?

This was the 60th F1 British Grand Prix.

POINTS

DRIVERS

1	Jenson Button	64
2	Rubens Barrichello	41
3	Sebastian Vettel	39
4	Mark Webber	35.5
5	Jarno Trulli	21.5
6	Felipe Massa	16
7	Nico Rosberg	15.5
8	Timo Glock	13
9	Fernando Alonso	11
10	Kimi Räikkönen	10
11	Lewis Hamilton	9
12	Nick Heidfeld	6
13	Heikki Kovalainen	4
14	Sébastien Buemi	3
15	Robert Kubica	2
16	Sébastien Bourdais	2

CONSTRUCTORS

1	Brawn	105
2	Red Bull	74.5
3	Toyota	34.5
4	McLaren	26
5	Renault	15.5
6	BMW Sauber	13
7	Ferrari	11
8	Williams	8
9	Toro Rosso	5

8	49	50	51	52	53	54	55	56	57	58	59	60	·	
5	15	15	15	15	15	15	15	15	15	15	15	15		1
4	14	14	14	14	14	14	14	14	14	14	14	14		2
2	22	23	23	23	23	23	23	23	23	23	23	23		3
3	23	3	3	3	3	3	3	3	3	3	3	3		4
3	3	16	16	16	16	16	16	16	16	16	16	16		5
6	16	22	22	22	22	22	22	22	22	22	22	22		6
0	9	9	9	9	9	9	9	9	9	9	9	9		7
9	4	4	4	4	4	4	4	4	4	4	4	4		8
4	10	10	10	10	10	10	10	10	10	10	10	10		
1	21	21	21	21	21	21	21	21	21	21	21	21		
7	17	17	17	17	17	17	17	17	17	17	17	17		
8	8	8	8	8	8	8	8	8	8	8	8	8		
5	5	5	5	5	5	5	5	5	5	5	5	5		
7	7	7	7	7	7	7	7	7	7	7	7	7		
6	6	6	6	6	6	6	6	6	6	6	6	6		
1	1	1	1	1	1	1	1	1	1	1	1	1		
0	20	20	20	20	20	20	20	20	20	20	20	20		
2	12	12	12	12	12	12	12	12	12	12	12	12		

21 Pit stop   *14 One lap or more behind*

RACE TYRE STRATEGIES

The tyre regulations stipulate that two dry tyre specifications must be used during the race.

The Soft compound Bridgestone Potenza tyre is marked with a green stripe on the sidewall of the tyre.

	Driver	Race Stint 1	Race Stint 2	Race Stint 3
1	Sebastian Vettel	Soft: 1-21	Soft: 22-44	Hard: 45-60
2	Mark Webber	Soft: 1-20	Soft: 21-47	Hard: 48-60
3	Rubens Barrichello	Soft: 1-19	Hard: 20-47	Soft: 48-60
4	Felipe Massa	Soft: 1-23	Soft: 24-45	Hard: 46-60
5	Nico Rosberg	Hard: 1-18	Hard: 19-43	Soft: 44-60
6	Jenson Button	Soft: 1-18	Hard: 19-49	Soft: 50-60
7	Jarno Trulli	Soft: 1-18	Soft: 19-46	Hard: 47-60
8	Kimi Räikkönen	Soft: 1-16	Soft: 17-42	Hard: 43-60
9	Timo Glock	Soft: 1-19	Soft: 20-48	Hard: 49-60
10	Giancarlo Fisichella	Soft: 1-21	Hard: 22-45	Soft: 46-60
11	Kazuki Nakajima	Hard: 1-15	Hard: 16-40	Soft: 41-60
12	Nelson Piquet	Hard: 1-29	Soft: 30-59	
13	Robert Kubica	Hard: 1-28	Soft: 29-47	Soft: 48-59
14	Fernando Alonso	Hard: 1-18	Hard: 19-38	Soft: 39-59
15	Nick Heidfeld	Soft: 1-21	Hard: 22-46	Soft: 47-59
16	Lewis Hamilton	Soft: 1-20	Soft: 21-43	Hard: 44-59
17	Adrian Sutil	Hard: 1-33	Soft: 34-59	
18	Sébastien Buemi	Hard: 1-22	Soft: 23-41	Soft: 42-59
	Sébastien Bourdais	Soft: 1-27	Soft: 28-34	Hard: 35-37 (dnf)
	Heikki Kovalainen	Soft: 1-33	Hard: 34	Hard: 35-36 (dnf)

GERMAN GRAND PRIX

NÜRBURGRING CIRCUIT

NÜRBURGRING QUALIFYING

HE knew he could have won at Silverstone, and now it looked as though he felt he must. Mark Webber's sense of purpose was manifest on Saturday. It wasn't the manner of his first Formula One pole position – just in front of the lightly-fuelled Brawns and 0.25 seconds clear of team-mate Sebastian Vettel – that reflected his resolve, but the way he dealt with the rain that blighted the beginning of Q2. He managed a 1m 38.038s on his first flying lap on intermediates, 1.5 seconds faster than anyone else mustered with the benefit of two.

It was a fabulous effort, but there were still a few minutes to go and the track was beginning to dry: slicks o'clock. "I knew that first lap was crucial," Webber said, "because you never know whether conditions might deteriorate. I was just trying to put in some sort of banker without going totally bananas. Of course, you have to push, but I had a good feeling for the car and the tyres straight away, and when you have that confidence you can obviously do reasonable lap times.

"I knew the time was competitive when I set it, but I was also aware the session wasn't really over because we might need to put slicks on, which we did, and I then almost crashed several times. I couldn't believe I was still fourth at the end of Q2, because it felt horrible driving around on slicks and I had so many moments. At the last corner, I was almost in my hotel room…"

It remained dry throughout Q3, and Webber delivered again. "I have been close to pole in the past and have achieved it on fuel-corrected times [at the same circuit, in 2006]," he said, "but that doesn't count. Today, though, I'm here. The team has done a great job, we've been quick all weekend and the conditions have really tested everyone. It was very, very chaotic, but to deliver the lap time when it mattered meant a lot to me."

Rubens Barrichello's dependably canny tyre judgment was evident in Q2, when everybody initially went out on slicks and, mostly, immediately came back in for intermediates. Uniquely, the Brazilian abandoned his first lap on inters because he felt that, by then, slicks were a better option. He was right, but it did lead to a fair amount of confusion on the Brawn radio channel; he ended up second, ahead of Jenson Button.

McLaren introduced what was, in all bar name, a B-spec version of the MP4-24, with new front wing, sidepods, engine cover, floor and diffuser. However, the team had only enough parts to furnish Lewis Hamilton with a full upgrade kit. "It feels great to have a car you can really push into corners," Hamilton said. "It just breeds confidence." He lined up fifth, a huge step forward since Silverstone, and Heikki Kovalainen was sixth in the standard chassis. "The parts situation actually indicates how hard the team is working," the Finn said, "and I understand that. People have been toiling night and day to get the new bits to the track, and it's just unfortunate that we don't yet have two complete sets."

Timo Glock struggled to generate any kind of tyre heat in his Toyota and failed to get beyond Q1, a major disappointment at his home race. Then he was handed a three-position penalty for blocking Fernando Alonso, but as he was 19th anyway – and the stewards weren't about to make him start from Koblenz – such details were largely irrelevant.

Opening spread: Mark Webber and the buoyant Red Bull team celebrate the Australian driver's long overdue maiden grand prix victory in front of the RBR Energy Station in the Nürburgring paddock.
Photo: Jad Sherif/WRi2

Right: Nico Rosberg impressed with a strong drive from 15th place on the grid, taking every opportunity that presented itself to climb through to fourth at the chequered flag.
Photo: Peter J. Fox

Below left: Sir Frank Williams looks pleased with his team's weekend.
Photo: Jean-François Galeron/WRi2

Below: Former triple world champion Niki Lauda demonstrated a 2.5-litre Mercedes W196 in a historic parade on race morning.
Photo: Peter J. Fox

SUNDAY, 16.59. The Red Bull Energy Station is surrounded by a photographic multitude. It's less than 90 minutes since the German Grand Prix finished, but the whole team is primed for action once more, albeit with less intense pursuits in mind. Only one element is missing...

Mark Webber's mood had been easy enough to assess during qualifying, and he was no less resolute come the race. He didn't get the best of starts from pole, and Rubens Barrichello, fuelled lightly for three stops, was swift to draw alongside from the outside of the front row. "I completely lost sight of him," Webber said. "I thought he'd gone to the left, so I went to the right and banged into him. I thought, 'Ah, that's where he is...'"

Formula One drivers forever complain about the relative uselessness of the mirrors attached to their cars, but the stewards eventually decided that Webber was guilty of causing an avoidable collision and summoned him for a drive-through penalty, although circumstances rendered the delay inconsequential. The Australian's maiden grand prix success – the first for his nation since Alan Jones triumphed at Las

Vegas in 1981 – owed much to his own endeavours, and quite a lot to Heikki Kovalainen.

While Barrichello bounced harmlessly off Webber to lead into Turn One, Lewis Hamilton used KERS to pull momentarily ahead of the Australian and the two cars touched when Webber moved across in the immediate aftermath of his scrape with Barrichello. It was the slightest of brushes, but the Red Bull's front wing endplate cut into Hamilton's right rear tyre and the Englishman slithered wide over the kerbs as it deflated. Webber's car suffered a minor nick, but Hamilton lost almost a lap while crawling to the pits, during which time flailing rubber inflicted serious damage to the MP4-24's revised floor, rendering the car more or less unusable. Hamilton thought it might be worth stopping for the sake of engine and gearbox preservation, but the team encouraged him to carry on. He eventually finished 18th – and last. "It felt as though I was driving on ice," Hamilton said. "I was pushing and pushing, but there was nothing I could do. It was a waste of time, but the good news from the weekend is that the latest updates have been successful." In the circumstances, though, it had

been impossible to assess their full benefits over a complete race distance.

While he was left to stew in his own despond, team-mate Kovalainen vaulted from sixth to third to lead Felipe Massa, Jenson Button, Sebastian Vettel, Kimi Räikkönen, Adrian Sutil (a career-best seventh in qualifying, having excelled, as always, in the mixed conditions that blighted Q2), Nico Rosberg, Robert Kubica, Fernando Alonso, Nick Heidfeld, Sébastien Buemi, Giancarlo Fisichella, Nelson Piquet, Jarno Trulli, Sébastien Bourdais, Timo Glock (who opted to start from the pits) and Kazuki Nakajima, sentenced to the tail of the pack after a nudge from Trulli had forced him wide.

Button outbraked Massa at the start of the second lap, but Kovalainen was a trickier proposition. "His pace was way off what we could have achieved at that point of the race," Button said, "but there was just no way through."

While the Finn lapped consistently in the 1m 36s bracket, Barrichello and Webber were able to pull away at more than a second per lap. The stewards didn't give notice of the Australian's punishment until

Right: Robert Kubica puts on a smile for his enthusiastic fans, briefly taking his mind off a disappointing weekend, which would yield him only 14th place in his BMW Sauber.

Below: Lewis Hamilton's hopes of capitalising on the McLaren MP4-24's aerodynamic upgrade were thwarted when he picked up a puncture in a first-corner brush with Webber.
Photos: Lukas Gorys

Below right: Sébastian Bourdais was driving his final race for Scuderia Toro Rosso, much to the Frenchman's disappointment.
Photo: Jad Sherif/WRi2

lap 11, and he stayed out on the track for another three laps, the maximum period allowed by the rules. Barrichello peeled in at the same time for his first scheduled stop and, with Kovalainen 17.6 seconds adrift, Webber took the race lead while serving his penalty. Barrichello moved back to the front once the leaders had completed their initial round of stops – Webber came in again on lap 19, this time by design – but the Brazilian's strategy made him easy prey. Webber was almost on Barrichello's tail just before the latter made his second stop, on lap 32, and then the Brawn's prospects were further compromised by a jammed fuel rig.

Rubens was stationary for so long that he assumed the team was switching him to a two-stop strategy, and wasn't best pleased to discover it hadn't. He dropped to fifth as a consequence, and lost another place to team-mate Button after the final stops. Later, clearly very angry, he indicated that he would rather go straight home than talk it through with the team.

Team principal Ross Brawn countered that the Brazilian was simply in a heightened emotional state, triggered by heat-of-the-moment disappointment. "Rubens set 11th fastest race lap," he said, "and that being the case, it didn't really matter what strategy he was on; he wasn't going to win."

Webber, in contrast, was able to press on serenely at the head of the field. He made his second stop on lap 43, ceding the lead for an instant to Vettel, who had vaulted Kovalainen and Massa during the first stops, but the German had lost so much time during the opening stint – shades of Webber behind Barrichello at Silverstone – that he posed no threat, and Webber was able to slip into cruise mode. After he crossed the line, still almost ten seconds clear of Vettel, his exultant cheers lasted long and loud: arguably, the pit radio was superfluous. "Towards the end, I was just trying to stay away from the kerbs," Webber said – not least because they were thought to have caused Vettel's wiring loom to work loose on Friday, which had led to his engine cutting suddenly during the first free practice session – "I just kept the car in the middle of the track and made sure I brought it home. There was no need to finish 20 seconds in front. As Jack Brabham used to

say, 'It's best to win at the slowest possible speed'. I was thinking about him today.

"I wanted this so badly after Silverstone, where I thought I had a good chance, and in the end the only thing I thought might beat me was the rain, but even that held off. It is really important to me that I wasn't handed victory, I had to work for it. I hope grand prix wins are like muscles, obviously: when you get one, you acquire a few more…"

During the early stages, Vettel made several attempts to pass Massa using novel methodology – the racetrack, rather than the pit lane – but his efforts were in vain. "Felipe was defending well with his special button," he said. "Even when I was in his tow, I couldn't get quite close enough. By the end of the straight, I'd go for the outside, but I was braking absolutely on the limit, and he had the line, so it was very tight and he did a good job. Sometimes it was very close and I knew I needed to be cautious, because of the wide front wings we have now."

Massa might have made a flying start, courtesy of KERS, but his pace was strong throughout a long first stint, which carried him past Kovalainen, and his afternoon's work was a model of consistency and maturity – a carbon copy of Silverstone, in fact. The only difference was that it earned him a place on the podium for the first time since Brazil 2008. "I've rather missed being up here," he said, "but if Sebastian would like to exchange a bit of his downforce for my KERS, I'd gladly swap now."

Nico Rosberg was equally flawless. He was one of a small group to start on the medium Bridgestone, which had looked much slower than the super-soft for the first two days, when track temperatures struggled to reach 20 degrees, although it was the better option in Sunday's warmer climate. After rising from 15th to ninth at the start, the German drove one of the longest first stints – 29 laps – and his heavy fuel load was not too punitive because the cars ahead were wedged behind Kovalainen. The true quality of his performance, though, was partially concealed. "Nico had a fuel system problem," said Williams technical director Sam Michael. "He had to come in early for both stops and carry an extra 15 kilos of fuel, worth

half a second per lap, from the first stop to the end of the race."

The Brawns were next, with Button ahead after the late positional swap that did little to calm the already agitated Barrichello. "My race started badly and didn't get much better," Button said. "We struggled with graining and tyre degradation throughout, and neither compound worked well for us."

Team principal Ross Brawn added, "We simply didn't have the pace to match the Red Bulls. We opted for three stops to give both drivers the best possible chance of achieving a podium position, but the problem with Rubens's fuel rig dropped him behind Rosberg, compromised his strategy and possibly prevented him finishing third."

Alonso started on super-softs, but effectively destroyed them by spinning on the formation lap while conducting his customarily extravagant warm-up exercises. Late in the race, however, he set fastest lap on the medium, which he felt was a better barometer of Renault's progress than his seventh place. He had paid the penalty, though, for failing to survive the quirky weather conditions in Q2. "Our car was good enough to finish on the podium this weekend," he said. "It is definitely faster than the Ferrari, and look what happened to Massa."

Kovalainen took the final point – just – after fending off a queue containing Glock (a decent drive on a one-stopper), Heidfeld (who lost time during his first stop, because he had to be held stationary to avoid a possible collision with the incoming Piquet), Nakajima and Fisichella, who passed more cars than anybody during the afternoon.

The Force India's gathering pace, though, had been obvious from Sutil's performance. The pit cycle promoted the German to second during his 27-lap opening salvo, but after his first stop, he rejoined adjacent to Räikkönen's Ferrari. The two cars ran together all the way to Turn One, where they touched. Sutil lost a front wing endplate, and his second stint lasted just a single lap before he came in for repairs. The delay dropped him to 15th, behind Nakajima, Piquet and Kubica, who complained that his tyre pressures were set too high during a gripless second stint.

Räikkönen survived the clash with Sutil, but retired soon afterwards with unrelated radiator damage. He'd collected some debris earlier in the race and had been losing power since lap 14.

Buemi finished an uneventful 16th, ahead of Trulli, who dropped back after pitting for a new nose on lap four, a consequence of hitting Nakajima. Hamilton was 18th. Bourdais retired with hydraulic failure, and when he pulled into the garage after 18 laps, it marked the last time he would do so as a Toro Rosso driver. The weekend had been rife with rumours that the Frenchman was about to be dropped – and Red Bull junior driver Jaime Alguersuari had been seen in the team's pit throughout the weekend. His presence wasn't entirely coincidental.

Having finally unshackled himself from the demands of a zillion TV crews, Mark Webber finally made it back through the paddock and reached the team motorhome, where a reception committee was waiting. Hugs and handshakes preceded a celebratory team photograph, the whole thing eventually descending into a good-natured champagne fight. There is always a feel-good factor when a driver scores his maiden F1 victory, but the warmth and affection seemed particularly acute at this time.

Simon Arron

Left: Competitive again. Felipe Massa's Ferrari gives chase to Sebastian Vettel's Red Bull as the Brazilian heads for a podium finish.
Photo: Peter J. Fox

Above: Rubens finished the race in a stressed frame of mind again, worrying about the Brawn team's even-handedness.
Photo: Jean-Francois Galeron/WRi2

EDITOR'S VIEW
BARRICHELLO LOSES HIS COOL

THERE were people inside the Brawn team during the 2009 season who hinted that, when all the emotion was stripped out of the equation, Rubens Barrichello, at his best, was as much a match for Jenson Button as he had been for Michael Schumacher at Ferrari. Indeed, some felt that Rubens was more of a racer than his English colleague. You could even find those who reckoned Rubens was quite simply a better bet than Jenson – at least on the basis of their respective performances in 2008.

Yet for all his consummate driving skill, Barrichello could still display a fragile streak. He'd done it once in Barcelona, and it was much the same situation at the Nürburgring. This time, he lost his patience with the Brawn-Mercedes team after he had dropped from an initial commanding lead of the German Grand Prix to an eventual fifth, behind his team-mate.

After qualifying second, Barrichello out-accelerated eventual winner Mark Webber's Red Bull into the first corner after the start, but his efforts were thwarted when the Brawn team switched both its drivers to three-stop refuelling strategies. Eventually, they finished fifth and sixth, the top four runners having been on two-stoppers.

"I'm terribly upset with the way things have gone today," the Brazilian veteran of nine career grand prix wins told the BBC, "because it was a very good show of how to lose a race. I did everything I had to. I had to go into the first corner first, and that's what I did.

"Then they [Brawn] made me lose the race basically. If we keep going like this, then we will end up losing both championships, which would be terrible."

He added, "To be honest, I wish I could just get on a plane and go home now. I don't want to talk to anybody in the team because it would just be a load of blah, blah, blah. And I don't want to hear that. I am just terribly upset."

After his Spanish outburst, Rubens had calmed down and accepted assurances from team principal Ross Brawn that the two drivers would always receive equal treatment. However, his annoyance was compounded in the German race when he suffered an additional delay at the second of his three refuelling stops, when the fuel rig malfunctioned and the back-up rig had to be pressed into action.

For his part, Brawn hinted that he did not think that Barrichello had been quite quick enough. "I think that is a frustrated racing driver," he said. "When you have put so much into a race and it has not worked out, that's what you get sometimes. If you get out of the car thinking that you should have won, and haven't got all the facts, then that can happen. Now he has the facts and understands what happened, he's fine.

"Rubens has been a very important member of the team. He's stuck through very difficult times, he has a lot of loyalty and that is not something that will be destroyed by a few frustrated words after a race."

Button, who saw his championship lead reduced, but remain intact, said he had regarded the closing stages of the race as something of a survival exercise.

Yet, for all this, Ross Brawn must have been starting to be aware of, if not quite worried about, the widely fluctuating inconsistencies in performance assailing his drivers. Suddenly, it seemed that the balmy days of Bahrain, Spain and Turkey were disappearing fast into their rear-view mirrors.

Alan Henry

NÜRBURGRING, NÜRBURG/EIFEL
Circuit: 3.199 miles/5.148km 60 laps

Dunlop-Kurve 103/64 ③
Ford-Kurve 127/79 ②
Schumacher 258/161 ⑥
206/128 ⑤
187/116 kmh/mph ⑭ Gear
Castrol-S 79/49 ①
Michelin 163/101 ④
Coca-Cola Kurve 70/113 ②
Mercedes - Arena 98/61 ②
Warsteiner-Kurve 100/161 ③
NGK-Schikane 66/106 ②
ADVAN-Bogen 180/290 ⑥

FIA F1 WORLD CHAMPIONSHIP ROUND 9
GROSSER PREIS SANTANDER VON DEUTSCHLAND
NÜRBURGRING 10-12 JULY 2009

Photos: Peter J. Fox

RACE DISTANCE: 60 laps, 191.919 miles/308.863km • RACE WEATHER: Partly cloudy/sunny/cloudy (track 21-24°C, air 19-20°C)

Pos.	Driver	Nat.	No.	Entrant	Car/Engine	Tyres	Laps	Time/Retirement	Speed (mph/ km/h)	Gap to leader	Fastest race lap
1	Mark Webber	AUS	14	Red Bull Racing	Red Bull RB5-Renault RS27 V8	B	60	1h 36m 43.310s	119.053/191.598		1m 34.003s 37
2	Sebastian Vettel	D	15	Red Bull Racing	Red Bull RB5-Renault RS27 V8	B	60	1h 36m 52.562s	118.864/191.293	+ 9.252s	1m 34.089s 42
3	Felipe Massa	BR	3	Scuderia Ferrari Marlboro	Ferrari F60-056 V8	B	60	1h 36m 59.216s	118.728/191.074	+ 15.906s	1m 34.458s 53
4	Nico Rosberg	D	16	AT&T Williams	Williams FW31-Toyota RVX-09 V8	B	60	1h 37m 04.409s	118.622/190.904	+ 21.099s	1m 34.403s 50
5	Jenson Button	GB	22	Brawn GP Formula 1 Team	Brawn BGP 001-Mercedes FO108W V8	B	60	1h 37m 06.919s	118.571/190.822	+ 23.609s	1m 34.252s 53
6	Rubens Barrichello	BR	23	Brawn GP Formula 1 Team	Brawn BGP 001-Mercedes FO108W V8	B	60	1h 37m 07.778s	118.554/190.794	+ 24.468s	1m 34.676s 54
7	Fernando Alonso	E	7	ING Renault F1 Team	Renault R29-RS27 V8	B	60	1h 37m 08.198s	118.545/190.780	+ 24.888s	1m 33.365s 49
8	Heikki Kovalainen	FIN	2	Vodafone McLaren Mercedes	McLaren MP4-24-Mercedes FO108W V8	B	60	1h 37m 42.002s	117.862/189.680	+ 58.692s	1m 35.524s 59
9	Timo Glock	D	10	Panasonic Toyota Racing	Toyota TF109-RVX-09 V8	B	60	1h 37m 44.767s	117.806/189.590	+ 1m 01.457s	1m 35.369s 40
10	Nick Heidfeld	D	6	BMW Sauber F1 Team	BMW Sauber F1.09-BMW P86/9 V8	B	60	1h 37m 45.235s	117.796/189.575	+ 1m 01.925s	1m 34.559s 42
11	Giancarlo Fisichella	I	21	Force India F1 Team	Force India VJM02-Mercedes FO108W V8	B	60	1h 37m 45.637s	117.788/189.562	+ 1m 02.327s	1m 35.301s 54
12	Kazuki Nakajima	J	17	AT&T Williams	Williams FW31-Toyota RVX-09 V8	B	60	1h 37m 46.186s	117.778/189.545	+ 1m 02.876s	1m 34.238s 49
13	Nelsinho Piquet	BR	8	ING Renault F1 Team	Renault R29-RS27 V8	B	60	1h 37m 51.638s	117.668/189.369	+ 1m 08.328s	1m 34.876s 46
14	Robert Kubica	PL	5	BMW Sauber F1 Team	BMW Sauber F1.09-BMW P86/9 V8	B	60	1h 37m 52.865s	117.644/189.329	+ 1m 09.555s	1m 34.537s 47
15	Adrian Sutil	D	20	Force India F1 Team	Force India VJM02-Mercedes FO108W V8	B	60	1h 37m 55.251s	117.596/189.252	+ 1m 11.941s	1m 35.366s 43
16	Sébastien Buemi	CH	12	Scuderia Toro Rosso	Toro Rosso STR04-Ferrari 056 V8	B	60	1h 38m 13.535s	117.231/188.665	+ 1m 30.225s	1m 36.279s 24
17	Jarno Trulli	I	9	Panasonic Toyota Racing	Toyota TF109-RVX-09 V8	B	60	1h 38m 14.280s	117.216/188.641	+ 1m 30.970s	1m 33.654s 52
18	Lewis Hamilton	GB	1	Vodafone McLaren Mercedes	McLaren MP4-24-Mercedes FO108W V8	B	59			+ 1 lap	1m 35.367s 46
	Kimi Räikkönen	FIN	4	Scuderia Ferrari Marlboro	Ferrari F60-056 V8	B	34	radiator damage			1m 36.080s 4
	Sébastien Bourdais	F	11	Scuderia Toro Rosso	Toro Rosso STR04-Ferrari 056 V8	B	18	hydraulics			1m 37.498s 10

Fastest race lap: Fernando Alonso on lap 49, 1m 33.365s, 123.341mph/198.498km/h.

Lap record: Juan Pablo Montoya (Williams FW23-BMW V10), 1m 18.354s, 130.070mph/209.326km (2001) (2.831-mile/4.556km circuit).

Lap record (current configuration): Michael Schumacher (Ferrari F2004 V10), 1m 29.468s, 128.714mph/207.144km/h (2004)

11	BOURDAIS · Toro Rosso
12	BUEMI · Toro Rosso
16	ROSBERG · Williams
17	NAKAJIMA · Williams
6	HEIDFELD · BMW Sauber
4	RÄIKKÖNEN · Ferrari
10	GLOCK · Toyota 3-place penalty for impeding - started from pit lane
21	FISICHELLA · Force India
5	KUBICA · BMW Sauber
9	TRULLI · Toyota
7	ALONSO · Renault
8	PIQUET · Renault

All results and data © FOM 2009

Grid order	1	2	3	4	5	6	7	8	9	10	11	12	13	14	15	16	17	18	19	20	21	22	23	24	25	26	27	28	29	30	31	32	33	34	35	36	37	38	39	40	41	42	43	44	45	46
14 WEBBER	23	23	23	23	23	23	23	23	23	23	23	23	23	14	14	14	14	14	3	3	3	3	3	23	23	23	23	23	23	14	14	14	14	14	14	14	14	14	14	14	15	14	14
23 BARRICHELLO	14	14	14	14	14	14	14	14	14	14	14	14	14	3	3	3	3	3	23	23	23	23	23	20	20	16	16	14	14	23	15	15	15	15	15	15	15	15	15	14	3	16
22 BUTTON	2	2	2	2	2	2	2	2	2	2	2	2	23	23	23	23	15	4	4	4	20	3	16	20	14	16	22	22	15	3	3	3	3	3	3	3	3	3	3	16	23
15 VETTEL	3	22	22	22	22	22	22	22	22	22	22	22	3	3	15	15	15	15	4	20	20	20	16	16	14	14	22	22	15	3	16	16	16	16	16	16	16	16	16	16	23	22
1 HAMILTON	22	3	3	3	3	3	3	3	3	3	15	15	2	4	4	4	4	20	15	16	16	4	14	22	22	15	15	3	3	16	23	23	23	23	23	23	23	23	23	23	22	15
2 KOVALAINEN	15	15	15	15	15	15	15	15	15	15	4	4	4	20	20	20	16	16	5	14	14	22	6	15	3	3	16	4	22	22	22	22	22	22	22	22	22	22	15	7
20 SUTIL	4	4	4	4	4	4	4	4	4	4	22	20	20	16	16	16	5	5	14	22	22	6	8	3	4	4	4	22	4	2	2	2	2	2	2	7	7	7	7	7	5
3 MASSA	20	20	20	20	20	20	20	20	20	20	16	16	5	5	14	14	22	5	6	8	15	4	2	2	2	2	21	7	7	7	7	2	6	6	6	6	6	8
4 RÄIKKÖNEN	16	16	16	16	16	16	16	16	16	16	5	21	21	21	22	22	6	6	8	15	3	2	17	17	21	10	10	5	5	6	6	6	8
8 PIQUET	5	5	5	5	5	5	5	5	5	5	21	7	7	6	22	12	12	8	15	4	4	17	21	21	10	10	7	21	5	10	5	5	5	5	8	8	17	17	17
6 HEIDFELD	7	7	7	7	7	7	7	7	7	7	21	7	7	6	22	12	12	8	15	2	2	21	20	10	10	17	7	7	5	6	8	8	17	17	5	20	20
7 ALONSO	6	6	6	6	6	6	21	21	7	6	12	22	12	8	8	12	2	2	17	17	7	10	7	7	5	12	6	12	12	17	17	20	20	20	2	2
17 NAKAJIMA	12	12	12	21	21	21	6	6	6	6	12	12	22	12	8	2	2	17	21	21	10	7	5	6	8	12	8	17	20	20	2	2	2	10	10
9 TRULLI	21	21	21	12	12	12	12	12	12	12	22	8	8	2	17	17	10	21	10	10	5	12	6	6	8	17	10	10	10	10	10	21	21
16 ROSBERG	8	8	8	8	8	8	8	8	8	8	2	17	10	10	10	7	7	12	12	6	4	17	20	20	10	21	21	21	21	21	5	5
5 KUBICA	9	10	10	10	10	10	10	10	10	10	17	10	21	21	7	7	5	5	6	6	8	6	8	8	9	9	9	9	9	9	9	9
12 BUEMI	11	11	17	17	17	17	17	17	17	17	10	9	9	9	9	9	5	8	20	20	20	20	9	9	12	12	12	12	12	12
21 FISICHELLA	10	17	11	11	11	11	11	11	11	11	9	9	7	9	9	9	9	9	9	9	9	9	9	1	1	1	1	1	1	1	1	1
11 BOURDAIS	17	9	9	9	9	9	9	9	9	9	9	9	11	1	1	1	1	1	1	1	1	1
10 GLOCK	1	1	1	1	1	1	1	1	1	1	1	1	1	1	1	1	1	1	1

14 Drive-thru pena*

TIME SHEETS

PRACTICE 1 (FRIDAY)
Cloudy/sunny
(track 13-18°C, air 13-18°C)

Pos.	Driver	Laps	Time
1	Mark Webber	19	1m 33.082s
2	Jenson Button	18	1m 33.463s
3	Felipe Massa	21	1m 33.745s
4	Jarno Trulli	23	1m 33.795s
5	Giancarlo Fisichella	26	1m 33.839s
6	Kimi Räikkönen	23	1m 33.840s
7	Nico Rosberg	26	1m 33.902s
8	Sebastian Vettel	13	1m 33.909s
9	Kazuki Nakajima	25	1m 33.952s
10	Fernando Alonso	16	1m 34.148s
11	Nick Heidfeld	25	1m 34.221s
12	Rubens Barrichello	17	1m 34.227s
13	Lewis Hamilton	14	1m 34.483s
14	Robert Kubica	23	1m 34.694s
15	Nelsinho Piquet	24	1m 34.738s
16	Sébastien Bourdais	27	1m 34.827s
17	Sébastien Buemi	28	1m 34.878s
18	Heikki Kovalainen	26	1m 34.893s
19	Timo Glock	23	1m 34.911s
20	Adrian Sutil	6	1m 35.092s

PRACTICE 2 (FRIDAY)
Cloudy/drizzle
(track 17-18°C, air 15-16°C)

Pos.	Driver	Laps	Time
1	Lewis Hamilton	23	1m 32.149s
2	Sebastian Vettel	31	1m 32.331s
3	Jenson Button	32	1m 32.369s
4	Mark Webber	28	1m 32.480s
5	Jarno Trulli	32	1m 32.511s
6	Adrian Sutil	32	1m 32.585s
7	Rubens Barrichello	26	1m 32.664s
8	Fernando Alonso	24	1m 32.774s
9	Kazuki Nakajima	32	1m 32.872s
10	Nelsinho Piquet	29	1m 32.992s
11	Nick Heidfeld	36	1m 33.012s
12	Felipe Massa	34	1m 33.052s
13	Nico Rosberg	34	1m 33.128s
14	Robert Kubica	28	1m 33.161s
15	Timo Glock	34	1m 33.172s
16	Kimi Räikkönen	29	1m 33.182s
17	Heikki Kovalainen	27	1m 33.724s
18	Sébastien Buemi	30	1m 33.903s
19	Sébastien Bourdais	30	1m 34.025s
20	Giancarlo Fisichella	3	1m 38.877s

PRACTICE 3 (SATURDAY)
Cloudy
(track 16-17°C, air 15°C)

Pos.	Driver	Laps	Time
1	Lewis Hamilton	16	1m 31.121s
2	Fernando Alonso	18	1m 31.340s
3	Felipe Massa	20	1m 31.351s
4	Sebastian Vettel	17	1m 31.542s
5	Mark Webber	16	1m 31.610s
6	Kimi Räikkönen	19	1m 31.615s
7	Jarno Trulli	23	1m 31.620s
8	Nico Rosberg	20	1m 31.690s
9	Kazuki Nakajima	20	1m 31.731s
10	Nick Heidfeld	21	1m 31.928s
11	Jenson Button	22	1m 32.009s
12	Timo Glock	20	1m 32.022s
13	Adrian Sutil	20	1m 32.104s
14	Rubens Barrichello	13	1m 32.124s
15	Giancarlo Fisichella	21	1m 32.135s
16	Nelsinho Piquet	15	1m 32.223s
17	Sébastien Buemi	23	1m 32.239s
18	Robert Kubica	20	1m 32.269s
19	Heikki Kovalainen	18	1m 32.742s
20	Sébastien Bourdais	21	1m 32.883s

QUALIFYING (SATURDAY)
Cloudy/drizzle (track 18-19° C, air 16-17° C)

Pos.	Driver	First	Second	Third	Weight
1	Mark Webber	**1m 31.257s**	1m 38.038s	**1m 32.230s**	661kg
2	Rubens Barrichello	1m 31.482s	**1m 34.455s**	1m 32.357s	647kg
3	Jenson Button	1m 31.568s	1m 39.032s	1m 32.473s	644kg
4	Sebastian Vettel	1m 31.430s	1m 39.504s	1m 32.480s	661kg
5	Lewis Hamilton	1m 31.473s	1m 39.149s	1m 32.616s	654.5kg
6	Heikki Kovalainen	1m 31.881s	1m 40.826s	1m 33.859s	664kg
7	Adrian Sutil	1m 32.015s	1m 36.740s	1m 34.316s	678.5g
8	Felipe Massa	1m 31.600s	1m 41.708s	1m 34.574s	673.5kg
9	Kimi Räikkönen	1m 31.869s	1m 41.730s	1m 34.710s	674kg
10	Nelsinho Piquet	1m 32.128s	1m 35.737s	1m 34.803s	676kg
11	Nick Heidfeld	1m 31.771s	1m 42.310s		681kg
12	Fernando Alonso	1m 31.302s	1m 42.318s		668.2kg
13	Kazuki Nakajima	1m 31.884s	1m 42.500s		683.6kg
14	Jarno Trulli	1m 31.760s	1m 42.771s		683.7kg
15	Nico Rosberg	1m 31.598s	1m 42.859s		689.5kg
16	Robert Kubica	1m 32.190s			673.5kg
17	Sébastien Buemi	1m 32.251s			674.5kg
18	Giancarlo Fisichella	1m 32.402s			662.5kg
19	Timo Glock	1m 32.423s			662.3kg
20	Sébastien Bourdais	1m 33.559s			689.5kg

DID YOU KNOW?

The last time pole was achieved by an Australian was in Germany 1980, and the last time an Australian won was in Las Vegas 1981 (both Alan Jones). Mark Webber became the third Australian pole position and winning driver, after Jack Brabham and Alan Jones.

This was the first grand prix where the Australian national anthem was played for the winner.

POINTS

DRIVERS

1	Jenson Button	68
2	Sebastian Vettel	47
3	Mark Webber	45.5
4	Rubens Barrichello	44
5	Felipe Massa	22
6	Jarno Trulli	21.5
7	Nico Rosberg	20.5
8	Timo Glock	13
9	Fernando Alonso	13
10	Kimi Räikkönen	10
11	Lewis Hamilton	9
12	Nick Heidfeld	6
13	Heikki Kovalainen	5
14	Sébastien Buemi	3
15	Robert Kubica	2
16	Sébastien Bourdais	2

CONSTRUCTORS

1	Brawn	112
2	Red Bull	92.5
3	Toyota	34.5
4	Ferrari	32
5	Williams	20.5
6	McLaren	14
7	Renault	13
8	BMW Sauber	8
9	Toro Rosso	5

20 SUTIL · Force India

1 HAMILTON · McLaren

22 BUTTON · Brawn

14 WEBBER · Red Bull

3 MASSA · Ferrari

2 KOVALAINEN · McLaren

15 VETTEL · Red Bull

23 BARRICHELLO · Brawn

8	49	50	51	52	53	54	55	56	57	58	59	60	
4	14	14	14	14	14	14	14	14	14	14	14	14	1
3	23	22	22	15	15	15	15	15	15	15	15	15	2
2	22	23	3	3	3	3	3	3	3	3	3	3	3
5	15	15	15	16	16	16	16	16	16	16	16	16	4
3	3	3	16	22	22	22	22	22	22	22	22	22	5
6	16	16	23	23	23	23	23	23	23	23	23	23	6
7	7	7	7	7	7	7	7	7	7	7	7	7	7
7	17	17	2	2	2	2	2	2	2	2	2	2	8
2	2	2	10	10	10	10	10	10	10	10	10	10	
0	10	10	6	6	6	6	6	6	6	6	6	6	
6	6	6	17	17	17	17	17	17	17	21	21	21	
1	21	21	21	21	21	21	21	21	21	17	17	17	
3	8	8	8	8	8	8	8	8	8	8	8	8	
5	5	5	5	5	5	5	5	5	5	5	5	5	
0	20	20	20	20	20	20	20	20	20	20	20	20	
9	9	12	12	12	12	12	12	9	12	12	12	12	
2	12	9	9	9	9	9	9	12	9	9	9	9	
1	1	1	1	1	1	1	1	1	1	1	1	1	

2 Pit stop   *1 One lap or more behind*

RACE TYRE STRATEGIES

The tyre regulations stipulate that two dry tyre specifications must be used during the race.

The Soft compound Bridgestone Potenza tyre is marked with a green stripe on the sidewall of the tyre.

	Driver	Race Stint 1	Race Stint 2	Race Stint 3	Race Stint 4
1	Mark Webber	Super Soft: 1-19	Medium: 20-43	Medium: 44-60	
2	Sebastian Vettel	Super Soft: 1-21	Medium: 22-44	Super Soft: 45-60	
3	Felipe Massa	Super Soft: 1-25	Super Soft: 26-45	Medium: 46-60	
4	Nico Rosberg	Hard: 1-26	Hard: 27-47	Soft: 48-60	
5	Jenson Button	Super Soft: 1-13	Super Soft: 14-31	Medium: 32-51	Super Soft: 52-60
6	Rubens Barrichello	Super Soft: 1-14	Super Soft: 15-32	Medium: 33-50	Medium: 51-60
7	Fernando Alonso	Super Soft: 1-17	Medium: 18-46	Medium: 47-60	
8	Heikki Kovalainen	Super Soft: 1-15	Medium: 16-40	Medium: 41-60	
9	Timo Glock	Medium: 1-37	Super Soft: 38-60		
10	Nick Heidfeld	Super Soft: 1-26	Super Soft: 27-47	Medium: 48-60	
11	Giancarlo Fisichella	Super Soft: 1-18	Super Soft: 19-35	Medium: 36-60	
12	Kazuki Nakajima	Medium: 1-31	Super Soft: 32-50	Super Soft: 51-60	
13	Nelson Piquet	Medium: 1-26	Medium: 27-47	Super Soft: 48-60	
14	Robert Kubica	Super Soft: 1-23	Medium: 24-44	Super Soft: 45-60	
15	Adrian Sutil	Medium: 1-27	Medium: 28	Medium: 29-46	Super Soft: 47-60
16	Sébastien Buemi	Super Soft: 1-21	Super Soft: 22-38	Medium: 39-60	
17	Jarno Trulli	Super Soft: 1-2	Super Soft: 3-21	Medium: 22-49	Super Soft: 50-60
18	Lewis Hamilton	Super Soft: 1	Medium: 2-37	Super Soft: 38-59	
	Kimi Räikkönen	Super Soft: 1-24	Super Soft: 25-34 (dnf)		
	Sébastien Bourdais	Soft: 1-18 (dnf)			

HUNGARIAN GRAND PRIX

HUNGARORING CIRCUIT

After his disappointment at the Nürburgring, Lewis Hamilton took full advantage of the McLaren's upgraded specification to produce a commanding victory in the Hungarian Grand Prix.
Photo: Peter J. Fox

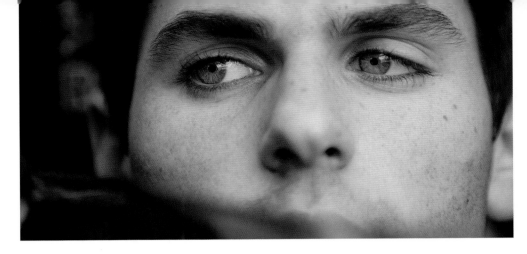

HUNGARORING QUALIFYING

ONE moment it was a routine discussion – track conditions, tyre performance, handling characteristics – but the airwaves fell suddenly silent. Up on the pit wall, Ferrari personnel were perplexed, but then the TV director focused on Felipe Massa's stationary F60, wedged in the Turn Four tyre wall, and the team radio chimed in again. There were no words, though, only cries of pain.

These were times of heightened sensitivity for motor racing, following the death six days previously of Henry Surtees, struck on the crash helmet by a stray wheel while competing in an FIA Formula Two race at Brands Hatch. That had been an accident in the term's truest sense, something that occurs by chance, and it seemed barely possible that a similar set of circumstances should arise so soon afterwards.

Aided by a thimble of fuel, Fernando Alonso took pole for Renault, ahead of the Red Bulls of Sebastian Vettel and Mark Webber, and Lewis Hamilton's McLaren, but a potentially interesting discussion point was completely overshadowed by events during Q2's closing moments.

Massa had just completed a timed lap and was approaching Turn Four at an estimated 160mph when he was struck on the head by an 800g coil spring that had tumbled from Rubens Barrichello's Brawn. Instantly rendered unconscious, Massa continued at significant speed, with his feet riding both throttle and brake, until he hit the tyre wall. The initial impact left the Brazilian with a fractured skull, an injury from which he subsequently recovered with remarkable speed, although it would sideline him for the balance of the season. A couple of inches one way, and the spring would have missed him; a couple of inches the other, and almost certainly the blow would have been fatal. Tiny margins, stark contrasts…

A couple of days beforehand, Massa had spoken eloquently about the hurdles facing Jaime Alguersuari, Toro Rosso's choice to replace the axed Sébastien Bourdais and poised to become the youngest driver ever to compete in a world championship grand prix, aged 19 years and 125 days. "I made my debut at 20," Massa said, "and that was way too soon. I committed far too many errors, and that was after spending all winter testing an F1 car. He has only driven the Toro Rosso in a straight line…"

The following morning, ironically, Massa went bounding off the track at the dawn of his first timed run while Alguersuari completed 82 laps without putting a foot wrong. He qualified last, predictably, but it was a performance without shame, albeit another talking point whose relevance had passed.

As a precaution, Brawn replaced the springs on championship leader Jenson Button's car ahead of Q3, leaving him with time for only a single run in a car that had already been fuelled to do two. He struggled to eighth, five positions ahead of Barrichello.

"It'll be tough starting from 13th at a circuit where overtaking is almost impossible," the Brazilian driver said, "but that is unimportant. My thoughts right now are with Felipe and his family."

THE moment was probably lost on a cluster of youngsters, who were busily pulling stunts with their radio-controlled Ferraris, executing doughnuts and, with unconscious irony, using the McLaren motorhome's underbelly as their temporary racetrack. They made it look blissfully simple, but then that had been the day's motif. As they played, they seemed wholly oblivious to the gathering tumult, wherein champagne flutes were the accessory of the moment. Most of those doing the drinking wore the day-glo orange T-shirts that symbolise a McLaren victory, the first time such apparel had been seen for nine months.

Fernando Alonso's wispy fuel load enabled him to make a clean break at the start, but he knew even then that he was racing for a top-three finish rather than victory: Renault's abacus suggested the podium was eminently achievable on a three-stop strategy.

Behind the Spaniard, the Red Bulls were swamped by the KERS bullies amassed in their wake. Lewis Hamilton, Heikki Kovalainen and Kimi Räikkönen sprinted through from fourth, sixth and seventh to hassle the Red Bulls of Sebastian Vettel and Mark Webber, initially second and third, but now distinctly vulnerable.

Hamilton's start was especially good, a simultaneous blend of attack, defence and improvisation. It carried him past Vettel and Webber, but he skated slightly wide at Turn One's exit and the Australian reclaimed second. Räikkönen annexed fourth, from Nico Rosberg and Kovalainen, and Vettel was the one left standing when the music stopped.

The German had started on soft Bridgestones, rather than the super-softs favoured by most, because lessons learned in Monaco – where he'd trashed a set of the latter within a handful of laps – had made him cautious. Despite a mediocre start from the dirtier side of the track, he was still alongside Räikkönen as they came out of Turn One, but the Finn edged across to avoid Webber and hit the other Red Bull's front left wheel. Given that F1 stewards tend to launch an investigation if anybody so much as sneezes in the paddock, this was duly examined, but was adjudged to be a simple racing incident and no action was taken. "I didn't even notice I'd touched somebody," Räikkönen said. "I was between, I think, Mark and somebody else, but didn't feel anything."

However, Vettel's afternoon was ruined. He would spend the first stint at the tail end of the leading group, in seventh place, but damage inflicted during the race's opening seconds caused his front left suspension to wilt, and the car would be withdrawn shortly before half-distance.

The first-corner squabble allowed Alonso to pull 1.2 seconds clear during the opening lap, with Webber heading Hamilton, Räikkönen, Rosberg, Vettel, Kazuki Nakajima, Jenson Button, Jarno Trulli, Nelson Piquet, Timo Glock, Robert Kubica, Sébastien Buemi, Nick Heidfeld, Rubens Barrichello (nudged wide at Turn Two by an anonymous assailant, which cost him several places and a scuffed left sidepod), Giancarlo Fisichella and Jaime Alguersuari, while Adrian Sutil headed straight for the pits. His water temperature read-out had displayed discouraging messages during the formation lap, and the numbers became even more critical within a single racing lap, so he retired to save the engine.

Alonso was three seconds clear within four laps, but the balance of power shifted at the start of the fifth, when Hamilton challenged Webber on the run down to Turn One, breezing by around the outside through the right-handed kink that follows.

"I used most of my KERS on the straight," Hamilton said. "I thought I'd be able to get Mark in Turn One, but he blocked me. I went to the outside and might have used a little bit of KERS at first, but then I ran out. Mark was in my blind spot eventually, so I couldn't really see him. I gave him plenty of room and eventually saw him fade into the background. It was quite a straightforward move, but clearly Mark was

Right: Kimi Räikkönen's strong run to second place gave Ferrari a little bit of a boost after Massa's dreadful shunt.

Below: Squeezing out the sparks. Kazuki Nakajima at full chat in his Williams-Toyota.
Photos: Peter J. Fox

Bottom: Alonso's pole winning pace heralded little when it came to the race, as his Renault shed an insecurely fastened front wheel after its first pit stop.
Photo: Peter Nygaard/GP Photo

very smart: he's got to score points and there's no real sense in taking silly risks. I needed to get past, but I was completely surprised that I'd even been able to keep up with him, let alone overtake and pull away while still looking after my tyres."

Hamilton immediately increased his pace by about 0.5 seconds per lap, and Alonso's advantage began to shrink. By the time the Spaniard came in for his first scheduled stop, on lap 12, the gap was little more than a second and his cameo was about to come to an abrupt end.

From the second lap, Alonso had been troubled by a fuel pump problem that the team was trying to manage remotely, but his pace masked the concerns. When he stopped, however, the team failed to secure his front right wheel properly and it wobbled for a few corners before unfastening itself and bouncing away down the road.

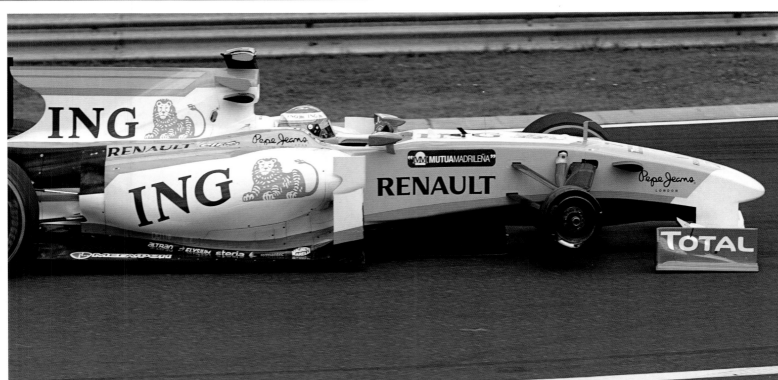

The image had a particular poignancy in the light of recent events *(see Qualifying)*. Although the errant rim didn't inflict any damage, subsequently Renault was banned from competing in the Grand Prix of Europe for sending the car out in an unsafe condition and then failing to instruct Alonso to stop when he radioed in to report what he thought was a puncture. The penalty was overturned on appeal, however, and instead Renault was issued with a $50,000 fine and a reprimand.

Alonso was able to return to the pits on three wheels and rejoin the race one lap in arrears, but the fuel pump malady obliged him to retire soon afterwards.

Hamilton would have eased ahead anyway after the opening round of stops, and the balance of the afternoon looked remarkably easy. He made scheduled stops on laps 20 and 46, and saw other cars only when he lapped them. Even in straitened times at the season's dawn, the McLaren had always been strong in tight, slow corners of the kind that proliferate in Budapest – he might also have challenged for victory in Monaco, remember, but for a qualifying accident. Given how desperate the team's situation had looked at Silverstone, only two races beforehand, the transformation was remarkable. The circuit character-

istics helped, although they weren't the only factor.

"It's an incredible feeling to be back here after what feels like such a long time and after such a struggle," Hamilton said. "I am so proud of the guys when I go to the factory and see how hard everyone is pushing. They all want to win just as much as I do and have never given up. Undoubtedly we have caught up quite a bit. The latest aero improvements have given the car a much better balance, but we never felt we had the pace to win this weekend."

It was something of a landmark success – the first in F1 for a car with KERS – but just how straightforward had it been? "The most pleasing thing," said McLaren team principal Martin Whitmarsh, "is that Lewis was in complete control. From about lap 20, he was saying, 'Tell me what lap time you want me to do and I'll set it.' He was in cruise mode."

Webber lost second place during the first round of stops. He and Räikkönen came in together, on lap 19, but Red Bull's lollipop man began to move slightly too early: Webber made a false start and lost a couple of seconds while his right rear wheel was secured properly. Then the two cars almost collided as Webber rejoined – subsequently, the team was reprimanded for allowing him to do so in an unsafe fashion – and Räikkönen was away.

Webber was further compromised by a last-minute change of heart over tyres – he had asked for softs, rather than the more suitable super-softs, and thus was destined to lose out for the next 31 laps. "That was my call," he said, "because I was worried about the length of the stint, and it was quite difficult to know which compound to choose."

It was Räikkönen's turn to lose a few seconds during the final stops. Ferrari was concerned about the temperature of the Finn's right-hand exhaust and asked him to restart manually, rather than relying on automated systems that generate supplementary heat. In the process, he accidentally triggered the anti-stall, but by then he was sufficiently far ahead of Webber for the delay to be inconsequential.

Rosberg, so often beneath the radar, drove solidly once again to take his second consecutive fourth place. A fuel rig problem at the first stop cost him a couple of seconds, just enough to ensure he remained behind Webber at that stage, but he was pleased with his afternoon's toil. "Today was quite tricky," he said, "especially against the KERS cars at the start. I had no chance off the line, but the first corner was quite a big mess and I managed to climb back to fifth, which was important. As the race settled down, I had to manage the tyres cautiously, because

of graining during the first and second stints, so given all these issues I have to be happy."

Kovalainen took fifth, which might have looked better had his team-mate not been more than half a minute up the road, and faced an unexpected challenge during the closing stages. Second here on merit one year before, Glock started only 13th, but shuffled up the order while underlining the super-soft Bridgestone's longevity during a 32-lap first stint that was impressive in its consistency. Then he stayed out for another 28 laps, during which he briefly put Räikkönen under a fair bit of pressure, before finally pitting again to complete the remaining ten laps on the soft Bridgestone. A triumph for strategy over speed, it was beautifully executed.

Team-mate Trulli claimed the final point, but the Toyotas were separated by Button, who maintained his 100-per-cent scoring record and was relieved to concede championship points to only Webber. "Overall the weekend has been a disappointment," he said. "When it was really hot on Friday, our car was really looking after its tyres and had less wear than anybody. Since the temperature dropped, though, we have been destroying the rears. I did all I could to look after them, but after five laps, they were shot. I lost a place to Nakajima at the start, but repassed him on lap two and tried to stick with the cars ahead,

because I was running a long stint and felt I could jump a few places after the stops. With the tyres the way they were, though, I couldn't keep up."

On Monday, as the circus filtered away from town, temperatures were back where they had been on Friday...

Nakajima and Barrichello were right on Trulli's tail throughout the final stint, with Heidfeld, Piquet and Kubica – the last unlapped runner – not far behind. A maudlin little trio, that, for BMW would announce four days later that it intended quitting F1 at the season's end. Piquet, meanwhile, was tipped to be dropped after a string of disappointing performances. It would be three weeks before Renault made any official announcement, but the Brazilian did the job for the team within a matter of days, issuing a press release that combined the confirmation of his departure with a blistering attack on team principal Flavio Briatore. A pity his driving hadn't shown quite that much venom during the previous 18 months.

Fisichella, Alguersuari and Buemi completed the finishers. It was a worthy effort by the young Spaniard, who had finally laid to rest the statistical curiosity about whether Mike Thackwell counted as F1's youngest ever starter. The New Zealander had been on the original grid for the 1980 Canadian Grand Prix, but was absent when the race was restarted over the

full distance following a shunt on the first lap.

Alguersuari had just become the definitive pub-quiz answer and silenced critics of Toro Rosso's embryo selection policy with a reassuring, error-free weekend. It had been team-mate Buemi who had spent almost as much time off the track as on it. "I just tried to be consistent," Alguersuari said. "My problems were probably more mental than physical, although my back was hurting and I felt absolutely destroyed with about five laps to go. My target was to finish, though, and it was important to achieve that." Any word for those who had questioned his graduation? "I know what I can do," he said, "and don't give a shit what they think."

That's them told, then.

While the champagne corks popped at McLaren and TV cameras swarmed around a stray Pussycat Doll who was leaping around by the motorhome entrance, Hamilton didn't allow the clamour to deflect his attention from what mattered most. "Despite our celebrations," he said, "it's important to remember that there's a guy lying in a hospital bed tonight. I think I speak on behalf of everyone when I say we had Felipe Massa in our hearts and minds today, and wish him a speedy recovery."

A worthy winner, and gracious with it.

Simon Arron

EDITOR'S VIEW
BMW TO QUIT FORMULA ONE, OTHER TEAMS TO FOLLOW?

THE not-altogether-surprising news that the woefully underperforming BMW Sauber team intended to withdraw from Formula One at the end of the 2009 season inevitably triggered speculation that others might follow the German car maker out of the sport, if not in 2009, at the end of 2010.

Toyota moved quickly to reassure everybody that its F1 plans were not currently under review and that it was committed to the sport long-term, although it wanted to see a structured programme of cost reductions introduced over the following couple of years. However, pit-lane speculation that Toyota had offered Jarno Trulli a one-year extension of his contract further fuelled suspicions that the team could – indeed would – withdraw in 2010.

FOTA, the F1 teams' association, sought to soften the blow dealt by BMW by making it clear that the association would offer all possible assistance to enable the team to continue, possibly as a privateer operation similar to Brawn, but the FIA issued a statement that effectively said, "We told you so."

"The FIA regrets the announcement of BMW's intended withdrawal from F1, but it is not surprised by it," ran the baldly unsympathetic statement, which continued, "It has been clear for some time that motor sport cannot ignore the world economic crisis. Car manufacturers cannot be expected to continue to pour large sums of money into F1 when their survival depends on redundancies, plant closures and the support of the taxpayer.

"This is why the FIA prepared regulations to reduce costs drastically. Had these regulations not been so strongly opposed by a number of team principals, the withdrawal of BMW and further such announcements in the future could have been avoided."

At the time of writing, no obvious potential buyers for the BMW Sauber team had emerged. The factory at Hinwil, near Zurich, is one of the best equipped in the F1 business, but, being based in Switzerland, it has a very high cost base.

Meanwhile, the fledgling Epislon Euskadi team, which failed to gain an entry in the 2010 World Championship, indicated that it would be interested in taking BMW Sauber's place on the starting grid for that season if there were a vacancy.

Truth be told, one could see the whole texture and character of F1 changing significantly over the coming years. The fact that Jarno Trulli was offered a one-year extension to his Toyota contract raises inevitable speculation that the manufacturer will follow rival Honda out of the sport at the end of 2010. As we would soon find out, Toyota would be making arrangements to pack up their traps and prepare their caravan for moving out at the end of the current season.

Thankfully Lewis Hamilton's victory at Budapest seemed certain to take the sting out of any pressure for Mercedes to re-think their fundamental commitment to F1, although the texture of this commitment would change dramatically when they bought the Brawn squad at the end of the year, signalling a gradual wind-down of their investment in the McLaren Group. But, on the other hand, it would be a brave man who risked a large amount of money betting that Renault stays in on an open-ended basis. As engine suppliers perhaps, as they have done in the past.

As Bob Dylan once sang, "The times they are a changing."

Alan Henry

Above: Rare sight in 2009, a podium without a Brawn driver somewhere on it!
Photo: Peter Nygaard/GP Photo

Above right: BMW called a halt to their Formula One programme.

Right: Jarno Trulli's prospects of remaining with Toyota in 2010 attracted a lot of debate and speculation.
Photos: Peter J. Fox

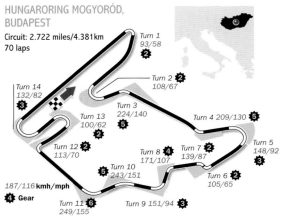

HUNGARORING MOGYORÓD, BUDAPEST

Circuit: 2.722 miles/4.381km
70 laps

Turn 1 93/58
Turn 2 108/67
Turn 3 224/140
Turn 4 209/130
Turn 5 148/92
Turn 6 105/65
Turn 7 139/87
Turn 8 171/107
Turn 9 151/94
Turn 10 243/151
Turn 11 249/155
Turn 12 113/70
Turn 13 100/62
Turn 14 132/82

187/116 kmh/mph
 Gear

FIA F1 WORLD CHAMPIONSHIP ROUND 10

ING
MAGYAR NAGYDÍJ

BUDAPEST 24-26 JULY 2009

RACE DISTANCE: 70 laps, 190.531 miles/306.630km • RACE WEATHER: Sunny (track 31-35°C, air 23°C)

Pos.	Driver	Nat.	No.	Entrant	Car/Engine	Tyres	Laps	Time/Retirement	Speed (mph/km/h)	Gap to leader	Fastest race lap	
1	Lewis Hamilton	GB	1	Vodafone McLaren Mercedes	McLaren MP4-24-Mercedes FO108W V8	B	70	1h 38m 23.876s	116.180/186.973		1m 22.479s	16
2	Kimi Räikkönen	FIN	4	Scuderia Ferrari Marlboro	Ferrari F60-056 V8	B	70	1h 38m 35.405s	115.953/186.609	+ 11.529s	1m 22.434s	70
3	Mark Webber	AUS	14	Red Bull Racing	Red Bull RB5-Renault RS27 V8	B	70	1h 38m 40.762s	115.848/186.440	+ 16.886s	1m 21.931s	65
4	Nico Rosberg	D	16	AT&T Williams	Williams FW31-Toyota RVX-09 V8	B	70	1h 38m 50.843s	115.651/186.123	+ 26.967s	1m 22.468s	65
5	Heikki Kovalainen	FIN	2	Vodafone McLaren Mercedes	McLaren MP4-24-Mercedes FO108W V8	B	70	1h 38m 58.268s	115.507/185.890	+ 34.392s	1m 22.958s	63
6	Timo Glock	D	10	Panasonic Toyota Racing	Toyota TF109-RVX-09 V8	B	70	1h 38m 59.113s	115.491/185.864	+ 35.237s	1m 22.506s	63
7	Jenson Button	GB	22	Brawn GP Formula 1 Team	Brawn BGP 001-Mercedes FO108W V8	B	70	1h 39m 18.964s	115.105/185.244	+ 55.088s	1m 22.706s	57
8	Jarno Trulli	I	9	Panasonic Toyota Racing	Toyota TF109-RVX-09 V8	B	70	1h 39m 32.048s	114.854/184.839	+ 1m 08.172s	1m 23.261s	65
9	Kazuki Nakajima	J	17	AT&T Williams	Williams FW31-Toyota RVX-09 V8	B	70	1h 39m 32.650s	114.842/184.820	+ 1m 08.774s	1m 23.180s	55
10	Rubens Barrichello	BR	23	Brawn GP Formula 1 Team	Brawn BGP 001-Mercedes FO108W V8	B	70	1h 39m 33.132s	114.833/184.805	+ 1m 09.256s	1m 23.024s	55
11	Nick Heidfeld	D	6	BMW Sauber F1 Team	BMW Sauber F1.09-BMW P86/9 V8	B	70	1h 39m 34.488s	114.806/184.763	+ 1m 10.612s	1m 23.282s	65
12	Nelsinho Piquet	BR	8	ING Renault F1 Team	Renault R29-RS27 V8	B	70	1h 39m 35.388s	114.789/184.735	+ 1m 11.512s	1m 23.418s	65
13	Robert Kubica	PL	5	BMW Sauber F1 Team	BMW Sauber F1.09-BMW P86/9 V8	B	70	1h 39m 37.922s	114.741/184.657	+ 1m 14.046s	1m 23.224s	65
14	Giancarlo Fisichella	I	21	Force India F1 Team	Force India VJM02-Mercedes FO108W V8	B	69			+ 1 lap	1m 23.174s	40
15	Jaime Alguersuari	E	11	Scuderia Toro Rosso	Toro Rosso STR04-Ferrari 056 V8	B	69			+ 1 lap	1m 23.444s	69
16	Sébastien Buemi	CH	12	Scuderia Toro Rosso	Toro Rosso STR04-Ferrari 056 V8	B	69			+ 1 lap	1m 22.955s	69
	Sebastien Vettel	D	15	Red Bull Racing	Red Bull RB5-Renault RS27 V8	B	29	accident/front suspension			1m 23.457s	18
	Fernando Alonso	E	7	ING Renault F1 Team	Renault R29-RS27 V8	B	15	fuel pump			1m 23.529s	4
	Adrian Sutil	D	20	Force India F1 Team	Force India VJM02-Mercedes FO108W V8	B	1	water temperature			no time	
NS	Felipe Massa	BR	3	Scuderia Ferrari Marlboro	Ferrari F60-056 V8	B		driver injured in qualifying			no time	

Fastest race lap: Mark Webber on lap 65, 1m 21.931s, 119.613mph/192.498km/h.

Lap record: Michael Schumacher (Ferrari F2004 V10), 1m 19.071s, 123.939mph/199.461km/h (2004).

All results and data © FOM 2009

11 ALGUERSUARI · Toro Rosso
20 SUTIL · Force India
6 HEIDFELD · BMW Sauber
10 GLOCK · Toyota
9 TRULLI · Toyota
17 NAKAJIMA · Williams
5 KUBICA · BMW Sauber
21 FISICHELLA · Force India
8 PIQUET · Renault
23 BARRICHELLO · Brawn
12 BUEMI · Toro Rosso

Grid order	1	2	3	4	5	6	7	8	9	10	11	12	13	14	15	16	17	18	19	20	21	22	23	24	25	26	27	28	29	30	31	32	33	34	35	36	37	38	39	40	41	42	43	44	45	46	47	48	49	50	51	52	53
7 ALONSO	7	7	7	7	7	7	7	7	7	7	1	1	1	1	1	1	1	1	2	1	1	1	1	1	1	1	1	1	1	1	1	1	1	1	1	1	1	1	1	1	1	1	1	1	1	1	1	1	1	1	1	1	1
15 VETTEL	14	14	14	14	1	1	1	1	1	1	7	14	14	14	14	14	14	16	15	22	22	22	9	9	9	9	4	4	4	4	4	4	4	4	4	4	4	4	4	4	4	4	4	14	14	14	14	14	4	4	4
14 WEBBER	1	1	1	1	14	14	14	14	14	14	14	4	4	4	4	4	4	2	1	9	9	9	22	4	4	4	10	10	10	14	14	14	14	14	14	14	14	14	14	14	14	14	16	16	16	16	4	10	10	10	1
1 HAMILTON	4	4	4	4	4	4	4	4	4	4	4	16	16	16	16	16	16	15	22	17	8	4	4	10	10	10	14	14	14	2	2	2	2	2	2	2	2	21	16	4	4	4	10	14	14	14	1
16 ROSBERG	16	16	16	16	16	16	16	16	16	16	16	2	2	2	2	2	22	17	8	4	10	10	14	14	2	2	2	16	16	16	16	16	16	16	16	2	10	10	10	10	10	16	16	16	16	1
2 KOVALAINEN	2	2	2	2	2	2	2	2	2	2	15	15	15	15	15	15	17	9	4	10	14	14	2	2	16	16	16	16	23	10	10	10	10	10	10	10	10	10	10	2	2	2	2	2	2	2	2
4 RÄIKKÖNEN	15	15	15	15	15	15	15	15	15	15	22	22	22	22	22	9	8	10	14	2	2	16	16	16	23	23	23	23	10	9	9	9	9	9	9	9	9	9	9	9	9	9	9	9	9	9
22 BUTTON	17	22	22	22	22	22	22	22	22	22	22	17	17	17	17	17	7	8	4	14	2	16	16	15	23	23	9	9	9	22	22	22	22	22	22	22	22	22	22	22	22	22	22	22	22	22
17 NAKAJIMA	22	17	17	17	17	17	17	17	17	17	17	9	9	9	9	9	9	4	10	2	16	15	15	23	21	21	21	22	22	22	22	8	8	8	8	8	8	8	8	8	8	17	17	17	17	17	1
12 BUEMI	9	9	9	9	9	9	9	9	9	9	8	8	8	8	8	8	8	10	14	16	15	12	12	21	22	22	22	8	8	8	17	17	17	17	17	17	17	17	17	17	6	6	5	5	23	23
9 TRULLI	8	8	8	8	8	8	8	8	8	8	10	10	10	10	10	10	10	14	16	15	12	23	23	1	2	15	8	8	17	17	17	6	6	6	6	6	6	6	6	6	8	5	23	23	5	6
23 BARRICHELLO	10	10	10	10	10	10	10	10	10	10	5	5	5	5	5	5	5	5	12	23	21	21	22	11	11	17	6	6	6	5	5	5	5	5	5	5	5	5	5	5	23	6	6	6	8
10 GLOCK	5	5	5	5	5	5	5	5	5	5	6	6	6	6	6	12	12	12	23	21	11	11	11	8	11	6	5	5	23	23	23	23	23	23	23	23	23	23	23	23	8	8	8	5
8 PIQUET	12	12	12	12	12	12	12	12	12	12	12	23	23	23	21	11	8	8	8	17	6	5	12	12	12	12	12	21	21	21	21	21	21	21	11	11	11	11	11	21
6 HEIDFELD	6	6	6	6	6	6	6	6	6	6	23	23	23	23	23	21	11	21	11	17	17	17	6	5	12	21	21	21	21	21	11	11	11	11	11	11	11	11	21	21	21	21	11
21 FISICHELLA	23	23	23	23	23	23	23	23	23	23	21	21	21	21	21	11	11	6	6	6	6	5	12	11	11	11	11	11	11	11	12	12	12	12	12	12	12	12	12	12	12	12	12	12
20 SUTIL	21	21	21	21	21	21	21	21	21	21	11	11	11	11	11	11	6	6	6	5	5	5	5	12	15	15
5 KUBICA	11	11	11	11	11	11	11	11	11	11	11	7	7	7
11 ALGUERSUARI	20

TIME SHEETS

PRACTICE 1 (FRIDAY)
Sunny
(track 30-38°C, air 26-30°C)

Pos.	Driver	Laps	Time
1	Heikki Kovalainen	21	1m 22.278s
2	Nico Rosberg	27	1m 22.337s
3	Lewis Hamilton	20	1m 22.554s
4	Mark Webber	21	1m 22.615s
5	Kazuki Nakajima	25	1m 22.619s
6	Jarno Trulli	17	1m 22.705s
7	Kimi Räikkönen	23	1m 22.796s
8	Felipe Massa	25	1m 22.855s
9	Fernando Alonso	28	1m 23.001s
10	Jenson Button	25	1m 23.130s
11	Robert Kubica	24	1m 23.146s
12	Nick Heidfeld	23	1m 23.154s
13	Rubens Barrichello	24	1m 23.209s
14	Timo Glock	30	1m 23.234s
15	Sebastian Vettel	25	1m 23.283s
16	Giancarlo Fisichella	20	1m 23.484s
17	Nelsinho Piquet	22	1m 23.678s
18	Adrian Sutil	18	1m 23.845s
19	Sébastien Buemi	37	1m 23.998s
20	Jaime Alguersuari	42	1m 24.228s

PRACTICE 2 (FRIDAY)
Sunny
(track 41-43°C, air 30°C)

Pos.	Driver	Laps	Time
1	Lewis Hamilton	36	1m 22.079s
2	Heikki Kovalainen	36	1m 22.126s
3	Nico Rosberg	47	1m 22.154s
4	Mark Webber	29	1m 22.369s
5	Kazuki Nakajima	40	1m 22.426s
6	Sebastian Vettel	30	1m 22.550s
7	Rubens Barrichello	38	1m 22.641s
8	Jarno Trulli	28	1m 22.663s
9	Nick Heidfeld	43	1m 22.690s
10	Timo Glock	45	1m 22.751s
11	Kimi Räikkönen	38	1m 22.763s
12	Fernando Alonso	37	1m 22.793s
13	Jenson Button	42	1m 22.806s
14	Robert Kubica	36	1m 22.870s
15	Nelsinho Piquet	36	1m 22.927s
16	Adrian Sutil	28	1m 22.978s
17	Giancarlo Fisichella	39	1m 23.029s
18	Felipe Massa	32	1m 23.156s
19	Sébastien Buemi	45	1m 23.176s
20	Jaime Alguersuari	40	1m 23.942s

PRACTICE 3 (SATURDAY)
Cloudy/sunny
(track 31-36°C, air 24°C)

Pos.	Driver	Laps	Time
1	Lewis Hamilton	19	1m 21.009s
2	Nick Heidfeld	23	1m 21.408s
3	Nico Rosberg	21	1m 21.509s
4	Heikki Kovalainen	20	1m 21.655s
5	Sébastien Buemi	23	1m 21.800s
6	Timo Glock	12	1m 21.849s
7	Felipe Massa	19	1m 21.911s
8	Kazuki Nakajima	19	1m 21.935s
9	Mark Webber	16	1m 21.936s
10	Sebastian Vettel	21	1m 21.971s
11	Robert Kubica	20	1m 22.076s
12	Jarno Trulli	25	1m 22.097s
13	Rubens Barrichello	22	1m 22.101s
14	Nelsinho Piquet	17	1m 22.210s
15	Kimi Räikkönen	20	1m 22.270s
16	Fernando Alonso	19	1m 22.274s
17	Jenson Button	22	1m 22.312s
18	Jaime Alguersuari	20	1m 22.391s
19	Giancarlo Fisichella	23	1m 22.684s
20	Adrian Sutil	16	1m 23.231s

QUALIFYING (SATURDAY)
Partly cloudy/sunny (track 31-36°C, air 24°C)

Pos.	Driver	First	Second	Third	Weight
1	Fernando Alonso	1m 21.313s	1m 20.826s	**1m 21.569s**	637.5kg
2	Sebastian Vettel	1m 21.178s	1m 20.604s	1m 21.607s	655kg
3	Mark Webber	1m 20.964s	**1m 20.358s**	1m 21.741s	652kg
4	Lewis Hamilton	1m 20.842s	1m 20.465s	1m 21.839s	650.5kg
5	Nico Rosberg	**1m 20.793s**	1m 20.862s	1m 21.890s	654kg
6	Heikki Kovalainen	1m 21.659s	1m 20.807s	1m 22.095s	655kg
7	Kimi Räikkönen	1m 21.500s	1m 20.647s	1m 22.468s	651.5kg
8	Jenson Button	1m 21.471s	1m 20.707s	1m 22.511s	664.5kg
9	Kazuki Nakajima	1m 21.407s	1m 20.525s	1m 22.835s	658kg
10	Felipe Massa	1m 21.420s	1m 20.823s	no time	
11	Sébastien Buemi	1m 21.571s	1m 21.002s		671.5kg
12	Jarno Trulli	1m 21.416s	1m 21.082s		671.3kg
13	Rubens Barrichello	1m 21.558s	1m 21.222s		689kg
14	Timo Glock	1m 21.584s	1m 21.242s		679.2kg
15	Nelsinho Piquet	1m 21.278s	1m 21.389s		667.7kg
16	Nick Heidfeld	1m 21.738s			658kg
17	Giancarlo Fisichella	1m 21.807s			680.5kg
18	Adrian Sutil	1m 21.868s			683.5kg
19	Robert Kubica	1m 21.901s			666kg
20	Jaime Alguersuari	1m 22.359s			675.5kg

4 — RÄIKKÖNEN · Ferrari

16 — ROSBERG · Williams

14 — WEBBER · Red Bull

7 — ALONSO · Renault

22 — BUTTON · Brawn

2 — KOVALAINEN · McLaren

1 — HAMILTON · McLaren

15 — VETTEL · Red Bull

FOR THE RECORD

10th WIN: **Lewis Hamilton**

50th GRAND PRIX START: **Robert Kubica**

1st FASTEST LAP: **Mark Webber**

1st GRAND PRIX START: **Jaime Alguersuari**
(the 11th Spaniard to start a Formula 1 GP)

30th FRONT ROW: **Fernando Alonso**

DID YOU KNOW?

Alguersuari became the youngest driver ever to start a Formula One World Championship race at the age of 19 years 4 months and 3 days (beating Mike Thackwell in 1980 by nearly two months).

For each of the drivers who led a lap in this race (Alonso, Hamilton and Kovalainen), it was their first of the season.

This was Alonso's first pole in 32 races (since Italy 2007).

POINTS

DRIVERS

1	Jenson Button	70
2	Mark Webber	51.5
3	Sebastian Vettel	47
4	Rubens Barrichello	44
5	Nico Rosberg	25.5
6	Jarno Trulli	22.5
7	Felipe Massa	22
8	Lewis Hamilton	19
9	Kimi Räikkönen	18
10	Timo Glock	16
11	Fernando Alonso	13
12	Heikki Kovalainen	9
13	Nick Heidfeld	6
14	Sébastien Buemi	3
15	Robert Kubica	2
16	Sébastien Bourdais	2

CONSTRUCTORS

1	Brawn	114
2	Red Bull	98.5
3	Ferrari	40
4	Toyota	38.5
5	McLaren	28
6	Williams	25.5
7	Renault	13
8	BMW Sauber	8
9	Toro Rosso	5

Lap chart

56	57	58	59	60	61	62	63	64	65	66	67	68	69	70		
1	1	1	1	1	1	1	1	1	1	1	1	1	1	1		1
4	4	4	4	4	4	4	4	4	4	4	4	4	4	4		2
10	10	10	10	10	14	14	14	14	14	14	14	14	14	14		3
14	14	14	14	14	16	16	16	16	16	16	16	16	16	16		4
16	16	16	16	16	2	2	2	2	2	2	2	2	2	2		5
2	2	2	2	2	10	10	10	10	10	10	10	10	10	10		6
9	9	9	22	22	22	22	22	22	22	22	22	22	22	22		7
7	23	22	9	9	9	9	9	9	9	9	9	9	9	9		8
3	22	17	17	17	17	17	17	17	17	17	17	17	17	17		
22	17	23	23	23	23	23	23	23	23	23	23	23	23	23		
6	6	6	6	6	6	6	6	6	6	6	6	6	6	6		
8	8	8	8	8	8	8	8	8	8	8	8	8	8	8		
5	5	5	5	5	5	5	5	5	5	5	5	5	5	5		
21	21	21	21	21	21	21	21	21	21	21	21	21	21	21		
11	11	11	11	11	11	11	11	11	11	11	11	11	11	11		
12	12	12	12	12	12	12	12	12	12	12	12	12	12	12		

_ Pit stop
» One lap or more behind

RACE TYRE STRATEGIES

The tyre regulations stipulate that two dry tyre specifications must be used during the race.

The Super-Soft compound Bridgestone Potenza tyre is marked with a green stripe on the sidewall of the tyre.

	Driver	Race Stint 1	Race Stint 2	Race Stint 3
1	Lewis Hamilton	Super-Soft: 1-20	Super-Soft: 21-46	Soft: 47-70
2	Kimi Räikkönen	Super-Soft: 1-21	Super-Soft: 22-45	Soft: 46-70
3	Mark Webber	Super-Soft: 1-19	Super-Soft: 20-50	Soft: 51-70
4	Nico Rosberg	Super-Soft: 1-20	Super-Soft: 21-49	Soft: 50-70
5	Heikki Kovalainen	Super-Soft: 1-21	Super-Soft: 22-44	Soft: 45-70
6	Timo Glock	Super-Soft: 1-32	Super-Soft: 33-60	Soft: 61-70
7	Jenson Button	Super-Soft: 1-25	Super-Soft: 26-55	Soft: 56-70
8	Jarno Trulli	Super-Soft: 1-28	Super-Soft: 29-58	Soft: 59-70
9	Kazuki Nakajima	Super-Soft: 1-22	Super-Soft: 23-56	Soft: 57-70
10	Rubens Barrichello	Soft: 1-33	Soft: 34-57	Super-Soft: 58-70
11	Nick Heidfeld	Super-Soft: 1-18	Super-Soft: 19-49	Soft: 50-70
12	Nelson Piquet	Super-Soft: 1-23	Super-Soft: 24-48	Soft: 49-70
13	Robert Kubica	Super-Soft: 1-21	Super-Soft: 22-52	Soft: 53-70
14	Giancarlo Fisichella	Super-Soft: 1-29	Super-Soft: 30-47	Soft: 48-69
15	Jaime Alguersuari	Super-Soft: 1-28	Super-Soft: 29-52	Soft: 53-69
16	Sébastien Buemi	Soft: 1-26	Super-Soft: 27-38	Soft: 39-69
	Sebastian Vettel	Soft: 1-21	Soft: 22-27	Soft: 28-29 (dnf)
	Fernando Alonso	Super-Soft: 1-12	Super-Soft: 13-14	Soft: 15 (dnf)
	Adrian Sutil	Soft: 0-1 (dnf)		
dns	Felipe Massa			

A winner again at last.
Not since the inaugural
Chinese GP at Shanghai,
where he won for Ferrari,
had Rubens Barrichello
occupied the top step of the
F1 podium.
Photo: Peter J. Fox

FIA FORMULA 1 WORLD CHAMPIONSHIP • ROUND 11

EUROPEAN
GRAND PRIX

VALENCIA CIRCUIT

VALENCIA QUALIFYING

IT was a question of pushing back boundaries – as well as the front suspension. McLaren came to Valencia with a car that was significantly different from the one Lewis Hamilton had used to dominate the Hungarian Grand Prix, but the potentially fragile consequences of Formula One's constant development race were all too apparent.

Not for the first time, Hamilton and team-mate Heikki Kovalainen were singing from different set-up sheets. The wheelbase of Hamilton's car had been shortened, the front suspension having been moved back 75mm in a bid to put more weight over the front tyres and give them extra purchase. Kovalainen, meanwhile, merely assessed some revised front wing endplates on Friday, although these would not be used in the race.

The perils of such ambition were apparent during the early moments of the second free practice session, when Hamilton brushed a wall. "It was only a graze and I barely felt the impact," he said, but the front wing was damaged and the team had no spares of that specification, so he was obliged to sit and watch for the balance of the day.

That would be no impediment. He and Kovalainen duly went on to lock out the front row, with Rubens Barrichello and Sebastian Vettel third and fourth, ahead of points leader Jenson Button.

"Every little bit of time you spend on the track makes a difference," Hamilton said. "You find out more about the car and do ever more fine-tuning, so after yesterday I was under quite a lot of pressure in terms of dialling in the chassis, but fortunately we did quite a good job this morning." Not that final free practice was particularly relaxing: 25 minutes of the session were lost when Vettel suffered a failed Renault V8 and coated the track with oil.

Enough parts arrived overnight to convert Kovalainen's car to short-wheelbase spec on Saturday, but he was happy with the balance as it was and, being lighter than Hamilton, had slightly more scope for playing around with weight distribution in a standard car. Thus the new bits remained in their crate, and Kovalainen was on course for provisional pole – until he locked an inside front at the penultimate corner and then ran wide at the final left-hander. By that stage, Hamilton was back on track and going faster still, although he was able to abort the lap and preserve some fuel in the wake of his team-mate's error.

Promoted from GP2 to replace the sacked Nelson Piquet Mk 2, Romain Grosjean belied his reputation for intermittent wildness with steady, methodical progress that carried him to within 0.323 seconds of team-mate – and peerless yardstick – Fernando Alonso during Q2.

There was a rather bigger gulf between Kimi Räikkönen, sixth, and Ferrari stand-in Luca Badoer. Having not raced anything for ten years and with no significant F1 mileage for ten months, the Italian was never likely to set the track alight. When Button set the pace in Q1, he was 1.394 seconds quicker than 19th-fastest Jaime Alguersuari – and the Spaniard was 1.488 seconds clear of Badoer. Four speeding offences confirmed, however, that the Italian was the man to beat in the pit lane.

Above: Pole-sitter Lewis Hamilton was in great form for McLaren, but had no answers for Barrichello in the race.
Photo: Lukas Gorys

Top right: A special message to Felipe from Rubens.
Photo: Studio Colombo/WRi2

Above right: Down by the water front docks. Heikki Kovalainen showed impressive speed throughout the weekend and could have fared better than fourth place had he not been fitted with the wrong tyres at his final stop.
Photo: Peter J. Fox

Left: It was hard to say whether Luca Badoer looked resigned to disappointment or simply out of his depth as he lined up for his F1 debut with Ferrari.
Photo: Peter J. Fox

TO those armed with only a television monitor, it was a humdrum sporting spectacle. To those with the added benefit of a timing screen, it was utterly compelling – a race in the purest sense of the term. It highlighted a common Formula One dilemma: fierce competition isn't always engaging to watch.

Those responsible for converting Valencia's harbour and fish market into a convincing racetrack have done a professional, plausible job, and the TV director's favourite shot – looking down from aloft, with yachts in the foreground – adds a suitably Mediterranean flourish. The cameras tend not to point the other way, where the backdrop is an industrial tapestry of cranes and container docks. The harbour was hardly a sell-out in 2009, either: allegedly, one or two folks were invited to park their boats for free, to help make the place look busy.

For a while, though, it had looked as though the European Grand Prix might be the campaign's most newsworthy event, with Michael Schumacher busily getting himself fit to take part in his 250th grand prix, three years after his 249th, as Felipe Massa's stand-in. A sore neck – the result of an accident while testing a Superbike at Cartagena, Spain, in February – forced him to abort his comeback, however, and

those who had rushed to buy tickets would be treated instead to Luca Badoer, a man who had last raced when Schumacher had won only two of his seven world titles. At least they were guaranteed a glimpse of Fernando Alonso, following Renault's successful appeal against the one-race ban imposed for misdemeanours in Budapest. Alonso, though, wouldn't be a factor – there were only two of those.

Lewis Hamilton made a clean start from pole while his most likely challenger, Rubens Barrichello, was forced to tuck in behind the second McLaren of Heikki Kovalainen. The opening lap was only mildly chaotic, with Kimi Räikkönen gaining two places to settle into fourth, ahead of Sebastian Vettel, Nico Rosberg, Alonso, Jenson Button, Mark Webber, Nick Heidfeld, Robert Kubica, Adrian Sutil, Giancarlo Fisichella, Kazuki Nakajima, Jarno Trulli, Jaime Alguersuari and Luca Badoer. The last had briefly risen to a KERS-assisted 14th, but then spun back to where he'd started following a nudge from Romain Grosjean, who subsequently pulled into the pits, even though he had no need to do so. Before tapping Badoer, he had seen a nose wing shatter in front of him on the track and assumed it was his own, although actually it was from Sébastien Buemi's Toro Rosso: the

Swiss claimed that Timo Glock had simply driven over him; Glock countered that he'd been rammed from behind. Either way, both had to pit for repairs.

There was trouble ahead for Button, too. He had briefly managed to pass Alonso during the course of the lap, but ran wide in the process and slipped back behind the Renault. Of more concern to the stewards, he shouldn't have been in a position to challenge the Spaniard, because he had bypassed the Turn Four chicane to oust Webber: on lap five, with Hamilton leading the field by three seconds, Button was ordered to hand the place back. The BMWs swapped places at this point, too, but that was due to tactical collusion rather than a sudden outbreak of racing. Sutil attempted to follow Kubica past Heidfeld, but was elbowed over the kerbs and got precisely nowhere.

On lap six, Hamilton began to put on a spurt and Kovalainen conveniently failed to respond. The upshot was that the leader was almost eight seconds clear of Barrichello by the time he made his first stop, on lap 16. Kovalainen came in one lap later, and Barrichello – who had started on Bridgestone's soft tyre, while both McLaren drivers went for super-softs – began setting a string of personal bests prior to pitting on lap

Right: Sebastian Vettel looked crest-fallen after qualifying only fourth, but things got worse in the race when he retired with an engine failure.

Below: In a spin. The hapless Romain Grosjean continued his error-strewn form.

Photos: Lukas Gorys

Far right: Lewis Hamilton's pit crew were wrong-footed by his arrival for his second refuelling stop, but it did not materially affect the outcome of the race.

Photo: Peter Nygaard/GP Photo

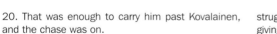

20. That was enough to carry him past Kovalainen, and the chase was on.

Both teams opted to continue with the tyre compounds on which they'd started. This might have been a mistake, as McLaren team principal Martin Whitmarsh later acknowledged, because the super-softs didn't hold up as well towards the end of a stint. Initially, however, there didn't appear to be much in it. Barrichello rejoined 3.2 seconds in arrears, dropped away a little while his tyres got up to temperature and then began reducing the deficit. Assuming he was running longer, it looked like his race. Hamilton responded by dipping into the 1m 39s range and staying there between laps 26 and 36, just before his second stop. Perhaps he still had the edge – or maybe not, because Barrichello conjured an even quicker sequence: from laps 28 to 39, his times ranged between 1m 39.810s and 1m 38.990s, with one fractionally slower interlude while he lapped the

struggling Badoer. This was the best bit: two blokes giving no quarter.

Acutely aware that it was fighting a losing battle, McLaren tried desperately to squeeze one more lightly fuelled lap from Hamilton's tank. The Englishman was due to pit on lap 37, when he had 3.5 seconds in hand, but the team decided at the last minute that a 38th was possible and told him as much by radio. "Unfortunately," Hamilton said, "I was already committed to coming in by then." The pit crew was ready on the apron, but his tyres weren't; had Hamilton continued for one more lap, Kovalainen would have been called in instead. About seven seconds were lost while the correct tyres were retrieved and fitted, but ultimately that was immaterial. McLaren's pit fumble made the headlines, but the prosaic truth is that Hamilton was on course to lose anyway.

Barrichello came in on lap 40, but only because by then he was far enough ahead to do so. He had

enough fuel on board for another four or five laps, each of which would have gained him a second or more over Hamilton, but the team felt there was no point in keeping him out in case a safety car interrupted the afternoon's smooth flow. Game over. The sport was about to welcome its fifth different winner in as many races.

It was Barrichello's first F1 World Championship success since China 2004, and the 100th for a Brazilian driver. "I don't care much about such numbers," he said. "I just care about my work." He dedicated his victory to the whole of Brazil, and particularly compatriot Felipe Massa, injured by the coil spring that had fallen from Barrichello's car in Hungary a month earlier. "I had two wishes," he said. "The first was that Felipe would still be the same guy after his accident, which he is, and secondly that he will be the same driver when he comes back, although I think he might be even tougher."

Hamilton was happy with his pace during the opening stint, but readily acknowledged that Barrichello had enjoyed the upper hand thereafter. "After a long season of finishing towards the back," he said, "I can't complain about being on the podium for two consecutive races. I'm very grateful to be here."

Their duel during the second stint had briefly given the afternoon some bite, but the rest was all rather straightforward. Desperately in need of a strong race to improve his prospects of retaining a seat alongside Hamilton, Kovalainen provided his team-mate with a useful buffer during the opening stint, but wasn't quite fast enough during the second, when Räikkönen ran two laps longer and posted a sequence of low 1m 39s laps just before making his stop. Kovalainen didn't put in times of that calibre until the race's penultimate lap, by which stage third place had long since been lost.

"I needed to go 100 per cent all the time," explained the Ferrari driver. "The car felt good on Friday and worked well during the long stints, so I was hoping it would be okay in the race. We are not really developing any more new parts this year, so we are a little bit behind the leaders, but once we get it running well, we can usually fight for third. We might even be able to challenge for victory if something weird happens…"

Vettel lost a huge amount of time with a fuel rig problem during his first stop – he only had just enough juice on board to make it back to the pits one lap later – and retired soon afterwards when he suffered his second engine failure of the weekend. Fortunately, unlike Saturday morning, he didn't coat the circuit with an oil slick on this occasion.

The balance of the order did not change too significantly between the first lap and the last, with the dependable Rosberg finishing fifth, ahead of Alonso, Button and Kubica, who passed Webber during the final pit stops, not least because Red Bull was being cautious following its earlier woes with Vettel. Button had finally passed Webber legitimately during the first stops and felt that his car had been every bit as good as Barrichello had demonstrated, but circumstances prevented him from making the most of it. "A small mistake in qualifying and getting caught in traffic really cost me," said the championship leader, "but at least we beat the Red Bulls, so I'm not too disappointed."

Sutil was tenth, a meritorious reflection of Force India's gathering momentum. "That was a good performance with no mistakes," he said. "It was a very tough race in the heat, but everything worked perfectly. I was behind the two BMWs for my first stint and couldn't get by on the track, but the team did a really good job in the pits and I was able to pass Heidfeld. I'm really looking forward to Spa now: I love the track and, with the pace we've shown this weekend, things

look promising for a good result there." For once, this wasn't mere PR spiel.

Fisichella trailed in behind Heidfeld, ahead of fellow one-stoppers Trulli and Glock – technically a two-stopper given his unscheduled repairs, but he only refuelled once. Grosjean, 15th, managed to set a faster race lap than team-mate Alonso, albeit when running on fumes, and pulled off the afternoon's only physical pass when he overtook Badoer in the pit exit lane. Ferrari personnel were on the radio to the Italian at the time, warning him about traffic: they meant the stuff on the track rather than the car immediately behind, but the rusty Luca swerved right and gifted a place to Renault's rookie. Then Badoer went too far to the left and crossed the pit exit line prematurely, which earned him a drive-through penalty to add to his earlier collection of pit speeding fines. He finished 17th and last, behind Alguersuari, who found the heat exhausting and could have done with a drinks bottle that worked properly.

Nakajima was classified 18th, but stopped three laps from the finish: he'd sustained a punctured left rear on the 39th lap and flailing debris damaged the gearbox, so he was withdrawn.

Buemi posted the only other retirement. His collision with Glock dropped him to the back, but unseen brake duct damage fried his front left disc, which subsequently shattered and sent him spinning off the track on lap 42, at Turn 12.

Badoer might have thought the chequered flag heralded the end of a painfully awkward weekend, but he was wrong: cooling-off lap complete, he pulled into *parc fermé* and shunted straight into Sutil's parked Force India…

Simon Arron

EDITOR'S VIEW
RETURN OF THE CHAMPION – ALMOST

THE month-long run-up to the European Grand Prix at Valencia left the Formula One community's nerves frayed, to say the least. Felipe Massa's accident during qualifying at the Hungaroring, coming as it did only a week after the death of Henry Surtees from injuries sustained in an F2 race at Brands Hatch, acted as a sobering reminder that front-line motor racing, for all its glamour and charisma, remains a potentially very hazardous pastime, even in an era when sophisticated technology and clever engineering have contributed so much to safety.

Ferrari had plenty of time between Budapest and Valencia to consider what to do about a stand-in for the injured Massa. Logic might have suggested that the team would opt for one of its test drivers, Luca Badoer or Marc Gené. Instead, Maranello tantalised us with an agreement to draft seven times world champion Michael Schumacher into the vacant cockpit for as long as Massa was out of action.

The regulations forbade any testing during the course of the season, apart from strictly controlled straight-line runs to check aerodynamic development. But the F1 community correctly anticipated that, on safety grounds, Ferrari would request that Schumacher be allowed to acquaint himself with his new machine before the meeting rather than being pitchforked into the frenzy of Friday's first qualifying session on a circuit he had not seen before.

Schumacher spent a couple of days testing at the Ferrari-owned Mugello circuit, near Florence, driving one of the F2007 machines in which Kimi Räikkönen had won the 2007 World Championship the year after the German had retired. Driving the earlier F1 car was not prohibited by the testing ban, which only applied to the current cars being used by the teams contesting the World Championship.

In the event, the expected road-block was erected by Williams with assistance from Red Bull Racing and Scuderia Toro Rosso.

"While we welcome Michael Schumacher back to Formula One, the fact is that any form of in-season circuit testing is strictly prohibited, a regulation clearly laid down by the FIA and adhered to by all of the teams," Frank Williams said. "It was for this reason that [Jaime] Alguersuari, who drove a Formula One car for the very first time in Hungary, did not have the opportunity to familiarise himself with the Toro Rosso before he made his race debut. Williams sees no distinction between Alguersuari's situation and Schumacher's, and feels that any deviation from the rule would create a precedent for the future."

Red Bull team owner Dietrich Mateschitz agreed. "We asked for permission to test for Alguersuari before the Hungarian Grand Prix, and it was turned down," he said. "So why should we approve an exemption for a seven-time champion after this?" Ferrari was left to fume quietly.

Meanwhile, Massa said that his old colleague was the best choice that Ferrari could have made as his substitute, but warned the former world champion not to become too comfortable, as he intended to be back behind the wheel again soon.

"Michael doesn't need my advice," joked Massa as he left Budapest for his home in Brazil. "It was him who gave me many tips during my career when we were racing together. He knows how to win, he knows how to drive and he's great. It was the best choice handing over the car to such a fantastic person, and I'm sure everybody will be happy to see him back on the track again. Although I hope I'll be back on the track with Ferrari as soon as possible."

In the event, of course, the fans were deprived of the opportunity of seeing Schumacher in action again, as he withdrew from the planned outing, complaining that he was still suffering from a neck injury sustained during a motorcycle accident earlier in the year. Given the intensely competitive nature of contemporary F1, and the speed at which things develop, there were many in the pit lane who felt that Michael had been saved from himself.

Alan Henry

Above: Michael Schumacher still had racing in his sights.

Above left: Dreamscape. Valencia's futuristic architecture provided a dramatic backdrop to the more prosaic track.

Left: Nico Rosberg speeds past the yachts in the harbour on his way to fifth place in the Williams-Toyota.

Photos: Peter J. Fox

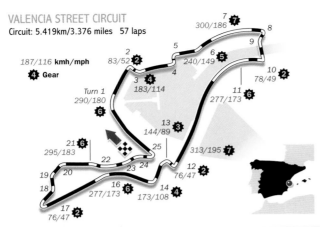

VALENCIA STREET CIRCUIT
Circuit: 5.419km/3.376 miles 57 laps

187/116 **kmh/mph**
4 Gear

Photos: Peter J. Fox

FIA F1 WORLD CHAMPIONSHIP ROUND 11
TELEFÓNICA
GRAND PRIX OF
EUROPE

VALENCIA 21-23 AUGUST 2009

RACE DISTANCE: 57 laps, 191.931 miles/308.883km • RACE WEATHER: Sunny (track 45-47°C, air 32°C)

Pos.	Driver	Nat.	No.	Entrant	Car/Engine	Tyres	Laps	Time/Retirement	Speed (mph/km/h)	Gap to leader	Fastest race lap
1	Rubens Barrichello	BR	23	Brawn GP Formula 1 Team	Brawn BGP 001-Mercedes FO108W V8	B	57	1h 35m 51.289s	120.138/193.344		1m 38.990s 39
2	Lewis Hamilton	GB	1	Vodafone McLaren Mercedes	McLaren MP4-24-Mercedes FO108W V8	B	57	1h 35m 53.647s	120.089/193.265	+ 2.358s	1m 39.056s 57
3	Kimi Räikkönen	FIN	4	Scuderia Ferrari Marlboro	Ferrari F60-056 V8	B	57	1h 36m 07.283s	119.805/192.808	+ 15.994s	1m 39.207s 39
4	Heikki Kovalainen	FIN	2	Vodafone McLaren Mercedes	McLaren MP4-24-Mercedes FO108W V8	B	57	1h 36m 11.321s	119.721/192.673	+ 20.032s	1m 39.341s 56
5	Nico Rosberg	D	16	AT&T Williams	Williams FW31-Toyota RVX-09 V8	B	57	1h 36m 12.159s	119.704/192.645	+ 20.870s	1m 39.329s 52
6	Fernando Alonso	E	7	ING Renault F1 Team	Renault R29-RS27 V8	B	57	1h 36m 19.033s	119.562/192.416	+ 27.744s	1m 39.494s 46
7	Jenson Button	GB	22	Brawn GP Formula 1 Team	Brawn BGP 001-Mercedes FO108W V8	B	57	1h 36m 26.202s	119.413/192.177	+ 34.913s	1m 38.874s 46
8	Robert Kubica	PL	5	BMW Sauber F1 Team	BMW Sauber F1.09-BMW P86/9 V8	B	57	1h 36m 27.956s	119.377/192.119	+ 36.667s	1m 39.374s 55
9	Mark Webber	AUS	14	Red Bull Racing	Red Bull RB5-Renault RS27 V8	B	57	1h 36m 36.199s	119.208/191.846	+ 44.910s	1m 39.528s 50
10	Adrian Sutil	D	20	Force India F1 Team	Force India VJM02-Mercedes FO108W V8	B	57	1h 36m 39.224s	119.145/191.746	+ 47.935s	1m 39.622s 36
11	Nick Heidfeld	D	6	BMW Sauber F1 Team	BMW Sauber F1.09-BMW P86/9 V8	B	57	1h 36m 40.111s	119.127/191.716	+ 48.822s	1m 39.704s 53
12	Giancarlo Fisichella	I	21	Force India F1 Team	Force India VJM02-Mercedes FO108W V8	B	57	1h 36m 54.903s	118.824/191.229	+ 1m 03.614s	1m 40.111s 53
13	Jarno Trulli	I	9	Panasonic Toyota Racing	Toyota TF109-RVX-09 V8	B	57	1h 36m 55.816s	118.806/191.199	+ 1m 04.527s	1m 39.941s 52
14	Timo Glock	D	10	Panasonic Toyota Racing	Toyota TF109-RVX-09 V8	B	57	1h 37m 17.808s	118.358/190.478	+ 1m 26.519s	1m 38.683s 55
15	Romain Grosjean	F	8	ING Renault F1 Team	Renault R29-RS27 V8	B	57	1h 37m 23.063s	118.251/190.307	+ 1m 31.774s	1m 39.428s 41
16	Jaime Alguersuari	E	11	Scuderia Toro Rosso	Toro Rosso STR04-Ferrari 056 V8	B	56			+ 1 lap	1m 40.935s 29
17	Luca Badoer	I	3	Scuderia Ferrari Marlboro	Ferrari F60-056 V8	B	56			+ 1 lap	1m 40.590s 52
18	Kazuki Nakajima	J	17	AT&T Williams	Williams FW31-Toyota RVX-09 V8	B	54	damage from puncture		+ 3 laps	1m 39.747s 53
	Sébastien Buemi	CH	12	Scuderia Toro Rosso	Toro Rosso STR04-Ferrari 056 V8	B	41	accident/brakes			1m 41.042s 37
	Sebastian Vettel	D	15	Red Bull Racing	Red Bull RB5-Renault RS27 V8	B	23	engine			1m 39.992s 13

Fastest race lap: Timo Glock on lap 55, 1m 38.683s, 122.837mph/197.687km/h. (record)

Previous Lap record: Felipe Massa (Ferrari F2008 V8), 1m 38.708s, 122.806mph/197.637km/h (2008)

All results and data © FOM 2009

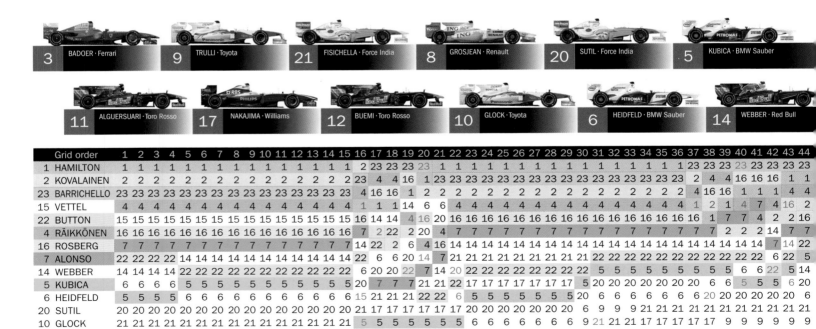

	Grid order	1	2	3	4	5	6	7	8	9	10	11	12	13	14	15	16	17	18	19	20	21	22	23	24	25	26	27	28	29	30	31	32	33	34	35	36	37	38	39	40	41	42	43	44
1	HAMILTON	1	1	1	1	1	1	1	1	1	1	1	1	1	1	1	1	2	23	23	23	23	1	1	1	1	1	1	1	1	1	1	1	1	1	1	1	1	23	23	23	23	23	23	23
2	KOVALAINEN	2	2	2	2	2	2	2	2	2	2	2	2	2	2	2	23	4	4	16	1	23	23	23	23	23	23	23	23	23	23	23	23	23	23	23	2	4	4	16	16	16	1	1	
23	BARRICHELLO	23	23	23	23	23	23	23	23	23	23	23	23	23	23	23	4	16	16	1	2	2	2	2	2	2	2	2	2	2	2	2	2	2	2	2	4	16	16	1	1	1	4	4	
15	VETTEL	4	4	4	4	4	4	4	4	4	4	4	4	4	4	4	1	1	1	14	6	6	4	4	4	4	4	4	4	4	4	4	4	4	4	4	1	2	1	4	7	4	16	2	
22	BUTTON	15	15	15	15	15	15	15	15	15	15	15	15	15	15	16	14	14	4	16	20	16	16	16	16	16	16	16	16	16	16	16	16	16	16	16	16	1	7	7	4	2	2	16	
4	RÄIKKÖNEN	16	16	16	16	16	16	16	16	16	16	16	16	16	16	7	2	22	2	20	4	7	7	7	7	7	7	7	7	7	7	7	7	7	7	7	7	7	2	2	2	14	14		
16	ROSBERG	7	7	7	7	7	7	7	7	7	7	7	7	7	7	14	22	2	6	4	16	14	14	14	14	14	14	14	14	14	14	14	14	14	14	14	14	14	14	14	7	14	22		
7	ALONSO	22	22	22	22	14	14	14	14	14	14	14	14	14	14	22	6	6	20	14	7	21	21	21	21	21	21	21	22	22	22	22	22	22	22	22	22	22	22	6	22	5			
14	WEBBER	14	14	14	14	22	22	22	22	22	22	22	22	22	22	6	20	20	22	7	14	20	22	22	22	22	22	22	5	5	5	5	5	5	5	5	5	6	6	22	5	14			
5	KUBICA	6	6	6	6	5	5	5	5	5	5	5	5	5	5	20	7	7	7	21	21	22	17	17	17	17	17	17	5	20	20	20	20	20	20	6	6	5	5	5	6	20			
6	HEIDFELD	5	5	5	5	6	6	6	6	6	6	6	6	6	6	15	21	21	21	22	22	6	5	5	5	5	5	5	20	6	6	9	6	20	20	20	20	20	20	20	20	6			
20	SUTIL	20	20	20	20	20	20	20	20	20	20	20	20	20	20	21	17	17	17	17	17	5	20	20	20	20	20	20	6	9	9	21	21	21	21	21	21	21	21	9	9				
10	GLOCK	21	21	21	21	21	21	21	21	21	21	21	21	21	21	5	5	5	5	5	5	6	6	6	6	6	6	6	9	21	21	17	17	17	17	17	9	9	9	9					
8	PIQUET	17	17	17	17	17	17	17	17	17	17	17	17	17	17	9	9	9	9	9	9	9	9	9	9	9	17	17	17	9	9	9	9	8	8	8	10	10	10						
12	BUEMI	9	9	9	9	9	9	9	9	9	9	9	9	9	9	15	11	11	11	11	15	3	3	3	3	11	11	11	11	8	8	8	8	8	8	10	10	10	8	8	8				
21	FISICHELLA	11	11	11	11	11	11	11	11	11	11	11	11	11	11	3	15	15	15	05	11	8	8	10	10	10	8	11	10	10	10	8	11	10	10	10	11	11	11	11	11				
17	NAKAJIMA	3	3	3	3	3	3	3	3	3	3	3	3	3	3	8	8	8	11	11	11	11	3	8	8	10	10	11	11	11	11	11	11	3	3	3	3	3	3						
9	TRULLI	8	8	8	8	8	8	8	8	8	8	8	8	8	8	11	11	10	10	10	8	3	3	3	3	3	3	3	3	3	12	12	12	12	17	17									
11	ALGUERSUARI	10	10	10	10	10	10	10	10	10	10	10	10	10	10	10	10	10	10	12	12	12	12	12	12	12	12	12	12	12	17	17	17												
3	BADOER	12	12	12	12	12	12	12	12	12	12	12	12	12	12	12	12	12	12	12	12																								

TIME SHEETS

PRACTICE 1 (FRIDAY)
Sunny
(track 31-39°C, air 28-30°C)

Pos.	Driver	Laps	Time
1	Rubens Barrichello	19	1m 42.460s
2	Heikki Kovalainen	16	1m 42.636s
3	Lewis Hamilton	18	1m 42.654s
4	Jenson Button	19	1m 43.074s
5	Sebastian Vettel	17	1m 43.088s
6	Adrian Sutil	13	1m 43.209s
7	Kazuki Nakajima	25	1m 43.225s
8	Mark Webber	19	1m 43.243s
9	Fernando Alonso	18	1m 43.345s
10	Kimi Räikkönen	23	1m 43.384s
11	Sébastien Buemi	30	1m 43.389s
12	Robert Kubica	20	1m 43.419s
13	Jaime Alguersuari	30	1m 43.637s
14	Nico Rosberg	22	1m 43.746s
15	Nick Heidfeld	23	1m 44.040s
16	Giancarlo Fisichella	17	1m 44.126s
17	Romain Grosjean	23	1m 44.356s
18	Jarno Trulli	26	1m 44.638s
19	Timo Glock	28	1m 44.732s
20	Luca Badoer	25	1m 45.840s

PRACTICE 2 (FRIDAY)
Sunny
(track 43-46°C, air 32-33°C)

Pos.	Driver	Laps	Time
1	Fernando Alonso	33	1m 39.404s
2	Jenson Button	33	1m 40.178s
3	Rubens Barrichello	34	1m 40.209s
4	Nico Rosberg	39	1m 40.385s
5	Kazuki Nakajima	35	1m 40.503s
6	Adrian Sutil	23	1m 40.596s
7	Robert Kubica	34	1m 40.643s
8	Giancarlo Fisichella	31	1m 40.681s
9	Sebastian Vettel	33	1m 40.723s
10	Heikki Kovalainen	31	1m 40.738s
11	Kimi Räikkönen	39	1m 40.739s
12	Jarno Trulli	32	1m 40.770s
13	Romain Grosjean	35	1m 40.787s
14	Mark Webber	37	1m 40.956s
15	Timo Glock	30	1m 40.985s
16	Sébastien Buemi	34	1m 41.156s
17	Nick Heidfeld	29	1m 41.350s
18	Luca Badoer	37	1m 42.017s
19	Jaime Alguersuari	34	1m 42.089s
20	Lewis Hamilton	3	1m 43.214s

PRACTICE 2 (FRIDAY)
Sunny
(track 37-41°C, air 29-30°C)

Pos.	Driver	Laps	Time
1	Adrian Sutil	12	1m 39.143s
2	Kazuki Nakajima	12	1m 39.247s
3	Robert Kubica	12	1m 39.513s
4	Heikki Kovalainen	8	1m 39.553s
5	Nico Rosberg	11	1m 39.732s
6	Giancarlo Fisichella	12	1m 39.764s
7	Jenson Button	10	1m 39.883s
8	Lewis Hamilton	12	1m 39.950s
9	Jarno Trulli	11	1m 40.017s
10	Romain Grosjean	11	1m 40.088s
11	Sébastien Buemi	12	1m 40.118s
12	Rubens Barrichello	10	1m 40.192s
13	Nick Heidfeld	12	1m 40.230s
14	Kimi Räikkönen	12	1m 40.260s
15	Fernando Alonso	9	1m 40.402s
16	Timo Glock	10	1m 40.443s
17	Mark Webber	10	1m 40.879s
18	Sebastian Vettel	6	1m 40.916s
19	Jaime Alguersuari	12	1m 41.125s
20	Luca Badoer	14	1m 42.198s

QUALIFYING (SATURDAY)
Sunny (track 45°C, air 31-32°C)

Pos.	Driver	First	Second	Third	Weight
1	Lewis Hamilton	1m 38.649s	1m 38.182s	1m 39.498s	653kg
2	Heikki Kovalainen	1m 38.816s	1m 38.230s	1m 39.532s	655kg
3	Rubens Barrichello	1m 39.019s	**1m 38.076s**	**1m 39.563s**	662.5kg
4	Sebastian Vettel	1m 39.295s	1m 38.273s	1m 39.789s	654kg
5	Jenson Button	**1m 38.531s**	1m 38.601s	1m 39.821s	661.5kg
6	Kimi Räikkönen	1m 38.843s	1m 38.782s	1m 40.144s	661.5kg
7	Nico Rosberg	1m 39.039s	1m 38.346s	1m 40.185s	665kg
8	Fernando Alonso	1m 39.155s	1m 38.717s	1m 40.236s	656.5kg
9	Mark Webber	1m 38.983s	1m 38.625s	1m 40.239s	664.5kg
10	Robert Kubica	1m 38.806s	1m 38.747s	1m 40.512s	657.5kg
11	Nick Heidfeld	1m 39.032s	1m 38.826s		677kg
12	Adrian Sutil	1m 39.145s	1m 38.846s		672.5kg
13	Timo Glock	1m 39.459s	1m 38.991s		694.7kg
14	Romain Grosjean	1m 39.322s	1m 39.040s		677.7kg
15	Sébastien Buemi	1m 38.912s	1m 39.514s		688.5kg
16	Giancarlo Fisichella	1m 39.531s			692.5kg
17	Kazuki Nakajima	1m 39.795s			702kg
18	Jarno Trulli	1m 39.807s			707.3kg
19	Jaime Alguersuari	1m 39.925s			678.5kg
20	Luca Badoer	1m 41.413s			690.5kg

7 ALONSO · Renault

4 RÄIKKÖNEN · Ferrari

15 VETTEL · Red Bull

2 KOVALAINEN · McLaren

16 ROSBERG · Williams

22 BUTTON · Brawn

23 BARRICHELLO · Brawn

1 HAMILTON · McLaren

FOR THE RECORD

150th GRAND PRIX START: Kimi Räikkönen

150th WIN: Bridgestone

10th WIN: Rubens Barrichello

300th FRONT ROW POSITION: McLaren

1st FASTEST LAP: Timo Glock

60th PODIUM: Kimi Räikkönen

DID YOU KNOW?

This was the 250th Grand Prix for the McLaren-Mercedes partnership, which has produced 59 victories.

It had been 85 races since Barrichello last won (China 2004). Only Patrese beats him on races between wins (99)

POINTS

DRIVERS
1	Jenson Button	72
2	Rubens Barrichello	54
3	Mark Webber	51.5
4	Sebastian Vettel	47
5	Nico Rosberg	29.5
6	Lewis Hamilton	27
7	Kimi Räikkönen	24
8	Jarno Trulli	22.5
9	Felipe Massa	22
10	Timo Glock	16
11	Fernando Alonso	16
12	Heikki Kovalainen	14
13	Nick Heidfeld	6
14	Robert Kubica	3
15	Sébastien Buemi	3
16	Sébastien Bourdais	2

CONSTRUCTORS
1	Brawn	126
2	Red Bull	98.5
3	Ferrari	46
4	McLaren	41
5	Toyota	38.5
6	Williams	29.5
7	Renault	16
8	BMW Sauber	9
9	Toro Rosso	5

(Lap chart)

46	47	48	49	50	51	52	53	54	55	56	57	·	
23	23	23	23	23	23	23	23	23	23	23	23		1
1	1	1	1	1	1	1	1	1	1	1	1		2
4	4	4	4	4	4	4	4	4	4	4	4		3
2	2	2	2	2	2	2	2	2	2	2	2		4
16	16	16	16	16	16	16	16	16	16	16	16		5
7	7	7	7	7	7	7	7	7	7	7	7		6
22	22	22	22	22	22	22	22	22	22	22	22		7
5	5	5	5	5	5	5	5	5	5	5	5		8
14	14	14	14	14	14	14	14	14	14	14	14		
20	20	20	20	20	20	20	20	20	20	20	20		
6	6	6	6	6	6	6	6	6	6	6	6		
21	21	21	21	21	21	21	21	21	21	21	21		
9	9	9	9	9	9	9	9	9	9	9	9		
10	10	10	10	10	10	10	10	10	10	10	10		
8	8	8	8	8	8	8	8	8	8	8	8		
11	11	11	11	11	11	11	11	11	11	11	11		
3	3	3	3	3	3	3	3	3	3	3			
17	17	17	17	17	17	17	17	17	17				

22 Pit stop   *17 One lap or more behind*

RACE TYRE STRATEGIES

The tyre regulations stipulate that the two dry tyre specifications must be used during the race.

The Super-Soft compound Bridgestone Potenza tyre is marked with a green stripe on the sidewall of the tyre.

	Driver	Race Stint 1	Race Stint 2	Race Stint 3	Race Stint 4
1	Rubens Barrichello	Super-Soft: 1-20	Super-Soft: 21-40	Soft: 41-57	
2	Lewis Hamilton	Super-Soft: 1-16	Super-Soft: 17-38	Soft: 39-57	
3	Kimi Räikkönen	Super-Soft: 1-19	Super-Soft: 20-40	Soft: 41-57	
4	Heikki Kovalainen	Super-Soft: 1-17	Super-Soft: 18-38	Super-Soft: 39-57	
5	Nico Rosberg	Soft: 1-20	Soft: 21-43	Super-Soft: 44-57	
6	Fernando Alonso	Soft: 1-17	Soft: 18-42	Super-Soft: 43-57	
7	Jenson Button	Soft: 1-19	Soft: 20-42	Super-Soft: 43-57	
8	Robert Kubica	Super-Soft: 1-16	Soft: 17-40	Super-Soft: 41-57	
9	Mark Webber	Soft: 1-20	Soft: 21-43	Super-Soft: 44-57	
10	Adrian Sutil	Soft: 1-22	Super-Soft: 23-38	Super-Soft: 39-57	
11	Nick Heidfeld	Super-Soft: 1-22	Super-Soft: 23-43	Soft: 44-57	
12	Giancarlo Fisichella	Soft: 1-31	Super-Soft: 32-57		
13	Jarno Trulli	Soft: 1-34	Super-Soft: 35-57		
14	Timo Glock	Soft: 0-1	Soft: 2-32	Super-Soft: 33-49	Super-Soft: 50-57
15	Romain Grosjean	Soft: 0-1	Soft: 2-28	Super-Soft: 29-42	Super-Soft: 43-57
16	Jaime Alguersuari	Soft: 1-22	Super-Soft: 23-33	Super-Soft: 34-56	
17	Luca Badoer	Super-Soft: 1-28	Super-Soft: 29-32	Super-Soft: 33-43	Super-Soft: 44-56
18	Kazuki Nakajima	Soft: 1-30	Soft: 31-39	Super-Soft: 40-54	
	Sébastien Buemi	Super-Soft: 0-1	Super-Soft: 2-23	Super-Soft: 24-41 (dnf)	
	Sebastian Vettel	Soft: 1-16	Soft: 17	Soft: 18-23 (dnf)	

BELGIAN GRAND PRIX

SPA-FRANCORCHAMPS CIRCUIT

Main photo: Kimi Räikkönen presses the KERS button on his Ferrari and is just about to vault in front of Giancarlo Fisichella's Force India to take the lead.
Photo: Fritz Van Eldik/WRi2

Inset: Second place for Fisi must have seemed almost as good as a win after such a long barren period.
Photo: Peter J. Fox

SPA-FRANCORCHAMPS QUALIFYING

THE on-line betting portals went into overdrive late on Saturday morning. Jenson Button hadn't looked particularly quick, and late August in Belgium amplified Brawn's traditional struggle to generate tyre temperature in cool conditions, but Button was rumoured to have been lumbering around with a handsome fuel cargo, and at 12/1 he was perceived as a fair-priced bet for pole. At no stage did anybody recommend a flutter on Giancarlo Fisichella, a 150/1 shot…

Given that Force India had only once qualified a car in the top ten, when Adrian Sutil had lined up seventh at the Nürburgring two months beforehand, and had yet to score its first championship point, this was as blue as bolts come. There had been clues, though: the team had taken a significantly upgraded aero package – front wing, floor and sidepods – to Valencia, where its performance had been better rather than sparkling, but the car had always worked well in low-drag configuration, a useful asset in sectors one and three at Spa. Furthermore, track temperature increased by seven degrees during qualifying, and in sector two that translated to slight gains for those who were already quick – the Red Bulls, for instance – and much riper fruit for the rest. Subsequently, Fisichella did not put a foot wrong, and a 1m 46.308s was just good enough for pole.

"I didn't expect that," he said, "especially when you consider our budget. It is unbelievable."

Button? He wound up 14th, and much cash was frittered. "The car hasn't felt quite right all weekend," he said, "and I wasn't able to get any more out of it today. Rubens and I are usually very closely matched, but he was quick on the option tyre, and I just couldn't find any grip. The rear end felt unstable and I had no confidence under braking, particularly in the middle sector." The team also briefly tried a Red Bull-style engine cover on Button's car, although it was swiftly discarded. "The numbers didn't add up in the wind tunnel," said team principal Ross Brawn. "The same turned out to be true on the track, and it weighs more, too…"

With the highly fancied Red Bulls only eighth (Sebastian Vettel, who was heavily fuelled and ran wide on what should have been his quickest lap) and ninth (Mark Webber, who missed all but three laps of Saturday morning after an electrical problem forced the team to replace a brand-new Renault V8), the grid was headed by Fisichella (whose team sorely needed fresh investment), Jarno Trulli (at a time when Toyota reportedly required a little encouragement to continue its participation in the sport) and Nick Heidfeld (for sale: F1 team, two careful owners).

Trulli, effectively on pole when fuel weight adjustments were factored in, was slightly perplexed by his emergence as a likely winner. "We haven't done anything to the car compared with the last few races, yet suddenly we are extremely competitive," he said. "It's a mystery."

Heidfeld added, "We have a couple of small updates here, but nothing major. I think one reason why the grid is a bit more mixed is that this is a completely different track; it's the first time we've used a medium-downforce package."

Having hit, and written off, a rabbit at the start of Saturday's final free practice session, Fisichella had other notions about the campaign's least predictable F1 grid. "My engineers told me that in England, when you do something with a rabbit, it brings you luck," he said. "It turned out to be true, so next time I'm on the track I will try to find another one."

His grasp of English folklore did not quite match his mastery of Spa.

Right: Heikki Kovalainen and his McLaren are just a small part of the majesty of Eau Rouge under typical Spa weather.

Below: Unexpected celebration for Fisichella after the Italian bagged a surprise pole for the Force India squad.
Photos: Peter J. Fox

THERE is a chip kiosk adjacent to the media car park at Spa, and it is one of the world's most rewarding places to stand, a chance to enjoy delicious, mayonnaise-laced local produce while watching Eau Rouge rising through the pines and on towards the horizon. In Valencia's immediate slipstream, it was nice to be back at an authentic racetrack.

Remember what Kimi Räikkönen had said in the Grand Prix of Europe's aftermath, one weekend beforehand? "We might even be able to challenge for victory if something weird happens…" The grid probably qualified as the sport's oddest for some time. Logic told you that Sebastian Vettel might win, if he could make up a few places at the start and stay in touch with the leading group. The romantics hoped that somehow Giancarlo Fisichella would conjure a victory for Force India. And simple maths dictated that this should really be Jarno Trulli's race, but arithmetic never accounts for circumstance…

Fisichella started brightly and led through La

Source, where Robert Kubica slotted into second and Räikkönen used the run-off area to give himself an extra head of steam on the drop down to Eau Rouge – more effective than legitimate, although he does have previous at Spa, having taken advantage of areas other than the track during his lead battle with Lewis Hamilton one year earlier. Trulli, though, was already out of contention: he'd been beaten away by Nick Heidfeld's BMW and then clipped the German under braking for the first corner, inflicting frontal wing damage that ruined his afternoon almost before it started. At the same point, Adrian Sutil, Nico Rosberg and Fernando Alonso banged wheels, Rosberg getting very sideways before a second biff from Sutil helpfully straightened him out.

Räikkönen used KERS to pass Kubica on the long drag to Les Combes, where the Finn ran wide before brushing wheels with the Pole as he rejoined. Heidfeld slithered across the grass, too, losing places to Timo Glock and Mark Webber, but more significant

chaos broke out behind. Championship leader Jenson Button turned in to the first part of Les Combes just as Romain Grosjean was contemplating the inside line. Each blamed the other for the ensuing contact, which forced both cars out on the spot – the first time Button had failed to score in 2009 – but the stewards ruled that it was a common-or-garden racing accident and took no further action. Immediately behind, meanwhile, Lewis Hamilton backed off to avoid becoming involved and was rammed by the unsighted Jaime Alguersuari. Neither went any further, and the safety car was sent out while the mess was cleared up.

"I made a really good start and gained a few places in the first couple of corners," Button said. "I had a good run going down the straight and turned in to Les Combes, but Romain simply outbraked himself and hit my back wheel. That was that. It's frustrating because I was in a reasonable position and had lots of fuel on board, but it's better to have my first retire-

ment of the season here, when I haven't been so competitive, than when I'm running at the front."

The assorted incidents and errors had allowed Fisichella to pull more than two seconds clear before the race was neutralised, but he completed the lap at reduced pace with Räikkönen, Kubica, Glock, Trulli (heading to the pits for a fresh front wing), Webber, Rosberg, Heidfeld, Vettel, Alonso, Heikki Kovalainen, Sébastien Buemi, Kazuki Nakajima, Rubens Barrichello, Luca Badoer and Sutil completing the order. Slow off the line because of an electronic clutch glitch, Barrichello pitted to replace his soft Bridgestones with mediums, taking on extra fuel and converting to what was now effectively a one-stopper, while Sutil came in for a replacement front wing – not for the first time in his career – after his brush with Alonso and co.

The safety car made a significant difference to the outcome, because Fisichella was rendered vulnerable when the race resumed at the start of lap five, when Räikkönen, aided and abetted by KERS, breezed ahead on the run to Les Combes and pulled 0.9 seconds clear by the end of the lap. Fisichella remained in touch, however. The official fuel weights suggested that the Italian should pit about two laps before Räikkönen, but in the end they came in simultaneously on lap 14. "Force India seems to be running those things on diesel," one rival team principal said.

The pattern remained unchanged during the second stint, with Fisichella hovering around one second behind the Ferrari. Both made their final stops on lap 31 and, once more, they rejoined without the gap having altered. "Once I was ahead," Räikkönen said, "I switched tactics with KERS and used it more in the later part of the lap, to make sure I had good speed down the back straight." That provided him with a protective cushion at the chicane and La Source, and guaranteed Ferrari's first victory of the campaign. Six different winners in six races: shades of 1982.

Fisichella's performance received warm applause

throughout the paddock, but even so he felt a tinge of regret about what might have been. "I was quicker than him and lost out only because of KERS and the safety car," he said. "I am a little bit sad about that. This is a great result, but it could have been a victory. I came here thinking it would be fantastic if we could score points and maybe finish eighth or something. In reality, though…"

In terms of raw pace, Vettel was the quickest man on the day, but he spent too much time in traffic, a situation that was compounded when he lost places to Webber and Rosberg on the opening lap, the second of those at Les Combes, where he admitted being too cautious amid the developing chaos. Once into his stride, though, he flew: he passed Rosberg shortly after the restart, and vaulted Heidfeld and Glock, who suffered a fuel rig malfunction, during the first stops. He was gifted a place, too, when Webber was handed a drive-through for rejoining "in an unsafe manner" after his first stop – the Australian almost collected Heidfeld, who was forced to perform

Above: Sebastian Vettel kept his championship hopes alive with a strong run to third place in his Red Bull-Renault.
Photo: Peter J. Fox

Right: Force India mechanics were justifiably proud of their second place.
Photo: Bernard Asset

Above right: Nick Heidfeld accelerates his BMW Sauber down the hill towards Eau Rouge.
Photo: Peter J. Fox

a virtual emergency stop. Mark had no qualms about that. "If I'd been Nick, I'd have been pretty hacked off," he said.

That put Vettel fourth, once the one-stoppers had moved aside, and then he passed Kubica by dint of running five laps longer during his second stint. "I just lost too much ground during the first part of the race," he said, "but in the second and third, the car was fantastic. I didn't make a single mistake and drove every lap as though it were a qualifying session. The car was a pleasure to drive and I was quicker than the guys at the front, but there was no way of making up the time I lost at the beginning."

Kubica and Heidfeld ended up fourth and fifth, a significant boost, given previous form, although the German admitted to being disappointed. "My thought pattern before the race went back and forth about whether I should use soft or medium tyres at the start," he said. "The medium was quicker but, obviously, not the best for generating tyre heat. I chose it though, because the sun was shining, and paid the penalty. I lost a few places because my tyres weren't warm enough, and then I ran wide at Les Combes…"

He was quick in the final stint and swiftly closed the gap to Kubica. "I couldn't overtake, though," he said, "because as soon as you are less than two seconds behind another car, you start sliding around due to

loss of downforce in the dirty air." He didn't make too much fuss about the incident with Webber in the pits, but then he'd passed the Australian moments later on the run to Les Combes.

Kovalainen drove well to convert his one-stopper to sixth place, reserving one of his finest drives of the campaign for a track that didn't particularly suit the car, while Barrichello took seventh after a wonderfully spirited recovery from the back of the field. "I had a lot of fun after the strategy change," he said, "and my move on Mark Webber at Blanchimont was definitely one of the highlights." He was chasing Kovalainen hard at the end, but with two laps to go, the team called him off because an oil leak had developed. Obligingly, the car didn't catch fire until after he'd taken the chequered flag.

Rosberg took eighth – "More than I could have hoped for, because the car was difficult to drive." – and Webber's early penalty dropped him into dense traffic, from which he was unable to recover. He was also told to adjust his line through Eau Rouge, because the telemetry displayed worrying signs of oil surge every time he rode the kerbs.

Glock completed the top ten, ahead of Sutil, Buemi (who thought his front wing had collected some debris shortly after the start and made vigorous use of the kerbs for a few laps to dislodge whatever it was, a ploy he claimed was successful), Nakajima

and Badoer, who promised he'd do better at Monza, although, having been up to three seconds off the pace, it wasn't clear why he thought he might still be needed.

Alonso drove a strong opening stint, but his first stop, on lap 24, was delayed because his wheel spinner – the formal name for the aesthetically displeasing discs no one likes – had been damaged in his collision with Sutil. The team called him in shortly afterwards, on safety grounds, but much larger clouds were gathering on the horizon. Brazilian TV had just broken the story that it had evidence of Renault arranging for the recently sacked Nelson Piquet to crash deliberately during the 2008 Singapore Grand Prix, to create a safety-car period that played into team-mate Alonso's hands. News of an official FIA investigation followed soon afterwards.

Trulli was the only other retirement, the team bringing him in because of excessive brake wear, but, unlike Barrichello, he'd made almost no progress in the wake of his early delays. At one point, when Barrichello and Sutil had dispatched Badoer in quick succession, on laps seven and nine, Toyota got on the radio and reminded Trulli how important it was to do likewise. "It's impossible," came the reply. "He's too quick."

Possibly a unique perspective, that.

Simon Arron

EDITOR'S VIEW
ENIGMATIC KIMI NO LONGER WANTED AT MARANELLO

KIMI Räikkönen's reputation as one of the most enigmatic of contemporary Formula One drivers was further accentuated by his drive to victory in the Belgian Grand Prix. After using his Ferrari F60's KERS system to great effect to gain a slender, but crucial, edge over Giancarlo Fisichella's Force India in the opening moments of the race, he paced himself to perfection to post his first win of the season – and, as it turned out, his last ever for the Prancing Horse.

The introspective Finn had always been a baffling cocktail of contradictions. He cut his F1 teeth at the wheel of a Sauber, honed that wild and woolly edge to winning perfection during a five-year stint at McLaren, and then demonstrated a great blend of tactical acuity and controlled aggression to overturn Lewis Hamilton's 17-point advantage to win the 2007 World Championship at the final hurdle.

There have been many fine drivers over the years who have risen to the occasion on an intermittent basis, but when Kimi won the 2004 Belgian Grand Prix for McLaren, edging out Michael Schumacher's Ferrari by just over three seconds, there was a definite sense in the paddock that we had witnessed something very special. Behind that curtain of apparent indifference, Räikkönen had truly sizzling star quality. You could tell by the expression on Schumacher's face when they were on the podium together: "This really shouldn't have happened. Not to me.

Not on a circuit like this."

Yet, for all that, Kimi always had a somewhat wilful quality to his character. At McLaren, where he was partnered first by David Coulthard and subsequently Juan Pablo Montoya, he demonstrated the same inconsistency that later he would carry over to Ferrari. He also had a self-contained nature, which made it difficult to identify his true character. Kimi marched very much to his own beat, of that there was no doubt.

Truth be told, Raikkonen was never really a team player in the sense that he fully integrated or allowed himself to be absorbed into the Maranello fraternity. Moreover, throughout the summer of 2009 it was a pretty open secret within the F1 community that Ferrari was discreetly negotiating behind the scenes in an effort to terminate the Finn's present contract a year before its expiry at the end of 2010.

This, of course, was to make room for the incoming Fernando Alonso who had been romanced by Ferrari almost since the day he had left McLaren at the end of 2007. Moving to Renault had been a temporary resting place, but Ferrari was the ultimate destination. Now it seemed a return to McLaren beckoned for the Kimster. Yet as things transpired even that would be thwarted at the 11th hour. Jenson Button would outbrake him for the seat alongside Lewis Hamilton and a sabbatical seemed the only choice for the Finn.

Alan Henry

Left: Ferrari celebrated its only win of the year in force, generously not forgetting the hapless and absent Felipe Massa.
Photo: Peter J. Fox

Below left: After his long run without a win, Kimi gets stuck into the bubbly.
Photo: Lukas Gorys

Below: Back to the Ferrari prop cupboard. Luca Badoer's understudy role lasted for just two performances.
Photo: Bernard Asset

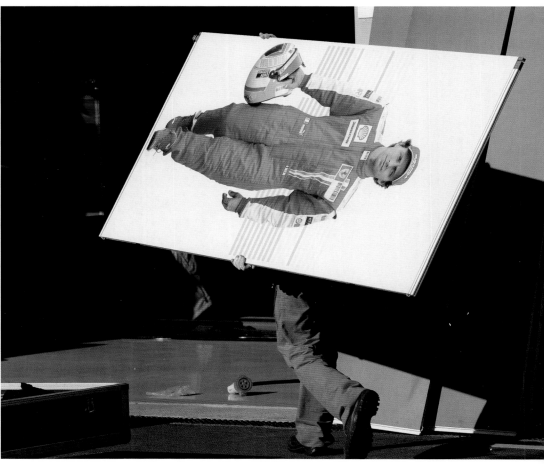

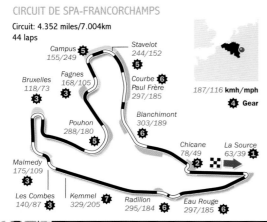

CIRCUIT DE SPA-FRANCORCHAMPS

Circuit: 4.352 miles/7.004km
44 laps

Campus **5** 155/249
Stavelot **5** 244/152
Fagnes **3** 168/105
Courbe Paul Frère **6** 297/185
Bruxelles **3** 118/73
187/116 **kmh/mph**
❀ Gear
Blanchimont **6** 303/189
Pouhon **5** 288/180
Chicane **2** 78/49
La Source **1** 63/39
Malmedy **3** 175/109
Les Combes **3** 140/87
Kemmel **7** 329/205
Radillon **6** 295/184
Eau Rouge **6** 297/185

FIA F1 WORLD CHAMPIONSHIP ROUND 12

ING
BELGIAN
GRAND PRIX

SPA-FRANCORCHAMPS 28-30 AUGUST 2009

RACE DISTANCE: 44 laps, 191.415 miles/308.052km • **RACE WEATHER:** Partly cloudy (track 24-26°C, air 17°C)

Pos.	Driver	Nat.	No.	Entrant	Car/Engine	Tyres	Laps	Time/Retirement	Speed (mph/km/h)	Gap to leader	Fastest race lap	
1	Kimi Räikkönen	FIN	4	Scuderia Ferrari Marlboro	Ferrari F60-056 V8	B	44	1h 23m 50.995s	136.969/220.430		1m 47.674s	42
2	Giancarlo Fisichella	I	21	Force India F1 Team	Force India VJM02-Mercedes FO108W V8	B	44	1h 23m 51.934s	136.943/220.389	+ 0.939s	1m 47.737s	43
3	Sebastian Vettel	D	15	Red Bull Racing	Red Bull RB5-Renault RS27 V8	B	44	1h 23m 54.870s	136.864/220.261	+ 3.875s	1m 47.263s	38
4	Robert Kubica	PL	5	BMW Sauber F1 Team	BMW Sauber F1.09-BMW P86/9 V8	B	44	1h 24m 00.961s	136.699/219.995	+ 9.966s	1m 47.664s	41
5	Nick Heidfeld	D	6	BMW Sauber F1 Team	BMW Sauber F1.09-BMW P86/9 V8	B	44	1h 24m 02.271s	136.663/219.938	+ 11.276s	1m 47.371s	35
6	Heikki Kovalainen	FIN	2	Vodafone McLaren Mercedes	McLaren MP4-24-Mercedes FO108W V8	B	44	1h 24m 23.758s	136.083/219.004	+ 32.763s	1m 48.348s	24
7	Rubens Barrichello	BR	23	Brawn GP Formula 1 Team	Brawn BGP 001-Mercedes FO108W V8	B	44	1h 24m 26.456s	136.011/218.888	+ 35.461s	1m 48.257s	37
8	Nico Rosberg	D	16	AT&T Williams	Williams FW31-Toyota RVX-09 V8	B	44	1h 24m 27.203s	135.990/218.855	+ 36.208s	1m 47.766s	41
9	Mark Webber	AUS	14	Red Bull Racing	Red Bull RB5-Renault RS27 V8	B	44	1h 24m 27.954s	135.970/218.823	+ 36.959s	1m 47.783s	39
10	Timo Glock	D	10	Panasonic Toyota Racing	Toyota TF109-RVX-09 V8	B	44	1h 24m 32.485s	135.849/218.627	+ 41.490s	1m 47.736s	40
11	Adrian Sutil	D	20	Force India F1 Team	Force India VJM02-Mercedes FO108W V8	B	44	1h 24m 33.631s	135.818/218.578	+ 42.636s	1m 47.859s	42
12	Sébastien Buemi	CH	12	Scuderia Toro Rosso	Toro Rosso STR04-Ferrari 056 V8	B	44	1h 24m 37.101s	135.725/218.429	+ 46.106s	1m 47.763s	42
13	Kazuki Nakajima	J	17	AT&T Williams	Williams FW31-Toyota RVX-09 V8	B	44	1h 24m 45.236s	135.508/218.079	+ 54.241s	1m 48.205s	42
14	Luca Badoer	I	3	Scuderia Ferrari Marlboro	Ferrari F60-056 V8	B	44	1h 25m 33.172s	134.243/216.043	+ 1m 42.177s	1m 49.803s	41
	Fernando Alonso	E	7	ING Renault F1 Team	Renault R29-RS27 V8	B	26	accident/front left wheel			1m 48.634s	23
	Jarno Trulli	I	9	Panasonic Toyota Racing	Toyota TF109-RVX-09 V8	B	21	brakes			1m 50.029s	16
	Lewis Hamilton	GB	1	Vodafone McLaren Mercedes	McLaren MP4-24-Mercedes FO108W V8	B	0	accident			no time	
	Jenson Button	GB	22	Brawn GP Formula 1 Team	Brawn BGP 001-Mercedes FO108W V8	B	0	accident			no time	
	Jaime Alguersuari	E	11	Scuderia Toro Rosso	Toro Rosso STR04-Ferrari 056 V8	B	0	accident			no time	
	Romain Grosjean	F	8	ING Renault F1 Team	Renault R29-RS27 V8	B	0	accident			no time	

Fastest race lap: Sebastian Vettel on lap 38, 1m 47.263s, 146.066 mph/235.070km/h.

Lap record: Kimi Räikkönen (McLaren MP4-19-Mercedes Benz V8), 1m 45.108s, 148.465mph/238.931km/h (2004) (4.335-mile/6.976km circuit)

Previous lap record (current configuration): Kimi Räikkönen (Ferrari F2008 V8), 1m 47.930s, 145.164mph/233.618km/h (2008)

3 BADOER · Ferrari
penalty for gearbox change

17 NAKAJIMA · Williams

12 BUEMI · Toro Rosso

22 BUTTON · Brawn

1 HAMILTON · McLaren

16 ROSBERG · Williams

8 GROSJEAN · Renault

11 ALGUERSUARI · Toro Rosso

2 KOVALAINEN · McLaren

7 ALONSO · Renault

20 SUTIL · Force India

14 WEBBER · Red Bull

Grid order	1	2	3	4	5	6	7	8	9	10	11	12	13	14	15	16	17	18	19	20	21	22	23	24	25	26	27	28	29	30	31	32	33	34	35	36	37	38	39	40	41	42	43	44	
21 FISICHELLA	21	21	21	21	4	4	4	4	4	4	4	4	4	4	4	15	15	16	4	4	4	4	4	4	4	4	4	4	4	4	4	4	15	15	15	15	4	4	4	4	4	4	4	4	1
9 TRULLI	4	4	4	4	21	21	21	21	21	21	21	21	21	21	16	16	4	21	21	21	21	21	21	21	21	21	21	21	21	6	4	4	4	21	21	21	21	21	21	21	21	21	21	21	2
6 HEIDFELD	5	5	5	5	5	5	5	5	5	5	5	5	14	14	4	4	21	16	7	7	7	7	7	5	5	5	5	5	5	15	15	4	21	21	21	15	15	15	15	15	15	15	15	15	3
23 BARRICHELLO	10	10	10	10	10	10	10	10	10	10	10	14	6	15	21	21	7	7	5	5	5	5	5	7	2	15	15	15	15	5	6	21	5	5	5	5	5	5	5	5	5	5	5	5	4
5 KUBICA	9	14	14	14	14	14	14	14	14	14	14	6	15	6	7	7	5	5	2	2	2	2	2	2	15	2	6	6	6	6	5	5	6	6	6	6	6	6	6	6	6	6	6	6	5
4 RÄIKKÖNEN	14	6	6	6	6	6	6	6	6	6	6	10	16	16	5	5	2	2	12	12	15	15	15	15	6	6	23	16	16	16	16	16	14	14	2	2	2	2	2	2	2	2	2	2	6
10 GLOCK	6	16	16	16	15	15	15	15	15	15	15	15	7	7	2	2	12	12	15	15	12	6	6	6	23	23	16	10	10	10	10	14	16	2	23	23	23	23	23	23	23	23	23	23	
15 VETTEL	16	15	15	15	16	16	16	16	16	16	16	16	5	5	12	12	15	15	6	6	23	23	23	20	16	10	14	14	14	14	10	2	23	16	16	16	16	16	16	16	16	16	16	16	
14 WEBBER	15	7	7	7	7	7	7	7	7	7	7	7	2	2	6	6	6	6	23	23	23	20	20	20	16	20	14	2	2	2	2	23	16	14	14	14	14	14	14	14	14	14	14	14	
16 ROSBERG	7	2	2	2	2	2	2	2	2	2	2	12	12	23	23	23	23	20	20	20	16	16	16	10	10	2	12	12	23	23	23	10	10	10	10	10	10	10	10	10	10	10	10	10	
20 SUTIL	2	12	12	12	12	12	12	12	12	12	12	23	23	14	14	14	14	16	16	16	10	10	10	14	14	12	23	23	12	20	20	20	12	12	12	12	12	20	20	20	20	20	20	20	
1 HAMILTON	12	17	17	17	17	17	23	23	23	23	23	20	20	20	20	20	10	10	10	10	14	14	14	12	12	17	20	20	12	12	12	12	12	12	12	12	12	12	12	12	12	12	12	12	
7 ALONSO	17	3	3	3	23	23	17	17	20	20	20	10	10	10	10	10	14	14	14	14	12	12	12	17	20	20	17	17	17	17	17	17	17	17	17	17	17	17	17	17	17	17	17	17	
22 BUTTON	23	9	9	9	3	3	20	20	17	17	17	17	17	17	17	17	17	17	17	17	17	17	17	7	7	3	3	3	3	3	3	3	3	3	3	3	3	3	3	3	3	3	3	3	
2 KOVALAINEN	3	23	23	23	9	20	3	3	3	3	3	3	3	3	3	3	3	3	3	3	3	3	3	3																					
12 BUEMI	20	20	20	20	20	9	9	9	9	9	9	9	9	9	9	9	9	9	9	9	9	9																						
11 ALGUERSUARI																																													
17 NAKAJIMA																																													
8 GROSJEAN																																													
3 BADOER																																													

14 One lap or more behind
22 Pit stop
Safety car deployed on laps shown

TIME SHEETS

PRACTICE 1 (FRIDAY)
Cloudy/drizzle/rain
(track 18-20ºC, air 16-19ºC)

Pos.	Driver	Laps	Time
1	Jarno Trulli	13	1m 49.675s
2	Jenson Button	18	1m 50.283s
3	Fernando Alonso	13	1m 50.368s
4	Sébastien Buemi	20	1m 51.045s
5	Jaime Alguersuari	24	1m 51.529s
6	Rubens Barrichello	18	1m 52.321s
7	Kimi Räikkönen	16	1m 52.930s
8	Heikki Kovalainen	11	1m 53.383s
9	Robert Kubica	12	1m 53.650s
10	Luca Badoer	20	1m 55.068s
11	Giancarlo Fisichella	11	2m 03.972s
12	Nico Rosberg	13	2m 04.505s
13	Romain Grosjean	13	2m 05.513s
14	Nick Heidfeld	14	2m 05.614s
15	Kazuki Nakajima	15	2m 05.705s
16	Adrian Sutil	10	2m 05.839s
17	Mark Webber	6	2m 06.181s
18	Timo Glock	15	2m 06.331s
19	Sebastian Vettel	1	no time
20	Lewis Hamilton	4	no time

PRACTICE 2 (FRIDAY)
Sunny
(track 26-29ºC, air 19-20ºC)

Pos.	Driver	Laps	Time
1	Lewis Hamilton	29	1m 47.201s
2	Timo Glock	29	1m 47.217s
3	Kimi Räikkönen	26	1m 47.285s
4	Mark Webber	31	1m 47.329s
5	Romain Grosjean	34	1m 47.333s
6	Giancarlo Fisichella	27	1m 47.506s
7	Jarno Trulli	33	1m 47.559s
8	Robert Kubica	33	1m 47.578s
9	Jaime Alguersuari	36	1m 47.579s
10	Sebastian Vettel	25	1m 47.602s
11	Sébastien Buemi	38	1m 47.702s
12	Heikki Kovalainen	33	1m 47.743s
13	Adrian Sutil	29	1m 47.790s
14	Fernando Alonso	30	1m 47.862s
15	Kazuki Nakajima	32	1m 47.961s
16	Nick Heidfeld	30	1m 48.017s
17	Jenson Button	34	1m 48.125s
18	Rubens Barrichello	37	1m 48.130s
19	Nico Rosberg	29	1m 48.360s
20	Luca Badoer	30	1m 49.211s

PRACTICE 3 (SATURDAY)
Sunny/partly cloudy
(track 18-20ºC, air 14-15ºC)

Pos.	Driver	Laps	Time
1	Nick Heidfeld	17	1m 45.388s
2	Jarno Trulli	18	1m 45.462s
3	Adrian Sutil	20	1m 45.677s
4	Romain Grosjean	18	1m 45.878s
5	Timo Glock	18	1m 45.908s
6	Robert Kubica	18	1m 45.987s
7	Nico Rosberg	19	1m 46.040s
8	Giancarlo Fisichella	21	1m 46.114s
9	Lewis Hamilton	17	1m 46.301s
10	Jenson Button	20	1m 46.406s
11	Kimi Räikkönen	19	1m 46.409s
12	Sébastien Buemi	19	1m 46.417s
13	Heikki Kovalainen	17	1m 46.462s
14	Sebastian Vettel	14	1m 46.747s
15	Jaime Alguersuari	22	1m 46.814s
16	Rubens Barrichello	19	1m 46.815s
17	Fernando Alonso	14	1m 46.926s
18	Luca Badoer	20	1m 47.055s
19	Kazuki Nakajima	19	1m 47.078s
20	Mark Webber	3	no time

QUALIFYING (SATURDAY)
Cloudy/sunny (track 20-27ºC, air 16-20ºC)

Pos.	Driver	First	Second	Third	Weight
1	Giancarlo Fisichella	**1m 45.102s**	1m 44.667s	**1m 46.308s**	648kg
2	Jarno Trulli	1m 45.140s	**1m 44.503s**	1m 46.395s	656.5kg
3	Nick Heidfeld	1m 45.566s	1m 44.709s	1m 46.500s	655kg
4	Rubens Barrichello	1m 45.237s	1m 44.834s	1m 46.513s	644.5kg
5	Robert Kubica	1m 45.655s	1m 44.557s	1m 46.586s	649kg
6	Kimi Räikkönen	1m 45.579s	1m 44.953s	1m 46.633s	655kg
7	Timo Glock	1m 45.450s	1m 44.877s	1m 46.677s	648.5kg
8	Sebastian Vettel	1m 45.372s	1m 44.592s	1m 46.761s	662.5kg
9	Mark Webber	1m 45.350s	1m 44.924s	1m 46.788s	658kg
10	Nico Rosberg	1m 45.486s	1m 45.047s	1m 47.362s	670kg
11	Adrian Sutil	1m 45.239s	1m 45.119s		678.5kg
12	Lewis Hamilton	1m 45.767s	1m 45.122s		693.5kg
13	Fernando Alonso	1m 45.707s	1m 45.136s		684.4kg
14	Jenson Button	1m 45.761s	1m 45.251s		694.2kg
15	Heikki Kovalainen	1m 45.705s	1m 45.259s		697kg
16	Sébastien Buemi	1m 45.951s			685kg
17	Jaime Alguersuari	1m 46.032s			704.5kg
18	Kazuki Nakajima	1m 46.307s			706.1kg
19	Romain Grosjean	1m 46.359s			604.7kg
20	Luca Badoer	1m 46.957s			691.5kg

FOR THE RECORD

1st POLE/PODIUM/POINT: **Force India**

50th GRAND PRIX START: **Luca Badoer**

200th POINT: **Red Bull**

100th POINT: **Heikki Kovalainen**

10th FRONT ROW POSITION: **Toyota**

POINTS

DRIVERS

1	Jenson Button	72
2	Rubens Barrichello	56
3	Sebastian Vettel	53
4	Mark Webber	51.5
5	Kimi Räikkönen	34
6	Nico Rosberg	30.5
7	Lewis Hamilton	27
8	Jarno Trulli	22.5
9	Felipe Massa	22
10	Heikki Kovalainen	17
11	Timo Glock	16
12	Fernando Alonso	16
13	Nick Heidfeld	10
14	Giancarlo Fisichella	8
15	Robert Kubica	8
16	Sébastien Buemi	3
17	Sébastien Bourdais	2

CONSTRUCTORS

1	Brawn	128
2	Red Bull	104.5
3	Ferrari	56
4	McLaren	44
5	Toyota	38.5
6	Williams	30.5
7	BMW Sauber	18
8	Renault	16
9	Force India	8
10	Toro Rosso	5

15 VETTEL · Red Bull

4 RÄIKKÖNEN · Ferrari

23 BARRICHELLO · Brawn

9 TRULLI · Toyota

10 GLOCK · Toyota

5 KUBICA · BMW Sauber

6 HEIDFELD · BMW Sauber

21 FISICHELLA · Force India

RACE TYRE STRATEGIES

The tyre regulations stipulate that two dry tyre specifications must be used during the race.

The Soft compound Bridgestone Potenza tyre is marked with a green stripe on the sidewall of the tyre.

	Driver	Race Stint 1	Race Stint 2	Race Stint 3
1	Kimi Räikkönen	Soft: 1-14	Medium: 15-31	Soft: 32-44
2	Giancarlo Fisichella	Soft: 1-14	Soft: 15-31	Medium: 32-44
3	Sebastian Vettel	Medium: 1-16	Medium: 17-35	Soft: 36-44
4	Robert Kubica	Soft: 1-12	Medium: 13-30	Soft: 31-44
5	Nick Heidfeld	Medium: 1-14	Medium: 15-32	Soft: 33-44
6	Heikki Kovalainen	Soft: 1-26	Medium: 27-44	
7	Rubens Barrichello	Soft: 1	Medium: 2-27	Medium: 28-44
8	Nico Rosberg	Medium: 1-18	Medium: 19-33	Soft: 34-44
9	Mark Webber	Medium: 1-14	Medium: 15-34	Soft: 35-44
10	Timo Glock	Medium: 1-12	Soft: 13-32	Soft: 33-44
11	Adrian Sutil	Medium: 1	Medium: 2-26	Soft: 27-44
12	Sébastien Buemi	Medium: 1-12	Medium: 13-30	Soft: 31-44
13	Kazuki Nakajima	Medium: 1-28	Soft: 29-44	
14	Luca Badoer	Soft: 1-24	Medium: 25-44	
	Fernando Alonso	Medium: 1-24	Soft: 25-26 (dnf)	
	Jarno Trulli	Medium: 1	Medium: 2-20	Soft: 21 (dnf)
	Jenson Button	Medium: 0 (dnf)		
	Romain Grosjean	Medium: 0 (dnf)		
	Lewis Hamilton	Medium: 0 (dnf)		
	Jaime Alguersuari	Medium: 0 (dnf)		

ITALIAN GRAND PRIX

MONZA CIRCUIT

Rubens Barrichello in the Brawn-Mercedes
at speed on his way to his third victory in
the Italian GP at Monza, following on from
his Ferrari wins in 2002 and 2004.
Photo: Peter J. Fox

MONZA QUALIFYING

"**T**HIS**," said Ross Brawn, "is the only track at which a one-stop strategy is definitely quicker…" At any other venue, his cars' presence in fifth and sixth positions, Rubens Barrichello ahead of Jenson Button, might have provided further evidence of a team still thrashing around in a bid to recapture its early-season form, but Brawn spoke with serene confidence.

Irrespective of ambient conditions, the generation of tyre temperature, the Brawns' oft-repeated bugbear, is rarely an issue at a dry Monza. High straight-line speeds, heavy braking and fierce lateral loads through the Parabolica guarantee that much, but this was a race of two grids – and McLaren took pole in both instances.

Lewis Hamilton, Adrian Sutil and Kimi Räikkönen plumped for double-stop strategies and, unsurprisingly, annexed the top three positions. It was the first time that Hamilton and Sutil had occupied the front row of a grid since they had been F3 team-mates in 2006 – and the world champion admitted that KERS assistance was a major plus.

"It gives us a little bit more in qualifying than it does during a race," he said, a reference to the fact that boost applied at the end of a warm-up lap provided a little extra oomph at the start of a qualifying run and still left a full – 6.7-second – allocation to play with over the next 3.6 miles.

"I think it makes up for the loss of downforce and, perhaps, drag that we have compared to others," he added. "Adrian is quicker than us down the main straight, even though we have KERS boosting us all the way, so it kind of compensates some of the bits that aren't so great on the car, and we are still working to improve those."

And even KERS might not have been enough if Sutil hadn't run slightly wide through the first Lesmo on his quickest run. "This has been a great day for me," the German said. "The car is amazing and it feels so different now, driving and knowing that you have a real chance. The good feeling you get from being a racing driver has returned."

The irony was that he revelled in the spotlight while former team-mate Giancarlo Fisichella – suddenly a major draw at Monza – was learning a host of new buttons and functions in his first weekend with Ferrari. Having been delayed by an accident at Parabolica on Saturday morning, however, the Italian lined up only 14th.

"Giancarlo has already acknowledged that his new car perhaps isn't as strong as ours," Sutil said. "He knows he could have won the last race, but you have to understand that an Italian driver's dream is to race in Formula One with Ferrari. Given the chance, anybody else would have done the same."

Fisichella's replacement, Vitantonio Liuzzi, built up steadily, didn't put a foot wrong and qualified a laudable seventh – or fourth on the 'Class B' grid, behind Heikki Kovalainen and the Brawns.

Kovalainen's was a particularly sweet lap, and, fuel corrected, it equated to the day's finest of all. "I think we're going to be strong," he said. "We're in good shape and have a solid, reliable car. I've been quick all weekend and felt the car actually worked better with a heavier fuel load. I'm focusing on victory and think that's a realistic target."

Above: Jackie Stewart celebrated the 40th anniversary of his first World Championship at Monza.
Photo: Paul-Henri Cahier

Left: Pat Symonds arrives in the paddock for what would prove to be his final race as the Renault team's executive director of engineering.
Photo: Lukas Gorys

Below: Under pressure. Flavio Briatore was feeling the heat at Monza in more ways than one.
Photo: Peter J. Fox

Below left: Pole-sitter Lewis Hamilton congratulates Adrian Sutil on his first ever front-row start.
Photo: Jad Sherif/WRi2

Right: Charge of the KERS brigade. Hamilton and Räikkönen make their moves at the start of the race.
Photo: Peter J. Fox

THE setting is traditional – crumbling pathways, flowing streams and, obviously, a goat farm – and so are many local customs. That's why, at 7.40 on race morning, nobody batted an eyelid as a teenage boy attempted to climb through a small gap in Monza's security fencing. Such opportunism, though, could not mask a horrible truth: when the cars lined up on Sunday afternoon, many grandstand seats remained conspicuously empty. In most countries, that would have been blamed on the recession or, in newer Formula One markets, simple disinterest, but at Monza it was mostly a reflection of Ferrari's generally mediocre form. Neither Kimi Räikkönen's recent Spa victory nor the recruitment of Giancarlo Fisichella had been enough to alter perceptions, but then you don't need people – or cars, come to that – to create atmosphere at Monza.

Shortly before the start, Brawn team manager Ron Meadows stood alone on the grid, in quiet contemplation of his own cars and those around them. Did he still think a one-stop strategy would pay dividends? "We'll finish first and second," he said, the tone of his response measured rather than brash. He also happened to be right.

The opening stint, though, was all about the charge of the light brigade, Lewis Hamilton tearing away into the lead and Räikkönen using a blast of KERS to usurp Adrian Sutil's Force India before they'd reached the first chicane. For the tactically advantaged Heikki Kovalainen, though, the afternoon began cataclysmically. While most of the field opted to start on soft Bridgestones, the Finn chose mediums. He failed to conjure sufficient tyre heat during the final formation lap, however, and didn't have anything like enough purchase as he left the line. And KERS doesn't much help when your wheels are spinning…

Rubens Barrichello, who was able to make the mediums work at the start, helped himself to fourth place straight away, and Kovalainen's lap deteriorated thereafter. He got very sideways on the way out of the second chicane, which allowed Jenson Button to draw alongside at the first Lesmo and pull ahead before the second. By the time he'd come out of Ascari, Kovalainen had returnee Tonio Liuzzi's Force India on his tail, and the Italian swept ahead before Parabolica.

By the lap's end, Hamilton led closest challenger Räikkönen by 1.277 seconds, Sutil by 1.805 seconds and main threat Barrichello by 3.426 seconds. Button lay fifth from Liuzzi, Kovalainen, Sebastian Vettel, Fernando Alonso, Robert Kubica, Giancarlo Fisichella, Nick Heidfeld, Jarno Trulli, Nico Rosberg, Kazuki Nakajima, Romain Grosjean, Timo Glock, Sébastien Buemi and Jaime Alguersuari.

Mark Webber's afternoon was already over by this stage. The Australian had edged Kubica on to the grass as they sprinted towards the first chicane, and the two cars brushed slightly when they got there. There was firmer contact as they came into the second chicane, which resulted in a bent front wing for the Pole and a gravel parking bay for Webber. "I was on Mark's left at the start and guess he didn't see me," Kubica said. "At the second chicane, he was on the outside and slightly ahead of me, but when we were going into the first apex I was unfortunately unable to avoid him."

Webber added, "It seems like Robert's front wheel was inside my left rear, but it was difficult to know he was there. We made contact, which flicked my car into the air a little bit and then nosed it into the guardrail."

It was undamaged, but stuck, and that heralded his first retirement of the campaign.

Alonso and Kubica passed Vettel on the second lap – the Pole's damaged front wing apparently no impediment – and the Spaniard elbowed Kovalainen aside going into the first chicane on lap three. The former champion had been expected to hassle the Brawns at the start, Renault having refitted KERS to its cars on a one-off basis, but the system didn't respond as anticipated and he made a disappointingly conventional start.

At the front, meanwhile, Hamilton was easing away at his leisure and was 5.205 seconds clear of Räikkönen after ten laps. Barrichello and Button were respectively 13.494 and 16.629 seconds in arrears at that stage – and lapping about seven-tenths slower than the leader. The mathematics, though, dictated that Hamilton needed to be 25–26 seconds clear by the time he made his second stop, but the balance of power altered early in his second stint, when he began dropping six- or seven-tenths per lap to the now lighter Brawns. Barrichello pitted on lap 29, one later than Button, and both were less than 20 seconds behind Hamilton when the early pace-setter made his final stop on lap 34. Thus was proven the benefit of a one-stop strategy, although Hamilton was an in-touch third when he rejoined.

The Brawn drivers chose reverse tyre strategies – Button started on softs because he had no fresh mediums available and feared used tyres would expose him to the risk of being jumped by Alonso – but it didn't make a great deal of difference, because the car worked well on both compounds. The Brawn team remained true to its principle of allowing its drivers to compete for the title without the imposition of subtle team orders, and the two cars ran like clockwork, about four seconds apart, as the race drew towards its conclusion.

"I struggled a little bit with my brakes at the start of the year," recounted Barrichello, "but since we changed things at Silverstone, I have been a lot happier. I love Monza, and to win here feels great, especially after I was thinking about my transmission for most of last night…"

The team hadn't been sure the Brazilian's gearbox would last, having been subjected to a momentary overdose of torque when the anti-stall kicked in during the previous race at Spa, but it opted not to take the five-position grid penalty that would have accompanied a change, and Barrichello reported no problems at all.

Button was gracious in defeat – and glad to be back on the podium for the first time since winning in Turkey. "I am happy with my performance," he said, "but Rubens just went one better, so well done to him. People asked why I was only 19th fastest on Friday, but we were doing race set-up work, and as you can see the team did it very well."

Towards the end, he was under increasing pressure from Hamilton, but Button wasn't unduly worried. "It might sound daft," he said, "but it really isn't that easy to overtake around here, even with KERS. If I didn't make a mistake, I don't think Lewis was going to get past me. My engineer was getting quite excited on the radio, but I was pretty much in control."

Which is more than could be said for Hamilton…

The Englishman's combative spirit is engaging, but it can also be costly. With half a lap to go, he felt he might be able to have a KERS-assisted shot at Button if he could just get close enough. That persuaded him to push a little bit harder through the first Lesmo, and he took just a little bit too much of the exit kerbing, which spat him back across the track and hard into

Above: A slightly delayed pitstop dented Adrian Sutil's hopes of a first podium.

Photo: Jean-François Galeron/WRi2

Right: Sheer delight as Rubens Barrichello takes the winner's applause for the second time in three races.

Photo: Peter J. Fox

the opposite tyre wall. "I wasn't on the optimal strategy and really had to push to make my two-stopper work," he said. "I got every tenth out of the car and didn't make any mistakes…until the last lap. I can only apologise to the team."

His lapse gifted Räikkönen a fourth consecutive podium finish and shuffled Sutil up to fourth, although both might have fallen prey to the one-stopping Liuzzi, whose impressive comeback ended when a driveshaft snapped on lap 23.

As at Spa, where Fisichella had coaxed extraordinary economy from a Force India, Sutil appeared to have topped up with diesel: his post-qualifying weight suggested that he had half a lap more fuel than Hamilton, yet he stayed out two laps longer.

He and Räikkönen made their second stops simultaneously, on lap 37, and the Finn lost a bit of time when his lollipop man began giving the 'go' signal a fraction too soon. Räikkönen recovered swiftly from a faltering restart, but the mistake was inconsequential because Sutil's stop was far worse. The German braked too late as he entered his pit and knocked over one of his crew, happily without injury.

"At the start, I knew it would be really difficult to defend against Kimi," Sutil said, "and then I was stuck behind him for the whole race. I was really quick, but couldn't find a way past because KERS had such a big effect."

Alonso's drive was yet another masterclass in making the most of what you've got. He shouldn't have been within a canton of the nearest McLaren, let alone ahead of one, and the vanquished Kovalainen

could only describe himself as "rather disappointed", which failed to paint the full, horrible truth. His sixth place at Spa had been the result of a solid job in difficult circumstances, yet at Monza he'd been running almost 35 seconds behind his team-mate, despite a theoretically favourable strategy. At least, though, he finished.

Hamilton's accident brought the safety car into play for the final half-lap, which didn't affect the Brawns, but caused a certain amount of confusion further back.

Nick Heidfeld put in a strong, steady drive to rise from 15th to seventh, ahead of Vettel, who accepted that Red Bull's shortcomings were only temporary. "The first five to ten laps were the biggest issue today," he said, "because I was sliding around all over the place and lost a lot of time. Overall, this wasn't the best track for our car, but in Singapore we will put more downforce on again and maybe we'll be better. The championship isn't over yet."

Fisichella was happy with his performance, if not with ninth place, and felt that Saturday morning's accident had been the weekend's pivotal setback. Nakajima completed the top ten, ahead of Glock – and this was actually one of the Japanese driver's finest F1 performances to date. He delivered it, though, during a weekend when the Williams cars were hopelessly off the pace: the team's low-drag configuration simply didn't work.

Nakajima survived a late passing attempt by Jarno Trulli, who launched himself over the first chicane kerbs at the start of a comedic 48th lap, in which he

committed a litany of errors and dropped places to both Glock and Buemi.

Technically, the latter didn't finish the race, because he followed the post-Hamilton safety car into the pits rather than taking the chequered flag. Consequently, he was classified 13th, behind Hamilton, but ahead of Trulli, Grosjean (whose car suffered punitive first-lap accident damage) and Rosberg, whose fine start – he gained four places off the line – was swiftly compromised. "Some debris hit my front left and the car suddenly felt very different, with lots of understeer," he said, "so I assumed I had punctured my tyre and requested to pit." When he came in, on lap four, he discovered that his tyres were fine. Instead, his aero balance, which hadn't been terribly good in the first place, was now even worse.

Toro Rosso withdrew Alguersuari after 19 laps, because of worsening gearbox problems, but Kubica's afternoon had ended earlier still. Although his sense of adventure hadn't been compromised by the front wing damage sustained when he hit Webber, the stewards considered the loose bodywork a potentially dangerous companion, given Monza's high speeds, and the black and orange warning flag made a rare appearance on lap seven. Kubica pitted for repairs two laps later, but retired with a gearbox oil leak soon afterwards. For the team, though, there was a bigger concern: with four races to go, it was beginning to run out of engines – and as the F1 programme was being disbanded, BMW didn't plan to make any new ones.

Simon Arron

EDITOR'S VIEW
FISICHELLA FAILS TO IMPRESS AT FERRARI

Left: Vitantonio Liuzzi returned to F1 action with Force India and qualified in a very impresssive seventh place. His race ended in dsappointment when well placed.

Photo: Fritz Van Eldik/WRi2

Below: Giancarlo Fisichella looked like a man who had taken on more than he bargained for with Ferrari.

Photo: Paul-Henri Cahier

THERE is a certain passion missing from Monza when Ferrari is doing badly, a curious "What-are-we-doing-here?" feeling. It's not unfamiliar, either, more's the pity, although Michael Schumacher did more for Maranello's credibility rating and strike rate over the past decade than pretty much all the drivers combined in the Prancing Horse's 60-year history.

In 2009, of course, we had the stuff of which legends are made – well, at least tall stories. An Italian driver was contesting the Italian Grand Prix at the wheel of a Ferrari. I can't begin to imagine what Enzo Ferrari would have thought of the genial former Force India driver who took over the role of Felipe Massa's stand-in from the hapless Luca Badoer. Most likely, the *Commendatore* would have been grumbling, "There you are, and you all wonder why I've never been particularly bothered about Italian drivers."

I'm not talking about ancient history here, of course.

Ferrari was a great fan of Antonio Ascari, whose son, Alberto, became the only Italian ever to win a world championship with the team, taking back-to-back titles in 1952 and 1953. Another 13 years would pass before Lodivico Scarfiotti joined Giuseppe Farina and Ascari as the only other Italian ever to win at Monza for Ferrari. But the relationship between Ferrari and his compatriots was always fraught with mutual tension, the Old Man bizarrely seeming to resent anybody who took attention away from his beloved racing cars. That habit died with him in 1988, but a residual sense of the slightly neurotic has lingered ever since.

The mood in the Ferrari camp at Monza in 2009 was one of uncomfortable transition, everybody knowing full well that the team was in a state of flux, that negotiations were continuing frantically behind the scenes to uncouple Kimi Räikkönen from the balance of his contract to make way for Fernando Alonso in 2010. In fairness to Kimi, while such a situation might have transformed many a driver into a gibbering basket case, the Finn just breezed through the weekend, apparently unconcerned as to how his future might unfold. The anaesthetising power of the dollar clearly played a crucial role in this process of mental insulation.

Kimi got on with the job in hand, starting third and finishing third, behind the two Brawns. For his part, Fisichella looked out of his depth and never at home in his new skin. Qualifying 14th and finishing ninth was a lousy way to kick off his Ferrari career. Forget testing limitations, lack of familiarity with the car and all the other indulgent excuses trotted out in Formula One to avoid calling a spade a spade. This was a guy in his 224th grand prix, and one could only sympathise with the slightly plaintive tones of his engineer, Rob Smedley, trying to infuse his man with the motivation to get on with it over the radio. It was a day when the whole team needed to dig deep, in terms of patience at any rate.

All the team could do was to take whatever succour it could from Räikkönen's drive to third place at the wheel of car that was only good enough to inherit that place after Lewis Hamilton crashed his McLaren spectacularly on the final lap.

All of which brings me to my favourite Monza story, which I believe to be apocryphal. I certainly hope so anyway. Legend has it that an hour or so after the main grandstand emptied following Ludovico Scarfiotti's victory, one spectator remained sitting there. On investigation, it emerged that he was dead, stabbed, presumably by a fan of Lorenzo Bandini, the other Italian driving a Ferrari in that race.

Can't imagine that happening at Silverstone, somehow. Or Monza, to be fair. Yet the story lingers on, becoming further embellished and exaggerated with the passing of the years. Like so much in the F1 business, you can never be *quite* sure whether it is true or not.

Alan Henry

Left: Fernando Alonso reminded the Ferrari fans that he was coming with a strong fifth place for Renault.

Photo: Bernard Asset

Right: The disused and decaying banking at Monza is just part of the circuit's unique atmosphere.

Photo: Paul-Henri Cahier

AUTODROMO NAZIONALE DI MONZA
Circuit: 3.600 miles/5.793km   53 laps

Lesmo 2
176/110 ❽

Lesmo 1
191/119 ❹

Curva del Serraglio
189/304 ❺

Curva Vialone
169/105 ❸

Variante
della Roggia
119/74 ❷

Variante Ascari
225/140 ❹

336/208 ⓫

Variante del
Rettifilo 85/53 ❶

Curva Grande
303/189 ❻

Rettifilo Tribune 298/186 ❼

Curva Parabolica
213/133 ❿

187/116 kmh/mph   ❹ Gear

FIA F1 WORLD CHAMPIONSHIP ROUND 13

GRAN PREMIO SANTANDER D'ITALIA

MONZA 11-13 SEPTEMBER 2009

Photos: Peter J. Fox

RACE DISTANCE: 53 laps, 190.587 miles/306.720km • RACE WEATHER: Sunny (track 36-38°C, air 26-27°C)

Pos.	Driver	Nat.	No.	Entrant	Car/Engine	Tyres	Laps	Time/Retirement	Speed (mph/km/h)	Gap to leader	Fastest race lap
1	Rubens Barrichello	BR	23	Brawn GP Formula 1 Team	Brawn BGP 001-Mercedes FO108W V8	B	53	1h 16m 21.706s	149.750/241.000		1m 24.967s 48
2	Jenson Button	GB	22	Brawn GP Formula 1 Team	Brawn BGP 001-Mercedes FO108W V8	B	53	1h 16m 24.572s	149.657/240.849	+ 2.866s	1m 24.935s 46
3	Kimi Räikkönen	FIN	4	Scuderia Ferrari Marlboro	Ferrari F60-056 V8	B	53	1h 16m 52.370s	148.754/239.397	+ 30.664s	1m 24.761s 36
4	Adrian Sutil	D	20	Force India F1 Team	Force India VJM02-Mercedes FO108W V8	B	53	1h 16m 52.837s	148.739/239.373	+ 31.131s	1m 24.739s 36
5	Fernando Alonso	E	7	ING Renault F1 Team	Renault R29-RS27 V8	B	53	1h 17m 20.888s	147.840/237.926	+ 59.182s	1m 25.199s 50
6	Heikki Kovalainen	FIN	2	Vodafone McLaren Mercedes	McLaren MP4-24-Mercedes FO108W V8	B	53	1h 17m 22.399s	147.793/237.849	+ 1m 00.693s	1m 25.109s 51
7	Nick Heidfeld	D	6	BMW Sauber F1 Team	BMW Sauber F1.09-BMW P86/9 V8	B	53	1h 17m 44.118s	147.104/236.741	+ 1m 22.412s	1m 25.488s 30
8	Sebastian Vettel	D	15	Red Bull Racing	Red Bull RB5-Renault RS27 V8	B	53	1h 17m 47.113s	147.010/236.589	+ 1m 25.407s	1m 25.194s 50
9	Giancarlo Fisichella	I	3	Scuderia Ferrari Marlboro	Ferrari F60-056 V8	B	53	1h 17m 48.562s	146.964/236.516	+ 1m 26.856s	1m 25.498s 28
10	Kazuki Nakajima	J	17	AT&T Williams	Williams FW31-Toyota RVX-09 V8	B	53	1h 19m 03.869s	144.631/232.761	+ 2m 42.163s	1m 25.976s 51
11	Timo Glock	D	10	Panasonic Toyota Racing	Toyota TF109-RVX-09 V8	B	53	1h 19m 05.631s	144.578/232.675	+ 2m 43.925s	1m 25.751s 50
12	Lewis Hamilton	GB	1	Vodafone McLaren Mercedes	McLaren MP4-24-Mercedes FO108W V8	B	52	accident		+ 1 lap	1m 24.802s 52
13	Sébastien Buemi	CH	12	Scuderia Toro Rosso	Toro Rosso STR04-Ferrari 056 V8	B	52			+ 1 lap	1m 25.564s 50
14	Jarno Trulli	I	9	Panasonic Toyota Racing	Toyota TF109-RVX-09 V8	B	52			+ 1 lap	1m 25.700s 49
15	Romain Grosjean	F	8	ING Renault F1 Team	Renault R29-RS27 V8	B	52			+ 1 lap	1m 25.609s 51
16	Nico Rosberg	D	16	AT&T Williams	Williams FW31-Toyota RVX-09 V8	B	51			+ 2 laps	1m 25.901s 50
	Vitantonio Liuzzi	I	21	Force India F1 Team	Force India VJM02-Mercedes FO108W V8	B	22	driveshaft			1m 26.041s 22
	Jaime Alguersuari	E	11	Scuderia Toro Rosso	Toro Rosso STR04-Ferrari 056 V8	B	19	gearbox			1m 27.846s 17
	Robert Kubica	PL	5	BMW Sauber F1 Team	BMW Sauber F1.09-BMW P86/9 V8	B	15	oil leak			1m 27.819s 12
	Mark Webber	AUS	14	Red Bull Racing	Red Bull RB5-Renault RS27 V8	B	0	accident			no time

Fastest race lap: Adrian Sutil on lap 36, 1m 24.739s, 152.923mph/246.106km/h.

Lap record: Rubens Barrichello (Ferrari F2004 V10), 1m 21.046s, 159.892mph/257.320km/h (2004)

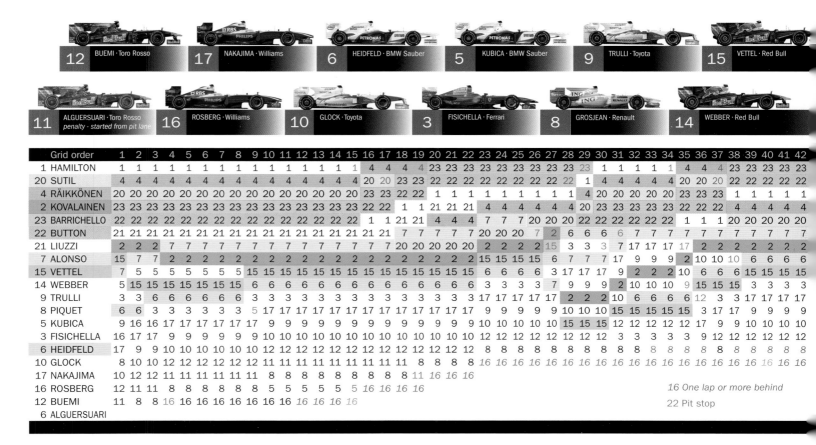

Grid order	1	2	3	4	5	6	7	8	9	10	11	12	13	14	15	16	17	18	19	20	21	22	23	24	25	26	27	28	29	30	31	32	33	34	35	36	37	38	39	40	41	42
1 HAMILTON	1	1	1	1	1	1	1	1	1	1	1	1	1	1	1	1	4	4	4	23	23	23	23	23	23	23	23	23	1	1	1	1	1	4	4	4	23	23	23	23
20 SUTIL	4	4	4	4	4	4	4	4	4	4	4	4	4	4	4	20	20	23	23	22	22	22	22	22	22	22	22	1	4	4	4	4	20	20	20	22	22	22	22
4 RÄIKKÖNEN	20	20	20	20	20	20	20	20	20	20	20	20	20	20	20	23	23	22	1	1	1	1	1	1	1	1	4	20	20	20	20	23	23	23	1	1	1	1
2 KOVALAINEN	23	23	23	23	23	23	23	23	23	23	23	23	23	23	23	22	1	1	21	21	4	4	4	4	4	20	23	23	23	23	22	22	4	4	4	4
23 BARRICHELLO	22	22	22	22	22	22	22	22	22	22	22	22	22	22	1	1	21	21	4	4	4	7	7	20	20	20	22	22	22	22	1	1	1	20	20	20	20
22 BUTTON	21	21	21	21	21	21	21	21	21	21	21	21	21	21	21	7	7	7	7	20	20	20	7	2	6	6	6	6	7	7	7	7	7	7	7	7	7
21 LIUZZI	2	2	2	7	7	7	7	7	7	7	7	7	7	7	7	20	20	20	20	2	2	2	2	15	3	3	3	7	17	17	17	17	2	2	2	2	2
7 ALONSO	15	7	7	2	2	2	2	2	2	2	2	2	2	2	2	2	2	15	15	15	15	6	7	7	17	9	9	9	2	10	10	10	6	6	6	6
15 VETTEL	7	5	5	5	5	5	5	15	15	15	15	15	15	15	15	15	15	6	6	6	6	3	17	17	17	9	2	2	10	6	6	6	15	15	15
14 WEBBER	5	15	15	15	15	15	15	6	6	6	6	6	6	6	6	6	6	6	3	3	3	3	7	9	9	9	2	10	10	10	9	15	15	15	3	3	3	3
9 TRULLI	3	3	6	6	6	6	6	3	3	3	3	3	3	3	3	3	3	3	17	17	17	17	2	2	10	6	6	6	6	12	3	3	17	17	17
8 PIQUET	6	6	3	3	3	3	3	5	17	17	17	17	17	17	17	17	17	9	9	9	9	10	10	10	15	15	15	15	3	17	19	9	9	9
5 KUBICA	9	16	16	17	17	17	17	17	9	9	9	9	9	9	9	9	10	10	10	10	15	15	15	12	12	12	7	9	10	10	10	10
3 FISICHELLA	12	12	12	9	9	9	9	9	12	12	12	12	12	12	12	12	9	9	9	8	8	12	12	3	3	3	12	12	12	12	12	12
6 HEIDFELD	17	9	9	10	10	10	10	10	10	12	12	12	12	12	12	12	8	8	8	8	8	8	8	3	8	8	8	8	8	8	8	8
10 GLOCK	8	10	10	12	12	12	12	12	11	11	11	11	11	11	11	8	16	16	16	16	16	16	16	16	16	16	16	16	16	16	16	16
17 NAKAJIMA	10	12	12	11	11	11	11	11	8	8	8	8	8	8	11	16	16	16														
16 ROSBERG	12	11	11	8	8	8	8	8	5	5	5	5	5	5	16	16	16	16														
12 BUEMI	11	8	8	16	16	16	16	16	16	16	16	16	16	16																		
6 ALGUERSUARI																																

16 One lap or more behind

22 Pit stop

TIME SHEETS

PRACTICE 1 (FRIDAY)
Sunny
(track 30-33ºC, air 23-25ºC)

Pos.	Driver	Laps	Time
1	Lewis Hamilton	26	1m 23.936s
2	Heikki Kovalainen	27	1m 24.332s
3	Adrian Sutil	24	1m 24.471s
4	Fernando Alonso	21	1m 24.477s
5	Nick Heidfeld	25	1m 24.683s
6	Sébastien Buemi	35	1m 24.703s
7	Jenson Button	21	1m 24.706s
8	Giancarlo Fisichella	24	1m 24.732s
9	Mark Webber	19	1m 24.759s
10	Kimi Räikkönen	26	1m 24.761s
11	Robert Kubica	20	1m 24.813s
12	Rubens Barrichello	24	1m 24.826s
13	Nico Rosberg	29	1m 24.927s
14	Kazuki Nakajima	28	1m 25.150s
15	Romain Grosjean	18	1m 25.612s
16	Vitantonio Liuzzi	29	1m 25.689s
17	Jaime Alguersuari	30	1m 25.742s
18	Sebastian Vettel	8	1m 25.951s
19	Jarno Trulli	23	1m 26.020s
20	Timo Glock	17	1m 26.325s

PRACTICE 2 (FRIDAY)
Sunny
(track 38-40ºC, air 28º-29ºC)

Pos.	Driver	Laps	Time
1	Adrian Sutil	28	1m 23.924s
2	Romain Grosjean	31	1m 24.163s
3	Fernando Alonso	35	1m 24.297s
4	Heikki Kovalainen	41	1m 24.482s
5	Robert Kubica	40	1m 24.622s
6	Timo Glock	36	1m 24.634s
7	Nick Heidfeld	34	1m 24.693s
8	Kimi Räikkönen	39	1m 24.796s
9	Kazuki Nakajima	36	1m 24.799s
10	Sébastien Buemi	44	1m 24.884s
11	Lewis Hamilton	32	1m 24.902s
12	Vitantonio Liuzzi	39	1m 24.921s
13	Jarno Trulli	40	1m 24.967s
14	Mark Webber	25	1m 24.979s
15	Jaime Alguersuari	34	1m 25.003s
16	Rubens Barrichello	35	1m 25.140s
17	Nico Rosberg	38	1m 25.215s
18	Sebastian Vettel	27	1m 25.386s
19	Jenson Button	32	1m 25.424s
20	Giancarlo Fisichella	36	1m 25.543s

PRACTICE 3 (SATURDAY)
Sunny
(track 31-35ºC, air 25-26ºC)

Pos.	Driver	Laps	Time
1	Adrian Sutil	21	1m 23.336s
2	Jenson Button	21	1m 23.404s
3	Nick Heidfeld	18	1m 23.490s
4	Rubens Barrichello	20	1m 23.575s
5	Lewis Hamilton	18	1m 23.633s
6	Heikki Kovalainen	20	1m 23.803s
7	Vitantonio Liuzzi	21	1m 23.849s
8	Fernando Alonso	17	1m 23.915s
9	Timo Glock	21	1m 23.959s
10	Robert Kubica	18	1m 23.996s
11	Romain Grosjean	15	1m 24.197s
12	Kimi Räikkönen	20	1m 24.302s
13	Jarno Trulli	17	1m 24.326s
14	Kazuki Nakajima	20	1m 24.392s
15	Sébastien Buemi	23	1m 24.572s
16	Nico Rosberg	21	1m 24.621s
17	Mark Webber	13	1m 25.154s
18	Sebastian Vettel	16	1m 25.244s
19	Jaime Alguersuari	10	1m 25.791s
20	Giancarlo Fisichella	10	1m 25.951s

QUALIFYING (SATURDAY)
Sunny (track 37-39ºC, air 27ºC)

Pos.	Driver	First	Second	Third	Weight
1	Lewis Hamilton	**1m 23.375s**	1m 22.973s	**1m 24.066s**	653.5kg
2	Adrian Sutil	1m 23.576s	1m 23.070s	1m 24.261s	655kg
3	Kimi Räikkönen	1m 23.349s	1m 23.426s	1m 24.523s	662kg
4	Heikki Kovalainen	1m 23.515s	1m 23.528s	1m 24.845s	683kg
5	Rubens Barrichello	1m 23.483s	1m 22.976s	1m 25.015s	688.5kg
6	Jenson Button	1m 23.403s	**1m 22.955s**	1m 25.030s	687kg
7	Vitantonio Liuzzi	1m 23.578s	1m 23.207s	1m 25.043s	679.5kg
8	Fernando Alonso	1m 23.708s	1m 23.497s	1m 25.072s	677.5kg
9	Sebastian Vettel	1m 23.558s	1m 23.545s	1m 25.180s	682kg
10	Mark Webber	1m 23.755s	1m 23.273s	1m 25.314s	683kg
11	Jarno Trulli	1m 24.014s	1m 23.611s		703kg
12	Romain Grosjean	1m 23.975s	1m 23.728s		699.8kg
13	Robert Kubica	1m 24.001s	1m 23.866s		697.5kg
14	Giancarlo Fisichella	1m 23.828s	1m 23.901s		690kg
15	Nick Heidfeld	1m 23.584s	1m 24.275s		697.5kg
16	Timo Glock	1m 24.036s			709.8k
17	Kazuki Nakajima	1m 24.074s			706.2kg
18	Nico Rosberg	1m 24.121s			708.6kg
19	Sébastien Buemi	1m 24.220s			706kg
20	Jaime Alguersuari	1m 24.951s			706kg

DID YOU KNOW?

This was the 80th Italian Grand Prix, the first having been run in 1921, and the 60th in the World Championship.

POINTS

DRIVERS

1	Jenson Button	80
2	Rubens Barrichello	66
3	Sebastian Vettel	54
4	Mark Webber	51.5
5	Kimi Räikkönen	40
6	Nico Rosberg	30.5
7	Lewis Hamilton	27
8	Jarno Trulli	22.5
9	Felipe Massa	22
10	Heikki Kovalainen	20
11	Fernando Alonso	20
12	Timo Glock	16
13	Nick Heidfeld	12
14	Giancarlo Fisichella	8
15	Robert Kubica	8
16	Adrian Sutil	5
17	Sébastien Buemi	3
18	Sébastien Bourdais	2

CONSTRUCTORS

1	Brawn	146
2	Red Bull	105.5
3	Ferrari	62
4	McLaren	47
5	Toyota	38.5
6	Williams	30.5
7	BMW Sauber	20
8	Renault	20
9	Force India	13
10	Toro Rosso	5

21 LIUZZI · Force India

23 BARRICHELLO · Brawn

4 RÄIKKÖNEN · Ferrari

1 HAMILTON · McLaren

7 ALONSO · Renault

22 BUTTON · Brawn

2 KOVALAINEN · McLaren

20 SUTIL · Force India

	44	45	46	47	48	49	49	50	51	52	53	
3	23	23	23	23	23	23	23	23	23	23	23	1
2	22	22	22	22	22	22	22	22	22	22	22	2
1	1	1	1	1	1	1	1	1	1	1	4	3
4	4	4	4	4	4	4	4	4	4	4	20	4
)	20	20	20	20	20	20	20	20	20	20	7	5
	7	7	7	7	7	7	7	7	7	2	2	6
2	2	2	2	2	2	2	2	2	2	6		7
6	6	6	6	6	6	6	6	6	6	15		8
5	15	15	15	15	15	15	15	15	15	3		
3	3	3	3	3	3	3	3	3	3	17		
7	17	17	17	17	17	17	17	17	17	10		
)	9	9	9	9	10	10	10	10	10	10		
)	10	10	10	10	12	12	12	12	12	12		
2	12	12	12	12	9	9	9	9	9	9		
3	8	8	8	8	8	8	8	8	8	8		
6	16	16	16	16	16	16	16	16	16			

◼ Safety car deployed on lap shown

RACE TYRE STRATEGIES

The tyre regulations stipulate that two dry tyre specifications must be used during the race.

The Soft compound Bridgestone Potenza tyre is marked with a green stripe on the sidewall of the tyre.

	Driver	Race Stint 1	Race Stint 2	Race Stint 3	Race Stint 4
1	Rubens Barrichello	Medium: 1-29	Soft: 30-53		
2	Jenson Button	Soft: 1-28	Medium: 29-53		
3	Kimi Räikkönen	Soft: 1-19	Soft: 20-37	Medium: 38-53	
4	Adrian Sutil	Soft: 1-20	Medium: 21-37	Soft: 38-53	
5	Fernando Alonso	Soft: 1-26	Medium: 27-53		
6	Heikki Kovalainen	Medium: 1-27	Soft: 28-53		
7	Nick Heidfeld	Soft: 1-31	Medium: 32-53		
8	Sebastian Vettel	Medium: 1-27	Soft: 28-53		
9	Giancarlo Fisichella	Soft: 1-30	Medium: 31-53		
10	Kazuki Nakajima	Soft: 1-30	Medium: 31-53		
11	Timo Glock	Soft: 1-38	Medium: 39-52		
12	Lewis Hamilton	Soft: 1-15	Medium: 16-34	Medium: 35-52 (dnf)	
13	Sebastien Buemi	Medium: 1-36	Soft: 37-52		
14	Jarno Trulli	Medium: 1-35	Soft: 36-52		
15	Romain Grosjean	Medium: 1-33	Soft: 34-52		
16	Nico Rosberg	Medium: 1-4	Soft: 5-15	Soft: 16-40	Soft: 41-51
	Vitantonio Liuzzi	Soft: 1-15 (dnf)			
	Jaime Alguersuari	Medium: 1-19 (dnf)			
	Robert Kubica	Soft: 1-9	Medium: 10-15 (dnf)		
	Mark Webber	Medium: 0 (dnf)			

FIA FORMULA 1 WORLD CHAMPIONSHIP · ROUND 14

SINGAPORE GRAND PRIX

MARINA BAY CIRCUIT

Lewis Hamilton uses every centimetre of the Marina Bay circuit, and a bit more besides, as his McLaren MP4-24 opens an early lead over Nico Rosberg's Williams, the young British driver determined to make amends for his last-lap shunt in the previous race at Monza.
Photo: Peter J. Fox

MARINA BAY QUALIFYING

FROM a mechanic's perspective, tradition dictates that an all-nighter means repairing to the hotel at four or five in the morning, if at all. In Singapore, the nocturnal schedule dictated that McLaren's troops had to toil until 10am to enhance Lewis Hamilton's prospects, but he rewarded their endeavours in full.

A potential problem with his KERS system's wiring loom was identified after Friday's two free practice sessions, and it was simpler to switch everything to a different tub than it was to effect a replacement, which would have involved drilling out parts that had been bonded to the carbon fibre.

Consequently, he switched from MP4-24 04 to chassis 02 – and a 1m 47.891s, delivered early in Q3, put pole beyond his rivals' reach. In the wake of his self-inflicted last-lap retirement at Monza, Hamilton admitted this felt like partial redemption. "I was very self-critical after the previous race," he said. "I wanted to lift myself back up, lift the team back up and, in a way, apologise. I really didn't know where we'd be this weekend. Obviously we have brought a few updates, but then so has everybody else..."

His cause was aided by Rubens Barrichello, who careered into the Turn Five wall and brought the session to a halt just as the majority were embarking on their second runs, while some had still to complete a lap on fresh super-softs. The session was restarted after Barrichello's splintered Brawn had been spirited away, but with only 26 seconds of the session remaining, it was a gesture without purpose.

The Red Bulls weren't expected to go particularly well at a stop-start circuit whose profile didn't suit their strengths, but Sebastian Vettel had just posted Q3's quickest first-sector time when the red flag flew, and his earlier 1m 48.204s, set on scrubbed options, was good enough for second, although he was due to start with a smaller – 9.5kg lighter – fuel load than Hamilton. Team-mate Mark Webber bounced back strongly after crashing at the final turn during Friday's second free practice to take fourth.

Nico Rosberg split the two title outsiders, but it was his Q2 time of 1m 46.197s that stood out; nobody else got within 0.271 second through the second sector. How had he managed that?

"He cut the chicane," suggested Hamilton, smiling, but the lap's author had no definitive explanation. "I just really got it together," he said. "Prior to that, there had always been a little mistake here and there, but on that lap I completely nailed every corner."

Barrichello's accident left him stranded in fifth, which became tenth when he was handed a five-position penalty for an unscheduled gearbox change. The unit used at Monza had already been suspect, and further risk was unwarranted.

That put him only two places ahead of teammate and championship leader Jenson Button, who was second to Hamilton in Q1 and felt a spot on the front row was feasible. "The car felt good at first," he said, "but in Q2 the grip had gone and I don't really know why." The team lowered the front tyre pressures in a bid to alleviate the problem, but then Button locked up at Turn Seven during his second run and flat-spotted both front tyres. His first run, on used tyres, hadn't been quick enough, and now the second had been irreparably compromised.

Right: Timo Glock drove extremely well to deliver his personal best result of the season with a strong second place for Toyota.
Photo: Peter J. Fox

Below: Nico Rosberg challenged hard for pole and ran second to Hamilton in the opening stages, before incurring a drive-through penalty for crossing the line delineating the pit exit road after his first re-fuelling stop. He wound up out of the points, a disappointing 11th.
Photo: Jean-François Galeron/WRi2

AIRPORT-STYLE security scanners at the paddock gate, baggage checks when you enter *and* leave the circuit, the need for a second mortgage to purchase a gin sling and a state ban on the sale of chewing gum… It's not just the nocturnal landscape that sets Singapore's grand prix apart.

Although 2008's inaugural event was regarded as a success in terms of culture and spectacle, it was widely accepted that extravagant TV images did not compensate for the absence of overtaking opportunities. To counteract this, minor changes were made to Turns One, 13 and 14, and, in addition, the pit exit and entry were reprofiled, largely to ensure that the latter was no longer indistinguishable from the racing line.

The major topic of conversation, though, concerned politics rather than cosmetics: on the Monday before the race, Renault F1 boss Flavio Briatore was banned from the sport indefinitely, and the team's popular engineering director, Pat Symonds, for five years, for the role they had played at Singapore one year before. It followed Nelson Piquet's recent admission that he'd deliberately crashed out of the race at Turn 17 to trigger a safety car that assisted team-mate Fernando Alonso's cause (although the Spaniard's subsequent victory owed a little to other factors – almost certainly Mark Webber would have beaten him had his Red Bull's gearbox electronics not been short-circuited by a passing tram). In his final submission to the FIA World Motor Sport Council, Symonds maintained that the idea had been devised by Piquet, but the Brazilian's whistle-blowing role enabled him to escape without censure.

For the balance of the campaign, Renault handed its management reins to technical director Bob Bell

– and there was no concealing his ironic grin on Friday evening, when Piquet's replacement, Romain Grosjean, slithered into the wall at Turn 17…

Eventually, though, from amid the political maelstrom, a motor race broke out.

Lewis Hamilton started strongly to lead away from pole and pull almost a second clear during the opening lap. Nico Rosberg pounced to pass Sebastian Vettel on the run to Turn One, where Alonso put all four wheels beyond the kerbs to annex fourth from Mark Webber. The Australian attempted to retaliate on the approach to Turn Seven, but was squeezed to the outside and obliged to use the run-off area as Alonso drifted wide towards the exit kerb. It was almost a carbon copy of their first-corner exchange, albeit in reverse: Webber kept his foot planted and reclaimed fourth, while Alonso lost sufficient momentum to become easy prey for Timo Glock at Turn Eight. Rubens Barrichello completed the lap in seventh place, ahead of Robert Kubica, Heikki Kovalainen, Jenson Button, Kazuki Nakajima, Sébastien Buemi, Kimi Räikkönen, Jaime Algersuari, Adrian Sutil, Giancarlo Fisichella, Jarno Trulli, Tonio Liuzzi, Grosjean and Nick Heidfeld.

Liuzzi passed Trulli cleanly on the second lap – and the initial word from race control was that the opening exchanges between Webber and Alonso had been acceptable, too. On lap six, however, officials decided that the Australian had been out of order and instructed him to surrender a place to Alonso. Given subsequent events, that meant dropping behind Glock as well.

"It seems we get penalised just for racing nowadays," Webber said. "I'm not sure where I was supposed to go, because I was alongside Fernando and he was heading off the road. I wouldn't mind

if these things were handled consistently, but Kimi [Räikkönen] gained an advantage by putting all four wheels off the track on the opening lap at Spa and nothing was done about that."

He had a point.

Hamilton was edging clear at the front, but his pace had altered almost imperceptibly on lap five. In the pits, the team had spotted a potential problem with the MP4-24's KERS and got on the radio. "The pump that circulates cooling fluid around the batteries wasn't working," said McLaren team principal Martin Whitmarsh. "They would have overheated if Lewis had continued using KERS, so we had to tell him how to reset the pump to get it going again, which he did." Scrolling through assorted steering wheel menus while maintaining impeccable precision, he was half a second slower on that lap than he had been on the previous one – and 0.757 seconds quicker than team-mate Kovalainen, who was only one lap heavier. Impediment over, Hamilton dipped straight into the high 1m 48s range and continued to pull clear.

The leader made his first scheduled stop on lap 20, two laps after Rosberg (who scarred his podium prospects by sliding over the pit exit kerbs and re-entering the circuit prematurely – he attempted to make amends by driving back to where he should have been, but subsequently the stewards slapped him with a drive-through), three after Vettel and one before the safety car appeared for the first and only time in the race.

Its intervention was triggered by a spectacular piece of misjudgement on Sutil's part. His attempt to pass Alguersuari's Toro Rosso at Turn 14 was an act of pure optimism, and it was no surprise that he spun harmlessly to a halt. Then he tried to rejoin,

however, by driving straight through Heidfeld's BMW. "I was already on the move and didn't see him," said Sutil, who claimed that it was just a racing accident, a theory that suggested a trip to the optician might be in order. "I think we need to find him a brain," said Heidfeld. The stewards took his side, reprimanding Sutil and fining him $20,000. Heidfeld retired on the spot, while Sutil attempted to continue with what remained of his car until failing rear brake pressure obliged him to stop soon afterwards. When he returned to the pits, he received a swift visit from a short, bearded German, who wished to convey a few basic points about circuit protocol.

With the field bunched up in the aftermath of the clash, Rosberg's harsh, but inevitable, penalty – served on lap 27, one after the restart – caused him to drop right down the order and out of contention. The safety car had assorted other consequences, too. Glock – third, in the wake of Rosberg's demotion – was able to wipe out a 15-second deficit to Vettel, while Button was obliged to make his first stop five laps ahead of schedule, which denied him a potentially useful stint of light running while the tanks of

several close adversaries were brimmed with fuel.

Once Rosberg had pitted and dropped to 14th, Hamilton led Vettel, Glock, Alonso, Barrichello, Kovalainen, Button and Webber. The order remained settled until the second round of stops, when it was Hamilton's turn to have his pit schedule altered by circumstance. Singapore takes a fierce toll on brakes, and Red Bull had noticed that Webber's wear rate was alarmingly high, a situation compounded by high temperatures generated while running in traffic, as he had been doing since he was ordered to drop behind Alonso.

The team called him in on lap 44, two ahead of schedule, and a check-up revealed that one brake duct had accumulated assorted debris. That was cleared and Webber rejoined, but the telemetry continued to indicate a serious problem, and there was no option but to withdraw the car. That message had still to percolate from pit to driver, however, when the RB5's front right disc exploded on the approach to Turn One. Webber spun backwards into the tyres, his faint title hopes finally extinguished, but he also felt mildly relieved. "It was probably the safest point on

the circuit for that to happen," he said. "It might have been a bit more, erm, interesting if the disc had gone on the approach to Turn Seven…"

Webber's car wasn't positioned too precariously, but McLaren promptly called in Hamilton a couple of laps early for his final stop, to allow for a possible safety-car intervention – which didn't materialise – and that meant running a slightly longer third stint on Bridgestone's super-soft, the durability of which was felt to be suspect. "That was a minor concern," said Whitmarsh, "but Lewis had plenty in hand, and was able to drive quickly and conservatively to look after the tyres."

Hamilton duly went on to score his second victory of the campaign after a performance that had been without blemish. "Generally, the race was pretty straightforward," he said, "but this is a tough circuit. The track is very bumpy, the temperatures are high and there is never much of a break: it's just corner after corner after corner. The focus you need here is probably the maximum."

And that KERS issue?

"I just had to make some switch changes," he said.

Left: Fernando Alonso heads towards third place and the Renault team's only podium of the year.
Photo: Paul-Henri Cahier

Below: The highest-placed Brawn driver was Jenson Button, who squeezed home fifth, just ahead of team-mate Rubens Barrichello as they continued their protracted title battle.
Photo: Peter J. Fox

Bottom: Looking wistful. Lewis Hamilton celebrates his second victory of the season.
Photo: Jean-François Galeron/WRi2

second stint that carried him past Kovalainen and, a crucial detail in championship terms, Barrichello, who didn't help his own cause by stalling in the pits during his second stop. Button briefly harried Vettel, too, but the team advised him to call off the chase in the interests of brake preservation. The same message went out to Barrichello, but oddly he appeared not to hear it and persisted with a frantic, but fruitless, pursuit of his team-mate.

Kubica secured the final point, behind Kovalainen, in BMW Sauber's extensively revised F1.09 – with new front wing, sidepods, diffuser and gearbox. "We had lots of rear tyre degradation problems," Kubica said, "and the final 10–15 laps of each stint were very slow, especially at the end of the race. I had to defend extremely hard, and it was probably the most difficult point I have ever scored."

Nakajima and Räikkönen completed the top ten, the Ferrari being uncompetitive all weekend and its lack of development ever more perceptible. "I had no grip and the car was sliding everywhere," Räikkönen said. "The situation improved late in the race, on the softer tyres, but by then it was too late. I don't expect the situation to be much different next week in Suzuka, because aerodynamically it is very demanding and we are lacking in that area."

The unfortunate Rosberg was 11th, from Trulli (whose efforts were a feeble contrast to those of Glock, in the same car), Fisichella and Liuzzi. The Toro Rossos retired almost simultaneously, after 47 laps, Buemi with a gearbox oil leak and Alguersuari with overheating brakes. Grosjean maintained a much lower profile than predecessor Piquet, retiring after three slow laps with a repetition of braking problems that had plagued him throughout the weekend.

The final word, though, went to his team-mate, Alonso. After the tumult of the previous ten days, third place felt as sweet as a victory to Renault, and he dedicated his podium finish to the man who had given him his first F1 opportunity. "This is for Flavio Briatore," he said, "because he is very much a part of the success we've had today."

Simon Arron

"I believe I had to disengage it and re-engage it or something like that, as if I don't already have enough things to think about in the car…"

The second round of stops proved costly to Vettel, albeit less so than the first had been to Rosberg. He was clocked at 101.4kph in the pit lane – 1.4kph above the limit – and received the inevitable drive-through, even though Red Bull insisted that its own data showed he had committed no offence. He might have escaped without positional penalty but for the earlier safety-car interruption, which ensured Glock and Alonso were too close for such things not to matter.

Glock admitted that he'd rather lost track of events as the evening wore on. "The team hadn't told me which position I was in," he said, "but suddenly came on the radio and informed me I was a safe second. That was a real surprise." It had been a delightful cameo from a driver who invariably thrives in difficult situations that demand an aggressive, sleeves-rolled-up approach.

Vettel was a safe, if frustrated, fourth, while Button rose to fifth after a quick and supremely consistent

EDITOR'S VIEW
RENAULT WEATHERS THE STORM

IT was one of the biggest scandals in recent Formula One history, and as the racing community gathered in the paddock at Singapore, there were many individuals who could not take it in. No matter how many times they read the stark words on the official communiqué from the Place de la Concorde, it all seemed like something plucked from the MGM cutting-room floor.

At a meeting of the FIA World Motor Sport Council in Paris earlier that week, Renault team principal Flavio Briatore had been banned indefinitely from any involvement in the sport, while the team's renowned executive director of engineering, Pat Symonds, had received a five-year suspension.

Their crime? Conspiring with their driver, Nelson Piquet Junior, to stage a deliberate accident in the 2008 Singapore Grand Prix, which tactically advantaged their number-one driver, Fernando Alonso, helping him climb through the field to win the race. It was hard to believe. I mean, even John Frankenheimer had stopped short of asking Pete Aron (aka James Garner) to crash a car deliberately in his movie blockbuster *Grand Prix* more than 40 years ago!

Renault had certainly come through the eye of a raging storm since last racing at Singapore 12 months previously. Then the team had been fêted as a worthy winner after Alonso had dodged every hazard on his way to what had seemed like a brilliantly opportunistic and tactically astute victory. Forget the fact that Piquet had spun into the wall after only 14 laps. These things happen, after all, particularly to novices. Nobody thought any more about it.

Yet unknown to its senior management, Renault was nursing a grubby little secret. Even as the dust settled and the raucous exhaust notes were stilled, there was already a suspicion in some peoples' minds that all was not quite as it should have been.

In fact, Piquet was ready to confess to his involvement in this race fixing scam shortly after the 2008 race. Word reached the FIA, but the governing body could not act on rumour and speculation alone. But helpfully it signalled that, in the event of Piquet making a formal complaint, he would be absolved from any penalty. He duly attended the offices of the governing body and made a legal statement.

As a corporate entity, Renault did not get away entirely unscathed. Sure enough, it was given a 'permanent' exclusion from the F1 business, but that was suspended for two years until the end of 2011. It would only be activated if the team transgressed the rules in a similarly serious manner during that period – which, of course, would be unlikely.

Yet it was still a very serious issue, as indicated by the fact that the French cars appeared without their ING and Mutua Madrilena logos following the decision by both backers to withdraw their sponsorship with only four races of the season left to go. It was hard to think of a more public display of disapproval about the sordid allegations that had decimated the upper reaches of this F1 team's management in the week before the second night race at the Marina Bay circuit.

To put things back on an even keel, Renault had announced that the positions of team principal and chief technical officer would be assumed by Bob Bell, previously the technical director, while Jean-Francois Caubet, formerly the director of marketing and communications, would step into the role of managing director. Both men would be reporting directly to Bernard Rey, the president of the Renault F1 team.

They may have been less glamorous and high profile than Briatore and Symonds, but Bell and Caubet were regarded as safe pairs of hands to steer Renault through to the end of the 2009 season.

Bell, a quiet and highly respected engineer, admitted that he was stunned by the revelations that had engulfed the Renault team

"It is a dream job obviously, but in very difficult circumstances," he said. " I am taking a very pragmatic and realistic approach to it. The team needed somebody to step in and see through the rest of the season.

"I have agreed to do that. I am very happy to do it. My motivation as ever is to see that the team continues and continues successfully, and I am very proud that I have been asked to do it, and I relish the challenge."

Caubet added that it was crucial that Renault's F1 team should embrace a change of culture to prevent anything like this from happening again. "We don't want to return to the 1980s, when Renault corporate [philosophy] controlled the team," he said, "but we do not want to make the same mistakes that have occurred by the team having 100 per cent control."

Not that staging a deliberate accident was ever likely to appear as a formal discussion item during a pre-race briefing, for goodness' sake.

Alan Henry

Left: The elated Panasonic Toyota crew welcome Timo Glock after his excellent drive.
Photo: Studio Colombo/WRi2

Right: Under scrutiny. The newly appointed Renault F1 team principal Bob Bell faces the media for the first time in his role as Flavio Briatore's successor. It was all a bit of a contrast to his engineering role.
Photo: Renault F1 Team

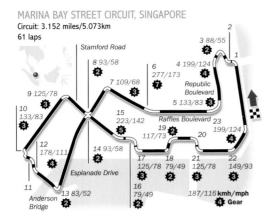

MARINA BAY STREET CIRCUIT, SINGAPORE
Circuit: 3.152 miles/5.073km
61 laps

Stamford Road
8 93/58
7 109/68
9 125/78
10 133/83
15 223/142
Raffles Boulevard
19 117/73
14 93/58
12 178/111
17 125/78
18 79/49
21 79/49
22 149/93
16 79/49
11
Anderson Bridge
13 83/52
Esplanade Drive
20
23 199/124
6 277/173
4 199/124
5 133/83
2
3 88/55
1
Republic Boulevard
187/116 kmh/mph
Gear

FIA F1 WORLD CHAMPIONSHIP ROUND 14
SINGTEL
SINGAPORE
GRAND PRIX
SINGAPORE 25-27 SEPTEMBER 2009

Photo: Peter J. Fox

RACE DISTANCE: 61 laps, 192.200 miles/309.316km • RACE WEATHER: Dry/dark (track 32-34°C, air 30-32°C)

Pos.	Driver	Nat.	No.	Entrant	Car/Engine	Tyres	Laps	Time/Retirement	Speed (mph/km/h)	Gap to leader	Fastest race lap
1	Lewis Hamilton	GB	1	Vodafone McLaren Mercedes	McLaren MP4-24-Mercedes FO108W V8	B	61	1h 56m 06.337s	99.323/159.845		1m 48.345s 36
2	Timo Glock	D	10	Panasonic Toyota Racing	Toyota TF109-RVX-09 V8	B	61	1h 56m 15.971s	99.186/159.624	+ 9.634s	1m 48.396s 34
3	Fernando Alonso	E	7	ING Renault F1 Team	Renault R29-RS27 V8	B	61	1h 56m 22.961s	99.086/159.464	+ 16.624s	1m 48.240s 53
4	Sebastian Vettel	D	15	Red Bull Racing	Red Bull RB5-Renault RS27 V8	B	61	1h 56m 26.598s	99.035/159.381	+ 20.261s	1m 48.398s 10
5	Jenson Button	GB	22	Brawn GP Formula 1 Team	Brawn BGP 001-Mercedes FO108W V8	B	61	1h 56m 36.352s	98.897/159.159	+ 30.015s	1m 48.369s 54
6	Rubens Barrichello	BR	23	Brawn GP Formula 1 Team	Brawn BGP 001-Mercedes FO108W V8	B	61	1h 56m 38.195s	98.871/159.117	+ 31.858s	1m 48.598s 50
7	Heikki Kovalainen	FIN	2	Vodafone McLaren Mercedes	McLaren MP4-24-Mercedes FO108W V8	B	61	1h 56m 42.494s	98.810/159.020	+ 36.157s	1m 49.283s 36
8	Robert Kubica	PL	5	BMW Sauber F1 Team	BMW Sauber F1.09-BMW P86/9 V8	B	61	1h 57m 01.391s	98.545/158.592	+ 55.054s	1m 48.847s 44
9	Kazuki Nakajima	J	17	AT&T Williams	Williams FW31-Toyota RVX-09 V8	B	61	1h 57m 02.391s	98.530/158.569	+ 56.054s	1m 49.371s 45
10	Kimi Räikkönen	FIN	4	Scuderia Ferrari Marlboro	Ferrari F60-056 V8	B	61	1h 57m 05.229s	98.490/158.505	+ 58.892s	1m 48.391s 54
11	Nico Rosberg	D	16	AT&T Williams	Williams FW31-Toyota RVX-09 V8	B	61	1h 57m 06.114s	98.478/158.485	+ 59.777s	1m 48.352s 9
12	Jarno Trulli	I	9	Panasonic Toyota Racing	Toyota TF109-RVX-09 V8	B	61	1h 57m 19.346s	98.293/158.187	+ 1m 13.009s	1m 48.816s 54
13	Giancarlo Fisichella	I	3	Scuderia Ferrari Marlboro	Ferrari F60-056 V8	B	61	1h 57m 26.227s	98.197/158.033	+ 1m 19.890s	1m 49.417s 49
14	Vitantonio Liuzzi	I	21	Force India F1 Team	Force India VJM02-Mercedes FO108W V8	B	61	1h 57m 39.839s	98.008/157.728	+ 1m 33.502s	1m 49.852s 48
	Jaime Alguersuari	E	11	Scuderia Toro Rosso	Toro Rosso STR04-Ferrari 056 V8	B	47	*brakes*			1m 52.483s 32
	Sébastian Buemi	CH	12	Scuderia Toro Rosso	Toro Rosso STR04-Ferrari 056 V8	B	47	*gearbox*			1m 50.636s 17
	Mark Webber	AUS	14	Red Bull Racing	Red Bull RB5-Renault RS27 V8	B	45	*brakes/accident*			1m 49.319s 35
	Adrian Sutil	D	20	Force India F1 Team	Force India VJM02-Mercedes FO108W V8	B	23	*brakes*			1m 52.623s 15
	Nick Heidfeld	D	6	BMW Sauber F1 Team	BMW Sauber F1.09-BMW P86/9 V8	B	19	*accident*			1m 51.346s 18
	Romain Grosjean	F	8	ING Renault F1 Team	Renault R29-RS27 V8	B	3	*brakes*			1m 57.192s 2

Fastest race lap: Fernando Alonso on lap 53, 1m 48.240s, 104.841mph/168.725km/h.

Lap record: Kimi Räikkönen (Ferrari F2008 V8), 1m 45.599s, 107.336mph/172.740km/h (2008) (3.148-mile/5.067km circuit).

All results and data © FOM 2009

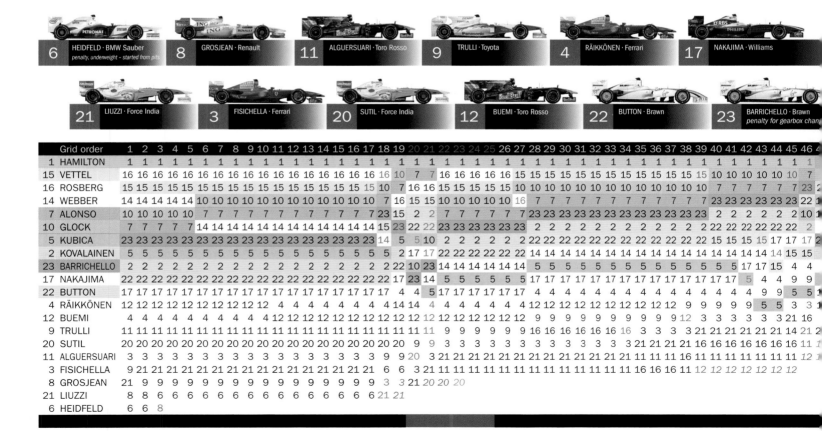

| | 6 | HEIDFELD · BMW Sauber *penalty, underweight - started from pits* | 8 | GROSJEAN · Renault | 11 | ALGUERSUARI · Toro Rosso | 9 | TRULLI · Toyota | 4 | RÄIKKÖNEN · Ferrari | 17 | NAKAJIMA · Williams |
| 21 | LIUZZI · Force India | 3 | FISICHELLA · Ferrari | 20 | SUTIL · Force India | 12 | BUEMI · Toro Rosso | 22 | BUTTON · Brawn | 23 | BARRICHELLO · Brawn *penalty for gearbox change* |

Grid order	1	2	3	4	5	6	7	8	9	10	11	12	13	14	15	16	17	18	19	20	21	22	23	24	25	26	27	28	29	30	31	32	33	34	35	36	37	38	39	40	41	42	43	44	45	46
1 HAMILTON	1	1	1	1	1	1	1	1	1	1	1	1	1	1	1	1	1	1	1	1	1	1	1	1	1	1	1	1	1	1	1	1	1	1	1	1	1	1	1	1	1	1	1	1	1	1
15 VETTEL	16	16	16	16	16	16	16	16	16	16	16	16	16	16	16	16	16	16	10	7	7	16	16	16	16	16	15	15	15	15	15	15	15	15	15	15	15	15	15	15	10	10	10	10	10	7
16 ROSBERG	15	15	15	15	15	15	15	15	15	15	15	15	15	15	15	15	15	10	7	16	16	15	15	15	15	10	10	10	10	10	10	10	10	10	10	10	10	10	7	7	7	7	7	7	23	2
14 WEBBER	14	14	14	14	14	10	10	10	10	10	10	10	10	10	10	10	10	7	16	15	15	10	10	10	10	10	16	7	7	7	7	7	7	7	7	7	7	7	23	23	23	23	23	23	22	1
7 ALONSO	10	10	10	10	10	7	7	7	7	7	7	7	7	7	7	7	7	23	15	2	2	7	7	7	7	7	23	23	23	23	23	23	23	23	23	23	2	2	2	2	2	10	1
10 GLOCK	7	7	7	7	14	14	14	14	14	14	14	14	14	14	14	14	14	23	22	22	23	23	23	23	23	2	2	2	2	2	2	2	2	2	2	22	22	22	22	22	2
5 KUBICA	23	23	23	23	23	23	23	23	23	23	23	23	23	23	23	23	14	5	5	10	2	2	2	2	2	22	22	22	22	22	22	22	22	22	15	15	15	15	17	17	17	2
2 KOVALAINEN	5	5	5	5	5	5	5	5	5	5	5	5	5	5	5	5	2	17	17	22	22	22	22	22	14	14	14	14	14	14	14	14	14	14	14	14	14	14	14	15	15
23 BARRICHELLO	2	2	2	2	2	2	2	2	2	2	2	2	2	2	2	2	22	10	23	14	14	14	14	14	5	5	5	5	5	5	5	5	5	5	5	17	17	15	4	4
17 NAKAJIMA	22	22	22	22	22	22	22	22	22	22	22	22	22	22	22	22	17	23	14	5	5	5	5	5	17	17	17	17	17	17	17	17	17	17	17	17	17	5	4	4	9	9
22 BUTTON	17	17	17	17	17	17	17	17	17	17	17	17	17	17	17	17	4	4	5	17	17	17	17	17	4	4	4	4	4	4	4	4	4	4	4	4	9	9	5	5	1
4 RÄIKKÖNEN	12	12	12	12	12	12	12	12	12	12	12	4	4	4	4	4	4	14	4	4	4	4	12	12	12	12	12	12	12	12	12	12	9	9	9	9	5	5	3	3	1
12 BUEMI	4	4	4	4	4	4	4	4	4	4	12	12	12	12	12	12	12	12	12	12	12	12	9	9	9	9	9	9	9	9	9	12	3	3	3	3	3	21	16
9 TRULLI	11	11	11	11	11	11	11	11	11	11	11	11	11	11	11	11	11	9	9	9	9	9	16	16	16	16	16	16	16	3	3	3	3	21	21	21	21	21	14	21	2
20 SUTIL	20	20	20	20	20	20	20	20	20	20	20	20	20	20	20	20	9	9	3	3	3	3	3	3	3	21	16	16	16	16	16	16	11	1
11 ALGUERSUARI	3	3	3	3	3	3	3	3	3	3	3	3	3	3	9	20	3	21	21	21	21	21	21	21	21	11	11	11	11	11	11	11	11	11	11	11	11	12	1
3 FISICHELLA	9	21	21	21	21	21	21	21	21	21	21	21	21	21	6	3	21	11	11	11	11	11	11	11	11	16	16	16	11	12	12	12	12	12	12	12
8 GROSJEAN	21	9	9	9	9	9	9	9	9	9	9	9	9	9	3	3	21	20	20	20
21 LIUZZI	8	8	6	6	6	6	6	6	6	6	6	6	6	21	21
6 HEIDFELD	6	6	8

TIME SHEETS

PRACTICE 1 (FRIDAY)
Dry
(track 35-37ºC, air 32ºC)

Pos.	Driver	Laps	Time
1	Rubens Barrichello	19	1m 50.179s
2	Jenson Button	22	1m 50.356s
3	Mark Webber	21	1m 50.416s
4	Fernando Alonso	16	1m 50.567s
5	Sebastian Vettel	16	1m 50.614s
6	Heikki Kovalainen	21	1m 50.699s
7	Lewis Hamilton	17	1m 50.715s
8	Robert Kubica	15	1m 50.815s
9	Kimi Räikkönen	19	1m 50.865s
10	Kazuki Nakajima	25	1m 51.089s
11	Nico Rosberg	23	1m 51.427s
12	Adrian Sutil	14	1m 51.544s
13	Sébastien Buemi	28	1m 51.643s
14	Nick Heidfeld	15	1m 51.656s
15	Timo Glock	20	1m 52.083s
16	Jarno Trulli	20	1m 52.135s
17	Giancarlo Fisichella	24	1m 52.390s
18	Vitantonio Liuzzi	23	1m 52.905s
19	Jaime Alguersuari	25	1m 53.232s
20	Romain Grosjean	9	1m 53.458s

PRACTICE 2 (FRIDAY)
Dry
(track 33-34ºC, air 31ºC)

Pos.	Driver	Laps	Time
1	Sebastian Vettel	31	1m 48.650s
2	Fernando Alonso	27	1m 48.924s
3	Heikki Kovalainen	30	1m 48.952s
4	Nick Heidfeld	31	1m 49.098s
5	Jenson Button	34	1m 49.311s
6	Mark Webber	14	1m 49.317s
7	Nico Rosberg	33	1m 49.333s
8	Timo Glock	30	1m 49.342s
9	Lewis Hamilton	28	1m 49.358s
10	Robert Kubica	24	1m 49.609s
11	Rubens Barrichello	30	1m 49.616s
12	Adrian Sutil	31	1m 49.710s
13	Jarno Trulli	29	1m 49.795s
14	Kimi Räikkönen	29	1m 49.941s
15	Kazuki Nakajima	34	1m 50.023s
16	Giancarlo Fisichella	31	1m 50.253s
17	Sébastien Buemi	29	1m 50.527s
18	Vitantonio Liuzzi	28	1m 50.605s
19	Romain Grosjean	17	1m 50.972s
20	Jaime Alguersuari	31	1m 51.423s

PRACTICE 3 (SATURDAY)
Dry
(track 33-34ºC, air 32-33ºC)

Pos.	Driver	Laps	Time
1	Lewis Hamilton	15	1m 47.632s
2	Sebastian Vettel	17	1m 47.909s
3	Nico Rosberg	18	1m 48.332s
4	Heikki Kovalainen	14	1m 48.420s
5	Robert Kubica	16	1m 48.501s
6	Nick Heidfeld	13	1m 48.526s
7	Rubens Barrichello	16	1m 48.551s
8	Timo Glock	17	1m 48.673s
9	Sébastien Buemi	17	1m 48.754s
10	Jarno Trulli	12	1m 48.757s
11	Kazuki Nakajima	17	1m 48.831s
12	Kimi Räikkönen	16	1m 48.864s
13	Mark Webber	15	1m 48.876s
14	Jenson Button	17	1m 48.921s
15	Fernando Alonso	15	1m 49.032s
16	Vitantonio Liuzzi	16	1m 49.055s
17	Adrian Sutil	17	1m 49.122s
18	Jaime Alguersuari	17	1m 49.399s
19	Romain Grosjean	16	1m 49.641s
20	Giancarlo Fisichella	21	1m 50.039s

QUALIFYING (SATURDAY)
Dry (track 32º C, air 31º C)

Pos.	Driver	First	Second	Third	Weight
1	Lewis Hamilton	**1m 46.977s**	1m 46.657s	**1m 47.891s**	660.5kg
2	Sebastian Vettel	1m 47.541s	1m 46.362s	1m 48.204s	651kg
3	Nico Rosberg	1m 47.390s	**1m 46.197s**	1m 48.348s	675.5kg
4	Mark Webber	1m 47.646s	1m 46.328s	1m 48.722s	654.5kg
5	Rubens Barrichello	1m 47.397s	1m 46.787s	1m 48.828s	655.5kg
6	Fernando Alonso	1m 47.757s	1m 46.767s	1m 49.054s	658kg
7	Timo Glock	1m 47.770s	1m 46.707s	1m 49.180s	660.5kg
8	Nick Heidfeld	1m 47.347s	1m 46.832s	1m 49.307s	650kg
9	Robert Kubica	1m 47.615s	1m 46.813s	1m 49.514s	664kg
10	Heikki Kovalainen	1m 47.542s	1m 46.842s	1m 49.778s	664.5kg
11	Kazuki Nakajima	1m 47.637s	1m 47.013s		680.7kg
12	Jenson Button	1m 47.180s	1m 47.141s		683kg
13	Kimi Räikkönen	1m 47.293s	1m 47.177s		680.5kg
14	Sébastien Buemi	1m 47.677s	1m 47.369s		678kg
15	Jarno Trulli	1m 47.690s	1m 47.413s		690.9kg
16	Adrian Sutil	1m 48.231s			693kg
17	Jaime Alguersuari	1m 48.340s			683.5kg
18	Giancarlo Fisichella	1m 48.350s			678.5kg
19	Romain Grosjean	1m 48.544s			683kg
20	Vitantonio Liuzzi	1m 48.792s			656kg

Photo: Renault F1 Team

2 KOVALAINEN · McLaren

10 GLOCK · Toyota

14 WEBBER · Red Bull

15 VETTEL · Red Bull

5 KUBICA · BMW Sauber

7 ALONSO · Renault

16 ROSBERG · Williams

1 HAMILTON · McLaren

FOR THE RECORD

100th POINT: Sebastian Vettel

50th POINT: Timo Glock

Photo: Peter J. Fox

POINTS

DRIVERS

1	Jenson Button	84
2	Rubens Barrichello	69
3	Sebastian Vettel	59
4	Mark Webber	51.5
5	Kimi Räikkönen	40
6	Lewis Hamilton	37
7	Nico Rosberg	30.5
8	Fernando Alonso	26
9	Timo Glock	24
10	Jarno Trulli	22.5
11	Felipe Massa	22
12	Heikki Kovalainen	22
13	Nick Heidfeld	12
14	Robert Kubica	9
15	Giancarlo Fisichella	8
16	Adrian Sutil	5
17	Sébastien Buemi	3
18	Sébastien Bourdais	2

CONSTRUCTORS

1	Brawn	153
2	Red Bull	110.5
3	Ferrari	62
4	McLaren	59
5	Toyota	46.5
6	Williams	30.5
7	Renault	26
8	BMW Sauber	21
9	Force India	13
10	Toro Rosso	5

	9	50	51	52	53	54	55	56	57	58	59	60	61	
	7	7	1	1	1	1	1	1	1	1	1	1	1	
	1	1	22	10	10	10	10	10	10	10	10	10	10	2
	2	22	10	7	7	7	7	7	7	7	7	7	7	3
	0	10	7	15	15	15	15	15	15	15	15	15	15	4
	5	15	15	22	22	22	22	22	22	22	22	22	22	5
	4	4	4	23	23	23	23	23	23	23	23	23	23	6
	3	23	23	4	2	2	2	2	2	2	2	2	2	7
	2	2	2	5	5	5	5	5	5	5	5	5	5	8
	9	9	5	5	17	17	17	17	17	17	17	17	17	
	5	5	9	17	4	4	4	4	4	4	4	4	4	
	7	17	17	16	16	16	16	16	16	16	16	16	16	
	6	16	16	9	9	9	9	9	9	9	9	9	9	
	3	3	3	3	3	3	3	3	3	3	3	3	3	
	1	21	21	21	21	21	21	21	21	21	21	21	21	

14 Drive thru
16 Pit stop
12 One lap or more behind
▮ Safety car deployed on laps shown

RACE TYRE STRATEGIES

The tyre regulations stipulate that two dry tyre specifications must be used during the race.

The Super-Soft compound Bridgestone Potenza tyre is marked with a green stripe on the sidewall of the tyre.

	Driver	Race Stint 1	Race Stint 2	Race Stint 3	Race Stint 3
1	Lewis Hamilton	Soft: 1-20	Soft: 21-46	Super-Soft: 47-61	
2	Timo Glock	Soft: 1-19	Soft: 20-45	Super-Soft: 46-61	
3	Fernando Alonso	Soft: 1-21	Soft: 22-50	Super-Soft: 51-61	
4	Sebastian Vettel	Soft: 1-17	Soft: 18-39	Super-Soft: 40-43	Super-Soft: 44-61
5	Jenson Button	Soft: 1-21	Soft: 22-51	Super-Soft: 52-61	
6	Rubens Barrichello	Soft: 1-19	Soft: 20-46	Super-Soft: 47-61	
7	Heikki Kovalainen	Soft: 1-21	Soft: 22-46	Super-Soft: 47-61	
8	Robert Kubica	Soft: 1-20	Soft: 21-42	Super-Soft: 43-61	
9	Kazuki Nakajima	Soft: 1-21	Soft: 22-46	Super-Soft: 47-61	
10	Kimi Räikkönen	Soft: 1-21	Soft: 22-52	Super-Soft: 53-61	
11	Nico Rosberg	Soft: 1-18	Soft: 19-27	Soft: 28-34	Super-Soft: 35-61
12	Jarno Trulli	Soft: 1-21	Soft: 22-51	Super-Soft: 52-61	
13	Giancarlo Fisichella	Soft: 1-18	Soft: 19-46	Super-Soft: 47-61	
14	Vitantonio Liuzzi	Super-Soft: 1-18	Super-Soft: 19-46	Soft: 47-61	
	Jaime Alguersuari	Soft: 1-21	Soft: 22-46	Super-Soft: 47 (dnf)	
	Sébastien Buemi	Soft: 1-21	Super-Soft: 22-38	Super-Soft: 39	Soft: 40-47 (dnf)
	Mark Webber	Soft: 1-18	Soft: 19-44	Super-Soft: 45 (dnf)	
	Adrian Sutil	Soft: 1-20	Soft: 21-46 (dnf)		
	Nick Heidfeld	Soft: 1-19 (dnf)			
	Romain Grosjean	Soft: 1-3 (dnf)			

JAPANESE GRAND PRIX

SUZUKA CIRCUIT

J. TRULLI

SUZUKA QUALIFYING

THE prosaic details? Sebastian Vettel qualified on pole position for the Japanese Grand Prix, with title rivals Rubens Barrichello and Jenson Button back in sixth and tenth – but such a simple sentence masks a litany of errors: this was a chaotic qualifying session that lasted longer than the race.

Formula One's return to Suzuka began in damp conditions during Friday's opening free practice, and spectators were utterly drenched during the afternoon, while the drivers huddled in their new pit garages for almost an hour. The weather perked up on Saturday, but by then driving standards had deteriorated...

The rot set in during final free practice, when Mark Webber skated off at Degner. It wasn't a particularly big accident – the car bottomed out and he was deprived of directional control momentarily – but the subsequent impact tore the steering rack from its mount and did sufficient damage to necessitate a fresh chassis. The Australian had felt sure he could win here, but a relatively minor impact obliged him to miss qualifying and start from the pits.

Sébastien Buemi was first to crash during qualifying, although he was able to make it back to the pits after hitting the tyres at Degner in Q1 and subsequently set a good time. His team-mate, Jaime Alguersuari, went off at the same point early in Q2, prompting the first red flag, and the session was stopped again after Timo Glock lost it at the right-hand kink leading on to the main straight. His Toyota's front wing pierced the tub and left him with a nasty gash in his left leg: the requisite 14 stitches would sideline him for the balance of the weekend. A high temperature had kept Glock away from the track on Friday, when Toyota reserve Kamui Kobayashi had taken over, but there was no provision for the Japanese driver to deputise in the race.

Buemi crashed again in the final moments of Q2, leaving a trail of debris that ran all the way from the point of impact, at Spoon Curve, to the pits. Finally, Heikki Kovalainen prompted another red flag early in Q3, when he became the latest driver to be snared by the Degner tyre wall.

Throughout all the commotion, Vettel kept his customary cool head and took pole, ahead of Jarno Trulli and Lewis Hamilton, in the only one of four Adrian Newey cars that remained in one piece. "I think I was lucky in Q2 and Q3," he said, "because when the red flags came out, I was able to come in and abort what was basically an out lap, so I wasn't yet on a flier. That means your tyres are obviously no longer new, but they're not that badly worn; the first sector is very demanding for tyres, and I hadn't yet been through there at speed. You don't know if there will be another yellow or red flag; it's out of your hands and down to pure luck."

Adrian Sutil was fourth and, initially, Barrichello and Button were fifth and seventh. The Brawn duo, though, were summoned to the stewards because they – along with Sutil and Fernando Alonso – were adjudged not to have slowed sufficiently at the scene of Buemi's second accident. "I didn't lift," admitted Button, "but the wreckage was on a straight and everything was under control. I didn't want to back off suddenly in case there was someone behind."

Right: Lewis Hamilton suffered problems with the KERS system on his McLaren and was unable to duplicate his previous weekend's success 'down the road' in Singapore.
Photo: Paul-Henri Cahier

Below: Timo Glock injured his leg when he took his eyes off the road and crashed heavily in qualifying.
Photo: Peter J. Fox

Below centre: Toyota reserve driver Kamui Kobayashi briefly stood in for the hapless Glock during the Friday free practice session when the German was unwell.
Photo: Lukas Gorys

Bottom: The Japanese GP celebrated its return to Suzuka for the first time since 2006 under blue skies.
Photo: Peter J. Fox

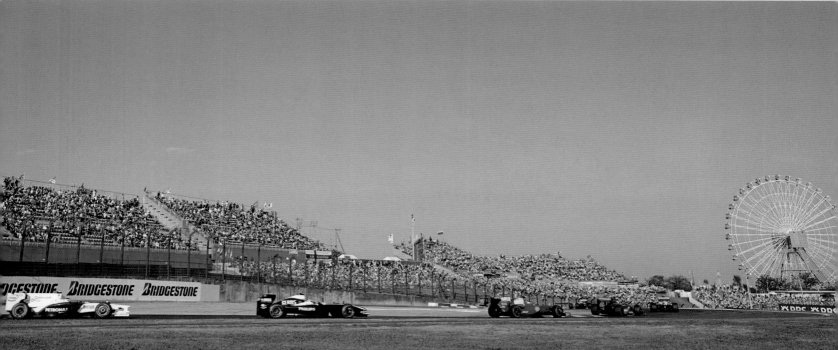

I N a simple sentence, Sebastian Vettel captured the weekend's true essence. "When I began my last lap," he said, "I felt slightly regretful that it was almost all over…"

Everybody appreciated Suzuka's return to the Formula One calendar for the first time since 2006 – except, perhaps, those who had to pick up the tab for qualifying's most destructive excesses. The circuit hadn't altered greatly during the intervening three seasons, with only minor tweaks to one or two run-off areas, but the infrastructure was much improved, with an imposing new pit complex, many extra grandstand seats and a few subtle home improvements around the track's immediate perimeter. The upgrade cost a reported $200m and achieved the desired effect without diluting the venue's character one iota – a masterclass in sympathetic renovation.

With most serious rivals hamstrung by the previous day's assorted mishaps and penalties, Vettel's most pressing concern was the KERS-assisted presence of Lewis Hamilton's McLaren. From third, the outgoing champion breezed past Jarno Trulli's Toyota on the approach to Turn One and duly began to pull

alongside the leader, but Vettel stuck to the middle of the road. "I made a good start," he said, "and was looking both left and right in my mirrors. I decided to stay where I was, ready to go to the inside in case Jarno or Lewis had made a really good start, then all of a sudden I saw a silver arrow to my left. He was almost alongside me, but I had the advantage of the inside line for Turn One. Fortunately, that was the only wheel-to-wheel racing I had all afternoon…"

He plunged into the first corner, pulled 1.1 seconds clear on the opening lap and would barely be seen again until the podium ceremony.

Behind Hamilton and Trulli, Nick Heidfeld settled into fourth, ahead of Kimi Räikkönen, Rubens Barrichello, Adrian Sutil, Nico Rosberg, Heikki Kovalainen, Robert Kubica, Jenson Button, Giancarlo Fisichella, Kazuki Nakajima, Jaime Alguersuari, Tonio Liuzzi, Fernando Alonso, Romain Grosjean and Sébastien Buemi, who struggled to get away on the formation lap – because of clutch trouble – and suffered a repeat when the race began in earnest. Having started from the pits, poor Mark Webber returned there within a lap because his Red Bull's headrest had worked

loose. The same thing happened to the Australian on lap two, and on the fourth he picked up a puncture. From that point on, the race was treated as a test session – during which a new front wing was evaluated – and the conquest of fastest lap was scant consolation at the end of a hellish weekend.

As Vettel pulled clear at the front, Rosberg and Kovalainen passed Sutil on the second lap, when Alguersuari and Alonso dispatched Nakajima and Liuzzi respectively. Next time around, Button reclaimed the place he'd lost at the start, by diving past Kubica going into the chicane, and on the fourth lap Buemi usurped Grosjean, although it was a short-term gain, as the Toro Rosso driver would soon be obliged to stop with terminal clutch problems. At the front, though, there was only inertia.

Sutil attempted to wrest eighth from Kovalainen by slicing down the inside at the chicane on lap 13: he got the first bit right, but rather assumed the Finn would back off in mid-corner and left his rival insufficient room at the exit. They duly brushed wheels, as a result of which Sutil spun, Kovalainen lost momentum and – of greater significance – Button was gifted two places.

Like Imola, Monaco, Silverstone and several other venues, Suzuka is a wonderful theatre in which to appreciate the artistry of an F1 driver, but it doesn't always produce a pulsating contest – and this was a prime example.

Vettel was almost 4.5 seconds clear of Hamilton when the Englishman made his first stop, on lap 15. The German came in three laps later and dropped a couple of seconds – previously the team had been penalised for some trigger-happy pit releases, and its lollipop man did not want to risk impeding Heidfeld's incoming BMW – but that was a minor distraction. Vettel's true rhythm would be broken only once – on lap 45, when the safety car was deployed shortly after Alguersuari crashed heavily at 130R. The Spaniard was on an out lap, having just made his final stop, and was perplexed by the incident. "I don't know what happened," he said. "I had been going well and felt as though it was the first proper day of my F1 career. And then the car just spun without warning…" The testing ban might have saved a few quid in some respects, but it was beginning to look costly in others.

When the race restarted on lap 50, Vettel was shielded from the rest by Grosjean's lapped Renault and was able to pull clear once more to cement the fourth success of his F1 career. "I had clean air for the whole race," he said, "so I was able to run at my own pace. The circuit is amazing, and 53 laps give you the chance to appreciate it even more. On the soft tyres, at the end, I had a very good feeling and pushed very hard to make sure I got fastest lap [except that Webber beat him to it]. My engineer came on the radio and told me not to do anything stupid with the tyres, in case the safety car came out, and two laps later it did… I got a good restart, though, and was able to pull away. For me, it was a very good race from start to finish."

Behind, Hamilton held off Trulli until their second and final stops, when the Italian ran two laps longer and was able to recover the position he'd lost at the start. "I really enjoyed that," Trulli said, "because we both had to drive as though we were doing a constant series of qualifying laps."

Hamilton's pace was compromised shortly before his second stop, however, when his KERS packed up. "The system has three primary components," said team principal Martin Whitmarsh, "the battery, the e-motor and the electronics. On this occasion,

it appears to have been an isolation problem on the e-motor. We did all sorts of checks to see if we could overcome it, but that wasn't possible. Lewis wasn't just losing the engine benefit, either, because KERS is an integral part of the drivetrain that alters brake balance and engine braking. He and his engineers had to work hard to make compensatory adjustments."

And while this was going on, he was unable to drive as quickly as was required towards the end of his second stint, on a light fuel load, and the battle was lost.

"As I exited the pits after my second stop," Hamilton said, "I lost time with a gearbox problem. I coasted for 100 metres, which cost me about a second, but to be honest it wasn't a surprise to be jumped by Jarno at the final stops. I needed every tenth to build a big enough gap, but I couldn't quite make it. When we were behind the safety car, I asked the team if they could get the KERS working again so that I could shoot past Jarno at the restart, but they couldn't do it and I wasn't close enough to get in his slipstream."

Räikkönen moved up to fourth after a stellar second stint on the soft Bridgestone, a cameo that proved

it was the most effective tyre option, even though it wasn't widely used at that stage of the race.

Heidfeld lost time with a jammed right rear wheel nut during his second stop; subsequently, he dropped behind Rosberg in mildly bizarre circumstances. Alguersuari caused the safety car to be scrambled just as Rosberg was due to make his second stop, on lap 45. In such situations, the cars' dash displays are supposed to show an advisory 'time delta', a safe pace at which to complete the lap while the event is neutralised. Rosberg had no such information, however, because it was overridden by his low-fuel alarm. Consequently, he returned to the pit slightly more briskly – by about one second – than was desirable, although telemetry revealed he had backed off adequately at the accident scene.

Rosberg had been 20.5 seconds clear of the Brawns, which were seventh and eighth, and a final stop – estimated time about 23 seconds – should have dropped him behind both, but with those further back spending more of lap 45 at a reduced pace, Rosberg was able to pit and rejoin without losing any positions, although he would have slipped behind

Heidfeld had the BMW driver not backed off significantly on the pit straight. Had Heidfeld kept his foot down until after the pit exit, as he was entitled to do, he'd have kept fifth. Later, the stewards investigated Rosberg's track protocol, but concluded that he'd behaved responsibly.

Kubica's interminable first stint – he did 26 laps to Button's 17 – put him on course to nick eighth place, but the Pole lost time, shortly before his final stop, because he was impeded by heavily fuelled teammate Heidfeld. That swung things Button's way, and the championship leader finished on Barrichello's tail to ensure that his advantage was cut by only a single point. "We are getting ourselves into tricky situations, but keep getting ourselves out of them," he said.

Kubica took ninth, ahead of Alonso, Kovalainen, Fisichella (who left the pits ahead of the second McLaren after the final stops before being bullied aside at Turn One), Sutil, Liuzzi, Nakajima, Grosjean and the distant Webber.

Had it been a great race? No, but it was great to be back...

Simon Arron

Above: Jarno Trulli had one of his excellent 'on days' with the Toyota, dicing expertly with Hamilton to finish second. Even so, the Toyota top brass made it clear it had been looking for a win.

Far left: Enthusiastic messages of support for Jenson, Rubens and the BBC!

Photos: Paul-Henri Cahier

THE DRIVERS WHO LISTEN AND LEARN

"That's how you handle Suzuka!"
The elated winner celebrates the
fact that he outgunned many of the
Japanese circuit's old hands to score
that memorable win.
Photo: Paul-Henri Cahier

MY highly respected journalistic colleague Peter Windsor, one of the
co-founders of the forthcoming Team US F1 operation, made a very
straightforward and obvious point in the aftermath of the Japanese
Grand Prix. The underlying message was that really clever racing drivers are
always sensible enough to heed good advice, wherever they may find it.

The point he was making was that on Sebastian Vettel's first full outing at
Suzuka, the German driver's ego was not inflated to the level where he was
unwilling to listen to every word that David Coulthard, his predecessor in
the Red Bull Racing ranks, had to offer about driving the luridly high-speed
circuit near Nagoya. In the same way, during his spell as Kimi Räikkönen's
team-mate at McLaren, Coulthard had allowed himself to be guided by driver
coach Rob Wilson when he ran into the mental barrier posed by the one-lap
Indy-style qualifying that briefly was an element of the GP format.

That training helped Coulthard outpace Räikkönen at Suzuka in 2003, and
essentially the same guidelines helped Vettel to outclass everybody at the
Japanese track in 2009. "I'll help the old team in any way I can," said DC.
"Those notes from 2003 are still valid today."

Not only did Vettel show himself to be clever in seeking such information,
but also he was not tardy in employing it to excellent effect. He qualified his
Red Bull on pole, and stormed away from the front row of the grid to clinch a
decisive and very convincing win. One could see from the sheer aplomb that
radiated from the young German's cockpit that he was absolutely relishing
every inch of the magnificent circuit, in no way constrained by the rather
disappointing undercurrent of complaint from several of his rivals suggesting that Suzuka needs a significant safety upgrade.

If that should prove to be the case, then such a step – minor as it might
seem in isolation – could come to be regarded as a 'litmus test' in how the
future of the show is to be shaped. Suzuka ranks right up there with Spa-
Francorchamps and Monza as one of the few remaining tests of driver skill
and ability. If messed with unnecessarily, there is a risk of banging another
unwanted nail into the coffin of politically incorrect F1 – raw, uninhibited and
potentially extremely dangerous.

Returning to the theme of really clever racing drivers briefly, in 1985, I
recall being very impressed when a young Brazilian called Ayrton Senna
accepted an invitation to drive for Lotus. In only his second F1 season, he
declined number-one status, reasoning that he could learn a lot from current
incumbent Elio de Angelis. It said much for Senna's racing nous.

It also said much for Elio's intelligence that he decided to leave Lotus
at the end of 1985, reasoning that Senna might make it his own private
fiefdom. If that has ever crossed Mark Webber's mind in relation to Vettel,
there's been no sign of it. And if it did cross his mind, Webber would be savvy
enough to keep his thoughts very much to himself.

Alan Henry

SUZUKA INTERNATIONAL RACING COURSE, SUZUKA CITY

Circuit: 3.387 miles/5.451km 53 laps
187/116 kmh/mph
⚙ Gear

Turn 14 138/86
Spoon
Turn 13 178/11
Turn 12 284/177
Degner 2 122/76
Turn 2 138/86
Degner 1 183/114
130R 308/192
Hairpin 63/39
S Curves 183/114
245/152
199/124
Casino Triangle 88/55
Turn 1 258/161
Dunlop 119/190

FIA F1 WORLD CHAMPIONSHIP ROUND 15

FUJI TELEVISION
JAPANESE
GRAND PRIX
SUZUKA 2-4 OCTOBER 2009

Photos: Peter J. Fox

RACE DISTANCE: 53 laps, 191.117 miles/307.573km • RACE WEATHER: Sunny (track 40-43°C, air 27-28°C)

Pos.	Driver	Nat.	No.	Entrant	Car/Engine	Tyres	Laps	Time/Retirement	Speed (mph/km/h)	Gap to leader	Fastest race lap	
1	Sebastian Vettel	D	15	Red Bull Racing	Red Bull RB5-Renault RS27 V8	B	53	1h 28m 20.443s	129.804/208.900		1m 32.572s	43
2	Jarno Trulli	I	9	Panasonic Toyota Racing	Toyota TF109-RVX-09 V8	B	53	1h 28m 25.320s	129.685/208.707	+ 4.877s	1m 33.152s	38
3	Lewis Hamilton	GB	1	Vodafone McLaren Mercedes	McLaren MP4-24-Mercedes FO108W V8	B	53	1h 28m 26.915s	129.646/208.645	+ 6.472s	1m 33.259s	13
4	Kimi Räikkönen	FIN	4	Scuderia Ferrari Marlboro	Ferrari F60-056 V8	B	53	1h 28m 28.383s	129.610/208.587	+ 7.940s	1m 32.999s	33
5	Nico Rosberg	D	16	AT&T Williams	Williams FW31-Toyota RVX-09 V8	B	53	1h 28m 29.236s	129.589/208.554	+ 8.793s	1m 33.595s	43
6	Nick Heidfeld	D	6	BMW Sauber F1 Team	BMW Sauber F1.09-BMW P86/9 V8	B	53	1h 28m 29.952s	129.571/208.525	+ 9.509s	1m 33.600s	13
7	Rubens Barrichello	BR	23	Brawn GP Formula 1 Team	Brawn BGP 001-Mercedes FO108W V8	B	53	1h 28m 31.084s	129.544/208.481	+ 10.641s	1m 33.910s	17
8	Jenson Button	GB	22	Brawn GP Formula 1 Team	Brawn BGP 001-Mercedes FO108W V8	B	53	1h 28m 31.917s	129.524/208.448	+ 11.474s	1m 33.251s	42
9	Robert Kubica	PL	5	BMW Sauber F1 Team	BMW Sauber F1.09-BMW P86/9 V8	B	53	1h 28m 32.220s	129.516/208.436	+ 11.777s	1m 33.334s	44
10	Fernando Alonso	E	7	ING Renault F1 Team	Renault R29-RS27 V8	B	53	1h 28m 33.508s	129.485/208.386	+ 13.065s	1m 33.946s	28
11	Heikki Kovalainen	FIN	2	Vodafone McLaren Mercedes	McLaren MP4-24-Mercedes FO108W V8	B	53	1h 28m 34.178s	129.469/208.360	+ 13.735s	1m 33.801s	35
12	Giancarlo Fisichella	I	3	Scuderia Ferrari Marlboro	Ferrari F60-056 V8	B	53	1h 28m 35.039s	129.448/208.326	+ 14.596s	1m 33.479s	33
13	Adrian Sutil	D	20	Force India F1 Team	Force India VJM02-Mercedes FO108W V8	B	53	1h 28m 35.402s	129.439/208.312	+ 14.959s	1m 33.668s	36
14	Vitantonio Liuzzi	I	21	Force India F1 Team	Force India VJM02-Mercedes FO108W V8	B	53	1h 28m 36.177s	129.420/208.281	+ 15.734s	1m 34.294s	36
15	Kazuki Nakajima	J	17	AT&T Williams	Williams FW31-Toyota RVX-09 V8	B	53	1h 28m 38.416s	129.366/208.194	+17.973s	1m 34.783s	26
16	Romain Grosjean	F	8	ING Renault F1 Team	Renault R29-RS27 V8	B	52			+ 1 lap	1m 34.643s	39
17	Mark Webber	AUS	14	Red Bull Racing	Red Bull RB5-Renault RS27 V8	B	51			+ 2 laps	1m 32.569s	50
	Jaime Alguersuari	E	11	Scuderia Toro Rosso	Toro Rosso STR04-Ferrari 056 V8	B	43	*accident*			1m 34.049s	34
	Sébastien Buemi	CH	12	Scuderia Toro Rosso	Toro Rosso STR04-Ferrari 056 V8	B	11	*clutch*			1m 35.392s	5
NS	Timo Glock	D	10	Panasonic Toyota Racing	Toyota TF109-RVX-09 V8			*driver injured in qualifying*				

Fastest lap: Mark Webber on lap 50, 1m 32.569s, 140.327mph/225.833km/h.

Lap record: Kimi Räikkönen (McLaren MP4-20-Mercedes Benz V10) on lap 44, 1m 31.540s, 141.904mph/228.372km/h (2005).

14	WEBBER · Red Bull *chassis change - started from pits*	8	GROSJEAN · Renault	17	NAKAJIMA · Williams	12	BUEMI · Toro Rosso *penalty for impeding*	2	KOVALAINEN · McLaren *penalty for gearbox change*	5	KUBICA · BMW Sauber
21	LIUZZI · Force India *penalty for gearbox change*	7	ALONSO · Renault *penalty - speeding under yellow flags*	3	FISICHELLA · Ferrari	11	ALGUERSUARI · Toro Rosso	22	BUTTON · Brawn *penalty - speeding under yellow flags*		

	Grid order	1	2	3	4	5	6	7	8	9	10	11	12	13	14	15	16	17	18	19	20	21	22	23	24	25	26	27	28	29	30	31	32	33	34	35	36	37	38	39	40	41	42
15	VETTEL	15	15	15	15	15	15	15	15	15	15	15	15	15	15	15	15	15	15	15	15	15	15	15	15	15	15	15	15	15	15	15	15	15	15	15	15	15	15	15	15	15	15
9	TRULLI	1	1	1	1	1	1	1	1	1	1	1	1	1	1	1	1	9	6	6	16	16	16	16	1	1	1	1	1	1	1	1	1	1	1	1	1	1	1	9	9	9	9
1	HAMILTON	9	9	9	9	9	9	9	9	9	9	9	9	9	9	9	9	6	4	4	1	1	1	1	9	9	9	9	9	9	9	9	9	9	9	9	9	1	1	1	1	1	1
6	HEIDFELD	6	6	6	6	6	6	6	6	6	6	6	6	6	6	6	6	4	23	23	9	9	9	9	6	6	6	6	6	6	6	6	6	6	6	6	6	6	23	23	23	23	23
4	RÄIKKÖNEN	4	4	4	4	4	4	4	4	4	4	4	4	4	4	4	4	23	16	16	6	6	6	6	2	5	5	4	4	4	4	4	4	4	4	23	16	16	16	16	16	16	16
23	BARRICHELLO	23	23	23	23	23	23	23	23	23	23	23	23	23	23	16	1	1	2	2	2	2	5	2	4	4	23	23	23	23	23	23	16	22	22	22	22	4	4
16	ROSBERG	20	16	16	16	16	16	16	16	16	16	16	16	16	16	16	1	9	5	5	5	4	4	23	16	16	16	16	16	16	16	16	22	4	4	4	4	5	6
20	SUTIL	16	2	2	2	2	2	2	2	2	2	2	22	22	22	22	22	2	4	4	4	23	23	16	16	7	7	7	22	22	22	22	22	22	4	6	6	5	5	6	22
5	KUBICA	2	20	20	20	20	20	20	20	20	20	20	2	2	2	2	5	23	23	23	23	16	16	17	17	17	22	22	7	5	5	5	5	5	6	6	22	11
22	BUTTON	5	5	22	22	22	22	22	22	22	22	22	5	5	5	5	11	11	11	11	17	17	7	7	22	5	5	2	2	2	2	2	2	2	2	11	11	5
2	KOVALAINEN	22	22	5	5	5	5	5	5	5	5	5	3	3	3	3	3	17	17	17	21	21	21	21	22	5	2	2	3	3	3	3	3	3	3	3	7	7	7
11	ALGUERSUARI	3	3	3	3	3	3	3	3	3	3	20	20	11	11	21	21	21	11	7	7	22	2	2	3	20	20	20	20	20	20	20	21	21	21
12	BUEMI	17	11	11	11	11	11	11	11	11	11	11	17	17	17	7	7	7	7	22	22	2	3	20	20	11	11	11	11	11	11	11	2	2	2
3	FISICHELLA	11	17	17	17	17	17	17	17	17	17	17	21	21	22	22	22	22	8	8	8	8	8	11	7	7	7	7	7	7	7	3	3	3
17	NAKAJIMA	21	7	7	7	7	7	7	7	7	21	21	21	8	8	8	8	3	3	20	20	11	8	17	17	21	21	21	21	21	21	20	20
7	ALONSO	7	21	21	21	21	21	21	21	21	7	7	7	7	7	3	3	3	3	20	20	20	11	11	21	17	17	17	17	17	17	17	17	17
8	GROSJEAN	8	8	8	12	12	12	12	12	12	12	8	8	20	20	20	20	20	20	11	11	11	21	21	8	8	8	8	8	8	8	8	8
21	LIUZZI	12	12	12	8	8	8	8	8	8	8	12	14	14	14	14	14	14	14	14	14	14	14	14	14	14	14	14	14	14	14	14	14	14
14	WEBBER	14	14	14	14	14	14	14	14	14	14																						

■ Safety car deployed on laps show

All results and data © FOM 2009

TIME SHEETS

PRACTICE 1 (FRIDAY)
Overcast
(track 23°C, air 21-22°C)

Pos.	Driver	Laps	Time
1	Heikki Kovalainen	24	1m 40.356s
2	Kazuki Nakajima	18	1m 40.648s
3	Adrian Sutil	14	1m 40.806s
4	Giancarlo Fisichella	27	1m 40.985s
5	Sébastien Buemi	26	1m 41.421s
6	Lewis Hamilton	15	1m 41.443s
7	Fernando Alonso	22	1m 41.532s
8	Kimi Räikkönen	25	1m 41.577s
9	Rubens Barrichello	19	1m 41.821s
10	Nico Rosberg	20	1m 42.188s
11	Mark Webber	10	1m 42.332s
12	Vitantonio Liuzzi	15	1m 42.475s
13	Jarno Trulli	13	1m 42.657s
14	Jaime Alguersuari	27	1m 42.667s
15	Robert Kubica	17	1m 42.833s
16	Nick Heidfeld	14	1m 42.977s
17	Sebastian Vettel	11	1m 43.218s
18	Jenson Button	17	1m 43.318s
19	Kamui Kobayashi	16	1m 43.407s
20	Romain Grosjean	22	1m 43.572s

PRACTICE 2 (FRIDAY)
Rain/drizzle
(track 23°C, air 22°C)

Pos.	Driver	Laps	Time
1	Adrian Sutil	5	1m 47.261s
2	Sebastian Vettel	6	1m 47.923s
3	Vitantonio Liuzzi	5	1m 47.931s
4	Lewis Hamilton	5	1m 47.983s
5	Kazuki Nakajima	8	1m 48.058s
6	Sébastien Buemi	9	1m 48.691s
7	Fernando Alonso	5	1m 48.693s
8	Jarno Trulli	7	1m 48.737s
9	Jaime Alguersuari	11	1m 48.802s
10	Robert Kubica	6	1m 48.861s
11	Kimi Räikkönen	5	1m 48.886s
12	Kamui Kobayashi	7	1m 49.054s
13	Mark Webber	7	1m 49.382s
14	Romain Grosjean	6	1m 49.405s
15	Giancarlo Fisichella	5	1m 49.553s
16	Nico Rosberg	8	1m 49.872s
17	Nick Heidfeld	10	1m 50.179s
	Rubens Barrichello		no time
	Jenson Button		no time
	Heikki Kovalainen		no time

PRACTICE 3 (SATURDAY)
Sunny
(track 36-39°C, air 27-28°C)

Pos.	Driver	Laps	Time
1	Jarno Trulli	24	1m 31.709s
2	Sébastien Buemi	26	1m 31.771s
3	Nico Rosberg	28	1m 32.343s
4	Sebastian Vettel	19	1m 32.414s
5	Kimi Räikkönen	26	1m 32.445s
6	Adrian Sutil	25	1m 32.467s
7	Rubens Barrichello	24	1m 32.488s
8	Heikki Kovalainen	22	1m 32.546s
9	Jenson Button	25	1m 32.668s
10	Jaime Alguersuari	20	1m 32.689s
11	Romain Grosjean	25	1m 32.717s
12	Nick Heidfeld	21	1m 32.736s
13	Fernando Alonso	21	1m 32.742s
14	Timo Glock	26	1m 32.749s
15	Kazuki Nakajima	23	1m 32.752s
16	Lewis Hamilton	19	1m 32.789s
17	Robert Kubica	20	1m 32.848s
18	Giancarlo Fisichella	26	1m 32.878s
19	Mark Webber	15	1m 32.930s
20	Vitantonio Liuzzi	18	1m 33.167s

QUALIFYING (SATURDAY)
Sunny (track 39-42°C, air 27-28°C)

Pos.	Driver	First	Second	Third	Weight
1	Sebastian Vettel	**1m 30.883s**	**1m 30.341s**	**1m 32.160s**	658.5kg
2	Jarno Trulli	1m 31.063s	1m 30.737s	1m 32.220s	655.5kg
3	Lewis Hamilton	1m 30.917s	1m 30.627s	1m 32.395s	656kg
4	Adrian Sutil	1m 31.386s	1m 31.222s	1m 32.466s	650kg
5	Rubens Barrichello	1m 31.272s	1m 31.055s	1m 32.660s	660.5kg
6	Nick Heidfeld	1m 31.501s	1m 31.260s	1m 32.945s	660kg
7	Jenson Button	1m 31.041s	1m 30.880s	1m 32.962s	658.5kg
8	Kimi Räikkönen	1m 31.228s	1m 31.052s	1m 32.980s	661kg
9	Heikki Kovalainen	1m 31.499s	1m 31.223s	no time	675kg
10	Sébastien Buemi	1m 31.196s	1m 31.103s	no time	665.4kg
11	Nico Rosberg	1m 31.286s	1m 31.482s		684.5kg
12	Fernando Alonso	1m 31.401s	1m 31.638s		689.5kg
13	Robert Kubica	1m 31.417s	1m 32.341s		686kg
14	Timo Glock	1m 31.550s	no time		dns
15	Jaime Alguersuari	1m 31.571s	no time		682.5kg
16	Giancarlo Fisichella	1m 31.704s			661.5kg
17	Kazuki Nakajima	1m 31.718s			695.7kg
18	Romain Grosjean	1m 32.073s			691.8kg
19	Vitantonio Liuzzi	1m 32.087s			682.5kg
	Mark Webber	no time			not declared

16	ROSBERG · Williams		4	RÄIKKÖNEN · Ferrari		1	HAMILTON · McLaren		15	VETTEL · Red Bull

20	SUTIL · Force India penalty - speeding under yellow flag		23	BARRICHELLO · Brawn penalty - speeding under yellow flag		6	HEIDFELD · BMW Sauber		9	TRULLI · Toyota

FOR THE RECORD

50th GRAND PRIX START: Lewis Hamilton/
Heikki Kovalainen/Adrian Sutil

600th POINT: Rubens Barrichello

250th POINT: Lewis Hamilton

DID YOU KNOW?

This was the 25th Japanese Grand Prix (the first
being in 1976 at Fuji when James Hunt clinched the
championship).

POINTS

DRIVERS

1	Jenson Button	85
2	Rubens Barrichello	71
3	Sebastian Vettel	69
4	Mark Webber	51.5
5	Kimi Räikkönen	45
6	Lewis Hamilton	43
7	Nico Rosberg	34.5
8	Jarno Trulli	30.5
9	Fernando Alonso	26
10	Timo Glock	24
11	Felipe Massa	22
12	Heikki Kovalainen	22
13	Nick Heidfeld	15
14	Robert Kubica	9
15	Giancarlo Fisichella	8
16	Adrian Sutil	5
17	Sébastien Buemi	3
18	Sébastien Bourdais	2

CONSTRUCTORS

1	Brawn	156
2	Red Bull	120.5
3	Ferrari	67
4	McLaren	65
5	Toyota	54.5
6	Williams	34.5
7	Renault	26
8	BMW Sauber	24
9	Force India	13
10	Toro Rosso	5

RACE TYRE STRATEGIES

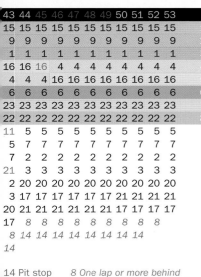

The tyre
regulations
stipulate that
two dry tyre
specifications
must be used
during the race.

The Soft
compound
Bridgestone
Potenza tyre is
marked with a
green stripe
on the sidewall
of the tyre.

	Driver	Race Stint 1	Race Stint 2	Race Stint 3	Race Stint 4	Race Stint 5	Race Stint 6
1	Sebastian Vettel	Hard: 1-18	Hard: 19-40	Soft: 41-53			
2	Jarno Trulli	Hard: 1-16	Hard: 17-39	Soft: 40-53			
3	Lewis Hamilton	Soft: 1-15	Hard: 16-37	Soft: 38-53			
4	Kimi Räikkönen	Hard: 1-18	Hard: 19-35	Soft: 36-53			
5	Nico Rosberg	Hard: 1-22	Hard: 23-45	Soft: 46-53			
6	Nick Heidfeld	Soft: 1-18	Hard: 19-36	Soft: 37-53			
7	Rubens Barrichello	Hard: 1-18	Hard: 19-42	Soft: 43-53			
8	Jenson Button	Hard: 1-17	Hard: 18-40	Soft: 41-53			
9	Robert Kubica	Hard: 1-26	Hard: 27-41	Soft: 42-53			
10	Fernando Alonso	Hard: 1-30	Soft: 31-53				
11	Heikki Kovalainen	Soft: 1-24	Hard: 25-39	Soft: 40-53			
12	Giancarlo Fisichella	Soft: 1-17	Soft: 18-39	Hard: 40-53			
13	Adrian Sutil	Soft: 1-15	Hard: 16-39	Soft: 40-53			
14	Vitantonio Liuzzi	Hard: 1-25	Hard: 26-43	Soft: 44-53			
15	Kazuki Nakajima	Hard: 1-27	Soft: 28-53				
16	Romain Grosjean	Hard: 1-29	Soft: 30-53				
17	Mark Webber	Soft: 1	Hard: 2	Hard: 4	Hard: 5-33	Soft: 34-45	Soft: 46-53
	Jaime Alguersuari	Hard: 1-22	Hard: 23-43	Soft: 44 (dnf)			
	Sébastien Buemi	Soft: 1-11 (dnf)					
dns	Timo Glock						

Race lap chart (positions lap 43-53):

43	44	45	46	47	48	49	50	51	52	53	
15	15	15	15	15	15	15	15	15	15	15	1
9	9	9	9	9	9	9	9	9	9	9	2
1	1	1	1	1	1	1	1	1	1	1	3
16	16	16	4	4	4	4	4	4	4	4	4
4	4	4	16	16	16	16	16	16	16	16	5
6	6	6	6	6	6	6	6	6	6	6	6
23	23	23	23	23	23	23	23	23	23	23	7
22	22	22	22	22	22	22	22	22	22	22	8
11	5	5	5	5	5	5	5	5	5		
5	7	7	7	7	7	7	7	7	7		
7	2	2	2	2	2	2	2	2	2		
21	3	3	3	3	3	3	3	3	3		
2	20	20	20	20	20	20	20	20	20		
3	17	17	17	17	17	21	21	21	21		
20	21	21	21	21	21	17	17	17	17		
17	8	8	8	8	8	8	8	8			
8	14	14	14	14	14	14	14	14			
14											

14 Pit stop   *8 One lap or more behind*

FIA FORMULA 1 WORLD CHAMPIONSHIP • ROUND 16

BRAZILIAN GRAND PRIX

INTERLAGOS CIRCUIT

Pole-sitter Rubens Barrichello's Brawn storms away from eventual winner Mark Webber's Red Bull as the pack piles through the second corner just after the start. Future champion Jenson Button is mired way down in the pack at this point.
Photo: Peter J. Fox

INTERLAGOS QUALIFYING

AS moments of opportunism go, it wasn't particularly subtle. Tonio Liuzzi's Force India had barely come to rest when a local marshal tried to make away with the steering wheel – potentially a £25,000 souvenir. Liuzzi swiftly claimed it back and refitted it, but his car was in urgent need of rather more wheels than that...

Q1 had taken place in the wet, and had claimed some unusual victims. Traditional rain maestros Sebastian Vettel and Lewis Hamilton were both eliminated, the German hitting traffic when the track was at its best – a relative term – and then being left with no chance to improve as the weather deteriorated. Hamilton described it as one of the worst sessions of his career. "The car had no grip at all," he said. "I couldn't even use full throttle on the straights." McLaren was running a dry set-up, in anticipation of better conditions for Sunday, but was not alone in that. The session was also briefly red-flagged when Giancarlo Fisichella spun at Turn Two: the Italian was unable to restart, largely because he had unwittingly hit the ignition cut-out switch – the error that caused him to lose control in the first place.

The rain delayed the start of Q2 briefly, but then the green light was given – and Liuzzi was just trying to start his first flying lap when he hit a puddle on the main straight. His car slewed into the pit wall and bounced across the road into the facing tyre wall. "I was just a passenger," he said. His gearbox being damaged beyond repair, he also had to take a five-position grid penalty.

The session was stopped once more and did not resume until 16.10. If you thought qualifying dragged on for a bit in Japan, it lasted fully 165 minutes in Brazil. This forced the Beeb to switch live coverage to BBC2, to pacify irate viewers waiting for *Strictly Come Dancing*...

Drivers plumped for Bridgestone wets when Q2 finally resumed, but Williams team-mates Nico Rosberg and Satoru Nakajima switched to intermediates once they had banker laps under their belts. It paid off – they were first and second – but it took three laps to conjure sufficient tyre heat to make the inters work properly. Time wasn't a luxury available to Jenson Button, though. He persisted with a single set of wets, convinced he'd be able to produce a decent lap, but... "We dropped the tyre pressures," he said, "and I had massive understeer at first. There was no balance at all, and then the rears began to go, too." Ross Brawn admitted that, at the very least, the team should have brought Button in for fresh wets, a ploy that worked well for others.

The World Championship leader was stranded in 14th, but Rubens Barrichello just scraped through to Q3, which was reasonably straightforward, with everybody using intermediates from the outset. And, as is so often the case in variable conditions, Barrichello excelled: he was fuelled lighter than main adversary Mark Webber, but a 1m 19.576s was just enough to eclipse the Australian – with Adrian Sutil a couple of tenths further adrift in third – and ensure that a Brazilian started his home race from pole position for the fourth straight year.

The architect of the previous three occasions, Ferrari driver Felipe Massa, was present at a grand prix for the first time since the accident he had suffered in Hungary, but only as an observer – and to wave the chequered flag on Sunday.

"You never knew what was going to happen next," Barrichello said. "It was very variable, but I am so happy. It might be that we have less fuel than Red Bull, but it is better to start at the front and run at your own pace than to be towards the middle of the pack. It is great that so many people stayed to see it, too."

The crowd's chanted response – "Rubinho! Rubinho!" – was both long and loud. The Interlagos grandstands provide scant weather protection, but such things matter not at moments like this.

Right: Where's my steering wheel? Liuzzi's crash threw qualifying into disarray for the other competitors
Photo: Jad Sherif/WRi2

Below right: Disgruntled trio. Jarno Trulli, Fernando Alonso and Adrian Sutil step out for home after their first-lap tangle. Trulli told Sutil his fortune in no uncertain terms, but candour became expensive when the Italian was given a $10,000 fine.
Photo: Jean-François Galeron/WRi2

Bottom right: The ever-youthful Roberto Moreno, no doubt itching to get back behind the wheel of an F1 car, at the ripe old age of 50!
Photo: Bernard Asset

Below left: Adrian Sutil splashes down the pit lane in his Force India.
Photo: Studio Colombo/WRi2

AS signs of the times go, it was quite striking. By 8am on Brazilian Grand Prix Sunday, there is usually a colossal human tailback along the hill that leads past some smart apartment blocks – built on the site of old *favelas* (slums) – and on towards the main gate at Interlagos. It is customarily a cheerful, colourful, noisy assembly, packed with a majority who have tickets and a few who intend simply to climb on their mates' shoulders to jump over the fence. This time, though, the pavements were thinly populated. Unlike the previous three seasons, this wasn't a guaranteed title decider. Rubens Barrichello might have been on pole, but the headgear of consumer choice was a Ferrari cap – and Felipe Massa wasn't racing. Or perhaps the locals had just studied the fuel weights and thought, "Actually, this looks like Mark Webber's race…"

Barrichello made a brisk start to lead unchallenged into the Senna Esses, but Webber – one of many who has pointed out the virtual uselessness of modern F1 mirrors – can't have failed to notice a bright red thing immediately behind as Kimi Räikkönen attempted to convert fifth into second with a helping prod from KERS.

The Australian survived the Finn's initial attack and was fully prepared for the next, at the end of the back straight leading into Turn Four. Webber's subsequent chop was, in his own words, "Firm, but fair, and Kimi would have done exactly the same to me." Additionally, Räikkönen attempted the move from so far back that he might as well have been in Bolivia, but the upshot was a clipped front wing that immediately fell apart, which consigned him to an early pit stop.

The consequences were more brutal for those behind. Räikkönen's sudden loss of momentum compromised the following Adrian Sutil, who was forced to slow, and that created an opportunity for Jarno Trulli. The Italian swooped around the outside of Turn Five, but Sutil, who claimed he hadn't seen his shadow, left absolutely no space to his right. Trulli was forced on to the grass, whereupon he spun back across the track, clipping one of Sutil's rear wheels in the process, and smashed into the opposite retaining wall.

Sutil, his trajectory deflected, speared off to the right and then slewed back on to the circuit directly in front of the innocent Fernando Alonso. The impact could have been horrible, but the Spaniard was able to reduce it to a glancing blow. All three cars finished up on the same side of the track, and Trulli sprinted along the run-off area to confront Sutil, ignoring marshals' requests that he should do so from the other side of the tyre wall. A comedy shoving match ensued – about as far from Ali v Frazier as you could get – and stewards later fined Trulli $10,000 for his conduct, although they felt that the trigger had been an ordinary racing incident and took no further action on that front.

The safety car was dispatched immediately, which persuaded McLaren to call Lewis Hamilton into the pits: they removed the super-soft rubber on which he'd started, brimmed him with fuel and converted him to what was effectively a one-stopper on the more durable Bridgestone medium. His team-mate, Heikki Kovalainen, had spun at the foot of the Ess-

es, forcing Giancarlo Fisichella to run wide on to the grass, and he was called in, too, for a fuel top-up, even though he had started on the medium tyre. In his case, however, the strategic switch became immaterial, because he was signalled to leave his pit too soon with half his fuel rig still attached and spewing its content on to the pit lane. Räikkönen, replacement front wing freshly fitted – and with super-softs swapped for mediums, for a 42-lap stint that was one longer than Hamilton's – drove straight through the slick of unleaded, and a few drops of petrol got into his eyes, leaving them sore for the balance of the afternoon. Heat from his exhaust ignited the spillage, too, so momentarily he had to drive through the flash fire he'd just created on the pit apron. Kovalainen pulled up at the Brawn pit, where the crew obligingly disconnected the rogue fuel hose and handed it back to McLaren, which had ample time to reconstruct its rig, although Kovalainen had lost several laps of fuel in the incident and would still have to make another two stops. All this and the race had been running for less than two minutes…

Tonio Liuzzi made two stops while the safety car was out, to complete a mandatory racing lap on the super-soft, and the race finally resumed on lap six, with Barrichello leading Webber, Nico Rosberg, Robert Kubica (who immediately passed the preceding Williams at Turn One), Sébastien Buemi, Kazuki Nakajima, newcomer Kamui Kobayashi (who had done a terrific job all weekend as stand-in for Timo Glock, because it had been discovered that the German had cracked a vertebra in his Suzuka accident), Romain Grosjean, Jenson Button, Jaime Alguersuari, Sebastian Vettel, Nick Heidfeld, Fisichella, Hamilton, Räikkönen, Kovalainen and Liuzzi.

Button passed Grosjean during the lap, taking no risks, despite the Franco-Swiss making things difficult, and outbraked Nakajima into Turn One at the start of the seventh. Kobayashi, though, would be a

more obstinate proposition. Button briefly outfumbled him once, at Turn One, but ran wide in the process. He would remain snared until the first round of stops: although he pitted on lap 29, one earlier than Kobayashi, his greater experience told and his in and out laps were, collectively, almost three seconds brisker. The battle was won, but Toyota's tyro had made his presence felt.

At the front, Barrichello led until the first round of stops, during which time Webber went into fuel conservation mode and managed to extend his first stint by two laps. When Barrichello came in on lap 21, four of Webber's next five laps were ultra-quick – 1m 14.050s, 1m 14.012s, 1m 14.501s, 1m 13.875s, 1m 13.733s – and pre-race expectations were fulfilled. It was more surprising that Kubica, who ran just two laps longer than Barrichello, was also able to vault the Brazilian.

The Pole's performance was unquestionably the drive of the day – and possibly of the season. As BMW Sauber had spent most of the campaign performing at a lesser level than plain old Sauber used to do, Kubica had little business being on the same continent as a Red Bull, let alone in its slipstream, although he had to keep ducking out of that, because his engine was running a little hot and he'd had to turn the revs down after 15 laps. That was not surprising, as this was his third race with the same V8 and if it blew, BMW didn't have any more left.

Webber admitted he'd been slightly alarmed when Kubica began catching him during the second stint, but the Pole was running lighter at that stage and the Australian eventually established a safe, five-second cushion: the race was won. Kubica was concerned about using super-softs for the final 28 laps, given that they had lasted for about five during practice on Friday, but he nursed them to the end. "I was impressed by Robert's pace," said Webber. He wasn't the only one.

With Barrichello third just after half-distance, ahead of the charging Hamilton – who'd saved his finest Brazilian GP drive for when it least mattered – Räikkönen and Button, the destiny of the world title appeared settled. Button had passed Buemi during the first stops, and another potential impediment vanished on lap 27, when gearbox failure obliged Rosberg to stop. The issue was put beyond doubt, however, when a puncture forced Barrichello to make a second stop on lap 63, just after Hamilton had passed him for third with a bold lunge as they came on to the pit straight. The two cars came extremely close – extremely as in just enough for the McLaren's wing to nick the Brazilian's left rear tyre.

Button lost out to Vettel during the final stops, but moved back ahead of Räikkönen, and so, for the second consecutive season, an Englishman driving a Mercedes-powered car bearing the number 22 clinched the world title by finishing fifth in Brazil. And he hadn't reversed into it, either. This was a drive with a champion's hallmark, a paragon of aggression, judgment and control. Webber and Kubica – the day's principal stars – were almost forgotten amid the pandemonium.

"After Friday, I was quite confident we could go for a victory," Webber said, before nodding in Hamilton's general direction. "Our pace was pretty good, but I was a little bit worried about this guy here because we knew the McLaren would do pretty well with KERS. Fortunately, things were mixed up yesterday and that's where the foundations were laid, particularly for Robert and I, when we managed to get through Q1 in those difficult conditions."

Hamilton admitted he was surprised to be third. "I had no idea I would even be able to get into the points," he said. "The team did a great job with the strategy, but I was on a knife edge all the way." He looked as tired as he sounded.

Räikkönen was sixth, behind Vettel and Button,

Left: Jenson Button came alive at Interlagos with a succession of inspired overtaking moves on his way to a title-clinching fifth place. Here he muscles aside Sébastien Buemi's Toro Rosso.
Photo: Lukas Gorys

Below: BMW found some pace and was rewarded with a second place after a very strong drive by Robert Kubica.
Photo: Peter J. Fox

while Buemi and Barrichello completed the scorers. The Brazilian was among the first to give Button a congratulatory hug afterwards, underlining the fact that friendships can be genuine in F1, even among team-mates. "I'm truly pleased for Jenson," he said, "because he is a great champion. We have a fantastic working relationship, and that has really shone through this year. We've had a true fight and I battled really hard, but really he won it during the first half of the season."

Kovalainen finished ninth on the road, but was handed a 25-second penalty as a result of his unsafe release from the pits. That dropped him to 12th, behind Kobayashi, Fisichella and Liuzzi. Kobayashi's copybook was blotted only by an incident on the 31st lap, when he simply barged Nakajima off the track – and out of the race – on the approach to Turn Four. The stewards didn't consider that incident worthy of investigation, bizarrely, but the early stages of the race had left a firm impression on Button. "That guy is crazy," he said. "I suppose it is just inexperience, but he moves around a lot in the braking zones, and that makes things very difficult, as Nakajima found out."

On the back of a hugely indifferent GP2 series campaign, however, Kobayashi was suddenly a serious contender for a Toyota seat in 2010. "Physically, it felt like a really long race and it was quite tough," he said. "My first target was to finish, and I am pleased to have achieved that, but after the start I was in a decent position to score points, so I am a little disappointed I didn't. The car felt good in the first stint, but when I changed tyres the balance felt different and I struggled a bit."

Grosjean and Alguersuari were the only other finishers, a lap down, and Heidfeld retired after his first scheduled stop, on lap 21, because no fuel was delivered and he didn't have enough to make it back to the pits.

They were but footnotes, though, as Button launched into karaoke mode during the cooling-off lap and began bellowing Queen's 'We Are The Champions' over the airwaves – the only thing he'd done badly all afternoon.

When Hamilton clinched the title in 2008, there was no formal conference for the champion, and the subsequent media stampede was somewhat unruly in the world's most cramped F1 paddock. The FIA had taken that lesson on board and, once traditional post-race formalities had been completed, Button was whisked upstairs for formal interrogation.

He repeated the same refrain throughout, his smile broadening with his every utterance: "I am the world champion. I am the world champion, and I'm going to keep saying it all night because I've heard my flight home is cancelled.

"I have had a very up-and-down season and haven't enjoyed the past few weeks," he added, "but I have come out on top and I am the world champion, or whatever word I can use. Perhaps that's getting boring…"

Then he paused for an instant and smiled again.

"No," he said. "It isn't."

Simon Arron

EDITOR'S VIEW
RUMOURS ABOUND ABOUT BUTTON'S FUTURE

Above: The Brawn team celebrates its remarkable feat of winning both the drivers' and constructors' titles in its debut year.

Above far left: Mark Webber took his second win of the season.

Above left: That's my boy! John Button, in his lucky pink shirt, poses with Jenson.
Photos: Peter J. Fox

Top left: After the race, the usual sunny disposition of Sebastian Vettel was not in evidence, despite the German's fighting drive to fourth place from his lowly grid position.

Left: Toyota's debutant Kamui Kobayashi certainly caught the eye with his robust driving. Here he battles wheel to wheel with Kazuki Nakajima. Later, he would clash with his fellow countryman, forcing the unlucky Williams driver on to the grass and into the barriers.
Photo: Lukas Gorys

IT is the very nature of the Formula One business that when a driver is on course to win the World Championship, his thoughts should turn towards how to capitalise on that achievement from a commercial standpoint in the year that follows his title winning success.

Think Niki Lauda, switching to Bernie Ecclestone's Brabham squad from Ferrari after winning the title in 1977. Think Nigel Mansell, opting to take a lucrative year in Indy cars rather than accepting Alain Prost as his Williams team-mate in 1993. Or even Damon Hill, asking for too much financially from the Williams squad and being – incomprehensibly – passed over in favour of Heinz-Harald Frentzen even before he'd got the 1996 championship in the bag.

Bearing all that in mind, it's no real surprise that, even before Jenson Button came pounding up the final hill at Interlagos to take that crucial fifth place in the Brazilian Grand Prix, his management team had already fired its first salvo in its negotiations with Ross Brawn for the 2010 season. This was a much more sharply defined debate than one might have expected in the normal course of events. In fact, that was the whole point. The backdrop against which the negotiations were set to take place was no 'normal course of events'.

Button had taken a significant pay cut to help Brawn GP rise, phoenix-like, from the ashes of the Honda squad. He had stayed because he wanted to, because he rightly believed in the car, the team and the key people involved. But given that he had won the World Championship, surely it was reasonable for him to expect a significant upward adjustment of his retainer.

On the other hand, one might surmise that he had been a lucky boy, that circumstances had conspired to give him a car that was the class of the field during the first half of the season.

Within days of his title success, the notion of a Button/Hamilton super-team at McLaren was occupying the F1 rumour mill. It was certainly a tantalising prospect. McLaren could afford it, both financially and technically; it could turn into a rerun of the Prost-Senna partnership, but without the unpleasant edge.

"There is more to being a top driver and selecting a team than simply getting into a fast car," said triple world champion Jackie Stewart. "You need to be in a position where you are really doing the best for yourself on every front. Take my situation in 1965, for example. I was invited to join Lotus alongside Jimmy Clark, but I declined the offer for two reasons. Firstly, Jimmy had already got his feet too far under the table. It was very much his team. And I didn't feel, anyway, that Lotus had the technical capacity to deliver two fully competitive cars. So I went to BRM instead, which I felt was one of the few teams who could do that. And it was right for me."

So would Stewart have recommended that Button seriously consider the possibility of going to McLaren? "Absolutely not," said the Scot firmly. "He's got everything he needs where he is. And, most importantly, he's got Ross Brawn. Why would he want to give up that special relationship?" Yet within a few weeks that is just what Jenson would do, brushing aside Sir Jackie's advice and signing for McLaren.

Alan Henry

AUTODROMO JOSÉ CARLOS PACE, INTERLAGOS SÃO PAULO
Circuit: 2.677 miles/4.309km · 71 LAPS

187/116 mph/kmh

Descida do Logo 143/89
Junção 177/110
290/181
Murgulho 240/150
Ferradura 115/85
Pinheirinho 110/69
Curva do Sol 205/125
Senna-S 148/92
Cotovelo 74/46
296/184
Arquibancadas 244/152
Laranja 99/62
Descida do Sol 88/54

FIA F1 WORLD CHAMPIONSHIP ROUND 16
GRANDE PRÊMIO PETROBRAS DO
BRASIL
SÃO PAULO 16-18 OCTOBER 2009

RACE DISTANCE: 71 laps, 190.083 miles/305.909km • RACE WEATHER: Partly cloudy/sunny (track 33-37°C, air 26°-27°C)

Pos.	Driver	Nat.	No.	Entrant	Car/Engine	Tyres	Laps	Time/Retirement	Speed (mph/km/h)	Gap to leader	Fastest race lap
1	Mark Webber	AUS	14	Red Bull Racing	Red Bull RB5-Renault RS27 V8	B	71	1h 32m 23.081s	123.451/198.675		1m 13.733s 25
2	Robert Kubica	PL	5	BMW Sauber F1 Team	BMW Sauber F1.09-BMW P86/9 V8	B	71	1h 32m 30.707s	123.281/198.402	+ 7.626s	1m 14.155s 38
3	Lewis Hamilton	GB	1	Vodafone McLaren Mercedes	McLaren MP4-24-Mercedes FO108W V8	B	71	1h 32m 42.025s	123.030/197.998	+ 18.944s	1m 14.345s 59
4	Sebastian Vettel	D	15	Red Bull Racing	Red Bull RB5-Renault RS27 V8	B	71	1h 32m 42.733s	123.015/197.973	+ 19.652s	1m 13.890s 59
5	Jenson Button	GB	22	Brawn GP Formula 1 Team	Brawn BGP 001-Mercedes FO108W V8	B	71	1h 32m 52.086s	122.808/197.640	+ 29.005s	1m 14.353s 46
6	Kimi Räikkönen	FIN	4	Scuderia Ferrari Marlboro	Ferrari F60-056 V8	B	71	1h 32m 56.421s	122.713/197.487	+ 33.340s	1m 14.558s 47
7	Sébastien Buemi	CH	12	Scuderia Toro Rosso	Toro Rosso STR04-Ferrari 056 V8	B	71	1h 32m 59.072s	122.654/197.393	+ 35.991s	1m 14.563s 58
8	Rubens Barrichello	BR	23	Brawn GP Formula 1 Team	Brawn BGP 001-Mercedes FO108W V8	B	71	1h 33m 08.535s	122.447/197.059	+ 45.454s	1m 13.950s 20
9	Kamui Kobayashi	I	10	Panasonic Toyota Racing	Toyota TF109-RVX-09 V8	B	71	1h 33m 26.405s	122.057/196.431	+ 1m 03.324s	1m 14.676s 71
10	Giancarlo Fisichella	I	3	Scuderia Ferrari Marlboro	Ferrari F60-056 V8	B	71	1h 33m 33.746s	121.897/196.174	+ 1m 10.665s	1m 14.931s 55
11	Vitantonio Liuzzi	I	21	Force India F1 Team	Force India VJM02-Mercedes FO108W V8	B	71	1h 33m 34.469s	121.881/196.148	+ 1m 11.388s	1m 14.990s 43
12*	Heikki Kovalainen	FIN	2	Vodafone McLaren Mercedes	McLaren MP4-24-Mercedes FO108W V8	B	71	1h 33m 36.580s	121.835/196.075	+ 1m 13.499s	1m 14.303s 68
13	Romain Grosjean	F	8	ING Renault F1 Team	Renault R29-RS27 V8	B	70			+ 1 lap	1m 14.789s 54
14	Jaime Alguersuari	E	11	Scuderia Toro Rosso	Toro Rosso STR04-Ferrari 056 V8	B	70			+ 1 lap	1m 14.861s 59
	Kazuki Nakajima	J	17	AT&T Williams	Williams FW31-Toyota RVX-09 V8	B	30	accident			1m 15.073s 21
	Nico Rosberg	D	16	AT&T Williams	Williams FW31-Toyota RVX-09 V8	B	27	gearbox			1m 14.370s 16
	Nick Heidfeld	D	6	BMW Sauber F1 Team	BMW Sauber F1.09-BMW P86/9 V8	B	21	out of fuel			1m 14.988s 19
	Adrian Sutil	D	20	Force India F1 Team	Force India VJM02-Mercedes FO108W V8	B	0	accident			no time
	Jarno Trulli	I	9	Panasonic Toyota Racing	Toyota TF109-RVX-09 V8	B	0	accident			no time
	Fernando Alonso	E	7	ING Renault F1 Team	Renault R29-RS27 V8	B	0	accident			no time

All results and data © FOM 2009

* includes 25-second penalty for dragging fuel hose and causing fire.

Fastest race lap: Mark Webber on lap 25, 1m 13.733s, 130.728mph/210.386km/h.

Lap record: Juan Pablo Montoya (Williams FW26-BMW V10), 1m 11.473s, 134.862mph/217.038km/h (2004)

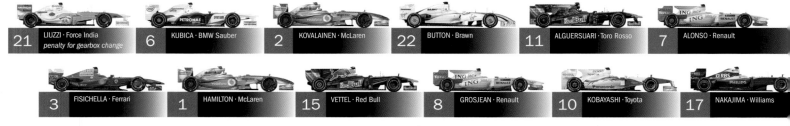

| 21 | LIUZZI · Force India penalty for gearbox change | 6 | KUBICA · BMW Sauber | 2 | KOVALAINEN · McLaren | 22 | BUTTON · Brawn | 11 | ALGUERSUARI · Toro Rosso | 7 | ALONSO · Renault |
| 3 | FISICHELLA · Ferrari | 1 | HAMILTON · McLaren | 15 | VETTEL · Red Bull | 8 | GROSJEAN · Renault | 10 | KOBAYASHI · Toyota | 17 | NAKAJIMA · Williams |

Grid order	1	2	3	4	5	6	7	8	9	10	11	12	13	14	15	16	17	18	19	20	21	22	23	24	25	26	27	28	29	30	31	32	33	34	35	36	37	38	39	40	41	42	43	44	45	46	47	48	49	50	51	52	53	54
23 BARRICHELLO	23	23	23	23	23	23	23	23	23	23	23	23	23	23	23	23	23	23	23	14	14	14	14	14	14	14	14	14	14	14	14	14	14	14	14	14	14	14	14	14	14	14	14	14	14	14	14	14	14	14	14	14	14	14
14 WEBBER	14	14	14	14	14	14	14	14	14	14	14	14	14	14	14	14	14	14	14	23		5	16	16	22	22	22	22	22	15	15	15	15	15	15	15		5	5	5	5	5	5	5	5	5	23	23	23	23		5	5	5
20 SUTIL	16	16	16	16	16		5	5	5	5	5	5	5	5	5	5	5	5	5	5	16		5	12	17	10	10	10	10		5	5	5	5	5	5	5	23	23	23	23	23	23	23	23		5	5	5	22	22	22	22	22
9 TRULLI	5	5	5	5		5	16	16	16	16	16	16	16	16	16	16	16	16	16	16	10	10	15	15	15	23	23	23	23	23	23	23	23		1	1	1	1		22	22	22	22	22	22	22	22	15	15	15	15
4 RÄIKKÖNEN	12	12	12	12	12	12	12	12	12	12	12	12	12	12	12	12	12	12	12	10	10	22	15		5	5	5	5		1	1	1	1	1	1	1	1		4	4	4	4		15	15	15	15	15	15	15	15	12	12	12
12 BUEMI	17	17	17	17	17	10	10	10	10	10	10	10	10	10	10	10	10	10	10	22	22	17		5	23	23	23	23	10	8	8	8	4	4	4	4	22	22	22	22		4	12	12	12	12	12	12	23	23	23	23
16 ROSBERG	10	10	10	10	10	17	22	22	22	22	22	22	22	22	22	22	22	22	17	17	15	23		1	1	1	1	8	4	4	4	22	22	22	22	15	15	15	15	15	12		1	1	1	1	1	1	1	1	1	1
5 KUBICA	8	8	8	8	8	22	17	17	17	17	17	17	17	17	17	17	17	17	17	15	15		5	1	17	2	2	2	4	12	12	12	12	12	12	12	12	12	21	10	10	10	10	10	10	10	10
17 NAKAJIMA	22	22	22	22	22	15	15	15	15	15	15	15	15	15	15	15	15	15	15		1	23	23		2	2	8	8	8	12	22	22	22	8	3	3	3	21	21	21	21	21		1	21	2	2	2	2	2	2	2	2
7 ALONSO	11	11	11	11	11	8	6	6	6	6	6	6	6	6	6	6	6	6		1	1	23		1	1	16	16	4	4	4	22	3	3	3	3	21	21	10	10	10	10	10	10	2	4	4	4	4	4	4	4	4	4
10 KOBAYASHI	15	15	15	15	15	6	1	1	1	1	1	1	1	1	1	1	1	1		1	2	2	2	2	8	12	12	12	3	21	21	21	10	10	10	2	2	2	2	2	8	8	8	8	8	8	8	8
11 ALGUERSUARI	1	6	6	6	6	11	8	8	2	2	2	2	2	2	2	2	2	2	6	6	8	8	4	11	11	11	21	10	10	10	10	2	2	2	8	8	8	8	8	21	3	3	3	3	3	3	3	3
8 GROSJEAN	21	21	3	3	3	1	11	2	8	8	8	8	8	8	8	8	8	8	4	4	4	12	3	3	11	2	2	8	8	8	3	3	3	11	11	11	11	21	21	21	21
22 BUTTON	6	3	1	1	1	4	2	11	11	4	4	4	4	4	4	4	4	4	11	11	21	21	11	11	11	11	11	11	11	11	11	11	11	21	21	21	21	11	11	11	11
15 VETTEL	3	1	4	4	4	2	4	4	11	11	11	11	11	11	11	11	11	11	3	3	3	3	17	17	17	2															
2 KOVALAINEN	4	4	2	2	2	3	3	3	3	3	3	3	3	3	3	3	3	3	21	21	21	21	21	16																
1 HAMILTON	2	2	21	21	21	21	21	21	21	21	21	21	21	21	21	21	21	6																						
6 HEIDFELD																																								
3 FISICHELLA																																								
22 LIUZZI																																								

TIME SHEETS

PRACTICE 1 (FRIDAY)
Cloudy/drizzle/cloudy
(track 21-26°C, air 19-21°C)

Pos.	Driver	Laps	Time
1	Mark Webber	29	1m 12.463s
2	Rubens Barrichello	32	1m 12.874s
3	Sebastian Vettel	27	1m 12.932s
4	Heikki Kovalainen	25	1m 12.989s
5	Lewis Hamilton	25	1m 13.048s
6	Kazuki Nakajima	21	1m 13.067s
7	Jenson Button	29	1m 13.141s
8	Nico Rosberg	23	1m 13.147s
9	Adrian Sutil	23	1m 13.232s
10	Kimi Räikkönen	24	1m 13.321s
11	Jarno Trulli	26	1m 13.326s
12	Nick Heidfeld	28	1m 13.464s
13	Sébastien Buemi	24	1m 13.503s
14	Robert Kubica	24	1m 13.563s
15	Giancarlo Fisichella	23	1m 13.619s
16	Fernando Alonso	28	1m 13.787s
17	Vitantonio Liuzzi	26	1m 13.829s
18	Kamui Kobayashi	27	1m 14.029s
19	Jaime Alguersuari	38	1m 14.040s
20	Romain Grosjean	23	1m 14.173s

PRACTICE 2 (FRIDAY)
Cloudy
(track 22-23°C, air 18-20°C)

Pos.	Driver	Laps	Time
1	Fernando Alonso	27	1m 12.314s
2	Sébastien Buemi	45	1m 12.357s
3	Rubens Barrichello	38	1m 12.459s
4	Mark Webber	41	1m 12.514s
5	Jenson Button	45	1m 12.523s
6	Jarno Trulli	37	1m 12.605s
7	Sebastien Vettel	45	1m 12.611s
8	Nico Rosberg	42	1m 12.633s
9	Adrian Sutil	35	1m 12.720s
10	Lewis Hamilton	39	1m 12.749s
11	Romain Grosjean	27	1m 12.806s
12	Robert Kubica	39	1m 12.862s
13	Kamui Kobayashi	40	1m 12.869s
14	Kazuki Nakajima	41	1m 12.929s
15	Nick Heidfeld	38	1m 12.948s
16	Vitantonio Liuzzi	36	1m 12.950s
17	Heikki Kovalainen	39	1m 12.992s
18	Kimi Räikkönen	42	1m 13.026s
19	Jaime Alguersuari	40	1m 13.041s
20	Giancarlo Fisichella	38	1m 13.275s

PRACTICE 3 (SATURDAY)
Wet/cloudy
(track 18-19°C, air 17-18°C)

Pos.	Driver	Laps	Time
1	Nico Rosberg	9	1m 23.182s
2	Kazuki Nakajima	7	1m 23.832s
3	Jenson Button	6	1m 24.122s
4	Fernando Alonso	5	1m 24.125s
5	Adrian Sutil	4	1m 24.149s
6	Romain Grosjean	5	1m 24.389s
7	Sébastien Buemi	5	1m 24.443s
8	Jarno Trulli	5	1m 24.859s
9	Nick Heidfeld	5	1m 24.867s
10	Mark Webber	5	1m 25.440s
11	Kimi Räikkönen	4	1m 25.508s
12	Heikki Kovalainen	5	1m 25.685s
13	Jaime Alguersuari	6	1m 26.224s
14	Rubens Barrichello	4	1m 26.530s
15	Sebastian Vettel	4	1m 27.047s
16	Vitantonio Liuzzi	4	1m 27.341s
17	Lewis Hamilton	4	1m 27.798s
18	Giancarlo Fisichella	4	1m 29.285s
19	Robert Kubica	3	1m 29.895s
20	Kamui Kobayashi	4	1m 30.259s

DID YOU KNOW?
Jenson Button became the 10th British world champion, (8th English).

This was the first time that British drivers have won back-to-back World Championships since 1968/69, when Hill and Stewart took the titles.

QUALIFYING (SATURDAY)
Wet/drizzle/cloudy (track 18-19°C, air 17-18°C)

Pos.	Driver	First	Second	Third	Weight
1	Rubens Barrichello	1m 24.100s	1m 21.659s	**1m 19.576s**	650.5kg
2	Mark Webber	1m 24.722s	1m 20.803s	1m 19.668s	656kg
3	Adrian Sutil	1m 24.447s	1m 20.753s	1m 19.912s	656.5kg
4	Jarno Trulli	1m 24.621s	1m 20.635s	1m 20.097s	658.5kg
5	Kimi Räikkönen	1m 23.047s	1m 21.378s	1m 20.168s	651.5kg
6	Sébastien Buemi	1m 24.591s	1m 20.701s	1m 20.250s	659kg
7	Nico Rosberg	**1m 22.828s**	**1m 20.368s**	1m 20.326s	657kg
8	Robert Kubica	1m 23.072s	1m 21.147s	1m 20.631s	656kg
9	Kazuki Nakajima	1m 23.161s	1m 20.427s	1m 20.674s	664kg
10	Fernando Alonso	1m 24.842s	1m 21.657s	1m 21.422s	652kg
11	Kamui Kobayashi	1m 24.335s	1m 21.960s		671.5kg
12	Jaime Alguersuari	1m 24.773s	1m 22.231s		671.5kg
13	Romain Grosjean	1m 24.394s	1m 22.477s		677.2kg
14	Jenson Button	1m 24.297s	1m 22.504s		672kg
15	Vitantonio Liuzzi	1m 24.645s	no time		680kg
16	Sebastian Vettel	1m 25.009s			683.5kg
17	Heikki Kovalainen	1m 25.052s			656.5kg
18	Lewis Hamilton	1m 25.192s			661kg
19	Nick Heidfeld	1m 25.515s			650.5kg
20	Giancarlo Fisichella	1m 40.703s			683.5kg

POINTS

DRIVERS

1	Jenson Button	89
2	Sebastian Vettel	74
3	Rubens Barrichello	72
4	Mark Webber	61.5
5	Lewis Hamilton	49
6	Kimi Räikkönen	48
7	Nico Rosberg	34.5
8	Jarno Trulli	30.5
9	Fernando Alonso	26
10	Timo Glock	24
11	Felipe Massa	22
12	Heikki Kovalainen	22
13	Robert Kubica	17
14	Nick Heidfeld	15
15	Giancarlo Fisichella	8
16	Adrian Sutil	5
17	Sébastien Buemi	5
18	Sébastien Bourdais	2

CONSTRUCTORS

1	Brawn	161
2	Red Bull	135.5
3	McLaren	71
4	Ferrari	70
5	Toyota	54.5
6	Williams	34.5
7	BMW Sauber	32
8	Renault	26
9	Force India	13
10	Toro Rosso	7

5 KUBICA · BMW Sauber

12 BUEMI · Toro Rosso

9 TRULLI · Toyota

14 WEBBER · Red Bull

16 ROSBERG · Williams

4 RÄIKKÖNEN · Ferrari

20 SUTIL · Force India

23 BARRICHELLO · Brawn

7	58	59	60	61	62	63	64	65	66	67	68	69	70	71	
4	14	14	14	14	14	14	14	14	14	14	14	14	14	14	1
5	5	5	5	5	5	5	5	5	5	5	5	5	5	5	2
3	23	23	23	23	1	1	1	1	1	1	1	1	1	1	3
1	1	1	1	1	23	15	15	15	15	15	15	15	15	15	4
5	15	15	15	15	15	23	22	22	22	22	22	22	22	22	5
2	2	22	22	22	22	22	4	4	4	4	4	4	4	4	6
22	2	2	4	4	4	4	12	12	12	12	12	12	12	12	7
4	4	4	12	12	12	12	23	23	23	23	23	23	23	23	8
2	12	12	2	2	2	2	2	2	2	2	2	2	2	2	
3	3	3	3	3	3	3	3	3	3	10	10	10	10	10	
0	10	10	10	10	10	10	10	10	10	3	3	3	3	3	
1	21	21	21	21	21	21	21	21	21	21	21	21	21	21	
8	8	8	8	*8*	*8*	*8*	*8*	*8*	*8*	*8*	*8*	*8*	*8*	*8*	
1	*11*	*11*	*11*	*11*	*11*	*11*	*11*	*11*	*11*	*11*	*11*	*11*	*11*	*11*	

1 Pit stop
1 One lap or more behind
█ Safety car deployed on laps shown

RACE TYRE STRATEGIES

The tyre regulations stipulate that two dry tyre specifications must be used during the race.

The Super-Soft compound Bridgestone Potenza tyre is marked with a green stripe on the sidewall of the tyre.

	Driver	Race Stint 1	Race Stint 2	Race Stint 3	Race Stint 4
1	Mark Webber	Medium: 1-26	Medium: 27-52	Super-Soft: 53-71	
2	Robert Kubica	Medium: 1-23	Medium: 24-46	Super-Soft: 47-71	
3	Lewis Hamilton	Super-Soft: 1	Medium: 2-42	Medium: 43-71	
4	Sebastian Vettel	Medium: 1-37	Medium: 38-56	Super-Soft: 57-71	
5	Jenson Button	Medium: 1-29	Medium: 30-55	Super-Soft: 56-71	
6	Kimi Räikkönen	Super-Soft: 1	Medium: 2-43	Super-Soft: 44-71	
7	Sébastien Buemi	Medium: 1-24	Medium: 25-54	Super-Soft: 55-71	
8	Rubens Barrichello	Medium: 1-30	Medium: 31-50	Super-Soft: 51-63	Super-Soft: 64-71
9	Kamui Kobayoshi	Medium: 1-19	Medium: 20-56	Super-Soft: 57-71	
10	Giancarlo Fisichella	Medium: 1-37	Super-Soft: 38-71		
11	Vitantonio Liuzzi	Medium: 1-2	Super-Soft: 3	Medium: 4-44	Medium: 45-71
12	Heikki Kovalainen	Medium: 1	Medium: 2-29	Super-Soft: 30-59	Super-Soft: 60-71
13	Romain Grosjean	Medium: 1-34	Medium: 35-55	Super-Soft: 56-70	
14	Jaime Alguersuari	Medium: 1-30	Medium: 31-50	Super-Soft: 51-70	
	Kazuki Nakajima	Medium: 1-26	Medium: 27-30 (dnf)		
	Nico Rosberg	Medium: 1-24	Medium: 25-27 (dnf)		
	Nick Heidfeld	Super-Soft: 1-20	Medium: 21 (dnf)		
	Adrian Sutil	Medium: 0 (dnf)			
	Jarno Trulli	Medium: 0 (dnf)			
	Fernando Alonso	Medium: 0 (dnf)			

ABU DHABI
GRAND PRIX

YAS MARINA CIRCUIT

YAS MARINA QUALIFYING

AN obvious clue was there almost straight away: Lewis Hamilton, 1m 39.873s. Not a bad marker on your fourth flying qualifying lap, that, when everybody else is struggling to break 1m 41s.

The contours of the new Yas Marina Circuit were every bit as impressive as the architecturally lavish facilities – and they were always likely to suit the McLaren MP4-24. In many ways, the sport's latest venue was something of a throwback: the corners might not have looked like much, beyond the opening series of fast, undulating sweeps, but some awkward cambers had been included, and the drivers had a little bit extra to contemplate. Throughout Friday's free practice sessions, cars could regularly be seen bouncing over kerbs and then slithering sideways: the backdrop might have had little in common with the 1960s or '70s, but certain elements of the sport's heritage were apparent.

When both McLaren drivers were asked to describe the circuit, Heikki Kovalainen gave a measured response, but Hamilton could barely wait to snatch the microphone from him.

"I thought it was great," he said. "It felt a bit like driving a kart through some of the corners: the sequence from Turns 11 to 13 reminds me of a kart track. You use a bit of kerb here, a bit more there, and then you slightly lose vision as you go over a brow and the car drops down before you get back on the power. It's cool. I really like it." The McLaren's appetite for slower corners and Hamilton's zest for any kind of corner complemented the circuit's long, KERS-friendly straight to perfection.

Kovalainen was almost a second adrift of his team-mate when his gearbox jammed in second during Q2, condemning him to yet another five-position penalty (and 18th on the grid), but his predicament was amplified by the extent to which Hamilton continued to flatter the chassis. "The car is much better than it was," he said, "but I still think it's a long way from being the best in the field. If we went back to Spa, with all its quick corners, we'd be a long way off."

His pole lap, well clear of the rest, was a thing of great beauty.

Sebastian Vettel and Mark Webber were customarily close – albeit 0.667 seconds and 0.778 seconds respectively behind Hamilton – but Vettel had the edge in terms of both speed and fuel weight. "We're both a little bit surprised by the gap," Vettel said. "Lewis has been strong all weekend, and generally McLaren looks very strong. We could see already in Q1 and Q2 that it would be difficult to match them, but the car is working well. We do have a KERS button on our steering wheel, of course, but it doesn't do anything…"

The Brawns of Rubens Barrichello and Jenson Button were fourth and fifth, a source of frustration to the freshly crowned champion, who was relishing his first tension-free race weekend for some time. "The car felt good," he said, "but I picked up a bit of a front-wheel vibration on my final run, hopefully nothing more than a balancing weight that's fallen out. Without that, I thought I could definitely have been on the front row, although I'd still probably have been half a second behind Lewis."

Opening spread: The dramatic new Yas Marina circuit provided a suitably surreal backdrop for F1's second fixture in the Gulf region.
Photo: Paul-Henri Cahier

Right: The three-storey pit complex provided an amazing level of opulence and viewing opportunities for the celebrity guests.
Photos: Paul-Henri Cahier

Below: Lewis Hamilton was the pace setter in both qualifying and the early stages of the race.

Below right: Everyone wanted to capture a bit of the action.

Bottom right: Robert Kubica prepares for his final race with the BMW Sauber squad.

Bottom right: Kamui Kobayashi was once again one of the stars of the show, but his efforts came too late to have any chance of influencing Toyota to reconsider its withdrawal from F1.
Photos: Peter J. Fox

Kimi Räikkönen   Giancarlo Fisichella

Above: The race began as daylight faded with Lewis Hamilton taking the early lead. His race would not go to plan, however, ending in retirement due to concerns over his McLaren's brakes.
Photo: Peter J. Fox

Above right: Ron Dennis attended a race for the first time since the season's opener in Melbourne.

Right: Pit stop for Jenson Button's third-place Brawn-Mercedes. Little did we know that this would be the new world champion's final outing for the Brackley based team.
Photos: Peter J. Fox

I N the paddock, a long line of limousines had just deposited their royal or presidential cargos. On the grid, newly elected FIA president Jean Todt was conducting a meet-and-greet tour, with cameras following almost every handshake. And Ron Dennis, dressed in civvies, rather than team uniform, was back in the McLaren pit for the first time since he had abdicated his Formula One responsibilities in the wake of the Melbourne 'liargate' scandal. At the first Abu Dhabi Grand Prix – the sport's inaugural day/night race – the pomp and ceremony stretched far beyond the frivolous architectural eye candy, notably the flashing, multi-coloured hotel roof, that lured many a wide-angle lens.

Beyond the Yas Marina Circuit's perimeter, much of the construction work had a distinctly unfinished air, but the vital core was complete. There was ample proof, too, that this was a circuit on which drivers could race – the six support events confirmed that much – but sometimes circumstance confounds expectation. Qualifying form led some to assume that Lewis Hamilton would be checking in for his flight home before anybody else had finished, but the script altered within a matter of laps. Hamilton made a good start, but his rate of escape wasn't as brisk as had been anticipated: he was 1.3 seconds clear within four laps, but then Sebastian Vettel pegged him back.

The Red Bulls had almost rubbed wheels at the start, Mark Webber contemplating a move around Vettel into Turn One, but the Australian tucked back in and was promptly thumped by Rubens Barrichello. The RB5 flicked sideways, but Webber maintained momentum, while Barrichello was forced to consider how to deal with the understeer that set in, because the incident had removed a slice of his front wing. He lost a place to team-mate Jenson Button a cou-

ple of corners later, but swiftly decided he could live with the frontal imbalance and opted not to have the damaged nose replaced. Robert Kubica ran sixth after elbowing Jarno Trulli aside during the opening lap's course – one of the campaign's more predictable developments, that – and Nick Heidfeld settled into eighth, ahead of Nico Rosberg, Sébastien Buemi, Kamui Kobayashi, Kimi Räikkönen, Heikki Kovalainen, Kazuki Nakajima, Tonio Liuzzi, Giancarlo Fisichella, Romain Grosjean, Fernando Alonso, Jaime Alguersuari (who lost several positions when he ran wide at Turn 19) and Adrian Sutil.

With Vettel due to run two laps longer than Hamilton during the opening stint, this was beginning to look like a finely balanced contest rather than the anticipated walkover – but the leader was feeling uncomfortable for reasons other than the German's proximity. "I realised very early on that something was wrong," Hamilton said. "After three or four laps, it became clear that there was a problem with my right rear brake."

From the pit wall, the situation looked bleak. "Drivers are sensitive souls," said McLaren team principal Martin Whitmarsh, "and Lewis could feel the yaw

action you get when one pad isn't grabbing as well as the others, so he lost a bit of the confidence the car had given him during qualifying."

The team had hoped he'd be able to pull away by about half a second per lap, but the reduced circumstances dictated that the gap was only 1.733 seconds after ten: next time around, that was halved when he locked up at Turn 17, flat-spotted his right front and ran wide.

Hamilton kept going, but it was clear that he would be unable to keep Vettel behind after they had made their initial stops – on laps 17 and 19 respectively. "We looked for brake dust when Lewis came in," Whitmarsh said, "but we couldn't see any. That suggested there wasn't a problem, but in the end you have to believe what the sensors tell you or there's no point having them on the car." On safety grounds, Hamilton was summoned back to the pits on his 20th lap and the car was withdrawn. "It's a shame we couldn't maintain the performance we'd shown throughout the weekend," he said, "but sometimes that's racing. I think we can be really proud of our efforts, though. At the start of the year, who'd have thought we'd finish third in the championship for constructors?" Fair question, well asked.

"We're not sure quite what happened," Whitmarsh added. "The other three pads were fine, so it looks as though some rogue material might have crept in during the manufacturing process."

With Hamilton gone, Vettel had little to do but reel off the laps – although there had been a momentary scare shortly before his first stop, not that he was aware of it...

Custody of two grand prix teams might confer cer-

tain marketing benefits, but it can also produce confusing side-effects. Running towards the tail of the field, Alguersuari had lost a couple of gears and pitted on lap 18 to have the problem checked. Unfortunately, the Toro Rosso driver mistook the Red Bull pit for his own and stopped in the wrong place a matter of seconds before Vettel was due to arrive. The Spaniard was swiftly waved away – his gearbox packed up completely before he'd managed to complete another lap – and Vettel was serviced without delay, but Red Bull sporting director Christian Horner admitted that the air had, momentarily, turned "slightly blue" on the pit counter.

Vettel had a slight speed advantage over Webber during the first two stints, on the medium Bridgestone, and the difference grew when the two switched to softs at the end. Once Hamilton had vanished, the result was never in doubt. "The car was absolutely fantastic from start to finish," Vettel said. "On the opening lap, it was quite shocking to see how much KERS was worth when Lewis pushed his button on the back straight, and it is not easy following another car, even when you are a couple of seconds behind, because it doesn't feel as though you are in your own clean air. It was unfortunate that he had to retire, though. I enjoyed our fight, even if we weren't wheel to wheel."

Red Bull's strategy had been to get Vettel ahead of Hamilton at the first stop, and to repeat the process with Webber at the second, but ultimately both objectives were handed to them on a plate. Webber, though, had other concerns. The team told him to wind down his revs at the start of the final stint – and then promptly told him to turn them up again, when

it became apparent how quickly Button was going on the soft Bridgestone.

"The prime tyre was not my favourite in the race," the new world champion said, "because it gave me a lot of understeer. On the softs, though, the front end came back and I got good initial turn-in, which meant I was able to carry a lot of speed through the corners. That's why I was able to close down Mark."

The Australian's situation, meanwhile, was completely the opposite. "I didn't have the same feel for the softer tyre," Webber said. "It was like that when I tried it on Friday and it was the same in the race. I was hoping things would be better once the circuit rubbered in, but I felt I couldn't commit properly to the corners, and it was probably costing me a tenth each time."

Webber made his final stop on lap 40, two before Button, and at that stage they were separated by 5.8 seconds. The gap closed inexorably, however, and was down to 0.6 second as the final lap began. Button managed to get into the Australian's tow on the long drag to Turn Eight, but Webber refused to yield as the Englishman attempted to slice down the inside. They remained as one most of the way to Turn 13, where Webber was finally able to cut across and snuff out any possibility of Red Bull losing its fourth 1-2 of the campaign. "I thought I could pull it off," Button said, "but Mark is always very hard to pass. We were on the edge, but it was good fun, and clean."

Barrichello managed to complete the distance without any need for a replacement front wing and took a safe fourth in his final race for Brawn – his transfer to Williams would be confirmed within a day of the season's conclusion. "I was quicker than Jen-

son during the middle stint," he said, "but it was very difficult to overtake, and even more so against your team-mate in the same car. There was nothing I could do, but I have to thank the team for giving me a competitive car and an opportunity to return to winning ways this year."

Barrichello had been shadowed for much of the second stint by Heidfeld, who passed Trulli and Kubica by running slightly longer prior to the first stops, and the German almost caught the Brawn after a quicker turn-around when they came in together on lap 41. Even so, fifth place – coupled with Kubica's stellar second in Brazil – represented a decent swansong for BMW Sauber.

During the race's immediate aftermath, team principal Dr Mario Theissen had a distinctly emotional tremor in his voice as he cradled a can of Heineken in the paddock. "We were hoping Barrichello might stop one lap earlier," he said, "but this was still a nice way to bow out." Heidfeld, who had completed seven of his ten F1 seasons with this team, in its different iterations, admitted it had been difficult to concentrate as the tale drew to its close. "I had to pull myself together," he said, "because things felt quite emotional."

While his was an unsung cameo, Kamui Kobayashi's was anything but. As in Brazil, he'd qualified respectably, making the unusual excuse that he was unfamiliar with the dry conditions, and went on to race exceptionally well on a one-stop strategy that worked to his advantage and enabled him to breeze past such as Kubica and Trulli. The Japanese was relatively lightly fuelled when he came up behind Button as the Englishman rejoined after his first stop – and Kobayashi calmly forced the sport's new king into an error at Turn Eight. "It's always very difficult to judge your braking point when you've just come out of the pits with a load of fuel on board," Button said, "and I slightly outfumbled myself by locking the rears, but it didn't make any difference to my race when Kamui got past because he was quicker at that point."

A few weeks earlier, Toyota's former reserve had assumed his career was over in the slipstream of a miserable GP2 campaign – and that his next job might involve working in his father's sushi restaurant back home – but now his name was on everybody's lips. And all because Timo Glock had run a touch too wide during qualifying for the Japanese GP.

"Kamui's GP2 performances hadn't really encouraged us to think about using him next year," admitted team principal John Howett, "but now... The thing that has most impressed me is the way he sits in debriefs and tells us that he doesn't think overtaking in F1 is a problem. I like his attitude." His prospects of a full-time Toyota seat would be dashed within a couple of days, however, when the Japanese manufacturer announced that it would follow Honda and BMW out of the sport.

Kobayashi finished six seconds clear of two-stopping team-mate Trulli, who explained that his race had been compromised by rapid rear tyre wear during his opening stint and the deterioration of his brakes.

Buemi claimed the final point for Toro Rosso after yet another impressive drive. The Swiss faced a brief challenge from Kubica immediately after his second stop, but closed the door very firmly. "I left him space," Buemi said, "and thought I was fair." Kubica described the move as "a bit dangerous", and the resultant spin dropped him to tenth, behind Rosberg.

Kovalainen, Räikkönen, Nakajima, Alonso, Liuzzi, Fisichella, Sutil and Grosjean completed the finishers on an afternoon that had been fairly quiet for all bar Grosjean, who spent almost as much of the weekend off the track as he had on it. Alonso's result, though, revealed everything you needed to know about the Renault's performance level.

On the morning after the race, Bridgestone announced that it would not be tendering for the deal to supply F1 tyres when its current contract expired at the end of 2010 – but there had been a more jocular bombshell during the previous evening's sweet-natured post-race press conference.

"I hear you're getting married," said Vettel to Button.

"Thanks for that, Seb," retorted the champ. "They write some great things in the press..." Later, when someone asked what the top three would be doing during the winter, Vettel tried again. "Jenson is getting married," he said, to which Webber added, "And we're all invited."

Button: "Next question."

Then, when Button attempted to answer a question about Brawn's ability to maintain its performance edge over such as McLaren and Ferrari, the Red Bull duo began chatting among themselves.

Button: "Excuse me, I'm trying to talk. You might want to listen."

Webber: "We're just chatting about your wedding day, mate, trying to clear our schedules."

Button: "I'm not getting married this year."

Vettel: "Why not? Don't you love her?"

It was the easy repartee of people who feel comfortable in each other's company, on or off the track – a feel-good end to a mostly feel-good campaign.

Simon Arron

EDITOR'S VIEW
A PASSING THOUGHT

Left: Night rider. Red Bull's Sebastian Vettel finished the season on a high, taking his fourth grand prix win in 2009.

Below: Sébastien Buemi drove another impressive race to score points for Toro Rosso in a season where he exceeded the expectations of many.
Photos: Peter J. Fox

YOU didn't have to look far to discern the uneasy juxtaposition of the new and old orders in Formula One throughout the weekend at the breathtaking Yas Marina circuit in Abu Dhabi. For those of us of a certain generation, who used to stand, soaked to the skin, in our plastic macs, munching ham sandwiches from greaseproof paper in the spectator areas at Copse or Clearways, it was almost too much to take in.

Damon Hill, every inch the English gentleman abroad, was present in his role as the president of the BRDC, trying to inch the negotiations along with Bernie Ecclestone to emphasise that just because Donington Park's chances of holding the British Grand Prix had collapsed, there was absolutely no reason for Silverstone's to go the same way.

Hill is a supremely intelligent individual who knows full well that there is no point in trying to exert any pressure on Mr E. But somehow the task of saving Silverstone's place on the F1 calendar took on a renewed urgency against the glitzy backdrop of the prosperous Gulf state. Impressive though Abu Dhabi certainly was, its arrival on the schedule seemed to make it even more imperative that the FIA World Championship exerts a strong effort to remain a 'broad church' as it goes forward into the future.

Of course, there are those within the F1 community who believe that it is running out of control in the fast lane, in endless pursuit of an elusive crock of gold somewhere beyond the horizon. Yet there is always a reality check lurking just around the corner, and on this occasion, it exploded on to the scene only three days after the final race of the season, when Japanese man-ufacturer Toyota announced its immediate withdrawal from F1.

Toyota's decision to quit after a lamentable record of under-achievement came as absolutely no surprise to me, although I must say that I will remember the team fondly for having introduced Kamui Kobayashi into F1, the very best Japanese driver I have ever seen.

Toyota's departure seemed, at least, to clear the way for Sauber to re-enter F1 as an independent team for 2010, but it soon became clear that the Japanese car maker might have to field a legal action from both the FIA and Ecclestone's Formula One Management organisation. Having signed the Concorde Agreement earlier in 2009, Toyota was technically committed to competing in the FIA World Championship until the end of 2012. So how will all that be sorted out?

Many were stunned by Toyota's decision, and eyes were cast a little nervously in the direction of the Renault squad, which had had a threadbare season, to say the least, as far as hard results were concerned. One hopes that the French car maker will not follow Honda, BMW and Toyota out of the sport, but the fear that it might do so cannot be discounted.

Worrying times for F1 in some ways, I fancy. That said, the cost cutting initiatives have tempted some new lower-budget teams to throw their hats into the ring for 2010.

As the sun set over Abu Dhabi, and the 2009 season passed into the history books, there were still some dark shadows lurking just down the road.

Alan Henry

Circuit: 3.451 miles/5.554km
55 laps

8 81/50
6 70/43
4 270/168
21 125/78
3 254/159
5 100/62
6 90/56
9 125/78
20 245/153
10 230/143
17 98/61
19 113/70
2 260/163
18 105/65
16 280/175
15 275/171
14 110/68
11 81/50
12&13 128/80

Turn 1
127/79
116/187 mph/kmh
Gear

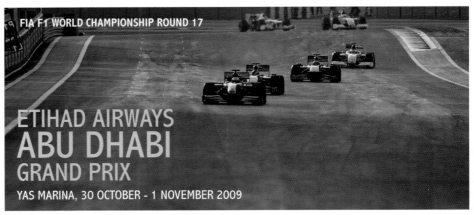

FIA F1 WORLD CHAMPIONSHIP ROUND 17

ETIHAD AIRWAYS
ABU DHABI
GRAND PRIX

YAS MARINA, 30 OCTOBER - 1 NOVEMBER 2009

Photos: Peter J. Fox

All results and data © FOM 2009

RACE DISTANCE: 55 laps, 189.739 miles/305.355km • RACE WEATHER: Sunny/dusk/dark (track 30-37°C, air 29-31°C)

Pos.	Driver	Nat.	No.	Entrant	Car/Engine	Tyres	Laps	Time/Retirement	Speed (mph/km/h)	Gap to leader	Fastest race lap	
1	Sebastian Vettel	D	15	Red Bull Racing	Red Bull RB5-Renault RS27 V8	B	55	1h 34m 03.414s	121.036/194.789		1m 40.279s	54
2	Mark Webber	AUS	14	Red Bull Racing	Red Bull RB5-Renault RS27 V8	B	55	1h 34m 21.271s	120.655/194.175	+ 17.857s	1m 40.571s	14
3	Jenson Button	GB	22	Brawn GP Formula 1 Team	Brawn BGP 001-Mercedes FO108W V8	B	55	1h 34m 21.881s	120.642/194.154	+ 18.467s	1m 40.642s	49
4	Rubens Barrichello	BR	23	Brawn GP Formula 1 Team	Brawn BGP 001-Mercedes FO108W V8	B	55	1h 34m 26.149s	120.550/194.007	+ 22.735s	1m 40.449s	54
5	Nick Heidfeld	D	6	BMW Sauber F1 Team	BMW Sauber F1.09-BMW P86/9 V8	B	55	1h 34m 29.667s	120.476/193.887	+ 26.253s	1m 40.672s	54
6	Kamui Kobayashi	J	10	Panasonic Toyota Racing	Toyota TF109-RVX-09 V8	B	55	1h 34m 31.757s	120.432/193.816	+ 28.343s	1m 40.779s	55
7	Jarno Trulli	I	9	Panasonic Toyota Racing	Toyota TF109-RVX-09 V8	B	55	1h 34m 37.780s	120.304/193.610	+ 34.366s	1m 40.723s	49
8	Sébastian Buemi	CH	12	Scuderia Toro Rosso	Toro Rosso STR04-Ferrari 056 V8	B	55	1h 34m 44.708s	120.157/193.374	+ 41.294s	1m 40.326s	55
9	Nico Rosberg	D	16	AT&T Williams	Williams FW31-Toyota RVX-09 V8	B	55	1h 34m 49.355s	120.059/193.216	+ 45.941s	1m 40.997s	49
10	Robert Kubica	PL	5	BMW Sauber F1 Team	BMW Sauber F1.09-BMW P86/9 V8	B	55	1h 34m 51.594s	120.012/193.140	+ 48.180s	1m 40.924s	54
11	Heikki Kovalainen	FIN	2	Vodafone McLaren Mercedes	McLaren MP4-24-Mercedes FO108W V8	B	55	1h 34m 56.212s	119.915/192.984	+ 52.798s	1m 41.316s	53
12	Kimi Räikkönen	FIN	4	Scuderia Ferrari Marlboro	Ferrari F60-056 V8	B	55	1h 34m 57.731s	119.882/192.932	+ 54.317s	1m 40.843s	54
13	Kazuki Nakajima	J	17	AT&T Williams	Williams FW31-Toyota RVX-09 V8	B	55	1h 35m 03.253s	119.766/192.745	+ 59.839s	1m 40.754s	54
14	Fernando Alonso	E	7	ING Renault F1 Team	Renault R29-RS27 V8	B	55	1h 35m 13.101s	119.560/192.413	+ 1m 09.687s	1m 40.757s	54
15	Vitantonio Liuzzi	I	21	Force India F1 Team	Force India VJM02-Mercedes FO108W V8	B	55	1h 35m 37.864s	119.044/191.583	+ 1m 34.450s	1m 41.277s	54
16	Giancarlo Fisichella	I	3	Scuderia Ferrari Marlboro	Ferrari F60-056 V8	B	54			+ 1 lap	1m 41.132s	54
17	Adrian Sutil	D	20	Force India F1 Team	Force India VJM02-Mercedes FO108W V8	B	54			+ 1 lap	1m 40.904s	34
18	Romain Grosjean	F	8	ING Renault F1 Team	Renault R29-RS27 V8	B	54			+ 1 lap	1m 42.274s	47
	Lewis Hamilton	GB	1	Vodafone McLaren Mercedes	McLaren MP4-24-Mercedes FO108W V8	B	20	rear brakes			1m 40.367s	16
	Jaime Alguersuari	E	11	Scuderia Toro Rosso	Toro Rosso STR04-Ferrari 056 V8	B	18	gearbox			1m 43.318s	16

Fastest race lap: Sebastian Vettel on lap 54, 1m 40.279s, 123.894 mph/199.387 km/h.

Lap record: No previous race.

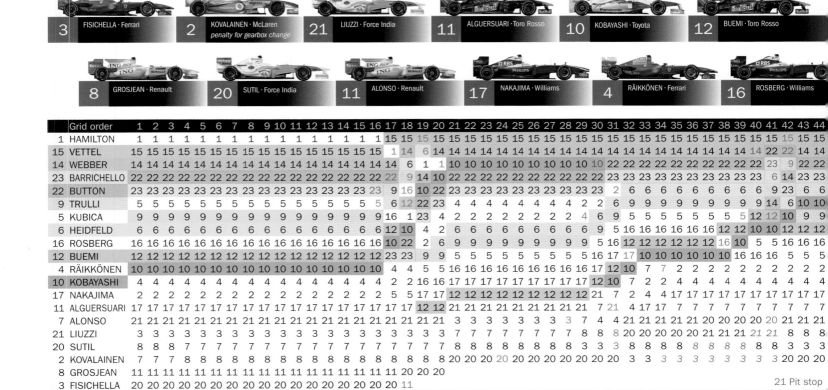

	3 FISICHELLA · Ferrari	2 KOVALAINEN · McLaren *penalty for gearbox change*	21 LIUZZI · Force India	11 ALGUERSUARI · Toro Rosso	10 KOBAYASHI · Toyota	12 BUEMI · Toro Rosso
	8 GROSJEAN · Renault	20 SUTIL · Force India	11 ALONSO · Renault	17 NAKAJIMA · Williams	4 RÄIKKÖNEN · Ferrari	16 ROSBERG · Williams

	Grid order	1	2	3	4	5	6	7	8	9	10	11	12	13	14	15	16	17	18	19	20	21	22	23	24	25	26	27	28	29	30	31	32	33	34	35	36	37	38	39	40	41	42	43	44
1	HAMILTON	1	1	1	1	1	1	1	1	1	1	1	1	1	1	1	1	15	15	15	15	15	15	15	15	15	15	15	15	15	15	15	15	15	15	15	15	15	15	15	15	15	15	15	15
15	VETTEL	15	15	15	15	15	15	15	15	15	15	15	15	15	15	15	1	14	6	14	14	14	14	14	14	14	14	14	14	14	14	14	14	14	14	14	14	14	14	22	22	14	14		
14	WEBBER	14	14	14	14	14	14	14	14	14	14	14	14	14	14	14	6	1	1	10	10	10	10	10	10	10	10	22	22	22	22	22	22	22	22	22	23	9	22	22					
23	BARRICHELLO	22	22	22	22	22	22	22	22	22	22	22	22	22	22	22	9	14	10	22	22	22	22	22	22	22	23	23	23	23	23	23	23	6	14	23									
22	BUTTON	23	23	23	23	23	23	23	23	23	23	23	23	23	23	23	9	16	10	22	23	23	23	23	23	23	2	6	6	6	6	6	6	6	9	23	6	6							
9	TRULLI	5	5	5	5	5	5	5	5	5	5	5	5	5	5	6	12	22	23	4	4	4	4	4	4	2	6	9	9	9	9	9	9	14	6	10	10								
5	KUBICA	9	9	9	9	9	9	9	9	9	9	9	9	9	16	1	23	4	2	2	2	2	2	4	6	9	5	5	5	5	5	12	12	10	9	9									
6	HEIDFELD	6	6	6	6	6	6	6	6	6	6	6	6	6	10	4	2	2	9	9	16	16	16	16	12	10	10	10	12	12															
16	ROSBERG	16	16	16	16	16	16	16	16	16	16	16	16	16	10	22	9	9	9	9	9	16	12	12	12	12	16	10	5	5	10														
12	BUEMI	12	12	12	12	12	12	12	12	12	12	12	12	23	23	9	9	5	16	17	10	10	10	10	10	16	16	5	5	5															
4	RÄIKKÖNEN	10	10	10	10	10	10	10	10	10	10	10	10	10	4	5	16	16	16	16	16	10	7	2	2	2	2	2	2	4	4														
10	KOBAYASHI	4	4	4	4	4	4	4	4	4	4	4	4	4	2	16	16	17	17	17	17	12	10	7	2	4	4	4	4	4	4														
17	NAKAJIMA	2	2	2	2	2	2	2	2	2	2	2	2	2	5	17	12	12	12	12	12	12	21	7	4	17	17	17	17	17	17	17	17	17											
11	ALGUERSUARI	17	17	17	17	17	17	17	17	17	17	17	17	17	12	12	21	21	21	21	21	7	21	4	17	7	7	7	7	7															
7	ALONSO	21	21	21	21	21	21	21	21	21	21	21	21	21	3	3	3	3	3	7	4	4	21	21	20	20	20	21	21																
21	LIUZZI	3	3	3	3	3	3	3	3	3	3	3	3	3	7	7	7	7	7	8	8	20	20	20	21	21	21	21	8	8															
20	SUTIL	8	8	7	7	7	7	7	7	7	7	7	7	7	8	8	8	8	2	20	20	8	8	8	8	8	8	8	3	3															
2	KOVALAINEN	7	7	8	8	8	8	8	8	8	8	8	8	8	20	20	20	20	20	20	20	20	3	3	3	3	3	3	3	20	20														
8	GROSJEAN	11	11	11	11	11	11	11	11	11	11	11	11	11	11	20	20																												
3	FISICHELLA	20	20	20	20	20	20	20	20	20	20	20	20	20	20	20	11																												

21 Pit stop

TIME SHEETS

FOR THE RECORD

1st GRAND PRIX: Abu Dhabi (UAE)

1st POINTS: Kamui Kobayashi

10th PODIUM: Mark Webber

DID YOU KNOW?

The United Arab Emirates became the 28th country to host a F1 World Championship Grand Prix.

PRACTICE 1 (FRIDAY)
Sunny
(track 46-50ºC, air 32-34ºC)

Pos.	Driver	Laps	Time
1	Lewis Hamilton	18	1m 43.939s
2	Jenson Button	20	1m 44.035s
3	Sebastian Vettel	28	1m 44.153s
4	Rubens Barrichello	23	1m 44.207s
5	Nick Heidfeld	23	1m 44.667s
6	Sébastien Buemi	32	1m 44.687s
7	Adrian Sutil	14	1m 44.688s
8	Mark Webber	25	1m 44.805s
9	Jaime Alguersuari	33	1m 44.955s
10	Jarno Trulli	25	1m 44.958s
11	Robert Kubica	22	1m 44.988s
12	Heikki Kovalainen	20	1m 45.123s
13	Nico Rosberg	27	1m 45.649s
14	Kazuki Nakajima	25	1m 45.679s
15	Kimi Räikkönen	27	1m 45.704s
16	Fernando Alonso	23	1m 45.865s
17	Vitantonio Liuzzi	22	1m 46.239s
18	Giancarlo Fisichella	26	1m 46.267s
19	Kamui Kobayashi	28	1m 46.364s
20	Romain Grosjean	27	1m 46.411s

PRACTICE 2 (FRIDAY)
Cloudy/dusk/dark
(track 32-35ºC, air 30ºC)

Pos.	Driver	Laps	Time
1	Heikki Kovalainen	35	1m 41.307s
2	Lewis Hamilton	34	1m 41.504s
3	Jenson Button	39	1m 41.541s
4	Sebastian Vettel	37	1m 41.591s
5	Kamui Kobayashi	34	1m 41.636s
6	Sébastien Buemi	37	1m 41.683s
7	Mark Webber	34	1m 41.684s
8	Rubens Barrichello	38	1m 41.831s
9	Nico Rosberg	39	1m 41.931s
10	Kimi Räikkönen	39	1m 41.987s
11	Adrian Sutil	28	1m 42.180s
12	Kazuki Nakajima	36	1m 42.245s
13	Nick Heidfeld	36	1m 42.278s
14	Jarno Trulli	30	1m 42.409s
15	Vitantonio Liuzzi	33	1m 42.530s
16	Fernando Alonso	29	1m 42.782s
17	Giancarlo Fisichella	37	1m 42.932s
18	Romain Grosjean	37	1m 43.021s
19	Jaime Alguersuari	39	1m 43.022s
20	Robert Kubica	13	1m 43.708s

PRACTICE 3 (SATURDAY)
Sunny
(track 48-51ºC, air 34ºC)

Pos.	Driver	Laps	Time
1	Jenson Button	21	1m 40.625s
2	Lewis Hamilton	18	1m 40.627s
3	Rubens Barrichello	20	1m 40.907s
4	Sébastien Buemi	22	1m 40.934s
5	Nick Heidfeld	18	1m 41.241s
6	Heikki Kovalainen	20	1m 41.263s
7	Jarno Trulli	23	1m 41.310s
8	Robert Kubica	20	1m 41.322s
9	Adrian Sutil	22	1m 41.372s
10	Kimi Räikkönen	23	1m 41.373s
11	Sebastian Vettel	19	1m 41.403s
12	Nico Rosberg	22	1m 41.478s
13	Kamui Kobayashi	24	1m 41.499s
14	Vitantonio Liuzzi	20	1m 41.675s
15	Mark Webber	15	1m 41.682s
16	Fernando Alonso	19	1m 41.782s
17	Kazuki Nakajima	21	1m 42.156s
18	Romain Grosjean	19	1m 42.213s
19	Giancarlo Fisichella	23	1m 42.351s
20	Jaime Alguersuari		no time

QUALIFYING (SATURDAY)
Sunny/dusk (track 31-35º C, air 29-30º C)

Pos.	Driver	First	Second	Third	Weight
1	Lewis Hamilton	**1m 39.873s**	**1m 39.695s**	**1m 40.948s**	658.5kg
2	Sebastian Vettel	1m 40.666s	1m 39.984s	1m 41.615s	663kg
3	Mark Webber	1m 40.667s	1m 40.272s	1m 41.726s	660kg
4	Rubens Barrichello	1m 40.574s	1m 40.421s	1m 41.786s	655kg
5	Jenson Button	1m 40.378s	1m 40.148s	1m 41.892s	657kg
6	Jarno Trulli	1m 40.517s	1m 40.373s	1m 41.897s	661kg
7	Robert Kubica	1m 40.520s	1m 40.545s	1m 41.992s	654.5kg
8	Nick Heidfeld	1m 40.558s	1m 40.635s	1m 42.343s	664kg
9	Nico Rosberg	1m 40.842s	1m 40.661s	1m 42.583s	665kg
10	Sébastien Buemi	1m 40.908s	1m 40.430s	1m 42.713s	661.5kg
11	Kimi Räikkönen	1m 41.100s	1m 40.726s		692kg
12	Kamui Kobayashi	1m 41.035s	1m 40.777s		694.3kg
13	Heikki Kovalainen	1m 40.808s	1m 40.983s		697kg
14	Kazuki Nakajima	1m 41.096s	1m 41.148s		704kg
15	Jaime Alguersuari	1m 41.503s	1m 41.689s		696.5kg
16	Fernando Alonso	1m 41.667s			708.3kg
17	Vitantonio Liuzzi	1m 41.701s			695kg
18	Adrian Sutil	1m 41.863s			696kg
19	Romain Grosjean	1m 41.950s			670.8kg
20	Giancarlo Fisichella	1m 42.184s			692.5kg

POINTS

DRIVERS

1	Jenson Button	95
2	Sebastian Vettel	84
3	Rubens Barrichello	77
4	Mark Webber	69.5
5	Lewis Hamilton	49
6	Kimi Räikkönen	48
7	Nico Rosberg	34.5
8	Jarno Trulli	32.5
9	Fernando Alonso	26
10	Timo Glock	24
11	Felipe Massa	22
12	Heikki Kovalainen	22
13	Nick Heidfeld	19
14	Robert Kubica	17
15	Giancarlo Fisichella	8
16	Sébastien Buemi	6
17	Adrian Sutil	5
18	Kamui Kobayashi	3
19	Sébastien Bourdais	2

CONSTRUCTORS

1	Brawn	172
2	Red Bull	153.5
3	McLaren	71
4	Ferrari	70
5	Toyota	59.5
6	BMW Sauber	36
7	Williams	34.5
8	Renault	26
9	Force India	13
10	Toro Rosso	8

6 HEIDFELD · BMW Sauber

9 TRULLI · Toyota

23 BARRICHELLO · Brawn

15 VETTEL · Red Bull

5 KUBICA · BMW Sauber

22 BUTTON · Brawn

14 WEBBER · Red Bull

1 HAMILTON · McLaren

45	46	47	48	49	50	51	52	53	54	55	
15	15	15	15	15	15	15	15	15	15	15	1
14	14	14	14	14	14	14	14	14	14	14	2
22	22	22	22	22	22	22	22	22	22	22	3
23	23	23	23	23	23	23	23	23	23	23	4
6	6	6	6	6	6	6	6	6	6	6	5
10	10	10	10	10	10	10	10	10	10	10	6
9	9	9	9	9	9	9	9	9	9	9	7
12	12	12	12	12	12	12	12	12	12	12	8
16	16	16	16	16	16	16	16	16	16	16	
5	5	5	5	5	5	5	5	5	5	5	
2	2	2	2	2	2	2	2	2	2	2	
4	4	4	4	4	4	4	4	4	4	4	
17	17	17	17	17	17	17	17	17	17	17	
7	7	7	7	7	7	7	7	7	7	7	
21	21	21	21	21	21	21	21	21	21	21	
8	8	8	8	8	8	8	8	3	3		
3	3	3	3	3	3	3	3	8	20		
20	20	20	20	20	20	20	20	20	8		

One lap or more behind

RACE TYRE STRATEGIES

The tyre regulations stipulate that two dry tyre specifications must be used during the race.

The Soft compound Bridgestone Potenza tyre is marked with a green stripe on the sidewall of the tyre.

	Driver	Race Stint 1	Race Stint 2	Race Stint 3
1	Sebastian Vettel	Medium: 1-19	Medium: 20-42	Soft: 43-55
2	Mark Webber	Medium: 1-18	Medium: 19-40	Soft: 41-55
3	Jenson Button	Medium: 1-17	Medium: 18-42	Soft: 43-55
4	Rubens Barrichello	Medium: 1-16	Medium: 17-41	Soft: 42-55
5	Nick Heidfeld	Medium: 1-19	Medium: 20-41	Soft: 42-55
6	Kamui Kobayoshi	Medium: 1-30	Soft: 31-55	
7	Jarno Trulli	Medium: 1-18	Medium: 19-42	Soft: 43-55
8	Sébastien Buemi	Medium: 1-18	Medium: 19-41	Soft: 42-55
9	Nico Rosberg	Medium: 1-18	Medium: 19-38	Soft: 39-55
10	Robert Kubica	Medium: 1-16	Medium: 17-39	Soft: 40-55
11	Heikki Kovalainen	Medium: 1-31	Soft: 32-55	
12	Kimi Räikkönen	Medium: 1-29	Soft: 30-55	
13	Kazuki Nakajima	Medium: 1-32	Soft: 33-55	
14	Fernando Alonso	Medium: 1-34	Soft: 35-55	
15	Tonio Liuzzi	Medium: 1-31	Soft: 32-55	
16	Giancarlo Fisichella	Soft: 1-28	Medium: 29-31	Medium: 32-54
17	Adrian Sutil	Medium: 1-24	Medium: 25-41	Soft: 42-54
18	Romain Grosjean	Medium: 1-31	Soft: 32-54	
	Lewis Hamilton	Medium: 1-17	Medium: 18-20 (dnf)	
	Jaime Alguersuari	Medium: 1-18	Medium: 19 (dnf)	

STATISTICS
DRIVERS' POINTS TABLE
Compiled by DAVID HAYHOE

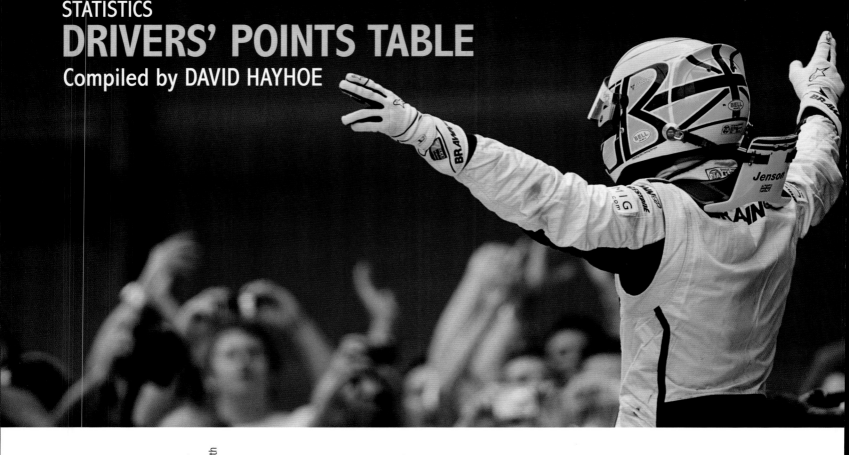

Place	Driver	Nationality	Date of birth	Car	Australia	Malaysia	China	Bahrain	Spain	Monaco	Turkey	Britain	Germany	Hungary	Europe	Belgium	Italy	Singapore	Japan	Brazil	Abu Dhabi	Points
1	Jenson BUTTON	GB	19/1/80	Brawn-Mercedes	1p	1pf	3	1	1p	1p	1f	6	5	7	7	R	2	5	8	5	3	95
2	Sebastian VETTEL	D	3/7/87	Red Bull-Renault	13*	15*	1p	2	4	R	3p	1pf	2	R	R	3f	8	4	1p	4	1f	84
3	Rubens BARRICHELLO	BR	23/5/72	Brawn-Mercedes	2	5	4f	5	2f	2	R	3	6	10	1	7	1	6	7	8p	4	77
4	Mark WEBBER	AUS	27/8/76	Red Bull-Renault	12	6	2	11	3	5	2	2	1p	3f	9	9	R	R	17f	1f	2	69.5
5	Lewis HAMILTON	GB	7/1/85	McLaren-Mercedes	DQ	7	6	4	9	12	13	16	18	1	2p	R	12*p	1p	3	3	Rp	49
6	Kimi RÄIKKÖNEN	FIN	17/10/79	Ferrari	15*	14	10	6	R	3	9	8	R	2	3	1	3	10	4	6	12	48
7	Nico ROSBERG	D	27/6/85	Williams-Toyota	6f	8	15	9	8	6	5	5	4	4	5	8	16	11	5	R	9	34.5
8	Jarno TRULLI	I	13/7/74	Toyota	3	4	R	3pf	R	13	4	7	17	8	13	R	14	12	2	R	7	32.5
9	Fernando ALONSO	E	29/7/81	Renault	5	11	9	8	5	7	10	14	7f	Rp	6	R	5	3f	10	R	14	26
10	Timo GLOCK	D	18/3/82	Toyota	4	3	7	7	10	10	8	9	9	6	14f	10	11	2	NS	-	-	24
11	Felipe MASSA	BR	25/4/81	Ferrari	R	9	R	14	6	4f	6	4	3	NS	-	-	-	-	-	-	-	22
12	Heikki KOVALAINEN	FIN	19/10/81	McLaren-Mercedes	R	R	5	12	R	R	14	R	8	5	4	6	6	7	11	12	11	22
13	Nick HEIDFELD	D	10/5/77	BMW Sauber-BMW	10	2	12	19	7	11	11	15	10	11	11	5	7	R	6	R	5	19
14	Robert KUBICA	PL	7/12/84	BMW Sauber-BMW	14*	R	13	18	11	R	7	13	14	13	8	4	R	8	9	2	10	17
15	Giancarlo FISICHELLA	I	14/1/73	Force India-Mercedes	11	18*	14	15	14	9	R	10	11	14	12	2p	-	-	-	-	-	8
				Ferrari	-	-	-	-	-	-	-	-	-	-	-	-	9	13	12	10	16	
16	Sébastien BUEMI	CH	31/10/88	Toro Rosso-Ferrari	7	16*	8	17	R	R	15	18	16	16	R	12	13	R	R	7	8	6
17	Adrian SUTIL	D	11/1/83	Force India-Mercedes	9	17	17*	16	R	14	17	17	15	R	10	11	4f	R	13	R	17	5
18	Kamui KOBAYASHI	J	13/9/86	Toyota	-	-	-	-	-	-	-	-	-	-	-	-	-	-	AP	9	6	3
19	Sébastien BOURDAIS	F	28/2/79	Toro Rosso-Ferrari	8	10	11	13	R	8	18	R	R	-	-	-	-	-	-	-	-	2
	Kazuki NAKAJIMA	J	11/1/85	Williams-Toyota	R	12	R	R	13	15*	12	11	12	9	18	13	10	9	15	R	13	
	Nelsinho PIQUET	BR	25/7/85	Renault	R	13	16	10	12	R	16	12	13	12	-	-	-	-	-	-	-	
	Vitantonio LIUZZI	I	6/8/80	Force India-Mercedes	-	-	-	-	-	-	-	-	-	-	-	-	R	14	14	11	15	
	Romain GROSJEAN	F	17/4/86	Renault	-	-	-	-	-	-	-	-	-	-	15	R	15	R	16	13	18	
	Jaime ALGUERSUARI	E	23/3/90	Toro Rosso-Ferrari	-	-	-	-	-	-	-	-	-	15	16	R	R	R	R	14	R	
	Luca BADOER	I	25/1/71	Ferrari	-	-	-	-	-	-	-	-	-	-	17	14	-	-	-	-	-	

KEY:

AP	Also practiced		*	Placed but retired
R	Retired		p	pole position
DQ	Disqualified		f	fastest lap
NS	Non-starter			

POINTS AND PERCENTAGES
Compiled by DAVID HAYHOE

GRID POSITIONS: 2009

Pos	Driver	Starts	Best	Worst	Average
1	Sebastian Vettel	17	1	15	4.41
2	Rubens Barrichello	17	1	12	4.53
3	Jenson Button	17	1	14	5.71
4	Mark Webber	17	1	19	6.71
5	Kimi Räikkönen	17	2	16	7.59
6	Nico Rosberg	17	3	18	8.06
7	Jarno Trulli	17	1	19	8.47
8	Felipe Massa	9	4	16	8.67
9	Fernando Alonso	17	1	16	8.88
10	Lewis Hamilton	17	1	19	9.18
11	Robert Kubica	17	4	18	10.71
12	Heikki Kovalainen	17	2	18	11.00
13	Kamui Kobayashi	2	11	12	11.50
14	Timo Glock	14	1	20	11.86
15	Nick Heidfeld	17	3	20	12.00
16	Kazuki Nakajima	17	5	18	12.18
17	Adrian Sutil	17	2	20	13.71
18	Nelsinho Piquet	10	10	17	14.10
19	Sébastien Buemi	17	6	20	14.18
20	Romain Grosjean	7	12	19	16.00
21	Vitantonio Liuzzi	5	7	20	16.00
22	Giancarlo Fisichella	17	1	20	16.06
23	Jaime Alguersuari	8	12	20	16.12
24	Sébastien Bourdais	9	14	20	17.11
25	Luca Badoer	2	20	20	20.00

RETIREMENTS: 2009

Number of cars to have retired

Grand Prix	starters	at 1/4 distance	at 1/2 distance	at 3/4 distance	at full distance	percentage of finishers
Australia	20	1	3	3	7	65.0
Malaysia	20	2	2	2	5	75.0
China	20	0	2	2	4	80.0
Bahrain	20	0	0	0	1	95.0
Spain	20	5	6	6	6	70.0
Monaco	20	3	4	5	6	70.0
Turkey	20	1	1	1	2	90.0
Britain	20	0	0	2	2	90.0
Germany	20	0	1	2	2	90.0
Hungary	19	2	3	3	3	84.2
Europe	20	0	1	2	2	90.0
Belgium	20	4	5	6	6	70.0
Italy	20	1	4	4	5	75.0
Singapore	20	1	3	4	6	70.0
Japan	19	1	1	1	2	89.5
Brazil	20	3	6	6	6	70.0
Abu Dhabi	20	0	2	2	2	90.0

LAP LEADERS: 2009

Grand Prix	Button	Vettel	Hamilton	Barrichello	Webber	Räikkönen	Rosberg	Alonso	Glock	Massa	Fisichella	Trulli	Kovalainen	Total
Australia	58	-	-	-	-	-	-	-	-	-	-	-	-	58
Malaysia	14	-	-	1	-	15	-	-	-	-	-	1	-	31
China	5	49	-	-	2	-	-	-	-	-	-	-	-	56
Bahrain	36	7	-	-	-	2	-	-	10	-	-	2	-	57
Spain	33	-	-	32	-	-	-	-	-	1	-	-	-	66
Monaco	77	-	-	-	1	-	-	-	-	-	-	-	-	78
Turkey	57	-	-	1	-	-	-	-	-	-	-	-	-	58
Britain	-	57	-	-	3	-	-	-	-	-	-	-	-	60
Germany	-	1	-	21	33	-	-	-	-	5	-	-	-	60
Hungary	-	-	58	-	-	-	-	11	-	-	-	-	1	70
Europe	-	-	31	25	-	-	-	-	-	-	-	-	1	57
Belgium	-	6	-	-	-	33	1	-	-	-	4	-	-	44
Italy	-	-	20	26	-	7	-	-	-	-	-	-	-	53
Singapore	-	-	57	-	-	-	-	4	-	-	-	-	-	61
Japan	-	53	-	-	-	-	-	-	-	-	-	-	-	53
Brazil	-	-	-	20	51	-	-	-	-	-	-	-	-	71
Abu Dhabi	-	39	16	-	-	-	-	-	-	-	-	-	-	55
Total	280	212	182	125	90	43	16	15	10	6	4	3	2	988
(Per cent)	28.3	21.5	18.4	12.7	9.1	4.4	1.6	1.5	1.0	0.6	0.4	0.3	0.2	100.0

CAREER PERFORMANCES: 2009 DRIVERS

Driver	Nationality	Races	Championships	Wins	2nd places	3rd places	4th places	5th places	6th places	7th places	8th places	Pole positions	Fastest laps	Points
Jaime Alguersuari	E	8	-	-	-	-	-	-	-	-	-	-	-	-
Fernando Alonso	E	139	2	21	19	13	14	9	5	6	4	18	13	577
Luca Badoer	I	51	-	-	-	-	-	-	-	1	3	-	-	-
Rubens Barrichello	BR	285	-	11	29	28	19	17	12	13	6	14	17	607
Sébastien Bourdais	F	27	-	-	-	-	-	-	-	2	2	-	-	6
Sébastien Buemi	CH	17	-	-	-	-	-	-	-	2	2	-	-	6
Jenson Button	GB	170	1	7	5	12	12	19	7	9	11	7	2	327
Giancarlo Fisichella	I	229	-	3	7	9	14	14	17	11	13	4	2	275
Timo Glock	D	36	-	-	2	1	3	-	2	5	1	-	1	51
Romain Grosjean	F	7	-	-	-	-	-	-	-	-	-	-	-	-
Lewis Hamilton	GB	52	1	11	8	8	2	4	1	3	-	17	3	256
Nick Heidfeld	D	167	-	-	8	4	10	9	16	12	9	1	2	219
Kamui Kobayashi	J	2	-	-	-	-	-	-	1	-	-	-	-	3
Heikki Kovalainen	FIN	52	-	1	2	1	4	7	3	5	6	1	2	105
Robert Kubica	PL	57	-	1	4	4	6	5	3	4	4	1	-	137
Vitantonio Liuzzi	I	44	-	-	-	-	-	-	1	-	2	-	-	5
Felipe Massa	BR	114	-	11	9	8	6	8	8	5	5	15	12	320
Kazuki Nakajima	J	36	-	-	-	-	-	-	1	2	2	-	-	9
Nelsinho Piquet	BR	28	-	-	1	-	1	-	1	1	1	-	-	19
Kimi Räikkönen	FIN	156	1	18	20	24	11	8	7	4	6	16	35	579
Nico Rosberg	D	70	-	-	1	1	3	4	5	5	6	-	2	75.5
Adrian Sutil	D	52	-	-	-	-	1	-	-	-	1	1	1	6
Jarno Trulli	I	216	-	1	4	6	16	14	14	15	13	4	1	246.5
Sebastian Vettel	D	43	-	5	2	2	5	3	2	-	4	5	3	125
Mark Webber	AUS	138	-	2	4	4	3	10	13	7	1	3	169.5

Note: As is now common practice, drivers retiring on the formation lap are not counted as having started.
Where races have been subject to a restart, those retiring during an initial race are included as having started.

ALL TIME RECORDS

STARTS
Rubens Barrichello	285
Riccardo Patrese	256
Michael Schumacher	249
David Coulthard	246
Giancarlo Fisichella	229
Jarno Trulli	216
Gerhard Berger	210
Andrea de Cesaris	208
Nelson Piquet	204
Jean Alesi	201
Alain Prost	199
Michele Alboreto	194

WINS
Michael Schumacher	91
Alain Prost	51
Ayrton Senna	41
Nigel Mansell	31
Jackie Stewart	27
Jim Clark	25
Niki Lauda	25
Juan Manuel Fangio	24
Nelson Piquet	23
Damon Hill	22
Fernando Alonso	21
Mika Häkkinen	20

POLE POSITIONS
Michael Schumacher	68
Ayrton Senna	65
Jim Clark	33
Alain Prost	33
Nigel Mansell	32
Juan Manuel Fangio	29
Mika Häkkinen	26
Niki Lauda	24
Nelson Piquet	24
Damon Hill	20

PODIUMS
Michael Schumacher	154
Alain Prost	106
Ayrton Senna	80
Rubens Barrichello	68
Kimi Räikkönen	62
David Coulthard	62
Nelson Piquet	60
Nigel Mansell	59
Niki Lauda	54
Fernando Alonso	53
Mika Häkkinen	51

YOUNGEST WINNERS
Sebastian Vettel	21y 02m 11d
Fernando Alonso	22y 00m 26d
Bruce McLaren	22y 03m 12d
Lewis Hamilton	22y 05m 03d
Kimi Räikkönen	23y 05m 06d
Robert Kubica	23y 06m 01d
Jacky Ickx	23y 06m 06d
Michael Schumacher	23y 07m 27d
Emerson Fittipaldi	23y 09m 22d
Mike Hawthorn	24y 02m 25d
Jody Scheckter	24y 04m 11d
Elio de Angelis	24y 04m 20d

YOUNGEST STARTERS
Jaime Alguersuari	19y 04m 03d
Mike Thackwell	19y 05m 29d
Ricardo Rodriguez	19y 06m 27d
Fernando Alonso	19y 07m 03d
Esteban Tuero	19y 10m 14d
Chris Amon	19y 10m 20d
Sebastian Vettel	19y 11m 14d
Eddie Cheever	20y 01m 22d
Jenson Button	20y 01m 22d
Tarso Marques	20y 02m 12d
Sébastien Buemi	20y 04m 29d
Peter Collins	20y 06m 12d
Nico Rosberg	20y 08m 13d
Rubens Barrichello	20y 09m 00d

FASTEST LAPS
Michael Schumacher	76
Alain Prost	41
Kimi Räikkönen	35
Nigel Mansell	30
Jim Clark	28
Mika Häkkinen	25
Niki Lauda	24
Juan Manuel Fangio	23
Nelson Piquet	23
Gerhard Berger	21
Stirling Moss	19
Damon Hill	19
Ayrton Senna	19

YOUNGEST ON POLE
Sebastian Vettel	21y 02m 11d
Fernando Alonso	21y 07m 23d
Rubens Barrichello	22y 03m 05d
Lewis Hamilton	22y 05m 03d
Andrea de Cesaris	22y 10m 04d
Robert Kubica	23y 03m 30d
Jacky Ickx	23y 07m 03d
Kimi Räikkönen	23y 08m 12d
David Coulthard	24y 00m 13d
Jenson Button	24y 03m 06d
Eugenio Castellotti	24y 07m 26d
Chris Amon	24y 09m 22d

YOUNGEST CHAMPIONS
Lewis Hamilton	23y 09m 26d
Fernando Alonso	24y 01m 27d
Emerson Fittipaldi	25y 08m 29d
Michael Schumacher	25y 10m 10d
Niki Lauda	26y 06m 16d
Jacques Villeneuve	26y 06m 17d
Jim Clark	27y 06m 04d
Kimi Räikkönen	28y 00m 04d
Jochen Rindt	28y 05m 16d
Ayrton Senna	28y 07m 09d
James Hunt	29y 01m 25d
Nelson Piquet	29y 02m 00d

WORLD CHAMPIONSHIPS
Michael Schumacher	7
Juan Manuel Fangio	5
Alain Prost	4
Jack Brabham	3
Niki Lauda	3
Nelson Piquet	3
Ayrton Senna	3
Jackie Stewart	3
Fernando Alonso	2
Alberto Ascari	2
Jim Clark	2
Emerson Fittipaldi	2
Mika Häkkinen	2
Graham Hill	2

GP2 REVIEW by MARK GLENDENNING

THE INCREDIBLE HULK

Nico Hülkenberg's unerring rise to the top continued unabated. The young German was due to move into Formula One with Williams in 2010.
Photo: GP2 Media Services

To win the 2009 GP2 crown, Nico Hülkenberg had to step up as a rookie and beat the most experienced field in the history of the series. Many front-runners from the previous season had found their efforts to progress up the ladder limited by lack of opportunity (Toro Rosso had the only Formula One drive available at the start of the year, a seat that was filled by Sébastien Buemi), so with the final rung on the ladder out of reach, most of the top GP2 seats were quickly filled by quick drivers embarking on their third or fourth campaigns. The most obvious exception was pre-season favourite Romain Grosjean, who was preparing for his second year with Barwa Addax, the former Campos team having changed ownership and name during the off-season.

Even for a debutant with such impeccable credentials as Hülkenberg, it presented a massive challenge. Yet not only did he go on to win the crown, he did it with a round to spare. It was a remarkable achievement, all the more so because over the first few race weekends, there was very little to suggest that the German would eventually triumph.

The season was fought out in two distinct phases, and the point at which one ended and the other began can be defined precisely by the moment that Grosjean vaulted into the barriers at Monaco. Having won the previous day's feature race, the Swiss driver was occupied in chasing down Andreas Zuber in Sunday morning's sprint race when he attempted an ill-judged move under braking for Tabac, and succeeded in launching himself off the back of Zuber's car and

slamming into the top section of the catch fencing.

Prior to the crash, Grosjean had been making the season look like a one-horse race – from three starts, he'd notched up two wins and a second. After the accident, however, he never made it back on to the podium. His best results were two fourths (at Silverstone and Hungary), and even they came in reversed-grid races.

Grosjean's early-season pace wasn't unexpected, but it was a surprise that nobody seemed capable of matching it. Veteran Lucas di Grassi, who'd teamed up with 2008 championship winning squad Racing Engineering and who was expected to challenge for the title, put up a reasonable fight during qualifying for the first round in Barcelona. But tyre degradation problems dropped him back during the feature race, and his misery was completed when he was caught up in a three-way accident and retired.

That left Grosjean to open his account with a comfortable win over Barwa Addax team-mate Vitaly Petrov, while DAMS' Jerome d'Ambrosio finished a distant third. Edoardo Mortara – who joined Sergio Perez in forming Arden's all-rookie line-up – was the first of the newcomers to get off the mark when he won the sprint race on Sunday, while Hülkenberg struggled for pace all weekend and left Spain without any points.

To begin with, it was more of the same in Monaco, with a dominant Grosjean again leading Petrov to Addax's second 1-2, leaving di Grassi in third. But then came Grosjean's unplanned aerobatics display

Left: Racing Engineering's Luca di Grassi took pole in Hungary *(left)*, but he never had the pace or consistency to mount a successful title challenge and finished third in the series, behind Hülkenberg and Petrov.

Below: Alberto Valeiro gave Piquet Sports a win in the feature race at Silversone.

Photos: Peter J. Fox

Right: Romain Grosjean was the early-season force, but after a crash at Monaco, the Frenchman's challenge dwindled somewhat, before he was whisked off to F1 with Renault.

Left: Alvaro Parente gave OceanGP its first win with a victory at Spa-Francorchamps.

Below left: Giedo van der Garde was a strong force for iSport International, notching wins in Budapest and Monza.

Photos: GP2 Media Services

on Sunday morning, during which his car hit the wall with such force that a 20cm hole was cracked in the tub. He had a new chassis for the following weekend, but never again looked as potent.

Meanwhile, Monaco's sprint race had been controlled initially by Karun Chandhok, driving for the new Ocean Racing Team. Victory had looked certain until the Indian was forced to pull over with a broken driveshaft, paving the way for ART's Pastor Maldonado to claim the win. It was an important race for his team-mate, too – Hülkenberg's third, behind d'Ambrosio, gave him the first GP2 podium of his career, backing up the points he'd earned for finishing fifth the previous day.

In highlighting Hülkenberg and Petrov as the men to beat, the next race in Turkey set the tone for the remainder of the season. Hülkenberg took pole, but was distracted while scrapping with Luca Filippi, which allowed Petrov to slip through and claim his first win of the year. Up to that point, the Russian had been very much in Grosjean's shadow, but as races progressed he asserted himself increasingly upon the

championship fight. By the time Grosjean left the series, after Hungary, there was a case to be made that Petrov had become Addax's *de facto* team leader.

Filippi claimed second – a decent, if belated, result from the fourth-year veteran running with the pedigree Super Nova team, while Davide Valsecchi was third for Durango. Hülkenberg, having led early on, eventually finished fifth.

Di Grassi won the sprint race, ahead of Javier Villa and Petrov, the Russian moving to the top of the points table after Grosjean failed to score in either race, while Hülkenberg kept things ticking over with fourth.

But the German's season was really only just starting. The series moved from Turkey to Silverstone, and it was this weekend that Hülkenberg later identified as the one when he and ART finally got their heads around the car.

Grosjean looked to be back to his early-season form when he took pole, but in the race he fell victim to an unexpected threat in the form of Piquet GP's Alberto Valerio, who'd qualified a surprise second and then carried that pace through to the race. The Brazilian harried Grosjean through the opening laps, and when the leader fell asleep momentarily at Abbey, on lap eight, Valerio was through for a popular maiden win. Di Grassi was second, ahead of Hülkenberg, who'd made his way through the pack after starting from seventh, while Grosjean eventually dropped to fifth. He did regain the series lead, however, after Petrov was pushed wide at the first corner and ended up 15th. Maldonado won Sunday's sprint race from Zuber and Chandhok, with Grosjean fourth, Hülkenberg fifth and Petrov again failing to score as a result of his awful grid position. Di Grassi also had a dreadful race, stalling at the start and falling to the back of the field. Even with half of the season still to come, the Brazilian's hopes of mounting a title charge were slipping.

Then came Germany, and Hülkenberg's loudest declaration of intent – in a single-spec series, walk-

Left: Vitaly Petrov points the way to the top. The Russian eventually had to settle for the runner-up position.

Below left: Andreas Zuber behind his ever-present-shades.

Below: ART Grand Prix's Pastor Maldolano was overshadowed by team-mate Hülkenberg, but he had his moment, highlighted by a win at Monaco.

Photos: GP2 Media Services

ing away from your home race having made a clean sweep of pole and two wins tends to get you noticed. Conditions had varied wildly over the course of the Nürburgring weekend, but irrespective of whether it was dry, wet or somewhere in between, Hülkenberg was untouchably fast. The points table at the end of the round showed him as the new championship leader, but his performance on the track was a clear message to his rivals that the bar had just been lifted. And over the races that followed, it gradually became apparent that no one was capable of carrying the fight to him.

Circumstance accounted for one rival following the next race at the Hungaroring, where the fall-out between the Renault F1 team and Nelson Piquet Jr meant that Grosjean's services were required to replace the ousted Brazilian at the top level. But by then, the die had been cast. Hülkenberg won the Hungary feature race, and from thereon his position became progressively stronger. Di Grassi never quite had the pace or consistency to mount a sustained challenge, and while Petrov kept needling away at Hülkenberg's lead, he was never able to gain a foothold. Even when the Russian won the feature race at the next round at Valencia, Hülkenberg limited the damage by finishing second.

Things came to a head at Spa, where Petrov desperately needed a strong weekend – and ideally, Hülkenberg to suffer some misfortune – to keep the championship alive. Instead, while Alvaro Parente dominated from pole to give Ocean its first GP2 win,

with Hülkenberg chasing him across the line for second, Petrov stopped at the side of the track with a blown engine. Even when Hülkenberg suffered his first DNF of the season the next day, courtesy of a turn one pile-up, Petrov was only able to salvage a single point for sixth.

In mathematical terms, the fight was still open going into Monza, but in reality it was all but decided. Hülkenberg was curiously off-song early in the weekend, finishing a relatively sedate sixth in the wet feature race, while up ahead iSport's Giedo van der Garde made a late pass on Petrov for the victory. But the German needed just one point on Sunday morning to confirm himself as champion, and with a third place behind first-time winner Luiz Razia and di Grassi, the mission was easily accomplished.

In terms of the drivers' championship, Hülkenberg's Monza success rendered the final round at the Algarve circuit – a new venue for the series – largely redundant. But ART still had the teams' championship to fight for, and Hülkenberg secured that with a dominant win on Saturday. Perversely, though, Sunday's season finale would deliver Hülkenberg's worst classified finish of the year when he was relegated to 16th after being one of eight drivers penalised for accidentally passing the safety car. But he still did better than Petrov, who stalled on the line and was rear-ended by DPR's Michael Herck. Amid all the mess, it was Filippi who took the honours as 2009's final race winner, the Italian finishing just ahead of Villa for a Super Nova 1-2

BAGUETTE ON A ROLL

AFTER three years of plying his trade in the World Series by Renault, Belgium's Bertrand Baguette finally earned his bread by clinching the title for stalwart International Draco Racing, although it required a strong end to a consistent season to avoid being left, once again, with the crumbs.

After the major upheaval that preceded the 2008 season – involving a new chassis, increased power and another change to the increasingly confused qualifying procedure – there was comparatively little tinkering ahead of 2009. True, the Dallara's aero package received 'minor enhancements inspired by the 2009 F1 regulations', but the other changes were confined to track time, the familiar pre-race test being scrapped in favour of extra sessions of Friday, and both races extended to 44 minutes plus a lap, despite the points for each continuing to differ to distinguish sprint and feature rounds.

The only alteration to the scoring saw a bonus point awarded to the driver who gained the most places during a race, while qualifying, often a bone of contention for World Series followers, retained the Superpole session and reversed top eight starters for the sprint race, as introduced in 2008.

More important than any rule changes, however, was the assurance that the World Series would con-

tinue to play a part in Renault's motorsport ladder. Despite the declining economic climate and involvement of the *regie* in GP2, the manufacturer appeared determined to maintain both two-litre Formula Renault and the 3.5-litre World Series as alternatives to new paths being set up to promote young talent, notably the Max Mosley driven F2, and the scheduled 2010 debut of GP3.

"The World Series by Renault is a key part of the brand's motorsport set-up," Renault Sport Technologies' managing director, Rémi Deconinck, claimed on the eve of the season. "The talent of the young drivers, who are the real stars of these events, is showcased in a unique manner in the media, for spectators and partners.

"The success of the various Renault categories is based on solid foundations, which enable us to offer a unique programme, a stepping stone to F1. Our greatest satisfaction lies in the ongoing loyalty of the teams, who have once again provided us with some superb line-ups in 2009, but the strength of our programme comes from our long-term strategy, which is based on performance, state-of-the-art technology, safety and reliability at reduced cost.

"And, in 2011, we will launch the new World Series car, with ever better performance levels!"

While the teams did, indeed, show commendable loyalty – only Kurt Mollekens' KTR bowed out, owing to a dearth of drivers, to be replaced eventually by ambitious FRenault Eurocup outfit KMP Group/SG Formula – there was the usual turnover of pedallers, both prior to round one and, in familiar World Series by Renault fashion, throughout the nine-round campaign.

Naturally, reigning champion Giedo van der Garde moved on, to GP2, while top-ten finishers Fabio Carbone, Esteban Guerrieri, Salvador Duran and Alvaro Barba all sought their thrills elsewhere, but the most notable departures involved 2008 runner-up Julien Jousse, fifth-placed Mikhail Aleshin and 12th placed Robert Wickens – plus pre-season pace setter Andy Soucek – all of whom plumped for the cheaper F2 option.

Whereas van der Garde had inherited top spot in 2008, the top five from the previous year having departed, Baguette had never finished a season higher than seventh, and still had the likes of Miguel Molina (fourth in '08) and Charles Pic (sixth) supposedly ahead of him. Remaining with Draco provided the Belgian with vital continuity, however, and Baguette married the 'family feel' of the Italian outfit to improved luck, retiring just once in 17 outings and never finishing lower than eighth when he saw the chequered flag.

Remarkably, though, he didn't win until the middle of July, but began the second half of the season in style, rising to the occasion with a double victory at Le Mans that precipitated a haul of five wins in the final eight races. Prior to that, the 23-year old had begun strongly, with second place in three of the opening four races – punctuated by that sole DNF, courtesy of clutch failure in the Barcelona feature – before tailing off slightly with fifth, third, sixth, eighth and fifth before arriving at La Sarthe.

At Le Mans, he enjoyed a stroke of good fortune that would help turn his season around, being promoted into the Superpole session after Dani Clos was penalised, and then qualifying sixth overall, which translated into third for Saturday's sprint race. Defying steering bent in a first-corner skirmish, the Belgian went on to win at last and, buoyed by his success, vaulted from sixth to second at the first turn in Sunday's feature. Helped further by a rapid mandatory pit stop from the Draco team, he claimed a second victory. With all his main rivals having suffered poor weekends, Baguette left Le Mans with a 19-point championship advantage.

"We have deserved this victory for quite a while, but winning two in one go, that's an excellent surprise," Baguette said at the time. "In Budapest, I was in the lead when the safety car ruined the entire race, and in Barcelona, the clutch gave up the ghost just as I was in a position to win. So, all in all, I reckon it was definitely our turn to win, but, at the same time, to come out so well for the championship..."

Once ahead, the veteran was not to be passed again. The next round, at the new Portimao circuit on Portugal's Algarve, yielded second and fifth places, before Baguette returned to the top step of the podium at the Nürburgring. Again, qualifying served up a modicum of fortune, as the cold temperatures limited him to seventh fastest time, enough for a front-row slot on Saturday. Despite dropping briefly to third, he recovered second spot and, although having vowed not to take risks with the crown in sight, duly overhauled Daniil Move for the victory.

Holding a 42-point advantage heading into the feature race, Baguette knew that he didn't have to improve much over his grid slot, and he did enough

Above: Britain's Jon Lancaster made an immediate impact on the World Series by Renault, taking two poles and winning third time out for Comtec Racing.

Left: Bertrand Baguette was the most successful driver in the 2009 World Series by Renault, taking five second-half wins to add to earlier consistency, and was crowned at the penultimate round in Germany.
Then a double win at the Aragon finale delivered the teams' title to International Draco.

Below: Marcos Martinez began 2009 with three wins in three races for Pons Racing – and later added a fourth at Silverstone – but his season was derailed by five DNFs.
Photos: World Series by Renault

Above: 1992 F1 world champion Nigel Mansell had a run in son Greg's Ultimate Motorsport Dallara during the Silverstone weekend.

Top: Oliver Turvey ended the 2009 World Series by Renault season as leading rookie, thanks in part to victory on the streets of Monaco.

Top right: Fairuz Fauzy returned to the World Series by Renault after his family bought into Fortec Motorsport. He rewarded the renamed Mofaz Racing team with victory in Hungary.

Centre right: Despite winning at Spa and finishing on the podium in Monaco *(pictured)*, James Walker saw his hopes go up in smoke when P1 Racing's premises burnt down.

Right: Reigning British F3 champion Jaime Alguersuari's early-season World Series form was solid if unspectacular, but it still led to an F1 seat with Scuderia Toro Rosso.

Photos: World Series by Renault

on the road to claim fifth – and the title – with the final double-header still to run.

"I feel rather strange grabbing the title before the final round, but I'm really proud to be able to offer Draco this championship," the Belgian admitted. "They spent the entire weekend checking and double-checking the car just to make sure that nothing could go seriously wrong. Mission accomplished, and in perfect style!"

Although the pressure was off, Baguette was determined to make it a double celebration for the Draco team – which had begun the year by adopting Force India F1 colours in place of its familiar yellow – and duly dominated the season finale at the new Motorland Aragon facility in Spain.

Despite managing only fourth in qualifying, having set the pace on both test sessions, the Belgian was not to be denied in either sprint or feature, attacking for pure pleasure and claiming victory on Saturday, before benefiting from another solid pit stop to repeat the feat in the final race of the year. Draco duly claimed the teams' title by 24 points over Carlin Motorsport, while Baguette eventually became drivers' champion by a massive 57-point margin.

If there was a gulf between first and second, the battle to be runner-up behind the Belgian was an altogether closer affair: just ten points – the equivalent of second in a sprint race or third in a feature – separated the next five drivers.

Fairuz Fauzy eventually emerged as Baguette's closest 'challenger', having achieved a breakthrough win in the Hungaroring sprint. The Malaysian had remained in the World Series after taking a controlling stake in the Fortec team through the family Mofaz concern, but did not appear to be a contender until Budapest, where his victory ended a run of 15th-place finishes. Second place on familiar ground at Silverstone maintained the upswing, but, despite a 100-per-cent finishing record, Fauzy's championship position wasn't confirmed until the home stretch, where he claimed three podiums in the final four races to vault from fifth to second.

That run was enough to deny Pic, who had entered 2009 as perhaps the most obvious title favourite, having finished sixth overall in the previous season. A slow beginning to the campaign was the Frenchman's undoing, however: he was a non-starter in the opening race after an accident on the warm-up lap and managed only sixth from pole the next day. Fourth and a DNF in Belgium ensued, with three lowly points finishes then preceding victory from pole – with fastest lap – in the Silverstone feature. Just two further podium visits, including feature race success at the Nürburgring, followed, leaving Pic to wonder what might have been as he contemplated the switch to GP2 for 2010.

The Frenchman edged leading rookie Oliver Turvey by a single point in the final reckoning, the British F3 runner-up having emerged as a genuine threat after breaking through with victory on the streets of Monaco in May. After qualifying on pole, the Carlin driver didn't put a wheel wrong all weekend, boosting his confidence and precipitating a run of third places mid-season, including both races on home soil at Silverstone. He may have had no answer to a fired-up Baguette after starting from pole at Aragon, but the Brit looks set to move up again with his reputation enhanced.

Turvey's performance allowed him to turn the tables on British F3 champion Jaime Alguersuari, who remained a team-mate at Carlin and looked set to achieve the better championship position, until Scuderia Toro Rosso came knocking on his door with an F1 contract in hand. Up to that point, the Red Bull prospect hadn't exactly looked like grand prix material, but had remained in WSbR "to gain experience" and had raised his game with back-to-back third places at Le Mans and Portimao, before claiming his first World Series win, from pole, in the Portuguese feature. He faded after that, with F1 commitments taking him out of Europe, but did enough to finish sixth overall.

That put Alguersuari one place behind another Brit, James Walker, who had started the season with great

intentions, having slipped into van der Garde's seat at P1 Motorsport, but ultimately he saw his ambitions, quite literally, go up in flames. Successive DNFs in races two and three made for a slow start to the year, but the Jerseyman bounced back with victory at Spa and four top-four results, punctuated by another retirement, to keep his title hopes intact at half-time. The following month, however, P1's Norfolk base – and everything in it – was destroyed by fire, leaving it in a race against time to field replacement cars for Walker and Move in Germany. The Brit responded with fourth place, to give himself an outside chance of second overall, but then failed to score in Spain.

If anyone had started the season looking likely to mount a championship challenge, it was Marcos Martinez, who appeared to be just about unbeatable in the opening two rounds. The Spaniard dominated on home soil in Barcelona and won the Spa sprint, but then his results took a turn for the worse. Although he added a fourth victory to his tally, at Silverstone, to become the most successful driver after Baguette and earn himself a prize drive in Renault's F1 car, he didn't manage another podium place, as his campaign was wrecked by a total of five DNFs and four other finishes outside the top ten.

Ironically, the other drivers to win races in 2009 tied for 12th overall, on 39 points, behind the likes of Miguel Molina, Marco Barba, Daniil Move and Chris van der Drift. Molina had finished fourth overall in 2008, but was derailed by a move to Ultimate Motorsport that yielded a handful of podium finishes. He failed to see out the campaign, however, while Barba could not match Draco bread-winner Baguette, a brace of seconds in Hungary being his best. Move and rookie van der Drift, meanwhile, achieved more than was expected of them, the Russian taking a couple of surprise third places for P1, and the Kiwi a similar result for Epsilon Euskadi second time out.

Series stalwart Pasquale di Sabatino and rookie Jon Lancaster were the only other winners, the Italian triumphing for RC Motorsport in the safety car affected Hungarian race that Baguette thought should have been his, but doing little else of note, except

finishing second at Le Mans. Lancaster, meanwhile, shook off a failed attempt to remain in the F3 Euroseries to shine with Comtec Racing. Having joined the WSbR at round four in Budapest, he claimed fastest lap third time out, before pole in France precipitated a repeat – and victory – in Portugal. Another fastest lap followed in Germany as the young Brit marked himself out as a hot property for 2010.

Lancaster's belated arrival in the series again highlighted its problem of fielding a settled line-up. No fewer than 42 drivers were named on the final list of starters, despite there being only 26 seats available at any given round, and only 14 of those contested each of the 17 races.

Having been a front-runner with big plans – including F1 – in 2008, Ultimate failed to appear at the last two rounds, while both RC and Interwetten.com had one car missing on occasion. Ultimate did gain media mileage, however, by fielding Greg Mansell, son of 1992 F1 world champion Nigel, in the first seven events before an acrimonious split led to the Brit missing the Nürburgring. He resurfaced with Comtec at Aragon and, despite managing just four points and 26th overall, hoped to return in 2010.

If he does come back, Mansell will find another mildly altered World Series, with slightly more power on tap from the Solution F-tuned Renault V8s and a 'light aerodynamic specification' mandated for Saturday sprint races. Race distances remain the same, while testing track time is increased, but it is qualifying that undergoes the biggest change again, with Superpole and the reversed grid abandoned in favour of separate timed sessions for each race. The calendar also receives a tweak, with Brno and Hockenheim making their WSbR debuts in place of Portimao and the Nürburgring respectively, and Magny-Cours returning to take over from Le Mans.

With Alguersuari already on board, and both Fauzy and Walker linked to F1 roles in 2010, the World Series continues to do something right – even if, ironically, its new champion may find his prize of an F1 test scuppered by uncertainty over Renault's continued participation in the top flight.

JULES IN THE CROWN

Above: A repeat of his 2008 Masters success eluded Jules Bianchi, but he more than made up for it with the Euroseries crown.
Photo: Formula 3 Euroseries

Above right: Art team-mates Valterri Bottas and Jules Bianchi share the podium at the October Hockenheim meeting.
Photos: Drew Gibson/LAT Photographic

Right: Experienced F3 racer Christian Vietoris provided the strongest opposition to Jules Bianchi, but won just one feature race, at the penultimate round, when it was a case of too little too late.
Photo: Formula 3 Euroseries

AS if to mirror the 2008 season, the globe's two foremost Formula Three championships kicked off once more with one man tipped to dominate in Europe, while the British series remained anyone's guess.

Jules Bianchi had outscored everyone in the final four rounds of the 2008 F3 Euroseries, adding a late-season run to victory in the prestigious Masters event at Zolder to cap an impressive rookie season. Remaining with the crack ART Grand Prix squad that had provided the previous five series champions gave the Frenchman an added edge over his rivals, and although occasionally he made life difficult for himself, he duly delivered.

Again, like predecessor Nico Hülkenberg – who would go on to clinch the GP2 series crown at his first attempt – Bianchi did not start as he meant to continue, claiming only fifth and third places at the season opener at Hockenheim, but thereafter he set about establishing a comfortable points advantage with at least one victory in seven of the remaining nine double-header rounds.

His return to the top step of the podium came in round two, at the Lausitzring, and set the tone for the rest of the season, as the familiar No 1 ART machine made a habit of crossing the line first in the opening race of the weekend. Repeat performances came at the Norisring, Zandvoort, Oschersleben and the

Nürburgring – the last three from pole – before a brief lull following a qualifying accident at Brands Hatch interrupted the sequence. Unfazed, Bianchi was back on form in Spain, taking another pole and feature race win, before rounding out the season with pole at Dijon and another pole/victory double at the Hockenheim finale.

The Frenchman, whose uncle Lucien had triumphed in the 1968 Le Mans 24 Hours, only twice failed to back up his Saturday success with points in Sunday's DTM supporting sprint event – at Lausitz and Brands – and frequently kept the pressure on his rivals by claiming one of the remaining podium positions. Third place at the Norisring, and seconds at Zandvoort and Dijon took his silverware haul for the season to 12; despite the title fight going to the penultimate round, he took the championship by a massive 39 points before heading for GP2 with ART.

Although there was a strong supporting cast at the French team – albeit composed of three rookies – Bianchi's closest opposition throughout the season came from fellow Euroseries 'veteran' Christian Vietoris, the German having finished sixth in his debut campaign in 2008. Remaining with Mücke Motorsport gave sometime A1GP driver Vietoris a degree of continuity, but he mirrored Bianchi's slower-than-expected start to the season, taking home one point fewer than his rival, despite sharing the sprint race podium at

three rounds. Despite that, he finished just 13 points shy of Vietoris in the final reckoning and will surely spearhead ART's assault in 2010.

The Finn, who did manage to claim overall rookie honours, could have come under threat from fellow newcomer Alexander Sims, had the Briton found his form a little quicker. Having stepped up from his national FRenault series, Sims had joined the Mücke ranks alongside Vietoris and, after netting just nine points in the opening three rounds, proceeded to rival both his team-mate and Bottas score for score over the remainder of the season.

Pole for round three was followed by a maiden podium in the feature, but the second half of the campaign provided a breakthrough victory at the Nürburgring. This was followed by successive podium finishes at Brands Hatch and in both races at the Circuit de Catalunya as Sims marked himself out as another to watch in 2010.

While Bianchi and Vietoris made sputtering starts to their campaigns, the early-season lead was fought over by Stefano Coletti and Jean-Karl Vernay, who left the Hockenheim opener with 12 and nine points respectively. Sadly, neither could maintain his initial

form through the year and, along with fellow round-one pace-setters Sam Bird, Mika Mäki and Roberto Mehri, fell away in the final standings.

Coletti added just seven points to his initial haul, all in round five at Oschersleben, after being distracted by overtures from teams in both the World Series by Renault and GP2, allowing Vernay to wind up as best of the rest, claiming fifth overall for 2008 runner-up Signature after finishing the year as he had started – with sprint race victory at Hockenheim. In between, the Frenchman had managed podium visits at Lausitz, the Norisring and on the return to Hockenheim, but had endured too long a scoreless run during the second half of the season to be a threat.

Bird claimed the first pole bonus of the year and finished on the podium four times, but he could not get his Mücke entry consistently into the top three, finishing the year eighth overall, behind Mäki, who disappointed in his second year with just one victory (at Brands Hatch), and Mehri, who didn't return Manor Motorsport to the top step, but took four podium finishes.

While ART's Esteban Gutierrez and Coletti rounded out the top ten overall, the remaining victories went to

Carlin Motorsport's Brendon Hartley and Renger van de Zande. The former had been tipped to do better than 11th overall, but had his season confused by regular outings in the World Series by Renault, while the latter, after finishing fourth overall in 2008, translated his sterling British series form into a rare success for the small Motopark Academy squad in the Barcelona sprint.

In the UK, meanwhile, reigning champion team Carlin appeared to have the strongest hand, but with many new faces and still unknown quantities making up a deep field, it was thought that the title could go all the way to the wire. That it didn't was thanks, in part, to the continued emergence of Australian Daniel Ricciardo who, having opened a few eyes with his performance in chasing Bottas throughout the 2008 FRenault Eurocup campaign, made himself instantly at home in F3.

Despite others in the field having greater experience, Ricciardo stamped his authority on the proceedings at the Oulton Park season-opener, claiming victory in both races, and then added a third success in four at Silverstone to establish a strong points platform. Although he didn't win again until round 13 at Spa-Francorchamps, regular top-five finishes – including a brace of seconds at Snetterton – kept the 20-year-old out front, and he rattled off a 1st-2nd-1st-3rd-1st-3rd-1st-3rd scoring sequence over the final eight races to wrap up the crown at the new Portimao circuit with a round still to run.

Just one non-finish all season was testament to Ricciardo's consistency, and his only apparent flaw – early-season qualifying – was laid to rest with a sequence of pole positions in the second half that contributed to his strong run of results.

Ricciardo's success also returned Volkswagen to the top of the British F3 tree 20 years after countryman David Brabham had led a Bowman team managed by Trevor Carlin to similar heights. Despite Carlin's now eponymous team running a four-strong VW-powered assault, however, it was Mercedes-propelled

Hitech Racing that provided the Australian's greatest opposition.

The 2007 season champion team would not have been singled out as a title contender based on team leader Walter Grubmüller's previous form, but the Austrian – whose father owns a sizeable stake in the operation – started solidly and accelerated once Euroseries veteran van der Zande was added to the line-up.

The Dutchman's greater pedigree should have seen *him* post the biggest threat to Ricciardo, but, controversially, he was hired simply to help Grubmüller and, despite taking victory first time out at Silverstone, and following that up with others at Snetterton and Silverstone again, he was frequently required to defer to the Austrian. As a result, potential podiums – and even race wins – at Donington Park, Spa, Silverstone and Portimao went begging; van der Zande didn't even appear at the Brands Hatch finale, eventually taking third overall, 97 points adrift of Ricciardo.

Grubmüller, meanwhile, went on to collect the runner's-up cheque on the strength of two mid-season wins at Hockenheim and, more significantly, Donington, but he wound up just ten points clear of his *aide victoire*. Both will be looking to move up to GP2 or World Series in 2010, where they can expect to face off against Ricciardo once more. Only then may the true impression of their relative strengths come to light.

Fourth and fifth in the standings went to Britons Max Chilton and Riki Christodoulou, who brought vastly differing levels of experience to the table, but left with the same tally of 'on-track' wins. Although Chilton was officially credited with the points for two victories, he only managed to cross the line first on one occasion – the season finale at Brands Hatch – despite being among the fastest drivers and best qualifiers. Somehow, the youngster failed to turn front row into top spot come race day, although his maximum point pursuit of Euroseries interlopers Bianchi and Bird, at Portimao, at least paved the way for

Brands. Christodoulou had graduated from FRenault and claimed a maiden win at Snetterton mid-season, but he failed to capitalise on that and wound up 41 points adrift of Chilton, let alone anyone higher.

Fellow rookie Adriano Buzaid's campaign proceeded in a similar manner, the Brazilian unable to build on victory in the rain at Spa, while his T-Sport team-mate, Wayne Boyd – the reigning Formula Ford UK champion – was expected to do better than 12th overall, even if an awe-inspiring win in the wet at Donington hinted at more to come in 2010.

The other wins in 2009 went to drivers who failed to see out the entire campaign. Marcus Ericsson took time out of his ultimately successful Japanese campaign to claim back-to-back victories at Rockingham and Hockenheim, while Nick Tandy provided a fitting tribute to brother Joe – tragically killed in a car accident in late April – by winning the opener at Rockingham in the unfancied JTR Mygale.

Tandy edged Ericsson for the final spot in the top ten by just three points, after switching to a fruitless Euroseries ride with the Kolles & Heinz Union team mid-season, while Räikkönen Robertson duo Daisuke Nakajima and Carlos Huertas, and Carlin's Henry Arundel also merited top-ten slots.

The National Class title came down to a battle between Fortec's Daniel McKenzie and T-Sport's Gabriel Dias, both of whom had stepped up from FRenault, but eventually it was decided by the Briton's superior finishing record as he backed up an 11-8 win tally with a string of strong points hauls.

If Bottas went empty-handed in the Euroseries, he did at least claim one important victory during his rookie season, retaining the Masters crown for ART in the first of the year's one-off events, which returned to its spiritual home at Zandvoort after a brief sojourn across the border in Belgium.

After finishing second in the pole-position shoot-out, the Finn was promoted to top spot when reigning champion Bianchi was docked places for blocking. He never looked back, leading from lights to flag to claim

Left: Daniel Ricciardo continued Red Bull's success, succeeding Jaime Alguersuari as British F3 champion.

Below: Australian born Ricciardo took to the British Formula 3 series from the off, and showing the way to some far more experienced competitors.

Below centre: Marcus Ericsson won in Britain and took the Japanese F3 Championship. The Swedish youngster, guided by Kenny Bräck, looks set to move into GP2 in 2010.

Photos: Jakob Ebrey/LAT Photographic

the first Masters title for his country in the 19-year history of the race.

Euroseries rivals Mäki and Coletti completed the podium as the UK runners struggled again to get to grips with the Kumho tyres provided. Bianchi and Sims rounded out the top five, before van der Zande took sixth for Hitech. Ricciardo, meanwhile, failed to complete a lap after his gearbox failed.

Elsewhere around the globe, Marcus Ericsson justified his decision to move east by winning the All-Japan F3 title by nine points over Petronas Team TOM's team-mate Takuto Iguchi, while Yuji Kunimoto completed a top-three lock-out for the perennial front-runner. Naoki Yamamoto, meanwhile, claimed an altogether more comfortable N-Class win for HFDP Racing.

Daniel Zampieri earned himself a test with Ferrari's F1 team after triumphing in a closely-fought Italian national series, eventually coming out on top by 15 points over BVM-Target Racing team-mate Marco Zipoli. Third-placed Pablo Sanchez-Lopez was scheduled to join the two Italians at Maranello over the winter after giving chase all season for Alan Racing, while fourth overall Sergio Campana missed out on a prize drive by just three points.

Germany's ATS Formel 3 Cup went the way of a Belgian driver again, Laurens Vanthoor dominating to succeed countryman Frederic Vervisch. The van Amersfoort driver won 11 times in the course of the season, taking at least one victory at every round, and

generally claiming a pole and fastest lap as well.

Vanthoor's team-mate – and leading Junior – Stef Dusseldorp was his closest rival, and the only other driver to make it over 100 points for the year, but he was 57 adrift at the end. Zettl Sportsline's Markus Pommer was third overall, but did not win a race, unlike fifth-placed Nico Monien and Euroseries refugee Tom Dillman.

In the only other titles decided as *AUTOCOURSE* went to press, Kimmo Joutvuo fended off countrymen Marko Vahamaki and Aki Sandberg to win the Finnish crown in an ageing Dallara-Mugen F396, while Italian Francesco Lopez defeated Christian Zeller to claim the Austrian series. Finland's Jani Tammi won the second NEZ Cup over three double-header rounds in northern Europe.

Competition continued to rage, meanwhile, in the Australian, South American and retitled European Open series. Tim Macrow and Briton Joey Foster headed to a Sandown showdown, locked in battle to succeed James Winslow in Australia, although promising youngster Tom Tweedie had already sewn up the National Class. Leonardo Cordeiro looked favourite to claim the Sud-Am crown, holding a 30-point lead over Claudio Cantelli, with double-headers at Campo Grande and Curitiba to run, while veteran Celso Miguez and Bruno Mendez were set to duke it out for the Euro Open crown in Barcelona. Team West-Tec's Callum Macleod held a 14-point advantage in the Copa d'Espana class for older machinery.

Above: Hitech Racing's driver pairing of Renger van der Zande and Walter Grubmüller *(behind)*.

Left: Max Chilton was the highest-placed British competitor, taking fourth overall in the series.

Photos: Jakob Ebrey/LAT Photographic

SPORTS & GT REVIEW by GARY WATKINS

TALES OF THE UNEXPECTED

The winning Marc Gené/Alex Wurz/David Brabham No 9 Peugeot 908 HDi, which finally ended the Audi domination of the Le Mans 24-hour race.

Photo: Kevin Wood/LAT Photographic

WAS Peugeot a surprise winner of the 2009 Le Mans 24 Hours? Probably not. The real shock was the manner of its victory over Audi in the 77th running of the annual endurance classic. The French manufacturer trounced its German rival, outperforming in every way a marque that had been beaten only once in a decade. No one had expected that.

Peugeot had made Audi the favourite in the run-up to the race, and Audi had returned the compliment. A close-fought Sebring 12 Hours, the only race in which the two teams of turbo-diesels had gone head to head prior to the 24 Hours, had gone to the wire. Everything looked set for another thriller at Le Mans.

Yet there would be no repeat of the 2008 classic for two reasons: Peugeot got it oh-so right; Audi got it very, very wrong. That's why the French manufacturer completed a 1-2 victory, with the unfancied crew of Alex Wurz, David Brabham and Marc Gené running out winners by one lap over the sister car of pole-winner Stephane Sarrazin, Franck Montagny and Sébastien Bourdais. The best Audi was six laps down in third.

Peugeot had the faster car in the latest evolution of the 908 HDi, just as it had done in 2008. Only this

time, it didn't squander that performance advantage. What's more, the French car proved more reliable than the new-for-2009 Audi R15 TDI. The in-house Peugeot Sport team was also quicker than the Joest Audi squad in the pits, it matched its German rival on fuel economy and tyre wear, and, crucially, made all the right tactical calls. This proved team manager Serge Saulnier's pre-race assertion that his organisation was ready to claim the biggest prize in sportscar racing, 16 years after its previous victory at La Sarthe.

Wurz, Brabham and Gené claimed the honours because they had the kind of untroubled run that had typified so many of Audi's victories down the years. Theirs wasn't the quickest of the Peugeots, but it was ahead in the small hours of Sunday morning when the prospect of any kind of challenge from Audi finally disappeared. Team orders were called at this point, effectively freezing the positions of the top two 908s late before the completion of the 14th hour.

The other two factory 'Pugs' ran into problems early in the race, hence the victory for Brabham and co. The car driven by Pedro Lamy, Nicolas Minassian and Christian Klien was delayed early on. Lamy was sent out of his pit stall and straight into the path of the factory assisted Pescarolo 908, driven by Jean-Chris-

tophe Boullion. The impact punctured the works car's left rear tyre, forcing a slow lap back to the pits, followed by a half-hour stop for repairs.

The pole-winning car hit problems shortly before quarter-distance. The left rear wheel nut became loose, which caused the studs on its disc bell to shear. Nine minutes were lost while the corner was replaced. This car had the legs of the winning Peugeot and had moved back on to the lead lap in the eighth hour, only for the comeback to be halted when Bourdais tangled with a slower car. The resulting stop to fix damaged bodywork put the car the better part of a lap behind. And it was still behind when the call to stop racing came.

Bourdais reckoned victory would have been within reach of the all-French crew. "We had everything necessary to win: we had the pace to come back again," he said, "but we always knew team orders were coming."

It emerged afterwards that there were extenuating circumstances for the sometimes baffling lack of pace of the winning car. It had a brake problem from early in the race, which meant that the drivers had to refrain from pushing to the limit to avoid the need for a change of brakes.

Audi was nowhere at Le Mans. It never looked a potential winner, except for a brief moment during the night, and then only with one of its three factory cars. McNish may have qualified second to Sarrazin, but in reality the R15 wasn't on the pace of the 908 in the race. By the time the Scot pitted for the first time, he was already 20 seconds down on the leading Peugeot.

A switch to a higher-downforce nose during the night threatened to revive Audi's fortunes. When McNish climbed aboard the No 1 car for a second time, it suddenly looked like it could compete with the Peugeots. "Now it's a real racing car," announced McNish. "We're in the ballpark." Not for long, however.

Just after 4am on Sunday morning, Capello had to stop for his R15's intercoolers to be cleaned out. A repeat just 20 minutes later effectively signalled the end of Audi's bid for victory. A further delay – to remedy an electrical glitch and a suspension problem – stretched the deficit to the winning Peugeot to a full six laps.

Audi and Joest never found what McNish called the "sweet spot" of the R15 during Le Mans week. The reasons for that were numerous: a winter test programme interrupted by poor weather and two major shunts; a very hot endurance run at Paul Ricard, which marque motorsport boss Wolfgang Ullrich admitted had "fooled" the team; the cancellation of the Le Mans Test Day; more rain in free practice on Wednesday; and some car niggles in qualifying on Thursday.

The last in the catalogue of problems for Audi brought the best of Aston Martin Racing's LMP1 coupes almost to within striking distance of a podium. The Lola-Aston B09/60 driven by Stefan Mücke, Tomas Enge and Jan Charouz achieved AMR's target of first in the unofficial petrol class with what Mücke described as "nearly the perfect race". One puncture and the addition of the odd drop of lubricant were all that interrupted the relentless progress of the Gulf-liveried car to fourth place.

The factory Chevrolet Corvette GT1 programme came to an end after ten successful seasons at the 24 Hours. The swansong for the C6.R resulted in Le Mans class victory number six for the Pratt & Miller-built 'Vette, honours going to Jan Magnussen, Johnny O'Connell and Antonio Garcia in what was admittedly a poorly-supported class. Porsche took LMP2 honours again, Team Essex from Denmark dominating the secondary prototype category, but the German marque lost out in the GT2 division to the Ferrari run by the US Risi Competizione team.

The Peugeot versus Audi battle spilled off the racetrack in 2009. The French team took offence to several areas of the R15's aerodynamic package, most notably its radical front end. It claimed the front splitter and a giant flap under the nose worked together like a front wing, something prohibited by the regulations.

Peugeot was ready to protest at Sebring, but backed away when the Automobile Club de l'Ouest at Le Mans promised to clarify the rules. When that clarification never materialised, it protested the Audi on the afternoon of first practice during Le Mans week. It appealed when that protest was thrown out, only to withdraw its action a few weeks later. The French manufacturer claimed it had received assurances over the "interpretation and implementation" of the rules for 2010, which appeared to suggest that the Audi's front end would be declared illegal.

That explained Peugeot Sport technical director Bruno Famin's reaction to an ACO compromise solution announced in September. Audi, which had been making noises about quitting the prototype arena, would be allowed to run the R15 with relatively subtle modifications to its front end.

The Le Mans 24 Hours was one of only two occa-

Above: Aston Martin came a strong fourth with the Tomas Enge/Stefan Mücke/Jan Charouz No 007 B09/60.
Photo: Drew Gibson/LAT Photographic

Above right: Perennial Le Mans LMGT1 class-winner, Jan Magnussen grabs some snapshots on his way to the gantry.
Photo: Kevin Wood/LAT Photographic

Right: Bourdais limps the No 7 Peugeot back to the pits, effectively putting victory out of the equation for the fastest car in the race.
Photo: Drew Gibson/LAT Photographic

This was the year the once impregnable Audi machines were forced to give best to their French rivals at Le Mans. The Allan McNish/Tom Kristensen/Rinaldo Capello No 1 Audi R15 TDI gives chase on the classic Circuit de La Sarthe.

Photo: Drew Gibson/LAT Photographic

Above: Michael Bartels and Andrea Bertolini were the FIA GT champions once again with the Vitaphone Racing Team Maserati MC12.

Photo: JakobEbrey/LAT Photographic

Top: The championship winning HighCroft Acura of David Brabham and Scott Sharp bathed in the sunset of Laguna Seca, California, USA.

Photo: Dan R. Boyd/LAT Photographic

Above right: The Daytona 24-hour race was won by the No 58 Brumos Riley-Porsche of Darren Law, David Donohue, Antonio Garcia and Buddy Rice after a thrilling finish.

Photo: F. Peirce Williams/LAT Photographic

Right: Tom Kristensen, Allan McNish and Renaldo Capello celebrate Audi's major success of the season after winning the Sebring 12-hour race.

Photo: Michael L. Levitt/LAT Photographic

Ferran and Simon Pagenaud, nor the Highcroft Racing Acura in which Dario Franchitti joined team regulars David Brabham and Scott Sharp, finished the race. Brabham and Sharp completed enough laps to be classified, and the points they gained won them the title, despite being outscored in victories five to three by de Ferran and Pagenaud.

Peugeot took in one LMS race, the Spa 1,000km in May, by way of a warm-up for Le Mans. Not surprisingly, it dominated, the car driven by Nicolas Minassian, Christian Klien and Simon Pagenaud collecting the winner's trophy. Meanwhile, the end-of-season silverware went to Aston Martin Racing after a textbook assault.

The best of the AMR Lola-Astons won when it had the opportunity, at Barcelona and the Nürburbring, and finished on the podium when it didn't, at Spa, the new Algarve circuit and Silverstone. That was more than enough to give Mücke, Enge and Charouz the LMP1 title, ahead of the Pescarolo Sport line-up of Jean-Christophe Boullion and Christophe Tinseau.

An era ended for the FIA GT Championship, prior to the series splitting in two for 2010 with the creation of the FIA GT1 World Championship and the FIA European GT2 Championship. Maserati and the German Vitaphone Racing team maintained their stranglehold on FIA GTs, notching up a fourth straight drivers' title with team boss Michael Bartels and Andrea Bertolini, and a fifth consecutive teams' crown.

Once again, the most professional team in the paddock won on consistency, in a championship where success ballast has traditionally kept things close. Vitaphone's critics, most notably the second-placed PK-Carsport Chevrolet team, and drivers Mike Hezemans and Anthony Kumpen, argued that the German squad effectively had bought its way to the overall FIA GT title. A third Vitaphone Maserati MC12 was entered for the second half of the series and undoubtedly played a part in sealing championship honours for Bartels and Bertolini.

How much of a role the extra car, driven by Alessandro Pier Guidi and Matteo Bobbi, played was due to be decided by the FIA International Court of Appeal. The Belgian PK squad accused Vitaphone of race fixing, or rather calling team orders to move Bartels and Bertolini up the order in the closing stages of two of the final three rounds.

Hezemans and Kumpen ultimately finished two points down, fewer than they reckoned the title winners had gained illicitly. Their consolation was victory in the blue-riband event of the championship, the Spa 24 Hours, in which they shared their Corvette C6.R with Jos Menten and Kurt Mollekens.

Briton Richard Westbrook claimed the FIA GT2 crown for Porsche. The ProSpeed Competition driver came from behind at the final round to grab the title from reigning champions Gianmaria Bruni and Toni Vilander in the AF Corse Ferrari 430 GT.

Over in Grand-Am, the GAINSCO/Bob Stallings Racing Riley-Pontiac team of Alex Gurney and Jon Fogarty reprised its 2007 championship success in the Daytona Prototype class. The highlight of the Grand-Am season came at the very start, with an amazing Daytona 24 Hours: four cars finished on the lead lap, victory eventually going to the Brumos Riley-Porsche driven by David Donohue, Darren Law, Antonio Garcia and Buddy Rice

It was the closest – and most exciting – finish in the history of the Daytona enduro. That said, the 2009 sportscar season will be remembered for the thriller that wasn't, the Le Mans 24 Hours, and Peugeot's domination.

sions when Peugeot and Audi went head to head in 2009: there was no repeat of their thrilling battle in the 2008 Le Mans Series in Europe. The economic downturn caused the German manufacturer to opt out of defending both its LMS and American Le Mans Series crowns, while the French marque decided that a full LMS campaign would detract from its efforts to win the big one at Le Mans.

The first confrontation between the 908 and the new R15 took place at Sebring in the opening ALMS round. Peugeot looked set for a win, only for the best of the R15s, driven by McNish, Capello and Kristensen, to come from behind to claim the laurels, ahead of the Peugeot driven by Sarrazin, Montagny and Bourdais.

The new Acura ARX-02a claimed pole position at Sebring in the hands of Scott Dixon, but the Honda brand's all-new LMP1 contender wasn't a match for the turbo-diesels on speed or reliability. Neither the De Ferran Motorsports entry Dixon shared with Gil de

Main photo: Yvan Muller's battle-scarred SEAT is chased by his team-mates, Gabriele Tarquini and Rikard Rydell, at Brno. The competition between them was just as closely fought throughout the rest of the year as the trio chased the championship.
Photo: Drew Gibson/LAT Photographic

Inset right: Audi's Timo Scheider was once again the man to beat in DTM, retaining his crown for the second year running.
Photo: Alastair Staley/LAT Photographic

Inset far right: Colin Turkington and BMW emerged victorious in the battle for the BTCC Championship. Here he lifts a wheel of his Team RAC BMW 320si E90 at Knockhill.
Photo: Jakob Ebrey/LAT Photographic

Above: Agusto Farfus carried BMW's title hopes into the final round at Macau. The Brazilian had much ground to make up.
Photo: BMW Motorsport

TOURING CAR REVIEW by MATT SALISBURY

CLOSE racing, action aplenty and title fights that went all the way to the wire. Yet again, in 2009, it was a dramatic season for fans of touring car racing.

As *AUTOCOURSE* went to press, the battle for the World Touring Car Championship had yet to be decided, with three drivers in contention to lift the crown on the streets of Macau. The British Touring Car Championship saw a new name added to its list of champions after Colin Turkington secured his maiden crown, while in Germany, Timo Scheider successfully defended the title he had won for the first time in 2008. Down under, the fight to secure the V8 Supercar Championship looked likely to go all the way to the end once again.

Heading to Macau, Italian driver Gabriele Tarquini was leading the way in the WTCC standings, but had SEAT team-mate Yvan Muller breathing down his neck, the pair separated by just two points. Had it not been for fellow SEAT drivers Rickard Rydell and Jordi Gené slowing on the final lap of race two at Okayama, allowing Tarquini to pick up extra places, the pair would have gone into the season finale level

on points. Augusto Farfus also retained hope of securing the title for BMW, but was 13 points off the pace. History has shown that anything can happen in Macau, however, and the Brazilian was sure to be a factor on the challenging street circuit.

The fight between Muller – who clinched the 2008 title in Macau – and Tarquini raged from the opening round in Brazil, where both took victory and scored 15 points from the weekend. While Muller put distance between the pair through the early part of the season, Tarquini battled back as the year wore on and took the points lead at Oschersleben; a more consistent campaign gave him the advantage, despite winning three races as opposed to Muller's four.

Farfus, meanwhile, was left to carry the hopes of BMW, picking up more wins than anyone else, with five trips to the top step of the podium. His first win didn't come until the fifth round of the season in Spain, however, which left the Brazilian playing catch-up as the year wore on. A double failure to score at Brno, after he had triggered a start-line accident in race one, could prove to be the deciding factor if he fails to overhaul the SEAT pair for the title...

The fight for the manufacturers' championship was just as close, with SEAT holding a slender three-point lead over BMW in the standings. As well as Tarquini and Muller, Rickard Rydell aided SEAT's challenge with a victory in Mexico, while Andy Priaulx, Alex Zanardi and Sergio Hernandez all took to the stop step of the podium for BMW.

The remaining wins went the way of Chevrolet as the manufacturer debuted the new Cruze: Rob Huff, Alain Menu and Nicola Larini all tasted victory, Larini for the first time. Ultimately, however, a slow start to the season prevented the team from launching a title challenge.

The 2009 campaign also saw a fourth manufacturer join the field in the shape of Lada, which stepped into the series with a full works team after a privateer entry with Russian Bears Motorsport in 2008. The ageing 110 model was well off the pace early on, but the introduction of the new Priora at Porto – and the addition of James Thompson to the driver line-up – saw a noticeable improvement in form. Thompson scored the team's first top-eight finish at Imola, while Jaap van Lagen had qualified an impressive fourth at

Above: The irrepressible Alex Zanardi (seen with his Team Italy-Spain boss, Roberto Ravaglia) was, as ever, a firm favourite with the crowds.
Photo: BMW Motorsport

Right: Gabriele Tarquini may not have a full head of hair any more, but the delightful Italian was still a force to be reckoned with on the track.
Photo: Drew Gibson/LAT Photographic

Not for Everyone.

For those who know real performance.

ADVAN. The leader in our product line-up. The name found only on our top-performing tyres.
Fast. Comfortable. Genuine. Spirited. ADVAN is for those satisfied only when leading the pack.
ADVAN. Performance cars wanted.

OKOHAMA supplier of ADVAN tyres to the WTCC since 2006

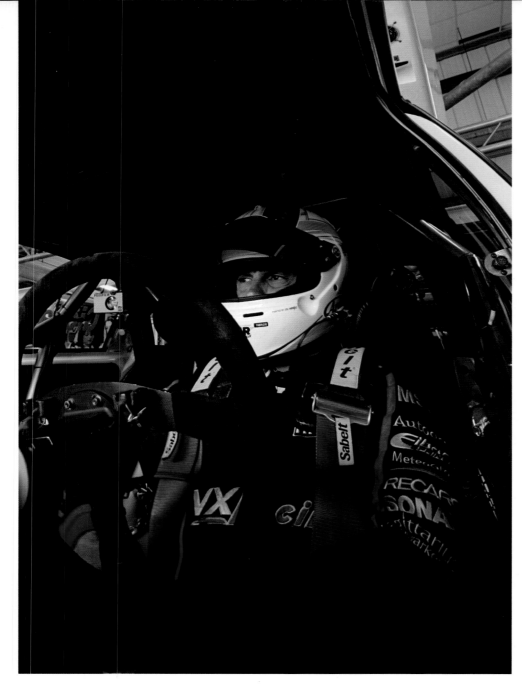

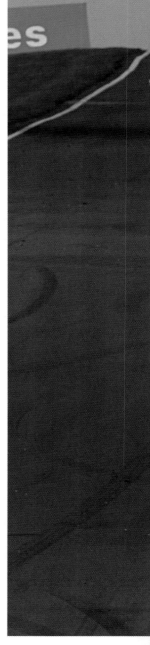

Oschersleben before being forced off the road while fighting for points on race day.

Ahead of 2010, rumours persisted about the future of both SEAT and BMW, while Chevrolet was reported to be considering expanding its programme for the new campaign. The calendar for 2010 sees a return to Belgium with a round at Zolder, while the new Portimao circuit in the Algarve will host the Portuguese event. There will be no event in France, however, which means that the famous Pau Grand Prix will not take place during the new season.

After back-to-back wins by Fabrizio Giovanardi, a new champion was crowned in the British Touring Car Championship when Colin Turkington lifted the title for the first time, following a dramatic conclusion to the season at Brands Hatch.

The Team RAC driver started the season among the title favourites, but faced a tough challenge from two of the most experienced touring car drivers around. As expected, Giovanardi was in the mix for honours again as he chased a title hat-trick, while Jason Plato – left without a drive when SEAT quit the championship – also emerged as a strong contender after inking a deal to drive a Chevrolet Lacetti for RML just days before the opening round.

Turkington started the season well with a double podium at Brands Hatch, then picked up his first win of the campaign at Thruxton. During the opening half of the season, the Northern Irishman set about exerting his authority on the title race, and by the mid-way

stage, he had picked up five wins to hold a 25-point lead over Vauxhall's Matt Neal. Giovanardi was third, four points further back, but was playing catch-up after a tough opener at Brands Hatch, while Plato had spent the first half of the year getting used to his new surroundings and was 36 points behind, in fourth, having taken one win during the opening rounds of the campaign.

As others dropped out of contention when the season resumed at Snetterton, the race for the crown quickly became a three-way fight. Giovanardi won twice, and Turkington once as the gap between them dropped to 17 points; Plato managed just a single podium. From Knockhill onwards, however, Plato's Chevrolet emerged as the car to beat, the 2001 champion winning in Scotland, and then at both Silverstone and Rockingham, ensuring that he went to Brands Hatch for the finale with an outside chance of the title. Turkington, who had been picking up points, but hadn't won again since the Snetterton rounds, remained out front, having survived an on-track skirmish with Plato at Rockingham, while Giovanardi was second, 13 points behind his BMW rival.

The finale threw up an early shock when Tom Chilton took pole in his Team Aon Ford Focus, and he led until the final corner of the first race, before Plato edged ahead to secure the closest victory in BTCC history. With Giovanardi third and Turkington down in eighth, suddenly just 14 points covered the top three. Then Plato doubled up in race two, with Giovanardi

and Turkington joining him on the podium, which meant that the three-way battle for the title would go to the 30th and final race of the year.

Eight points behind, Plato knew he had to win to stand any chance of taking a second title, and he came through the field from eighth on the grid to become only the second driver – after Dan Eaves in 2005 – to win all three races on the same day. Despite Neal attempting to back up the pack early on, Turkington took second place, which was enough to give him the title, while Giovanardi finished fourth; the Italian not only lost his grip on the crown, but also dropped to third in the standings, behind Plato.

"My ambition in life has been to win this," an emotional Turkington said after receiving his trophy. "To finally achieve your dream is an unbelievable feeling. I have been with West Surrey Racing [the team behind Team RAC] for all but one season in the BTCC, and I'm so happy for them as well. Fighting with Fabrizio was hard enough without throwing Jason in as well. They are two tough guys, and we had to be at the top of our game."

As well as crowning a new champion, the season finale marked the end of an era for the BTCC, as Vauxhall bowed out after 20 years of continuous support, which had included numerous titles along the way. While the drivers' title proved to be elusive, Vauxhall did manage to pick up two trophies as it secured both the manufacturers'/constructors' championship and the teams' title. Turkington added a third straight In-

dependents' Trophy to his overall honours, while Team RAC secured the Independents' Team Trophy.

Between them, the top three in the title race secured 18 wins during the season, with Mat Jackson emerging as 'best of the rest' after joining the field as Plato's team-mate at Thruxton. He picked up four wins and enjoyed a fine second half to the season, which included a run of eight successive podium finishes. Former champion James Thompson returned for a part-campaign with Team Dynamics and won three times in his Honda Civic, while there were two wins apiece for Rob Collard and Stephen Jelley. Both had reason to cheer, as Collard secured the first victories for the Motorbase team, while Jelley's double success at Rockingham marked his first visits to the top step of the podium. Neal was the other driver to taste victory, but he failed to build on his win in the first race of the year and his championship bid tailed off dramatically. Rookies Jonathan Adam and James Nash both won 'on the road' before subsequently being stripped of their victories for incidents on track.

Elsewhere, one of the BTCC's most popular figures returned to the track when Paul O'Neill launched a comeback with Team sunshine.co.uk with Tech-Speed and continually punched above his weight in an older BTC-spec Honda Integra. Bad luck cost him possible victories at Thruxton and Croft, but an emotional podium finish at Snetterton saw him voted as the fans' favourite driver at the end of the year. Chilton also earned special mention, the Arena-run Focus going

Above: Former champion Gary Paffett regularly starred with the Salzgitter AMG Mercedes C-Klasse. Even a win in the final round at Hockenheim was not enough, however, as he finished just five points shy of champion Timo Scheider.

Above right: Mercedes-Benz drivers Gary Paffett and Paul di Resta do the honours for Timo Scheider as the Audi Sport Team Abt celebrates winning the championship on the Hockenheim podium.

Photos: Drew Gibson/LAT Photographic

Right: Canadian Bruno Spengler works his Mercedes-Benz Bank AMG C-Klasse on the Catalunya kerbing.

Photo: Andrew Ferraro/LAT Photographic

from being well off the pace at the start of the year to a podium contender by the end of the campaign, while former F1 racer Johnny Herbert joined the grid with Team Dynamics for the final three meetings, hoping to return full-time in 2010.

As the credit crunch bit, the BTCC took steps to ensure its long-term future by announcing new rules that will come into play from 2011. Under those new regulations, teams will be offered the opportunity of using a spec engine, and that engine could be brought into the series in 2010, depending on the outcome of discussions that were still ongoing as AUTOCOURSE closed for press.

While a new champion was crowned in Britain, there was repeat success in Germany as Timo Scheider defended his DTM crown, making him only the second driver to achieve the feat since the series was relaunched in 2000.

The 2009 campaign proved to be a hard-fought affair, as no fewer than six drivers tasted victory during the ten-race season, although the battle for the title had become a two-driver affair by the time the field headed to Hockenheim for the season finale.

Scheider had held the points lead early in the season, before slipping behind Mercedes man Gary Paffett, following the fourth round of the campaign at Zandvoort – the only time he would fail to score all season. A first win of the year at Oschersleben and a podium at the Nürburgring in round six saw Scheider hit the front again; his second victory of the year arrived in Spain, putting the German 12 points clear with two rounds to go.

Paffett took victory in the penultimate race of the year in France, closing to within seven points of Scheider, and despite the Brit winning again in the final round of the campaign, Scheider followed him home in second to make it back-to-back titles.

"The first title involved the highest amount of pressure," the double champion said. "The second one is more enjoyable. I'm incredibly happy that we did it again, and it's great that we managed to win the title again. Thanks to the Audi squad, my Abt team and my family, It's been a fantastic season!"

Scheider ended the season five points clear of Paffett, despite winning twice compared to the four wins enjoyed by his Mercedes rival. With both drivers only failing to score once all season, ultimately Scheider's consistency would prove to be the deciding factor, as he picked up four additional podium finishes. Aside from his victories, Paffett failed to make it on to the podium in any of the other races.

Paul di Resta, having finished second to Scheider in 2008, had to settle for third place in the standings; the Scot was one of four drivers who took a single win during the season. Martin Tomczyk, Jamie Green and Tom Kristensen also enjoyed victories, the latter bowing out of the series at the end of the year.

In an effort to reduce costs and encourage participation by new manufacturers, the DTM implemented a development freeze, which came into play after the race at the Nürburgring in August and was scheduled to continue into 2010. That freeze came as work continued on finalising new regulations for 2011.

The three-way fight for the 2008 V8 Supercar Championship title was decided in favour of Jamie Whincup, who beat Mark Winterbottom and Garth Tander to his maiden championship crown after AUTOCOURSE 2008-09 went to press.

Team Vodafone ace Whincup was once again the man to beat, and with two rounds remaining and 600 points up for grabs, Whincup had eked out a small lead over Davison again of 122 points. Davison's team-mate Garth Tander still remained an outside chance, 340 points behind Whincup in third, while Whincup's team-mate Craig Lowndes' title hopes were over, 613 points off his team-mate's total.

While a Ford driver was heading the field, Holden had enjoyed success in the two big events on the calendar, Tander and Davison having taken victory at both Phillip Island and Bathurst, the two races ending in equally dramatic fashion. Bathurst also saw the V8 debut of former World Superbike title winner Troy Bayliss, although he failed to finish.

While the current season had yet to come to an end, a number of changes were already confirmed for 2010, including Team Vodafone making the switch from Ford to Holden. The calendar will also feature an additional race meeting, and the year will start with two events in the Middle East, in Abu Dhabi and Bahrain.

UNITED STATES RACING REVIEW by GORDON KIRBY

TROUBLED TIMES

The grids are still full, but even NASCAR has felt the chill winds of recession. It seems better placed to meet the economic downturn than other forms of motorsport in the USA.
Photo: Tyler Barrick/LAT Photographic

NO doubt about it, these are lean times for American motor racing. Indy car, ALMS and Grand-Am sports car racing have been hit hard by the tough economic times, while NASCAR has also struggled, with declining crowds and substantial job losses as the effects of the bankruptcies of General Motors and Chrysler spilled across the industry. Many people, from crewmen and car builders to race fans and journalists lost their jobs. Ticket sales fell by as much as a third at some NASCAR tracks, as did TV ratings for the premier Sprint Cup series. The average viewing figure per race in 2009 was 6.1 million, compared to 6.9 million in 2008.

During the winter of 2008/9, both General Motors and Chrysler used America's Chapter 11 bankruptcy laws and US$62bn in bail-out funds from the United States Treasury to restructure and reduce costs. GM began selling off its most troubled brands and closed 2,600 dealerships across the USA, reducing its debt by US$17bn. As a result, most NASCAR teams laid off 10–20 per cent of their workforces over the winter. In recent years, four factory-supported Chevrolet teams – Hendrick Motorsports, Richard Childress Racing, Stewart-Haas Racing and Earnhardt-Ganassi Racing – competed in NASCAR's top series, fielding

11 cars in all. Each of these teams received annual financial support of between $10m and $20m, with Hendrick Motorsport and Stewart-Haas at the upper end of the spectrum, but now all that has gone

Four-time NASCAR champion Jeff Gordon is the team leader of Rick Hendrick's four-car Chevrolet team and co-owner of defending champion Jimmie Johnson's car. Gordon said all aspects of NASCAR, including souvenir sales, had been damaged by the bad economic times. "Souvenir sales have been hurt dramatically by the economy," he explained. "The die-cast car model business is not what it used to be, and that is an important business to the teams and even to the sponsors, who used to look at it as a form of income that could offset some of their costs. So we've got to be more creative to find out how we can grow that business and get it back up to where it was in the late nineties and early 2000s."

Richard Petty Motorsports, whose roots go back to the beginning of NASCAR in 1949, ran four Dodges in 2009 for Kasey Kahne, Elliott Sadler, Reed Sorenson and A.J. Allmendinger. But Petty decided to switch to Fords for 2010 in a new partnership with Robert Yates Racing. This was the second merger Petty's team had gone through in the previous two years in a continuing

attempt to find the right financial support and technical resources. Over the decades, Petty's team had endured three separate manufacturer cutbacks or pull-outs, and the 'King' was not seriously disturbed by the current conditions. "We've been through all this stuff before two or three times at Petty Enterprises," he remarked. "The factories came in and we kind of really depended on them, and then the factories went home and we survived. So whether the factories are involved or not in the near future, we're going to survive."

Petty pointed out that NASCAR's top teams had developed their own engineering programmes and facilities. "It used to be, and lately too, most everybody has depended on the factories for a lot of technical support," he said. "But over a period of time, we've been able to get our own engineers and do our own wind-tunnel programmes, and do the mechanical part of the engines and chassis. So we really don't look at the factories as strong as we did in the past.

"Today, the basic thing that the factories do is design the engines and build some of the engine parts that we so far have not developed in-house. So we're just going to have to play it by ear and continue to do what we're going to do."

Toyota Racing Development's NASCAR racing boss, Lee White, said that Toyota was not interested in expanding beyond its collection of three teams and nine cars. "Our goal, when we came into this sport, was to have 25 per cent of the field," White commented. "We've said that over and over again, and as long as there are four manufacturers, that's still where we'd like to settle in. We're not recruiting teams. We're not pursuing teams or offering teams anything to leave other manufacturers. In fact, we've never done that. We're very happy with the organisations and partners we're with now in Joe Gibbs Racing, Red Bull and Michael Waltrip."

White explained that Toyota had made substantial budget cuts, but that the NASCAR programme had been tremendously successful for the Japanese manufacturer. "We were faced with budget challenges a year ago, before everyone else thought about taking bankruptcy," White continued. "The company was that far out ahead of it. TRD has worked very hard over the past year and we've managed to reduce our budget by about 20 per cent without laying off a single person. Nor, in my opinion, have we given up anything in any way that we provide the teams. Our marketing group has cut their budget with their activation around the racing activities by about 50 per cent, which is about the same story you'll hear from every manufacturer.

"But at the very highest level of Toyota across America and around the world, this programme has been an absolute home run," White added. "By every metric we use to measure our success and return on investment to the company, our two years in Cup racing have improved the consideration for purchase among fans by 20 points. We came in 20–25 points behind Chevrolet and Ford, but right now we're equal to, or ahead of, all of our competition among NASCAR fans. So we consider it a great success." NASCAR's vice president of competition, Robin Pemberton, also discussed the GM and Chrysler cutbacks. "In today's world, the industry has grown so that there are a lot of available rolling-road wind tunnels in the United States and Europe, and a lot of seven-post machines," Pemberton observed. "There are a lot of nice engineering facilities around the country, and those facilities will still be available for the teams to use, whether they be the mega-teams or the independent teams.

"We'll take it step by step," Pemberton added. "We'll be here for the manufacturers when they decide to increase their support again, and we surely support them. We're racing and car guys. We enjoy our involvement with the manufacturers and we feel like NASCAR is a good platform to advertise their product. Things go up and down over the years and we have to go with the flow."

NASCAR had its problems but it was still way ahead of any other form of American racing, with 43-car fields and a handful of non-qualifiers at every Sprint Cup race. Much of NASCAR's strength lies in its ladder system and grass-roots reach. American open-wheel and road racing will never come close to NASCAR unless IRL, ALMS, Grand-Am, etc work together to develop a similar defined, well-promoted and marketed ladder system. NASCAR's broad-based system comprises a dozen different championships, all with sponsors, and these grass-roots series bring a massive base of drivers, teams, car and engine builders, sponsors and media to NASCAR. It's a true ladder system in a class of its own.

CHASING THE CUP

Despite GM's bankruptcy, NASCAR's premier Sprint Cup championship was dominated in 2009 by Chevrolet teams and drivers. Tony Stewart led the points for most of the season in his first year as a team owner, but by mid-November he had dropped down to fifth in the championship battle, behind three other Chevrolets, driven by Jimmie Johnson, Mark Martin and Jeff Gordon, and the Dodge of Kurt Busch. Stewart scored his first win as an owner/driver at Pocono in June.

After ten years with Joe Gibbs's top-ranked team, including 33 wins and two championships (2002 and 2005), Stewart decided in 2008 to take the plunge into team ownership. With Chevrolet's help and no up-front investment, he was able to acquire a half-interest in Gene Haas's unsuccessful team. Haas's business is the USA's largest manufacturer of CNC machinery, but he recently spent two years in a federal jail for tax evasion.

Stewart, 38, had come up through midget and sprint cars, winning USAC's midget championship in

Above: Pit stop under lights for defending Sprint Cup champion Jimmie Johnson's Chevy at Charlotte
Photo: Michael Levitt/LAT Photographic

Right: Perhaps no longer unstoppable, Jeff Gordon still remains a powerful force.
Photo: Brian Czobat/LAT Photographic

Above: Tony Stewart ran his own team for the first time and looked a likely championship winner before losing out in the 'Chase'.
Photo: Nigel Kinrade/LAT Photographic

Above right: Mid-November, Avondale, Arizona, and with the championship still up for grabs, Mark Martin leans on Jimmie Johnson during a restart.
Photo: Brian Czobat/LAT Photographic

Right: Veteran Mark Martin defied the years to become a real force once more after joining the Hendricks team. However, the four-time runner-up was still looking for that elusive NASCAR crown.
Photo: Nigel Kinrade/LAT Photographic

1994 and becoming the first driver to win all three of USAC's midget, sprint car and Silver Crown titles in 1995. He graduated to the IRL series in 1996 and won the IRL championship in 1997, before moving to NASCAR with Joe Gibbs in 1999. Today, Stewart also owns the legendary Eldora Speedway dirt track in Ohio and a USAC midget team.

A key element in Stewart's decision to become a partner with Gene Haas in Stewart-Haas Racing was the guarantee of a supply of cars and engines from Hendrick Motorsports, equal to those provided to Hendrick's team. With top equipment, Stewart was a ferocious competitor in most races. His team-mate in the new venture is Ryan Newman, also an Indiana native, who started in midget and sprint cars. Newman drove for Roger Penske for eight years, but decided he had more chance for success with Stewart's team. Sure enough, Newman also ran well through most of the first half of 2009 and also made the 'Chase for the Cup'.

With just two races to go, defending champion Jimmie Johnson remained the odds-on favourite to beat veteran Mark Martin to the championship. Johnson had won the previous three NASCAR titles, and was chasing an unprecedented fourth consecutive title. Driving for Rick Hendrick's four-car team, Johnson was frequently the man to beat, having won 26 races over the previous four years. A quiet, unassuming fellow who grew up in California racing motorcycles and dirt cars, Johnson is a cool, analytical driver who often has the best-handling car for the final laps of a race.

Top seed in the 2009 'Chase' was 50-year-old Mark Martin, who enjoyed a resurgence during the season, his first with the all-powerful Hendrick team. Martin started racing Cup cars in 1981 and has been a regular in NASCAR's top series since 1988, when he joined Jack Roush's fledgling team. He has finished second in the championship four times and placed third in four more years, but has never won

the championship. In 2006, Martin decided to run less than the full NASCAR schedule to help his son pursue a racing career. But in 2008, after his son turned his back on racing, he determined to enter all 36 races once again and joined Rick Hendrick's superteam. Right away, he reminded everyone how quick and relentless he is, and with the equipment to fight for the championship, Martin was without doubt the sentimental favourite.

Making the 'Chase' for the first time was Juan Pablo Montoya, who was very competitive in many races. The 2009 season was Montoya's third in NASCAR with Chip Ganassi's team, which merged during the winter with Dale Earnhardt Incorporated. The merger resulted in Montoya switching from Dodges to Chevrolets, and JPM truly earned his NASCAR spurs, often running near the front and showing plenty of racing moxie. Had he not exceeded the pit-lane speed limit at Indianapolis in July, he would have scored his first NASCAR oval-track victory. In mid-October, he was an impressive fourth in points with a serious chance of winning the championship.

Other 2009 championship contenders included Johnson's and Martin's Hendrick team-mate, Jeff Gordon, who was very competitive in many races. Also qualifying for the 'Chase' were Kurt Busch (Penske Dodge), Denny Hamlin (Joe Gibbs Toyota), Carl Edwards and Greg Biffle aboard two of five Roush-Fenway Fords, Brian Vickers (Red Bull Toyota) and Kasey Kahne in a Richard Petty Motorsports Dodge.

Biggest surprise among those who failed to make the 'Chase' was Kyle Busch. In 2008, Busch won eight races and was rated as a top championship contender for 2009. Everyone concedes that he is one of NASCAR's fastest drivers, but luck and reliability were not on his side. By mid-October, he had won four races, but finished the regular season in thirteenth place, eight points short of qualifying for the 'Chase'.

Also failing to make the 'Chase' were 2003 Cup champion Matt Kenseth and NASCAR's most popular driver, Dale Earnhardt Jr. While Kenseth was in and out of the top 12 in points all year, fighting hard to get into the 'Chase', Earnhardt never looked at all like a serious contender. In fact, it was Dale Jr's worst year on record, as he didn't come close to winning a race and finished outside the top 20 in points, in stark contrast to his three Hendrick team-mates, Johnson, Martin and Gordon.

LOVING LIFE IN NASCAR

For his part, Montoya was enjoying life in NASCAR more than ever and had become a big fan of the latest, ill-handling Cup car, referred to as the 'Car of Tomorrow' on its introduction two years ago. "I'm loving it," Juan grinned. "As a car to drive compared to the other cars I've driven, it handles horrible, but for racing it's the best car I've driven. If you could combine the way an open-wheel car drives with the racing that we have in NASCAR, it would be the ideal racing. That's what you want. I've driven all the great cars, but the racing has always been terrible. And this racing is incredible! I love it. I get a kick out of it.

"Here, you race close with everybody all the time. You pass cars, other cars pass you, and everything happens. It's very exciting. But in Formula One nothing happens. You come in [to the pits], you go out. You drive around on your own, come in again, go out, and that's it. You never even come into the pits together with anybody!

"In Formula One, when you've got the best car, you've got to win, and when you don't have the best

car, you don't win. It's that simple. Here, every week you've got a shot at winning, and you've got to try to do the best to take it. It's hard, because on any given Sunday there are four or five cars out there that can actually win the race. It comes down to pit stops and strategy and all that stuff."

Steve Hmiel is Earnhardt-Ganassi's director of competition. He has worked in NASCAR for 35 years, having started in the mid-seventies with Petty Enterprises. "We've got better engines this year than we've ever had," Hmiel explained. "But we have a race car driver who I think is on top of his game in a stock car. He was always on top of his game in anything else and now he's learned how to be on top of his game in these cars."

Montoya added, "It's good that we are competitive now. It sucks when you're not. But when you're not, it doesn't mean you are not trying. Last year, when we finished 15th or 16th, that was an awesome day. Now, we finish 15th and we suck. This year we achieved what we wanted to do, and making the 'Chase' is like a little bonus for us. It's a plus. We're

bringing our best cars and equipment every week to make sure that we don't leave anything on the table, and the team is incredible. They're pumped up, they're excited. They can see that we can do it."

Marcos Ambrose raced Formula Fords and F3 cars in Europe, and won the Australian V8 championship in 2003 and 2004. He came to America in 2005 and worked his way through NASCAR's Truck and Nationwide series before landing a full-time Sprint Cup ride for 2009 with JTG Daugherty's Toyota. In his first full Cup season, it looked as though he would finish well within the top 20 in points, ahead of such top NASCAR drivers as Jeff Burton, Kevin Harvick and Earnhardt Jr, and he says the tremendous depth to NASCAR's fields has made him a better driver.

"The level of competition is just incredible," Ambrose grinned. "It looks big on TV, but when you get in there and see how talented the field is, and how much money is invested, and how intense the racing is, it's just lifted up my level of performance no end. I'm a much better driver than I was before I came to America because you have to. The depth of talent is

so big that it's just remarkable. Anyone from Australia or Europe has just got to come here and see it for themselves. You can't appreciate it from TV. They will be amazed at how tough it is and how deep the talent goes.

"There are a lot of very talented race car drivers from open-wheel that have come in and struggled," Ambrose went on. "Montoya has adapted very, very well, but a lot of talented drivers have had a hard time adapting to stock cars. The cars handle like a school bus at 200mph. They're really a bad handling car, and you've got to trick them to make them go. One weekend you've got an eighteen-hundred-pound right rear spring, and the next week you've got a three-hundred-pound right rear spring. There's so much variation in the set-ups and what it takes to get these cars to run, and that's what the challenge really is, getting it to run right."

Ambrose has developed great respect for NASCAR's top drivers. "There's a special set of drivers who are the best in Cup cars, and it's a never-ending quest for me to find out what they do and how they

do it. To turn up every weekend with a competitive car for every track takes real talent, and it's a skill set that very few people have got."

American racing great Parnelli Jones fervently believes that all types of racing should ban "all that electronic junk" like NASCAR, and not allow any data gathering on race weekends. Ambrose has become a great believer in this maxim, as well as the ugly handling of NASCAR's current Cup car. "I think it's wonderful," Ambrose glowed. "For the driver, you know you've won the race and no one else knows how you did it. NASCAR's trying really hard to keep it out of the hands of the engineers. They don't want the car to handle well. Their mission was to make this the toughest race car in the world to drive, and they've done that. It's a real challenge for all of us.

"Whenever you get driver aids like ABS brakes, sequential gearboxes and paddle shifts, the racing deteriorates," Ambrose added. "NASCAR want the best driver to win the race, and they do that every week. And you can't say that Formula One does that every week."

Above: Dario Franchitti returned from an unhappy spell in the NASCAR arena to drive for Target Ganassi. The canny Scot used all of his considerable experience to take the title from team-mate Scott Dixon and Penske's Ryan Briscoe.

Photo: Phillip Abbott/LAT Photographic

Right: That's three! Helio Castroneves made a fairytale return to action to win a third Indianapolis 500 in commanding style.

Photo: Michael Levitt/LAT Photographic

GANASSI v PENSKE

The 2009 IRL IndyCar series was dominated by the Ganassi and Penske teams, Dario Franchitti winning his second Indy car championship with Ganassi. The only non-Penske or non-Ganassi winner was Justin Wilson at Watkins Glen in July with Dale Coyne's renowned little-guy operation. Ganassi's drivers led the points through most of the year, with defending champion Scott Dixon and new team-mate Franchitti winning five races apiece. Across the board, Dixon and Franchitti were the class of the field, and it was rare when they didn't run at the front.

Of course, Franchitti turned his back on Indy car racing after winning the 2007 IRL title and Indy 500 with Andretti-Green. He tried his hand at NASCAR in 2008 with Chip Ganassi's team, but near the end of the year he decided to accept Ganassi's offer of a return to Indy car racing with Chip's IRL team, where he was paired with Dixon.

Late in the season, Ryan Briscoe was able to edge ahead of Dixon and Franchitti, thanks to a string of eight second places and three first-rate wins. After a couple of unsuccessful years trying to break into the IRL, Aussie Briscoe joined Roger Penske's ALMS Porsche LMP2 team in 2007 and was promoted in 2008 to Penske's Indy car team. He won three IRL races in 2008 and finished fifth in the championship, but in 2009 he became Penske's *de facto* lead driver as Helio Castroneves recovered from his income tax evasion trial.

Castroneves had a turbulent year, his trial in April being followed by an anxious acquittal and a return to action at Long Beach. Then he enjoyed a dreamlike month of May at Indianapolis, qualifying on the pole and winning his third 500. But the rest of the season didn't go so well. He endured a series of incidents and accidents, and often he wasn't quite able to match Briscoe's pace. Meanwhile, Will Power, Penske's new third driver showed his stuff by winning at Edmonton in July, only to crash at Sonoma (Sears Point) the following month, breaking three vertebra. Power was out for the rest of the year, compelled to wear a back brace for four months.

At Indianapolis, there was no stopping Castroneves, who qualified on the pole and was in a class of his own at the end of the 500, beating 2005 winner Dan Wheldon by a shade under two seconds, a lifetime on a big speedway like Indy. It was Castroneves's third win at Indianapolis and Penske's 15th Indy 500 win, ten more than any other owner in history. It was also Team Penske's fifth win in the last nine 500s, following Roger's decision to desert CART – an organisation he had co-founded in 1979 with Pat Patrick – to return to the Speedway in 2001.

In the wake of Tony George's creation of the Indy Racing League, Penske's team missed five years at Indianapolis, from 1996 to 2000, and the team famously failed to qualify any of its cars for the race in 1995, the last year that CART's teams raced at the

Speedway. Over 41 years, therefore, starting in 1969, Penske's team has raced in 35 Indy 500s and won more than 40 per cent of them!

The 93rd running of the 500 was dominated by Penske's and Chip Ganassi's cars. Castroneves and team-mate Briscoe led 77 of the 200 laps, while 2008 winner Dixon and 2007 winner Franchitti combined to lead 123 laps for Ganassi. Nobody else led a single lap. Franchitti and Dixon looked very strong through the first two-thirds of the 500, but both ran into 'snafus' on their final pit stops and wound up stuck in the pack, unable to pass at the end when it counted. Dixon came home sixth, with Franchitti directly behind in seventh.

GEORGE DEPOSED AS IMS PRESIDENT

Three days after the 2009 500, the IRL's many problems were underlined when news broke that Tony George had been ousted from the Indianapolis Motor Speedway's presidency by the board of directors – his mother, three sisters and the family's two attorneys. The IMS issued a statement denying the story, but a formal announcement arrived on the last day in June, confirming that George had been replaced by veteran IMS executives Jeffrey Belskus and Curtis Brighton. Belskus took over from George as president and CEO of the Indianapolis Motor Speedway Corporation, while Brighton became president and CEO of Hulman & Company (owner of the Speedway). Tony George remains a board member of the Hulman-George companies, but has no executive power.

Belskus has been with the IMS since 1987, having moved rapidly up the company's hierarchy, from treasurer to chief financial officer, then vice president and executive vice president before being promoted to the top job. Brighton joined Hulman & Company in 1994 as vice president and legal counsel before being promoted in 2002 to executive vice president and general counsel. He also served in similar capacities with the IMS and the Indy Racing League before taking charge of Hulman & Company.

So it was that Tony George's 19-year reign at the helm of the Indianapolis Motor Speedway came to an end as the track began its 100th anniversary celebrations. The Speedway was opened in August 1909, and the first 500-mile race was run in May 1911. By all accounts, the new regime placed the track and the Hulman-George family companies in solidly unadventurous, corporate hands.

Since founding the IRL in 1996, George spent more than US$600m bankrolling IRL race purses, teams, cars, engines and parts, as well as starting his own IRL team, Vision Racing, and remodelling the Speedway to accommodate F1 for eight fleeting years. During a motor sports business conference in New York in the winter, George – rather ominously, and perhaps incausitiously – said that he might be compelled to close down the IRL series in four or five years if it failed to pick up in fan and commercial interest.

Despite 2008's unification of the dying Champ Car organisation with the IRL, Indy car racing continues to struggle with a serious shortage of major media coverage so that the teams have great difficulty in selling sponsorship. Many IRL races struggle to draw crowds and TV ratings, particularly as most races are televised on Versus, a satellite network with a small market reach. Quite a few 2009 IRL races drew abysmal TV ratings: around 0.10–0.12, which translates to barely 100,000 viewers, in a country of some 320 million.

Sadly, Indy car racing has become one of America's least-watched sports. The 2009 Indy 500, telecast as always on ABC, drew only 3.9 per cent of American households, down 13 per cent from 2008, and 40 per cent from four years ago. It was the lowest TV rating since the race was first televised live from start to finish in 1986, and less than one-quarter the audience from those days. Many IRL teams are worried about the 2010 season and 2011 in particular, with existing sponsor contracts not expected to be renewed and sponsorship all but impossible to sell. As the IRL works to pull together its new formula for 2012, at least half its teams are wondering how on earth they will be able to afford a switch to new chassis and engines. After 15 years of bitter squabbling, Tony George's failed revolution, aimed at wresting control of Indy car racing from CART's team owners, has been a calamitous failure, ending with a barely audible whimper.

Remember George's exhortations about bringing American drivers back to the centre of Indy car racing? Well, in 2009, the smallest number of American drivers competed in Indy car racing in the sport's 100-year history. Only five Americans raced Indy cars on a regular basis during the year: Graham Rahal, Danica Patrick, Marco Andretti, Ryan Hunter-Reay and Ed Carpenter – and for the first time ever, not a single American won an Indy car race.

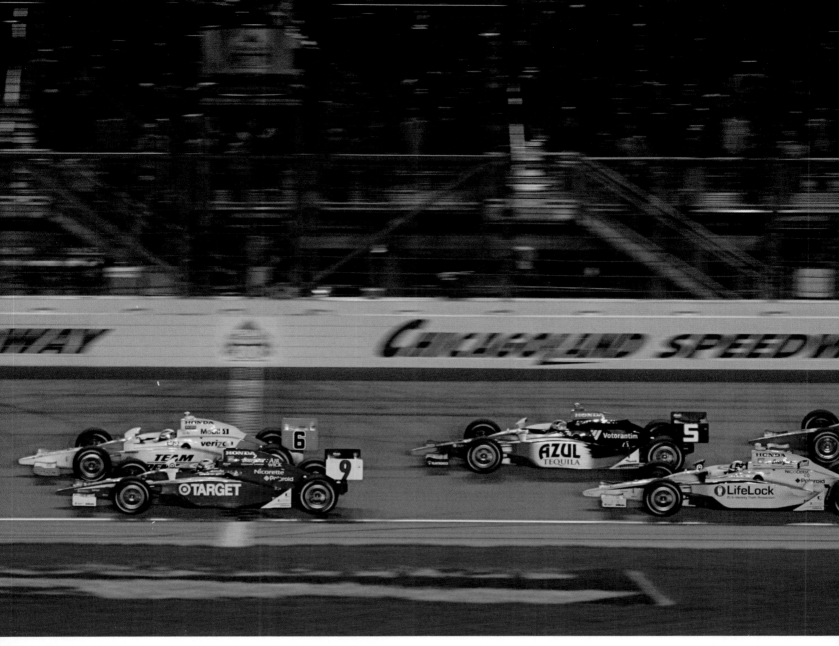

SPORTS CAR BLUES

It was also a tough year for the American Le Mans Series. Following the pull-out of both the Audi and Penske/Porsche teams, the ALMS featured a pair of Acura ARX-02a LMP1 cars run by Duncan Dayton's Highcroft Racing and de Ferran Motorsports, plus a pair of Lola-Mazda P2 cars fielded by long-time IMSA/ALMS stalwart Rob Dyson. The Acuras dominated the races, duelling among themselves well clear of the rest of the field. With David Brabham and Scott Sharp driving, Dayton's Highcroft team won the P1 championship from de Ferran's car driven by Gil de Ferran and Simon Pagenaud.

De Ferran's car won five races, while Highcroft scored four wins. Acura also won the P2 championship with Adrian Fernandez's lone entry for Fernandez and Luis Diaz, handily beating Dyson's pair of new Lolas. The Lola-Mazdas started the season without any testing, but were made quicker and more reliable by Dyson's team as the year wore on.

However, Acura has withdrawn its factory support for 2010, and ALMS boss Scott Atherton announced in August that his series would combine the P1 and

P2 categories for the coming season. Detail changes were planned to minimum weights, air restrictor sizes and fuel capacity in an attempt to equalise the P1 and P2 cars. The new Formula Le Mans Challenge Oreca spec car will also be permitted to race in the ALMS, and Atherton said that as many as four FLM Orecas could be on the grid in 2010.

The ALMS's GT2 category grew stronger in 2009 with the addition of Rahal-Letterman's factory BMW M3s, and from mid-summer, the new GT2 Corvette. Both the Rahal/BMW and Corvette teams scored their first GT2 wins in August, BMW at Elkhart Lake and the Corvette at Mosport the following weekend. But the GT2 championship was fought out by the Flying Lizard Porsche 911GT3 driven by Jörg Bergmeister and Patrick Long, and Risi Competizione's Ferrari 430GT handled by Jamie Melo and Pierre Kafer with Mika Salo's occasional assistance. Nor is there any doubt that Porsche v Ferrari v BMW v Corvette is a pretty good draw for GT2, with Jaguar set to join the fray in 2010.

The rival Grand-Am series, godfathered by NAS-

Below left: Sunrise at Daytona, and a photographer waits for something more interesting than a GT3 Porsche to capture with his lens.
Photo: R D Ethan/LAT Photographic

Below: A night watch for 'The Captain'. Roger Penske oversees race operations during the Daytona 24-hour race.
Photo: Autostock/LAT Photographic

CAR's Jim France, produced another tight battle, with three teams in the thick of the fight. The 2007 champions, Alex Gurney and Jon Fogarty, won four races and took their second Grand-Am championship driving Bob Stalling's Gainsco Riley-Pontiac. The championship went down to the wire, with Gurney/Fogarty beating defending champions Scott Pruett and Memo Rojas in Chip Ganassi's Riley-Lexus, and Max Angelelli and Brian Friselle aboard Wayne Taylor's Dallara-Ford. The Grand-Am's GT championship was taken by Dirk Werner and Leh Keen's Farnbacher/Loles Porsche 911GT3.

But even in the NASCAR-style, cost-contained Grand-Am, teams are struggling to survive, and when it comes to overall media coverage and TV ratings, both the ALMS and Grand-Am series are in even worse shape than the IRL. Nor does the Grand-Am draw much in the way of crowds. The ALMS, at least, enjoys a reasonable fan base and good crowds, although without Acura, the series won't have much pulling power in 2010.

The Indy Lights championship was won by J.R. Hildebrand, 21, from Aussie James Davison (grandson of four-time Australian GP winner Lex) and 19-year-old Colombian Sebastian Saavedra. Hildebrand won the SCCA's Formula Russell championship in 2004 and took the Cooper Tires F2000 championship two years later, winning 12 of 14 races. He raced Atlantic cars

with Newman/Wachs in 2007 before moving to Indy Lights with RLR/Andersen Racing in 2008 and then joining Andretti-Green's Lights team for the successful run at the championship.

Swiss Simona de Silvestro, 21, led the Atlantic series all season in her third year in the formula. She won four races, but crashed on the opening lap of the last race, while Newman/Wachs team-mates John Edwards and Jonathan Summerton finished 1-2 in the race and the championship. Edwards, 18, won the Star-Mazda championship in 2008 and is one of America's most promising open-wheel talents. Summerton is a favourite for a USF1 testing seat during 2010.

Following the demise of Champ Car racing at the end of 2006, the Atlantic series has run primarily with the ALMS. Without the million-dollar champion's prize it boasted a few years ago under Champ Car, the series struggled with ten- or twelve-car fields in 2008 and 2009. Vickie O'Connor has run North America's Atlantic series since 1985. "It's just survival," she remarked. "I dream for the mid-nineties. Hopefully, things will turn around. There are a bunch of Atlantic cars that are just sitting around. People haven't sold them. They're keeping them, but nobody's running them. I haven't seen it this bad since '91 Hopefully, we can get through this and come out stronger later."

Above: David Brabham and Scott Sharp brought the LMP1 ALMS title to Highcroft Racing. Here Brabham steers his Acura ARX-02a through the gloom to sixth place in the Petit Le Mans at Road Atlanta, Braselton, Georgia. It was enough to consolidate the team's leading championship position.

Left: Highcroft's main competition came from the similar de Ferran Motorsports Acura driven by Gil de Ferran and Simon Pagenaud. At Laguna Seca the car was reliveried in white to mirror the legendary Chaparral sports cars as a tribute to de Ferran's former IndyCar team boss, Jim Hall.

Photos: Dan R. Boyd/LAT Photographic

KARTING REVIEW by RUSSELL ATKINS

COMING OF AGE

Main photo: James Singleton (4) leads Harry Crawley (5) away from the grid in the 2009 FKS finale at Whilton Mill. Eventual champion Jack Barlow lies in wait behind.

Inset centre left: Singleton, Crawley and Barlow celebrate at the end of a season in which they expertly turned the Mini Max title fight into a strict three-way affair.

Inset left: Ultimate Motorsport star George Russell proudly shows off the 'No. 1' plate he earned by way of Formula Kart Stars Cadet title glory – as BTCC ace Rob Collard's son Ricky celebrates victory in the final outing of 2009 at Whilton Mill.

Inset far left: Ash Hand pips 2009 FKS Junior Max Champion Matt Parry to the chequered flag following a thrilling final lap at Whilton Mill – in a race that was described as arguably the most exciting of the season

Photos: Chris Walker/www.kartpix.net

For so long a successful breeding ground for Formula 1, touring car, IndyCar and sportscar stars the world over, 2009 was arguably the year when karting really came of age – with two of the biggest names in international motorsport, Bernie Ecclestone and Lewis Hamilton, pledging their support through first-hand involvement as the legendary Michael Schumacher returned to the track and the leading names of tomorrow duelled it out for supremacy in an effort to one day follow in the German's footsteps.

F1 ringmaster and Formula One Management (FOM) chief executive Ecclestone and 2008 world champion Hamilton caused a major stir when they bestowed their backing upon the championship previously called BRDC Stars of Tomorrow – henceforth to be known as Formula Kart Stars (FKS), with an official F1-style logo to match.

For one of the two leading karting series in Britain – and the one that had first discovered Hamilton himself just over a decade earlier – it was a considerable pre-season boost, immediately thrusting FKS into the international spotlight. And the racing – as ever – was absolutely first-rate. The four classes in the championship – Cadets, Mini Max, Junior Max and KF3 – produced deserving champions in the shape of respectively George Russell, Jack Barlow, Matt Parry and Alex Albon, and all manner of on-track thrills and spills along the way.

Ultimate Motorsport ace Russell thoroughly dominated the Cadet action – and was particularly impressive in the wet, when he was in a class all of his own – and it was only towards the end of the campaign that the 11-year-old's rivals finally began to peg him back in. Other drivers to shine with successes of their own were Josh White, Matthew Graham, Harry Webb – who arguably could have given Russell a run for his money had he not suffered an injury that ruled him out of the final meeting – Adam Mackay, Ricky Collard – son of BTCC Airwaves BMW front-runner Rob – and

Welsh hotshot Tom Harvey, and if the damage had already been done in terms of the 2009 title chase, 2010 is shaping up to be a classic.

Stepping up a gear to the Mini Max class, Barlow, Harry Crawley and James Singleton swiftly turned proceedings into a tight three-way tussle, as they divided up eight of the nine victories between them in a crushing display of dominance – four for Crawley, three for Singleton and one for Barlow. All three headed into the Whilton Mill double-header finale in with a shout of glory, but despite Singleton triumphing on the first day and Crawley replicating the feat on the second, it was the ever-consistent Barlow who won out in the end. Crawley could point to a clutch failure at Rowrah that arguably cost him the crown, whilst Singleton ended the season as incontrovertibly the form man as the trio all graduate to Junior Max in 2010. Others to catch the eye along the way were Danny Sweeney – the sole other driver to win a final, at Genk in Belgium – and Jay Goodwin, the only competitor to twice be awarded the prestigious Lewis Hamilton 'True Grit' accolade for his overtaking prowess.

The Junior Max laurels deservedly went the way of the peerless Parry, but behind the Paul Carr Racing speed demon there was a battle royale for the remaining top ten spots. The runner-up position was finally clinched by Henry Hunter, whilst others to make a name for themselves included Ollie Varney, Ash Hand – who got the better of Parry during the course of a thrilling, nail-biting duel in the final meeting at Whilton Mill, and also lifted the trophy in the prestigious annual Kartmasters outing at PF International in the summer – Andy King, Lee Napolitano, Alex Magee and Josh Parker. The victories went the way of Parry (four), Hand (two), Hunter (two) and King (one).

FKS' flagship class KF3, finally, was something of a one-horse race in that none of Albon's rivals were ever able to consistently take the fight to the experienced Red Bull-backed star, who similarly shone on

the European stage, finishing as highest-placed Brit in the fiercely-contested WSK International Series. Peterborough ace Callum Bowyer came closest in his maiden season of KF3 with a number of gutsy performances against the odds – struggling for budget in comparison with many of his adversaries – to clinch the runner-up honours at the last gasp, after being cruelly deprived of the top step of the podium on the series' overseas trip to Genk by an electrical failure. Russ Danzey and Macaulay Walsh, meanwhile, became two of the very first drivers in Britain to campaign the new Birel-based RK chassis, with the initials standing for 2008 Canadian Grand Prix winner Robert Kubica. Danzey drove superbly throughout for JM Racing after beginning the season with a kart some two seconds shy of the leading pace – fairly decimating the field when the heavens opened at Rowrah, and similarly prevailing at Glan Y Gors – whilst an unstoppable double victory for Walsh at Whilton sent out a warning shot for 2010.

In launching his own chassis, Kubica followed in the wheel tracks of his F1 rivals Fernando Alonso, Jarno Trulli and Hamilton, with the latter similarly debuting his own mount in 2009. McLaren-Mercedes Young Driver Programme member Oliver Rowland was privileged enough to get his hands on the first example – making good use of it by following up his 2008 World Cup glory in the KF2 class with a string of front-running performances on the international stage.

Rowland is a former Super 1 JICA (now KF3) champion, and the rival national series echoed FKS in taking a significant step forward this year – credited largely to the stellar efforts and unstinting hard work of new championship director John Hoyle of JKH. On the MSA package, it was many of the same suspects in the hunt for honours, only this time Russell did not have things all his own way in Cadets. The Wisbech ace was a front-runner throughout, but only triumphed once as chief rival Alex Gill reached the highest step of the rostrum on no fewer than six occasions – or, to put it into perspective, almost half of the finals – to put the destiny of the laurels beyond reach of any of his pursuers. The success also helped to atone for the lack of a single victory for the Yorkshireman in FKS, where four podiums earned him third in the end-of-season standings, whilst Russell could at least console himself with Kartmasters glory, seeing off the challenge of Graham by the slimmest of margins. Sam Webster, Max Vaughan, Harry Woodhead and Graham were similarly well in attendance for the leading Super 1 positions throughout.

Albon again ruled the roost in KF3 – wrapping up the laurels one round early to leave his challengers to fight it out amongst themselves for the honour of triumphing in the final outing at Fulbeck. Bowyer succeeded in breaking his KF3 duck at the Lincolnshire circuit courtesy of a truly flawless performance – sealing an impressive fourth spot in the end-of-season rankings into the bargain – whilst Racing Steps Foundation-backed Jake Dennis ran Albon closest for championship glory, as Sennan Fielding, Walsh and the ever-consistent Jordan King rounded out the leading half dozen at the close of play. King, indeed, enjoyed a strong season both at home and abroad, with an opening meeting triumph in FKS, front-running form in Super 1 and victory at Kartmasters, getting the better of Dennis following a scintillating scrap for supremacy.

Jordan Chamberlain swept to the British title in KF2, with only Shaun Carter and early pace-setter Jake Ball really able to keep with the Welshman, as

the trio practically monopolised the top step of the podium throughout, with seven wins for Chamberlain, one for Carter and two for Ball. Only Chris Lock, Josh Fielding and Jake Lloyd succeeded in interrupting their dominance, but none of the three was consistent enough to truly challenge. Arguably an even bigger accolade for Chamberlain, though, was the European KF2 crown he clinched at Essay in France – defeating more than 200 rivals of international calibre through the qualifying and final stages to lift one of the most coveted trophies in global karting. The 17-year-old is bidding to graduate to cars in 2010, but the eternal bugbear of funding is unfortunately proving to be quite a stumbling-block.

There may have only been 14 drivers entered in KF1, meanwhile, but the class provided the most controversy when the title tussle between Ben Cooper, Robert Foster-Jones and KF2 Kartmasters king Mark Litchfield ended in tears in a bad-tempered Fulbeck finale. Runaway WSK International Series KF2 Champion Cooper went into the weekend looking to be in control – with Foster-Jones nursing only a mathematical chance – but the latter was the quickest of the trio on the track and prevailed in the first final after backing Cooper up into the baying pack behind and causing the points leader to fall to fifth. In the second – and decisive – final, it was Cooper who got the early jump as Foster-Jones languished, but a searing, all-out charge by the RFM star enabled him to both catch and pass his championship rival. Realising that victory alone was not enough, Foster-Jones then set about backing Cooper up once more – and as the tension

mounted, the inevitable occurred. Cooper went for a move, Foster-Jones gave no quarter, the former was sent spinning out and the latter survived to finish third and with it claim the crown. Cooper was subsequently excluded from the meeting, dropping him to 13th in the standings, with Litchfield annexing the runner-up spot ahead of Luke Wright, Richard Bradley and Jordon Lennox-Lamb.

On Super 1's Rotax bill, Nathan Harrison proved one of the benefits of focussing solely on one national championship rather than two, as he narrowly pipped Wavertree Motorsport rival and Kartmasters and FKS Champion Barlow to the honours, the pair triumphing three times apiece along the way. The consistent Harrison Scott wound up third, with FKS leading lights Crawley and Singleton again demonstrating their talent right up at the sharp end to claim fourth and fifth, and Jordan Houghton completing the front-running competitors in sixth. Like Barlow, Parry in Junior Max came up just short of doing the double as he found himself defeated by 'O' Plate winner Ed Brand, with Jack Dex the only driver to really get in on the action, winning both finals at Larkhall in Scotland and again tasting victory at Shenington the following time out.

Chamberlain aside, a number of other British drivers shone on the worldwide stage too, and chief amongst them was undoubtedly Jack Hawksworth. The Bradford star had already marked himself out in 2008 as one to watch and his nation's leading representative at gearbox level in Europe – and in 2009 he took another step forward again. A front-runner in both WSK and CIK-FIA competitions season-long

Left: Russ Danzey spent much of the year performing minor miracles with an uncompetitive kart, but after switching mounts to the all-new Robert Kubica chassis mid-season, he fairly flew.

Centre left: Jordan Chamberlain successfully flew the flag for Wales in 2009, by triumphing in both the European and British KF2 Championships.

Below left: Callum Bowyer gives free rein to his jubilation after finally breaking his duck in the KF3 class with an unchallenged victory in the last Super 1 outing of 2009 at Fulbeck.

Opposite page, far left: Robert Foster-Jones leads chief title rival Ben Cooper before the battle for 2009 Super 1 Series KF1 glory unravelled in epic style in the final round at Fulbeck.

Opposite page, top: Jordan King shows off the spoils of his success after producing arguably the performance of the season in the KF3 class of the WSK International Series at Genk in Belgium, storming through the field from the very back into third place as the heavens did their worst.

Opposite page, centre: Aside from walking away with the KF3 title in both Formula Kart Stars and Super 1 in Britain, Red Bull-backed Alex Albon represented his country in style on the European stage too, finishing a superb fifth in the WSK International Series.

Photos: Chris Walker/www.kartpix.net

Above: Frenchman Arnaud Kozlinski celebrates victory in the prestigious CIK-FIA World Championship at Macau, ahead of star 2009 breakthrough performer Aaro Vainio and leading Brit Ben Hanley.
Photo: Chris Walker/www.kartpix.net

Top: Jack Hawksworth once again proved himself to be the leading British gearbox competitor on the international stage, and claimed the biggest victory of his impressive career to-date when he triumphed in the 20th edition of the prestigious Margutti Trophy in Italy.
Photo: KSP

– with a superb second place in the WSK curtain-raiser at Sarno in Italy and a searing charge up through the order in the KZ1 World Cup at the same circuit to finish 13th from the back of the grid, and out of 76 initial entrants – the Energy Corse ace also turned heads across the Pond with victory on his first outing in the Florida Winter Tour at Homestead Karting. The 18-year-old's greatest success, however, was back on European shores, as he defeated the crème de la crème of international gearbox opposition to lift the coveted Trofeo Margutti on the 20th anniversary of the illustrious Italian event.

Elsewhere overseas, Jordan King converted his impressive British form to superb results in the WSK International Series, with a win at Sarno – evidently a happy hunting ground for UK competitors – and podiums at Castelletto and Genk, on the latter occasion belying his comparative lack of experience to storm through the field following an opening lap knock, lapping more than a second quicker than anybody else on the track as the rain fell to seal an incredible third place. A couple more laps and few were in any doubt that the Warwickshire star would have been toasting a famous victory. The crowning glory of the 15-year-old's year, though, was without doubt success in the CIK-FIA Asia-Pacific KF3 Championship in Macau, when he brilliantly overcame a torrential downpour, crumbling track surface and ailing engine to dominate one of the highest-profile karting events the world over.

Other drivers to make a name for themselves in Europe were WSK and CIK-FIA European KF3 Champion Nyck de Vries, who was pushed all the way by Danil Kyvat and Carlos Sainz Jnr – son of rallying legend Carlos Sainz, and winner of the 2009 KF3 Monaco Kart Cup – as Alex Albon similarly shared the limelight. Chris Lock made it a British one-two at KF2 level behind Cooper, with Joel Johansson and former WSK KF3 Champion Matteo Viganò also hitting the headlines, whilst Bas Lammers and former World and European KF1 Champion Marco Ardigò battled it out for KZ2 glory, the Belgian leapfrogging the Italian at the

last by way of a maximum score in the Zuera finale to add to his CIK-FIA KZ1 European Championship crown.

Frenchman Arnaud Kozlinski narrowly saw off the bid of Italian rival Sauro Cesetti for the WSK Super KF trophy, and defeated Aaro Vainio – who really sprang to prominence in 2009, with Super KF World Championship success at Essay in France – for the CIK-FIA World Championship crown in Macau, arguably the greatest prize in international competition. Ben Hanley was the leading Brit in third. Other major CIK-FIA trophies were claimed by David Da Luz (KF2 World Cup), Giuliano Maria Niceta – who saw off an inspired Jake Dennis for KF3 World Cup honours – Jonathan Thonon (KZ1 World Cup), Yannick De Brabander (Super KF World Cup), Felice Tiene (Asia-Pacific KF2 Championship), Angelo Lombardo (KZ2 European Championship) and Anthony Abbasse (KZ2 Monaco Kart Cup).

Lennox-Lamb, meanwhile, was unlucky to miss out on glory in the annual Bridgestone Cup at Lonato in Italy, when after overhauling both Birel team-mate Viganò and Nicolaj Møller Madsen and looking to be on-course for victory, the Bedford ace was struck down by an engine failure almost within sight of the chequered flag.

Having begun with an F1 link, finally, it seems only apt to come full circle and conclude with one too. Hamilton and Kubica might have launched their own karts in 2009, but 'Singapore-gate' protagonist Nelsinho Piquet, Scuderia Toro Rosso team-mates Jaime Alguersuari and Sébastien Buemi and record-breaking multiple world champion Schumacher all went one better still. Piquet entered into the Monaco Kart Cup endurance challenge, Alguersuari challenged at the front in the CIK-FIA KZ1 World Cup at Sarno and Buemi and Schumacher both threw their names into the hat to participate in the SKUSA Super Nationals outing at Las Vegas. In the glitziest city of them all, arguably the greatest driver of them all returned to his roots. Unquestionably, 2009 was the year in which karting truly arrived.

MAJOR RESULTS

OTHER CHAMPIONSHIP RACING SERIES WORLDWIDE

Compiled by DAVID HAYHOE and JOÃO PAULO CUNHA — www.forix.com

MAJOR RESULTS

OTHER CHAMPIONSHIP RACING SERIES WORLDWIDE

GP2 Series

All cars are Dallara GP2-08-Renault.

GP2 SERIES, Circuit de Catalunya, Montmeló, Barcelona, Spain, 9/10 May. Round 1. 39 and 26 laps of the 2.892-mile/4.655km circuit.

Race 1 (112.729 miles/181.419km).

1 Romain Grosjean, F, 1h 02m 22.709s, 108.430mph/174.501km/h; **2** Vitaly Petrov, RUS, 1h 02m 25.168s; **3** Jérôme D'Ambrosio, B, 1h 02m 29.058s; **4** Luca Filippi, I, 1h 02m 31.055s; **5** Pastor Maldonado, YV, 1h 02m 31.450s; **6** Edoardo Mortara, I, 1h 02m 35.238s; **7** Giedo van der Garde, NL, 1h 02m 35.457s; **8** Kamui Kobayashi, J, 1h 02m 36.772s; **9** Nico Hülkenberg, D, 1h 02m 36.969s; **10** Javier Villa, E, 1h 02m 37.909s; **11** Diego Nunes, BR, 1h 02m 39.378s; **12** Nelson Panciatici, F, 1h 02m 40.465s; **13** Michael Herck, RO, 1h 02m 41.154s; **14** Sergio Pérez, MEX, 1h 02m 41.304s; **15** Alberto Valério, BR, 1h 02m 54.338s; **16** Luiz Razia, BR, 38 laps; **17** Davide Rigon, I, 38; **18** Lucas Di Grassi, BR, 32 (DNF-accident); **19** Álvaro Parente, P, 32 (DNF-accident); **20** Daniel Clos, E, 31 (DNF-engine); **21** Karun Chandhok, IND, 27 (DNF-spin); **22** Roldán Rodríguez, E, 25 (DNF-accident); **23** Davide Valsecchi, I, 16 (DNF-clutch); **24** Ricardo Teixeira, ANG, 11 (DNF-spin); **25** Andreas Zuber, A, 5 (DNF-electrics); **26** Giacomo Ricci, I, 1 (DNF-accident).

Fastest race lap: Grosjean, 1m 31.070s, 114.340mph/184.012km/h.

Pole position: Grosjean, 1m 27.510s, 118.991mph/191.498km/h.

Race 2 (75.126 miles/120.904km).

1 Edoardo Mortara, I, 39m 55.235s, 112.913mph/181.716km/h; **2** Romain Grosjean, F, 39m 56.486s; **3** Jérôme D'Ambrosio, B, 40m 01.753s; **4** Giedo van der Garde, NL, 40m 09.873s; **5** Kamui Kobayashi, J, 40m 12.405s; **6** Pastor Maldonado, YV, 40m 15.334s; **7** Luca Filippi, I, 40m 24.206s; **8** Diego Nunes, BR, 40m 24.493s; **9** Vitaly Petrov, RUS, 40m 24.668s; **10** Lucas Di Grassi, BR, 40m 26.273s; **11** Álvaro Parente, P, 40m 27.261s; **12** Luiz Razia, BR, 40m 28.402s; **13** Alberto Valério, BR, 40m 29.024s; **14** Nico Hülkenberg, D, 40m 29.513s; **15** Giacomo Ricci, I, 40m 34.148s; **16** Davide Valsecchi, I, 40m 36.046s; **17** Sergio Pérez, MEX, 40m 37.493s; **18** Nelson Panciatici, F, 40m 54.899s; **19** Daniel Clos, E, 40m 54.982s; **20** Ricardo Teixeira, ANG, 40m 55.287s; **21** Davide Rigon, I, 25 laps (DNF-accident); **22** Karun Chandhok, IND, 21; **23** Javier Villa, E, 17 (DNF-gearbox); **24** Michael Herck, RO, 13 (DNF-accident damage); **25** Andreas Zuber, A, 8 (DNF-accident); **26** Roldán Rodríguez, E, 0 (DNF-accident).

Fastest race lap: Clos, 1m 30.063s, 115.618mph/186.069km/h.

Pole position: Kobayashi.

Championship points – Drivers: 1 Grosjean, 18; **2** Mortara, 10; **3** D'Ambrosio, 10; **4** Petrov, 8; **5** van der Garde, 5; **5** Filippi, 5.

Teams: 1 Barwa Addax Team, 26; **2** DAMS, 13; **3** Telmex Arden International.

GP2 SERIES, Monte Carlo Street Circuit, Monaco, 22/23 May. Round 2. 45 and 27 laps of the 2.075-mile/3.340km circuit.

Race 1 (93.392 miles/150.300km).

1 Romain Grosjean, F, 1h 03m 06.299s, 88.796mph/142.904km/h; **2** Vitaly Petrov, RUS, 1h 03m 12.899s; **3** Andreas Zuber, A, 1h 03m 37.339s; **4** Lucas Di Grassi, BR, 1h 03m 54.283s*; **5** Nico Hülkenberg, D, 1h 03m 55.742s*; **6** Jérôme D'Ambrosio, B, 1h 04m 06.076s; **7** Karun Chandhok, IND, 1h 04m 08.088s; **8** Pastor Maldonado, YV, 1h 04m 26.535s; **9** Davide Rigon, I, 1h 04m 27.547s; **10** Javier Villa, E, 1h 04m 41.388s*; **11** Roldán Rodríguez, E, 1h 04m 42.845s*; **12** Sergio Pérez, MEX, 44 laps; **13** Luiz Razia, BR, 44; **14** Giacomo Ricci, I, 44; **15** Davide Valsecchi, I, 43 (DNF-accident); **16** Michael Herck, RO, 43; **17** Giedo van der Garde, NL, 38; **18** Álvaro Parente, P, 36 (DNF-accident); **19** Edoardo Mortara, I, 35 (DNF-accident); **20** Luca Filippi, I, 34 (DNF-accident); **21** Kamui Kobayashi, J, 18 (DNF-accident); **22** Daniel Clos, E, 16 (DNF-acciodent); **23** Diego Nunes, BR, 13 (DNF-clutch); **24** Alberto Valério, BR, 5 (DNF-accident); **25** Nelson Panciatici, F, 4 (DNF-accident).

* includes 25-sec penalty for cutting corner.

Fastest race lap: Grosjean, 1m 21.823s, 91.311mph/146.951km/h.

Pole position: Grosjean, 1m 19.498s, 93.982mph/151.249km/h.

Race 2 (56.035 miles/90.180km).

1 Pastor Maldonado, YV, 39m 02.772s, 86.106mph/138.574km/h; **2** Jérôme D'Ambrosio, B, 39m 04.277s; **3** Nico Hülkenberg, D, 39m 06.317s; **4** Lucas Di Grassi, BR, 39m 07.252s; **5** Andreas Zuber, A, 39m 09.266s; **6** Vitaly Petrov, RUS, 39m 12.121s; **7** Davide Rigon, I, 39m 13.220s; **8** Javier Villa, E, 39m 56.006s; **9** Sergio Pérez, MEX, 39m 59.009s; **10** Luiz Razia, BR, 40m 00.542s; **11** Giedo van der Garde, NL, 40m 01.354s; **12** Kamui Kobayashi, J, 40m 02.468s; **13** Edoardo Mortara, I, 40m 06.482s; **14** Diego Nunes, BR, 40m 07.612s; **15** Nelson Panciatici, F, 40m 10.453s; **16** Michael Herck, RO, 26 laps; **17** Romain Grosjean, F, 25 (DNF-accident); **18** Davide Valsecchi, I, 25; **19** Daniel Clos, E, 23 (DNF-accident); **20** Alberto Valério, BR, 23 (DNF-accident); **21** Luca Filippi, I, 23 (DNF-withdrew); **22** Karun Chandhok, IND, 21 (DNF-driveshaft); **23** Giacomo Ricci, I, 18 (DNF-lost power); **24** Álvaro Parente, P, 15 (DNF-tyre); **25** Roldán Rodríguez, E, 2 (DNF-accident).

Fastest race lap: Petrov, 1m 22.045s, 91.064mph/146.553km/h.

Pole position: Maldonado.

Championship points – Drivers: 1 Grosjean, 31; **2** Petrov, 18; **3** D'Ambrosio, 18; **4** Maldonado, 12; **5** Mortara, 10; **6** Hülkenberg, 8.

Teams: 1 Barwa Addax Team, 49; **2** DAMS, 21; **3** ART Grand Prix, 20.

GP2 SERIES, Istanbul Speed Park, Tuzla, Turkey, 6/7 June. Round 3. 34 and 23 laps of the 3.317-mile/5.338km circuit.

Race 1 (112.645 miles/181.284km).

1 Vitaly Petrov, RUS, 57m 57.260s, 116.620mph/187.682km/h; **2** Luca Filippi, I, 58m 03.823s; **3** Davide Valsecchi, I, 58m 04.415s; **4** Alberto Valério, BR, 58m 16.909s; **5** Nico Hülkenberg, D, 58m 17.208s; **6** Pastor Maldonado, YV, 58m 21.227s; **7** Javier Villa, E, 58m 24.271s; **8** Lucas Di Grassi, BR, 58m 25.768s; **9** Andreas Zuber, A, 58m 26.095s; **10** Davide Rigon, I, 58m 26.572s; **11** Diego Nunes, BR, 58m 26.972s; **12** Daniel Clos, E, 58m 29.109s; **13** Karun Chandhok, IND, 58m 31.819s; **14** Ricardo Teixeira, ANG, 58m 36.261s; **15** Giedo van der Garde, NL, 58m 47.476s*; **16** Roldán Rodríguez, E, 26 laps (DNF-mechanical); **17** Romain Grosjean, F, 25 (DNF-hydraulics); **18** Edoardo Mortara, I, 20 (DNF-accident); **19** Nelson Panciatici, F, 18 (DNF-engine); **20** Álvaro Parente, P, 15 (DNF-spin); **21** Giacomo Ricci, I, 14 (DNF-accident); **22** Luiz Razia, BR, 13 (DNF-electrics); **23** Jérôme D'Ambrosio, B, 7 (DNF-engine); **24** Michael Herck, RO, 4 (DNF-spin); **25** Sergio Pérez, MEX, 1 (DNF-accident); **26** Kamui Kobayashi, J, 1 (DNF-accident).

* includes 25-sec penalty for overtaking safety car.

Fastest race lap: Chandhok, 1m 36.679s, 123.509mph/198.769km/h.

Pole position: Hülkenberg, 1m 34.404s, 126.486mph/203.559km/h.

Race 2 (76.159 miles/122.566km).

1 Lucas Di Grassi, BR, 37m 17.705s, 122.524mph/197.183km/h; **2** Javier Villa, E, 37m 21.558s; **3** Vitaly Petrov, RUS, 37m 23.056s; **4** Nico Hülkenberg, D, 37m 26.696s; **5** Pastor Maldonado, YV, 37m 28.131s; **6** Alberto Valério, BR, 37m 28.902s; **7** Daniel Clos, E, 37m 33.986s; **8** Davide Rigon, I, 37m 37.771s; **9** Edoardo Mortara, I, 37m 42.073s; **10** Álvaro Parente, P, 37m 42.401s; **11** Diego Nunes, BR, 37m 46.376s; **12** Romain Grosjean, F, 37m 50.471s; **13** Giedo van der Garde, NL, 37m 52.336s; **14** Karun Chandhok, IND, 37m 53.151s; **15** Jérôme D'Ambrosio, B, 37m 57.728s; **16** Sergio Pérez, MEX, 37m 58.876s; **17** Roldán Rodríguez, E, 38m 00.018s; **18** Ricardo Teixeira, ANG, 38m 09.943s; **19** Andreas Zuber, A, 38m 20.037s; **20** Luiz Razia, BR, 38m 55.473s; **21** Kamui Kobayashi, J, 19 laps; **22** Luca Filippi, I, 18 (DNF-withdrew); **23** Giacomo Ricci, I, 14 (DNF-mechanical); **24** Nelson Panciatici, F, 12 (DNF-accident damage); **25** Michael Herck, RO, 3 (DNF-spin); **26** Davide Valsecchi, I, 0 (DNF-accident).

Fastest race lap: Di Grassi, 1m 36.725s, 123.451mph/198.674km/h.

Pole position: Di Grassi.

Championship points – Drivers: 1 Petrov, 33; **2** Grosjean, 31; **3** D'Ambrosio, 18; **4** Maldonado, 17; **5** Hülkenberg, 17; **6** Di Grassi, 16.

Teams: 1 Barwa Addax Team, 64; **2** ART Grand Prix, 34; **3** DAMS, 21.

GP2 SERIES, Silverstone Grand Prix Circuit, Towcester, Northamptonshire, Great Britain, 20/21 June. Round 4. 36 and 23 laps of the 3.194-mile/5.141km circuit.

Race 1 (114.936 miles/184.971km).

1 Alberto Valério, BR, 55m 32.255s, 124.170mph/199.833km/h; **2** Lucas Di Grassi, BR, 55m 33.493s; **3** Nico Hülkenberg, D, 55m 37.544s; **4** Sergio Pérez, MEX, 55m 37.805s; **5** Romain Grosjean, F, 55m 46.664s; **6** Karun Chandhok, IND, 55m 48.647s; **7** Pastor Maldonado, YV, 55m 54.439s; **8** Andreas Zuber, A, 55m 59.144s; **9** Michael Herck, RO, 56m 08.576s; **10** Davide Valsecchi, I, 56m 11.970s; **11** Diego Nunes, BR, 56m 12.764s; **12** Roldán Rodríguez, E, 56m 13.734s; **13** Daniel Clos, E, 56m 17.856s; **14** Luca Filippi, I, 56m 18.502s; **15** Vitaly Petrov, RUS, 56m 18.670s; **16** Davide Rigon, I, 56m 29.351s; **17** Giacomo Ricci, I, 56m 43.015s; **18** Nelson Panciatici, F, 56m 48.506s; **19** Jérôme D'Ambrosio, B, 56m 51.404s; **20** Luiz Razia, BR, 35 laps (DNF-accident damage); **21** Javier Villa, E, 30 (DNF-engine); **22** Giedo van der Garde, NL, 29 (DNF-spin); **23** Ricardo Teixeira, ANG, 8 (DNF-engine); **24** Álvaro Parente, P, 1 (DNF-accident); **25** Kamui Kobayashi, J, 0 (DNF-accident); **26** Edoardo Mortara, I, 0 (DNF-accident).

Fastest race lap: Hülkenberg, 1m 29.914s, 127.901mph/205.836km/h.

Pole position: Grosjean, 1m 25.899s, 133.879mph/215.457km/h.

Race 2 (73.408 miles/118.138km).

1 Pastor Maldonado, YV, 35m 27.955s, 124.188mph/199.861km/h; **2** Andreas Zuber, A, 35m 28.573s; **3** Karun Chandhok, IND, 35m 31.372s; **4** Romain Grosjean, F, 35m 31.402s; **5** Nico Hülkenberg, D, 35m 31.811s; **6** Sergio Pérez, MEX, 35m 31.891s; **7** Alberto Valério, BR, 35m 32.271s; **8** Michael Herck, RO, 35m 32.479s; **9** Roldán Rodríguez, E, 35m 32.985s; **10** Vitaly Petrov, RUS, 35m 33.418s; **11** Álvaro Parente, P, 35m 33.871s; **12** Jérôme D'Ambrosio, B, 35m 34.508s; **13** Giedo van der Garde, NL, 35m 35.143s; **14** Davide Valsecchi, I, 35m 36.294s; **15** Javier Villa, E, 35m 43.199s; **16** Luca Filippi, I, 36m 02.824s; **17** Kamui Kobayashi, J, 36m 04.180s; **18** Ricardo Teixeira, ANG, 36m 04.643s; **19** Lucas Di Grassi, BR, 22 laps; **20** Davide Rigon, I, 22; **21** Edoardo Mortara, I, 19 (DNF-engine); **22** Daniel Clos, E, 19 (DNF-spin); **23** Nelson Panciatici, F, 17 (DNF-mechanical); **24** Luiz Razia, BR, 11 (DNF-accident); **25** Diego Nunes, BR, 0 (DNF-spin).

Did not start: Giacomo Ricci, I, 0 (fuel pump).

Fastest race lap: Di Grassi, 1m 29.069s, 129.114mph/207.789km/h.

Pole position: Zuber.

Championship points – Drivers: 1 Grosjean, 40; **2** Petrov, 33; **3** Maldonado, 26; **4** Hülkenberg, 26; **5** Di Grassi, 24; **6** D'Ambrosio, 18.

Teams: 1 Barwa Addax Team, 73; **2** ART Grand Prix, 52; **3** Fat Burner Racing Engineering, 24.

GP2 SERIES, Nürburgring, Nürburg/Eifel, Germany, 11/12 July. Round 5. 35 and 24 laps of the 3.199-mile/5.148km circuit.

Race 1 (111.948 miles/180.163km).

1 Nico Hülkenberg, D, 1h 00m 10.875s, 111.611mph/179.620km/h; **2** Roldán Rodríguez, E, 1h 00m 24.806s; **3** Andreas Zuber, A, 1h 00m 32.640s; **4** Vitaly Petrov, RUS, 1h 00m 39.991s; **5** Javier Villa, E, 1h 00m 42.409s; **6** Álvaro Parente, P, 1h 00m 58.875s; **7** Lucas Di Grassi, BR, 1h 01m 01.241s; **8** Sergio Pérez, MEX, 1h 01m 01.992s; **9** Kamui Kobayashi, J, 1h 01m 15.289s; **10** Jérôme D'Ambrosio, B, 1h 01m 16.101s; **11** Karun Chandhok, IND, 1h 01m 19.941s; **12** Giedo van der Garde, NL, 1h 01m 20.784s; **13** Davide Valsecchi, I, 1h 01m 25.981s; **14** Michael Herck, RO, 1h 01m 26.596s; **15** Rodolfo Gonzalez, YV, 1h 01m 33.596s; **16** Daniel Clos, E, 34 laps; **17** Edoardo Mortara, I, 34; **18** Romain Grosjean, F, 33 (DNF-hydraulics); **19** Nelson Panciatici, F, 33; **20** Alberto Valério, BR, 24 (DNF-mechanical); **21** Franck Perera, F, 21 (DNF-mechanical); **22** Diego Nunes, BR, 10 (DNF-accident); **23** Pastor Maldonado, YV, 10 (DNF-accident); **24** Ricardo Teixeira, ANG, 6 (DNF-brakes); **25** Luca Filippi, I, 0 (DNF-accident); **26** Luiz Razia, BR, 0 (DNF-accident).

Fastest race lap: Mortara, 1m 41.119s, 113.883mph/183.277km/h.

Pole position: Hülkenberg, 1m 38.161s, 117.315mph/188.800km/h.

Race 2 (76.761 miles/123.535km).

1 Nico Hülkenberg, D, 46m 49.622s, 98.354mph/158.286km/h; **2** Álvaro Parente, P, 47m 16.076s; **3** Kamui Kobayashi, J, 47m 23.123s; **4** Vitaly Petrov, RUS, 47m 23.310s; **5** Romain Grosjean, F, 47m 34.376s; **6** Javier Villa, E, 47m 39.697s; **7** Jérôme D'Ambrosio, B, 47m 42.142s; **8** Daniel Clos, E, 47m 43.583s; **9** Pastor Maldonado, YV, 47m 46.576s; **10** Davide Valsecchi, I, 48m 03.983s; **11** Diego Nunes, BR, 48m 19.204s; **12** Michael Herck, RO, 48m 22.708s; **13** Nelson Panciatici, F, 48m 24.292s; **14** Luiz Razia, BR, 48m 24.802s; **15** Ricardo Teixeira, ANG, 48m 29.192s; **16** Franck Perera, F, 23 laps; **17** Alberto Valério, BR, 23; **18** Luca Filippi, I, 22 (DNF-accident); **19** Rodolfo Gonzalez, YV, 22; **20** Sergio Pérez, MEX, 21 (DNF-spin); **21** Roldán Rodríguez, E, 14 (DNF-accident); **22** Andreas Zuber, A, 11 (DNF-spin); **23** Edoardo Mortara, I, 7 (DNF-accident); **24** Giedo van der Garde, NL, 1 (DNF-spin); **25** Lucas Di Grassi, BR, 0 (DNF-accident); **26** Karun Chandhok, IND, 0 (DNF-accident).

Fastest race lap: Valério, 1m 46.200s, 108.435mph/174.508km/h.

Pole position: Pérez.

Championship points – Drivers: 1 Hülkenberg, 46; **2** Grosjean, 42; **3** Petrov, 41; **4** Maldonado, 26; **5** Di Grassi, 26; **6** Zuber, 20.

Teams: 1 Barwa Addax Team, 83; **2** ART Grand Prix, 72; **3** Fat Burner Racing Engineering, 26.

GP2 SERIES, Hungaroring, Mogyorod, Budapest, Hungary, 25/26 July. Round 6. 42 and 28 laps of the 2.722-mile/4.381km circuit.

Race 1 (114.309 miles/183.962km).

1 Nico Hülkenberg, D, 1h 04m 46.079s, 105.893mph/170.419km/h; **2** Lucas Di Grassi, BR, 1h 05m 01.417s; **3** Javier Villa, E, 1h 05m 02.449s; **4** Pastor Maldonado, YV, 1h 05m 03.172s; **5** Davide Valsecchi, I, 1h 05m 03.235s; **6** Luca Filippi, I, 1h 05m 09.181s; **7** Giedo van der Garde, NL, 1h 05m 18.044s; **8** Davide Rigon, I, 1h 05m 18.635s; **9** Álvaro Parente, P, 1h 05m 20.253s; **10** Romain Grosjean, F, 1h 05m 24.714s; **11** Daniel Clos, E, 1h 05m 32.132s; **12** Edoardo Mortara, I, 1h 05m 37.056s; **13** Kamui Kobayashi, J, 1h 05m 37.348s; **14** Nelson Panciatici, F, 1h 05m 57.234s; **15** Michael Herck, RO, 1h 05m 57.309s; **16** Jérôme D'Ambrosio, B, 1h 05m 58.076s; **17** Karun Chandhok, IND, 40 laps (DNF-tyres); **18** Diego Nunes, BR, 36 (DNF-throttle); **19** Ricardo Teixeira, ANG, 33 (DNF-spin); **20** Vitaly Petrov, RUS, 20 (DNF-engine); **21** Roldán Rodríguez, E, 1 (DNF-accident); **22** Andreas Zuber, A, 0 (DNF-accident); **23** Alberto Valério, BR, 0 (DNF-accident); **24** Sergio Pérez, MEX, 0 (DNF-accident); **25** Luiz Razia, BR, 0 (DNF-accident).

Excluded: Franck Perera, F (caused accident in qualifying).

Fastest race lap: Hülkenberg, 1m 30.531s, 108.250mph/174.212km/h.

Pole position: Di Grassi, 1m 27.867s, 111.532mph/179.494km/h.

Race 2 (76.198 miles/122.628km).

1 Giedo van der Garde, NL, 44m 17.552s, 103.219mph/166.115km/h; **2** Luca Filippi, I, 44m 17.937s; **3** Lucas Di Grassi, BR, 44m 18.630s; **4** Romain Grosjean, F, 44m 19.251s; **5** Javier Villa, E, 44m 19.645s; **6** Álvaro Parente, P, 44m 21.013s; **7** Nico Hülkenberg, D, 44m 21.300s; **8** Kamui Kobayashi, J, 44m 21.641s; **9** Davide Valsecchi, I, 44m 22.372s; **10** Karun Chandhok, IND, 44m 27.893s; **11** Daniel Clos, E, 44m 29.283s; **12** Vitaly Petrov, RUS, 44m 29.374s; **13** Roldán Rodríguez, E, 44m 29.905s; **14** Edoardo Mortara, I, 44m 30.664s; **15** Diego Nunes, BR, 44m 31.214s; **16** Sergio Pérez, MEX, 44m 32.709s; **17** Andreas Zuber, A, 44m 39.279s; **18** Franck Perera, F, 44m 39.598s; **19** Ricardo Teixeira, ANG, 44m 42.837s; **20** Nelson Panciatici, F, 44m 57.377s; **21** Alberto Valério, BR, 26 laps; **22** Jérôme D'Ambrosio, B, 19 (DNF-exhaust); **23** Luiz Razia, BR, 18 (DNF-spin); **24** Pastor Maldonado, YV, 9 (DNF-suspension); **25** Davide Rigon, I, 0 (DNF-accident).

Did not start: Michael Herck, RO.

Fastest race lap: Filippi, 1m 29.788s, 109.146mph/175.653km/h.

Pole position: Rigon.

Championship points – Drivers: 1 Hülkenberg, 57; **2** Grosjean, 45; **3** Petrov, 41; **4** Di Grassi, 40; **5** Maldonado, 31; **6** Filippi, 22.

Teams: 1 ART Grand Prix, 88; **2** Barwa Addax Team, 86; **3** Super Nova Racing, 42.

GP2 SERIES, Valencia Street Circuit, Spain, 22/23 August. Round 7. 31 and 23 laps of the 3.367-mile/5.419km circuit.

Race 1 (104.384 miles/167.989km).

1 Vitaly Petrov, RUS, 56m 24.157s, 111.041mph/178.703km/h; **2** Nico Hülkenberg, D, 56m 24.553s; **3** Sergio Pérez, MEX, 56m 40.161s; **4** Álvaro Parente, P, 56m 47.079s; **5** Roldán Rodríguez, E, 56m 51.048s; **6** Edoardo Mortara, I, 57m 02.601s; **7** Luca Filippi, I, 57m 08.310s; **8** Kamui Kobayashi, J, 57m 23.621s; **9** Jérôme D'Ambrosio, B, 57m 24.116s; **10** Davide Valsecchi, I, 57m 29.160s; **11** Diego Nunes, BR, 57m 31.353s; **12** Davide Rigon, I, 57m 31.769s; **13** Michael Herck, RO, 57m 38.974s; **14** Giedo van der Garde, NL, 57m 40.511s; **15** Franck Perera, F, 57m 41.515s; **16** Andreas Zuber, A, 57m 43.993s; **17** Alberto Valério, BR, 58m 08.197s; **18** Javier Villa, E, 30 laps (DNF-accident); **19** Lucas Di Grassi, BR, 28 (DNF-gearbox); **20** Karun Chandhok, IND, 26 (DNF-suspension); **21** Stefano Coletti, MC, 16 (DNF-clutch); **22** Luiz Razia, BR, 3 (DNF-accident); **23** Nelson Panciatici, F, 3 (DNF-accident); **24** Ricardo Teixeira, ANG, 2 (DNF-accident); **25** Daniel Clos, E, 0 (DNF-accident).

Disqualified: Pastor Maldonado, YV, finished 8th in 57m 16.653s (bodywork irregularity).

Fastest race lap: Hülkenberg, 1m 47.041s, 113.246mph/182.251km/h.

Pole position: Hülkenberg, 1m 45.025s, 115.420mph/185.750km/h.

Race 2 (77.446 miles/124.637km).

1 Nico Hülkenberg, D, 44m 36.084s, 104.183mph/167.667km/h; **2** Sergio Pérez, MEX, 44m 47.693s; **3** Vitaly Petrov, RUS, 44m 49.313s; **4** Jérôme D'Ambrosio, B, 45m 04.664s; **5** Diego Nunes, BR, 45m 05.279s; **6** Karun Chandhok, IND, 45m 07.692s; **7** Davide Rigon, I, 45m 08.185s; **8** Pastor Maldonado, YV, 45m 08.826s; **9** Javier Villa, E, 45m 10.648s; **10** Alberto Valério, BR, 45m 11.868s; **11** Kamui Kobayashi, J, 45m 15.500s; **12** Edoardo Mortara, I, 45m 17.050s; **13** Luiz Razia, BR, 45m 21.198s; **14** Ricardo Teixeira, ANG, 45m 24.944s; **15** Nelson Panciatici, F, 45m 54.862s; **16** Franck Perera, F, 21 laps; **17** Daniel Clos, E, 11 (DNF-accident damage); **18** Stefano Coletti, MC, 10 (DNF-accident); **19** Álvaro Parente, P, 5 (DNF-accident); **20** Roldán Rodríguez, E, 2 (DNF-accident); **21** Luca Filippi, I, 1 (DNF-accident damage); **22** Davide Valsecchi, I, 0 (DNF-driveshaft); **23** Michael Herck, RO, 0 (DNF-accident); **24** Giedo van der Garde, NL, 0 (DNF-accident); **25** Andreas Zuber, A, 0 (DNF-accident); **26** Lucas Di Grassi, BR, 0 (DNF-accident).

Fastest race lap: Hülkenberg, 1m 46.487s, 113.835mph/183.199km/h.

Pole position: Kobayashi.

Championship points – Drivers: 1 Hülkenberg, 75; **2** Petrov, 55; **3** Grosjean, 45; **4** Di Grassi, 40; **5** Maldonado, 31; **6** Filippi, 24.

Teams: 1 ART Grand Prix, 106; **2** Barwa Addax Team, 100; **3** Super Nova Racing, 44.

GP2 SERIES, Circuit de Spa-Francorchamps, Stavelot, Belgium, 29/30 August. Round 8. 25 and 18 laps of the 4.352-mile/7.004km circuit.

Race 1 (108.725 miles/174.976km).

1 Álvaro Parente, P, 54m 12.997s, 120.323mph/193.641km/h; **2** Nico Hülkenberg, D, 54m 13.940s; **3** Lucas Di Grassi, BR, 54m 16.176s; **4** Pastor Maldonado, YV, 54m 16.465s; **5** Roldán Rodríguez, E, 54m 17.346s; **6** Giedo van der Garde, NL, 54m 17.684s; **7** Kamui Kobayashi, J, 54m 18.466s; **8** Edoardo Mortara, I, 54m 18.969s; **9** Diego Nunes, BR, 54m 42.102s*; **10** Daniel Clos, E, 54m 45.312s**; **11** Nelson Panciatici, F, 54m 48.471s**; **12** Stefano Coletti, MC, 23 laps; **13** Javier Villa, E, 22; **14** Jérôme D'Ambrosio, B, 20 (DNF-accident damage); **15** Luca Filippi, I, 13 (DNF-accident); **16** Davide Valsecchi, I, 13 (DNF-accident); **17** Karun Chandhok, IND, 7 (DNF-accident); **18** Davide Rigon, I, 7 (DNF-accident); **19** Vitaly Petrov, RUS, 6 (DNF-engine); **20** Michael Herck, RO, 0 (DNF-clutch); **21** Alberto Valério, BR, 0 (DNF-accident); **22** Ricardo Teixeira, ANG, 0 (DNF-clutch).

* includes 25-sec penalty for cutting corner.

** includes 25-sec penalty for speeding under yellow flags.

Did not start: Sergio Pérez, MEX, 0 (hydraulics).

Did not qualify: Franck Perera, F

Excluded from meeting: Andreas Zuber, A; Luiz Razla, BR.

Fastest race lap: Parente, 1m 57.468s, 133.377mph/214.649km/h.

Pole position: Parente, 1m 54.970s, 136.274mph/219.312km/h.

Race 2 (78.260 miles/125.948km).

1 Giedo van der Garde, NL, 37m 54.281s, 123.880mph/199.365km/h; **2** Roldán Rodríguez, E, 37m 57.383s; **3** Diego Nunes, BR, 37m 59.279s; **4** Sergio Pérez, MEX, 38m 00.573s; **5** Davide Rigon, I, 38m 08.090s; **6** Vitaly Petrov, RUS, 38m 11.740s; **7** Karun Chandhok, IND, 38m 13.081s; **8** Davide Valsecchi, I, 38m 14.320s; **9** Michael Herck, RO, 38m 15.684s; **10** Javier Villa, E, 38m 17.141s; **11** Kamui Kobayashi, J, 38m 19.572s; **12** Alberto Valério, BR, 38m 30.326s; **13** Nelson Panciatici, F, 38m 43.027s; **14** Ricardo Teixeira, ANG, 38m 49.060s; **15** Edoardo Mortara, I, 4 laps (DNF-accident); **16** Lucas Di Grassi, BR, 4 (DNF-accident); **17** Álvaro Parente, P, 2 (DNF-engine); **18** Pastor Maldonado, YV, 1 (DNF-accident); **19** Nico Hülkenberg, D, 0 (DNF-accident); **20** Daniel Clos, E, 0 (DNF-accident); **21** Jérôme D'Ambrosio, B, 0 (DNF-accident); **22** Luca Filippi, I, 0 (DNF-clutch).

Did not start: Coletti.

Did not qualify: Perera

Excluded: Zuber; Razla.

Fastest race lap: Pérez, 1m 56.731s, 134.219mph/216.004km/h.

Pole position: Mortara.

Championship points – Drivers: 1 Hülkenberg, 83; **2** Petrov, 56; **3** Di Grassi, 46; **4** Grosjean, 45; **5** Maldonado, 36; **6** Parente, 27.

Teams: 1 ART Grand Prix, 119; **2** Barwa Addax Team, 101; **3** Fat Burner Racing Engineering, 46.

GP2 SERIES, Autodromo Nazionale di Monza, Milan, Italy, 12/13 September. Round 9. 32 and 21 laps of the 3.600-mile/5.793km circuit.
Race 1 (114.995 miles/185.067km).
1 Giedo van der Garde, NL, 1h 03m 18.437s, 108.987mph/175.398km/h; **2** Vitaly Petrov, RUS, 1h 03m 20.757s; **3** Lucas Di Grassi, BR, 1h 03m 31.718s; **4** Jérôme D'Ambrosio, B, 1h 03m 32.807s; **5** Edoardo Mortara, I, 1h 03m 43.105s; **6** Nico Hülkenberg, D, 1h 03m 43.404s; **7** Javier Villa, E, 1h 03m 52.494s; **8** Luiz Razia, BR, 1h 03m 59.021s; **9** Davide Rigon, I, 1h 04m 02.307s; **10** Diego Nunes, BR, 1h 04m 06.102s; **11** Álvaro Parente, P, 1h 04m 14.222s*; **12** Andreas Zuber, A, 1h 04m 27.948s; **13** Roldán Rodríguez, E, 1h 04m 29.526s; **14** Davide Valsecchi, I, 1h 04m 30.431s; **15** Daniel Clos, E, 1h 05m 06.576s; **16** Ricardo Teixeira, ANG, 31 laps; **17** Kamui Kobayashi, J, 31; **18** Johnny Cecotto Jr., YV, 30 (DNF-accident); **19** Karun Chandhok, IND, 29 (DNF-spin); **20** Michael Herck, RO, 28 (DNF-accident); **21** Luca Filippi, I, 18 (DNF-engine); **22** Sergio Pérez, MEX, 6 (DNF-accident); **23** Pastor Maldonado, YV, 6 (DNF-accident); **24** Alberto Valério, BR, 0 (DNF-accident).
* includes 25-sec penalty for speeding in pit lane.
Fastest race lap: Mortara, 1m 43.283s, 125.467mph/201.919km/h.
Pole position: Petrov, 1m 30.007s, 143.972mph/231.701km/h.

Race 2 (75.400 miles/121.344km).
1 Luiz Razia, BR, 35m 12.921s, 128.466mph/206.746km/h; **2** Lucas Di Grassi, BR, 35m 15.497s; **3** Nico Hülkenberg, D, 35m 17.876s; **4** Jérôme D'Ambrosio, B, 35m 20.295s; **5** Vitaly Petrov, RUS, 35m 20.841s; **6** Giedo van der Garde, NL, 35m 21.608s; **7** Roldán Rodríguez, E, 35m 22.054s; **8** Davide Rigon, I, 35m 26.316s; **9** Davide Valsecchi, I, 35m 37.730s; **10** Javier Villa, E, 35m 38.413s; **11** Alberto Valério, BR, 35m 39.175s; **12** Karun Chandhok, IND, 35m 46.447s; **13** Michael Herck, RO, 35m 48.241s; **14** Ricardo Teixeira, ANG, 36m 12.543s; **15** Pastor Maldonado, YV, 19 laps (DNF-accident); **16** Johnny Cecotto Jr., YV, 18 (DNF-accident); **17** Kamui Kobayashi, J, 18 (DNF-electrics); **18** Luca Filippi, I, 15 (DNF-engine); **19** Andreas Zuber, A, 11 (DNF-accident); **20** Álvaro Parente, P, 6 (DNF-spin); **21** Edoardo Mortara, I, 6 (DNF-accident); **22** Sergio Pérez, MEX, 1 (DNF-engine); **23** Diego Nunes, BR, 0 (DNF-accident); **24** Daniel Clos, E, 0 (DNF-accident).
Fastest race lap: Filippi, 1m 32.553s, 140.012mph/225.328km/h.
Pole position: Razia.
Championship points – Drivers: 1 Hülkenberg, 90; **2** Petrov, 68; **3** Di Grassi, 57; **4** Grosjean, 45; **5** Maldonado, 36; **6** van der Garde, 33.
Teams: 1 ART Grand Prix, 126; **2** Barwa Addax Team, 113; **3** Fat Burner Racing Engineering, 57.

GP2 SERIES, Autódromo Internacional do Algarve, Portimão, Portugal, 19/20 September. Round 10. 37 and 24 laps of the 2.911-mile/4.684km circuit.
Race 1 (107.540 miles/173.069km).
1 Nico Hülkenberg, D, 1h 03m 43.837s, 101.245mph/162.938km/h; **2** Luca Filippi, I, 1h 03m 53.567s; **3** Lucas Di Grassi, BR, 1h 03m 53.773s; **4** Vitaly Petrov, RUS, 1h 03m 54.197s; **5** Roldán Rodríguez, E, 1h 03m 58.932s; **6** Kamui Kobayashi, J, 1h 04m 07.934s; **7** Davide Valsecchi, I, 1h 04m 13.174s; **8** Andreas Zuber, A, 1h 04m 16.138s; **9** Daniel Clos, E, 1h 04m 18.310s; **10** Luiz Razia, BR, 1h 04m 18.933s; **11** Pastor Maldonado, YV, 1h 04m 21.388s; **12** Diego Nunes, BR, 1h 04m 22.315s; **13** Javier Villa, E, 1h 04m 23.857s; **14** Davide Rigon, I, 1h 04m 41.849s*; **15** Ricardo Teixeira, ANG, 1h 04m 46.980s*; **16** Álvaro Parente, P, 22 laps (DNF-accident); **17** Sergio Pérez, MEX, 22 (DNF-accident); **18** Giedo van der Garde, NL, 22 (DNF-hydraulics); **19** Alberto Valério, BR, 4 (DNF-accident); **20** Jérôme D'Ambrosio, B, 4 (DNF-accident); **21** Karun Chandhok, IND, 1 (DNF-engine); **22** Edoardo Mortara, I, 0 (DNF-accident); **23** Johnny Cecotto Jr., YV, 0 (DNF-accident).
* includes 25-sec penalty for cutting corner.
Disqualified: Michael Herck, RO, finished 6th in 1h 03m 59.255s (ride-height breach).
Fastest race lap: Nunes, 1m 32.113s, 113.750mph/183.062km/h.
Pole position: Petrov, 1m 30.819s, 115.370mph/185.670km/h.

Race 2 (69.704 miles/112.177km).
1 Luca Filippi, I, 1h 01m 55.822s, 67.531mph/108.680km/h; **2** Javier Villa, E, 1h 02m 04.173s; **3** Daniel Clos, E, 1h 02m 04.848s; **4** Álvaro Parente, P, 1h 02m 05.252s; **5** Diego Nunes, BR, 1h 02m 09.468s; **6** Giedo van der Garde, NL, 1h 02m 09.754s; **7** Alberto Valério, BR, 1h 02m 15.179s; **8** Edoardo Mortara, I, 1h 02m 17.496s; **9** Davide Rigon, I, 1h 02m 17.704s; **10** Jérôme D'Ambrosio, B, 1h 02m 19.853s; **11** Sergio Pérez, MEX, 1h 02m 24.963s*; **12** Andreas Zuber, A, 1h 02m 26.066s; **13** Karun Chandhok, IND, 1h 02m 29.247s; **14** Davide Valsecchi, I, 1h 02m 29.691s; **15** Lucas Di Grassi, BR, 1h 02m 30.612s; **16** Nico Hülkenberg, D, 1h 02m 30.858s; **17** Luiz Razia, BR, 1h 02m 35.368s; **18** Johnny Cecotto Jr., YV, 1h 02m 46.506s; **19** Kamui Kobayashi, J, 1h 02m 47.550s; **20** Pastor Maldonado, YV, 1h 02m 48.379s; **21** Ricardo Teixeira, ANG, 23 laps; **22** Roldán Rodríguez, E, 5 (DNF-mechanical); **23** Vitaly Petrov, RUS, 0 (DNF-accident); **24** Michael Herck, RO, 0 (DNF-accident).
* includes 25-sec penalty for overtaking behind safety car.
Fastest race lap: Hülkenberg, 1m 32.388s, 113.411mph/182.517km/h.
Pole position: Zuber.

Final championship points
Drivers
1 Nico Hülkenberg, D, 100; **2** Vitaly Petrov, RUS, 75; **3** Lucas Di Grassi, BR, 63; **4** Romain Grosjean, F, 45; **5** Luca Filippi, I, 40; **6** Pastor Maldonado, YV, 36; **7** Giedo van der Garde, NL, 34; **8** Álvaro Parente, P, 30; **9** Jérôme D'Ambrosio, B, 29; **10** Javier Villa, E, 27; **11** Roldán Rodríguez, E, 25; **12** Sergio Pérez, MEX, 22; **13** Andreas Zuber, A, 21; **14** Edoardo Mortara, I, 19; **15** Alberto Valério, BR, 16; **16** Kamui Kobayashi, J, 13; **17** Davide Valsecchi, I, 12; **18** Karun Chandhok, IND, 10; **19** Luiz Razia, BR, 8; **20** Diego Nunes, BR, 8; **21** Daniel Clos, E, 4; **22** Davide Rigon, I, 3.

Teams
1 ART Grand Prix, 136; **2** Barwa Addax Team, 122; **3** Super Nova Racing, 67; **4** Fat Burner Racing Engineering, 67; **5** iSport International, 42; **6** DAMS, 42; **7** Piquet GP, 41; **8** Telmex Arden International, 41; **9** Ocean Racing Technology, 40; **10** Party Poker Racing.Com Scuderia Coloni, 29; **11** Durango, 10; **12** Trident Racing, 3.

GP2 Asia Series

All cars are Dallara-Renault.

2008–2009

The following races were run after AUTOCOURSE 2008–2009 went to press.

GP2 ASIA SERIES, Dubai Autodrome, United Arab Emirates, 5/6 December. Round 2. 34 and 23 laps of the 3.349-mile/5.390km circuit.
Race 1 (113.872 miles/183.260km).
1 Kamui Kobayashi, J, 1h 00m 26.439s, 113.042mph/181.923km/h; **2** Davide Valsecchi, I, 1h 00m 40.817s; **3** Roldán Rodríguez, E, 1h 00m 41.979s; **4** Giedo van der Garde, NL, 1h 00m 45.842s; **5** Vitaly Petrov, RUS, 1h 00m 53.980s; **6** Sergio Pérez, MEX, 1h 00m 55.473s; **7** Jérôme D'Ambrosio, B, 1h 01m 00.451s; **8** Sakon Yamamoto, J, 1h 01m 02.519s; **9** Javier Villa, E, 1h 01m 18.658s; **10** Luiz Razia, BR, 1h 01m 23.394s; **11** Renger van der Zande, NL, 1h 01m 25.182s; **12** James Jakes, GB, 1h 01m 28.656s; **13** Giacomo Ricci, I, 1h 01m 29.293s; **14** Fabrizio Crestani, I, 1h 01m 40.513s; **15** Michael Herck, RO, 1h 02m 01.077s; **16** Alberto Valério, BR, 1h 02m 08.385s; **17** Michael Dalle Stelle, I, 33 laps; **18** Kevin Chen, USA, 33; **19** Pastor Maldonado, YV, 30; **20** Earl Bamber, NZ, 30; **21** Andreas Zuber, A, 30; **22** Yelmer Buurman, NL, 15 (DNF); **23** Diego Nunes, BR, 15 (DNF); **24** Chris van der Drift, NZ, 13 (DNF); **25** Alex Yoong, MAL, 4 (DNF); **26** Hamad Al Fardan, BRN, 3 (DNF).
Fastest race lap: Kobayashi, 1m 43.079s, 116.969mph/188.243km/h.
Pole position: Kobayashi, 1m 41.091s, 119.269mph/191.945km/h.

Race 2 (77.031 miles/123.970km).
Cancelled due to flooding.
Pole position: Yamamoto.
Championship points – Drivers: 1 Kobayashi, 22; **2** Rodríguez, 19; **3** Valsecchi, 15; **4** Villa, 10; **5** Bamber, 8; **6** Petrov, 8.
Teams: 1 DAMS, 26; **2** Piquet GP, 19; **3** Durango, 15.

GP2 ASIA SERIES, Bahrain International Circuit, Sakhir, Bahrain, 23/24 January. Round 3. 34 and 23 laps of the 3.363-mile/5.412km circuit.
Race 1 (114.184 miles/183.762km).
1 Kamui Kobayashi, J, 1h 00m 10.318s, 113.858mph/183.236km/h; **2** Jérôme D'Ambrosio, B, 1h 00m 16.210s; **3** Edoardo Mortara, I, 1h 00m 28.888s; **4** Nico Hülkenberg, D, 1h 00m 29.754s; **5** Davide Valsecchi, I, 1h 00m 30.686s; **6** Roldán Rodríguez, E, 1h 00m 34.394s; **7** Giedo van der Garde, NL, 1h 00m 35.066s; **8** Sergio Pérez, MEX, 1h 00m 37.780s; **9** Javier Villa, E, 1h 00m 41.005s; **10** Vitaly Petrov, RUS, 1h 00m 47.020s; **11** Earl Bamber, NZ, 1h 00m 48.360s; **12** Hamad Al Fardan, BRN, 1h 01m 01.742s; **13** Diego Nunes, BR, 1h 01m 05.878s; **14** Luiz Razia, BR, 1h 01m 17.294s; **15** Frankie Provenzano, I, 1h 01m 24.902s; **16** Rodolfo Gonzalez, YV, 1h 01m 28.657s; **17** Sakon Yamamoto, J, 1h 01m 28.709s; **18** Michael Herck, RO, 1h 01m 28.877s; **19** Michael Dalle Stelle, I, 1h 01m 56.503s; **20** Marco Bonanomi, I, 33 laps; **21** Kevin Chen, USA, 32; **22** James Jakes, GB, 31; **23** Giacomo Ricci, I, 21 (DNF); **24** Adrián Vallés, E, 13 (DNF); **25** Fabrizio Crestani, I, 0 (DNF).
Did not start: Yelmer Buurman, NL.
Fastest race lap: Kobayashi, 1m 43.604s, 116.852mph/188.054km/h.
Pole position: Hülkenberg, 1m 41.351s, 119.449mph/192.234km/h.

Race 2 (77.193 miles/124.230km).
1 Sergio Pérez, MEX, 40m 14.642s, 115.087mph/185.215km/h; **2** Davide Valsecchi, I, 40m 15.391s; **3** Jérôme D'Ambrosio, B, 40m 22.723s; **4** Nico Hülkenberg, D, 40m 23.317s; **5** Javier Villa, E, 40m 25.175s; **6** Kamui Kobayashi, J, 40m 25.758s; **7** Earl Bamber, NZ, 40m 30.083s; **8** Edoardo Mortara, I, 40m 30.872s; **9** Luiz Razia, BR, 40m 31.855s; **10** Marco Bonanomi, I, 40m 32.463s; **11** Sakon Yamamoto, J, 40m 32.965s; **12** Vitaly Petrov, RUS, 40m 40.108s; **13** Yelmer Buurman, NL, 40m 43.925s; **14** Giedo van der Garde, NL, 40m 51.492s; **15** Frankie Provenzano, I, 40m 55.884s; **16** Giacomo Ricci, I, 40m 59.319s; **17** Fabrizio Crestani, I, 41m 00.031s; **18** Michael Herck, RO, 41m 05.106s; **19** Adrián Vallés, E, 41m 10.555s; **20** Michael Dalle Stelle, I, 41m 18.940s; **21** Kevin Chen, USA, 41m 21.877s; **22** Diego Nunes, BR, 41m 23.714s; **23** Roldán Rodríguez, E, 22 laps; **24** Rodolfo Gonzalez, YV, 14 (DNF); **25** Hamad Al Fardan, BRN, 12 (DNF); **26** James Jakes, GB, 8 (DNF).
Fastest race lap: Nunes, 1m 43.913s, 116.504mph/187.495km/h.
Pole position: Pérez.
Championship points – Drivers: 1 Kobayashi, 34; **2** Valsecchi, 24; **3** Rodríguez, 22; **4** D'Ambrosio, 17; **5** Villa, 12; **6** Pérez, 10.
Teams: 1 DAMS, 51; **2** Durango, 24; **3** Piquet GP, 22.

GP2 ASIA SERIES, Losail International Circuit, Doha, Qatar, 13/14 February. Round 4. 34 and 23 laps of the 3.343-mile/5.380km circuit.
Race 1 (113.661 miles/182.920km).
1 Nico Hülkenberg, D, 1h 10m 38.323s, 96.542mph/155.370km/h; **2** Sergio Pérez, MEX, 1h 10m 51.618s; **3** Vitaly Petrov, RUS, 1h 10m 52.666s; **4** Kamui Kobayashi, J, 1h 10m 53.069s; **5** Jérôme D'Ambrosio, B, 1h 11m 01.742s; **6** Davide Valsecchi, I, 1h 11m 12.242s; **7** Edoardo Mortara, I, 1h 11m 13.537s; **8** Luiz Razia, BR, 1h 11m 13.664s; **9** James Jakes, GB, 1h 11m 19.485s; **10** Fabrizio Crestani, I, 1h 11m 22.097s; **11** Diego Nunes, BR, 1h 11m 23.420s; **12** Giedo van der Garde, NL, 1h 11m 25.950s; **13** Javier Villa, E, 1h 11m 26.150s; **14** Davide Rigon, I, 1h 11m 45.767s; **15** Michael Herck, RO, 1h 11m 47.647s; **16** Marco Bonanomi, I, 1h 11m 58.324s; **17** Álvaro Parente, P, 1h 12m 10.309s; **18** Kevin Chen, USA, 32 laps; **19** Frankie Provenzano, I, 30; **20** Michael Dalle Stelle, I, 30; **21** Giacomo Ricci, I, 27 (DNF); **22** Roldán Rodríguez, E, 10 (DNF); **23** Hamad Al Fardan, BRN, 9 (DNF); **24** Sakon Yamamoto, J, 0 (DNF); **25** Rodolfo Gonzalez, YV, 0 (DNF); **26** Yelmer Buurman, NL, 0 (DNF).
Fastest race lap: Parente, 1m 38.699s, 121.933mph/196.232km/h.
Pole position: Hülkenberg, 1m 35.741s, 125.700mph/202.295km/h.

Race 2 (76.888 miles/123.740km).
1 Sergio Pérez, MEX, 39m 13.229s, 117.624mph/189.299km/h; **2** Vitaly Petrov, RUS, 39m 15.584s; **3** Nico Hülkenberg, D, 39m 25.158s; **4** Edoardo Mortara, I, 39m 32.683s; **5** Davide Valsecchi, I, 39m 34.964s; **6** Luiz Razia, BR, 39m 35.847s; **7** Jérôme D'Ambrosio, B, 39m 37.258s; **8** Giedo van der Garde, NL, 39m 37.575s; **9** James Jakes, GB, 39m 38.482s; **10** Javier Villa, E, 39m 39.303s; **11** Marco Bonanomi, I, 39m 39.443s; **12** Diego Nunes, BR, 39m 41.171s; **13** Giacomo Ricci, I, 39m 53.075s; **14** Sakon Yamamoto, J, 39m 53.620s; **15** Davide Rigon, I, 39m 54.379s; **16** Álvaro Parente, P, 39m 57.769s; **17** Roldán Rodríguez, E, 39m 58.673s; **18** Kamui Kobayashi, J, 40m 00.966s; **19** Rodolfo Gonzalez, YV, 40m 00.990s; **20** Frankie Provenzano, I, 40m 25.571s; **21** Fabrizio Crestani, I, 40m 32.668s; **22** Michael Dalle Stelle, I, 40m 41.973s; **23** Kevin Chen, USA, 22 laps; **24** Michael Herck, RO, 16 (DNF); **25** Hamad Al Fardan, BRN, 11 (DNF).
Fastest race lap: Pérez, 1m 39.527s, 120.919mph/194.600km/h.
Pole position: Razia.
Championship points – Drivers: 1 Kobayashi, 39; **2** Valsecchi, 29; **3** Hülkenberg, 27; **4** Pérez, 25; **5** Rodríguez, 22; **6** D'Ambrosio, 21.
Teams: 1 DAMS, 60; **2** Barwa International Campos Team, 44; **3** ART Grand Prix, 34.

GP2 ASIA SERIES, Sepang International Circuit, Jalan Pekeliling, Kuala Lumpur, Malaysia, 4/5 April. Round 5. 33 and 20 laps of the 3.444-mile/5.543km circuit.
Race 1 (113.661 miles/182.919km).
1 Diego Nunes, BR, 1h 00m 46.668s, 112.206mph/180.578km/h; **2** Kamui Kobayashi, J, 1h 00m 55.029s; **3** James Jakes, GB, 1h 00m 55.818s; **4** Roldán Rodríguez, E, 1h 01m 00.542s; **5** Yelmer Buurman, NL, 1h 01m 03.473s; **6** Vitaly Petrov, RUS, 1h 01m 28.125s; **7** Pastor Maldonado, YV, 1h 01m 28.675s; **8** Davide Valsecchi, I, 1h 01m 29.049s; **9** Hamad Al Fardan, BRN, 1h 01m 37.820s; **10** Rodolfo Gonzalez, YV, 1h 01m 39.908s; **11** Álvaro Parente, P, 1h 01m 41.103s; **12** Sakon Yamamoto, J, 1h 01m 46.626s; **13** Michael Herck, RO, 1h 01m 48.141s; **14** Giedo van der Garde, NL, 1h 01m 49.186s; **15** Fabrizio Crestani, I, 1h 01m 58.626s; **16** Giacomo Ricci, I, 1h 02m 20.986s; **17** Ricardo Teixeira, ANG, 1h 02m 37.096s; **18** Michael Dalle Stelle, I, 1h 02m 38.123s; **19** Javier Villa, E, 32 laps; **20** Kevin Chen, USA, 32; **21** Marco Bonanomi, I, 16 (DNF); **22** Sergio Pérez, MEX, 14 (DNF); **23** Luiz Razia, BR, 10 (DNF); **24** Jérôme D'Ambrosio, B, 0 (DNF-transmission); **25** Davide Rigon, I, 0 (DNF); **26** Edoardo Mortara, I, 0 (DNF).
Fastest race lap: Villa, 1m 48.208s, 114.587mph/184.411km/h.
Pole position: D'Ambrosio, 1m 45.410s, 117.629mph/189.306km/h.

Race 2 (68.885 miles/110.860km).
1 Vitaly Petrov, RUS, 45m 41.349s, 90.461mph/145.583km/h; **2** Pastor Maldonado, YV, 45m 44.263s; **3** Davide Valsecchi, I, 45m 45.688s; **4** Diego Nunes, BR, 45m 47.706s; **5** Hamad Al Fardan, BRN, 46m 02.888s; **6** Sergio Pérez, MEX, 46m 05.838s; **7** Kamui Kobayashi, J, 46m 05.871s; **8** Rodolfo Gonzalez, YV, 46m 07.457s; **9** Álvaro Parente, P, 46m 08.305s; **10** Giedo van der Garde, NL, 46m 17.074s; **11** Yelmer Buurman, NL, 46m 18.655s; **12** Roldán Rodríguez, E, 46m 19.032s; **13** Davide Rigon, I, 46m 25.739s; **14** Marco Bonanomi, I, 46m 27.707s; **15** Giacomo Ricci, I, 46m 29.167s; **16** Fabrizio Crestani, I, 46m 29.825s; **17** Edoardo Mortara, I, 46m 29.989s; **18** Javier Villa, E, 46m 51.198s; **19** Ricardo Teixeira, ANG, 47m 02.906s; **20** Michael Dalle Stelle, I, 47m 37.886s; **21** Jérôme D'Ambrosio, B, 14 laps (DNF); **22** Sakon Yamamoto, J, 14 (DNF); **23** Michael Herck, RO, 9 (DNF); **24** Luiz Razia, BR, 9 (DNF); **25** Kevin Chen, USA, 5 (DNF); **26** James Jakes, GB, 4 (DNF).
Fastest race lap: Parente, 2m 03.508s, 100.392mph/161.566km/h.
Pole position: Valsecchi.
Championship points – Drivers: 1 Kobayashi, 47; **2** Valsecchi, 34; **3** Petrov, 28; **4** Hülkenberg, 27; **5** Rodríguez, 27; **6** Pérez, 26.
Teams: 1 DAMS, 70; **2** Barwa International Campos Team, 54; **3** ART Grand Prix, 41.

GP2 ASIA SERIES, Bahrain International Circuit, Sakhir, Bahrain, 25/26 April. Round 6. 33 and 23 laps of the 3.363-mile/5.412km circuit.
Race 1 (110.822 miles/178.350km).
1 Diego Nunes, BR, 59m 59.025s, 110.851mph/178.398km/h; **2** Roldán Rodríguez, E, 1h 00m 03.931s; **3** Jérôme D'Ambrosio, B, 1h 00m 06.930s; **4** Kamui Kobayashi, J, 1h 00m 14.307s; **5** Giedo van der Garde, NL, 1h 00m 19.799s; **6** Sakon Yamamoto, J, 1h 00m 30.649s; **7** Davide Rigon, I, 1h 00m 47.035s; **8** Luiz Razia, BR, 1h 00m 49.948s; **9** Karun Chandhok, IND, 1h 00m 54.709s; **10** James Jakes, GB, 1h 00m 54.878s; **11** Giacomo Ricci, I, 1h 00m 56.596s; **12** Sergio Pérez, MEX, 1h 00m 56.903s; **13** Michael Herck, RO, 1h 00m 57.147s; **14** Marco Bonanomi, I, 1h 01m 04.353s; **15** Javier Villa, E, 1h 01m 14.770s; **16** Davide Valsecchi, I, 1h 01m 17.504s; **17** Ricardo Teixeira, ANG, 1h 01m 27.533s; **18** Fabrizio Crestani, I, 32 laps; **19** Vitaly Petrov, RUS, 31; **20** Rodolfo Gonzalez, YV, 16 (DNF); **21** Edoardo Mortara, I, 12 (DNF); **22** Álvaro Parente, P, 12 (DNF); **23** Hamad Al Fardan, BRN, 7 (DNF); **24** Kevin Chen, USA, 4 (DNF); **25** Pastor Maldonado, YV, 0 (DNF); **26** Michael Dalle Stelle, I, 0 (DNF).
Fastest race lap: D'Ambrosio, 1m 46.954s, 113.191mph/182.164km/h.
Pole position: Kobayashi, 1m 43.863s, 116.560mph/187.585km/h.
Fastest qualifier: D'Ambrosio, 1m 43.752s, 116.685mph/187.786km/h (10 place grid penalty).

Race 2 (77.193 miles/124.230km).
1 Luiz Razia, BR, 43m 47.690s, 105.756mph/170.198km/h; **2** Jérôme D'Ambrosio, B, 43m 59.184s; **3** Davide Rigon, I, 44m 00.336s; **4** Sakon Yamamoto, J, 44m 01.039s; **5** Kamui Kobayashi, J, 44m 01.582s; **6** Diego Nunes, BR, 44m 07.052s; **7** Giedo van der Garde, NL, 44m 10.873s; **8** Marco Bonanomi, I, 44m 15.503s; **9** Sergio Pérez, MEX, 44m 19.679s; **10** Giacomo Ricci, I, 44m 22.118s; **11** Vitaly Petrov, RUS, 44m 23.942s; **12** Javier Villa, E, 44m 24.356s; **13** Álvaro Parente, P, 44m 24.920s; **14** James Jakes, GB, 44m 26.956s; **15** Fabrizio Crestani, I, 44m 28.812s; **16** Edoardo Mortara, I, 44m 29.801s; **17** Hamad Al Fardan, BRN, 44m 39.779s; **18** Kevin Chen, USA, 44m 53.107s; **19** Michael Dalle Stelle, I, 44m 57.865s; **20** Michael Herck, RO, 16 laps (DNF); **21** Ricardo Teixeira, ANG, 13 (DNF); **22** Roldán Rodríguez, E, 0 (DNF); **23** Karun Chandhok, IND, 0 (DNF); **24** Davide Valsecchi, I, 0 (DNF); **25** Rodolfo Gonzalez, YV, 0 (DNF); **26** Pastor Maldonado, YV, 0 (DNF).
Fastest race lap: D'Ambrosio, 1m 46.648s, 113.516mph/182.686km/h.
Pole position: Razia.

Final championship points
Drivers
1 Kamui Kobayashi, J, 56; **2** Jérôme D'Ambrosio, B, 36; **3** Roldán Rodríguez, E, 35; **4** Davide Valsecchi, I, 34; **5** Vitaly Petrov, RUS, 28; **6** Nico Hülkenberg, D, 27; **7** Sergio Pérez, MEX, 26; **8** Diego Nunes, BR, 24; **9** Sakon Yamamoto, J, 13; **10** Javier Villa, E, 12; **11** Edoardo Mortara, I, 11; **12** Giedo van der Garde, NL, 11; **13** Luiz Razia, BR, 9; **14** Earl Bamber, NZ, 8; **15** Pastor Maldonado, YV, 7; **16** James Jakes, GB, 7; **17** Davide Rigon, I, 6; **18** Chris van der Drift, NZ, 5; **19** Yelmer Buurman, NL, 4; **20** Hamad Al Fardan, BRN, 2; **21** Álvaro Parente, P, 1.

Teams
1 DAMS, 92; **2** Piquet GP, 59; **3** Barwa International Campos Team, 54; **4** ART Grand Prix, 47; **5** Durango, 34; **6** Arden International Motorsport, 20; **7** Super Nova Racing, 19; **8** GFH Team iSport, 13; **9** Trident Racing, 11; **10** My Qi-Meritus.Mahara, 9; **11** Ocean Racing Technology, 4.

FIA Formula Two Championship

All cars are Williams-Audi turbo.

FIA FORMULA TWO CHAMPIONSHIP, Circuit de la Comunitat Valenciana Ricardo Tormo, Cheste, Valencia, Spain, 30/31 May. Round 1. 23 and 17 laps of the 2.489-mile/4.005km circuit.
Race 1 (57.238 miles/92.115km).
1 Robert Wickens, CDN, 37m 03.621s, 92.666mph/149.132km/h; **2** Carlos Iaconelli, BR, 37m 07.491s; **3** Kazim Vasiliauskas, LT, 37m 08.862s; **4** Mikhail Aleshin, RUS, 37m 12.175s; **5** Julien Jousse, F, 37m 13.543s; **6** Mirko Bortolotti, I, 37m 14.525s; **7** Henry Surtees, GB, 37m 14.940s; **8** Alex Brundle, GB, 37m 15.947s; **9** Nicola de Marco, I, 37m 16.534s; **10** Sebastian Hohenthal, S, 37m 17.597s.
Fastest race lap: Wickens, 1m 29.166s, 100.474mph/161.698km/h.
Pole position: Wickens, 1m 27.775s, 102.066mph/164.260km/h.

Race 2 (42.306 miles/68.085km).
1 Robert Wickens, CDN, 25m 22.024s, 100.065mph/161.039km/h; **2** Mirko Bortolotti, I, 25m 27.935s; **3** Philipp Eng, A, 25m 29.905s; **4** Andy Soucek, E, 25m 30.639s; **5** Nicola de Marco, I, 25m 31.804s; **6** Mikhail Aleshin, RUS, 25m 33.731s; **7** Edoardo Piscopo, I, 25m 35.625s; **8** Carlos Iaconelli, BR, 25m 38.640s; **9** Tobias Hegewald, D, 25m 40.850s; **10** Julien Jousse, F, 25m 43.601s.
Fastest race lap: Vasiliauskas, 1m 28.322s, 101.434mph/163.243km/h.
Pole position: Wickens, 1m 27.488s, 102.401mph/164.799km/h.

FIA FORMULA TWO CHAMPIONSHIP, Automotodrom Brno Masaryk Circuit, Brno, Czech Republic, 20/21 June. Round 2. 22 and 14 laps of the 3.357-mile/5.403km circuit.
Race 1 (73.860 miles/118.866km).
1 Mirko Bortolotti, I, 42m 32.103s, 104.186mph/167.672km/h; **2** Mikhail Aleshin, RUS, 42m 36.778s; **3** Philipp Eng, A, 42m 44.433s; **4** Henri Karjalainen, FIN, 42m 44.716s; **5** Julien Jousse, F, 42m 49.494s; **6** Armaan Ebrahim, IND, 42m 58.174s; **7** Edoardo Piscopo, I, 42m 58.458s; **8** Tom Gladdis, GB, 43m 06.158s; **9** Robert Wickens, CDN, 43m 07.212s; **10** Jolyon Palmer, GB, 43m 11.986s.
Fastest race lap: Wickens, 1m 49.747s, 110.127mph/177.233km/h.
Pole position: Nicola de Marco, I, 2m 03.484s, 97.876mph/157.516km/h.

Race 2 (47.002 miles/75.642km).
1 Andy Soucek, E, 30m 43.788s, 91.771mph/147.691km/h; **2** Julien Jousse, F, 30m 45.953s; **3** Nicola de Marco, I, 30m 50.863s; **4** Edoardo Piscopo, I, 30m 53.832s; **5** Milos Pavlovic, SRB, 30m 55.286s; **6** Armaan Ebrahim, IND, 30m 58.214s; **7** Tobias Hegewald, D, 31m 01.986s; **8** Kazim Vasiliauskas, LT, 31m 02.652s; **9** Philipp Eng, A, 31m 03.265s; **10** Tom Gladdis, GB, 31m 04.513s.
Fastest race lap: de Marco, 1m 50.011s, 109.863mph/176.807km/h.
Pole position: Henry Surtees, GB, 1m 48.006s, 111.902mph/180.089km/h.

FIA FORMULA TWO CHAMPIONSHIP, Circuit de Spa-Francorchamps, Stavelot, Belgium, 27/28 June. Round 3. 11 and 15 laps of the 4.351-mile/7.003km circuit.
Race 1 (47.866 miles/77.033km).
1 Tobias Hegewald, D, 25m 59.481s, 110.496mph/177.827km/h; **2** Milos Pavlovic, SRB, 26m 07.377s; **3** Julien Jousse, F, 26m 08.100s; **4** Andy Soucek, E, 26m 13.630s; **5** Jack Clarke, GB, 26m 18.887s; **6** Tom Gladdis, GB, 26m 19.436s; **7** Henri Karjalainen, FIN, 26m 21.201s; **8** Edoardo Piscopo, I, 26m 26.484s; **9** Mirko Bortolotti, I, 26m 33.674s; **10** Kazim Vasiliauskas, LT, 26m 35.871s.
Fastest race lap: Hegewald, 2m 09.812s, 120.676mph/194.210km/h.
Pole position: Hegewald, 2m 08.890s, 121.539mph/195.599km/h.

Race 2 (65.272 miles/105.045km).
1 Tobias Hegewald, D, 33m 04.856s, 118.385mph/190.523km/h; **2** Andy Soucek, E, 33m 11.711s; **3** Robert Wickens, CDN, 33m 13.734s; **4** Milos Pavlovic, SRB, 33m 19.833s; **5** Alex Brundle, GB, 33m 22.494s; **6** Julien Jousse, F, 33m 23.014s; **7** Kazim Vasiliauskas, LT, 33m 24.457s; **8** Mikhail Aleshin, RUS, 33m 25.307s; **9** Mirko Bortolotti, I, 33m 25.967s; **10** Carlos Iaconelli, BR, 33m 32.659s.
Fastest race lap: Hegewald, 2m 11.012s, 119.571mph/192.431km/h.

Pole position: Hegewald, 2m 08.233s, 122.162mph/196.601km/h.

FIA FORMULA TWO CHAMPIONSHIP, Brands Hatch Grand Prix Circuit, West Kingsdown, Dartford, Kent, Great Britain, 18/19 July. Round 4. 28 and 15 laps of the 2.301-mile/3.703km circuit.

Race 1 (64.408 miles/103.654km).

1 Philipp Eng, A, 39m 01.642s, 99.019mph/159.355km/h; **2** Andy Soucek, E, 39m 02.136s; **3** Henry Surtees, GB, 39m 03.336s; **4** Robert Wickens, CDN, 39m 04.642s; **5** Kazim Vasiliauskas, LT, 39m 04.913s; **6** Carlos Iaconelli, BR, 39m 09.040s; **7** Milos Pavlovic, SRB, 39m 09.584s; **8** Edoardo Piscopo, I, 39m 10.058s; **9** Nicola de Marco, I, 39m 10.595s; **10** Mikhail Aleshin, RUS, 39m 13.742s.

Fastest race lap: Mirko Bortolotti, I, 1m 18.705s, 105.245mph/169.376km/h.

Pole position: Eng, 1m 17.445s, 106.958mph/172.132km/h.

Race 2 (34.495 miles/55.515km).

1 Andy Soucek, E, 52m 23.670s, 39.502mph/63.573km/h; **2** Robert Wickens, CDN, 52m 24.921s; **3** Mikhail Aleshin, RUS, 52m 28.433s; **4** Philipp Eng, A, 52m 30.528s; **5** Mirko Bortolotti, I, 52m 30.957s; **6** Tobias Hegewald, D, 52m 31.346s; **7** Edoardo Piscopo, I, 52m 32.113s; **8** Jason Moore, GB, 52m 33.491s; **9** Julien Jousse, F, 52m 34.063s; **10** Armaan Ebrahim, IND, 52m 34.592s.

Fastest race lap: Soucek, 1m 17.810s, 106.456mph/171.325km/h.

Pole position: Soucek, 1m 16.947s, 107.650mph/173.246km/h.

FIA FORMULA TWO CHAMPIONSHIP, Donington Park National Circuit, Castle Donington, Great Britain, 16 August. Round 5. 2 x 25 laps of the 2.500-mile/4.023km circuit.

Race 1 (62.494 miles/100.575km).

1 Andy Soucek, E, 35m 26.366s, 105.804mph/170.276km/h; **2** Mikhail Aleshin, RUS, 35m 36.165s; **3** Tobias Hegewald, D, 35m 38.342s; **4** Edoardo Piscopo, I, 35m 39.214s; **5** Philipp Eng, A, 35m 40.422s; **6** Sebastian Hohenthal, S, 35m 42.126s; **7** Julien Jousse, F, 35m 42.655s; **8** Armaan Ebrahim, IND, 35m 55.962s; **9** Jack Clarke, GB, 36m 06.105s; **10** Mirko Bortolotti, I, 36m 07.880s.

Fastest race lap: Jousse, 1m 24.293s, 106.760mph/171.814km/h.

Pole position: Hegewald, 1m 23.116s, 108.272mph/174.248km/h.

Race 2 (62.494 miles/100.575km).

1 Julien Jousse, F, 38m 28.770s, 97.445mph/156.823km/h; **2** Kazim Vasiliauskas, LT, 38m 43.886s; **3** Mirko Bortolotti, I, 38m 46.628s; **4** Andy Soucek, E, 38m 47.088s; **5** Sebastian Hohenthal, S, 38m 48.085s; **6** Tobias Hegewald, D, 38m 48.718s; **7** Mikhail Aleshin, RUS, 38m 49.153s; **8** Milos Pavlovic, SRB, 38m 50.210s; **9** Carlos Iaconelli, BR, 38m 52.656s; **10** Philipp Eng, A, 38m 53.071s.

Fastest race lap: Jousse, 1m 24.135s, 106.961mph/172.137km/h.

Pole position: Jousse, 1m 23.507s, 107.765mph/173.432km/h.

FIA FORMULA TWO CHAMPIONSHIP, Motorsport Arena Oschersleben, Germany, 5/6 September. Round 6. 24 and 18 laps of the 2.297-mile/3.696km circuit.

Race 1 (55.118 miles/88.704km).

1 Andy Soucek, E, 38m 15.756s, 86.431mph/139.097km/h; **2** Mirko Bortolotti, I, 38m 22.222s; **3** Kazim Vasiliauskas, LT, 38m 26.925s; **4** Carlos Iaconelli, BR, 38m 33.550s; **5** Mikhail Aleshin, RUS, 38m 34.503s; **6** Nicola de Marco, I, 38m 34.973s; **7** Jack Clarke, GB, 38m 44.526s; **8** Robert Wickens, CDN, 38m 45.107s; **9** Armaan Ebrahim, IND, 38m 50.746s; **10** Ollie Hancock, GB, 38m 53.001s.

Fastest race lap: Soucek, 1m 21.449s, 101.507mph/163.361km/h.

Pole position: Soucek, 1m 20.402s, 102.829mph/165.488km/h.

Race 2 (41.339 miles/66.528km).

1 Mikhail Aleshin, RUS, 24m 50.757s, 99.827mph/160.657km/h; **2** Andy Soucek, E, 24m 51.236s; **3** Julien Jousse, F, 24m 51.818s; **4** Robert Wickens, CDN, 24m 53.671s; **5** Nicola de Marco, I, 24m 54.399s; **6** Tobias Hegewald, D, 24m 55.184s; **7** Kazim Vasiliauskas, LT, 24m 56.138s; **8** Edoardo Piscopo, I, 25m 04.047s; **9** Sebastian Hohenthal, S, 25m 05.950s; **10** Carlos Iaconelli, BR, 25m 07.873s.

Fastest race lap: Milos Pavlovic, SRB, 1m 21.731s, 101.157mph/162.797km/h.

Pole position: Aleshin, 1m 22.131s, 100.664mph/162.004km/h.

FIA FORMULA TWO CHAMPIONSHIP, Autodromo Enzo e Dino Ferrari, Imola, Italy, 19/20 September. Round 7. 21 and 15 laps of the 3.050-mile/4.909km circuit.

Race 1 (63.914 miles/102.860km).

1 Kazim Vasiliauskas, LT, 38m 03.024s, 100.783mph/162.195km/h; **2** Mirko Bortolotti, I, 38m 10.527s; **3** Andy Soucek, E, 38m 11.202s; **4** Robert Wickens, CDN, 38m 12.023s; **5** Philipp Eng, A, 38m 12.550s; **6** Milos Pavlovic, SRB, 38m 14.964s; **7** Mikhail Aleshin, RUS, 38m 21.316s; **8** Germán Sánchez, E, 38m 25.805s; **9** Sebastian Hohenthal, S, 38m 26.606s; **10** Julien Jousse, F, 38m 26.899s.

Fastest race lap: Vasiliauskas, 1m 38.959s, 110.966mph/178.583km/h.

Pole position: Vasiliauskas, 1m 38.468s, 111.519mph/179.473km/h.

Race 2 (45.612 miles/73.406km).

1 Andy Soucek, E, 30m 12.572s, 90.592mph/145.793km/h; **2** Robert Wickens, CDN, 30m 14.979s; **3** Milos Pavlovic, SRB, 30m 20.484s; **4** Tobias Hegewald, D, 30m 28.961s; **5** Carlos Iaconelli, BR, 30m 32.735s; **6** Jolyon Palmer, GB, 30m 36.082s; **7** Jason Moore, GB, 30m 38.067s; **8** Germán Sánchez, E, 30m 39.786s; **9** Nicola de Marco, I, 30m 39.860s; **10** Philipp Eng, A, 30m 40.643s.

Fastest race lap: Wickens, 1m 38.576s, 111.397mph/179.276km/h.

Pole position: Wickens, 1m 37.401s, 112.741mph/181.439km/h.

FIA FORMULA TWO CHAMPIONSHIP, Circuit de Catalunya, Montmeló, Barcelona, Spain, 31 October/1 November. Round 8. 2 x 20 laps of the 2.892-mile/4.655km circuit.

Race 1 (57.850 miles/93.100km).

1 Andy Soucek, E, 33m 53.492s, 102.414mph/164.819km/h; **2** Mikhail Aleshin, RUS, 33m 57.881s; **3** Tristan Vautier, F, 34m 01.137s; **4** Julien Jousse, F, 34m 01.472s; **5** Philipp Eng, A, 34m 06.821s; **6** Mirko Bortolotti, I, 34m 07.317s; **7** Natacha Gachnang, CH, 34m 10.469s; **8** Kazim Vasiliauskas, LT, 34m 10.968s; **9** Tobias Hegewald, D, 34m 12.743s; **10** Milos Pavlovic, SRB, 34m 17.995s.

Fastest race lap: Jason Moore, GB, 1m 40.931s, 103.168mph/166.034km/h.

Pole position: Robert Wickens, CDN, 1m 39.020s, 105.159mph/169.238km/h.

Race 2 (57.850 miles/93.100km).

1 Andy Soucek, E, 33m 46.273s, 102.779mph/165.407km/h; **2** Nicola de Marco, I, 33m 53.811s; **3** Robert Wickens, CDN, 33m 55.918s; **4** Kazim Vasiliauskas, LT, 33m 56.470s; **5** Tobias Hegewald, D, 34m 00.925s; **6** Tristan Vautier, F, 34m 05.899s; **7** Mikhail Aleshin, RUS, 34m 07.802s; **8** Julien Jousse, F, 34m 08.165s; **9** Philipp Eng, A, 34m 10.474s; **10** Armaan Ebrahim, IND, 34m 11.891s.

Fastest race lap: Soucek, 1m 39.704s, 104.438mph/168.077km/h.

Pole position: Wickens, 1m 38.096s, 106.150mph/170.832km/h.

Final championship points

1 Andy Soucek, E, 115; **2** Robert Wickens, CDN, 64; **3** Mikhail Aleshin, RUS, 59; **4** Mirko Bortolotti, I, 50; **5** Julien Jousse, F, 49; **6** Tobias Hegewald, D, 46; **7** Kazim Vasiliauskas, LT, 45; **8** Philipp Eng, A, 39; **9** Milos Pavlovic, SRB, 29; **10** Nicola de Marco, I, 25; **11** Carlos Iaconelli, BR, 21; **12** Edoardo Piscopo, I, 19; **13** Tristan Vautier, F, 9; **14** Henry Surtees, GB, 8; **15** Henri Karjalainen, FIN, 7; **16** Sebastian Hohenthal, S, 7; **17** Armaan Ebrahim, IND, 7; **18** Jack Clarke, GB, 6; **19** Alex Brundle, GB, 5; **20** Tom Gladdis, GB, 4; **21** Jolyon Palmer, GB, 3; **22** Jason Moore, GB, 3; **23** Natacha Gachnang, CH, 2; **24** Germán Sánchez, E, 2.

All-Japan Formula Nippon Championship

All cars are Swift FN09.

ALL-JAPAN FORMULA NIPPON CHAMPIONSHIP, Fuji International Speedway, Sunto-gun, Shizuoka Prefecture, Japan, 5 April. Round 1. 55 laps of the 2.835-mile/4.563km circuit, 155.942 miles/250.965km.

1 Benoît Treluyer, F (-Toyota), 1h 21m 59.897s, 114.107mph/183.637km/h; **2** Takuya Izawa, J (-Honda), 1h 22m 05.877s; **3** Kohei Hirate, J (-Toyota), 1h 22m 06.625s; **4** Loïc Duval, F (-Honda), 1h 22m 07.800s; **5** Yuji Tachikawa, J (-Toyota), 1h 22m 21.171s; **6** Koudai Tsukakoshi, J (-Honda), 1h 22m 27.136s; **7** Kazuya Oshima, J (-Toyota), 1h 22m 28.006s; **8** Takashi Kogure, J (-Honda), 1h 22m 29.604s; **9** Keisuke Kunimoto, J (-Toyota), 1h 22m 42.184s; **10** André Lotterer, D (-Toyota), 1h 23m 01.877s.

Fastest race lap: Lotterer, 1m 27.011s, 117.309mph/188.790km/h.

Pole position: Hirate, 1m 24.653s, 120.576mph/194.049km/h.

ALL-JAPAN FORMULA NIPPON CHAMPIONSHIP, Suzuka International Racing Course, Suzuka-shi, Mie Prefecture, Japan, 17 May. Round 2. 43 laps of the 3.608-mile/5.807km circuit, 155.157 miles/249.701km.

1 Loïc Duval, F (-Honda), 1h 26m 44.751s, 107.318mph/172.712km/h; **2** Benoît Treluyer, F (-Toyota), 1h 27m 05.356s; **3** André Lotterer, D (-Toyota), 1h 27m 21.348s; **4** Kohei Hirate, J (-Toyota), 1h 27m 31.365s; **5** Koudai Tsukakoshi, J (-Honda), 1h 27m 39.067s; **6** Richard Lyons, GB (-Honda), 1h 27m 52.638s; **7** Takuya Izawa, J (-Honda), 1h 28m 02.823s; **8** Hiroaki Ishiura, J (-Toyota), 42 laps; **9** Keisuke Kunimoto, J (-Toyota), 40; **10** Kazuya Oshima, J (-Toyota), 19 (DNF).

Fastest race lap: Duval, 1m 58.144s, 109.950mph/176.947km/h.

Pole position: Treluyer, 1m 59.106s, 109.062mph/175.518km/h.

ALL-JAPAN FORMULA NIPPON CHAMPIONSHIP, Twin Ring Motegi, Motegi-machi, Haga-gun, Tochigi Prefecture, Japan, 31 May. Round 3. 52 laps of the 2.983-mile/4.801km circuit, 155.127 miles/249.652km.

1 Takashi Kogure, J (-Honda), 1h 41m 02.832s, 92.111mph/148.239km/h; **2** Benoît Treluyer, F (-Toyota), 1h 41m 11.606s; **3** Hiroaki Ishiura, J (-Toyota), 1h 41m 26.580s; **4** Koudai Tsukakoshi, J (-Honda), 1h 41m 27.864s; **5** André Lotterer, D (-Toyota), 1h 41m 28.400s; **6** Tsugio Matsuda, J (-Toyota), 1h 41m 28.988s; **7** Richard Lyons, GB (-Honda), 1h 41m 35.680s; **8** Yuji Tachikawa, J (-Toyota), 29 laps (DNF); **9** Kohei Hirate, J (-Toyota), 22 (DNF); **10** Kazuya Oshima, J (-Toyota), 10 (DNF).

Fastest race lap: Tsukakoshi, 1m 37.466s, 110.187mph/177.330km/h.

Pole position: Kogure, 1m 33.772s, 114.528mph/184.315km/h.

ALL-JAPAN FORMULA NIPPON CHAMPIONSHIP, Fuji International Speedway, Sunto-gun, Shizuoka Prefecture, Japan, 28 June. Round 4. 55 laps of the 2.835-mile/4.563km circuit, 155.942 miles/250.965km.

1 Loïc Duval, F (-Honda), 1h 43m 02.140s, 90.809mph/146.143km/h; **2** Kazuya Oshima, J (-Toyota), 1h 43m 42.700s; **3** Richard Lyons, GB (-Honda), 1h 43m 44.561s; **4** Hiroaki Ishiura, J (-Toyota), 1h 43m 47.158s; **5** Kohei Hirate, J (-Toyota), 1h 43m 48.882s; **6** Koudai Tsukakoshi, J (-Honda), 1h 43m 50.028s; **7** Takashi Kogure, J (-Honda), 1h 43m 55.191s; **8** André Lotterer, D (-Toyota), 1h 43m 56.428s; **9** Yuji Tachikawa, J (-Toyota), 1h 44m 12.394s; **10** Keisuke Kunimoto, J (-Toyota), 54 laps.

Fastest race lap: Duval, 1m 40.822s, 101.239mph/162.929km/h.

Pole position: Duval, 1m 25.626s, 119.206mph/191.844km/h.

ALL-JAPAN FORMULA NIPPON CHAMPIONSHIP, Suzuka International Racing Course, Suzuka-shi, Mie Prefecture, Japan, 12 July. Round 5. 43 laps of the 3.608-mile/5.807km circuit, 155.157 miles/249.701km.

1 Loïc Duval, F (-Honda), 1h 17m 25.650s, 120.234mph/193.498km/h; **2** Takashi Kogure, J (-Honda), 1h 17m 36.689s; **3** Benoît Treluyer, F (-Toyota), 1h 17m 48.287s; **4** Hiroaki Ishiura, J (-Toyota), 1h 17m 57.788s; **5** Kohei Hirate, J (-Toyota), 1h 18m 12.803s; **6** Yuji Tachikawa, J (-Toyota), 1h 18m 20.066s; **7** André Lotterer, D (-Toyota), 1h 18m 20.689s; **8** Takuya Izawa, J (-Honda), 1h 18m 29.654s; **9** Koudai Tsukakoshi, J (-Honda), 1h 18m 30.234s; **10** Kazuya Oshima, J (-Toyota), 1h 18m 52.381s.

Fastest race lap: Kogure, 1m 45.191s, 123.489mph/198.736km/h.

Pole position: Duval, 1m 41.214s, 128.341mph/206.545km/h.

ALL-JAPAN FORMULA NIPPON CHAMPIONSHIP, Twin Ring Motegi, Motegi-machi, Haga-gun, Tochigi Prefecture, Japan, 9 August. Round 6. 52 laps of the 2.983-mile/4.801km circuit, 155.127 miles/249.652km.

1 André Lotterer, D (-Toyota), 1h 26m 41.317s, 107.368mph/172.792km/h; **2** Loïc Duval, F (-Honda), 1h 26m 43.576s; **3** Benoît Treluyer, F (-Toyota), 1h 27m 23.061s; **4** Hiroaki Ishiura, J (-Toyota), 1h 27m 29.230s; **5** Tsugio Matsuda, J (-Toyota), 1h 27m 31.777s; **6** Takashi Kogure, J (-Honda), 1h 27m 34.228s; **7** Yuji Tachikawa, J (-Toyota), 1h 27m 53.433s; **8** Kohei Hirate, J (-Toyota), 1h 27m 56.960s; **9** Takuya Izawa, J (-Honda), 1h 28m 16.171s; **10** Koudai Tsukakoshi, J (-Honda), 48 laps.

Fastest race lap: Kogure, 1m 37.612s, 110.023mph/177.064km/h.

Pole position: Kogure, 1m 33.979s, 114.276mph/183.909km/h.

ALL-JAPAN FORMULA NIPPON CHAMPIONSHIP, Autopolis International Racing Course, Kamit-sue-mura, Hita-gun, Oita Prefecture, Japan, 30 August. Round 7. 54 laps of the 2.904-mile/4.674km circuit, 156.832 miles/252.396km.

1 Takashi Kogure, J (-Honda), 1h 28m 38.994s, 106.147mph/170.827km/h; **2** André Lotterer, D (-Toyota), 1h 28m 58.620s; **3** Loïc Duval, F (-Honda), 1h 29m 16.402s; **4** Kohei Hirate, J (-Toyota), 1h 29m 16.977s; **5** Hiroaki Ishiura, J (-Toyota), 1h 29m 17.514s; **6** Takuya Izawa, J (-Honda), 1h 29m 22.258s; **7** Tsugio Matsuda, J (-Toyota), 1h 29m 27.268s; **8** Benoît Treluyer, F (-Toyota), 1h 29m 30.688s; **9** Kazuya Oshima, J (-Toyota), 1h 29m 31.276s; **10** Richard Lyons, GB (-Honda), 1h 29m 39.672s.

Fastest race lap: Keisuke Kunimoto, J, 1m 35.336s, 109.669mph/176.496km/h.

Pole position: Kogure, 1m 32.556s, 112.963mph/181.797km/h.

ALL-JAPAN FORMULA NIPPON CHAMPIONSHIP, Sportsland-SUGO International Course, Shibata-gun, Miyagi Prefecture, Japan, 27 September. Round 8. 62 laps of the 2.302-mile/3.704256km circuit, 142.707 miles/229.664km.

1 Loïc Duval, F (-Honda), 1h 25m 52.893s, 99.700mph/160.452km/h; **2** André Lotterer, D (-Toyota), 1h 25m 58.216s; **3** Kohei Hirate, J (-Toyota), 1h 26m 20.957s; **4** Koudai Tsukakoshi, J (-Honda), 1h 26m 40.654s; **5** Hiroaki Ishiura, J (-Toyota), 1h 26m 46.173s; **6** Kazuya Oshima, J (-Toyota), 1h 27m 05.195s; **7** Tsugio Matsuda, J (-Toyota), 1h 27m 09.708s; **8** Keisuke Kunimoto, J (-Toyota), 61 laps; **9** Benoît Treluyer, F (-Toyota), 61; **10** Takashi Kogure, J (-Honda), 61.

Fastest race lap: Duval, 1m 09.220s, 119.708mph/192.651km/h.

Pole position: Duval, 1m 06.540s, 124.529mph/200.411km/h.

Final championship points

Drivers

1 Loïc Duval, F, 62; **2** Benoît Treluyer, F, 40; **3** André Lotterer, D, 39; **4** Takashi Kogure, J, 37; **5** Kohei Hirate, J, 32; **6** Hiroaki Ishiura, J, 30; **7** Koudai Tsukakoshi, J, 20; **8** Takuya Izawa, J, 14; **9** Kazuya Oshima, J, 13; **10** Richard Lyons, GB, 11; **11** Tsugio Matsuda, J, 11; **12** Yuji Tachikawa, J, 9; **13** Keisuke Kunimoto, J, 1.

Teams

1 Nakajima Racing, 93; **2** Petronas Team Tom's, 52; **3** Lawson Team Impul, 50; **4** ahead Impul, 31; **5** Team LeMans, 31; **6** DoCoMo Dandelion, 25; **7** HFDP Racing, 20; **8** Cerumo/Inging, 9.

British Formula 3 International Series

BRITISH FORMULA 3 INTERNATIONAL SERIES, Oulton Park Circuit, Tarporley, Cheshire, Great Britain, 13 April. 20 and 16 laps of the 2.692-mile/4.332km circuit.

Round 1 (53.840 miles/86.647km).

1 Daniel Ricciardo, AUS (Dallara F308-Volkswagen), 29m 53.932s, 108.044mph/173.880km/h; **2** Nick Tandy, GB (Mygale M-09F3-Mercedes Benz), 29m 56.391s; **3** Walter Grubmüller, A (Dallara F308-Mercedes Benz), 30m 03.088s; **4** Daisuke Nakajima, J (Dallara F308-Mercedes Benz), 30m 10.421s; **5** Riki Christodoulou, GB (Dallara F308-Mercedes Benz), 30m 11.122s; **6** Adriano Buzaid, BR (Dallara F309-Volkswagen), 30m 16.189s; **7** Wayne Boyd, GB (Dallara F309-Volkswagen), 30m 17.929s; **8** Hywel Lloyd, GB (Dallara F309-Mugen Honda), 30m 19.185s; **9** Oliver Oakes, GB (Dallara F308-Volkswagen), 30m 19.733s; **10** Victor Garcia, E (Dallara F308-Mercedes Benz), 30m 28.199s.

National class winner: Daniel McKenzie, GB (Dallara F307-Mugen Honda), 30m 33.512s (11th).

Fastest race lap: Tandy, 1m 28.772s, 109.169mph/175.691km/h.

Pole position: Max Chilton, GB (Dallara F308-Volkswagen), 1m 27.830s, 110.340mph/177.575km/h.

Round 2 (43.072 miles/69.318km).

1 Daniel Ricciardo, AUS (Dallara F308-Volkswagen), 23m 57.693s, 107.852mph/173.572km/h; **2** Walter Grubmüller, A (Dallara F308-Mercedes Benz), 24m 00.318s; **3** Nick Tandy, GB (Mygale M-09F3-Mercedes Benz), 24m 02.147s; **4** Max Chilton, GB (Dallara F308-Volkswagen), 24m 08.345s; **5** Daisuke Nakajima, J (Dallara F308-Mercedes Benz), 24m 13.605s; **6** Riki Christodoulou, GB (Dallara F308-Mercedes Benz), 24m 14.414s; **7** Adriano Buzaid, BR (Dallara F309-Volkswagen), 24m 15.316s; **8** Oliver Oakes, GB (Dallara F308-Volkswagen), 24m 19.074s; **9** Henry Arundel, GB (Dallara F308-Volkswagen), 24m 19.866s; **10** Victor Garcia, E (Dallara F308-Mercedes Benz), 24m 27.065s.

National class winner: Daniel McKenzie, GB (Dallara F307-Mugen Honda), 24m 35.598s (12th).

Fastest race lap: Grubmüller, 1m 29.177s, 108.673mph/174.893km/h.

Pole position: Grubmüller, 1m 27.921s, 110.226mph/177.391km/h.

BRITISH FORMULA 3 INTERNATIONAL SERIES, Silverstone Grand Prix Circuit, Towcester, Northamptonshire, Great Britain, 3 May. 2 x 18 laps of the 3.194-mile/5.140km circuit.

Round 3 (57.489 miles/92.520km).

1 Renger van der Zande, NL (Dallara F308-Mercedes Benz), 30m 52.430s, 111.724mph/179.802km/h; **2** Max Chilton, GB (Dallara F308-Volkswagen), 30m 52.883s; **3** Adriano Buzaid, BR (Dallara F309-Volkswagen), 30m 54.151s; **4** Riki Christodoulou, GB (Dallara F308-Mercedes Benz), 30m 56.713s; **5** Daniel Ricciardo, AUS (Dallara F308-Volkswagen), 30m 57.239s; **6** Daisuke Nakajima, J (Dallara F308-Mercedes Benz), 30m 58.729s; **7** Walter Grubmüller, A (Dallara F308-Mercedes Benz), 31m 00.923s; **8** Nick Tandy, GB (Mygale M-09F3-Mercedes Benz), 31m 01.477s; **9** Henry Arundel, GB (Dallara F308-Volkswagen), 31m 08.846s; **10** Carlos Huertas, CO (Dallara F308-Mercedes Benz), 31m 09.279s.

National class winner: Gabriel Dias, BR (Dallara F307-Mugen Honda), 31m 25.586s (13th).

Fastest race lap: van der Zande, 1m 41.703s, 113.053mph/181.941km/h.

Pole position: Chilton, 1m 39.798s, 115.211mph/185.414km/h.

Round 4 (57.489 miles/92.520km).

1 Daniel Ricciardo, AUS (Dallara F308-Volkswagen), 30m 46.091s, 112.107mph/180.420km/h; **2** Riki Christodoulou, GB (Dallara F308-Mercedes Benz), 30m 48.054s; **3** Max Chilton, GB (Dallara F308-Volkswagen), 30m 50.846s; **4** Daisuke Nakajima, J (Dallara F308-Mercedes Benz), 30m 51.137s; **5** Nick Tandy, GB (Mygale M-09F3-Mercedes Benz), 30m 59.413s; **6** Henry Arundel, GB (Dallara F308-Volkswagen), 31m 08.098s; **7** Walter Grubmüller, A (Dallara F308-Mercedes Benz), 31m 09.861s; **8** Carlos Huertas, CO (Dallara F308-Mercedes Benz), 31m 11.525s; **9** Oliver Oakes, GB (Dallara F308-Volkswagen), 31m 12.872s; **10** Adriano Buzaid, BR (Dallara F309-Volkswagen), 31m 13.530s.

National class winner: Gabriel Dias, BR (Dallara F307-Mugen Honda), 31m 18.644s (14th).

Fastest race lap: Tandy, 1m 41.282s, 113.523mph/182.697km/h.

Pole position: Chilton, 1m 39.781s, 115.230mph/185.446km/h.

BRITISH FORMULA 3 INTERNATIONAL SERIES, Rockingham Motor Speedway, Corby, Northamptonshire, Great Britain, 31 May. 25 and 22 laps of the 1.940-mile/3.122km circuit.

Round 5 (48.500 miles/78.053km).

1 Nick Tandy, GB (Mygale M-09F3-Mercedes Benz), 30m 57.771s, 93.983mph/151.251km/h; **2** Marcus Ericsson, S (Dallara F308-Mercedes Benz), 31m 06.379s; **3** Daisuke Nakajima, J (Dallara F308-Mercedes Benz), 31m 15.081s; **4** Carlos Huertas, CO (Dallara F308-Mercedes Benz), 31m 15.997s; **5** Max Chilton, GB (Dallara F308-Volkswagen), 31m 16.571s; **6** Riki Christodoulou, GB (Dallara F308-Mercedes Benz), 31m 17.412s; **7** Henry Arundel, GB (Dallara F308-Volkswagen), 31m 20.947s; **8** Victor Garcia, E (Dallara F308-Mercedes Benz), 31m 24.740s; **9** Wayne Boyd, GB (Dallara F309-Volkswagen), 31m 26.557s; **10** Jay Bridger, GB (Mygale M-09F3-Mugen Honda), 31m 30.680s.

National class winner: Daniel McKenzie, GB (Dallara F307-Mugen Honda), 31m 37.136s (11th).

Fastest race lap: Renger van der Zande, NL (Dallara F308-Mercedes Benz), 1m 13.001s, 95.669mph/153.965km/h.

Pole position: Daniel Ricciardo, AUS (Dallara F308-Volkswagen), 1m 12.334s, 96.552mph/155.385km/h.

Round 6 (42.680 miles/68.687km).

1 Marcus Ericsson, S (Dallara F308-Mercedes Benz), 30m 01.530s, 85.287mph/137.256km/h; **2** Henry Arundel, GB (Dallara F308-Volkswagen), 30m 05.456s; **3** Adriano Buzaid, BR (Dallara F309-Volkswagen), 30m 06.401s; **4** Daisuke Nakajima, J (Dallara F308-Mercedes Benz), 30m 07.695s; **5** Daniel Ricciardo, AUS (Dallara F308-Volkswagen), 30m 08.874s; **6** Walter Grubmüller, A (Dallara F308-Mercedes Benz), 30m 09.567s; **7** Victor Garcia, E (Dallara F308-Mercedes Benz), 30m 14.618s; **8** Jay Bridger, GB (Mygale M-09F3-Mugen Honda), 30m 15.482s; **9** Hywel Lloyd, GB (Dallara F309-Mugen Honda), 30m 15.939s; **10** Max Chilton, GB (Dallara F308-Volkswagen), 30m 17.560s.

National class winner: Daniel McKenzie, GB (Dallara F307-Mugen Honda), 30m 28.677s (13th).

Fastest race lap: Tandy, 1m 13.644s, 94.835mph/152.621km/h.

Pole position: Ericsson, 1m 12.443s, 96.406mph/155.151km/h.

BRITISH FORMULA 3 INTERNATIONAL SERIES, Hockenheimring Grand Prix Circuit, Heidelberg, Germany, 6/7 June. 19 and 18 laps of the 2.842-mile/4.574km circuit.

Round 7 (54.001 miles/86.906km).

1 Marcus Ericsson, S (Dallara F308-Mercedes Benz), 30m 20.552s, 106.782mph/171.849km/h; **2** Renger van der Zande, NL (Dallara F308-Mercedes Benz), 30m 21.740s; **3** Walter Grubmüller, A (Dallara F308-Mercedes Benz), 30m 27.830s; **4** Daniel Ricciardo, AUS (Dallara F308-Volkswagen), 30m 30.327s; **5** Max Chilton, GB (Dallara F308-Volkswagen), 30m 34.135s; **6** Adriano Buzaid, BR (Dallara F309-Volkswagen), 30m 35.078s; **7** Carlos Huertas, CO (Dallara F308-Mercedes Benz), 30m 36.833s; **8** Wayne Boyd, GB (Dallara F309-Volkswagen), 30m 50.831s; **9** Victor Garcia, E (Dallara F308-Mercedes Benz), 30m 56.932s; **10** Hywel Lloyd, GB (Dallara F309-Mugen Honda), 30m 57.581s.

Disqualified: Nick Tandy, GB (Mygale M-09F3-Mercedes Benz), finished 8th in 30m 46.322s.

National class winner: Victor Correa, BR (SLC-Mugen Honda), 31m 31.885s (12th).

Fastest race lap: van der Zande, 1m 34.763s, 107.971mph/173.764km/h.

Pole position: van der Zande, 1m 32.965s, 110.060mph/177.124km/h.

Round 8 (51.159 miles/82.332km).

1 Walter Grubmüller, A (Dallara F308-Mercedes Benz), 30m 05.203s, 102.022mph/164.189km/h; **2** Renger van der Zande, NL (Dallara F308-Mercedes Benz), 30m 06.242s; **3** Robert Wickens, CDN (Dallara F308-Volkswagen), 30m 06.651s; **4** Marcus Ericsson, S (Dallara F308-Mercedes Benz),

30m 07.040s; **5** Riki Christodoulou, GB (Dallara F308-Mercedes Benz), 30m 13.978s; **6** Nick Tandy, GB (Mygale M-09F3-Mercedes Benz), 30m 18.284s; **7** Adriano Buzaid, BR (Dallara F309-Volkswagen), 30m 19.447s; **8** Daniel Ricciardo, AUS (Dallara F308-Volkswagen), 30m 19.749s; **9** Henry Arundel, GB (Dallara F308-Volkswagen), 30m 20.685s; **10** Daniel McKenzie, GB (Dallara F307-Mugen Honda), 30m 22.484s (1st National class).
Fastest race lap: Tandy, 1m 35.879s, 106.715mph/171.741km/h.
Pole position: Grubmüller, 1m 34.451s, 108.328mph/174.338km/h.

BRITISH FORMULA 3 INTERNATIONAL SERIES, Snetterton Circuit, Thetford, Norfolk, Great Britain, 5 July. 2 x 29 laps of the 1.952-mile/3.141km circuit.
Round 9 (56.608 miles/91.102km).
1 Renger van der Zande, NL (Dallara F308-Mercedes Benz), 30m 39.225s, 110.801mph/178.317km/h; **2** Daniel Ricciardo, AUS (Dallara F308-Volkswagen), 30m 43.095s; **3** Henry Arundel, GB (Dallara F308-Volkswagen), 30m 49.468s; **4** Walter Grubmüller, A (Dallara F308-Mercedes Benz), 30m 49.874s; **5** Riki Christodoulou, GB (Dallara F308-Mercedes Benz), 30m 53.494s; **6** Max Chilton, GB (Dallara F308-Volkswagen), 30m 53.899s; **7** Jay Bridger, GB (Mygale M-09F3-Mugen Honda), 30m 54.314s; **8** Daniel McKenzie, GB (Dallara F307-Mugen Honda), 30m 54.946s (1st National class); **9** Adriano Buzaid, BR (Dallara F309-Volkswagen), 30m 55.865s; **10** Daisuke Nakajima, J (Dallara F308-Mercedes Benz), 30m 59.183s.
Fastest race lap: van der Zande, 1m 02.645s, 112.174mph/180.528km/h.
Pole position: van der Zande, 1m 02.071s, 113.212mph/182.197km/h.

Round 10 (56.608 miles/91.102km).
1 Riki Christodoulou, GB (Dallara F308-Mercedes Benz), 30m 42.827s, 110.584mph/177.969km/h; **2** Daniel Ricciardo, AUS (Dallara F308-Volkswagen), 30m 43.979s; **3** Walter Grubmüller, A (Dallara F308-Mercedes Benz), 30m 44.630s; **4** Renger van der Zande, NL (Dallara F308-Mercedes Benz), 30m 45.922s; **5** Adriano Buzaid, BR (Dallara F309-Volkswagen), 30m 50.217s; **6** Wayne Boyd, GB (Dallara F309-Volkswagen), 30m 52.040s; **7** Max Chilton, GB (Dallara F308-Volkswagen), 30m 52.594s; **8** Henry Arundel, GB (Dallara F308-Volkswagen), 30m 58.743s; **9** Jay Bridger, GB (Mygale M-09F3-Mugen Honda), 30m 59.090s; **10** Victor Garcia, E (Dallara F308-Mercedes Benz), 30m 59.992s.
National class winner: Gabriel Dias, BR (Dallara F307-Mugen Honda), 31m 01.411s (11th).
Fastest race lap: van der Zande, 1m 02.863s, 111.785mph/179.902km/h.
Pole position: van der Zande, 1m 02.098s, 113.163mph/182.118km/h.

BRITISH FORMULA 3 INTERNATIONAL SERIES, Donington Park National Circuit, Castle Donington, Great Britain, 19 July. 28 and 24 laps of the 1.9573-mile/3.150km circuit.
Round 11 (54.804 miles/88.198km).
1 Walter Grubmüller, A (Dallara F308-Mercedes Benz), 30m 28.106s, 107.923mph/173.685km/h; **2** Renger van der Zande, NL (Dallara F308-Mercedes Benz), 30m 28.762s; **3** Daniel Ricciardo, AUS (Dallara F308-Volkswagen), 30m 29.288s; **4** Carlos Huertas, CO (Dallara F308-Mercedes Benz), 30m 34.766s; **5** Adriano Buzaid, BR (Dallara F309-Volkswagen), 30m 37.988s; **6** Max Chilton, GB (Dallara F308-Volkswagen), 30m 39.351s; **7** Riki Christodoulou, GB (Dallara F308-Mercedes Benz), 30m 40.585s; **8** Daisuke Nakajima, J (Dallara F308-Mercedes Benz), 30m 41.203s; **9** Jay Bridger, GB (Mygale M-09F3-Mugen Honda), 30m 45.866s; **10** Wayne Boyd, GB (Dallara F309-Volkswagen), 30m 48.798s.
National class winner: Daniel McKenzie, GB (Dallara F307-Mugen Honda), 30m 49.913s (12th).
Fastest race lap: Ricciardo, 1m 02.296s, 113.110mph/182.032km/h.
Pole position: van der Zande, 1m 02.260s, 113.175mph/182.138km/h.

Round 12 (46.975 miles/75.599km).
1 Wayne Boyd, GB (Dallara F309-Volkswagen), 30m 13.649s, 93.243mph/150.060km/h; **2** Adriano Buzaid, BR (Dallara F309-Volkswagen), 30m 19.731s; **3** Walter Grubmüller, A (Dallara F308-Mercedes Benz), 30m 21.011s; **4** Carlos Huertas, CO (Dallara F308-Mercedes Benz), 30m 21.957s; **5** Daniel Ricciardo, AUS (Dallara F308-Volkswagen), 30m 24.101s; **6** Henry Arundel, GB (Dallara F308-Volkswagen), 30m 25.643s; **7** Max Chilton, GB (Dallara F308-Volkswagen), 30m 27.111s; **8** Jay Bridger, GB (Mygale M-09F3-Mugen Honda), 30m 27.817s; **9** Daisuke Nakajima, J (Dallara F308-Mercedes Benz), 30m 28.954s; **10** Riki Christodoulou, GB (Dallara F308-Mercedes Benz), 30m 30.152s.
van der Zande finished 4th in 30m 21.585s, but penalised 25-sec for causing accident.
National class winner: Daniel McKenzie, GB (Dallara F307-Mugen Honda), 30m 43.666 (12th).
Fastest race lap: Ricciardo, 1m 04.596s, 109.082mph/175.551km/h.
Pole position: Ricciardo, 1m 02.066s, 113.529mph/182.707km/h.

BRITISH FORMULA 3 INTERNATIONAL SERIES, Circuit de Spa-Francorchamps, Stavelot, Belgium, 24/25 July. 12 and 11 laps of the 4.352-mile/7.004km circuit.
Round 13 (52.225 miles/84.048km).
1 Daniel Ricciardo, AUS (Dallara F308-Volkswagen), 32m 06.562s, 97.588mph/157.053km/h; **2** Jules Bianchi, F (Dallara F308-Mercedes Benz), 32m 08.071s; **3** Valtteri Bottas, FIN (Dallara F308-Mercedes Benz), 32m 15.431s; **4** Renger van der Zande, NL (Dallara F308-Mercedes Benz), 32m 16.379s; **5** Jake Rosenzweig, USA (Dallara F308-Volkswagen), 32m 26.091s; **6** Esteban Gutierrez, MEX (Dallara F308-Mercedes Benz), 32m 32.507s; **7** Victor Garcia, E (Dallara F308-Mercedes Benz), 32m 35.085s; **8** Max Chilton, GB (Dallara F308-Volkswagen), 32m 35.379s; **9** Hywel Lloyd, GB (Dallara F309-Mugen Honda), 32m 39.287s; **10** Philip Major, CDN (Dallara F308-Volkswagen), 32m 41.104s.
National class winner: Daniel McKenzie, GB (Dallara F307-Mugen Honda), 32m 46.399s (14th).
Fastest race lap: Bianchi, 2m 14.254s, 116.700mph/187.811km/h.
Pole position: Ricciardo, 2m 14.937s, 116.109mph/186.860km/h.

Round 14 (47.873 miles/77.044km).
1 Adriano Buzaid, BR (Dallara F309-Volkswagen), 27m 34.731s, 104.151mph/167.615km/h; **2** Daniel Ricciardo, AUS (Dallara F308-Volkswagen), 27m 40.631s; **3** Walter Grubmüller, A (Dallara F308-Mercedes Benz), 27m 55.346s; **4** Renger van der Zande, NL (Dallara F308-Mercedes Benz), 27m 56.978s; **5** Henry Arundel, GB (Dallara F308-Volkswagen), 27m 57.250s; **6** Max Chilton, GB (Dallara F308-Volkswagen), 27m 57.883s; **7** Carlos Huertas, CO (Dallara F308-Mercedes Benz), 28m 00.591s; **8** Daisuke Nakajima, J (Dallara F308-Mercedes Benz), 28m 14.126s; **9** Hywel Lloyd, GB (Dallara F309-Mugen Honda), 28m 30.869s; **10** Esteban Gutierrez, MEX (Dallara F308-Mercedes Benz), 28m 31.926s.
National class winner: Gabriel Dias, BR (Dallara F307-Mugen Honda), 28m 35.274s (11th).
Fastest race lap: Bianchi, 2m 17.194s, 114.199mph/183.786km/h.
Pole position: Buzaid, 2m 37.214s, 99.657mph/160.382km/h.

BRITISH FORMULA 3 INTERNATIONAL SERIES, Silverstone International Circuit, Towcester, Northamptonshire, Great Britain, 16 August. 2 x 23 laps of the 2.249-mile/3.619km circuit.
Round 15 (51.727 miles/83.247km).
1 Daniel Ricciardo, AUS (Dallara F308-Volkswagen), 29m 08.610s, 106.494mph/171.386km/h; **2** Walter Grubmüller, A (Dallara F308-Mercedes Benz), 29m 18.459s; **3** Renger van der Zande, NL (Dallara F308-Mercedes Benz), 29m 19.596s; **4** Max Chilton, GB (Dallara F308-Volkswagen), 29m 20.453s; **5** Henry Arundel, GB (Dallara F308-Volkswagen), 29m 29.574s; **6** Carlos Huertas, CO (Dallara F308-Mercedes Benz), 29m 30.022s; **7** Wayne Boyd, GB (Dallara F309-Volkswagen), 29m 33.043s; **8** Riki Christodoulou, GB (Dallara F308-Mercedes Benz), 29m 34.522s; **9** Daisuke Nakajima, J (Dallara F308-Mercedes Benz), 29m 35.299s; **10** Adriano Buzaid, BR (Dallara F309-Volkswagen), 29m 36.422s.
National class winner: Gabriel Dias, BR (Dallara F307-Mugen Honda), 29m 45.968s (11th).
Fastest race lap: Ricciardo, 1m 15.200s, 107.664mph/173.269km/h.
Pole position: Ricciardo, 1m 14.783s, 108.265mph/174.236km/h.

Round 16 (51.727 miles/83.247km).
1 Renger van der Zande, NL (Dallara F308-Mercedes Benz), 29m 39.462s, 104.648mph/168.414km/h; **2** Daisuke Nakajima, J (Dallara F308-Mercedes Benz), 29m 50.659s; **3** Daniel Ricciardo, AUS (Dallara F308-Volkswagen), 29m 51.894s; **4** Walter Grubmüller, A (Dallara F308-Mercedes Benz), 29m 52.186s; **5** Carlos Huertas, CO (Dallara F308-Mercedes Benz), 29m 57.340s; **6** Riki Christodoulou, GB (Dallara F308-Mercedes Benz), 29m 57.762s; **7** Max Chilton, GB (Dallara F308-Volkswagen), 29m 58.270s; **8** Wayne Boyd, GB (Dallara F309-Volkswagen), 30m 00.022s; **9** Henry Arundel, GB (Dallara F308-Volkswagen), 30m 00.760s; **10** Victor Garcia, E (Dallara F308-Mercedes Benz), 30m 00.841s.
National class winner: Gabriel Dias, BR (Dallara F307-Mugen Honda), 30m 16.163s (14th).
Fastest race lap: Chilton, 1m 16.309s, 106.100mph/170.751km/h.
Pole position: Nakajima, 1m 15.090s, 107.822mph/173.523km/h.

BRITISH FORMULA 3 INTERNATIONAL SERIES, Autódromo Internacional do Algarve, Portimão, Portugal, 13 September. 16 and 17 laps of the 2.891-mile/4.6528km circuit.
Round 17 (46.091 miles/74.177km).
1 Jules Bianchi, F (Dallara F308-Mercedes Benz), 30m 14.666s, 91.437mph/147.154km/h; **2** Esteban Gutierrez, MEX (Dallara F309-Mercedes Benz), 30m 16.834s; **3** Daniel Ricciardo, AUS (Dallara F308-Volkswagen), 30m 19.103s; **4** Renger van der Zande, NL (Dallara F308-Mercedes Benz), 30m 19.111s; **5** Carlos Huertas, CO (Dallara F308-Mercedes Benz), 30m 19.595s; **6** Max Chilton, GB (Dallara F308-Volkswagen), 30m 20.336s; **7** Riki Christodoulou, GB (Dallara F308-Mercedes Benz), 30m 21.279s; **8** Adrien Tambay, F (Dallara F309-Mercedes Benz), 30m 30.103s; **9** Pedro Nunes, BR (Dallara F309-Mercedes Benz), 30m 30.630s; **10** Hywel Lloyd, GB (Dallara F309-Mugen Honda), 30m 31.583s.
National class winner: Daniel McKenzie, GB (Dallara F307-Mugen Honda), 30m 43.179s (14th).
Fastest race lap: Gutierrez, 1m 39.197s, 104.922mph/168.856km/h.
Pole position: van der Zande, 1m 37.729s, 106.498mph/171.393km/h.

Round 18 (48.982 miles/78.830km).
1 Jules Bianchi, F (Dallara F309-Mercedes Benz), 31m 35.286s, 93.039mph/149.732km/h; **2** Sam Bird, GB (Dallara F308-Mercedes Benz), 31m 39.952s; **3** Max Chilton, GB (Dallara F308-Volkswagen), 31m 41.345s; **4** Carlos Huertas, CO (Dallara F308-Mercedes Benz), 31m 44.190s; **5** Daniel Ricciardo, AUS (Dallara F308-Volkswagen), 31m 54.503s; **6** Henry Arundel, GB (Dallara F308-Volkswagen), 31m 54.830s; **7** Hywel Lloyd, GB (Dallara F309-Mugen Honda), 31m 55.009s; **8** Adrien Tambay, F (Dallara F309-Mercedes Benz), 31m 55.618s; **9** Jay Bridger, GB (Mygale M-09F3-Mugen Honda), 31m 56.530s; **10** Esteban Gutierrez, MEX (Dallara F309-Mercedes Benz), 31m 56.620s*.
* includes 10-sec penalty for overtaking behind safety car.
Adriano Buzaid, BR (Dallara F309-Volkswagen) finished 5th in 31m 53.243s, but penalised 10-sec for overtaking behind safety car (placed 16th).
National class winner: Gabriel Dias, BR (Dallara F307-Mugen Honda), 31m 58.530s (13th).
Fastest race lap: Bianchi, 1m 38.904s, 105.233mph/169.356km/h.
Pole position: Chilton, 1m 37.538s, 106.707mph/171.728km/h.

BRITISH FORMULA 3 INTERNATIONAL SERIES, Brands Hatch Grand Prix Circuit, West Kingsdown, Dartford, Kent, Great Britain, 20 September. 22 and 21 laps of the 2.3009-mile/3.703km circuit.
Round 19 (50.620 miles/81.465km).
1 Daniel Ricciardo, AUS (Dallara F308-Volkswagen), 28m 47.041s, 105.516mph/169.812km/h; **2** Max Chilton, GB (Dallara F308-Volkswagen), 29m 02.572s; **3** Riki Christodoulou, GB (Dallara F308-Mercedes Benz), 29m 03.176s; **4** Marcus Ericsson, S (Dallara F308-Mercedes Benz), 29m 04.931s; **5** Walter Grubmüller, A (Dallara F308-Mercedes Benz), 29m 15.902s; **6** Carlos Huertas, CO (Dallara F308-Mercedes Benz), 29m 17.287s; **7** Henry Arundel, GB (Dallara F308-Volkswagen), 29m 17.583s; **8** Adriano Buzaid, BR (Dallara F309-Volkswagen), 29m 23.953s; **9** Daniel McKenzie, GB (Dallara F307-Mugen Honda), 29m 42.348s (1st National class); **10** Hywel Lloyd, GB (Dallara F309-Mugen Honda), 29m 44.986s.
Jay Bridger, GB (Mygale M-09F3-Mugen Honda) finished 10th in 29m 42.649s, but penalised 10-sec for not respecting track limits.
Fastest race lap: Ricciardo, 1m 17.793s, 106.477mph/171.359km/h.
Pole position: Ricciardo, 1m 17.207s, 107.286mph/172.660km/h.

Round 20 (48.319 miles/77.762km).
1 Max Chilton, GB (Dallara F308-Volkswagen), 31m 16.848s, 92.680mph/149.155km/h; **2** Riki Christodoulou, GB (Dallara F308-Mercedes Benz), 31m 17.815s; **3** Marcus Ericsson, S (Dallara F308-Mercedes Benz), 31m 19.400s; **4** Daniel Ricciardo, AUS (Dallara F308-Volkswagen), 31m 20.424s; **5** Walter Grubmüller, A (Dallara F308-Mercedes Benz), 31m 32.151s; **6** Daisuke Nakajima, J (Dallara F308-Mercedes Benz), 31m 32.642s; **7** Wayne Boyd, GB (Dallara F309-Volkswagen), 31m 33.310s; **8** Adriano Buzaid, BR (Dallara F309-Volkswagen), 31m 38.598s; **9** Carlos Huertas, CO (Dallara F308-Mercedes Benz), 31m 38.851s; **10** Victor Garcia, E (Dallara F308-Mercedes Benz), 31m 39.370s.
Arundel finished 5th in 31m 31.735s, but penalised 20-sec for jumping the start.
National class winner: Gabriel Dias, BR (Dallara F307-Mugen Honda), 31m 47.461s (11th).
Fastest race lap: Chilton, 1m 18.253s, 105.852mph/170.352km/h.
Pole position: Ricciardo, 1m 17.151s, 107.364mph/172.785km/h.

Final championship points
1 Daniel Ricciardo, AUS, 275; **2** Walter Grubmüller, A, 188; **3** Renger van der Zande, NL, 178; **4** Max Chilton, GB, 171; **5** Riki Christodoulou, GB, 130; **6** Adriano Buzaid, BR, 109; **7** Daisuke Nakajima, J, 95; **8** Carlos Huertas, CO, 95; **9** Henry Arundel, GB, 90; **10** Nick Tandy, GB, 68; **11** Marcus Ericsson, S, 65; **12** Wayne Boyd, GB, 50; **13** Hywel Lloyd, GB, 33; **14** Victor Garcia, E, 30; **15** Jay Bridger, GB, 28; **16** Robert Wickens, CDN, 12; **17** Philip Major, CDN, 10; **18** Oliver Oakes, GB, 7; **19** Stéphane Richelmi, MC, 4; **20** Kevin Chen, USA, 2.

National Class
1 Daniel McKenzie, GB, 351; **2** Gabriel Dias, BR, 295; **3** Victor Corrêa, BR, 184; **4** Maxim Snegirev, RUS, 108.

Formula 3 Euro Series

FORMULA 3 EURO SERIES, Hockenheimring Grand Prix Circuit, Heidelberg, Germany, 16/17 May. 16 and 24 laps of the 2.842-mile/4.574km circuit.
Round 1 (45.474 miles/73.184km).
1 Stefano Coletti, MC (Dallara F308-Mercedes Benz), 25m 20.955s, 107.635mph/173.222km/h; **2** Roberto Merhi, E (Dallara F308-Mercedes Benz), 25m 22.025s; **3** Sam Bird, GB (Dallara F308-Mercedes Benz), 25m 22.489s; **4** Mika Mäki, FIN (Dallara F308-Volkswagen), 25m 24.204s; **5** Jules Bianchi, F (Dallara F308-Mercedes Benz), 25m 28.793s; **6** Jean-Karl Vernay, F (Dallara F308-Volkswagen), 25m 32.189s; **7** Christian Vietoris, D (Dallara F308-Mercedes Benz), 25m 34.284s; **8** Atte Mustonen, FIN (Dallara F308-Mercedes Benz), 25m 40.127s; **9** Matteo Chinosi, I (Dallara F308-Mercedes Benz), 25m 44.215s; **10** Tiago Geronimi, BR (Dallara F308-Volkswagen), 25m 45.652s.
Fastest race lap: Alexander Sims, GB (Dallara F308-Mercedes Benz), 1m 34.174s, 108.647mph/174.851km/h.
Pole position: Bird, 1m 33.657s, 109.247mph/175.816km/h.

Round 2 (68.212 miles/109.776km).
1 Jean-Karl Vernay, F (Dallara F308-Volkswagen), 41m 01.954s, 99.743mph/160.520km/h; **2** Christian Vietoris, D (Dallara F308-Mercedes Benz), 41m 03.243s; **3** Jules Bianchi, F (Dallara F308-Mercedes Benz), 41m 10.163s; **4** Mika Mäki, FIN (Dallara F308-Volkswagen), 41m 10.652s; **5** Stefano Coletti, MC (Dallara F308-Mercedes Benz), 41m 11.675s; **6** Sam Bird, GB (Dallara F308-Mercedes Benz), 41m 11.844s; **7** Atte Mustonen, FIN (Dallara F308-Mercedes Benz), 41m 13.134s; **8** Alexander Sims, GB (Dallara F308-Mercedes Benz), 41m 19.127s; **9** Henkie Waldschmidt, NL (Dallara F308-Mercedes Benz), 41m 23.819s; **10** Roberto Merhi, E (Dallara F308-Mercedes Benz), 41m 30.972s.
Fastest race lap: Mäki, 1m 34.554s, 108.211mph/174.148km/h.
Pole position: Mustonen.

FORMULA 3 EURO SERIES, EuroSpeedway Lausitz, Klettwitz, Dresden, Germany, 30/31 May. 23 and 31 laps of the 2.161-mile/3.478km circuit.
Round 3 (49.706 miles/79.994km).
1 Jules Bianchi, F (Dallara F308-Mercedes Benz), 30m 18.861s, 98.381mph/158.329km/h; **2** Valtteri Bottas, FIN (Dallara F308-Mercedes Benz), 30m 21.637s; **3** Jean-Karl Vernay, F (Dallara F308-Volkswagen), 30m 23.467s; **4** Brendon Hartley, NZ (Dallara F308-Volkswagen), 30m 24.684s; **5** Sam Bird, GB (Dallara F308-Mercedes Benz), 30m 25.733s; **6** Roberto Merhi, E (Dallara F308-Mercedes Benz), 30m 26.657s; **7** Henkie Waldschmidt, NL (Dallara F308-Mercedes Benz), 30m 30.694s; **8** Christian Vietoris, D (Dallara F308-Mercedes Benz), 30m 31.464s; **9** Tiago Geronimi, BR (Dallara F308-Volkswagen), 30m 34.379s; **10** Matteo Chinosi, I (Dallara F308-Mercedes Benz), 30m 46.420s.
Fastest race lap: Stefano Coletti, MC (Dallara F308-Mercedes Benz), 1m 18.022s, 99.716mph/160.478km/h.
Pole position: Bottas, 1m 31.308s, 85.207mph/137.127km/h.

Round 4 (66.995 miles/107.818km).
1 Christian Vietoris, D (Dallara F308-Mercedes Benz), 40m 45.948s, 98.605mph/158.689km/h; **2** Roberto Merhi, E (Dallara F308-Mercedes Benz), 40m 50.767s; **3** Sam Bird, GB (Dallara F308-Mercedes Benz), 40m 51.717s; **4** Brendon Hartley, NZ (Dallara F308-Volkswagen), 40m 57.329s; **5** Henkie Waldschmidt, NL (Dallara F308-Mercedes Benz), 41m 01.649s; **6** Mika Mäki, FIN (Dallara F308-Volkswagen), 41m 14.377s; **7** Adrien Tambay, F (Dallara F308-Mercedes Benz), 41m 16.095s; **8** Christopher Zanella, CH (Dallara F308-Mercedes Benz), 41m 17.255s; **9** Marco Wittmann, D (Dallara F308-Mercedes Benz), 41m 20.271s; **10** Atte Mustonen, FIN (Dallara F308-Mercedes Benz), 41m 23.582s.
Fastest race lap: Waldschmidt, 1m 18.244s, 99.433mph/160.022km/h.
Pole position: Vietoris.

FORMULA 3 EURO SERIES, Norisring, Nürnberg (Nuremberg), Germany, 27/28 June. 20 and 44 laps of the 1.429-mile/2.300km circuit.
Round 5 (28.583 miles/46.000km).
1 Jules Bianchi, F (Dallara F308-Mercedes Benz), 32m 03.917s, 53.484mph/86.074km/h; **2** Alexander Sims, GB (Dallara F308-Mercedes Benz), 32m 04.400s; **4** Esteban Gutierrez, MEX (Dallara F308-Mercedes Benz), 32m 05.344s; **5** Roberto Merhi, E (Dallara F308-Mercedes Benz), 32m 06.022s; **6** Christian Vietoris, D (Dallara F308-Mercedes Benz), 32m 06.607s; **7** Jean-Karl Vernay, F (Dallara F308-Volkswagen), 32m 07.260s; **8** Sam Bird, GB (Dallara F308-Mercedes Benz), 32m 07.805s; **9** Henkie Waldschmidt, NL (Dallara F308-Mercedes Benz), 32m 08.754s; **10** Marco Wittmann, D (Dallara F308-Mercedes Benz), 32m 09.288s.
Disqualified: Stefano Coletti, MC (Dallara F308-Mercedes Benz), finished 3rd in 32m 04.871s (3rd place left vacant).
Fastest race lap: Valtteri Bottas, FIN (Dallara F308-Mercedes Benz), 49.443s, 104.058mph/167.466km/h.
Pole position: Sims, 55.367s, 92.925mph/149.548km/h.

Round 6 (62.883 miles/101.200km).
1 Christian Vietoris, D (Dallara F308-Mercedes Benz), 40m 44.425s, 92.610mph/149.041km/h; **2** Jean-Karl Vernay, F (Dallara F308-Volkswagen), 40m 48.165s; **3** Jules Bianchi, F (Dallara F308-Mercedes Benz), 40m 48.799s; **4** Atte Mustonen, FIN (Dallara F308-Mercedes Benz), 40m 49.349s; **5** Tiago Geronimi, BR (Dallara F308-Volkswagen), 40m 50.112s; **6** Henkie Waldschmidt, NL (Dallara F308-Mercedes Benz), 40m 50.788s; **7** Adrien Tambay, F (Dallara F308-Mercedes Benz), 40m 50.884s; **8** Roberto Merhi, E (Dallara F308-Mercedes Benz), 40m 51.255s; **9** Matteo Chinosi, I (Dallara F308-Mercedes Benz), 40m 51.711s; **10** César Ramos, BR (Dallara F308-Mercedes Benz), 40m 53.158s.
Fastest race lap: Vernay, 49.352s, 104.250mph/167.774km/h.
Pole position: Bird.

FORMULA 3 EURO SERIES, Circuit Park Zandvoort, Netherlands, 18/19 July. 17 and 26 laps of the 2.676-mile/4.307km circuit.
Round 7 (45.496 miles/73.219km).
1 Jules Bianchi, F (Dallara F308-Mercedes Benz), 31m 04.337s, 87.852mph/141.385km/h; **2** Valtteri Bottas, FIN (Dallara F308-Mercedes Benz), 31m 06.446s; **3** Christian Vietoris, D (Dallara F308-Mercedes Benz), 31m 07.341s; **4** Jean-Karl Vernay, F (Dallara F308-Volkswagen), 31m 09.189s; **5** Esteban Gutierrez, MEX (Dallara F308-Mercedes Benz), 31m 09.535s; **6** Henkie Waldschmidt, NL (Dallara F308-Mercedes Benz), 31m 11.274s; **7** Jake Rosenzweig, USA (Dallara F308-Volkswagen), 31m 11.869s; **8** Sam Bird, GB (Dallara F308-Mercedes Benz), 31m 12.038s; **9** Atte Mustonen, FIN (Dallara F308-Mercedes Benz), 31m 12.485s; **10** Brendon Hartley, NZ (Dallara F308-Volkswagen), 31m 13.610s.
Fastest race lap: Bianchi, 1m 31.076s, 105.785mph/170.245km/h.
Pole position: Bianchi, 1m 30.431s, 106.540mph/171.459km/h.

Round 8 (69.582 miles/111.982km).
1 Jules Bianchi, F (Dallara F308-Mercedes Benz), 40m 34.182s, 102.908mph/165.614km/h; **2** Sam Bird, GB (Dallara F308-Mercedes Benz), 40m 40.387s; **3** Jake Rosenzweig, USA (Dallara F308-Volkswagen), 40m 41.757s; **4** Christian Vietoris, D (Dallara F308-Mercedes Benz), 40m 42.100s; **5** Jean-Karl Vernay, F (Dallara F308-Volkswagen), 40m 42.814s; **6** Valtteri Bottas, FIN (Dallara F308-Mercedes Benz), 40m 43.637s; **7** Esteban Gutierrez, MEX (Dallara F308-Mercedes Benz), 40m 47.250s; **8** Brendon Hartley, NZ (Dallara F308-Volkswagen), 40m 56.282s; **9** Alexander Sims, GB (Dallara F308-Mercedes Benz), 40m 58.602s; **10** Marco Wittmann, D (Dallara F308-Mercedes Benz), 40m 59.801s.
Fastest race lap: Bianchi, 1m 32.051s, 104.665mph/168.441km/h.
Pole position: Bird.

FORMULA 3 EURO SERIES, Motorsport Arena Oschersleben, Germany, 1/2 August. 22 and 29 laps of the 2.297-mile/3.696km circuit.
Round 9 (50.525 miles/81.312km).
1 Jules Bianchi, F (Dallara F308-Mercedes Benz), 30m 13.182s, 100.315mph/161.442km/h; **2** Valtteri Bottas, FIN (Dallara F308-Mercedes Benz), 30m 23.373s; **3** Roberto Merhi, E (Dallara F308-Mercedes Benz), 30m 29.155s; **4** Christian Vietoris, D (Dallara F308-Mercedes Benz), 30m 31.985s; **5** Alexander Sims, GB (Dallara F308-Mercedes Benz), 30m 36.861s; **6** Jean-Karl Vernay, F (Dallara F308-Volkswagen), 30m 38.767s; **7** Stefano Coletti, MC (Dallara F308-Mercedes Benz), 30m 39.415s; **8** Mika Mäki, FIN (Dallara F308-Volkswagen), 30m 44.205s; **9** Esteban Gutierrez, MEX (Dallara F308-Mercedes Benz), 30m 44.850s; **10** Marco Wittmann, D (Dallara F308-Mercedes Benz), 30m 49.401s.
Fastest race lap: Bianchi, 1m 21.296s, 101.699mph/163.669km/h.
Pole position: Bianchi, 1m 20.706s, 102.442mph/164.865km/h.

Round 10 (66.601 miles/107.184km).
1 Christian Vietoris, D (Dallara F308-Mercedes Benz), 40m 33.472s, 98.527mph/158.565km/h; **2** Stefano Coletti, MC (Dallara F308-Mercedes Benz), 40m 51.042s; **3** Mika Mäki, FIN (Dallara F308-Volkswagen), 40m 59.490s; **4** Alexander Sims, GB (Dallara F308-Mercedes Benz), 41m 00.159s; **5** Roberto Merhi, E (Dallara F308-Mercedes Benz), 41m 00.884s; **6** Jules Bianchi, F (Dallara F308-Mercedes Benz), 41m 02.017s; **7** Jean-Karl Vernay, F (Dallara F308-Volkswagen), 41m 02.494s; **8** Valtteri Bottas, FIN (Dallara F308-Mercedes Benz), 41m 04.505s; **9** Esteban Gutierrez, MEX (Dallara F308-Mercedes Benz), 41m 05.021s; **10** Henkie Waldschmidt, NL (Dallara F308-Mercedes Benz), 41m 13.169s.
Fastest race lap: Coletti, 1m 22.440s, 100.288mph/161.397km/h.
Pole position: Mäki.

FORMULA 3 EURO SERIES, Nürburgring, Nürburg/Eifel, Germany, 15/16 August. 22 and 27 laps of the 2.255-mile/3.629km circuit.
Round 11 (49.609 miles/79.838km).
1 Jules Bianchi, F (Dallara F308-Mercedes Benz), 31m 01.013s, 95.965mph/154.441km/h; **2** Valtteri Bottas, FIN (Dallara F308-Mercedes Benz), 31m 14.735s; **3** Esteban Gutierrez, MEX (Dallara F308-Mercedes Benz), 31m 15.706s; **4** Sam Bird, GB (Dallara F308-Mercedes Benz), 31m 16.651s; **5** Mika Mäki, FIN (Dallara F308-Volkswagen), 31m 20.469s; **6** Jean-Karl Vernay, F (Dallara F308-Volkswagen), 31m 21.151s; **7** Alexander Sims, GB (Dallara F308-Mercedes Benz), 31m 21.435s; **8** Christian Vietoris, D (Dallara F308-Mercedes Benz), 31m 22.769s; **9** Stefano Coletti, MC (Dallara F308-Mercedes Benz), 31m 23.488s; **10** Henkie Waldschmidt, NL (Dallara F308-Mercedes Benz), 31m 27.794s.
Fastest race lap: Bianchi, 1m 23.851s, 96.813mph/155.805km/h.
Pole position: Bianchi, 1m 22.823s, 98.014mph/157.739km/h.

Round 12 (60.884 miles/97.983km).
1 Alexander Sims, GB (Dallara F308-Mercedes Benz), 41m 08.747s, 88.783mph/142.882km/h; **2** Christian Vietoris, D (Dallara F308-Mercedes Benz), 41m 12.451s; **3** Mika Mäki, FIN (Dallara F308-Volkswagen), 41m 18.501s; **4** Valtteri Bottas, FIN (Dallara F308-Mercedes Benz), 41m 19.543s; **5** Jules Bianchi, F (Dallara F308-Mercedes Benz), 41m 21.476s; **6** Esteban Gutierrez, MEX (Dallara F308-Mercedes Benz), 41m 21.548s; **7** Henkie Waldschmidt, NL (Dallara F308-Mercedes Benz), 41m 28.673s; **8** Sam Bird, GB (Dallara F308-Mercedes Benz), 41m 32.016s; **9** Marco Wittmann, D (Dallara F308-Mercedes Benz), 41m 33.647s; **10** Stefano Coletti, MC (Dallara F308-Mercedes Benz), 41m 34.291s.
Fastest race lap: Sims, 1m 24.443s, 96.134mph/154.713km/h.
Pole position: Vietoris.

FORMULA 3 EURO SERIES, Brands Hatch Indy Circuit, West Kingsdown, Dartford, Kent, Great Britain, 5/6 September. 39 and 52 laps of the 1.199-mile/1.929km circuit.
Round 13 (46.746 miles/75.231km).
1 Mika Mäki, FIN (Dallara F308-Volkswagen), 4h 43m 59.183s, 9.876mph/15.895km/h; **2** Valtteri Bottas, FIN (Dallara F308-Mercedes Benz), 4h 43m 59.732s; **3** Christian Vietoris, D (Dallara F308-Mercedes Benz), 4h 44m 01.027s; **4** Alexander Sims, GB (Dallara F308-Mercedes Benz), 4h 44m 04.333s; **5** Christopher Zanella, CH (Dallara F308-Mercedes Benz), 4h 44m 05.053s; **6** Sam Bird, GB (Dallara F308-Mercedes Benz), 4h 44m 05.857s; **7** Esteban Gutierrez, MEX (Dallara F308-Mercedes Benz), 4h 44m 06.272s; **8** Brendon Hartley, NZ (Dallara F308-Volkswagen), 4h 44m 09.399s; **9** Roberto Merhi, E (Dallara F308-Mercedes Benz), 4h 44m 10.125s; **10** Jake Rosenzweig, USA (Dallara F308-Volkswagen), 4h 44m 12.257s.
Race times include inactive period after an accident.
Fastest race lap: Vietoris, 42.183s, 102.294mph/164.626km/h.
Pole position: Bottas, 41.438s, 104.133mph/167.585km/h.

Round 14 (62.329 miles/100.308km).
1 Brendon Hartley, NZ (Dallara F308-Volkswagen), 40m 23.598s, 92.582mph/148.997km/h; **2** Alexander Sims, GB (Dallara F308-Mercedes Benz), 40m 23.957s; **3** Sam Bird, GB (Dallara F308-Mercedes Benz), 40m 24.520s; **4** Christian Vietoris, D (Dallara F308-Mercedes Benz), 40m 25.290s; **5** Esteban Gutierrez, MEX (Dallara F308-Mercedes Benz), 40m 27.012s; **6** Mika Mäki, FIN (Dallara F308-Volkswagen), 40m 28.886s; **7** Christopher Zanella, CH (Dallara F308-Mercedes Benz), 40m 29.752s; **8** Jean-Karl Vernay, F (Dallara F308-Volkswagen), 40m 32.124s; **9** Tim Sandtler, D (Dallara F308-Mercedes Benz), 40m 36.769s; **10** Marco Wittmann, D (Dallara F308-Mercedes Benz), 40m 37.268s.
Fastest race lap: Bird, 42.087s, 102.527mph/165.001km/h.
Pole position: Hartley.

FORMULA 3 EURO SERIES, Circuit de Catalunya, Montmeló, Barcelona, Spain, 19/20 September. 25 and 36 laps of the 1.850-mile/2.977km circuit.
Round 15 (46.246 miles/74.425km).
1 Jules Bianchi, F (Dallara F308-Mercedes Benz), 30m 22.894s, 91.329mph/146.981km/h; **2** Alexander Sims, GB (Dallara F308-Mercedes Benz), 30m 23.965s; **3** Andrea Caldarelli, I (Dallara F308-Mercedes Benz), 30m 26.106s; **4** Valtteri Bottas, FIN (Dallara F308-Mercedes Benz), 30m 26.771s; **5** Henkie Waldschmidt, NL (Dallara F308-Mercedes Benz), 30m 28.454s; **6** Christian Vietoris, D (Dallara F308-Mercedes Benz), 30m 32.832s; **7** Basil Shaaban, RL (Dallara F308-Mercedes Benz), 30m 43.032s; **8** Renger van der Zande, NL (Dallara F308-Mercedes Benz), 30m 43.848s; **9** Roberto Merhi, E (Dallara F308-Mercedes Benz), 30m 47.746s; **10** Mika Mäki, FIN (Dallara F308-Volkswagen), 30m 51.059s.
Fastest race lap: Caldarelli, 1m 07.062s, 99.302mph/159.810km/h.
Pole position: Bianchi, 1m 07.007s, 99.383mph/159.941km/h.

Round 16 (66.594 miles/107.172km).
1 Renger van der Zande, NL (Dallara F308-Mercedes Benz), 40m 43.958s, 98.094mph/157.867km/h; **2** Alexander Sims, GB (Dallara F308-Mercedes Benz), 40m 48.234s; **3** Basil Shaaban, RL (Dallara F308-Mercedes Benz), 40m 52.594s; **4** Christian Vietoris, D (Dallara F308-Mercedes Benz), 40m 56.005s; **5** Jules Bianchi, F (Dallara F308-Mercedes Benz), 40m 56.941s; **6** Valtteri Bottas, FIN (Dallara F308-Mercedes Benz), 40m 57.676s; **7** Henkie Waldschmidt, NL (Dallara F308-Mercedes Benz), 40m 59.488s; **8** Tiago Geronimi, BR (Dallara F308-Volkswagen), 41m 04.487s; **9** Esteban Gutierrez, MEX (Dallara F308-Mercedes Benz), 41m 05.352s; **10** Andrea Caldarelli, I (Dallara F308-Mercedes Benz), 41m 06.101s.
Fastest race lap: Bianchi, 1m 07.384s, 98.827mph/159.047km/h.
Pole position: van der Zande.

FORMULA 3 EURO SERIES, Circuit de Dijon-Prenois, Fontaine-les-Dijon, France, 10/11 October. 21 and 20 laps of the 2.362-mile/3.801km circuit.
Round 17 (49.598 miles/79.821km).
1 Christian Vietoris, D (Dallara F308-Mercedes Benz), 27m 15.927s, 109.146mph/175.653km/h; **2** Jules Bianchi, F (Dallara F308-Mercedes Benz), 27m 18.809s; **3** Mika Mäki, FIN (Dallara F308-Volkswagen), 27m 20.323s; **4** Andrea Caldarelli, I (Dallara F308-Mercedes Benz), 27m 21.107s; **5** Roberto Merhi, E (Dallara F308-Mercedes Benz), 27m 22.540s; **6** Sam Bird, GB (Dallara F308-Mercedes Benz), 27m 26.187s; **7** Christopher Zanella, CH (Dallara F308-Mercedes Benz), 27m 29.333s; **8** Alexander Sims, GB (Dallara F308-Mercedes Benz), 27m 30.039s; **9** Tiago Geronimi, BR (Dallara F308-Volkswagen), 27m 30.535s; **10** Basil Shaaban, RL (Dallara F308-Mercedes Benz), 27m 38.320s.
Fastest race lap: Bianchi, 1m 11.067s, 119.642mph/192.545km/h.
Pole position: Bianchi, 1m 10.111s, 121.273mph/195.171km/h.

Round 18 (47.237 miles/76.020km).
1 Jules Bianchi, F (Dallara F308-Mercedes Benz), 40m 50.023s, 69.408mph/111.702km/h; **2** Roberto Merhi, E (Dallara F308-Mercedes Benz), 40m 51.067s; **3** Esteban Gutierrez, MEX (Dallara F308-Mercedes Benz), 40m 55.062s; **4** Alexander Sims, GB (Dallara F308-Mercedes Benz), 40m 57.004s; **5** Sam Bird, GB (Dallara F308-Mercedes Benz), 41m 20.374s*; **6** Christian Vietoris, D (Dallara F308-Mercedes Benz), 41m 27.225s*; **7** Robert Wickens, CDN (Dallara F308-Volkswagen), 41m 29.030s*; **8** Tiago Geronimi, BR (Dallara F308-Volkswagen), 41m 30.256s*; **9** Johan Jokinen, DK (Dallara F309-Volkswagen), 41m 33.605s*; **10** Adrien Tambay, F (Dallara F308-Mercedes Benz), 41m 34.426s*.
* received drive-through substitute penalty of 30-sec.
Fastest race lap: Bird, 1m 11.163s, 119.481mph/192.285km/h.
Pole position: Sims.

FORMULA 3 EURO SERIES, Hockenheimring Grand Prix Circuit, Heidelberg, Germany, 24/25 October. 18 and 23 laps of the 2.842-mile/4.574km circuit.
Round 19 (51.159miles/82.332km).
1 Jules Bianchi, F (Dallara F308-Mercedes Benz), 28m 36.645s, 107.286mph/172.660km/h; **2** Valtteri Bottas, FIN (Dallara F308-Mercedes Benz), 28m 44.161s; **3** Jean-Karl Vernay, F (Dallara F308-Volkswagen), 28m 46.684s; **4** Roberto Merhi, E (Dallara F308-Mercedes Benz), 28m 48.116s; **5** Mika Mäki, FIN (Dallara F308-Volkswagen), 28m 56.979s; **6** Alexander Sims, GB (Dallara F308-Mercedes Benz), 28m 57.934s; **7** Marco Wittmann, D (Dallara F308-Mercedes Benz), 28m 58.549s; **8** Henkie Waldschmidt, NL (Dallara F308-Mercedes Benz), 29m 01.727s; **9** Victor Garcia, E (Dallara F308-Volkswagen), 29m 05.150s; **10** Stefano Coletti, MC (Dallara F309-Mercedes Benz), 29m 09.791s.
Fastest race lap: Bianchi, 1m 34.315s, 108.485mph/174.589km/h.
Pole position: Bianchi, 1m 48.890s, 93.964mph/151.220km/h.

Round 20 (65.369 miles/105.202km).
1 Jean-Karl Vernay, F (Dallara F308-Volkswagen), 40m 50.329s, 96.040mph/154.562km/h; **2** Christopher Zanella, CH (Dallara F308-Mercedes Benz), 40m 51.052s; **3** Mirko Bortolotti, I (Dallara F308-Volkswagen), 40m 59.630s; **4** Marco Wittmann, D (Dallara F308-Mercedes Benz), 41m 03.384s; **5** Valtteri Bottas, FIN (Dallara F308-Mercedes Benz), 41m 11.277s; **6** Esteban Gutierrez, MEX (Dallara F308-Mercedes Benz), 41m 21.258s; **7** Jules Bianchi, F (Dallara F308-Mercedes Benz), 41m 32.159s; **8** Henkie Waldschmidt, NL (Dallara F308-Mercedes Benz), 41m 35.117s; **9** Stefano Coletti, MC (Dallara F309-Mercedes Benz), 41m 44.638s; **10** Adrien Tambay, F (Dallara F308-Mercedes Benz), 41m 44.852s.
Fastest race lap: Vernay, 1m 36.390s, 106.149mph/170.831km/h.
Pole position: Waldschmidt.

Final championship points
Drivers
1 Jules Bianchi, F, 114; **2** Christian Vietoris, D, 75; **3** Valtteri Bottas, FIN, 62; **4** Alexander Sims, GB, 54; **5** Jean-Karl Vernay, F, 47; **6** Mika Mäki, FIN, 43; **7** Roberto Merhi, E, 42; **8** Sam Bird, GB, 40; **9** Esteban Gutierrez, MEX, 26; **10** Stefano Coletti, MC, 19; **11** Brendon Hartley, NZ, 15; **12** Henkie Waldschmidt, NL, 13; **13** Christopher Zanella, CH, 11; **14** Andrea Caldarelli, I, 11; **15** Renger van der Zande, NL, 7; **16** Basil Shaaban, RL, 6; **17** Jake Rosenzweig, USA, 6; **18** Marco Wittmann, D, 6; **19** Atte Mustonen, FIN, 4; **20** Tiago Geronimi, BR, 2.

Rookies
1 Valtteri Bottas, FIN, 62; **2** Alexander Sims, GB, 54; **3** Christopher Zanella, CH, 11; **4** Andrea Caldarelli, I, 11.

Teams
1 ART Grand Prix, 183; **2** Mücke Motor.sport, 163; **3** Signature, 92.

Nations
1 France, 155; **2** Finland, 108; **3** Great Britain, 92.

ATS Formel-3-Cup

ATS FORMEL-3-CUP, Motorsport Arena Oschersleben, Germany, 12/13 April. 18 and 22 laps of the 2.297-mile/3.696km circuit.
Round 1 (41.339 miles/66.528km).
1 Laurens Vanthoor, B (Dallara F307-Volkswagen), 31m 01.316s, 79.954mph/128.673km/h; **2** Stef Dusseldorp, NL (Dallara F307-Volkswagen), 31m 03.923s; **3** Rahel Frey, CH (Dallara F307-Mercedes Benz), 31m 10.752s; **4** Rafael Suzuki, BR (Dallara F307-Volkswagen), 31m 14.038s; **5** Marco Oberhauser, A (Dallara F307-Mercedes Benz), 31m 22.762s; **6** Markus Pommer, D (Dallara F307-Mercedes Benz), 31m 24.124s; **7** Bernd Herndlhofer, A (Dallara F307-Mercedes Benz), 31m 24.426s; **8** Max Nilsson, S (Dallara F307-Opel), 31m 31.156s; **9** Adderly Fong, HK (Dallara F307-Volkswagen), 31m 31.583s; **10** Sergey Chukanov, UA (ARTTech F24-Opel), 31m 45.762s.
Fastest race lap: Vanthoor, 1m 21.785s, 101.091mph/162.690km/h.
Pole position: Vanthoor, 1m 21.228s, 101.784mph/163.806km/h.

Round 2 (50.525 miles/81.312km).
1 Stef Dusseldorp, NL (Dallara F307-Volkswagen), 30m 16.978s, 100.106 mph/161.104 km/h; **2** Bernd Herndlhofer, A (Dallara F307-Mercedes Benz), 30m 28.101s; **3** Rafael Suzuki, BR (Dallara F307-Volkswagen), 30m 34.451s; **4** Rahel Frey, CH (Dallara F307-Mercedes Benz), 30m 37.498s; **5** Max Nilsson, S (Dallara F307-Opel), 30m 49.738s; **6** Willi Steindl, A (Dallara F307-Mercedes Benz), 30m 52.492s; **7** Markus Pommer, D (Dallara F307-Mercedes Benz), 30m 56.874s; **8** Nico Monien, D (Dallara F307-Mercedes Benz), 30m 59.493s; **9** Gary Hauser, L (Dallara F307-Mercedes Benz), 30m 59.893s; **10** Vladimir Semenov, RUS (Dallara F307-Mercedes Benz), 31m 00.783s.
Fastest race lap: Dusseldorp, 1m 21.575s, 101.351mph/163.109km/h.
Pole position: Vanthoor, 1m 20.258s, 103.014mph/165.785km/h.

ATS FORMEL-3-CUP, Nürburgring, Nürburg/Eifel, Germany, 22/23 May. 2 x 18 laps of the 2.882-mile/4.638km circuit.
Round 3 (51.875 miles/83.484km).
1 Laurens Vanthoor, B (Dallara F307-Volkswagen), 30m 05.328s, 103.443mph/166.475km/h; **2** Rahel Frey, CH (Dallara F307-Mercedes Benz), 30m 06.649s; **3** Bernd Herndlhofer, A (Dallara F307-Mercedes Benz), 30m 07.266s; **4** Rafael Suzuki, BR (Dallara F307-Volkswagen), 30m 15.920s; **5** Markus Pommer, D (Dallara F307-Mercedes Benz), 30m 20.810s; **6** Willi Steindl, A (Dallara F307-Mercedes Benz), 30m 21.431s; **7** Nico Monien, D (Dallara F307-Mercedes Benz), 30m 28.575s; **8** Nicolas Marroc, F (Dallara F307-Mercedes Benz), 30m 31.267s; **9** Adderly Fong, HK (Dallara F307-Volkswagen), 30m 32.056s; **10** Marco Oberhauser, A (Dallara F307-Mercedes Benz), 30m 35.894s.
Fastest race lap: Frey, 1m 39.380s, 104.396mph/168.010km/h.
Pole position: Vanthoor, 1m 39.187s, 104.599mph/168.337km/h.

Round 4 (51.875 miles/83.484km).
1 Rahel Frey, CH (Dallara F307-Mercedes Benz), 30m 15.574s, 102.859 mph/165.536 km/h; **2** Laurens Vanthoor, B (Dallara F307-Volkswagen), 30m 22.056s; **3** Nico Monien, D (Dallara F307-Mercedes Benz), 30m 29.537s; **4** Bernd Herndlhofer, A (Dallara F307-Mercedes Benz), 30m 31.086s; **5** Stef Dusseldorp, NL (Dallara F307-Volkswagen), 30m 31.910s; **6** Max Nilsson, S (Dallara F307-Opel), 30m 41.975s; **7** Rafael Suzuki, BR (Dallara F307-Volkswagen), 30m 43.495s; **8** Markus Pommer, D (Dallara F307-Mercedes Benz), 30m 45.710s; **9** Adderly Fong, HK (Dallara F307-Volkswagen), 30m 50.899s; **10** Gary Hauser, L (Dallara F307-Mercedes Benz), 30m 51.603s.
Fastest race lap: Dusseldorp, 1m 40.000s, 103.749mph/166.968km/h.
Pole position: Frey, 1m 38.359s, 105.480mph/169.754km/h.

ATS FORMEL-3-CUP, Hockenheimring Grand Prix Circuit, Heidelberg, Germany, 6/7 June. 19 and 17 laps of the 2.842-mile/4.574km circuit.
Round 5 (54.001 miles/86.906km).
1 Stef Dusseldorp, NL (Dallara F307-Volkswagen), 30m 28.762s, 106.303mph/171.078km/h; **2** Laurens Vanthoor, B (Dallara F307-Volkswagen), 30m 31.390s; **3** Rahel Frey, CH (Dallara F307-Mercedes Benz), 30m 43.044s; **4** Markus Pommer, D (Dallara F307-Mercedes Benz), 30m 55.540s; **5** Gary Hauser, L (Dallara F307-Mercedes Benz), 31m 00.797s; **6** Willi Steindl, A (Dallara F307-Mercedes Benz), 31m 02.735s; **7** Max Nilsson, S (Dallara F307-Opel), 31m 03.866s; **8** Nicolas Marroc, F (Dallara F307-Mercedes Benz), 31m 04.399s; **9** Marco Oberhauser, A (Dallara F307-Mercedes Benz), 31m 20.705s; **10** Sergey Chukanov, UA (ARTTech F24-Opel), 31m 27.615s.
Fastest race lap: Dusseldorp, 1m 35.248s, 107.422mph/172.879km/h.
Pole position: Rafael Suzuki, BR (Dallara F307-Volkswagen, 1m 34.341s, 108.455mph/174.541km/h.

Round 6 (48.317 miles/77.758 km).
1 Laurens Vanthoor, B (Dallara F307-Volkswagen), 27m 28.801s, 105.495 mph/169.777 km/h; **2** Stef Dusseldorp, NL (Dallara F307-Volkswagen), 27m 32.581s; **3** Nico Monien, D (Dallara F307-Mercedes Benz), 27m 36.243s; **4** Rafael Suzuki, BR (Dallara F307-Volkswagen), 27m 40.007s; **5** Markus Pommer, D (Dallara F307-Mercedes Benz), 27m 40.811s; **6** Willi Steindl, A (Dallara F307-Mercedes Benz), 27m 49.189s; **7** Max Nilsson, S (Dallara F307-Opel), 27m 51.413s; **8** Marco Oberhauser, A (Dallara F307-Mercedes Benz), 27m 52.593s; **9** Bernd Herndlhofer, A (Dallara F307-Mercedes Benz), 27m 53.270s; **10** Adderly Fong, HK (Dallara F307-Volkswagen), 27m 55.290s.
Fastest race lap: Dusseldorp, 1m 36.122s, 106.445mph/171.307km/h.
Pole position: Vanthoor, 1m 52.499s, 90.950mph/146.369km/h.

ATS FORMEL-3-CUP, Motorsport Arena Oschersleben, Germany, 20/21 June. 2 x 22 laps of the 2.297-mile/3.696km circuit.
Round 7 (50.525 miles/81.312km).
1 Laurens Vanthoor, B (Dallara F307-Volkswagen), 30m 28.208s, 99.491mph/160.115km/h; **2** Markus Pommer, D (Dallara F307-Mercedes Benz), 30m 41.091s; **3** Nico Monien, D (Dallara F307-Mercedes Benz), 30m 41.832s; **4** Rafael Suzuki, BR (Dallara F307-Volkswagen), 30m 44.316s; **5** Willi Steindl, A (Dallara F307-Mercedes Benz), 30m 58.259s; **6** Stef Dusseldorp, NL (Dallara F307-Volkswagen), 30m 59.470s; **7** Rahel Frey, CH (Dallara F307-Mercedes Benz), 31m 02.723s; **8** Marco Oberhauser, A (Dallara F307-Mercedes Benz), 31m 06.302s; **9** Max Nilsson, S (Dallara F307-Opel), 31m 06.625s; **10** Bernd Herndlhofer, A (Dallara F307-Mercedes Benz), 31m 07.237s.
Fastest race lap: Vanthoor, 1m 21.919s, 100.926mph/162.423km/h.
Pole position: Dusseldorp, 1m 21.945s, 100.893mph/162.372km/h.

Round 8 (50.525 miles/81.312km).
1 Laurens Vanthoor, B (Dallara F307-Volkswagen), 30m 32.566s, 99.254mph/159.734km/h; **2** Nico Monien, D (Dallara F307-Mercedes Benz), 30m 45.120s; **3** Rafael Suzuki, BR (Dallara F307-Volkswagen), 30m 48.446s; **4** Bernd Herndlhofer, A (Dallara F307-Mercedes Benz), 30m 56.455s; **5** Markus Pommer, D (Dallara F307-Mercedes Benz), 31m 02.662s; **6** Willi Steindl, A (Dallara F307-Mercedes Benz), 31m 14.675s; **7** Nicolas Marroc, F (Dallara F307-Mercedes Benz), 31m 17.657s; **8** Shirley van der Lof, NL (Dallara F307-Mercedes Benz), 31m 27.969s; **9** Stef Dusseldorp, NL (Dallara F307-Volkswagen), 31m 34.630s; **10** Jesse Krohn, FIN (ARTTech F24-Opel), 31m 40.974s.
Fastest race lap: Vanthoor, 1m 22.186s, 100.598mph/161.896km/h.
Pole position: Vanthoor, 1m 21.925s, 100.918mph/162.412km/h.

ATS FORMEL-3-CUP, EuroSpeedway Lausitz, Klettwitz, Dresden, Germany, 4/5 July. 24 and 23 laps of the 2.139-mile/3.442km circuit.
Round 9 (51.330 miles/82.608km).
1 Laurens Vanthoor, B (Dallara F307-Volkswagen), 31m 14.306s, 98.591mph/158.666km/h; **2** Rafael Suzuki, BR (Dallara F307-Volkswagen), 31m 26.749s; **3** Nico Monien, D (Dallara F307-Mercedes Benz), 31m 35.137s; **4** Max Nilsson, S (Dallara F307-Opel), 31m 38.930s; **5** Bernd Herndlhofer, A (Dallara F307-Mercedes Benz), 31m 39.039s; **6** Markus Pommer, D (Dallara F307-Mercedes Benz), 31m 43.157s; **7** Rahel Frey, CH (Dallara F307-Mercedes Benz), 31m 49.768s; **8** Adderly Fong, HK (Dallara F307-Volkswagen), 31m 54.790s; **9** David Hauser, L (Dallara F307-Mercedes Benz), 32m 02.390s; **10** Stef Dusseldorp, NL (Dallara F307-Volkswagen), 32m 04.719s.
Fastest race lap: Vanthoor, 1m 16.979s, 100.021mph/160.969km/h.
Pole position: Vanthoor, 1m 16.581s, 100.541mph/161.805km/h.

Round 10 (49.191 miles/79.166km).
1 Nico Monien, D (Dallara F307-Mercedes Benz), 30m 05.642s, 98.076 mph/157.837 km/h; **2** Laurens Vanthoor, B (Dallara F307-Volkswagen), 30m 06.731s; **3** Stef Dusseldorp, NL (Dallara F307-Volkswagen), 30m 07.496s; **4** Markus Pommer, D (Dallara F307-Mercedes Benz), 30m 07.993s; **5** Rahel Frey, CH (Dallara F307-Mercedes Benz), 30m 12.206s; **6** Rafael Suzuki, BR (Dallara F307-Volkswagen), 30m 13.707s; **7** Bernd Herndlhofer, A (Dallara F307-Mercedes Benz), 30m 18.769s; **8** Max Nilsson, S (Dallara F307-Opel), 30m 18.977s; **9** Sergey Chukanov, UA (ARTTech F24-Opel), 30m 39.476s; **10** David Hauser, L (Dallara F307-Mercedes Benz), 30m 44.531s.
Fastest race lap: Vanthoor, 1m 17.726s, 99.060mph/159.422km/h.
Pole position: Vanthoor, 1m 16.291s, 100.923mph/162.420km/h.

ATS FORMEL-3-CUP, Nationale Circuit Assen, Netherlands, 8/9 August. 2 x 18 laps of the 2.830-mile/4.555km circuit.
Round 11 (50.946 miles/81.990km).
1 Laurens Vanthoor, B (Dallara F307-Volkswagen), 30m 52.470s, 99.006mph/159.335km/h; **2** Stef Dusseldorp, NL (Dallara F307-Volkswagen), 30m 56.601s; **3** Max Nilsson, S (Dallara F307-Opel), 31m 08.471s; **4** Rafael Suzuki, BR (Dallara F307-Mercedes Benz), 31m 09.336s; **5** Sergey Chukanov, UA (ARTTech F24-Opel), 31m 16.355s; **6** Harald Schlegelmilch, LV (Dallara F307-Mercedes Benz), 31m 21.124s; **7** Jesse Krohn, FIN (ARTTech F24-Opel), 31m 33.620s; **8** Marco Oberhauser, A (Dallara F307-Mercedes Benz), 31m 33.996s; **9** Bernd Herndlhofer, A (Dallara F307-Volkswagen), 31m 34.301s; **10** Adderly Fong, HK (Dallara F307-Volkswagen), 31m 34.731s.
Fastest race lap: Vanthoor, 1m 32.736s, 109.874mph/176.825km/h.
Pole position: Vanthoor, 1m 34.073s, 108.312mph/174.311km/h.

Round 12 (50.946 miles/81.990km).
1 Laurens Vanthoor, B (Dallara F307-Volkswagen), 30m 52.463s, 99.007mph/159.336km/h; **2** Harald Schlegelmilch, LV (Dallara F307-Mercedes Benz), 31m 07.133s; **3** Rafael Suzuki, BR (Dallara F307-Mercedes Benz), 31m 07.728s; **4** Stef Dusseldorp, NL (Dallara F307-Volkswagen), 31m 09.780s; **5** Adderly Fong, HK (Dallara F307-Volkswagen), 31m 13.190s; **6** Nico Monien, D (Dallara F307-Mercedes Benz), 31m 13.415s; **7** Nicolas Marroc, F (Dallara F307-Mercedes Benz), 31m 15.791s; **8** Max Nilsson, S (Dallara F307-Opel), 31m 18.683s; **9** Sergey Chukanov, UA (ARTTech F24-Opel), 31m 23.652s; **10** Gary Hauser, L (Dallara F307-Mercedes Benz), 31m 33.555s.
Fastest race lap: Vanthoor, 1m 32.327s, 110.360mph/177.608km/h.
Pole position: Vanthoor, 1m 33.401s, 109.091mph/175.566km/h.

ATS FORMEL-3-CUP, Nürburgring, Nürburg/Eifel, Germany, 22 August. 2 x 16 laps of the 3.192-mile/5.137km circuit.
Round 13 (51.072 miles/82.192km).
1 Laurens Vanthoor, B (Dallara F307-Volkswagen), 30m 03.648s, 101.937mph/164.052km/h; **2** Stef Dusseldorp, NL (Dallara F307-Volkswagen), 30m 07.511s; **3** Tom Dillmann, F (Dallara F307-Mercedes Benz), 30m 13.090s; **4** Markus Pommer, D (Dallara F307-Mercedes Benz), 30m 26.438s; **5** Gary Hauser, L (Dallara F307-Mercedes Benz), 30m 32.090s; **6** Rafael Suzuki, BR (Dallara F307-Mercedes Benz), 30m 36.704s; **7** Harald Schlegelmilch, LV (Dallara F307-Mercedes Benz), 30m 47.093s; **8** Sergey Chukanov, UA (ARTTech F24-Opel), 30m 49.445s; **9** Jesse Krohn, FIN (ARTTech F24-Opel), 30m 50.459s; **10** Willi Steindl, A (Dallara F307-Mercedes Benz), 30m 50.642s.
Fastest race lap: Vanthoor, 1m 51.462s, 103.095mph/165.915km/h.
Pole position: Vanthoor, 1m 52.365s, 102.266mph/164.581km/h.

Round 14 (51.072 miles/82.192km).
1 Tom Dillmann, F (Dallara F307-Mercedes Benz), 30m 02.455s, 102.004mph/164.160km/h; **2** Tim Sandtler, D (Dallara F307-Mercedes Benz), 30m 14.954s; **3** Stef Dusseldorp, NL (Dallara F307-Volkswagen), 30m 15.361s; **4** Harald Schlegelmilch, LV (Dallara F307-Mercedes Benz), 30m 22.621s; **5** Nico Monien, D (Dallara F307-Mercedes Benz), 30m 29.930s; **6** Rafael Suzuki, BR (Dallara F307-Mercedes Benz), 30m 30.824s; **7** Adderly Fong, HK (Dallara F307-Volkswagen), 30m 36.850s; **8** Markus Pommer, D (Dallara F307-Mercedes Benz), 30m 37.467s; **9** Jesse Krohn, FIN (ARTTech F24-Opel), 30m 43.020s; **10** Max Nilsson, S (Dallara F307-Opel), 30m 49.051s.
Fastest race lap: Dillmann, 1m 51.362s, 103.187mph/166.064km/h.
Pole position: Dillmann, 2m 12.867s, 86.486mph/139.186km/h.

ATS FORMEL-3-CUP, Sachsenring, Oberlungwitz, Germany, 19/20 September. 2 x 24 laps of the 2.265-mile/3.645km circuit.
Round 15 (54.358 miles/87.480km).
1 Tom Dillmann, F (Dallara F307-Mercedes Benz), 30m 04.275s, 108.458mph/174.545km/h; **2** Stef Dusseldorp, NL (Dallara F307-Volkswagen), 30m 08.591s; **3** Harald Schlegelmilch, LV (Dallara F307-Mercedes Benz), 30m

26.537s; **4** Joey Foster, GB (Dallara F307-Mercedes Benz), 30m 34.202s; **5** Markus Pommer, D (Dallara F307-Mercedes Benz), 30m 39.056s; **6** David Hauser, L (Dallara F307-Mercedes Benz), 30m 42.626s; **7** Sergey Chukanov, UA (ARTTech F24-Opel), 30m 54.805s; **8** Max Nilsson, S (Dallara F307-Opel), 30m 55.694s; **9** Rafael Suzuki, BR (Dallara F307-Opel), 30m 55.867s; **10** Nico Monien, D (Dallara F307-Mercedes Benz), 30m 56.395s.
Fastest race lap: Dillmann, 1m 14.821s, 108.975mph/175.379km/h.
Pole position: Dillmann, 1m 14.245s, 109.821mph/176.739km/h.

Round 16 (54.358 miles/87.480km).
1 Laurens Vanthoor, B (Dallara F307-Volkswagen), 29m 59.290s, 108.758mph/175.029km/h; **2** Peter Elkmann, D (Dallara F307-Volkswagen), 30m 09.145s; **3** Tom Dillmann, F (Dallara F307-Mercedes Benz), 30m 09.677s; **4** Harald Schlegelmilch, LV (Dallara F307-Mercedes Benz), 30m 19.858s; **5** Joey Foster, GB (Dallara F307-Mercedes Benz), 30m 23.591s; **6** Stef Dusseldorp, NL (Dallara F307-Volkswagen), 30m 29.117s; **7** Nico Monien, D (Dallara F307-Mercedes Benz), 30m 31.410s; **8** Markus Pommer, D (Dallara F307-Mercedes Benz), 30m 35.409s; **9** Max Nilsson, S (Dallara F307-Opel), 30m 48.333s; **10** Rafael Suzuki, BR (Dallara F307-Opel), 31m 03.467s.
Fastest race lap: Vanthoor, 1m 14.232s, 109.840mph/176.770km/h.
Pole position: Vanthoor, 1m 13.349s, 111.162mph/178.898km/h.

ATS FORMEL-3-CUP, Motorsport Arena Oschersleben, Germany, 17/18 October. 16 and 22 laps of the 2.297-mile/3.696km circuit.
Round 17 (36.745 miles/59.136km).
1 Laurens Vanthoor, B (Dallara F307-Volkswagen), 30m 34.831s, 72.096mph/116.027km/h; **2** Markus Pommer, D (Dallara F307-Mercedes Benz), 30m 37.156s; **3** Stef Dusseldorp, NL (Dallara F307-Volkswagen), 30m 38.146s; **4** Joey Foster, GB (Dallara F307-Mercedes Benz), 30m 38.393s; **5** Nicolas Marroc, F (Dallara F307-Mercedes Benz), 30m 46.188s; **6** Nico Monien, D (Dallara F307-Mercedes Benz), 30m 47.403s; **7** Jesse Krohn, FIN (ARTTech F24-Opel), 30m 55.352s; **8** Gary Hauser, L (Dallara F307-Mercedes Benz), 31m 09.696s; **9** Max Nilsson, S (Dallara F307-Opel), 31m 16.521s; **10** Armaan Ebrahim, IND (Dallara F307-Volkswagen), 31m 23.855s.
Fastest race lap: Monien, 1m 44.058s, 79.453mph/127.867km/h.
Pole position: Pommer, 1m 42.740s, 80.472mph/129.507km/h.

Round 18 (50.525 miles/81.312km).
1 Tom Dillmann, F (Dallara F307-Mercedes Benz), 30m 51.896s, 98.218mph/158.067km/h; **2** Laurens Vanthoor, B (Dallara F307-Volkswagen), 31m 02.514s; **3** Stef Dusseldorp, NL (Dallara F307-Volkswagen), 31m 22.552s; **4** Markus Pommer, D (Dallara F307-Mercedes Benz), 32m 02.926s; **5** Sergey Chukanov, UA (ARTTech F24-Opel), 32m 20.258s; **6** Nicolas Marroc, F (Dallara F307-Mercedes Benz), 32m 28.037s; **7** Daniel Abt, D (Dallara F307-Volkswagen), 32m 32.471s; **8** Gary Hauser, L (Dallara F307-Mercedes Benz), 32m 37.629s; **9** David Hauser, L (Dallara F307-Mercedes Benz), 32m 47.894s; **10** Harald Schlegelmilch, LV (Dallara F307-Mercedes Benz), 33m 00.396s.
Fastest race lap: Vanthoor, 1m 22.075s, 100.734mph/162.115km/h.
Pole position: Dillmann, 1m 31.903s, 89.961mph/144.779km/h.

Final championship points
Formel-3-Cup
1 Laurens Vanthoor, B, 163; **2** Stef Dusseldorp, NL, 106; **3** Markus Pommer, D, 67; **4** Rafael Suzuki, BR, 65; **5** Nico Monien, D, 61; **6** Tom Dillmann, F, 49; **7** Rahel Frey, CH, 45; **8** Bernd Herndlhofer, A, 32; **9** Harald Schlegelmilch, LV, 30; **10** Max Nilsson, S, 30; **11** Willi Steindl, A, 19; **12** Nicolas Marroc, F, 14; **13** Sergey Chukanov, UA, 12; **14** Gary Hauser, L, 12; **15** Tim Sandtler, D, 8; **16** Adderly Fong, HK, 7; **17** Marco Oberhauser, A, 7; **18** David Hauser, L, 5; **19** Jesse Krohn, FIN, 5; **20** Shirley van der Lof, NL, 1.

Formel-3-Trophy
1 Sergey Chukanov, UA, 158; **2** Mika Vähämäki, FIN, 115; **3** Francesco Lopez, D, 89.

Rookie Cup
1 Stef Dusseldorp, NL, 149; **2** Markus Pommer, D, 130; **3** Nico Monien, D, 112.

Italian Formula 3 Championship

ITALIAN FORMULA 3 CHAMPIONSHIP, Autodromo Adria International Raceway, Adria, Italy, 9/10 May. Round 1. 2 x 20 laps of the 1.679-mile/2.702km circuit.
Race 1 (33.579 miles/54.040km).
1 Daniel Zampieri, I (Dallara F309-FIAT), 24m 16.698s, 82.984mph/133.551km/h; **2** Daniel Campos-Hull, E (Dallara F309-FIAT), 24m 17.929s; **3** Sergio Campana, I (Dallara F309-FIAT), 24m 22.951s; **4** Marco Zipoli, I (Dallara F309-FIAT), 24m 23.977s; **5** Pablo Sánchez, MEX (Mygale M-09F3-FIAT), 24m 27.860s; **6** Stefanos Kamitsakis, GR (Dallara F309-FIAT), 24m 29.082s; **7** Francesco Castellacci, I (Dallara F309-FIAT), 24m 42.859s; **8** Kevin Ceccon, I (Dallara F309-FIAT), 24m 43.658s; **9** Giovanni Nava, I (Dallara F309-FIAT), 24m 44.130s; **10** Michele Faccin, I (Dallara F309-FIAT), 24m 44.642s.
Fastest race lap: Campos-Hull, 1m 12.155s, 83.766mph/134.809km/h.
Pole position: Zampieri, 1m 11.606s, 84.409mph/135.843km/h.

Race 2 (33.579 miles/54.040km).
1 Stefanos Kamitsakis, GR (Dallara F309-FIAT), 24m 30.381s, 82.212mph/132.308km/h; **2** Marco Zipoli, I (Dallara F309-FIAT), 24m 31.122s; **3** Pablo Sánchez, MEX (Mygale M-09F3-FIAT), 24m 31.879s; **4** Sergio Campana, I (Dallara F309-FIAT), 24m 34.952s; **5** Daniel Zampieri, I (Dallara F309-FIAT), 24m 36.136s; **6** Daniel Campos-Hull, E (Dallara F309-FIAT), 24m 36.773s; **7** Kevin Ceccon, I (Dallara F309-FIAT), 24m 41.872s; **8** Francesco Castellacci, I (Dallara F309-FIAT), 24m 42.334s; **9** Giovanni Nava, I (Dallara F309-FIAT), 24m 46.915s; **10** Alessandro Cicognani, I (Dallara F309-FIAT), 24m 50.293s.
Fastest race lap: Campos-Hull, 1m 12.358s, 83.531mph/134.431km/h.
Pole position: Kamitsakis.

ITALIAN FORMULA 3 CHAMPIONSHIP, Autodromo Mario Umberto Borzacchini, Magione, Perugia, Italy, 7 June. Round 2. 22 and 20 laps of the 1.558-mile/2.507km circuit.
Race 1 (34.271 miles/55.154km).
1 Daniel Campos-Hull, E (Dallara F309-FIAT), 24m 57.748s, 82.374mph/132.568km/h; **2** Sergio Campana, I (Dallara F309-FIAT), 25m 01.229s; **3** Pablo Sánchez, MEX (Mygale M-09F3-FIAT), 25m 01.706s; **4** Francesco Castellacci, I (Dallara F309-FIAT), 25m 08.028s; **5** Marco Zipoli, I (Dallara F309-FIAT), 25m 11.430s; **6** Daniel Zampieri, I (Dallara F309-FIAT), 25m 13.853s; **7** Stefanos Kamitsakis, GR (Dallara F309-FIAT), 25m 14.601s; **8** Riccardo Cinti, I (Dallara F309-FIAT), 25m 21.153s; **9** Salvatore Cicatelli, I (Dallara F309-FIAT), 25m 24.779s; **10** Francesco Prandi, I (Dallara F309-FIAT), 25m 28.244s.
Fastest race lap: Zampieri, 1m 07.331s, 83.290mph/134.042km/h.
Pole position: Zampieri, 1m 06.579s, 84.230mph/135.556km/h.

Race 2 (31.156 miles/50.140km).
1 Daniel Zampieri, I (Dallara F309-FIAT), 25m 38.655s, 72.894mph/117.312km/h; **2** Sergio Campana, I (Dallara F309-FIAT), 25m 53.386s; **3** Marco Zipoli, I (Dallara F309-FIAT), 26m 06.340s; **4** Francesco Castellacci, I (Dallara F309-FIAT), 26m 06.999s; **5** Salvatore Cicatelli, I (Dallara F309-FIAT), 26m 07.709s; **6** Daniel Campos-Hull, E (Dallara F309-FIAT), 26m 28.339s; **7** Riccardo Cinti, I (Dallara F309-FIAT), 26m 28.450s; **8** Francesco Prandi, I (Dallara F309-FIAT), 26m 46.949s; **9** Angelo Comi, I (Mygale M-09F3-FIAT), 27m 07.992s; **10** Giovanni Nava, I (Dallara F309-FIAT), **19** laps.
Fastest race lap: Zampieri, 1m 07.548s, 83.022mph/133.611km/h.
Pole position: Zampieri.

ITALIAN FORMULA 3 CHAMPIONSHIP, Autodromo Internazionale del Mugello, Scarperia, Firenze (Florence), Italy, 20/21 June. Round 3. 15 and 12 laps of the 3.259-mile/5.245km circuit.
Race 1 (48.886 miles/78.675km).
1 Daniel Zampieri, I (Dallara F309-FIAT), 26m 24.782s, 111.050mph/178.718km/h; **2** Marco Zipoli, I (Dallara F309-FIAT), 26m 26.642s; **3** Pablo Sánchez, MEX (Mygale M-09F3-FIAT), 26m 32.189s; **4** Daniel Campos-Hull, E (Dallara F309-FIAT), 26m 34.125s; **5** Sergio Campana, I (Dallara F309-FIAT), 26m 36.261s; **6** Francesco Castellacci, I (Dallara F309-FIAT), 26m 42.854s; **7** Stéphane Richelmi, MC (Dallara F309-FIAT), 26m 46.265s; **8** Edoardo Liberati, I (Dallara F309-FIAT), 26m 52.184s; **9** Francesco Prandi, I (Dallara F309-FIAT), 26m 55.598s; **10** Giovanni Nava, I (Dallara F309-FIAT), 26m 57.792s.
Fastest race lap: Campana, 1m 44.287s, 112.504mph/181.058km/h.
Pole position: Campana, 1m 43.284s, 113.596mph/182.816km/h.

Race 2 (39.109 miles/62.940km).
1 Sergio Campana, I (Dallara F309-FIAT), 25m 14.614s, 92.956mph/149.598km/h; **2** Pablo Sánchez, MEX (Mygale M-09F3-FIAT), 25m 16.353s; **3** Daniel Zampieri, I (Dallara F309-FIAT), 25m 17.104s; **4** Marco Zipoli, I (Dallara F309-FIAT), 25m 17.323s; **5** Daniel Campos-Hull, E (Dallara F309-FIAT), 25m 18.533s; **6** Francesco Castellacci, I (Dallara F309-FIAT), 25m 19.650s; **7** Francesco Prandi, I (Dallara F309-FIAT), 25m 24.503s; **8** Giovanni Nava, I (Dallara F309-FIAT), 25m 24.919s; **9** Federico Glorioso, I (Dallara F309-FIAT), 25m 26.855s; **10** Edoardo Liberati, I (Dallara F309-FIAT), 25m 28.284s.
Fastest race lap: Campana, 1m 44.255s, 112.538mph/181.113 km/h.
Pole position: Castellacci.

ITALIAN FORMULA 3 CHAMPIONSHIP, Autodromo Internazionale di Misano, Misano Adriatico, Rimini, Italy, 18/19 July. Round 4. 2 x 16 laps of the 2.626-mile/4.226km circuit.
Race 1 (42.015 miles/67.616km).
1 Sergio Campana, I (Dallara F309-FIAT), 24m 49.848s, 101.522mph/163.384km/h; **2** Daniel Zampieri, I (Dallara F309-FIAT), 24m 59.565s; **3** Francesco Castellacci, I (Dallara F309-FIAT), 25m 00.362s; **4** Stéphane Richelmi, MC (Dallara F309-FIAT), 25m 00.854s; **5** Marco Zipoli, I (Dallara F309-FIAT), 25m 03.977s; **6** Pablo Sánchez, MEX (Mygale M-09F3-FIAT), 25m 04.395s; **7** Salvatore Cicatelli, I (Dallara F309-FIAT), 25m 04.884s; **8** Francesco Prandi, I (Dallara F309-FIAT), 25m 16.048s; **9** Riccardo Cinti, I (Dallara F309-FIAT), 25m 20.332s; **10** Alessandro Cicognani, I (Dallara F309-FIAT), 25m 20.798s.
Fastest race lap: Campana, 1m 32.012s, 102.739mph/165.343km/h.
Pole position: Daniel Campos-Hull, E, 1m 31.149s, 103.712mph/166.909km/h.

Race 2 (42.015 miles/67.616km).
1 Pablo Sánchez, MEX (Mygale M-09F3-FIAT), 25m 11.085s, 100.095mph/161.087km/h; **2** Marco Zipoli, I (Dallara F309-FIAT), 25m 25.177s; **3** Salvatore Cicatelli, I (Dallara F309-FIAT), 25m 26.148s; **4** Francesco Castellacci, I (Dallara F309-FIAT), 25m 26.479s; **5** Stéphane Richelmi, MC (Dallara F309-FIAT), 25m 28.827s; **6** Daniel Campos-Hull, E (Dallara F309-FIAT), 25m 29.540s; **7** Alessandro Cicognani, I (Dallara F309-FIAT), 25m 40.095s; **8** Riccardo Cinti, I (Dallara F309-FIAT), 25m 40.718s; **9** Kevin Ceccon, I (Dallara F308-FIAT), 25m 42.359s; **10** Angelo Comi, I (Mygale M-09F3-FIAT), 25m 43.601s.
Fastest race lap: Sánchez, 1m 33.521s, 101.082mph/162.675km/h.
Pole position: Sánchez.

ITALIAN FORMULA 3 CHAMPIONSHIP, Autodromo Riccardo Paletti, Varano dei Melegari, Parma, Italy, 2 August. Round 5. 2 x 20 laps of the 1.476-mile/2.375km circuit.
Race 1 (29.515 miles/47.500km).
1 Daniel Zampieri, I (Dallara F309-FIAT), 24m 17.263s, 72.913mph/117.343km/h; **2** Daniel Campos-Hull, E (Dallara F309-FIAT), 24m 20.044s; **3** Salvatore Cicatelli, I (Dallara F309-FIAT), 24m 22.953s; **4** Stéphane Richelmi, MC (Dallara F309-FIAT), 24m 23.857s; **5** Riccardo Cinti, I (Dallara F309-FIAT), 24m 27.111s; **6** Marco Zipoli, I (Dallara F309-FIAT), 24m 27.978s; **7** Pablo Sánchez, MEX (Mygale M-09F3-FIAT), 24m 29.126s; **8** Francesco Castellacci, I (Dallara F309-FIAT), 24m 36.094s; **9** Francesco Prandi, I (Dallara F309-FIAT), 24m 40.424s; **10** Alessandro Cicognani, I (Dallara F309-FIAT), 24m 41.674s.
Fastest race lap: Zampieri, 1m 03.618s, 83.509mph/134.395km/h.
Pole position: Zampieri, 1m 02.750s, 84.664mph/136.254km/h.

Race 2 (29.515 miles/47.500km).
1 Marco Zipoli, I (Dallara F309-FIAT), 24m 37.607s, 71.909mph/115.727km/h; **2** Stéphane Richelmi, MC (Dallara F309-FIAT), 24m 38.058s; **3** Riccardo Cinti, I (Dallara F309-FIAT), 24m 38.977s; **4** Daniel Campos-Hull, E (Dallara F309-FIAT), 24m 39.429s; **5** Pablo Sánchez, MEX (Mygale M-09F3-FIAT), 24m 46.722s; **6** Alessandro Cicognani, I (Dallara F309-FIAT), 24m 47.803s; **7** Edoardo Liberati, I (Dallara F309-FIAT), 24m 51.087s; **8** Sergio Campana, I (Dallara F309-FIAT), 24m 51.563s; **9** Kevin Ceccon, I (Dallara F308-FIAT), 24m 52.473s; **10** Francesco Castellacci, I (Dallara F309-FIAT), 24m 53.954s.
Fastest race lap: Campos-Hull, 1m 04.344s, 82.567mph/132.879km/h.
Pole position: Zipoli.

ITALIAN FORMULA 3 CHAMPIONSHIP, Autodromo Enzo e Dino Ferrari, Imola, Italy, 6 September. Round 6. 2 x 15 laps of the 3.050-mile/4.909km circuit.
Race 1 (45.755 miles/73.635km).
1 Pablo Sánchez, MEX (Mygale M-09F3-FIAT), 25m 46.903s, 106.481mph/171.365km/h; **2** Daniel Campos-Hull, E (Dallara F308-FIAT), 25m 47.744s; **3** Salvatore Cicatelli, I (Dallara F308-FIAT), 25m 52.743s; **4** Stéphane Richelmi, MC (Dallara F308-FIAT), 25m 58.105s; **5** Sergio Campana, I (Dallara F308-FIAT), 26m 03.006s; **6** Marco Zipoli, I (Dallara F308-FIAT), 26m 03.674s; **7** Daniel Zampieri, I (Dallara F308-FIAT), 26m 06.464s; **8** Riccardo Cinti, I (Dallara F309-FIAT), 26m 13.215s; **9** Edoardo Liberati, I (Dallara F309-FIAT), 26m 14.111s; **10** Angelo Comi, I (Mygale M-09F3-FIAT), 26m 26.347s.
Fastest race lap: Sánchez, 1m 42.191s, 107.456mph/172.934km/h.
Pole position: Campos-Hull, 1m 42.189s, 107.458mph/172.938km/h.

Race 2 (45.755 miles/73.635km).
1 Marco Zipoli, I (Dallara F308-FIAT), 26m 07.318s, 105.094mph/169.133km/h; **2** Pablo Sánchez, MEX (Mygale M-09F3-FIAT), 26m 07.730s; **3** Stéphane Richelmi, MC (Dallara F308-FIAT), 26m 10.868s; **4** Daniel Zampieri, I (Dallara F308-FIAT), 26m 13.841s; **5** Salvatore Cicatelli, I (Dallara F308-FIAT), 26m 17.508s; **6** Daniel Campos-Hull, E (Dallara F308-FIAT), 26m 17.893s; **7** Riccardo Cinti, I (Dallara F309-FIAT), 26m 22.415s; **8** Edoardo Liberati, I (Dallara F309-FIAT), 26m 23.486s; **9** Alessandro Cicognani, I (Dallara F308-FIAT), 26m 37.521s; **10** Federico Glorioso, I (Dallara F308-FIAT), 26m 40.816s.
Fastest race lap: Zipoli, 1m 43.039s, 106.572mph/171.511km/h.
Pole position: Zipoli.

ITALIAN FORMULA 3 CHAMPIONSHIP, Autodromo di Vallelunga, Campagnano di Roma, Italy, 20 September. Round 7. 17 and 14 laps of the 2.538-mile/4.085km circuit.
Race 1 (43.151 miles/69.445km).
1 Sergio Campana, I (Dallara F308-FIAT), 25m 59.202s, 99.630mph/160.339km/h; **2** Daniel Zampieri, I (Dallara F308-FIAT), 26m 03.034s; **3** Marco Zipoli, I (Dallara F308-FIAT), 26m 05.635s; **4** Daniel Campos-Hull, E (Dallara F308-FIAT), 26m 06.017s; **5** Stéphane Richelmi, MC (Dallara F308-FIAT), 26m 09.358s; **6** Salvatore Cicatelli, I (Dallara F308-FIAT), 26m 11.874s; **7** Francesco Castellacci, I (Dallara F309-FIAT), 26m 13.781s; **8** Alessandro Cicognani, I (Dallara F308-FIAT), 26m 27.548s; **9** Pablo Sánchez, MEX (Mygale M-09F3-FIAT), 26m 27.965s; **10** Francesco Prandi, I (Dallara F308-FIAT), 26m 28.808s.
Fastest race lap: Campana, 1m 30.850s, 100.582mph/161.871km/h.
Pole position: Zampieri, 1m 29.966s, 101.570mph/163.461km/h.

Race 2 (35.536 miles/57.190km).
1 Daniel Campos-Hull, E (Dallara F308-FIAT), 24m 48.894s, 85.923 mph/138.279 km/h; **2** Stéphane Richelmi, MC (Dallara F308-FIAT), 24m 54.578s; **3** Daniel Zampieri, I (Dallara F308-FIAT), 25m 08.575s; **4** Sergio Campana, I (Dallara F308-FIAT), 25m 12.002s; **5** Pablo Sánchez, MEX (Mygale M-09F3-FIAT), 25m 14.060s; **6** Marco Zipoli, I (Dallara F308-FIAT), 25m 22.156s; **7** Riccardo Cinti, I (Dallara F309-FIAT), 25m 25.836s; **8** Alessandro Cicognani, I (Dallara F308-FIAT), 25m 30.124s; **9** Giulio Glorioso, I (Dallara F308-FIAT), 25m 41.162s; **10** Gianmarco Raimondo, CDN (Dallara F308-FIAT), 25m 41.685s.
Fastest race lap: Campos-Hull, 1m 44.160s, 87.729mph/141.186km/h.
Pole position: Cicatelli.

ITALIAN FORMULA 3 CHAMPIONSHIP, Autodromo Nazionale di Monza, Milan, Italy, 17/18 October. Round 8. 2 x 14 laps of the 3.600-mile/5.793km circuit.
Race 1 (50.394 miles/81.102km).
1 Pablo Sánchez, MEX (Mygale M-09F3-FIAT), 25m 10.319s, 120.120mph/193.314km/h; **2** Marco Zipoli, I (Dallara F308-FIAT), 25m 12.338s; **3** Daniel Zampieri, I (Dallara F308-FIAT), 25m 12.636s; **4** Sergio Campana, I (Dallara F308-FIAT), 25m 15.359s; **5** Stéphane Richelmi, MC (Dallara F308-FIAT), 25m 18.216s; **6** Salvatore Cicatelli, I (Dallara F308-FIAT), 25m 18.555s; **7** Giulio Glorioso, I (Dallara F308-FIAT), 25m 38.326s; **8** Francesco Prandi, I (Dallara F308-FIAT), 25m 41.642s; **9** Riccardo Cinti, I (Dallara F309-FIAT), 25m 42.164s; **10** Angelo Comi, I (Mygale M-09F3-FIAT), 25m 48.004s.
Fastest race lap: Zipoli, 1m 46.830s, 121.300mph/195.214km/h.
Pole position: Zampieri, 1m 45.634s, 122.674mph/197.425km/h.

Race 2 (50.394 miles/81.102km).
1 Pablo Sánchez, MEX (Mygale M-09F3-FIAT), 25m 16.804s, 119.606mph/192.488km/h; **2** Sergio Campana, I (Dallara F308-FIAT), 25m 18.769s; **3** Daniel Campos-Hull, E (Dallara F308-FIAT), 25m 19.556s; **4** Daniel Zampieri, I (Dallara F308-FIAT), 25m 20.120s; **5** Marco Zipoli, I (Dallara F308-FIAT), 25m 25.411s; **6** Stéphane Richelmi, MC (Dallara F308-FIAT), 25m 26.058s; **7** Salvatore Cicatelli, I (Dallara F308-FIAT), 25m 26.092s; **8** Francesco Prandi, I (Dallara F308-FIAT), 25m 31.182s; **9** Giulio Glorioso, I (Dallara F308-FIAT), 25m 45.984s; **10** Angelo Comi, I (Mygale M-09F3-FIAT), 25m 51.009s.
Fastest race lap: Campos-Hull, 1m 47.201s, 120.881mph/194.539km/h.
Pole position: Cicatelli.

Final championship points
1 Daniel Zampieri, I, 173; **2** Marco Zipoli, I, 158; **3** Pablo Sánchez, MEX, 155; **4** Sergio Campana, I, 152; **5** Daniel Campos-Hull, E, 148; **6** Stéphane Richelmi, MC, 92; **7** Salvatore Cicatelli, I, 67; **8** Francesco Castellacci, I, 64; **9** Riccardo Cinti, I, 42; **10** Stefanos Kamitsakis, GR, 23; **11** Francesco Prandi, I, 22; **12** Alessandro Cicognani, I, 20; **13** Edoardo Liberati, I, 13; **14** Kevin Ceccon, I, 11; **15** Giovanni Nava, I, 9; **16** Giulio Glorioso, I, 8; **17** Angelo Comi, I, 6; **18** Federico Glorioso, I, 3; **19**= Michele Faccin, I, 1; **19**= Gianmarco Raimondo, CDN, 1.

Rookies
1 Daniel Zampieri, I, 227; **2** Sergio Campana, I, 206; **3** Riccardo Cinti, I, 126.

All-Japan Formula 3 Championship

ALL-JAPAN FORMULA 3 CHAMPIONSHIP, Fuji International Speedway, Sunto-gun, Shizuoka Prefecture, Japan, 4/5 April. 15 and 21 laps of the 2.835-mile/4.563km circuit.
Round 1 (42.341 miles/68.141km).
1 Takuto Iguchi, J (Dallara F308-Toyota), 26m 08.401s, 97.186mph/156.406km/h; **2** Marcus Ericsson, S (Dallara F308-Toyota), 26m 08.437s; **3** Yuji Kunimoto, J (Dallara F308-Toyota), 26m 13.148s; **4** Kei Cozzolino, I (Dallara F308-Mugen Honda), 26m 15.262s; **5** Kouki Saga, J (Dallara F308-Toyota), 26m 33.075s; **6** Yuki Iwasaki, J (Dallara F308-Toyota), 26m 35.295s; **7** Hironobu Yasuda, J (Dallara F309-Nissan), 26m 36.132s; **8** Yuhi Sekiguchi, J (Dallara F307-Toyota), 26m 38.754s; **9** Takashi Kobayashi, J (Dallara F307-Toyota), 26m 44.364s; **10** Katsumasa Chiyo, J (Dallara F306-Toyota), 26m 44.663s.
Fastest race lap: Ericsson, 1m 38.996s, 103.107mph/165.934km/h.
Pole position: Ericsson, 1m 34.019s, 108.565mph/174.718km/h.

Round 2 (59.353 miles/95.519km).
1 Takuto Iguchi, J (Dallara F308-Toyota), 33m 25.198s, 106.558mph/171.489km/h; **2** Yuji Kunimoto, J (Dallara F308-Toyota), 33m 28.485s; **3** Marcus Ericsson, S (Dallara F308-Toyota), 33m 31.102s; **4** Kei Cozzolino, I (Dallara F308-Mugen Honda), 33m 55.432s; **5** Kouki Saga, J (Dallara F308-Toyota), 33m 56.259s; **6** Yuki Iwasaki, J (Dallara F308-Toyota), 34m 03.038s; **7** Yuhi Sekiguchi, J (Dallara F307-Toyota), 34m 11.604s; **8** Naoki Yamamoto, J (Dallara F307-Toyota), 34m 12.559s; **9** Kimiya Sato, J (Dallara F306-Toyota), 34m 23.853s; **10** Alexandre Imperatori, CH (Dallara F307-Toyota), 34m 29.727s.
Fastest race lap: Ericsson, 1m 34.755s, 107.721mph/173.361km/h.
Pole position: Iguchi, 1m 33.451s, 109.225mph/175.780km/h.

ALL-JAPAN FORMULA 3 CHAMPIONSHIP, Okayama International Circuit (TI Circuit Aida), Aida Gun, Okayama Prefecture, Japan, 25/26 April. 18 and 25 laps of the 2.301-mile/3.703km circuit.
Round 3 (41.417 miles/66.654km).
1 Takuto Iguchi, J (Dallara F308-Toyota), 30m 17.067s, 82.056mph/132.056km/h; **2** Yuji Kunimoto, J (Dallara F308-Toyota), 30m 36.129s; **3** Yuhi Sekiguchi, J (Dallara F307-Toyota), 30m 37.803s; **4** Kei Cozzolino, I (Dallara F308-Mugen Honda), 30m 46.677s; **5** Hironobu Yasuda, J (Dallara F309-Nissan), 30m 48.299s; **6** Takashi Kobayashi, J (Dallara F307-Toyota), 30m 59.630s; **7** Kimiya Sato, J (Dallara F306-Toyota), 31m 04.450s; **8** Alexandre Imperatori, CH (Dallara F307-Toyota), 31m 05.062s; **9** Yuki Iwasaki, J (Dallara F308-Toyota), 31m 06.616s; **10** Marcus Ericsson, S (Dallara F308-Toyota), 31m 07.531s.
Fastest race lap: Ericsson, 1m 39.259s, 83.452mph/134.303km/h.
Pole position: Yasuda, 1m 42.833s, 80.552mph/129.635km/h.

Round 4 (57.523 miles/92.575km).
1 Hironobu Yasuda, J (Dallara F309-Nissan), 42m 20.246s, 81.521mph/131.196km/h; **2** Yuki Iwasaki, J (Dallara F308-Toyota), 42m 40.138s; **3** Kimiya Sato, J (Dallara F306-Toyota), 24 laps; **4** Kei Cozzolino, I (Dallara F308-Mugen Honda), 24; **5** Yuhi Sekiguchi, J (Dallara F307-Toyota), 24; **6** Naoki Yamamoto, J (Dallara F307-Toyota), 24; **7** Takashi Kobayashi, J (Dallara F307-Toyota), 24; **8** Yuji Kunimoto, J (Dallara F308-Toyota), 24; **9** Takuto Iguchi, J (Dallara F308-Toyota), 24; **10** Marcus Ericsson, S (Dallara F308-Toyota), 24.
Fastest race lap: Sato, 1m 38.794s, 83.845mph/134.935km/h.
Pole position: Kunimoto, 1m 42.915s, 80.488mph/129.532km/h.

ALL-JAPAN FORMULA 3 CHAMPIONSHIP, Suzuka International Racing Course, Suzuka-shi, Mie Prefecture, Japan, 16/17 May. 12 and 17 laps of the 3.608-mile/5.807km circuit.
Round 5 (43.300 miles/69.684km).
1 Marcus Ericsson, S (Dallara F308-Toyota), 26m 33.905s, 97.797mph/157.389km/h; **2** Takuto Iguchi, J (Dallara F308-Toyota), 26m 35.075s; **3** Yuji Kunimoto, J (Dallara F308-Toyota), 26m 41.113s; **4** Hironobu Yasuda, J (Dallara F309-Nissan), 26m 51.030s; **5** Kei Cozzolino, I (Dallara F308-Mugen Honda), 26m 56.674s; **6** Alexandre Imperatori, CH (Dallara F307-Toyota), 26m 58.676s; **7** Kimiya Sato, J (Dallara F306-Toyota), 26m 59.493s; **8** Naoki Yamamoto, J (Dallara F307-Toyota), 27m 02.064s; **9** Katsumasa Chiyo, J (Dallara F306-Toyota), 27m 08.773s; **10** Yoshitaka Kuroda, J (Dallara F307-Toyota), 27m 09.192s.
Fastest race lap: Kunimoto, 2m 10.189s, 99.777mph/160.576km/h.
Pole position: Imperatori, 2m 11.069s, 99.107mph/159.498km/h.

Round 6 (61.341 miles/98.719km).
1 Yuji Kunimoto, J (Dallara F308-Toyota), 32m 46.944s, 112.270mph/180.680km/h; **2** Marcus Ericsson, S (Dallara

F308-Toyota), 32m 47.852s; **3** Takuto Iguchi, J (Dallara F308-Toyota), 32m 48.317s; **4** Hironobu Yasuda, J (Dallara F309-Nissan), 33m 03.806s; **5** Kei Cozzolino, I (Dallara F308-Mugen Honda), 33m 04.281s; **6** Kouki Saga, J (Dallara F308-Toyota), 33m 04.499s; **7** Naoki Yamamoto, J (Dallara F307-Toyota), 33m 31.227s; **8** Katsumasa Chiyo, J (Dallara F306-Toyota), 33m 40.288s; **9** Alexandre Imperatori, CH (Dallara F307-Toyota), 33m 40.827s; **10** Takashi Kobayashi, J (Dallara F307-Toyota), 33m 42.229s.
Fastest race lap: Iguchi, 1m 55.005s, 112.951mph/181.776km/h.
Pole position: Kunimoto, 2m 07.840s, 101.611mph/163.526km/h.

ALL-JAPAN FORMULA 3 CHAMPIONSHIP, Fuji International Speedway, Sunto-gun, Shizuoka Prefecture, Japan, 27/28 June. 15 and 21 laps of the 2.835-mile/4.563km circuit.
Round 7 (42.341 miles/68.141km).
1 Yuji Kunimoto, J (Dallara F308-Toyota), 24m 07.218s, 105.324mph/169.503km/h; **2** Marcus Ericsson, S (Dallara F308-Toyota), 24m 08.758s; **3** Takuto Iguchi, J (Dallara F308-Toyota), 24m 17.248s; **4** Kouki Saga, J (Dallara F308-Toyota), 24m 23.542s; **5** Kei Cozzolino, I (Dallara F308-Mugen Honda), 24m 23.689s; **6** Yuki Iwasaki, J (Dallara F308-Toyota), 24m 32.794s; **7** Naoki Yamamoto, J (Dallara F307-Toyota), 24m 36.610s; **8** Alexandre Imperatori, CH (Dallara F307-Toyota), 24m 37.796s; **9** Takashi Kobayashi, J (Dallara F307-Toyota), 24m 49.233s; **10** Kimiya Sato, J (Dallara F306-Toyota), 24m 51.353s.
Fastest race lap: Ericsson, 1m 35.913s, 106.421mph/171.268km/h.
Pole position: Kunimoto, 1m 35.873s, 106.465mph/171.339km/h.

Round 8 (59.353 miles/95.519km).
1 Marcus Ericsson, S (Dallara F308-Toyota), 38m 23.509s, 92.758mph/149.280km/h; **2** Takuto Iguchi, J (Dallara F308-Toyota), 38m 26.615s; **3** Yuji Kunimoto, J (Dallara F308-Toyota), 38m 30.856s; **4** Hironobu Yasuda, J (Dallara F309-Nissan), 38m 45.588s; **5** Kouki Saga, J (Dallara F308-Toyota), 38m 53.748s; **6** Kimiya Sato, J (Dallara F306-Toyota), 39m 03.920s; **7** Katsumasa Chiyo, J (Dallara F306-Toyota), 39m 12.018s; **8** Naoki Yamamoto, J (Dallara F307-Toyota), 39m 19.251s; **9** Takashi Kobayashi, J (Dallara F307-Toyota), 39m 20.825s; **10** Yoshitaka Kuroda, J (Dallara F307-Toyota), 39m 26.601s.
Fastest race lap: Kunimoto, 1m 48.086s, 94.435mph/151.979km/h.
Pole position: Ericsson, 1m 35.752s, 106.600mph/171.556km/h.

ALL-JAPAN FORMULA 3 CHAMPIONSHIP, Suzuka International Racing Course, Suzuka-shi, Mie Prefecture, Japan, 11/12 July. 12 and 17 laps of the 3.608-mile/5.807km circuit.
Round 9 (43.300 miles/69.684km).
1 Yuji Kunimoto, J (Dallara F308-Toyota), 23m 21.946s, 111.187mph/178.939km/h; **2** Kei Cozzolino, I (Dallara F308-Mugen Honda), 23m 22.984s; **3** Hironobu Yasuda, J (Dallara F309-Nissan), 23m 24.177s; **4** Kouki Saga, J (Dallara F308-Toyota), 23m 26.907s; **5** Marcus Ericsson, S (Dallara F308-Toyota), 23m 27.291s; **6** Takuto Iguchi, J (Dallara F308-Toyota), 23m 38.078s; **7** Yuki Iwasaki, J (Dallara F308-Toyota), 23m 40.558s; **8** Alexandre Imperatori, CH (Dallara F307-Toyota), 23m 50.281s; **9** Takashi Kobayashi, J (Dallara F307-Toyota), 23m 52.184s; **10** Kimiya Sato, J (Dallara F306-Toyota), 23m 55.202s.
Fastest race lap: Ericsson, 1m 55.301s, 112.661mph/181.310km/h.
Pole position: Cozzolino, 1m 54.325s, 113.622mph/182.858km/h.

Round 10 (61.341 miles/98.719km).
1 Marcus Ericsson, S (Dallara F308-Toyota), 32m 59.227s, 111.573mph/179.559km/h; **2** Takuto Iguchi, J (Dallara F308-Toyota), 33m 02.859s; **3** Kouki Saga, J (Dallara F308-Toyota), 33m 15.269s; **4** Yuji Kunimoto, J (Dallara F308-Toyota), 33m 15.386s; **5** Kei Cozzolino, I (Dallara F308-Mugen Honda), 33m 26.885s; **6** Yuki Iwasaki, J (Dallara F308-Toyota), 33m 34.118s; **7** Naoki Yamamoto, J (Dallara F307-Toyota), 33m 52.370s; **8** Kimiya Sato, J (Dallara F306-Toyota), 33m 59.508s; **9** Takashi Kobayashi, J (Dallara F307-Toyota), 34m 02.640s; **10** Yoshitaka Kuroda, J (Dallara F307-Toyota), 34m 14.503s.
Fastest race lap: Ericsson, 1m 55.696s, 112.276mph/180.691km/h.
Pole position: Ericsson, 1m 54.000s, 113.946mph/183.379km/h.

ALL-JAPAN FORMULA 3 CHAMPIONSHIP, Twin Ring Motegi, Motegi-machi, Haga-gun, Tochigi Prefecture, Japan, 8/9 August. 14 and 20 laps of the 2.983-mile/4.80138km circuit.
Round 11 (41.768 miles/67.219km).
1 Marcus Ericsson, S (Dallara F308-Toyota), 25m 12.755s, 99.398mph/159.965km/h; **2** Kei Cozzolino, I (Dallara F308-Mugen Honda), 25m 15.212s; **3** Takuto Iguchi, J (Dallara F308-Toyota), 25m 16.438s; **4** Hironobu Yasuda, J (Dallara F309-Nissan), 25m 19.576s; **5** Yuji Kunimoto, J (Dallara F308-Toyota), 25m 20.748s; **6** Kouki Saga, J (Dallara F308-Toyota), 25m 26.808s; **7** Yuki Iwasaki, J (Dallara F308-Toyota), 25m 47.684s; **8** Naoki Yamamoto, J (Dallara F307-Toyota), 25m 51.423s; **9** Alexandre Imperatori, CH (Dallara F307-Toyota), 25m 54.475s; **10** Yuhi Sekiguchi, J (Dallara F307-Toyota), 25m 55.944s.
Fastest race lap: Ericsson, 1m 47.252s, 100.142mph/161.162km/h.
Pole position: Ericsson, 1m 46.499s, 100.850mph/162.302km/h.

Round 12 (59.669 miles/96.028km).
1 Kei Cozzolino, I (Dallara F308-Mugen Honda), 36m 10.369s, 98.973mph/159.282km/h; **2** Yuji Kunimoto, J (Dallara F308-Toyota), 36m 15.362s; **3** Hironobu Yasuda, J (Dallara F309-Nissan), 36m 17.004s; **4** Takuto Iguchi, J (Dallara F308-Toyota), 36m 17.311s; **5** Marcus Ericsson, S (Dallara F308-Toyota), 36m 18.966s; **6** Kouki Saga, J (Dallara F308-Toyota), 36m 27.318s; **7** Yuki Iwasaki, J (Dallara F308-Toyota), 36m 34.144s; **8** Naoki Yamamoto, J (Dallara F307-Toyota), 36m 54.254s; **9** Alexandre Imperatori, CH (Dallara F307-Toyota), 37m 07.492s; **10** Kimiya Sato, J (Dallara F306-Toyota), 37m 08.061s.
Fastest race lap: Cozzolino, 1m 47.855s, 99.582mph/160.261km/h.
Pole position: Cozzolino, 1m 46.442s, 100.904mph/162.389km/h.

ALL-JAPAN FORMULA 3 CHAMPIONSHIP, Autopolis International Racing Course, Kamit-sue-mura, Hita-gun, Oita Prefecture, Japan, 29/30 August. 14 and 20 laps of the 2.904-mile/4.674km circuit.
Round 13 (40.660 miles/65.436km).
1 Takuto Iguchi, J (Dallara F308-Toyota), 30m 32.408s, 79.882mph/128.557km/h; **2** Marcus Ericsson, S (Dallara F308-Toyota), 30m 36.008s; **3** Kouki Saga, J (Dallara F308-Toyota), 30m 43.818s; **4** Kei Cozzolino, I (Dallara F308-Mugen Honda), 30m 45.642s; **5** Yuji Kunimoto, J (Dallara F308-Toyota), 30m 48.916s; **6** Hironobu Yasuda, J (Dallara F309-Nissan), 30m 49.517s; **7** Yuki Iwasaki, J (Dallara F308-Toyota), 30m 58.046s; **8** Naoki Yamamoto, J (Dallara F307-Toyota), 31m 02.402s; **9** Kimiya Sato, J (Dallara F306-Toyota), 31m 04.434s; **10** Katsumasa Chiyo, J (Dallara F306-Toyota), 31m 08.546s.
Fastest race lap: Iguchi, 1m 41.911s, 102.594mph/165.109km/h.
Pole position: Iguchi, 1m 40.159s, 104.388mph/167.997km/h.

Round 14 (58.086 miles/93.480km).
1 Takuto Iguchi, J (Dallara F308-Toyota), 34m 36.298s, 100.712mph/162.081km/h; **2** Hironobu Yasuda, J (Dallara F309-Nissan), 34m 41.249s; **3** Kei Cozzolino, I (Dallara F308-Mugen Honda), 34m 58.235s; **4** Kouki Saga, J (Dallara F308-Toyota), 34m 58.778s; **5** Yuki Iwasaki, J (Dallara F308-Toyota), 35m 09.429s; **6** Marcus Ericsson, S (Dallara F308-Toyota), 35m 11.019s; **7** Yuji Kunimoto, J (Dallara F308-Toyota), 35m 14.686s; **8** Naoki Yamamoto, J (Dallara F307-Toyota), 35m 26.315s; **9** Alexandre Imperatori, CH (Dallara F307-Toyota), 35m 31.185s; **10** Takashi Kobayashi, J (Dallara F307-Toyota), 35m 32.159s.
Fastest race lap: Iguchi, 1m 42.689s, 101.817mph/163.858km/h.
Pole position: Iguchi, 1m 40.328s, 104.213mph/167.714km/h.

ALL-JAPAN FORMULA 3 CHAMPIONSHIP, Sportsland-SUGO International Course, Shibata-gun, Miyagi Prefecture, Japan, 26/27 September. 18 and 25 laps of the 2.302-mile/3.704256km circuit.
Round 15 (41.431 miles/66.677km).
1 Yuji Kunimoto, J (Dallara F308-Toyota), 22m 48.044s, 109.026mph/175.460km/h; **2** Marcus Ericsson, S (Dallara F308-Toyota), 22m 48.425s; **3** Takuto Iguchi, J (Dallara F308-Toyota), 22m 50.350s; **4** Kei Cozzolino, I (Dallara F308-Mugen Honda), 22m 56.230s; **5** Hironobu Yasuda, J (Dallara F309-Nissan), 23m 04.609s; **6** Kouki Saga, J (Dallara F308-Toyota), 23m 06.562s; **7** Yuki Iwasaki, J (Dallara F308-Toyota), 23m 13.775s; **8** Kimiya Sato, J (Dallara F306-Toyota), 23m 22.166s; **9** Alexandre Imperatori, CH (Dallara F307-Toyota), 23m 24.158s; **10** Yoshitaka Kuroda, J (Dallara F307-Toyota), 23m 33.686s.
Fastest race lap: Ericsson, 1m 14.714s, 110.905mph/178.485km/h.
Pole position: Kunimoto, 1m 14.157s, 111.738mph/179.826km/h.

Round 16 (57.543 miles/92.606km).
1 Marcus Ericsson, S (Dallara F308-Toyota), 34m 07.125s, 101.193mph/162.854km/h; **2** Hironobu Yasuda, J (Dallara F309-Nissan), 34m 09.858s; **3** Yuji Kunimoto, J (Dallara F308-Toyota), 34m 10.709s; **4** Kei Cozzolino, I (Dallara F308-Mugen Honda), 34m 13.776s; **5** Naoki Yamamoto, J (Dallara F307-Toyota), 34m 18.035s; **6** Katsumasa Chiyo, J (Dallara F306-Toyota), 34m 19.035s; **7** Takashi Kobayashi, J (Dallara F307-Toyota), 34m 19.619s; **8** Kimiya Sato, J (Dallara F306-Toyota), 34m 19.829s; **9** Ryuji Yamamoto, J (Dallara F307-Toyota), 34m 20.950s; **10** Yoshitaka Kuroda, J (Dallara F307-Toyota), 34m 22.454s.
Fastest race lap: Ericsson, 1m 15.264s, 110.095mph/177.181km/h.
Pole position: Ericsson, 1m 14.245s, 111.606mph/179.612km/h.

Final championship points
Championship Class
1 Marcus Ericsson, S, 112; **2** Takuto Iguchi, J, 103; **3** Yuji Kunimoto, J, 97; **4** Kei Cozzolino, I, 66; **5** Hironobu Yasuda, J, 53; **6** Kouki Saga, J, 30; **7** Yuki Iwasaki, J, 18.

National Class
1 Naoki Yamamoto, J, 121; **2** Kimiya Sato, J, 89; **3** Alexandre Imperatori, CH, 75; **4** Takashi Kobayashi, J, 62.

Major Non-Championship Formula 3

2008

The following races were run after AUTOCOURSE 2008–2009 went to press.

WINDSOR ARCH 55th FORMULA 3 MACAU GRAND PRIX, Circuito Da Guia, Macau, 16 November. 10 and 15 laps of the 3.803-mile/6.120km circuit.
Qualification race (38.028 miles/61.200km).
1 Edoardo Mortara, I (Dallara F308-Volkswagen), 29m 20.769s, 77.750mph/125.127km/h; **2** Keisuke Kunimoto, J (Dallara F308-Toyota), 29m 21.958s; **3** Roberto Streit, BR (Dallara F308-Mercedes Benz), 29m 23.673s; **4** Oliver Turvey, GB (Dallara F308-Mercedes Benz), 29m 24.133s; **5** Sam Bird, GB (Dallara F308-Mercedes Benz), 29m 24.753s; **6** Jaime Alguersuari, E (Dallara F308-Mercedes Benz), 29m 25.392s; **7** Stefano Coletti, MC (Dallara F308-Mercedes Benz), 29m 25.721s; **8** Marcus Ericsson, S (Dallara F308-Mercedes Benz), 29m 29.568s; **9** Daniel Campos-Hull, E (Dallara F308-Mercedes Benz), 29m 43.217s; **10** Kai Cozzolino, I (Dallara F308-Toyota), 29m 43.825s.
Fastest race lap: Brendon Hartley, NZ (Dallara F308-Mercedes Benz), 2m 13.169s, 102.802mph/165.443km/h.
Pole position: Carlo van Dam, NL (Dallara F308-Toyota), 2m 11.846s, 103.833mph/167.104km/h.

Feature race (57.042 miles/91.800km).
1 Keisuke Kunimoto, J (Dallara F308-Toyota), 41m 01.864s, 83.412mph/134.239km/h; **2** Edoardo Mortara, I (Dallara F308-Volkswagen), 41m 03.574s; **3** Brendon Hartley, NZ (Dallara F308-Mercedes Benz), 41m 05.870s; **4** Mika Mäki, FIN (Dallara F308-Mercedes Benz), 41m 10.306s; **5** Renger Van Der Zande, NL (Dallara F308-Mercedes Benz), 41m 12.140s; **6** Laurens Banthoor, GB (Dallara F308-Volkswagen), 41m 14.839s; **7** Oliver Turvey, GB (Dallara F308-Mercedes Benz), 41m 14.998s; **8** Walter Grubmuller, A (Dallara F308-Mercedes Benz), 41m 16.559s; **9** Jules Bianchi, F (Dallara F308-Mercedes Benz), 41m 20.589s; **10** Jaime Alguersuari, E (Dallara F308-Mercedes Benz), 41m 22.665s.
Fastest race lap: Hartley, 2m 12.565s, 103.270mph/166.197km/h.
Pole position: Mortara.

2009

TANGO MASTERS OF FORMULA 3, Circuit Park Zandvoort, Netherlands, 14 June. 25 laps of the 2.676-mile/4.307km circuit, 66.906 miles/107.675km.
1 Valtteri Bottas, FIN (Dallara F308-Mercedes Benz), 39m 12.544s, 102.383mph/164.770km/h; **2** Mika Mäki, FIN (Dallara F308-Volkswagen), 39m 15.154s; **3** Stefano Coletti, MC (Dallara F308-Mercedes Benz), 39m 30.792s; **4** Jules Bianchi, F (Dallara F308-Mercedes Benz), 39m 31.293s; **5** Alexander Sims, GB (Dallara F308-Mercedes Benz), 39m 41.280s; **6** Renger van der Zande, NL (Dallara F308-Mercedes Benz), 39m 45.382s; **7** Christian Vietoris, D (Dallara F308-Mercedes Benz), 39m 46.222s; **8** Sam Bird, GB (Dallara F308-Mercedes Benz), 39m 48.725s; **9** Tiago Geronimi, BR (Dallara F308-Volkswagen), 39m 57.897s; **10** Roberto Merhi, E (Dallara F308-Mercedes Benz), 39m 58.709s.
Fastest race lap: Bottas, 1m 33.251s, 103.318mph/166.273km/h.
Pole position: Bottas, 1m 31.175s, 105.670mph/170.059km/h.
Fastest qualifying lap: Bianchi,1m 31.143s, 105.707mph/170.119km/h (received 5-place grid penalty).

Results of the Macau races will be given in AUTOCOURSE 2010–2011.

World Series by Renault Formula Renault 3.5

All cars are Dallara-Renault.

FORMULA RENAULT 3.5, Circuit de Catalunya, Montmeló, Barcelona, Spain, 18/19 April. Round 1. 29 and 22 laps of the 2.892-mile/4.655km circuit.
Race 1 (83.882 miles/134.995km).
1 Marcos Martinez, E, 47m 05.443s, 106.877mph/172.002km/h; **2** Bertrand Baguette, B, 47m 06.886s; **3** Adrián Vallés, E, 47m 07.150s; **4** Oliver Turvey, GB, 47m 10.207s; **5** Jaime Alguersuari, E, 47m 10.975s; **6** James Walker, GB, 47m 11.883s; **7** Chris van der Drift, NZ, 47m 14.272s; **8** Fairuz Fauzy, MAL, 47m 15.982s; **9** Miguel Molina, E, 47m 25.933s; **10** Adrian Zaugg, ZA, 47m 27.221s.
Fastest race lap: Molina, 1m 35.751s, 108.750mph/175.016km/h.
Pole position: Vallés.

Race 2 (63.635 miles/102.410km).
1 Marcos Martinez, E, 41m 20.462s, 92.355mph/148.631km/h; **2** Sten Pentus, EST, 41m 22.281s; **3** Chris van der Drift, NZ, 41m 23.370s; **4** Adrián Vallés, E, 41m 24.796s; **5** Adrian Zaugg, ZA, 41m 26.776s; **6** Charles Pic, F, 41m 27.676s; **7** Fairuz Fauzy, MAL, 41m 28.495s; **8** Pasquale Di Sabatino, I, 41m 33.559s; **9** Brendon Hartley, NZ, 41m 34.144s; **10** Greg Mansell, GB, 41m 39.655s.
Fastest race lap: Pic, 1m 35.690s, 108.819mph/175.128km/h.
Pole position: Pic, 1m 32.584s, 112.470mph/181.003km/h.

FORMULA RENAULT 3.5, Circuit de Spa-Francorchamps, Stavelot, Belgium, 2/3 May. Round 2. 22 and 21 laps of the 4.351-mile/7.003km circuit.
Race 1 (95.732 miles/154.066km).
1 Marcos Martinez, E, 46m 36.943s, 123.218mph/198.301km/h; **2** Bertrand Baguette, B, 46m 40.759s; **3** Miguel Molina, E, 46m 47.995s; **4** Charles Pic, F, 46m 51.611s; **5** Daniil Move, RUS, 46m 51.830s; **6** Oliver Turvey, GB, 46m 52.205s; **7** Marco Barba, E, 46m 56.200s; **8** Pasquale Di Sabatino, I, 46m 56.718s; **9** Chris van der Drift, NZ, 46m 56.994s; **10** Jaime Alguersuari, E, 47m 07.780s.
Fastest race lap: Baguette, 2m 06.518s, 123.818mph/199.266km/h.
Pole position: Barba.

Race 2 (91.381 miles/147.063km).
1 James Walker, GB, 47m 45.056s, 114.821mph/184.787km/h; **2** Bertrand Baguette, B, 47m 51.477s; **3** Miguel Molina, E, 47m 57.039s; **4** Daniil Move, RUS, 48m 03.122s; **5** Marcos Martinez, E, 48m 04.038s; **6** Jaime Alguersuari, E, 48m 04.064s; **7** Adrian Zaugg, ZA, 48m 07.701s; **8** Pasquale Di Sabatino, I, 48m 08.895s; **9** Greg Mansell, GB, 48m 09.418s; **10** Brendon Hartley, NZ, 48m 12.040s.
Fastest race lap: Walker, 2m 04.030s, 126.302mph/203.263km/h.
Pole position: Baguette, 2m 02.862s, 127.502mph/205.196km/h.

FORMULA RENAULT 3.5, Monte-Carlo Street Circuit, Monaco, 24 May. Round 3. 25 laps of the 2.075-mile/3.340km circuit, 51.884 miles/83.500km.
1 Oliver Turvey, GB, 39m 24.975s, 78.979mph/127.104km/h; **2** Adrian Zaugg, ZA, 39m 25.636s; **3** James Walker, GB, 39m 28.570s; **4** Miguel Molina, E, 39m 33.263s; **5** Bertrand Baguette, B, 39m 34.312s; **6** Jaime Alguersuari, E, 39m 35.014s; **7** Chris van der Drift, NZ, 39m 35.406s; **8** Adrián Vallés, E, 39m 36.098s; **9** Charles Pic, F, 39m 36.437s; **10** Stefano Coletti, MC, 39m 38.831s.
Fastest race lap: Brendon Hartley, NZ, 1m 26.609s, 86.265mph/138.830km/h.
Pole position: Turvey, 1m 26.657s, 86.217mph/138.753km/h.

FORMULA RENAULT 3.5, Hungaroring, Mogyorod, Budapest, Hungary, 13/14 June. Round 4. 28 and 25 laps of the 2.722-mile/4.381km circuit.
Race 1 (76.222 miles/122.668km).
1 Fairuz Fauzy, MAL, 46m 28.278s, 98.412mph/158.379km/h; **2** Marco Barba, E, 46m 30.247s; **3** Bertrand Baguette, B, 46m 31.660s; **4** James Walker, GB, 46m 32.170s; **5** Jaime Alguersuari, E, 46m 34.006s; **6** Marcos Martinez, E, 46m 36.394s; **7** Miguel Molina, E, 46m 38.363s; **8** Oliver Turvey, GB, 46m 38.860s; **9** Jon Lancaster, GB, 46m 39.416s; **10** Adrian Zaugg, ZA, 46m 45.108s.
Fastest race lap: Brendon Hartley, NZ, 1m 34.529s, 103.672mph/166.844km/h.
Pole position: Fauzy.

Race 2 (68.056 miles/109.525km).
1 Pasquale Di Sabatino, I, 46m 54.069s, 87.062mph/140.113km/h; **2** Marco Barba, E, 46m 54.995s; **3** Ómar Leal, CO, 47m 06.060s; **4** Chris van der Drift, NZ, 47m 06.514s; **5** Michael Herck, RO, 47m 09.375s; **6** Bertrand Baguette, B, 47m 11.113s; **7** Fairuz Fauzy, MAL, 47m 11.415s; **8** Charles Pic, F, 47m 12.398s; **9** Daniil Move, RUS, 47m 13.246s; **10** Jon Lancaster, GB, 47m 21.765s.
Fastest race lap: Fauzy, 1m 34.027s, 104.225mph/167.734km/h.
Pole position: Martinez, 1m 31.285s, 107.356mph/172.773km/h.

FORMULA RENAULT 3.5, Silverstone Grand Prix Circuit, Towcester, Northamptonshire, Great Britain, 4/5 July. Round 5. 2 x 28 laps of the 3.194-mile/5.140km circuit.
Race 1 (89.428 miles/143.920km).
1 Marcos Martinez, E, 45m 49.264s, 117.100mph/188.454km/h; **2** Fairuz Fauzy, MAL, 45m 50.491s; **3** Oliver Turvey, GB, 45m 52.482s; **4** James Walker, GB, 45m 54.369s; **5** Brendon Hartley, NZ, 45m 55.375s; **6** Jaime Alguersuari, E, 45m 55.981s; **7** Charles Pic, F, 46m 01.242s; **8** Bertrand Baguette, B, 46m 04.765s; **9** Miguel Molina, E, 46m 05.157s; **10** Marco Barba, E, 46m 07.442s.
Fastest race lap: Jon Lancaster, GB, 1m 35.585s, 120.289mph/193.586km/h.
Pole position: Baguette.

Race 2 (89.428 miles/143.920km).
1 Charles Pic, F, 45m 45.997s, 117.239mph/188.679km/h; **2** James Walker, GB, 45m 50.270s; **3** Oliver Turvey, GB, 45m 50.556s; **4** Fairuz Fauzy, MAL, 45m 51.380s; **5** Bertrand Baguette, B, 46m 07.603s; **6** Marcos Martinez, E, 46m 09.335s; **7** Sten Pentus, EST, 46m 09.704s; **8** Daniil Move, RUS, 46m 18.555s; **9** Jaime Alguersuari, E, 46m 21.521s; **10** Marco Barba, E, 46m 24.648s.
Fastest race lap: Pic, 1m 36.018s, 119.746mph/192.713km/h.
Pole position: Pic, 1m 33.073s, 123.535mph/198.811km/h.

FORMULA RENAULT 3.5, Le Mans Bugatti Circuit, Les Raineries, Le Mans, France, 18/19 July. Round 6. 30 and 31 laps of the 2.600-mile/4.185km circuit.
Race 1 (78.013 miles/125.550km).
1 Bertrand Baguette, B, 46m 14.448s, 101.226mph/162.908km/h; **2** Pasquale Di Sabatino, I, 46m 19.318s; **3** Oliver Turvey, GB, 46m 21.259s; **4** Jaime Alguersuari, E, 46m 21.826s; **5** Marco Barba, E, 46m 25.123s; **6** Charles Pic, F, 46m 25.268s; **7** Fairuz Fauzy, MAL, 46m 32.487s; **8** Jon Lancaster, GB, 46m 33.217s; **9** Miguel Molina, E, 46m 36.372s; **10** Daniel Clos, E, 46m 38.840s.
Fastest race lap: Baguette, 1m 27.626s, 106.835mph/171.935km/h.
Pole position: Barba.

Race 2 (80.614 miles/129.735km).
1 Bertrand Baguette, B, 46m 08.636s, 104.820mph/168.691km/h; **2** Miguel Molina, E, 46m 09.784s; **3** Jaime Alguersuari, E, 46m 12.394s; **4** Fairuz Fauzy, MAL, 46m 23.555s; **5** Jon Lancaster, GB, 46m 24.922s; **6** Edoardo Mortara, I, 46m 25.171s; **7** Marco Barba, E, 46m 25.435s; **8** Pasquale Di Sabatino, I, 46m 25.801s; **9** James Walker, GB, 46m 29.055s; **10** Oliver Turvey, GB, 46m 30.897s.
Fastest race lap: Molina, 1m 26.982s, 107.626mph/173.208km/h.
Pole position: Lancaster, 1m 25.677s, 109.265mph/175.846km/h.

FORMULA RENAULT 3.5, Autódromo Internacional do Algarve, Portimão, Portugal, 1 August. Round 7. 21 and 22 laps of the 2.891-mile/4.653km circuit.
Race 1 (60.716 miles/97.713km).
1 Jon Lancaster, GB, 36m 45.926s, 99.086mph/159.464km/h; **2** Bertrand Baguette, B, 36m 46.494s; **3** Jaime Alguersuari, E, 36m 47.036s; **4** Charles Pic, F, 36m 47.370s; **5** Guillaume Moreau, F, 36m 48.068s; **6** James Walker, GB, 36m 50.532s; **7** Miguel Molina, E, 36m 51.166s; **8** Fairuz Fauzy, MAL, 36m 52.612s; **9** Sten Pentus, EST, 36m 53.636s; **10** Filip Salaquarda, CZ, 36m 56.758s.
Fastest race lap: Pic, 1m 34.834s, 109.754mph/176.632km/h.
Pole position: Lancaster.

Race 2 (63.607 miles/102.366km).
1 Jaime Alguersuari, E, 37m 57.020s, 100.563mph/161.842km/h; **2** Charles Pic, F, 37m 58.468s; **3** Guillaume Moreau, F, 37m 58.868s; **4** Miguel Molina, E, 38m 00.232s; **5** Bertrand Baguette, B, 38m 01.412s; **6** Oliver Turvey, GB, 38m 02.140s; **7** Chris van der Drift, NZ, 38m 02.716s; **8** James Walker, GB, 38m 03.352s; **9** Daniel Clos, E, 38m 03.836s; **10** Daniil Move, RUS, 38m 04.728s.
Fastest race lap: Alguersuari, 1m 34.472s, 110.175mph/177.309km/h.
Pole position: Alguersuari, 1m 33.462s, 111.365mph/179.225km/h.

FORMULA RENAULT 3.5, Nürburgring, Nürburg/Eifel, Germany, 19/20 September. Round 8. 23 and 25 laps of the 3.199-mile/5.148km circuit.
Race 1 (73.573 miles/118.404km).
1 Bertrand Baguette, B, 45m 01.920s, 98.027mph/157.759km/h; **2** Fairuz Fauzy, MAL, 45m 05.919s; **3** Daniil Move, RUS, 45m 08.618s; **4** Oliver Turvey, GB, 45m 09.084s; **5** Jaime Alguersuari, E, 45m 10.085s; **6** Charles Pic, F, 45m 10.696s; **7** John Martin, AUS, 45m 13.553s; **8** Marco Barba, E, 45m 14.296s; **9** Jon Lancaster, GB, 45m 14.404s; **10** Pasquale Di Sabatino, I, 45m 14.989s.
Fastest race lap: Lancaster, 1m 49.027s, 105.622mph/169.983km/h.
Pole position: Move.

Race 2 (79.970 miles/128.700km).
1 Charles Pic, F, 45m 59.547s, 104.326mph/167.897km/h; **2** Brendon Hartley, NZ, 46m 00.242s; **3** Fairuz Fauzy, MAL, 46m 13.494s; **4** James Walker, GB, 46m 14.377s; **5** Bertrand

Baguette, B, 46m 22.038s; **6** Jaime Alguersuari, E, 46m 26.055s; **7** Marco Barba, E, 46m 36.207s; **8** John Martin, AUS, 46m 42.494s; **9** Daniil Move, RUS, 46m 42.846s; **10** Chris van der Drift, NZ, 46m 45.357s.
Fastest race lap: Hartley, 1m 48.151s, 106.478mph/171.360km/h.
Pole position: Hartley, 1m 45.581s, 109.070mph/175.531km/h.

FORMULA RENAULT 3.5, MotorLand Aragón, Alcañiz, Aragon, Spain, 24/25 October. Round 9. 2 x 26 laps of the 3.321-mile/5.344km circuit.
Race 1 (86.336 miles/138.944km).
1 Bertrand Baguette, B, 46m 17.280s, 111.911mph/180.103km/h; **2** Oliver Turvey, GB, 46m 18.914s; **3** Jon Lancaster, GB, 46m 25.030s; **4** Daniil Move, RUS, 46m 25.762s; **5** Esteban Guerrieri, RA, 46m 28.521s; **6** Fairuz Fauzy, MAL, 46m 37.676s; **7** Federico Leo, I, 46m 41.019s; **8** Jaime Alguersuari, E, 46m 42.599s; **9** Chris van der Drift, NZ, 46m 42.969s; **10** Greg Mansell, GB, 46m 43.273s.
Fastest race lap: Guerrieri, 1m 45.507s, 113.302mph/182.342km/h.
Pole position: Turvey.

Race 2 (86.336 miles/138.944km).
1 Bertrand Baguette, B, 46m 28.831s, 111.447mph/179.357km/h; **2** Fairuz Fauzy, MAL, 46m 32.055s; **3** Daniil Move, RUS, 46m 43.309s; **4** Esteban Guerrieri, RA, 46m 49.802s; **5** Oliver Turvey, GB, 46m 51.309s; **6** Marco Barba, E, 46m 51.837s; **7** Federico Leo, I, 46m 53.132s; **8** Chris van der Drift, NZ, 46m 53.512s; **9** James Walker, GB, 46m 58.357s; **10** Sten Pentus, EST, 47m 00.693s.
Fastest race lap: Walker, 1m 44.833s, 114.030mph/183.514km/h.
Pole position: Fauzy, 1m 44.070s, 114.866mph/184.860km/h.

Final championship points
Drivers
1 Bertrand Baguette, B, 155; **2** Fairuz Fauzy, MAL, 98; **3** Charles Pic, F, 94; **4** Oliver Turvey, GB, 93; **5** James Walker, GB, 89; **6** Jaime Alguersuari, E, 88; **7** Marcos Martinez, E, 73; **8** Miguel Molina, E, 64; **9** Marco Barba, E, 50; **10** Daniil Move, RUS, 49; **11** Chris van der Drift, NZ, 41; **12** Pasquale Di Sabatino, I, 39; **13** Jon Lancaster, GB, 39; **14** Adrian Zaugg, ZA, 27; **15** Brendon Hartley, NZ, 26; **16** Sten Pentus, EST, 23; **17** Adrián Vallés, E, 19; **18** Guillaume Moreau, F, 18; **19** Esteban Guerrieri, RA, 15; **20** Ómar Leal, CO, 11; **21** Federico Leo, I, 8; **22** John Martin, AUS, 8; **23** Michael Herck, RO, 7; **24** Edoardo Mortara, I, 6; **25** Daniel Clos, E, 5; **26** Greg Mansell, GB, 4; **27** Filip Salaquarda, CZ, 1; **28** Stefano Coletti, MC, 1; **29** Anton Nebylitskiy, RUS, 1.

Teams
1 International Draco Racing, 205; **2** Carlin Motorsport, 181; **3** P1 Motorsport, 138.

FIA GT Championship 2008

The following race was run after AUTOCOURSE 2008–2009 went to press.

FIA GT CHAMPIONSHIP, Potrero de los Funes, San Luis, Argentina, 23 November. Round 10. 51 laps of the 3.896-mile/6.270km circuit, 198.470 miles/319.407km.
1 Anthony Kumpen/Bert Longin, B/B (Saleen S7R-Ford), 2h 00m 02.994s, 99.193mph/159.637km/h; **2** Mike Hezemans/Fabrizio Gollin, NL/I (Chevrolet Corvette C6.R), 2h 00m 03.555s; **3** Maxime Soulet/Christian Ledesma/Armand Fumal, B/RA/B (Chevrolet Corvette C6.R), 2h 00m 37.205s; **4** José Maria López/Esteban Tuero, RA/RA (Ferrari 550-GTS Maranello), 2h 01m 45.304s; **5** Andrea Bertolini/Michael Bartels, I/D (Maserati MC 12 GT1), 2h 02m 16.990s; **6** Matias Russo/Luis Pérez-Companc, RA/RA (Ferrari 430 GT2), 50 laps (1st GT2 class); **7** Toni Vilander/Gianmaria Bruni, FIN/I (Ferrari 430 GT2), 50; **8** Thomas Biagi/Christian Montanari, I/SM (Ferrari 430 GT2), 50; **9** Andrew Kirkaldy/Robert Bell, GB/GB (Ferrari 430 GT2), 49 (DNF-accident); **10** Mikael Forsten/Markus Palttala, FIN/FIN (Porsche 997 GT2 RSR), 49 (DNF-accident).
Fastest race lap: Marcel Fässler, CH (Chevrolet Corvette Z06), 2m 14.345s, 104.399mph/168.015km/h.
Pole position: Marcel Fässler/Ricardo Risatti, CH/RA, 2m 13.236s, 105.268mph/169.413km/h.

Final championship points
GT1 Drivers
1 Andrea Bertolini/Michael Bartels, I/D, 70; **2** Mike Hezemans/Fabrizio Gollin, NL/I, 66; **3** Alexandre 'Xandinho' Negrão/Miguel Ramos, BR/P, 52.5; **4** Marcel Fässler, CH, 48.5; **5** Jean-Denis Deletraz, CH/CH, 45.5; **6** Karl Wendlinger/Ryan Sharp, D/GB, 44; **7** Allan Simonsen/Philipp Peter, DK/A, 40; **8** Christophe Bouchut/Xavier Maassen, F/NL, 32.5; **9** Stéphane Sarrazin/Eric van de Poele, F/B, 20; **10** Anthony Kumpen/Bert Longin, B/B, 18.5.

GT1 Teams
1 Vitaphone Racing Team, 122.5; **2** Phoenix Carsport Racing, 107; **3** Jetalliance Racing, 59; **4** Gigawave Motorsport, 40; **5** Selleslagh Racing Team, 38.5.

GT2 Drivers
1 Toni Vilander/Gianmaria Bruni, FIN/I, 93; **2** Paolo Ruberti/Matteo Malucelli, I/I, 60.5; **3** Richard Westbrook, GB, 51; **4** Christian Montanari/Thomas Biagi, RSM/I, 45; **5** Emmanuel Collard, F, 41; **6** Robert Bell/Andrew Kirkaldy, GB/GB, 37; **7** Joël Camathias, CH, 35.5; **8** Davide Rigon, F, 33.5; **9** Tim Mullen, GB, 27; **10** Matias Russo, RA, 25.5.

GT2 Teams
1 AF Corse, 138; **2** BMS Scuderia Italia, 76; **3** Prospeed Competition, 69.5; **4** CR Scuderia, 61.

2009

FIA GT CHAMPIONSHIP, Silverstone Grand Prix Circuit, Towcester, Northamptonshire, Great Britain, 3 May. Round 1. 65 laps of the 3.194-mile/5.140km circuit, 207.630 miles/334.148km.
1 Karl Wendlinger/Ryan Sharp, A/GB (Saleen S7R-Ford), 2h 00m 10.556s, 103.662mph/166.829km/h; **2** Michael Bartels/Andrea Bertolini, D/I (Maserati MC 12 GT1), 2h 00m 16.055s; **3** Xavier Maassen/Guillaume Moreau, NL/F (Chevrolet Corvette C6.R), 2h 00m 36.512s; **4** Mike Hezemans/Anthony Kumpen, NL/B (Chevrolet Corvette C6.R), 2h 00m 41.120s; **5** Adam Lacko/Mario Dominguez, CZ/MEX (Saleen S7R-Ford), 2h 01m 10.184s; **6** Bert Longin/James Ruffier, B/F (Chevrolet Corvette C6.R), 2h 01m 54.380s; **7** Jos Menten/Markus Palttala, NL/FIN (Chevrolet Corvette C6.R), 64 laps; **8** Thomas Mutsch/Thomas Biagi, D/I (Ford GT), 64; **9** Stéphane Lemeret/Luke Hines, B/GB (Saleen S7 Twin Turbo-Ford), 64; **10** Bas Leinders/Renaud Kuppens, B/B (Ford GT), 63.
Fastest race lap: Wendlinger, 1m 44.687s, 109.830mph/176.755km/h.
Pole position: Wendlinger/Sharp, 1m 42.216s, 112.485mph/181.028km/h.

FIA GT CHAMPIONSHIP, Autodromo Adria International Raceway, Rovigo, Adria, Italy, 16 May. Round 2. 96 laps of the 1.679-mile/2.702km circuit, 161.082 miles/259.237km.
1 Michael Bartels/Andrea Bertolini, D/I (Maserati MC 12 GT1), 2h 00m 22.680s, 80.288mph/129.211km/h; **2** Mike Hezemans/Anthony Kumpen, NL/B (Chevrolet Corvette C6.R), 2h 00m 32.848s; **3** Miguel Ramos/Alex Müller, P/D (Maserati MC 12 GT1), 2h 00m 43.145s; **4** Xavier Maassen/Guillaume Moreau, NL/F (Chevrolet Corvette C6.R), 95 laps; **5** Bert Longin/James Ruffier, B/F (Chevrolet Corvette C6.R), 95; **6** Stéphane Lemeret/Luke Hines, B/GB (Saleen S7 Twin Turbo-Ford), 94; **7** Emmanuel Collard/Richard Westbrook, F/GB (Porsche 997 GT2 RSR), 92 (1st GT2 class); **8** Toni Vilander/Gianmaria Bruni, FIN/I (Ferrari 430 GT2), 92; **9** Alvaro Barba/Niki Cadei, E/I (Ferrari 430 GT2), 92; **10** Darryl O'Young/Marco Holzer, HK/D (Porsche 997 GT2 RSR), 92.
Fastest race lap: Moreau, 1m 13.018s, 82.776mph/133.216km/h.
Pole position: Bartels/Bertolini, 1m 12.086s, 83.847mph/134.938km/h.

FIA GT CHAMPIONSHIP, Motorsport Arena Oschersleben, Germany, 21 June. Round 3. 71 laps of the 2.297-mile/3.696km circuit, 163.058 miles/262.416km.
1 Mike Hezemans/Anthony Kumpen, NL/B (Chevrolet Corvette C6.R), 2h 00m 42.748s, 81.047mph/130.433km/h; **2** Michael Bartels/Andrea Bertolini, D/I (Maserati MC 12 GT1), 2h 00m 51.955s; **3** Miguel Ramos/Alex Müller, P/D (Maserati MC 12 GT1), 2h 01m 18.444s; **4** Bert Longin/James Ruffier, B/F (Chevrolet Corvette C6.R), 2h 02m 30.424s; **5** Xavier Maassen/Thomas Biagi, NL/I (Chevrolet Corvette C6.R), 70 laps; **6** Bas Leinders/Renaud Kuppens, B/B (Ford GT), 70; **7** Thomas Mutsch/Marc Hennerici, D/D (Ford GT), 70; **8** Stéphane Lemeret/Luke Hines, B/GB (Saleen S7R-Ford), 69; **9** Toni Vilander/Gianmaria Bruni, FIN/I (Ferrari 430 GT2), 69 (1st GT2 class); **10** Frédéric Makowiecki/Stéfan Mücke, F/D (Aston Martin V8 Vantage), 69.
Disqualified: Sean Edwards/Marco Holzer, GB/D (Porsche 997 GT2 RSR), 69, finished 10th (illegal engine).
Fastest race lap: Müller, 1m 26.205s, 95.907mph/154.348km/h.
Pole position: Ramos/Müller, 1m 24.546s, 97.789mph/157.377km/h.

24 HOURS OF SPA, Circuit de Spa-Francorchamps, Stavelot, Belgium, 25 July. Round 4. 559 laps of the 4.352-mile/7.004km circuit, 2432.738 miles/3915.112km.
1 Mike Hezemans/Anthony Kumpen/Jos Menten/Kurt Mollekens, NL/B/NL/B (Chevrolet Corvette C6.R), 24h 00m 03.458s, 101.360mph/163.123km/h; **2** Alessandro Pier Guidi/Stéphane Lemeret/Carl Rosenblad/Vincent Vosse, I/B/S/B (Maserati MC 12 GT1), 548 laps; **3** Marcel Fässler/Henri Moser/Alexandros Margaritis/Marc Basseng, CH/CH/GR/D (Audi R8 LMS), 544 (1st G2 class); **4** Toni Vilander/Gianmaria Bruni/Jaime Melo Jr./Luis Pérez-Companc, FIN/I/BR/RA (Ferrari 430 GT2), 540 (1st GT2 class); **5** Andrew Kirkaldy/Robert Bell/Peter Kox/Antonio Garcia, GB/GB/NL/E (Ferrari 430 GT2), 528; **6** Chris Niarchos/Tim Mullen/Phil Quaife/Chris Goodwin, CDN/GB/GB/GB (Ferrari 430 GT2), 525; **7** Thomas Mutsch/Maxime Martin/Peter Wyss/Marc Hennerici, D/B/CH/D (Ford GT), 519 (1st G3 class); **8** Christian Lefort/François Verbist/Rodney Forbes, B/B/AUS (Porsche 997 GT3 Cup S), 518; **9** Niki Lanik/Markus Palttala/Oskar Slingerland/David Loix, A/FIN/NL/B (Porsche 997 GT3 Cup S), 517; **10** Michael Krumm/Darren Turner/Anthony Davidson, D/GB/GB (Nissan GT-R), 513.
Disqualified: Luigi Lucchini/Martin Ragginger/Marco Holzer/Bryce Miller, I/A/D/USA (Porscge 997 GT2 RSR), 535 (finished 5th); Paul van Splunteren/Raymond Coronel/Niek Hommerson/Louis Machiels, NL/NL/NL/B (Porsche 997 GT2 RSR), 527 (finished 7th); Emmanuel Collard/Richard Westbrook/Dartryl O'Young/Sean Edwards, F/GB/HK/GB (Porsche 997 GT2 RSR), 526 (finished 8th).
Fastest race lap: Oliver Gavin, GB (Chevrolet Corvette C6.R), 2m 15.423s, 115.693mph/186.189km/h.
Pole position: Miguel Ramos/Alex Müller/Pedro Lamy/Eric van de Poele, P/D/P/B (Maserati MC12 GT1), 2m 18.030s, 113.507mph/182.673km/h.

FIA GT CHAMPIONSHIP, Hungaroring, Mogyorod, Budapest, Hungary, 30 August. Round 5. 67 laps of the 2.722-mile/4.381km circuit, 182.365 miles/293.488km.
1 Michael Bartels/Andrea Bertolini, D/I (Maserati MC 12 GT1), 2h 00m 50.589s, 90.546mph/145.720km/h; **2** Alessandro Pier Guidi/Matteo Bobbi, I/I (Maserati MC 12 GT1), 2h 00m 50.928s; **3** Enrique Bernoldi/Roberto Streit, BR/BR (Chevrolet Corvette C6.R), 2h 00m 51.409s; **4** Xavier Maassen/Thomas Biagi, NL/I (Chevrolet Corvette C6.R), 2h 00m 55.307s; **5** Mike Hezemans/Anthony Kumpen, NL/B (Chevrolet Corvette C6.R), 2h 01m 10.257s; **6** Bert Longin/James Ruffier, B/F (Chevrolet Corvette C6.R), 66 laps; **7** Emmanuel Collard/Richard Westbrook, F/GB (Porsche 997 GT3 Cup S), 65 (1st GT2 class); **8** Toni Vilander/Gianmaria Bruni, FIN/I (Ferrari 430 GT2), 65; **9** Matteo Malucelli/Paolo Ruberti, I/I (Ferrari 430 GT2), 65; **10** Bas Leinders/Renaud Kuppens, B/B (Ford GT), 65.
Disqualified: Karl Wendlinger/Ryan Sharp, A/GB (Saleen S7R-Ford), finished 1st in 2h 00m 17.422s.
Fastest race lap: Bernoldi, 1m 43.340s, 94.832mph/152.618km/h.
Pole position: Miguel Ramos/Alex Müller, P/D (Maserati MC 12 GT1), 1m 41.815s, 96.253mph/154.904km/h.

FIA GT CHAMPIONSHIP, Autódromo Internacional do Algarve, Portimão, Portugal, 20 September. Round 6. 66 laps of the 2.891-mile/4.653km circuit, 190.647 miles/306.817km.
1 Bert Longin/James Ruffier, B/F (Chevrolet Corvette C6.R), 2h 01m 39.556s, 94.023mph/151.316km/h; **2** Mike Hezemans/Anthony Kumpen, NL/B (Chevrolet Corvette C6.R), 2h 02m 12.778s; **3** Miguel Ramos/Alex Müller, P/D (Maserati MC 12 GT1), 2h 02m 31.466s; **4** Enrique Bernoldi/Roberto Streit/Xavier Maassen, BR/BR/NL (Chevrolet Corvette C6.R), 2h 02m 37.575s; **5** Michael Bartels/Andrea Bertolini, D/I (Maserati MC 12 GT1), 2h 02m 37.866s; **6** Alessandro Pier Guidi/Matteo Bobbi, I/I (Maserati MC 12 GT1), 2h 02m 38.110s; **7** Alvaro Barba/Niki Cadei, E/I (Ferrari 430 GT2), 64 laps (1st GT2 class); **8** Emmanuel Collard/Richard Westbrook, F/GB (Porsche 997 GT3 Cup S), 64; **9** Matteo Malucelli/Paolo Ruberti, I/I (Ferrari 430 GT2), 64; **10** Luis Pérez-Companc/Matias Russo, RA/RA (Ferrari 430 GT2), 64.
Fastest race lap: Müller, 1m 41.828s, 102.211mph/164.493km/h.
Pole position: Bernoldi/Streit/Maassen, 1m 40.664s, 103.393mph/166.395km/h.

FIA GT CHAMPIONSHIP, Circuit ASA Paul Ricard, Le Beausset, France, 4 October. Round 7. 57 laps of the 3.630-mile/5.842km circuit, 206.913 miles/332.994km.
1 Enrique Bernoldi/Roberto Streit, BR/BR (Chevrolet Corvette C6.R), 2h 00m 27.312s, 103.065mph/165.867km/h; **2** Miguel Ramos/Alex Müller, P/D (Maserati MC 12 GT1), 2h 00m 42.824s; **3** Bert Longin/James Ruffier, B/F (Chevrolet Corvette C6.R), 2h 00m 44.132s; **4** Xavier Maassen/Thomas Biagi, NL/I (Chevrolet Corvette C6.R), 2h 00m 52.932s; **5** Michael Bartels/Andrea Bertolini, D/I (Maserati MC 12 GT1), 2h 01m 22.316s; **6** Alessandro Pier Guidi/Matteo Bobbi, I/I (Maserati MC 12 GT1), 2h 01m 35.404s; **7** Ange Barde/Olivier Panis, F/F (Ferrari 550-GTS Maranello), 55 laps; **8** Thomas Mutsch/Henri Moser, D/CH (Ford GT), 55; **9** Toni Vilander/Gianmaria Bruni, FIN/I (Ferrari 430 GT2), 55 (1st GT2 class); **10** Emmanuel Collard/Richard Westbrook, F/GB (Porsche 997 GT3 Cup S), 54.
Fastest race lap: Bernoldi, 2m 02.659s, 106.540mph/171.460km/h.
Pole position: Ramos/Müller, 2m 01.856s, 107.242mph/172.590km/h.

FIA GT CHAMPIONSHIP, Circuit Zolder, Heusden-Zolder, Belgium, 25 October. Round 8. 79 laps of the 2.600-mile/4.184km circuit, 205.386 miles/330.536km.
1 Alessandro Pier Guidi/Matteo Bobbi, I/I (Maserati MC 12 GT1), 2h 01m 07.362s, 101.740mph/163.736km/h; **2** Mike Hezemans/Anthony Kumpen, NL/B (Chevrolet Corvette C6.R), 2h 01m 27.716s; **3** Michael Bartels/Andrea Bertolini, D/I (Maserati MC 12 GT1), 2h 02m 12.919s*; **4** Xavier Maassen/Thomas Biagi, NL/I (Chevrolet Corvette C6.R), 2h 02m 17.165s; **5** Enrique Bernoldi/Roberto Streit, BR/BR (Chevrolet Corvette C6.R), 78 laps; **6** Bert Longin/James Ruffier, B/F (Chevrolet Corvette C6.R), 78; **7** Richard Westbrook/Marco Holzer, GB/D (Porsche 997 GT3 Cup S), 76 (1st GT2 class); **8** Matteo Malucelli/Paolo Ruberti, I/I (Ferrari 430 GT2), 76; **9** Andrew Kirkaldy/Robert Bell, GB/GB (Ferrari 430 GT2), 76; **10** Toni Vilander/Gianmaria Bruni, FIN/I (Ferrari 430 GT2), 76.
* includes 30-sec penalty (fuel irregularity).
Fastest race lap: Bartels, 1m 26.220s, 108.551mph/174.697km/h.
Pole position: Pier Guidi/Bobbi, 1m 27.589s, 106.855mph/171.966km/h.
Fastest qualifying lap: Kumpen, 1m 27.399s, 107.088mph/172.340km/h (grid penalty for setting time under yellow flags).

Final championship points
GT1 Drivers
1 Michael Bartels/Andrea Bertolini,D/ I, 55; **2** Anthony Kumpen/Mike Hezemans, B/NL, 53; **3** Bert Longin/James Ruffier, B/ F, 38; **4** Xavier Maassen, NL, 35; **5** Alessandro Pier Guidi, I, 32; **6** Miguel Ramos/Alex Müller, P/D, 31; **7** Roberto Streit/Enrique Bernoldi, BR/BR, 25; **8** Matteo Bobbi, I, 24; **9** Thomas Biagi, I, 20; **10** Stéphane Lemeret, B, 13.

GT1 Teams
1 Vitaphone Racing Team, 86; **2** PK Carsport, 53; **3** Selleslagh Racing Team, 35; **4** Vitaphone Racing Team DHL, 32; **5** Luc Alphand Aventures, 30.

GT2 Drivers
1 Richard Westbrook, GB, 56; **2** Gianmaria Bruni/Toni Vilander, I/FIN, 54; **3** Emmanuel Collard, F, 49; **4** Niki Cadei/Alvaro Barba, I/E, 34; **5** Robert Bell/Andrew Kirkaldy, GB/GB, 34; **6** Luis Pérez-Companc, RA, 30; **7** Matteo Malucelli/Paolo Ruberti, I/ I, 27; **8** Marco Holzer, D, 23; **9** Tim Mullen/Chris Niarchos, GB/CDN, 21; **10** Matias Russo, RA, 20.

GT2 Teams
1 AF Corse, 88; **2** Prospeed Competition, 70; **3** CRS Racing, 55; **4** BMS Scuderia Italia, 28; **5** Pecom Racing, 20.

Le Mans Series

1000KM DE CATALUNYA, Circuit de Catalunya, Montmeló, Barcelona, Spain, 5 April. Round 1. 209 laps of the 2.892-mile/4.655km circuit, 604.529 miles/972.895km.
1 Jan Charouz/Tomas Enge/Stefan Mücke, CZ/CZ/D (Lola B09/60-Aston Martin), 6h 00m 05.674s, 100.728mph/162.106km/h; **2** Jean-Christophe Boullion/Christophe Tinseau, F/F (Pescarolo 01-Judd), 6h 00m 20.568s; **3** Stéphane Ortelli/Bruno Senna, MC/BR (Courage-Oreca LC70-AIM), 206 laps; **4** Pierre Ragues/Franck Mailleux, F/F (Courage-Oreca LC70-Judd), 206; **5** Peter Hardman/Nick Leventis/Danny Watts, GB/GB/GB (Ginetta-Zytek 09S-Zytek), 205; **6** Bruce Jouanny/João Barbosa, F/P (Pescarolo 01-Judd), 203; **7** Matteo Bobbi/Andrea Piccini/Thomas Biagi, I/I/I (Lola B08/80-Judd), 201; **8** Miguel Pais do Amaral/Olivier Pla, P/F (Ginetta-Zytek 09S-Zytek), 201; **9** Filippo Francioni/Andrea Ceccato/Giacomo Piccini, I/I/I (Lola B08/80-Judd), 195; **10** Pierre Bruneau/Nigel Greensall/Stuart Moseley, F/GB/GB (Radical SR9-AER), 193.
Fastest race lap: Mücke, 1m 34.094s, 110.665mph/178.098km/h.
Pole position: Hardman/Leventis/Watts, 1m 32.492s, 112.582mph/181.183km/h.

1000KM DE SPA, Circuit de Spa-Francorchamps, Stavelot, Belgium, 10 May. Round 2. 143 laps of the 4.352-mile/7.004km circuit, 622.348 miles/1001.572km.
1 Nicolas Minassian/Christian Klien/Simon Pagenaud, F/A/F (Peugeot 908), 5h 45m 35.429s, 108.049mph/173.888km/h; **2** Jean-Christophe Boullion/Christophe Tinseau, F/F (Pescarolo 01-Judd), 5h 46m 03.051s; **3** Jan Charouz/Tomas Enge/Stefan Mücke, CZ/CZ/D (Lola B09/60-Aston Martin), 142 laps; **4** Olivier Panis/Nicolas Lapierre, F/F (Courage-Oreca LC70-AIM), 142; **5** Harold Primat/Miguel Ramos/Darren Turner, CH/P/GB (Lola B09/60-Aston Martin), 142; **6** Andrew Meyrick/Charles Zwolsman/Narain Karthikeyan, GB/NL/IND (Audi R10 TDI), 141; **7** Christijan Albers/Christian Bakkerud/Giorgio Mondini, NL/DK/CH (Audi R10 TDI), 139; **8** Casper Elgaard/Kristian Poulsen/Emmanuel Collard, DK/DK/F (Porsche RS Spyder Evo), 139; **9** Jonny Kane/Benjamin Leuenberger/Xavier Pompidou, GB/CH/F (Lola B08/80-Judd), 139; **10** Andrea Belicchi/Marcel Fässler/Nicolas Prost, I/CH/F (Lola B08/60-Aston Martin), 139.
Fastest race lap: Pagenaud, 2m 02.569s, 127.825mph/205.715km/h.
Pole position: Minassian/Klien/Pagenaud, 2m 01.056s, 129.423mph/208.287km/h.

1000KM DO ALGARVE, Autódromo Internacional do Algarve, Portimão, Portugal, 1 August. Round 3. 215 laps of the 2.891-mile/4.653km circuit, 621.617 miles/1000.395km.
1 Jean-Christophe Boullion/Christophe Tinseau, F/F (Pescarolo 01-Judd), 5h 49m 04.176s, 106.846mph/171.953km/h; **2** Jan Charouz/Tomas Enge/Stefan Mücke, CZ/CZ/D (Lola B09/60-Aston Martin), 5h 50m 29.724s; **3** Bruno Senna/Tiago Monteiro, BR/P (Courage-Oreca LC70-AIM), 214 laps; **4** Olivier Panis/Nicolas Lapierre, F/F (Courage-Oreca LC70-AIM), 212; **5** Harold Primat/Darren Turner/Miguel Ramos, CH/GB/P (Lola B09/60-Aston Martin), 211; **6** Miguel Pais do Amaral/Olivier Pla, P/F (Ginetta-Zytek 09S-Zytek), 207; **7** Filippo Francioni/Andrea Ceccato/Giacomo Piccini, I/I/I (Lola B08/80-Judd), 205; **8** Karim Ojjeh/Claude-Yves Gosselin/Philipp Peter, SA/F/A (Zytek 07S), 205; **9** Matteo Bobbi/Andrea Piccini/Thomas Biagi, I/I/I (Lola B08/80-Judd), 203; **10** Pierre Ragues/Franck Mailleux, F/F (Courage-Oreca LC70-Judd), 202.
Fastest race lap: Lapierre, 1m 32.376s, 112.674mph/181.332km/h.
Pole position: Panis/Lapierre, 1m 31.020s, 114.353mph/184.034km/h.

ADAC 1000KM OF THE NÜRBURGRING, Nürburgring, Nürburg/Eifel, Germany, 23 August. Round 4. 195 laps of the 3.192-mile/5.137km circuit, 622.437 miles/1001.715km.
1 Jan Charouz/Tomas Enge/Stefan Mücke, CZ/CZ/D (Lola B09/60-Aston Martin), 5h 57m 26.595s, 104.481mph/168.146km/h; **2** Harold Primat/Darren Turner, CH/GB (Lola B09/60-Aston Martin), 5h 58m 31.451s; **3** Miguel Ramos/Stuart Hall/Chris Buncombe, P/GB/GB (Lola B09/60-Aston Martin), 193 laps; **4** Narain Karthikeyan/Andrew Meyrick/Charles Zwolsman, IND/GB/NL (Audi R10 TDI), 193; **5** Pierre Ragues/Franck Mailleux, F/F (Courage-Oreca LC70-Judd), 190; **6** Miguel Pais do Amaral/Olivier Pla, P/F (Ginetta-Zytek 09S-Zytek), 189; **7** Filippo Francioni/Andrea Ceccato/Giacomo Piccini, I/I/I (Lola B08/80-Judd), 187; **8** Mathieu Lahaye/Karim Ajlani, F/CH (Pescarolo 01-Mazda), 185; **9** Jacques Nicolet/Richard Hein, F/MC (Pescarolo 01-Mazda), 184; **10** Karim Ojjeh/Claude-Yves Gosselin/Philipp Peter, SA/F/A (Zytek 07S), 183.
Fastest race lap: Mücke, 1m 44.125s, 110.359mph/177.605km/h.
Pole position: Charouz/Enge/Mücke, 1m 41.944s, 112.720mph/181.405km/h.

AUTOSPORT 1000 KM OF SILVERSTONE, Silverstone Grand Prix Circuit, Towcester, Northamptonshire, Great Britain, 13 September. Round 5. 195 laps of the 3.194-mile/5.140km circuit, 622.800 miles/1002.300km.
1 Olivier Panis/Nicolas Lapierre, F/F (Courage-Oreca LC70-AIM), 5h 29m 12.688s, 113.507mph/182.672km/h; **2** Andrea Belicchi/Marcel Fässler/Nicolas Prost, I/CH/F (Lola B08/60-Aston Martin), 5h 30m 04.448s; **3** Jan Charouz/Tomas Enge/Stefan Mücke, CZ/CZ/D (Lola B09/60-Aston Martin), 5h 30m 14.418s; **4** Harold Primat/Darren Turner, CH/GB (Lola B09/60-Aston Martin), 5h 30m 16.028s; **5** Christijan Albers/Christian Bakkerud, NL/DK (Audi R10 TDI), 194 laps; **6** Narain Karthikeyan/Andrew Meyrick/Charles Zwolsman, IND/GB/NL (Audi R10 TDI), 193; **7** Pierre Ragues/Franck Mailleux, F/F (Courage-Oreca LC70-Judd), 193; **8** Jonny Kane/Benjamin Leuenberger/Xavier Pompidou, GB/CH/F (Lola B08/80-Judd), 190; **9** Nick Leventis/Danny Watts, GB/GB (Ginetta-Zytek 09S-Zytek), 189; **10** Tommy Erdos/Mike Newton, BR/GB (Lola B09/86-Mazda), 186.
Fastest race lap: Jean-Christophe Boullion, F (Pescarolo 01-Judd), 1m 34.316s, 121.907mph/196.191km/h.
Pole position: Panis/Lapierre, 1m 32.798s, 123.901mph/199.400km/h.

Final championship points
P1 Drivers
1 Jan Charouz/Tomas Enge/Stefan Mücke, CZ/CZ/D, 39; **2** Jean-Christophe Boullion/Christophe Tinseau, F/F, 26; **3** Olivier Panis/Nicolas Lapierre, F/F, 22; **4** Harold Primat/Darren Turner, CH/GB, 21; **5** Andrea Belicchi/Marcel Fässler/Nicolas Prost, I/CH/F, 14; **6** Miguel Ramos, P, 14; **7** Pierre Ragues/Franck Mailleux, F/F, 14; **8** Bruno Senna, BR, 12; **9** Andrew Meyrick/Charles Zwolsman, GB/NL, 12; **10** Nicolas Minassian/Christian Klien/Simon Pagenaud, F/A/F, 11; **11** Narain Karthikeyan, IND, 11.

P2 Drivers
1 Miguel Amaral/Olivier Pla, P/F, 33; **2** Jonny Kane/Xavier Pompidou, GB//F, 24; **3** Andrea Ceccato/Filippo Francioni/Giacomo Piccini, I/I/I, 23; **4** Benjamin Leuenberger, CH, 22.

GT1 Drivers
1 Yann Clairay/Patrice Goueslard, F/F, 44; **2** Roland Berville, F, 34; **3** Peter Kox, NL, 28.

GT2 Drivers
1 Marc Lieb/Richard Lietz, D/A, 36; **2** Robert Bell/Bruno Gianmaria,GB/ I, 35; **3** Antonio Garcia/Leo Mansell, E/GB, 24.

P1 Manufacturers
1 Lola Aston Martin, 65; **2** Oreca AIM, 34; **3** Pescarolo Judd, 29; **4** Audi, 18; **5** Oreca Judd, 14; **6** Peugeot, 11.

P2 Manufacturers
1 Lola Judd, 57; **2** Ginetta Zytek, 33; **3** Pescarolo Mazda, 22.

GT1 Manufacturers
1 Corvette, 44; **2** Saleen, 34; **3** Lamborghini, 18.

GT2 Manufacturers
1 Ferrari, 72; **2** Porsche, 57; **3** Spyker, 14.

P1 Teams
1 Aston Martin Racing, 39; **2** Pescarolo Sport, 26; **3** Team Oreca Matmut AIM, 23.

P2 Teams
1 Quifel ASM Team, 33; **2** Speedy Racing Team Sebah, 24; **3** Racing Box, 23.

GT1 Teams
1 Luc Alphand Aventures, 44; **2** Larbre Competition, 34; **3** IPB Spartak Racing, 18.

GT2 Teams
1 Team Felbermayr -Proton, 36; **2** JMW Motorsport, 35; **3** Team Modena, 24.

American Le Mans Series

57th MOBIL 1 TWELVE HOURS OF SEBRING, Sebring International Raceway, Florida, USA, 21 March. Round 1. 383 laps of the 3.700-mile/5.955km circuit, 1417.100 miles/ 2280.601km.
1 Rinaldo Capello/Tom Kristensen/Allan McNish, I/DK/GB (Audi R15), 12h 00m 38.638s, 117.986mph/189.880km/h (1st P1 class); **2** Stéphane Sarrazin/Franck Montagny/Sébastien Bourdais, F/F/F (Peugeot 908), 12h 01m 00.917s; **3** Lucas Luhr/Mike Rockenfeller/Marco Werner, D/D/D (Audi R15), 381 laps; **4** Adrián Fernández/Luis Diaz, MEX/MEX (Acura ARX-01B), 360 (1st P2 class); **5** Nicolas Minassian/Pedro Lamy/Christian Klien, F/P/A (Peugeot 908), 356 (DNF-gearbox); **6** Jan Magnussen/Johnny O'Connell/Antonio Garcia, DK/USA/E (Chevrolet Corvette C6.R), 349 (1st GT1 class); **7** Olivier Beretta/Oliver Gavin/Marcel Fässler, MC/GB/CH (Chevrolet Corvette C6.R), 348; **8** Jaime Melo Jr./Pierre Kaffer/Mika Salo, BR/D/FIN (Ferrari 430 GT2), 332 (1st GT2 class); **9** Luis Pérez-Companc/Matias Russo/Gianmaria Bruni, RA/RA/I (Ferrari 430 GT2), 330; **10** Dominik Farnbacher/Ian James, D/GB (Panoz Esperante GT-LM-Ford), 329.
Fastest race lap: Bourdais, 1m 43.274s, 128.977mph/ 207.568km/h.
Pole position: Gil de Ferran/Simon Pagenaud/Scott Dixon, BR/F/NZ (Acura ARX-02a), 1m 45.278s, 126.522mph/ 203.617km/h.

ACURA SPORTS CAR CHALLENGE OF ST. PETERSBURG, St. Petersburg Street Circuit, Florida, USA, 4 April. Round 2. 93 laps of the 1.800-mile/2.897km circuit, 167.400 miles/ 269.404km.
1 David Brabham/Scott Sharp, AUS/USA (Acura ARX-02a), 1h 55m 53.705s, 86.664 mph/139.473 km/h (1st P1 class); **2** Adrián Fernández/Luis Diaz, MEX/MEX (Acura ARX-01B), 1h 56m 25.855s (1st P2 class); **3** Chris Dyson/Guy Smith, USA/GB (Lola B09/86-Mazda), 92 laps; **4** Butch Leitzinger/Marino Franchitti, USA/GB (Lola B08/86-Mazda), 91; **5** Jörg Bergmeister/Patrick Long, D/USA (Porsche 997 GT3 RSR), 88 (1st GT2 class); **6** Jon Field/Clint Field/Chapman Ducote, USA/USA/USA (Lola B06/10-AER), 88; **7** Dirk Müller/Tom Milner, D/USA (BMW M3 E92), 86; **8** Dominik Farnbacher/Ian James, D/GB (Panoz Esperante GT-LM-Ford), 86; **9** Lou Gigliotti/Eric Curran, USA/USA (Chevrolet Corvette C6), 85; **10** Darren Law/Seth Neiman, CDN/USA (Porsche 997 GT3 RSR), 84.
Fastest race lap: Gil de Ferran, BR (Acura ARX-02a), 1m 06.959s, 96.775mph/155.745km/h.
Pole position: Gil de Ferran/Simon Pagenaud, BR/F, 1m 03.776s, 101.605mph/163.518km/h.

TEQUILA PATRÓN ALMS AT LONG BEACH, Long Beach Street Circuit, California, USA, 18 April. Round 3. 76 laps of the 1.968-mile/3.167km circuit, 149.568 miles/ 240.706km.
1 Gil de Ferran/Simon Pagenaud, BR/F (Acura ARX-02a), 1h 41m 42.927s, 88.227mph/141.988km/h (1st P1 class); **2** David Brabham/Scott Sharp, AUS/USA (Acura ARX-02a), 1h 41m 43.943s; **3** Adrián Fernández/Luis Diaz, MEX/MEX (Acura ARX-01B), 75 laps (1st P2 class); **4** Chris Dyson/Guy Smith, USA/GB (Lola B09/86-Mazda), 75; **5** Butch Leitzinger/Marino Franchitti, USA/GB (Lola B08/86-Mazda), 74; **6** Olivier Beretta/Oliver Gavin, MC/GB (Chevrolet Corvette C6.R), 73 (1st GT1 class); **7** Jon Field/Clint Field/Chapman Ducote, USA/USA/USA (Lola B06/10-AER), 71; **8** Jörg Bergmeister/Patrick Long, D/USA (Porsche 997 GT3 RSR), 71 (1st GT2 class); **9** Jaime Melo Jr./Pierre Kaffer, BR/D (Ferrari 430 GT2), 71; **10** Dirk Müller/Tom Milner, D/USA (BMW M3 E92), 70.
Fastest race lap: Brabham, 1m 14.053s, 95.672mph/ 153.969km/h.
Pole position: Brabham/Sharp, 1m 11.627s, 98.912mph/ 159.184km/h.

LARRY H. MILLER DEALERSHIPS UTAH GRAND PRIX, Miller Motorsports Park, Tooele, Utah, USA, 17 May. Round 4. 103 laps of the 3.048-mile/4.905km circuit, 313.944 miles/505.244km.
1 Gil de Ferran/Simon Pagenaud, BR/F (Acura ARX-02a), 2h 46m 14.913s, 113.304mph/182.345km/h (1st P1 class); **2** David Brabham/Scott Sharp, AUS/USA (Acura ARX-02a), 2h 47m 28.606s; **3** Adrián Fernández/Luis Diaz, MEX/MEX (Acura ARX-01B), 100 laps (1st P2 class); **4** Butch Leitzinger/Marino Franchitti, USA/GB (Lola B08/86-Mazda), 100; **5** Jon Field/Clint Field/Chapman Ducote, USA/USA/USA (Lola B06/10-AER), 93; **6** Chris Dyson/Guy Smith, USA/GB (Lola B09/86-Mazda), 92; **7** Jörg Bergmeister/Patrick Long, D/USA (Porsche 997 GT3 RSR), 90 (1st GT2 class); **8** Wolf Henzler/Dirk Werner, D/D (Porsche 997 GT3 RSR), 90; **9** Jaime Melo Jr./Pierre Kaffer, BR/D (Ferrari 430 GT2), 89; **10** Dominik Farnbacher/Ian James, D/GB (Panoz Esperante GT-LM-Ford), 89.
Fastest race lap: Pagenaud, 1m 32.815s, 118.222mph/ 190.260km/h.
Pole position: de Ferran/Pagenaud, 1m 30.645s, 121.052mph/194.815km/h.

AMERICAN LE MANS NORTHEAST GRAND PRIX, Lime Rock Park, Lakeville, Connecticut, USA, 18 July. Round 5. 184 laps of the 1.500-mile/2.414km circuit, 276.000 miles/ 444.179km.
1 Gil de Ferran/Simon Pagenaud, BR/F (Acura ARX-02a), 2h 45m 14.053s, 100.221mph/161.290km/h (1st P1 class); **2** David Brabham/Scott Sharp, AUS/USA (Acura ARX-02a), 2h 45m 57.829s; **3** Johnny Mowlem/Stefan Johansson, GB/S (Ginetta-Zytek 09S-Zytek), 177 laps; **4** Butch Leitzinger/Marino Franchitti, USA/GB (Lola B08/86-Mazda), 172 (1st P2 class); **5** Jörg Bergmeister/Patrick Long, D/USA (Porsche 997 GT3 RSR), 167 (1st GT2 class); **6** Tony Burgess/Chris McMurry, CDN/USA (Lola B06/10-AER), 166; **7** Adrián Fernández/Luis Diaz, MEX/MEX (Acura ARX-01B), 166; **8** Jaime Melo Jr./Pierre Kaffer, BR/D (Ferrari 430 GT2), 166; **9** Joey Hand/Bill Auberlen, USA/USA (BMW M3 E92), 166; **10** Wolf Henzler/Bryce Miller, D/USA (Porsche 997 GT3 RSR), 165.
Fastest race lap: Pagenaud, 47.791s, 112.991mph/ 181.842km/h.
Pole position: de Ferran/Pagenaud, 46.971s, 114.964mph/ 185.017km/h.

ACURA SPORTS CAR CHALLENGE, Mid-Ohio Sports Car Course, Lexington, Ohio, USA, 8 August. Round 6. 118 laps of the 2.258-mile/3.634km circuit, 266.444 miles/ 428.800km.
1 Gil de Ferran/Simon Pagenaud, BR/F (Acura ARX-02a), 2h 45m 27.326s, 96.622mph/155.498km/h (1st P1 class); **2** David Brabham/Scott Sharp, AUS/USA (Acura ARX-02a), 2h 45m 35.684s; **3** Adrián Fernández/Luis Diaz, MEX/MEX (Acura ARX-01B), 116 laps (1st P2 class); **4** Greg Pickett/Klaus Graf, USA/D (Porsche RS Spyder Evo), 116; **5** Jon Field/Clint Field, USA/USA (Lola B06/10-AER), 116; **6** Johnny Mowlem/Stefan Johansson, GB/S (Ginetta-Zytek 09S-Zytek), 114; **7** Jörg Bergmeister/Patrick Long, D/USA (Porsche 997 GT3 RSR), 108 (1st GT2 class); **8** Jan Magnussen/Johnny O'Connell, DK/USA (Chevrolet Corvette C6.R), 108; **9** Dirk Müller/Tom Milner, D/USA (BMW M3 E92), 107; **10** Olivier Beretta/Oliver Gavin, MC/GB (Chevrolet Corvette C6.R), 107.
Fastest race lap: Pagenaud, 1m 11.105s, 114.321mph/ 183.981km/h.
Pole position: de Ferran/Pagenaud, 1m 09.443s, 117.057mph/188.385km/h.

TIME WARNER CABLE ROAD RACE SHOWCASE, Road America, Elkhart Lake, Wisconsin, USA, 16 August. Round 7. 71 laps of the 4.048-mile/6.515km circuit, 287.408 miles/ 462.538km.
1 David Brabham/Scott Sharp, AUS/USA (Acura ARX-02a), 2h 45m 49.618s, 103.990mph/167.356km/h (1st P1 class); **2** Gil de Ferran/Simon Pagenaud, BR/F (Acura ARX-02a), 2h 45m 50.079s; **3** Adrián Fernández/Luis Diaz, MEX/MEX (Acura ARX-01B), 2h 46m 05.427s (1st P2 class); **4** Butch Leitzinger/Marino Franchitti, USA/GB (Lola B08/86-Mazda), 2h 46m 12.169s; **5** Greg Pickett/Klaus Graf, USA/D (Porsche RS Spyder Evo), 2h 46m 13.532s; **6** Jon Field/Clint Field, USA/USA (Lola B06/10-AER), 2h 46m 38.128s; **7** Johnny Mowlem/Stefan Johansson, GB/S (Ginetta-Zytek 09S-Zytek), 70 laps; **8** Bryan Willman/Chris McMurry, USA/USA (Lola B06/10-AER), 70; **9** Joey Hand/Bill Auberlen, USA/USA (BMW M3 E92), 69 (1st GT2 class); **10** Dirk Müller/Tom Milner, D/USA (BMW M3 E92), 68.
Fastest race lap: de Ferran, 1m 50.873s, 131.436mph/ 211.527km/h.
Pole position: de Ferran/Pagenaud, 1m 48.216s, 134.664mph/216.720km/h.

MOBIL 1 PRESENTS GRAND PRIX OF MOSPORT, Mosport International Raceway, Bowmanville, Ontario, Canada, 30 August. Round 8. 131 laps of the 2.459-mile/3.957km circuit, 322.129 miles/518.416km.
1 David Brabham/Scott Sharp, AUS/USA (Acura ARX-02a), 2h 45m 03.171s, 117.100mph/188.454km/h (1st P1 class); **2** Gil de Ferran/Simon Pagenaud, BR/F (Acura ARX-02a), 130 laps; **3** Adrián Fernández/Luis Diaz, MEX/MEX (Acura ARX-01B), 127 (1st P2 class); **4** Jon Field/Clint Field, USA/USA (Lola B06/10-AER), 125; **5** Butch Leitzinger/Marino Franchitti, USA/GB (Lola B08/86-Mazda), 118 (DNF-mechanical); **6** Jan Magnussen/Johnny O'Connell, DK/USA (Chevrolet Corvette C6.R), 117 (1st GT2 class); **7** Jaime Melo Jr./Pierre Kaffer, BR/D (Ferrari 430 GT2), 117; **8** Olivier Beretta/Oliver Gavin, MC/GB (Chevrolet Corvette C6.R), 116; **9** Wolf Henzler/Dirk Werner, D/D (Porsche 997 GT3 RSR), 116; **10** Jörg Bergmeister/Patrick Long, D/USA (Porsche 997 GT3 RSR), 115.
Disqualified: Gunnar van der Stuer/Adam Pecorari, DK/USA (Radical SR9-AER), 116 (finished 10th).
Fastest race lap: Pagenaud, 1m 06.376s, 133.367mph/ 214.634km/h.
Pole position: Brabham/Sharp, 1m 05.323s, 135.517mph/ 218.094km/h.

PETIT LE MANS, Road Atlanta Motorsports Center, Braselton, Georgia, USA, 26 September. Round 9. 184 laps of the 2.540-mile/4.088km circuit, 467.360 miles/ 752.143km.
1 Franck Montagny/Stéphane Sarrazin, F/F (Peugeot 908), 8h 44m 22.872s, 97.302mph/156.592km/h (1st P1 class); **2** Nicolas Minassian/Pedro Lamy, F/P (Peugeot 908), 8h 44m 24.883s; **3** Rinaldo Capello/Allan McNish, I/GB (Audi R15), 8h 44m 26.337s; **4** Lucas Luhr/Marco Werner, D/D (Audi R15), 183 laps; **5** Olivier Panis/Nicolas Lapierre/Romain Dumas, F/F/F (Courage-Oreca LC70-AIM), 181; **6** David Brabham/Scott Sharp/Dario Franchitti, AUS/USA/GB (Acura ARX-02a), 180; **7** Chris Dyson/Guy Smith, USA/GB (Lola B09/86-Mazda), 177; **8** Jaime Melo Jr./Pierre Kaffer/Mika Salo, BR/D/FIN (Ferrari 430 GT2), 170; **9** Dirk Müller/Tom Milner/Jörg Müller, D/USA/D (BMW M3 E92), 169; **10** Wolf Henzler/Dirk Werner, D/D (Porsche 997 GT3 RSR), 169.
Race times include period between the race being red-flagged up to the point when it was decided not to restart.
Race speeds are calculated on the time of the race, 4h 48m 11.484s.
Fastest race lap: McNish, 1m 08.063s, 134.346mph/ 216.209km/h.
Pole position: Minassian/Lamy, 1m 06.937s, 136.606mph/ 219.846km/h.

MONTEREY SPORTS CAR CHAMPIONSHIPS, Mazda Raceway Laguna Seca, Monterey, California, USA, 10 October. Round 10. 168 laps of the 2.238-mile/3.602km circuit, 375.984 miles/605.088km.
1 Gil de Ferran/Simon Pagenaud, BR/F (Acura ARX-02a), 4h 00m 51.966s, 93.658mph/150.727km/h (1st P1 class); **2** Adrián Fernández/Luis Diaz, MEX/MEX (Acura ARX-01B), 4h 00m 52.628s (1st P2 class); **3** David Brabham/Scott Sharp, AUS/USA (Acura ARX-02a), 164 laps; **4** Tony Burgess/Chris McMurry/Bryan Willman, CDN/USA/USA (Lola B06/10-AER), 159; **5** Johnny Mowlem/Stefan Johansson, GB/S (Ginetta-Zytek 09S-Zytek), 158; **6** Jörg Bergmeister/Patrick Long, D/USA (Porsche 997 GT3 RSR), 155 (1st GT2 class); **7** Jan Magnussen/Johnny O'Connell, DK/USA (Chevrolet Corvette C6.R), 155; **8** Wolf Henzler/Pierre Ehret, D/D (Porsche 997 GT3 RSR), 154; **9** Dominik Farnbacher/Ian James, D/GB (Panoz Esperante GT-LM-Ford), 154; **10** Johannes van Overbeek/Seth Neiman, USA/USA (Porsche 997 GT3 RSR), 153.
Fastest race lap: Pagenaud, 1m 13.281s, 109.943mph/ 176.937km/h.
Pole position: de Ferran/Pagenaud, 1m 11.206s, 113.147mph/182.093km/h.

Final championship points
P1 Drivers
1 David Brabham/Scott Sharp, AUS/USA, 179; **2** Gil de Ferran/Simon Pagenaud, BR/F, 162; **3** Jon Field/Clint Field, USA/USA, 116; **4** Johnny Mowlem/Stefan Johansson, GB/S, 58; **5** Franck Montagny/Stéphane Sarrazin, F/F, 56; **6** Rinaldo Capello/Allan McNish, I/GB, 53; **7** Bryan Willman/Chris McMurry, USA/USA, 49; **8** Nicolas Minassian/Pedro Lamy, F/P, 46; **9** Lucas Luhr/Marco Werner, D/D, 43; **10** Chapman Ducote, USA, 42.

P2 Drivers
1 Adrián Fernández/Luis Diaz, MEX/MEX, 217; **2** Butch Leitzinger/Marino Franchitti, USA/GB, 137; **3** Klaus Graf, D, 73; **4** Chris Dyson/Guy Smith, USA/GB, 55; **5** Greg Pickett, USA, 50.

GT1 Drivers
1 Olivier Beretta/Oliver Gavin, MC/GB, 46; **2** Jan Magnussen/Johnny O'Connell/Antonio Garcia, DK/USA/E, 30; **3** Marcel Fässler, CH, 26.

GT2 Drivers
1 Jörg Bergmeister/Patrick Long, D/USA, 181; **2** Jaime Melo Jr./Pierre Kaffer, BR/D,137; **3** Wolf Henzler, D, 102.

P1 Chassis Manufacturers
1 Acura, 199; **2** Lola, 123; **3** Ginetta-Zytek, 58.

P2 Chassis Manufacturers
1 Acura, 217; **2** Lola, 143; **3** Porsche, 73.

GT1 Automobile Manufacturers
1 Chevrolet, 50.

GT2 Automobile Manufacturers
1 Porsche, 188; **2** Ferrari, 137; **3** BMW, 118.

P1 Engines
1 Acura, 199; **2** AER, 123; **3** Zytek, 58.

P2 Engines
1 Acura, 217; **2** Mazda, 143; **3** Porsche, 73.

Asian Le Mans Series

ASIAN LE MANS SERIES, Okayama International Circuit (TI Circuit Aida), Aida Gun, Okayama Prefecture, Japan, 31 October/1 November. 126 and 128 laps of the 2.301-mile/ 3.703km circuit.
Race 1 (289.918 miles/466.578km).
1 Christophe Tinseau/Shinji Nakano, F/J (Pescarolo 01-Judd), 3h 00m 24.018s, 96.424mph/155.180km/h; **2** Nicolas Lapierre/Loïc Duval, F/F (Courage-Oreca LC70-AIM), 3h 00m 30.948s; **3** Stefan Mücke/Harold Primat, D/CH (Lola B09/60-Aston Martin), 124 laps; **4** Oliver Jarvis/Christian Bakkerud, GB/DK (Audi R10), 124; **5** Matteo Cressoni/Hideki Noda/Christijan Albers, I/J/NL (Audi R10), 122; **6** Paul Drayson/Jonathan Cocker, GB/GB (Lola B09/60-Judd), 121; **7** Jacques Nicolet/Richard Hein/Mathieu Lahaye, F/MC/F (Pescarolo 01-Mazda), 116; **8** Damien Toulemonde/Frédéric Da Rocha/José Ibanez, F/F/F (Courage LC75-AER), 116; **9** Shigekazu Wakisaka/Shogo Mitsuyama, J/J (Courage-Oreca LC70-YGK), 115; **10** Atsushi Yogo/Hiroyuki Iiri, J/J (Lamborghini Murcielago), 113.
Fastest race lap: Cocker, 1m 21.735s, 101.344mph/ 163.097km/h.
Pole position: Drayson/Cocker, 1m 19.143s, 104.663mph/ 168.439km/h.

Race 2 (294.520 miles/473.984km).
1 Stefan Mücke/Harold Primat, D/CH (Lola B09/60-Aston Martin), 3h 01m 08.944s, 97.550mph/156.992km/h; **2** Christophe Tinseau/Shinji Nakano, F/J (Pescarolo 01-Judd), 3h 02m 09.121s; **3** Nicolas Lapierre/Loïc Duval, F/F (Courage-Oreca LC70-AIM), 3h 02m 17.423s; **4** Paul Drayson/Jonathan Cocker, GB/GB (Lola B09/60-Judd), 127 laps; **5** Oliver Jarvis/Christian Bakkerud, GB/DK (Audi R10), 127; **6** Matteo Cressoni/Hideki Noda/Christijan Albers, I/J/NL (Audi R10), 125; **7** Jacques Nicolet/Richard Hein/Mathieu Lahaye, F/MC/F (Pescarolo 01-Mazda), 118; **8** Akihiro Tsuzuki/Takeshi Tsuchiya, J/J (Aston Martin DBR9), 115; **9** Atsushi Yogo/Hiroyuki Iiri, J/J (Lamborghini Murcielago), 114; **10** Roland Berville/Stéphane Lemeret/Carlo van Dam, F/B/NL (Saleen S7R-Ford), 114.
Fastest race lap: Cocker, 1m 20.561s, 102.821mph/ 165.474km/h.
Pole position: Drayson/Cocker.

Final championship points
P1
1 no.17 Sora Racing, 18; **2** no.007 Aston Martin Racing, 15; **3** no.10 Team ORECA Matmut AIM, 14; **4** no.15 Kolles, 10; **5** no.87 Drayson Racing, 9; **6** no.14 Kolles, 7; **7** no.11 Tokai University YGK Power, 2;

P2
1 no.24 Oak Racing, 21; **2** no.28 Jose Ibanez, 16.

GT1
1 no.69 JLOC, 18; **2** no.61 Hitotsuyama Team Nova, 15; **3** no.50 Larbre Competition, 14; **4** no.68 JLOC, 10.

GT2
1 no.89 Hankook Team Farnbacher, 16; **2** no.92 Rahal Letterman Racing Team, 14; **3** no.88 Team Felbermayr-Proton, 13; **4** no.77 Team Felbermayr-Proton, 9; **5** no.71 Team Daishin, 9.

Super GT Series (Japan)

2008

The following race was run after AUTOCOURSE 2008–2009 went to press.

FUJI GT 300km, Fuji International Speedway, Sunto-gun, Shizuoka Prefecture, Japan, 9 November. Round 9. 66 laps of the 2.835-mile/4.563km circuit, 187.131 miles/ 301.158km.
1 Tsugio Matsuda/Sébastien Philippe, J/F (Nissan GT-R), 1h 57m 09.624s, 95.833mph/154.228km/h; **2** Yuji Tachikawa/Richard Lyons, J/GB (Lexus SC430), 1h 57m 21.894s; **3** Daisuke Ito/Björn Wirdheim, J/S (Lexus SC430), 1h 57m 23.551s; **4** Loïc Duval/Katsuyuki Hiranaka, F/J (Honda NSX), 1h 57m 50.801s; **5** Toranosuke Takagi/André Couto, J/P (Lexus SC430), 1h 57m 52.539s; **6** Peter Dumbreck/Tatsuya Kataoka, GB/J (Lexus SC430), 1h 58m 08.515s; **7** Juichi Wakisaka/André Lotterer, J/D (Lexus SC430), 1h 58m 56.685s; **8** Takeshi Tsuchiya/Hiroaki Ishiura, J/J (Lexus SC430), 65 laps; **9** Satoshi Motoyama/Benoît Treluyer, J/F (Nissan GT-R), 65; **10** Katsutomo Kaneishi/Toshihiro Kaneishi, J/J (Honda NSX), 65.
Fastest race lap: Wirdheim, 1m 36.436s, 105.844mph/ 170.339km/h.
Pole position: Kaneishi/Kaneishi, 1m 42.661s, 99.426mph/ 160.010km/h.

Final championship points
Drivers (GT500)
1 Satoshi Motoyama/Benoît Tréluyer, J/F, 76; **2** Yuji Tachikawa/Richard Lyons, J/GB, 72; **3** Juichi Wakisaka/Andre Lotterer, J/D, 63; **4** Sébastien Philippe, F, 61; **5** Tsugio Matsuda, J, 61; **6** Ryo Michigami/Takashi Kogure, J/J, 60; **7** Michael Krumm/Masataka Yanagida, D/J, 57; **8** Ralph Firman/Takuya Izawa, IRL/J, 49; **9** Peter Dumbreck/Tatsuya Kataoka, GB/J, 45; **10** Loïc Duval/Katsuyuki Hiranaka, F/J, 43.

Drivers (GT300)
1 Hironobu Yasuda/Kazuki Hoshino, J/J, 78; **2** Morio Nitta/Shinichi Takagi, J/J, 77; **3** Nobuteru Taniguchi, J, 71.

2009

OKAYAMA GT300km, Okayama International Circuit (TI Circuit Aida), Aida Gun, Okayama Prefecture, Japan, 22 March. Round 1. 82 laps of the 2.301-mile/3.703km circuit, 188.677 miles/303.646km.
1 João Paulo de Oliveira/Seiji Ara, BR/J (Nissan), 2h 20m 54.071s, 80.344mph/129.301km/h; **2** Ryo Michigami/Takashi Kogure, J/J (Honda), 2h 21m 15.716s; **3** Ralph Firman/Takuya Izawa, IRL/J (Honda), 2h 22m 01.050s; **4** Tsugio Matsuda/Sébastien Philippe, J/F (Nissan), 2h 22m 26.502s; **5** Toshihiro Kaneishi/Koudai Tsukakoshi, J/J (Honda), 81 laps; **6** Yuji Tachikawa/Richard Lyons, J/GB (Lexus), 81; **7** Loïc Duval/Yuki Nakayama, F/J (Honda), 81; **8** Yuji Ide/Shinya Hosokawa, J/J (Honda), 81; **9** Hiroaki Ishiura/Kazuya Oshima, J/J (Lexus), 81; **10** Daisuke Ito/Björn Wirdheim, J/S (Lexus), 80.
Fastest race lap: André Lotterer, D (Lexus), 1m 37.940s, 84.576mph/136.111km/h.
Pole position: Tachikawa/Lyons,1m 24.069s, 98.531mph/ 158.570km/h.

KEIHIN SUZUKA 2 & 4 RACE, Suzuka International Racing Course, Ino-Cho, Suzuka-shi, Mie Prefecture, Japan, 19 April. Round 2. 52 laps of the 3.608-mile/5.807km circuit, 187.632 miles/301.964km.
1 Yuji Tachikawa/Richard Lyons, J/GB (Lexus), 1h 54m 52.997s, 97.994mph/157.706km/h; **2** Juichi Wakisaka/André Lotterer, J/D (Lexus), 1h 54m 54.885s; **3** Tsugio Matsuda/Sébastien Philippe, J/F (Nissan), 1h 54m 58.207s; **4** Daisuke Ito/Björn Wirdheim, J/S (Lexus), 1h 55m 02.582s; **5** Ryo Michigami/Takashi Kogure, J/J (Honda), 1h 55m 06.894s; **6** Toshihiro Kaneishi/Koudai Tsukakoshi, J/J (Honda), 1h 55m 08.351s; **7** Hiroaki Ishiura/Kazuya Oshima, J/J (Lexus), 1h 55m 10.529s; **8** João Paulo de Oliveira/Seiji Ara, BR/J (Nissan), 1h 55m 13.327s; **9** Loïc Duval/Yuki Nakayama, F/J (Honda), 1h 55m 17.060s; **10** André Couto/Kohei Hirate, P/J (Lexus), 1h 55m 18.901s.
Fastest race lap: Lyons, 1m 56.817s, 111.198mph/ 178.956km/h.
Pole position: Satoshi Motoyama/Benoît Treluyer, J/F (Nissan), 1m 53.487s, 111.199mph/178.957km/h.

FUJI GT 400km, Fuji International Speedway, Sunto-gun, Shizuoka Prefecture, Japan, 4 May. Round 3. 88 laps of the 2.835-mile/4.563km circuit, 249.508 miles/ 401.544km.
1 Satoshi Motoyama/Benoît Treluyer, J/F (Nissan), 2h 26m 09.788s, 102.423mph/164.833km/h; **2** Juichi Wakisaka/André Lotterer, J/D (Lexus), 2h 26m 10.007s; **3** Ralph Firman/Takuya Izawa, IRL/J (Honda), 2h 26m 28.785s; **4** João Paulo de Oliveira/Seiji Ara, BR/J (Nissan), 2h 26m 48.983s; **5** Hiroaki Ishiura/Kazuya Oshima, J/J (Lexus), 2h 26m 55.763s; **6** Daisuke Ito/Björn Wirdheim, J/S (Lexus), 2h 26m 57.195s; **7** Ronnie Quintarelli/Hironobu Yasuda, I/J (Nissan), 2h 27m 23.073s; **8** Loïc Duval/Yuki Nakayama, F/J (Honda), 2h 27m 23.303s; **9** Yuji Tachikawa/Richard Lyons, J/GB (Lexus), 2h 27m 43.974s; **10** André Couto/Kohei Hirate, P/J (Lexus), 2h 27m 48.387s.
Fastest race lap: Wirdheim, 1m 36.343s, 105.945mph/ 170.503km/h.
Pole position: Motoyama/ Treluyer, 1m 34.522s, 107.987mph/173.788km/h.

SUPER GT INTERNATIONAL SERIES MALAYSIA, Sepang International Circuit, Jalan Pekeliling, Kuala Lumpur, Malaysia, 21 June. Round 4. 54 laps of the 3.444-mile/5.542km circuit, 185.957 miles/299.268km.
1 Ronnie Quintarelli/Hironobu Yasuda, I/J (Nissan), 1h 52m 02.010s, 99.589mph/160.274km/h; **2** Toshihiro Kaneishi/Koudai Tsukakoshi, J/J (Honda), 1h 52m 13.504s; **3** Ralph Firman/Takuya Izawa, IRL/J (Honda), 1h 52m 18.216s; **4** Yuji Ide/Shinya Hosokawa, J/J (Honda), 1h 52m 18.575s; **5** João Paulo de Oliveira/Seiji Ara, BR/J (Nissan), 1h 52m 36.799s; **6** Juichi Wakisaka/André Lotterer, J/D (Lexus), 1h 52m 37.125s; **7** Tsugio Matsuda/Sébastien Philippe, J/F (Nissan), 1h 52m 42.173s; **8** Satoshi Motoyama/Benoît Treluyer, J/F (Nissan), 1h 52m 42.407s; **9** Hiroaki Ishiura/Kazuya Oshima, J/J (Lexus), 1h 53m 25.109s; **10** Yuji Tachikawa/Richard Lyons, J/GB (Lexus), 1h 54m 03.686s.
Fastest race lap: Daisuke Ito, J (Lexus), 2m 01.369s, 102.143mph/164.384km/h.
Pole position: Motoyama/Treluyer, 1m 58.124s, 104.950mph/ 168.900km/h.

SUGO GT 300km, Sportsland-SUGO International Course, Shibata-gun, Miyagi Prefecture, Japan, 26 July. Round 5. 81 laps of the 2.302-mile/3.704km circuit, 186.436 miles/ 300.040km.
1 Satoshi Motoyama/Benoît Treluyer, J/F (Nissan), 1h 59m 33.479s, 93.562mph/150.574km/h; **2** André Couto/Kohei Hirate, P/J (Lexus), 1h 59m 54.541s; **3** Ryo Michigami/Takashi Kogure, J/J (Honda), 1h 59m 58.491s; **4** Yuji Ide/Shinya Hosokawa, J/J (Honda), 1h 59m 59.954s; **5** Daisuke Ito/Björn

Wirdheim, J/S (Lexus), 2h 00m 28.343s; **6** Toshihiro Kaneishi/Koudai Tsukakoshi, J/J (Honda), 2h 00m 55.829s; **7** Juichi Wakisaka/André Lotterer, J/D (Lexus), 80 laps; **8** Tsugio Matsuda/Sébastien Philippe, J/F (Nissan), 80; **9** Ronnie Quintarelli/Hironobu Yasuda, I/J (Nissan), 80; **10** Yuji Tachikawa/Richard Lyons, J/GB (Lexus), 80.
Fastest race lap: Wirdheim, 1m 19.178s, 104.651mph/168.419km/h.
Pole position: Quintarelli/Yasuda, 1m 16.248s, 108.672mph/174.891km/h.

38th INTERNATIONAL POKKA GT SUMMER SPECIAL, Suzuka International Racing Course, Ino-Cho, Suzuka-shi, Mie Prefecture, Japan, 23 August. Round 6. 121 laps of the 3.608-mile/5.807km circuit, 436.605 miles/702.647km.
1 Hiroaki Ishiura/Kazuya Oshima, J/J (Lexus), 4h 16m 02.744s, 102.310mph/164.653km/h; **2** Ronnie Quintarelli/Hironobu Yasuda, I/J (Nissan), 4h 16m 13.425s; **3** Yuji Tachikawa/Richard Lyons, J/GB (Lexus), 4h 16m 21.194s; **4** Ryo Michigami/Takashi Kogure, J/J (Honda), 4h 16m 23.672s; **5** Tsugio Matsuda/Sébastien Philippe, J/F (Nissan), 4h 16m 39.649s; **6** Satoshi Motoyama/Michael Krumm, J/D (Nissan), 4h 16m 39.933s; **7** André Couto/Kohei Hirate, P/J (Lexus), 4h 16m 52.269s; **8** Juichi Wakisaka/André Lotterer, J/D (Lexus), 4h 17m 03.711s; **9** Yuji Ide/Shinya Hosokawa, J/J (Honda), 4h 17m 47.104s; **10** Toshihiro Kaneishi/Koudai Tsukakoshi/Katsutomo Kaneishi, J/J/J (Honda), 120 laps.
Fastest race lap: Ishiura, 1m 58.093s, 109.997mph/177.023km/h.
Pole position: Ishiura/Oshima, 1m 55.724s, 112.249mph/180.647km/h.

FUJI GT 300km, Fuji International Speedway, Sunto-gun, Shizuoka Prefecture, Japan, 13 September. Round 7. 66 laps of the 2.835-mile/4.563km circuit, 187.131 miles/301.158km.
1 Ralph Firman/Takuya Izawa, IRL/J (Honda), 1h 49m 39.143s, 102.394mph/164.788km/h; **2** Satoshi Motoyama/Benoît Treluyer, J/F (Nissan), 1h 49m 40.904s; **3** Juichi Wakisaka/André Lotterer, J/D (Lexus), 1h 49m 42.294s; **4** Toshihiro Kaneishi/Koudai Tsukakoshi, J/J (Honda), 1h 49m 58.762s; **5** Daisuke Ito/Björn Wirdheim, J/S (Lexus), 1h 50m 08.696s; **6** Ronnie Quintarelli/Hironobu Yasuda, I/J (Nissan), 1h 50m 17.258s; **7** Hiroaki Ishiura/Kazuya Oshima, J/J (Lexus), 1h 50m 24.475s; **8** Ryo Michigami/Takashi Kogure, J/J (Honda), 1h 50m 49.902s; **9** Loïc Duval/Yuki Nakayama, F/J (Honda), 1h 51m 05.990s; **10** Yuji Tachikawa/Richard Lyons, J/GB (Lexus), 65 laps.
Fastest race lap: Wirdheim, 1m 37.093s, 105.127mph/169.186km/h.
Pole position: Duval/ Nakayama, 1m 46.111s, 96.193mph/154.808km/h.

KYUSHU 300km, Autopolis International Racing Course, Kamit-sue-mura, Hita-gun, Oita Prefecture, Japan, 18 October. Round 8. 65 laps of the 2.904-mile/4.674km circuit, 188.779 miles/303.810km.
1 Juichi Wakisaka/André Lotterer, J/D (Lexus), 1h 57m 37.259s, 96.298mph/154.977km/h; **2** Satoshi Motoyama/Benoît Treluyer, J/F (Nissan), 1h 57m 40.169s; **3** João Paulo de Oliveira/Seiji Ara, BR/J (Nissan), 1h 58m 13.501s; **4** Ralph Firman/Takuya Izawa, IRL/J (Honda), 1h 58m 13.689s; **5** Ryo Michigami/Takashi Kogure, J/J (Honda), 1h 58m 15.227s; **6** Yuji Ide/Kosuke Matsuura, J/J (Honda), 1h 58m 15.915s; **7** Hiroaki Ishiura/Kazuya Oshima, J/J (Lexus), 1h 58m 27.297s; **8** Ronnie Quintarelli/Hironobu Yasuda, I/J (Nissan), 1h 58m 19.304s; **9** Loïc Duval/Yuki Nakayama, F/J (Honda), 64 laps; **10** Daisuke Ito/Björn Wirdheim, J/S (Lexus), 64.
Fastest race lap: Richard Lyons, GB (Lexus), 1m 44.842s, 99.725 mph/160.492 km/h.
Pole position: Yuji Tachikawa/Richard Lyons, J/GB (Lexus), 1m 41.609s, 102.899mph/165.600km/h.

MOTEGI GT 250km, Twin Ring Motegi, Motegi-machi, Haga-gun, Tochigi Prefecture, Japan, 8 November. Round 9. 53 laps of the 2.983-mile/4.8013km circuit, 158.120 miles/254.469km.
1 Ralph Firman/Takuya Izawa, IRL/J (Honda), 1h 43m 30.913s, 91.650mph/147.496km/h; **2** Juichi Wakisaka/André Lotterer, J/D (Lexus), 1h 43m 39.742s; **3** Toshihiro Kaneishi/Koudai Tsukakoshi, J/J (Honda), 1h 43m 39.923s; **4** Daisuke Ito/Björn Wirdheim, J/S (Lexus), 1h 43m 41.353s; **5** André Couto/Kohei Hirate, P/J (Lexus), 1h 43m 43.566s; **6** Loïc Duval/Yuki Nakayama, F/J (Honda), 1h 43m 44.330s; **7** Tsugio Matsuda/Sébastien Philippe, J/F (Nissan), 1h 43m 50.126s; **8** Yuji Ide/Shinya Hosokawa, J/J (Honda), 1h 43m 56.315s; **9** Hiroaki Ishiura/Kazuya Oshima, J/J (Lexus), 1h 43m 57.813s; **10** Ryo Michigami/Takashi Kogure, J/J (Honda), 1h 43m 58.724s.
Fastest race lap: Lotterer, 1m 47.602s, 99.814mph/160.635km/h.
Pole position: Firman/Izawa, 1m 44.390s, 102.885mph/165.577km/h.

Final championship points
Drivers (GT500)
1 André Lotterer/Juichi Wakisaka, D/J, 88; **2** Ralph Firman/Takuya Izawa, IRL/J, 81; **3** Satoshi Motoyama, J, 78; **4** Benoît Treluyer, F, 73; **5** Koudai Tsukakoshi/Toshihiro Kaneishi, J, 51; **6** Takashi Kogure/Ryo Michigami, J/J, 50; **7** Hironobu Yasuda/Ronnie Quintarelli, J/I, 49; **8** João Paulo de Oliveira/Seiji Ara, J, 48; **9** Hiroaki Ishiura/Kazuya Oshima, K/J, 44; **10** Richard Lyons/Yuji Tachikawa, GB/J, 41.

Drivers (GT300)
1 Manabu Orido/Tatsuya Kataoka, J, 85; **2** Ryo Orime/Nobutero Taniguchi, J/J, 82; **3** Tetsuya Tanaka/Katsuyuki Hiranaka, J, 79.

Other Sports Car races

ROLEX 24 AT DAYTONA, Daytona International Speedway, Daytona Beach, Florida, U.S.A., 24-25 January. 735 laps of the 3.560-mile/5.729km circuit, 2616.600 miles/4211.010km (Grand-Am round 1).
1 David Donohue/Antonio Garcia/Darren Law/Buddy Rice, USA/E/CDN/USA (Riley MkXI-Porsche), 24h 00m 26.465s, 108.992mph/175.405km/h; **2** Scott Pruett/Juan Pablo Montoya/Memo Rojas, USA/CO/MEX (Riley MkXI/XX-Lexus), 24h 00m 26.632s; **3** João Barbosa/Terry Borcheller/J.C. France/Hurley Haywood, P/USA/USA/USA (Riley MkXI-Porsche), 24h 00m 31.969s; **4** Max Angelelli/Pedro Lamy/Brian Frisselle/Wayne Taylor, I/P/USA/ZA (Dallara DP01-Ford), 24h 00m 37.054s; **5** Scott Dixon/Dario Franchitti/Alex Lloyd, NZ/GB/GB (Riley MkXI-Lexus), 731 laps; **6** Timo Bernhard/Romain Dumas/Ryan Briscoe, D/F/AUS (Riley MkXX-Porsche), 717; **7** Alex Gurney/Jon Fogarty/Jimmie Johnson/Jimmy Vasser, USA/USA/USA/USA (Riley MkXI/XX-Pontiac), 714; **8** Andy Wallace/Rob Finlay/Casey Mears/Danica Patrick, GB/USA/USA/USA (Crawford DP03-Pontiac), 702; **9** Andy Lally/Jörg Bergmeister/Patrick Long/Justin Marks/RJ Valentine, USA/D/USA/USA/USA (Porsche GT3 Cup), 695; **10** Spencer Pumpelly/Emmanuel Collard/Richard Lietz/Ted Ballou/Tim George Jr., USA/F/A/USA/USA (Porsche GT3 Cup), 694.
Fastest race lap: Dumas, 1m 41.537s, 126.220mph/203.131km/h.
Pole position: Donohue/Garcia/Law/Rice, 1m 40.540s, 127.472mph/205.146km/h.

ADAC-ZÜRICH-24h-RENNEN, Nürburgring Nordschleife Circuit, Nürburg/Eifel, Germany, 23-24 May. 155 laps of the 15.769-mile/25.378km circuit, 2555.220 miles/3933.5906km.
1 Timo Bernhard/ Marc Lieb/ Romain Dumas (Porsche 911 GT3 RSR), 24h 05m 01.412s, 101.488mph/163.330km/h; **2** Christian Abt/ Jean-Francois Hemroulle/ Pierre Kaffer/ Lucas Luhr (Audi R8 LMS), 154 Laps; **3** Emmanuel Collard/ Wolf Henzler/ Richard Lietz/ Dirk Werner (Porsche 911 GT3R Cup S), 152; **4** Uwe Alzen/ Sascha Bert/ Lance David Arnold/ Christophe Mies (Porsche 997 GT3 Cup), 150; **5** Marc Basseng/ Marcel Fässler/ Mike Rockenfeller/ Frank Stippler (Audi R8 LMS), 149; **6** Sabine Schmitz/ Klaus Abbelen/ Edgar Althoff/ Kenneth Heyer (Porsche 997 GT3 Cup), 149; **7** Frank Kräling/ Marc Grindorf/ Peter Scharmach/ Marco Holzer (Porsche 911 GT3 Cup), 149; **8** Heinz-Josef Bermes/ Oliver Kainz/ Frank Schmickler/ Jorg Bergmeister (Porsche 997 GT3 Cup), 148; **9** Anthony Quinn/ Klark Quinn/ Craig Baird/ Grant Denyer (Porsche 997 GT3 RSR), 146; **10** Rudi Adams/ Luca Ludwig/ Arnd Meier/ Markus Grossman (BMW Z4-M Coupe), 145.
Fastest race lap: Bernhard/Lieb/Dumas, 8m 36.768s, 109.854mph/176.793km/h.
Pole position: Dirk Adorf (Ford GT), 8m 36.536s, 109.903mph/176.872km/h.

77th 24 HEURES DU MANS, Circuit International Du Mans, Les Raineries, Le Mans, France, 13-14 June. 382 laps of the 8.469-mile/13.629km circuit, 3235.031 miles/5206.278km.
1 David Brabham/Marc Gené/Alexander Wurz, AUS/E/A (Peugeot 908), 24h 01m 45.442s, 134.629mph/216.664km/h (1st LMP1 class); **2** Sébastien Bourdais/Franck Montagny/Stéphane Sarrazin, F/F/F (Peugeot 908), 381 laps; **3** Rinaldo Capello/Tom Kristensen/Allan McNish, I/DK/GB (Audi R15), 376; **4** Jan Charouz/Tomas Enge/Stefan Mücke, CZ/CZ/D (Lola B09/60-Aston Martin), 373; **5** Olivier Panis/Nicolas Lapierre/Soheil Ayari, F/F/F (Courage-Oreca LC70-AIM), 370; **6** Christian Klien/Pedro Lamy/Nicolas Minassian, A/P/F (Peugeot 908), 369; **7** Narain Karthikeyan/André Lotterer/Charles Zwolsman, IND/D/NL (Audi R10), 369; **8** Christophe Tinseau/João Barbosa/Bruce Jouanny, F/P/F (Pescarolo 01-Judd), 368; **9** Christijan Albers/Christian Bakkerud/Giorgio Mondini, NL/DK/CH (Audi R10), 360; **10** Casper Elgaard/Kristian Poulsen/Emmanuel Collard, DK/DK/F (Porsche RS Spyder Evo), 357 (1st LMP2 class); **11** Pierre Ragues/Franck Mailleux/Didier André, F/F/F (Courage-Oreca LC70-Judd), 344; **12** Jonny Kane/Benjamin Leuenberger/Xavier Pompidou, GB/CH/F (Lola B09/80-Judd), 343; **13** Anthony Davidson/Darren Turner/Jos Verstappen, GB/GB/NL (Lola B09/60-Aston Martin), 342; **14** Andrea Belicchi/Neel Jani/Nicolas Prost, I/CH/F (Lola B09/60-Aston Martin), 342; **15** Jan Magnussen/Johnny O'Connell/Antonio Garcia, DK/USA/E (Chevrolet Corvette C6.R), 342 (1st LMGT1 class); **16** Yann Clairay/Xavier Maassen/Julien Jousse, F/NL/F (Chevrolet Corvette C6.R), 336; **17** Timo Bernhard/Romain Dumas/Alexandre Prémat, D/F/F (Audi R15), 333; **18** Jaime Melo Jr./Mika Salo/Pierre Kaffer, BR/FIN/D (Ferrari 430 GT2), 329 (1st LMGT2 class); **19** Fabio Babini/Matteo Malucelli/Paolo Ruberti, I/I/I (Ferrari 430 GT2), 327; **20** Jacques Nicolet/Richard Hein/Jean-François Yvon, F/MC/F (Pescarolo 01-Mazda), 325; **21** Peter Hardman/Nick Leventis/Danny Watts, GB/GB/GB (Ginetta-Zytek 09S-Zytek), 325; **22** Tracy Krohn/Nic Jönsson/Eric van de Poele, USA/S/B (Ferrari 430 GT2), 323; **23** Robert Bell/Andrew Kirkaldy/Tim Sugden, GB/GB/GB (Ferrari 430 GT2), 320; **24** Jamie Campbell-Walter/Vanina Ickx/Roman Iannetta, GB/B/F (Creation CA07-Judd), 319; **25** Tom Coronel/Jarek Janis/Jeroen Bleekemolen, NL/CZ/NL (Spyker C8 Laviolette GT2-R-Audi), 319; **26** Gianmaria Bruni/Luis Pérez-Companc/Matias Russo, I/RA/RA (Ferrari 430 GT2), 317; **27** Pierre Ehret/Leo Mansell/Roman Rusinov, D/GB/RUS (Ferrari 430 GT2), 314; **28** Juan Barazi/Stuart Moseley/Phil Bennett, DK/GB/GB (Zytek 07S), 306; **29** Christophe Bouchut/Yvan Lebon/Manuel Rodrigues, F/F/F (Ferrari 430 GT2), 304; **30** Patrick Dempsey/Joe Foster/Don Kitch Jr., USA/USA/USA (Ferrari 430 GT2), 301; **31** Lukas Lichtner-Hoyer/Alex Müller/Thomas Grüber, A/D/A (Aston Martin DBR9), 294; **32** Michael McInerney/Sean McInerney/Michael Vergers, GB/GB/NL (Ferrari 430 GT2), 280; **33** Seiji Ara/Keisuke Kunimoto/Sascha Maassen, J/J/D (Porsche RS Spyder Evo), 339 (DNF-accident); **34** Oliver Gavin/Olivier Beretta/Marcel Fässler, GB/MC/CH (Chevrolet Corvette C6.R), 311 (DNF-gearbox); **35** Tommy Erdos/Mike Newton/Chris Dyson, BR/GB/USA (Lola B09/86-Mazda), 273 (DNF-engine); **36** Jonathan Cocker/Paul Drayson/Marino Franchitti, GB/GB/GB (Aston Martin V8 Vantage), 272 (DNF-electrics); **37** Patrick Long/Patrick Pilet/Raymond Narac, USA/F/F (Porsche 997 GT3 RSR), 265 (DNF-gearbox); **38** Hideki Noda/Jean de Pourtales/Matthew Marsh, J/F/GB (Lola B09/86-Mazda), 261 (DNF-oil leak); **39** Stuart Hall/Peter Kox/Harold Primat, GB/NL/CH (Lola B09/60-Aston Martin), 252 (DNF-accident); **40** Bruno Senna/Stéphane Ortelli/Tiago Monteiro, BR/MC/P (Courage-Oreca LC70-AIM), 219 (DNF-bellhousing); **41** Jean-Christophe Boullion/Simon Pagenaud/Benoît Treluyer, F/F/F (Peugeot 908), 210 (DNF-accident); **42** Mathieu Lahaye/Karim Ajlani/Guillaume Moreau, F/CH/F (Pescarolo 01-Mazda), 208 (DNF-engine); **43** Thomas Biagi/Matteo Bobbi/Andrea Piccini, I/I/I (Lola B09/80-Judd), 203 (DNF-electrics); **44** Seth Neiman/Darren Law/Jörg Bergmeister, USA/CDN/D (Porsche 997 GT3 RSR), 194 (DNF-accident); **45** Darryl O'Young/Philippe Hesnault Jr./Plamen Kralev, HK/F/BG (Porsche 997 GT3 RSR), 186; **46** Allan Simonsen/Dominik Farnbacher/Christian Montanari, DK/D/SM (Ferrari 430 GT2), 183 (DNF-engine); **47** Lawrence Tomlinson/Richard Dean/Nigel Moore, GB/GB/GB (Ginetta-Zytek 09S-Zytek), 178 (DNF-fire); **48** Lucas Luhr/Mike Rockenfeller/Marco Werner, D/D/D (Audi R15), 104 (DNF-accident); **49** Karim Ojjeh/Claude-Yves Gosselin/Philipp Peter, SA/F/A (Zytek 07S), 102 (DNF-engine); **50** Horst Felbermayr Jr./Horst Felbermayr Sr./Michel Lecourt, A/A/F (Porsche 997 GT3 RSR), 102 (DNF-clutch); **51** Luc Alphand/Patrice Gouesland/Stéphane Grégoire, F/F/F (Chevrolet Corvette C6.R), 99 (DNF-accident); **52** Pierre Bruneau/Tim Greaves/Marc Rostan, F/GB/F (Radical SR9-AER), 91 (DNF-engine); **53** Miguel Pais do Amaral/Olivier Pla/Guy Smith, P/F/GB (Ginetta-Zytek 09S-Zytek), 46 (DNF-accident damage); **54** Marc Lieb/Richard Lietz/Wolf Henzler, D/A/D (Porsche 997 GT3 RSR), 24 (DNF-fuel pump); **55** Marco Apicella/Atsushi Yogo/Yutaka Yamagishi, I/J/J (Lamborghini Murciélago R-GT), 1 (DNF-engine).
Fastest race lap: Minassian, 3m 24.352s, 149.190mph/240.097km/h.
Pole position: Bourdais/Montagny/Sarrazin, 3m 22.888s, 150.266mph/241.830km/h.

V8 Supercar Championship Series

2008

The following races were run after AUTOCOURSE 2008–2009 went to press.

GULF AIR DESERT 400, Bahrain International Circuit, Sakhir, Bahrain, 7/8 November. Round 12. 3 x 32 laps of the 2.386-mile/3.840km circuit.
Race 1 (76.354 miles/122.880km).
1 Jamie Whincup, AUS (Ford Falcon BF), 50m 29.8677s, 90.721mph/146.002km/h; **2** Craig Lowndes, AUS (Ford Falcon BF), 50m 40.3307s; **3** Lee Holdsworth, AUS (Holden Commodore VE), 50m 43.4542s; **4** Russell Ingall, AUS (Holden Commodore VE), 50m 44.1632s; **5** James Courtney, AUS (Ford Falcon BF), 50m 45.7492s; **6** Steven Johnson, AUS (Ford Falcon BF), 50m 47.7845s; **7** Shane van Gisbergen, NZ (Ford Falcon BF), 50m 52.2450s; **8** Steven Richards, NZ (Ford Falcon BF), 50m 53.1133s; **9** Rick Kelly, AUS (Holden Commodore VE), 50m 56.7179s; **10** Greg Murphy, NZ (Holden Commodore VE), 50m 57.5350s.
Fastest race lap: Whincup, 1m 25.2678s, 100.739mph/162.124km/h.
Pole position: Whincup, 1m 25.0415s, 101.007mph/162.555km/h.

Race 2 (76.354 miles/122.880km).
1 Jamie Whincup, AUS (Ford Falcon BF), 49m 37.2508s, 92.325mph/148.582km/h; **2** Russell Ingall, AUS (Holden Commodore VE), 49m 43.9667s; **3** Craig Lowndes, AUS (Ford Falcon BF), 49m 44.9679s; **4** Mark Winterbottom, AUS (Ford Falcon BF), 49m 45.2293s; **5** Steven Richards, NZ (Ford Falcon BF), 49m 50.2147s; **6** Todd Kelly, AUS (Holden Commodore VE), 49m 52.2756s; **7** James Courtney, AUS (Ford Falcon BF), 49m 54.7224s; **8** Steven Johnson, AUS (Ford Falcon BF), 49m 57.4138s; **9** Paul Morris, AUS (Holden Commodore VE), 49m 59.0259s; **10** Will Davison, AUS (Ford Falcon BF), 49m 59.4156s.
Fastest race lap: Lowndes, 1m 25.5661s, 100.388mph/161.559 km/h.
Pole position: Whincup.

Race 3 (76.354 miles/122.880km).
1 Jamie Whincup, AUS (Ford Falcon BF), 51m 07.5065s, 89.608mph/144.210km/h; **2** James Courtney, AUS (Ford Falcon BF), 51m 13.5515s; **3** Craig Lowndes, AUS (Ford Falcon BF), 51m 14.0226s; **4** Mark Winterbottom, AUS (Ford Falcon BF), 51m 14.9899s; **5** Russell Ingall, AUS (Holden Commodore VE), 51m 17.3990s; **6** Will Davison, AUS (Ford Falcon BF), 51m 18.5694s; **7** Fabian Coulthard, NZ (Ford Falcon BF), 51m 19.4432s; **8** Lee Holdsworth, AUS (Holden Commodore VE), 51m 20.1479s; **9** Steven Richards, NZ (Ford Falcon BF), 51m 22.3787s; **10** Shane van Gisbergen, NZ (Ford Falcon BF), 51m 23.2587s.
Fastest race lap: Whincup, 1m 25.7817s, 100.135mph/161.153km/h.
Pole position: Whincup.

FALKEN TASMANIA CHALLENGE, Symmons Plains Raceway, Launceston, Tasmania, Australia, 22/23 November. Round 13. 3 x 50 laps of the 1.498-mile/2.411km circuit.
Race 1 (74.906 miles/120.550km).
1 Todd Kelly, AUS (Holden Commodore VE), 52m 25.8991s, 85.718mph/137.951km/h; **2** Jamie Whincup, AUS (Ford Falcon BF), 52m 26.9285s; **3** Mark Winterbottom, AUS (Ford Falcon BF), 52m 27.3095s; **4** Will Davison, AUS (Ford Falcon BF), 52m 33.2138s; **5** Shane van Gisbergen, NZ (Ford Falcon BF), 52m 33.6954s; **6** Craig Lowndes, AUS (Ford Falcon BF), 52m 40.7405s; **7** Jason Bright, AUS (Ford Falcon BF), 52m 42.1608s; **8** Steven Johnson, AUS (Ford Falcon BF), 52m 58.2160s; **9** Fabian Coulthard, NZ (Ford Falcon BF), 53m 01.9825s; **10** Lee Holdsworth, AUS (Holden Commodore VE), 53m 02.8942s.
Fastest race lap: Kelly (Todd), 53.1947s, 101.387mph/163.166km/h.
Pole position: Garth Tander, AUS (Holden Commodore VE), 51.8338s, 104.049mph/167.450km/h.

Race 2 (74.906 miles/120.550km).
1 Jamie Whincup, AUS (Ford Falcon BF), 46m 05.2365s, 97.518mph/156.941km/h; **2** Craig Lowndes, AUS (Ford Falcon BF), 46m 05.5530s; **3** Todd Kelly, AUS (Holden Commodore VE), 46m 05.8481s; **4** Mark Winterbottom, AUS (Ford Falcon BF), 46m 06.0570s; **5** Will Davison, AUS (Ford Falcon BF), 46m 07.5620s; **6** Steven Johnson, AUS (Ford Falcon BF), 46m 08.8270s; **7** Lee Holdsworth, AUS (Holden Commodore VE), 46m 10.2893s; **8** Garth Tander, AUS (Holden Commodore VE), 46m 10.6747s; **9** Rick Kelly, AUS (Holden Commodore VE), 46m 16.6796s; **10** Fabian Coulthard, NZ (Ford Falcon BF), 46m 18.4656s.
Fastest race lap: Whincup, 52.9857s, 101.786mph/163.810km/h.
Pole position: Kelly (Todd).

Race 3 (74.906 miles/120.550km).
1 Jamie Whincup, AUS (Ford Falcon BF), 48m 22.3812s, 92.910mph/149.525km/h; **2** Craig Lowndes, AUS (Ford Falcon BF), 48m 22.4850s; **3** Todd Kelly, AUS (Holden Commodore VE), 48m 23.4284s; **4** Mark Winterbottom, AUS (Ford Falcon BF), 48m 23.9305s; **5** Garth Tander, AUS (Holden Commodore VE), 48m 24.2231s; **6** Will Davison, AUS (Ford Falcon BF), 48m 26.7465s; **7** Steven Johnson, AUS (Ford Falcon BF), 48m 27.4823s; **8** Rick Kelly, AUS (Holden Commodore VE), 48m 27.9999s; **9** Lee Holdsworth, AUS (Holden Commodore VE), 48m 28.3732s; **10** James Courtney, AUS (Ford Falcon BF), 48m 28.8889s.
Fastest race lap: Whincup, 52.6742s, 102.388mph/164.778km/h.
Pole position: Whincup.

NRMA MOTORING & SERVICES GRAND FINALE, Oran Park Raceway, Narellan, New South Wales, Australia, 6/7 December. Round 14. 3 x 46 laps of the 1.628-mile/2.620km circuit.
Race 1 (74.888 miles/120.520km).
1 Jamie Whincup, AUS (Ford Falcon BF), 56m 12.2480s, 79.945mph/128.659km/h; **2** Craig Lowndes, AUS (Ford Falcon BF), 56m 18.8987s; **3** Russell Ingall, AUS (Holden Commodore VE), 56m 20.8253s; **4** Steven Richards, NZ (Ford Falcon BF), 56m 24.3870s; **5** James Courtney, AUS (Ford Falcon BF), 56m 25.1869s; **6** Garth Tander, AUS (Holden Commodore VE), 56m 25.3874s; **7** Todd Kelly, AUS (Holden Commodore VE), 56m 33.1419s; **8** Michael Caruso, AUS (Holden Commodore VE), 56m 43.9055s; **9** Rick Kelly, AUS (Holden Commodore VE), 56m 44.8900s; **10** Will Davison, AUS (Ford Falcon BF), 56m 45.6335s.
Fastest race lap: Ingall, 1m 10.6998s, 82.896mph/133.409km/h.
Pole position: Tander, 1m 09.4562s, 84.380mph/135.797km/h.

Race 2 (74.888 miles/120.520km).
1 Garth Tander, AUS (Holden Commodore VE), 57m 04.0467s, 78.735mph/126.713km/h; **2** Russell Ingall, AUS (Holden Commodore VE), 57m 04.5667s; **3** Steven Richards, NZ (Ford Falcon BF), 57m 05.1758s; **4** Rick Kelly, AUS (Holden Commodore VE), 57m 09.0118s; **5** Craig Lowndes, AUS (Ford Falcon BF), 57m 10.4681s; **6** James Courtney, AUS (Ford Falcon BF), 57m 11.2554s; **7** Jason Bright, AUS (Ford Falcon BF), 57m 15.3372s; **8** Todd Kelly, AUS (Holden Commodore VE), 57m 24.7458s; **9** Steven Johnson, AUS (Ford Falcon BF), 57m 27.4517s; **10** Fabian Coulthard, NZ (Ford Falcon BF), 57m 28.1224s.
Fastest race lap: Whincup, 1m 10.5408s, 83.083mph/133.709km/h.
Pole position: Whincup.

Race 3 (74.888 miles/120.520km).
1 Rick Kelly, AUS (Holden Commodore VE), 57m 03.6766s, 78.744mph/126.726km/h; **2** Garth Tander, AUS (Holden Commodore VE), 57m 04.8280s; **3** Craig Lowndes, AUS (Ford Falcon BF), 57m 09.5112s; **4** James Courtney, AUS (Ford Falcon BF), 57m 10.9877s; **5** Shane van Gisbergen, NZ (Ford Falcon BF), 57m 11.8098s; **6** Lee Holdsworth, AUS (Holden Commodore VE), 57m 12.7802s; **7** Jason Bright, AUS (Ford Falcon BF), 57m 23.4710s; **8** Fabian Coulthard, NZ (Ford Falcon BF), 57m 25.7515s; **9** Paul Morris, AUS (Holden Commodore VE), 57m 26.5981s; **10** Michael Caruso, AUS (Holden Commodore VE), 57m 36.1796s.
Fastest race lap: Lowndes, 1m 10.9847s, 82.563mph/132.873km/h.
Pole position: Tander.

Final championship points
Drivers
1 Jamie Whincup, AUS, 3332; **2** Mark Winterbottom, AUS, 3079; **3** Garth Tander, AUS, 3048; **4** Craig Lowndes, AUS, 2871; **5** Will Davison, AUS, 2495; **6** James Courtney, AUS, 2446; **7** Rick Kelly, AUS, 2430; **8** Steven Richards, NZ, 2416; **9** Russell Ingall, AUS, 2236; **10** Steven Johnson, AUS, 2163; **11** Lee Holdsworth, AUS, 2065; **12** Todd Kelly, AUS, 2053; **13** Fabian Coulthard, NZ, 1823; **14** Mark Skaife, AUS, 1644; **15** Shane van Gisbergen, NZ, 1614; **16** Greg Murphy, NZ, 1572; **17** Jason Richards, NZ, 1548; **18** Michael Caruso, AUS, 1439; **19** Jason Bright, AUS, 1438; **20** Paul Morris, AUS, 1436.

Teams
1 Team Vodafone, 5867; **2** Ford Performance Racing, 5308; **3** Jim Beam Racing, 4478.

2009

CLIPSAL 500, Adelaide Steet Circuit, South Australia, Australia, 21/22 March.Round 1. 2 x 78 laps of the 2.001-mile/3.220km circuit.
Race 1 (156.064 miles/251.160km).
1 Jamie Whincup, AUS (Ford Falcon FG), 1h 59m 06.5279s, 78.615mph/126.519km/h; **2** Lee Holdsworth, AUS (Holden Commodore VE), 1h 59m 20.5552s; **3** Will Davison, AUS (Holden Commodore VE), 1h 59m 32.6039s; **4** Steven Johnson, AUS (Ford Falcon FG), 1h 59m 35.4559s; **5** Jason Richards, NZ (Holden Commodore VE), 1h 59m 37.0436s; **6** Shane van Gisbergen, NZ (Ford Falcon FG), 1h 59m 42.4383s; **7** Todd Kelly, AUS (Holden Commodore VE), 1h 59m 42.8291s; **8** Russell Ingall, AUS (Holden Commodore VE), 1h 59m 48.0255s; **9** Cameron McConville, AUS (Holden Commodore VE), 1h 59m 49.6857s; **10** Rick Kelly, AUS (Holden Commodore VE), 1h 59m 54.0898s.
Fastest race lap: Whincup, 1m 23.0017s, 86.780mph/139.659km/h.
Pole position: Whincup, 1m 21.8123s, 88.042mph/141.690km/h.

Race 2 (156.064 miles/251.160km).
1 Jamie Whincup, AUS (Ford Falcon FG), 2h 00m 39.5887s, 77.605mph/124.893km/h; **2** Will Davison, AUS (Holden Commodore VE), 2h 00m 40.3366s; **3** Garth Tander, AUS (Holden Commodore VE), 2h 00m 43.9844s; **4** Craig Lowndes, AUS (Ford Falcon FG), 2h 00m 44.4449s; **5** Lee Holdsworth, AUS (Holden Commodore VE), 2h 00m 46.4651s; **6** Steven Johnson, AUS (Ford Falcon FG), 2h 00m 48.2497s; **7** Jason Richards, NZ (Holden Commodore VE), 2h 00m 54.3727s; **8** Greg Murphy, NZ (Holden Commodore VE), 2h 00m 55.1985s; **9** Steven Richards, NZ (Ford Falcon FG), 2h 00m 55.7524s; **10** Rick Kelly, AUS (Holden Commodore VE), 2h 01m 00.8034s.
Fastest race lap: Lowndes, 1m 22.3221s, 87.496mph/140.812km/h.
Pole position: Whincup.

HAMILTON 400, Hamilton City Street Circuit, New Zealand, 18/19 April. Round 2. 2 x 59 laps of the 2.113-mile/3.400km circuit.
Race 1 (124.647 miles/200.600km).
1 Jamie Whincup, AUS (Ford Falcon FG), 1h 27m 20.3645s, 85.629mph/137.807km/h; **2** Mark Winterbottom, AUS (Ford Falcon FG), 1h 27m 21.9023s; **3** Lee Holdsworth, AUS (Holden Commodore VE), 1h 27m 22.6768s; **4** Will Davison, AUS (Holden Commodore VE), 1h 27m 25.9300s; **5** Steven Johnson, AUS (Ford Falcon FG), 1h 27m 28.4542s; **6** Fabian Coulthard, NZ (Ford Falcon FG), 1h 27m 28.9387s; **7** Rick Kelly, AUS (Holden Commodore VE), 1h 27m 30.2290s; **8** Todd Kelly, AUS (Holden Commodore VE), 1h 27m 31.9427s; **9** Alex Davison, AUS (Ford Falcon FG), 1h 27m 34.4832s; **10** Jason

Richards, NZ (Holden Commodore VE), 1h 27m 35.7744s.
Fastest race lap: Whincup, 1m 24.4701s, 90.038mph/144.903km/h.
Pole position: Winterbottom, 1m 23.8053s, 90.753mph/146.052km/h.

Race 2 (124.647 miles/200.600km).
1 Jamie Whincup, AUS (Ford Falcon FG), 1h 27m 34.7215s, 85.395mph/137.430km/h; **2** James Courtney, AUS (Ford Falcon FG), 1h 27m 40.7534s; **3** Steven Johnson, AUS (Ford Falcon FG), 1h 27m 43.2754s; **4** Lee Holdsworth, AUS (Holden Commodore VE), 1h 27m 43.9627s; **5** Fabian Coulthard, NZ (Ford Falcon FG), 1h 27m 46.4034s; **6** Michael Caruso, AUS (Holden Commodore VE), 1h 27m 46.9920s; **7** Will Davison, AUS (Holden Commodore VE), 1h 27m 52.7761s; **8** Greg Murphy, NZ (Holden Commodore VE), 1h 27m 56.0521s; **9** Garth Tander, AUS (Holden Commodore VE), 1h 27m 56.6073s; **10** Alex Davison, AUS (Ford Falcon FG), 1h 28m 03.3037s.
Fastest race lap: Courtney, 1m 24.4944s, 90.012mph/144.861km/h.
Pole position: Steven Johnson, 1m 24.1606s, 90.369mph/145.436km/h.

V8 SUPERCAR CHAMPIONSHIP SERIES, Winton Motor Raceway, Benalla, Victoria, Australia, 2/3 May. Round 3. 33 and 66 laps of the 1.864-mile/3.000km circuit.
Race 1 (61.516 miles/99.000km).
1 Craig Lowndes, AUS (Ford Falcon FG), 49m 26.6167s, 74.649mph/120.136km/h; **2** Jamie Whincup, AUS (Ford Falcon FG), 49m 30.7838s; **3** Steven Richards, NZ (Ford Falcon FG), 49m 31.0035s; **4** Rick Kelly, AUS (Holden Commodore VE), 49m 36.7001s; **5** Cameron McConville, AUS (Holden Commodore VE), 49m 37.2875s; **6** Shane van Gisbergen, NZ (Ford Falcon FG), 49m 40.9352s; **7** Will Davison, AUS (Holden Commodore VE), 49m 43.5075s; **8** Garth Tander, AUS (Holden Commodore VE), 49m 43.5494s; **9** Russell Ingall, AUS (Holden Commodore VE), 49m 43.5592s; **10** Michael Caruso, AUS (Holden Commodore VE), 49m 44.8156s.
Fastest race lap: Tander, 1m 23.2003s, 80.658mph/129.807km/h.
Pole position: Mark Winterbottom, AUS (Ford Falcon FG), 1m 23.0906s, 80.764mph/129.978km/h.

Race 2 (123.031 miles/198.000km).
1 Craig Lowndes, AUS (Ford Falcon FG), 1h 37m 06.3464s, 76.019mph/122.340km/h; **2** Mark Winterbottom, AUS (Ford Falcon FG), 1h 37m 08.8584s; **3** Garth Tander, AUS (Holden Commodore VE), 1h 37m 25.4171s; **4** Paul Dumbrell, AUS (Holden Commodore VE), 1h 37m 27.1034s; **5** Will Davison, AUS (Holden Commodore VE), 1h 37m 27.4586s; **6** James Courtney, AUS (Ford Falcon FG), 1h 37m 30.4986s; **7** Rick Kelly, AUS (Holden Commodore VE), 1h 37m 51.2141s; **8** David Reynolds, AUS (Holden Commodore VE), 1h 37m 51.4618s; **9** Marcus Marshall, AUS (Ford Falcon BF), 1h 37m 51.9506s; **10** Jason Bargwanna, AUS (Holden Commodore VE), 1h 37m 52.0011s.
Fastest race lap: Marcus Marshall, AUS (Ford Flacon BF), 1m 22.9813s, 80.871mph/130.149km/h.
Pole position: Whincup, 1m 23.1687s, 80.689mph/129.856km/h.

FALKEN TASMANIA CHALLENGE, Symmons Plains Raceway, Launceston, Tasmania, Australia, 30/31 May. Round 4. 42 and 84 laps of the 1.498-mile/2.411km circuit.
Race 1 (62.921 miles/101.262km).
1 Garth Tander, AUS (Holden Commodore VE), 37m 13.9662s, 101.396mph/163.182km/h; **2** Russell Ingall, AUS (Holden Commodore VE), 37m 14.0956s; **3** Steven Johnson, AUS (Ford Falcon FG), 37m 22.6997s; **4** Will Davison, AUS (Holden Commodore VE), 37m 24.5697s; **5** Todd Kelly, AUS (Holden Commodore VE), 37m 25.1462s; **6** Shane van Gisbergen, NZ (Ford Falcon FG), 37m 28.8352s; **7** Craig Lowndes, AUS (Ford Falcon FG), 37m 30.3638s; **8** Jamie Whincup, AUS (Ford Falcon FG), 37m 35.3755s; **9** Greg Murphy, NZ (Holden Commodore VE), 37m 36.1441s; **10** Lee Holdsworth, AUS (Holden Commodore VE), 37m 36.5017s.
Fastest race lap: Kelly (Rick), 51.4713s, 104.781mph/168.629km/h.
Pole position: Tander, 51.7043s, 104.309mph/167.869km/h.

Race 2 (125.843 miles/202.524km).
1 Jamie Whincup, AUS (Ford Falcon FG), 1h 22m 07.8219s, 91.933mph/147.953km/h; **2** Will Davison, AUS (Holden Commodore VE), 1h 22m 08.2613s; **3** Fabian Coulthard, NZ (Ford Falcon FG), 1h 22m 08.4376s; **4** Mark Winterbottom, AUS (Ford Falcon FG), 1h 22m 11.4237s; **5** Lee Holdsworth, AUS (Holden Commodore VE), 1h 22m 12.2661s; **6** Russell Ingall, AUS (Holden Commodore VE), 1h 22m 15.6348s; **7** Jason Bright, AUS (Ford Falcon BF), 1h 22m 16.7048s; **8** Jason Bargwanna, AUS (Holden Commodore VE), 1h 22m 17.3259s; **9** Michael Patrizi, AUS (Ford Falcon BF), 1h 22m 17.8549s; **10** Craig Lowndes, AUS (Ford Falcon FG), 1h 22m 19.4529s.
Tim Slade, AUS (Holden Commodore VE), finished 9th in 1h 22m 17.5383s, but penalised 5 places.
Fastest race lap: Winterbottom, 51.8066s, 104.103mph/167.538km/h.
Pole position: Whincup, 51.4898s, 51m 4898s, 104.744mph/168.569km/h.

SKYCITY TRIPLE CROWN, Hidden Valley Raceway, Darwin, Northern Territory, Australia, 20/21 June. Round 5. 34 and 69 laps of the 1.783-mile/2.870km circuit.
Race 1 (60.633 miles/97.580km).
1 Jamie Whincup, AUS (Ford Falcon FG), 41m 09.7792s, 88.380mph/142.234km/h; **2** Mark Winterbottom, AUS (Ford Falcon FG), 41m 23.9785s; **3** Will Davison, AUS (Holden Commodore VE), 41m 25.2733s; **4** Garth Tander, AUS (Holden Commodore VE), 41m 25.7385s; **5** Todd Kelly, AUS (Holden Commodore VE), 41m 29.4064s; **6** Craig Lowndes, AUS (Ford Falcon FG), 41m 32.0275s; **7** Jason Richards, NZ (Holden Commodore VE), 41m 32.7427s; **8** James Courtney, AUS (Ford Falcon FG), 41m 32.7525s; **9** Cameron McConville, AUS (Holden Commodore VE), 41m 32.8604s; **10** Lee Holdsworth, AUS (Holden Commodore VE), 41m 33.6280s.
Fastest race lap: Tander, 1m 09.6076s, 92.231mph/148.432km/h.
Pole position: Richards, 1m 09.4908s, 92.386mph/148.681km/h.

Race 2 (123.050 miles/198.030km).
1 Michael Caruso, AUS (Holden Commodore VE), 1h 25m 24.6054s, 86.441mph/139.114km/h; **2** Alex Davison, AUS (Ford Falcon FG), 1h 25m 25.2133s; **3** Craig Lowndes, AUS (Ford Falcon FG), 1h 25m 27.8015s; **4** Rick Kelly, AUS (Holden Commodore VE), 1h 25m 33.3794s; **5** Garth Tander, AUS (Holden Commodore VE), 1h 25m 33.9331s; **6** Paul Dumbrell, AUS (Holden Commodore VE), 1h 25m 34.6079s; **7** Lee Holdsworth, AUS (Holden Commodore VE), 1h 25m 36.5151s; **8** Russell Ingall, AUS (Holden Commodore VE), 1h 25m 37.5280s; **9** Shane van Gisbergen, NZ (Ford Falcon FG), 1h 25m 39.8141s; **10** Jamie Whincup, AUS (Ford Falcon FG), 1h 25m 40.3215s.
Fastest race lap: Davison, 1m 09.5276s, 92.337mph/148.602km/h.
Pole position: Tander, 1m 09.7929s, 91.986mph/148.037km/h.

DUNLOP TOWNSVILLE 400, Townsville Street Circuit, Queensland, Australia, 11/12 July. Round 6. 71 and 72 laps of the 1.783-mile/2.870km circuit.
Race 1 (126.617 miles/203.770km).
1 Jamie Whincup, AUS (Ford Falcon FG), 1h 35m 37.4475s, 79.446mph/127.856km/h; **2** Will Davison, AUS (Holden Commodore VE), 1h 35m 38.8969s; **3** Garth Tander, AUS (Holden Commodore VE), 1h 35m 39.1939s; **4** Craig Lowndes, AUS (Ford Falcon FG), 1h 35m 40.4901s; **5** Michael Caruso, AUS (Holden Commodore VE), 1h 35m 41.8697s; **6** Russell Ingall, AUS (Holden Commodore VE), 1h 35m 42.2786s; **7** Rick Kelly, AUS (Holden Commodore VE), 1h 35m 46.9849s; **8** Mark Winterbottom, AUS (Ford Falcon FG), 1h 35m 47.2321s; **9** Cameron McConville, AUS (Holden Commodore VE), 1h 35m 47.4951s; **10** Todd Kelly, AUS (Holden Commodore VE), 1h 35m 47.6842s.
Fastest race lap: Lee Holdsworth, AUS (Holden Commodore VE), 1m 13.4727s, 87.379mph/140.623km/h.
Pole position: Holdsworth, 1m 12.7327s, 88.268mph/142.054km/h.

Race 2 (128.400 miles/206.640km).
1 James Courtney, AUS (Ford Falcon FG), 1h 35m 03.3900s, 81.046mph/130.431km/h; **2** Jamie Whincup, AUS (Ford Falcon FG), 1h 35m 04.2974s; **3** Garth Tander, AUS (Holden Commodore VE), 1h 35m 05.5854s; **4** Will Davison, AUS (Holden Commodore VE), 1h 35m 09.6024s; **5** Steven Johnson, AUS (Ford Falcon FG), 1h 35m 12.4442s; **6** Mark Winterbottom, AUS (Ford Falcon FG), 1h 35m 13.7996s; **7** Lee Holdsworth, AUS (Holden Commodore VE), 1h 35m 14.3019s; **8** Paul Dumbrell, AUS (Holden Commodore VE), 1h 35m 15.0490s; **9** Craig Lowndes, AUS (Ford Falcon FG), 1h 35m 21.7146s; **10** Michael Caruso, AUS (Holden Commodore VE), 1h 35m 22.5962s.
Fastest race lap: Fabian Coulthard, NZ (Ford Falcon FG), 1m 13.4470s, 87.410mph/140.672km/h.
Pole position: Tander, 1m 12.4700s, 88.588mph/142.569km/h.

NORTON 360 SANDOWN CHALLENGE, Sandown International Motor Raceway, Melbourne, Victoria, Australia, 1/2 August. Round 7. 33 and 65 laps of the 1.926-mile/3.100km circuit.
Race 1 (63.566 miles/102.300km).
1 Will Davison, AUS (Holden Commodore VE), 39m 34.9720s, 96.354mph/155.067km/h; **2** James Courtney, AUS (Ford Falcon FG), 39m 41.3923s; **3** Craig Lowndes, AUS (Ford Falcon FG), 39m 42.4524s; **4** Todd Kelly, AUS (Holden Commodore VE), 39m 53.3344s; **5** Michael Caruso, AUS (Holden Commodore VE), 39m 53.7490s; **6** Jamie Whincup, AUS (Ford Falcon FG), 39m 54.0765s; **7** Russell Ingall, AUS (Holden Commodore VE), 39m 54.4256s; **8** Steven Johnson, AUS (Ford Falcon FG), 39m 59.8925s; **9** David Reynolds, AUS (Holden Commodore VE), 40m 00.5078s; **10** Fabian Coulthard, NZ (Ford Falcon FG), 40m 02.5956s.
Fastest race lap: Davison, 1m 10.0743s, 98.959mph/159.259km/h.
Pole position: Davison, 1m 09.7185s, 99.464mph/160.072km/h.

Race 2 (125.206 miles/201.500km).
1 Garth Tander, AUS (Holden Commodore VE), 1h 27m 49.5475s, 85.537mph/137.658km/h; **2** Will Davison, AUS (Holden Commodore VE), 1h 27m 49.8975s; **3** Jamie Whincup, AUS (Ford Falcon FG), 1h 27m 56.5977s; **4** Cameron McConville, AUS (Holden Commodore VE), 1h 27m 59.6195s; **5** Craig Lowndes, AUS (Ford Falcon FG), 1h 28m 01.3357s; **6** Jason Richards, NZ (Holden Commodore VE), 1h 28m 02.4272s; **7** Tony D'Alberto, AUS (Holden Commodore VE), 1h 28m 03.5134s; **8** James Courtney, AUS (Ford Falcon FG), 1h 28m 06.1474s; **9** Jason Bargwanna, AUS (Holden Commodore VE), 1h 28m 09.4882s; **10** Paul Dumbrell, AUS (Holden Commodore VE), 1h 28m 10.1350s.
Fastest race lap: Tander, 1m 09.8573s, 99.266mph/159.754km/h.
Pole position: Davison, 1m 09.7472s, 99.423mph/160.006km/h.

QUEENSLAND HOUSE AND LAND.COM 300, Queensland Raceway, Ipswich, Queensland, Australia, 22/23 August. Round 8. 33 and 65 laps of the 1.942-mile/3.126km circuit.
Race 1 (64.099 miles/103.158km).
1 Jamie Whincup, AUS (Ford Falcon FG), 40m 43.7708s, 94.426mph/151.965km/h; **2** James Courtney, AUS (Ford Falcon FG), 40m 44.3571s; **3** Mark Winterbottom, AUS (Ford Falcon FG), 40m 58.2970s; **4** Steven Johnson, AUS (Ford Falcon FG), 41m 01.0157s; **5** Fabian Coulthard, NZ (Ford Falcon FG), 41m 01.9571s; **6** Todd Kelly, AUS (Holden Commodore VE), 41m 02.4063s; **7** Lee Holdsworth, AUS (Holden Commodore VE), 41m 03.3208s; **8** Jason Bright, AUS (Ford Falcon BF), 41m 04.3714s; **9** Shane van Gisbergen, NZ (Ford Falcon FG), 41m 05.0493s; **10** Tim Slade, AUS (Holden Commodore VE), 41m 25.7447s.
Fastest race lap: Slade, 1m 10.8948s, 98.634mph/158.736km/h.
Pole position: Whincup, 1m 10.8529s, 98.692mph/158.830km/h.

Race 2 (126.256 miles/203.190km).
1 Will Davison, AUS (Holden Commodore VE), 1h 20m 30.0744s, 94.102mph/151.443km/h; **2** Craig Lowndes, AUS (Ford Falcon FG), 1h 20m 44.1460s; **3** Russell Ingall, AUS (Holden Commodore VE), 1h 20m 46.8632s; **4** Mark Winterbottom, AUS (Ford Falcon FG), 1h 20m 55.8640s; **5** Paul Dumbrell, AUS (Holden Commodore VE), 1h 20m 58.4387s; **6** Michael Caruso, AUS (Holden Commodore VE), 1h 21m 01.3922s; **7** Steven Richards, NZ (Ford Falcon FG), 1h 21m 05.7356s; **8** James Courtney, AUS (Ford Falcon FG), 1h 21m 06.5186s; **9** Jason Bright, AUS (Ford Falcon BF), 1h 21m 08.9036s; **10** Rick Kelly, AUS (Holden Commodore VE), 1h 21m 09.1353s.
Fastest race lap: Ingall, 1m 10.7640s, 98.816mph/159.030km/h.
Pole position: Winterbottom, 1m 10.5290s, 99.145mph/159.559km/h.

L&H 500, Phillip Island Grand Prix Circuit, Cowes, Victoria, Australia, 12/13 September. Round 9. 14, 14 and 113 laps of the 2.764-mile/4.448km circuit.
Qualifying Race A (38.694 miles/62.272km).
1 Todd Kelly, AUS (Holden Commodore VE), 22m 29.2630s, 103.240mph/166.149km/h; **2** Craig Lowndes, AUS (Ford Falcon FG), 22m 29.6756s; **3** Will Davison, AUS (Holden Commodore VE), 22m 35.6976s; **4** Shane van Gisbergen, NZ (Ford Falcon FG), 22m 38.6006s; **5** Russell Ingall, AUS (Holden Commodore VE), 22m 42.1099s; **6** Paul Dumbrell, AUS (Holden Commodore VE), 22m 42.2688s; **7** David Reynolds, AUS (Holden Commodore VE), 22m 42.8352s; **8** Dean Canto, AUS (Ford Falcon FG), 22m 48.3967s; **9** Steve Owen, AUS (Holden Commodore VE), 22m 49.9463s; **10** Allan Simonsen, DK (Ford Falcon FG), 22m 50.2859s.
Fastest race lap: Lowndes, 1m 34.8390s, 104.913mph/168.841km/h.
Pole position: Dumbrell, 1m 33.3204s, 106.620mph/171.589km/h.

Qualifying Race B (38.694 miles/62.272km).
1 Mark Winterbottom, AUS (Ford Falcon FG), 23m 56.1139s, 96.996mph/156.101km/h; **2** Fabian Coulthard, NZ (Ford Falcon FG), 23m 57.6790s; **3** Jason Bright, AUS (Ford Falcon BF), 23m 58.1030s; **4** James Courtney, AUS (Ford Falcon FG), 24m 02.4175s; **5** David Besnard, AUS (Holden Commodore VE), 24m 05.6149s; **6** Jason Bargwanna, AUS (Holden Commodore VE), 24m 08.9249s; **7** Andrew Thompson, AUS (Holden Commodore VE), 24m 09.6157s; **8** John McIntyre, AUS (Ford Falcon FG), 24m 11.2213s; **9** Jonathon Webb, AUS (Ford Falcon FG), 24m 13.1725s; **10** Jason Richards, NZ (Holden Commodore VE), 24m 13.6116s.
Fastest race lap: Winterbottom, 1m 34.3803s, 105.423mph/169.662km/h.
Pole position: Winterbottom, 1m 33.1970s, 106.761mph/171.816km/h.

Race (312.316 miles/502.624km).
1 Will Davison/Garth Tander, AUS/AUS (Holden Commodore VE), 3h 09m 47.8436s, 98.731mph/158.892km/h; **2** Craig Lowndes/Jamie Whincup, AUS/AUS (Ford Falcon FG), 3h 09m 50.5165s; **3** Steven Richards/Mark Winterbottom, NZ/AUS (Ford Falcon FG), 3h 09m 58.1831s; **4** Steven Johnson/James Courtney, AUS/AUS (Ford Falcon FG), 3h 10m 01.1871s; **5** Todd Kelly/Rick Kelly, AUS/AUS (Holden Commodore VE), 3h 10m 39.8538s; **6** Warren Luff/Jonathon Webb, AUS/AUS (Ford Falcon FG), 3h 10m 47.7280s; **7** Russell Ingall/Tim Slade, AUS/AUS (Holden Commodore VE), 3h 10m 56.3564s; **8** Paul Dumbrell/Craig Baird, AUS/NZ (Holden Commodore VE), 3h 10m 59.2325s; **9** Dean Canto/Luke Youlden, AUS/AUS (Ford Falcon FG), 3h 11m 02.7487s; **10** Shane van Gisbergen/Alex Davison, NZ/AUS (Ford Falcon FG), 3h 11m 05.1013s.
Fastest race lap: Craig Lowndes/Jamie Whincup, 1m 34.8224s, 104.931mph/168.871km/h.
Pole position: Richards/Winterbottom.

SUPERCHEAP AUTO BATHURST 1000, Mount Panorama, Bathurst, New South Wales, Australia, 11 October. Round 10. 161 laps of the 3.861-mile/6.213km circuit, 621.553 miles/1000.293km.
1 Will Davison/Garth Tander, AUS/AUS (Holden Commodore VE), 6h 40m 02.4884s, 93.223mph/150.028km/h; **2** Cameron McConville/Jason Richards, AUS/NZ (Holden Commodore VE), 6h 40m 03.2483s; **3** Lee Holdsworth/Michael Caruso, AUS/AUS (Holden Commodore VE), 6h 40m 05.8726s; **4** Mark Skaife/Greg Murphy, AUS/NZ (Holden Commodore VE), 6h 40m 05.8768s; **5** Craig Lowndes/Jamie Whincup, AUS/AUS (Ford Falcon FG), 6h 40m 07.1466s; **6** Mark Noske/Jason Bargwanna, AUS/AUS (Holden Commodore VE), 6h 40m 08.4374s; **7** Paul Morris/Tim Slade, AUS/AUS (Holden Commodore VE), 6h 40m 10.5204s; **8** Todd Kelly/Rick Kelly, AUS/AUS (Holden Commodore VE), 6h 40m 12.8296s; **9** Greg Ritter/David Besnard, AUS/AUS (Holden Commodore VE), 6h 40m 12.9586s; **10** Tony D'Alberto/Andrew Thompson, AUS/AUS (Holden Commodore VE), 6h 40m 13.2086s.
Fastest race lap: McConville/Richards, 2m 08.9972s, 107.739mph/173.389km/h.
Pole position: Davison/Tander, 2m 07.9463s, 108.624mph/174.813km/h.

V8 SUPERCAR CHALLENGE, Surfer's Paradise Street Circuit, Queensland, Australia, 24/25 October. Round 11. 4 x 34 laps of the 2.794-mile/4.496km circuit.
Race 1a (94.985 miles/152.864km).
1 Mark Winterbottom, AUS (Ford Falcon FG), 1h 16m 43.8908s, 74.273mph/119.531km/h; **2** Garth Tander, AUS (Holden Commodore VE), 1h 16m 45.1760s; **3** Will Davison, AUS (Holden Commodore VE), 1h 16m 46.3133s; **4** Craig Lowndes, AUS (Ford Falcon FG), 1h 16m 46.9755s; **5** Shane van Gisbergen, NZ (Ford Falcon FG), 1h 16m 48.2419s; **6** Greg Murphy, NZ (Holden Commodore VE), 1h 16m 49.1429s; **7** Steven Richards, NZ (Ford Falcon FG), 1h 16m 50.0073s; **8** Paul Dumbrell, AUS (Holden Commodore VE), 1h 16m 51.8172s; **9** Russell Ingall, AUS (Holden Commodore VE), 1h 16m 51.9997s; **10** Steven Johnson, AUS (Ford Falcon FG), 1h 16m 52.4899s.
Fastest race lap: Winterbottom, 1m 51.3251s, 90.341mph/145.390km/h.
Pole position: Winterbottom, 1m 50.9325s, 90.661mph/145.904km/h.

Race 1b (94.985 miles/152.864km).
1 Garth Tander, AUS (Holden Commodore VE), 1h 04m 08.7239s, 88.846mph/142.985km/h; **2** Mark Winterbottom, AUS (Ford Falcon FG), 1h 04m 10.9865s; **3** Will Davison, AUS (Holden Commodore VE), 1h 04m 11.9156s; **4** Craig Lowndes, AUS (Ford Falcon FG), 1h 04m 12.1954s; **5** Greg Murphy, NZ (Holden Commodore VE), 1h 04m 19.6161s; **6** Steven Richards, NZ (Ford Falcon FG), 1h 04m 20.1076s; **7** Shane van Gisbergen, NZ (Ford Falcon FG), 1h 04m 22.2998s; **8** Jamie Whincup, AUS (Ford Falcon FG), 1h 04m 24.2295s; **9** Rick Kelly, AUS (Holden Commodore VE), 1h 04m 24.9791s; **10** Jason Bargwanna, AUS (Holden Commodore VE), 1h 04m 39.6943s.
Fastest race lap: Whincup, 1m 50.7233s, 90.832mph/146.180km/h.
Pole position: Winterbottom.

Race 2a (94.985 miles/152.864km).
1 Craig Lowndes, AUS (Ford Falcon FG), 1h 13m 55.2217s, 77.098mph/124.077km/h; **2** Mark Winterbottom, AUS (Ford Falcon FG), 1h 13m 57.4557s; **3** Garth Tander, AUS (Holden Commodore VE), 1h 13m 58.8328s; **4** Russell Ingall, AUS (Holden Commodore VE), 1h 14m 01.4744s; **5** James Courtney, AUS (Ford Falcon FG), 1h 14m 06.6642s; **6** Steven Johnson, AUS (Ford Falcon FG), 1h 14m 11.0837s; **7** David Reynolds, AUS (Holden Commodore VE), 1h 14m 12.9497s; **8** Jason Bright, AUS (Ford Falcon BF), 1h 14m 16.1826s; **9** Jason Bargwanna, AUS (Holden Commodore VE), 1h 14m 19.6956s; **10** Jason Richards, NZ (Holden Commodore VE), 1h 14m 20.5966s.
Fastest race lap: Lowndes, 1m 50.9442s, 90.651mph/145.889km/h.
Pole position: Bargwanna, 1m 49.9887s, 91.439mph/147.156km/h.

Race 2b (94.985 miles/152.864km).
1 Mark Winterbottom, AUS (Ford Falcon FG), 1h 16m 02.2312s, 74.951mph/120.623km/h; **2** Garth Tander, AUS (Holden Commodore VE), 1h 16m 04.8065s; **3** James Courtney, AUS (Ford Falcon FG), 1h 16m 08.1524s; **4** Jason Bright, AUS (Ford Falcon BF), 1h 16m 11.8342s; **5** Steven Johnson, AUS (Ford Falcon FG), 1h 16m 12.0672s; **6** Jamie Whincup, AUS (Ford Falcon FG), 1h 16m 12.4602s; **7** Greg Murphy, NZ (Holden Commodore VE), 1h 16m 13.5367s; **8** Jason Richards, NZ (Holden Commodore VE), 1h 16m 14.8898s; **9** Rick Kelly, AUS (Holden Commodore VE), 1h 16m 15.1732s; **10** Will Davison, AUS (Holden Commodore VE), 1h 16m 16.3142s.
Fastest race lap: Winterbottom, 1m 50.1712s, 91.287mph/146.913km/h.
Pole position: Lowndes.

THE ISLAND 300, Phillip Island Grand Prix Circuit, Cowes, Victoria, Australia, 7/8 November. Round 12. 22 and 44 laps of the 2.764-mile/4.448km circuit.
Race 1 (60.805 miles/97.856km).
1 Jamie Whincup, AUS (Ford Falcon FG), 38m 06.6490s, 95.728mph/154.060km/h; **2** Will Davison, AUS (Holden Commodore VE), 38m 08.4983s; **3** Rick Kelly, AUS (Holden Commodore VE), 38m 08.9845s; **4** Garth Tander, AUS (Holden Commodore VE), 38m 11.1649s; **5** Shane van Gisbergen, NZ (Ford Falcon FG), 38m 12.1978s; **6** Mark Winterbottom, AUS (Ford Falcon FG), 38m 12.9718s; **7** Lee Holdsworth, AUS (Holden Commodore VE), 38m 13.3552s; **8** Steven Johnson, AUS (Ford Falcon FG), 38m 13.7981s; **9** James Courtney, AUS (Ford Falcon FG), 38m 15.5699s; **10** Jason Richards, NZ (Holden Commodore VE), 38m 16.1984s.
Fastest race lap: Whincup, 1m 35.7592s, 103.905mph/167.219km/h.
Pole position: Jason Bright, AUS (Ford Falcon BF), 1m 33.6487s, 106.246mph/170.987km/h.

Race 2 (121.610 miles/195.712km).
1 Jamie Whincup, AUS (Ford Falcon FG), 1h 17m 54.0865s, 93.664mph/150.738km/h; **2** Rick Kelly, AUS (Holden Commodore VE), 1h 17m 59.2994s; **3** Garth Tander, AUS (Holden Commodore VE), 1h 18m 07.4356s; **4** James Courtney, AUS (Ford Falcon FG), 1h 18m 09.1696s; **5** Jason Bright, AUS (Ford Falcon BF), 1h 18m 12.8037s; **6** Shane van Gisbergen, NZ (Ford Falcon FG), 1h 18m 14.1153s; **7** Craig Lowndes, AUS (Ford Falcon FG), 1h 18m 20.2387s; **8** Paul Dumbrell, AUS (Holden Commodore VE), 1h 18m 21.4934s; **9** Fabian Coulthard, NZ (Ford Falcon FG), 1h 18m 22.8070s; **10** Michael Caruso, AUS (Holden Commodore VE), 1h 18m 25.3524s.
Fastest race lap: Whincup, 1m 36.1299s, 103.504mph/166.574km/h.
Pole position: Whincup, 1m 35.1992s, 104.516mph/168.203km/h.

Provisional championship points
Drivers
1 Jamie Whincup, AUS, 2905; **2** Will Davison, AUS, 2783; **3** Garth Tander, AUS, 2565; **4** Craig Lowndes, AUS, 2292; **5** Mark Winterbottom, AUS, 1964; **6** Steven Johnson, AUS, 1961; **7** Rick Kelly, AUS, 1925; **8** Lee Holdsworth, AUS, 1817; **9** James Courtney, AUS, 1790; **10** Shane van Gisbergen, NZ, 1679; **11** Russell Ingall, AUS, 1676; **12** Michael Caruso, AUS, 1623; **13** Paul Dumbrell, AUS, 1585; **14** Jason Richards, NZ, 1579; **15** Steven Richards, NZ, 1504; **16** Cameron McConville, AUS, 1451; **17** Todd Kelly, AUS, 1423; **18** Alex Davison, AUS, 1423; **19** Fabian Coulthard, NZ, 1350; **20** Jason Bright, AUS, 1343.

Teams
1 Toll Holden Racin, 5038; **2** TeamVodafone, 4829; **3** Jim Beam Racing, 3661.

Results of the Barbagallo and Sydney races will be given in AUTOCOURSE 2010–2011.

Non-Championship Australian V8 race

MANUFACTURERS CHALLENGE, Albert Park Circuit, Melbourne, Victoria, Australia, 27-29 March. 3 x 15 laps of the 3.295-mile/5.303km circuit.
Race 1 (49.427 miles/79.545km).
1 Craig Lowndes, AUS (Ford Falcon FG), 29m 53.5736s, 99.208mph/159.660km/h; **2** Mark Winterbottom, AUS (Ford Falcon FG), 29m 59.3395s; **3** Will Davison, AUS (Holden Commodore VE), 30m 03.0346s; **4** Steven Johnson, AUS (Ford Falcon FG), 30m 03.6279s; **5** Jason Richards, NZ (Holden Commodore VE), 30m 04.1147s; **6** Fabian Coulthard, NZ (Ford Falcon FG), 30m 08.8646s; **7** Jamie Whincup, AUS (Ford Falcon FG), 30m 11.9788s; **8** Shane van Gisbergen, NZ (Ford Falcon FG), 30m 12.8461s; **9** Todd Kelly, AUS (Holden Commodore VE), 30m 15.4517s; **10** Paul Dumbrell, AUS (Holden Commodore VE), 30m 16.0441s.
Fastest race lap: Lowndes, 1m 58.4183s, 100.174mph/161.215km/h.
Pole position: Lowndes, 1m 57.7400s, 100.751mph/162.144km/h.

Race 2 (49.427 miles/79.545km).
1 Mark Winterbottom, AUS (Ford Falcon FG), 31m 54.3485s,

92.949mph/149.587km/h; **2** Will Davison, AUS (Holden Commodore VE), 31m 54.6969s; **3** Craig Lowndes, AUS (Ford Falcon FG), 31m 56.3244s; **4** Steven Johnson, AUS (Ford Falcon FG), 31m 57.1996s; **5** Jason Richards, NZ (Holden Commodore VE), 31m 58.5369s; **6** Jamie Whincup, AUS (Ford Falcon FG), 31m 59.2260s; **7** Shane van Gisbergen, NZ (Ford Falcon FG), 32m 01.8374s; **8** Paul Dumbrell, AUS (Holden Commodore VE), 32m 03.5805s; **9** Fabian Coulthard, NZ (Ford Falcon FG), 32m 05.2516s; **10** Jason Bright, AUS (Ford Falcon BF), 32m 06.8320s.
Fastest race lap: Whincup, 1m 58.5904s, 100.029mph/160.981km/h.

Race 3 (49.427 miles/79.545km).
1 Craig Lowndes, AUS (Ford Falcon FG), 30m 02.1388s, 75.972mph/122.265km/h; **2** Mark Winterbottom, AUS (Ford Falcon FG), 30m 12.0612s; **3** Russell Ingall, AUS (Holden Commodore VE), 30m 20.4387s; **4** Will Davison, AUS (Holden Commodore VE), 30m 21.4783s; **5** Jason Richards, NZ (Holden Commodore VE), 30m 21.7404s; **6** Steven Johnson, AUS (Ford Falcon FG), 30m 25.7356s; **7** Garth Tander, AUS (Holden Commodore VE), 30m 26.0545s; **8** Shane van Gisbergen, NZ (Ford Falcon FG), 30m 26.4403s; **9** Fabian Coulthard, NZ (Ford Falcon FG), 30m 26.9526s; **10** Jamie Whincup, AUS (Ford Falcon FG), 30m 27.3087s.
Fastest race lap: Lowndes, 1m 58.8579s, 99.804mph/160.619km/h.

Overall
1 Craig Lowndes, AUS (Ford Falcon FG); **2** Mark Winterbottom, AUS (Ford Falcon FG); **3** Will Davison, AUS (Holden Commodore VE); **4** Steven Johnson, AUS (Ford Falcon FG); **5** Jason Richards, NZ (Holden Commodore VE); **6** Shane van Gisbergen, NZ (Ford Falcon FG); **7** Jamie Whincup, AUS (Ford Falcon FG); **8** Fabian Coulthard, NZ (Ford Falcon FG); **9** Paul Dumbrell, AUS (Holden Commodore VE); **10** Todd Kelly, AUS (Holden Commodore VE).

FIA World Touring Car Championship

2008

The following races were run after AUTOCOURSE 2008–2009 went to press.

RACE OF MACAU, Circuito Da Guia, Macau, 16 November. 2 x 9 laps of the 3.803-mile/6.120km circuit.
Round 23 (34.225 miles/55.080km).
1 Alain Menu, CH (Chevrolet Lacetti), 23m 10.203s, 88.627mph/142.632km/h; **2** Andy Priaulx, GB (BMW 320si), 23m 10.726s; **3** Yvan Muller, F (SEAT Leon TDI), 23m 18.784s; **4** Augusto Farfus Jr., BR (BMW 320si), 23m 19.538s; **5** Robert Huff, GB (Chevrolet Lacetti), 23m 20.074s; **6** Jordi Gené, E (SEAT Leon TDI), 23m 20.895s; **7** Gabriele Tarquini, I (SEAT Leon TDI), 23m 21.421s; **8** James Thompson, GB (Honda Accord Euro R), 23m 22.283s; **9** Nicola Larini, I (Chevrolet Lacetti), 23m 23.112s; **10** Jörg Müller, D (BMW 320si), 23m 24.428s.
Fastest race lap: Priaulx, 2m 33.327s, 89.286mph/143.692km/h.
Pole position: Menu, 2m 30.285s, 91.093mph/146.601km/h.

Round 24 (34.225 miles/55.080km).
1 Robert Huff, GB (Chevrolet Lacetti), 23m 23.216s, 87.805mph/141.309km/h; **2** Yvan Muller, F (SEAT Leon TDI), 23m 30.469s; **3** Andy Priaulx, GB (BMW 320si), 23m 31.173s; **4** Rickard Rydell, S (SEAT Leon TDI), 23m 41.336s; **5** Alessandro 'Alex' Zanardi, I (BMW 320si), 24m 14.943s; **6** Franz Engstler, D (BMW 320si), 24m 16.179s; **7** Manabu Orido, J (Chevrolet Lacetti), 24m 21.530s; **8** Matthew Marsh, GB (BMW 320si), 24m 25.839s; **9** Andrey Romanov, RUS (BMW 320si), 24m 39.569s; **10** Ibrahim Okyay, TR (BMW 320si), 24m 56.757s.
Fastest race lap: Farfus Jr., 2m 32.933s, 89.516mph/144.063km/h.
Pole position: Thompson.

Final championship points
Drivers
1 Yvan Muller, F, 114; **2** Gabriele Tarquini, I, 88; **3** Robert Huff, GB, 87; **4** Andy Priaulx, GB, 81; **5** Rickard Rydell, S, 77; **6** Augusto Farfus Jr., BR, 63; **7** Jörg Müller, D, 60; **8** Jordi Gené, E, 56; **9** Alain Menu, CH, 54; **10** Felix Porteiro, E, 51; **11** Nicola Larini, I, 48; **12** Tiago Monteiro, P, 43; **13** Alessandro 'Alex' Zanardi, I, 36; **14** Tom Coronel, NL, 35; **15** James Thompson, GB, 25; **16** Sergio Hernández, E, 9; **17** Franz Engstler, D, 3; **18** Stefano d'Aste, I, 2; **19** Manabu Orido, J, 2; **20** Olivier Tielemans, NL, 1; **21** Matthew Marsh, GB, 1.

Manufacturers
1 SEAT, 326; **2** BMW, 274; **3** Chevrolet, 238; **4** Honda, 60.

Yokohama Independents' Trophy
1 Sergio Hernández, E, 186; **2** Franz Engstler, D, 149; **3** Stefano d'Aste, I, 137; **4** Pierre-Yves Corthals, B, 112; **5** Andrey Romanov, RUS, 83.

Yokohama Teams' Trophy
1 Proteam Motorsport, 334; **2** Liqui Moly Team Engstler, 228; **3** Exagon Engineering, 112; **4** Wirchers-Sport, 105; **5** Borusan Otomotiv Motorsport, 51.

2009

RACE OF BRAZIL, Autódromo Internacional de Curitiba, Brazil, 8 March. 2 x 16 laps of the 2.296-mile/3.695km circuit.
Round 1 (36.735 miles/59.120km).
1 Yvan Muller, F (SEAT Leon TDI), 26m 45.799s, 82.356mph/132.539km/h; **2** Jordi Gené, E (SEAT Leon TDI), 26m 47.897s; **3** Rickard Rydell, S (SEAT Leon TDI), 26m 48.679s; **4** Gabriele Tarquini, I (SEAT Leon TDI), 26m 49.300s; **5** Augusto Farfus Jr., BR (BMW 320si), 26m 53.565s; **6** Sergio Hernández, E (BMW 320si), 26m 53.951s; **7** Andy Priaulx, GB (BMW 320si), 26m 57.927s; **8** Felix Porteiro, E (BMW 320si), 26m 59.240s; **9** Tom Coronel, NL (SEAT Leon), 27m 01.770s; **10** Alessandro Zanardi, I (BMW 320si), 27m 01.904s.
Fastest race lap: Muller (Yvan), 1m 25.662s, 96.489mph/155.284km/h.
Pole position: Muller (Yvan), 1m 24.196s, 98.169mph/157.988km/h.

Round 2 (36.735 miles/59.120km).
1 Gabriele Tarquini, I (SEAT Leon TDI), 27m 44.649s, 79.444mph/127.853km/h; **2** Rickard Rydell, S (SEAT Leon TDI), 27m 45.459s; **3** Jordi Gené, E (SEAT Leon TDI), 27m 50.518s; **4** Yvan Muller, F (SEAT Leon TDI), 27m 51.806s; **5** Jörg Müller, D (BMW 320si), 27m 54.565s; **6** Augusto Farfus Jr., BR (BMW 320si), 27m 56.408s; **7** Felix Porteiro, E (BMW 320si), 27m 58.370s; **8** Tom Coronel, NL (SEAT Leon), 27m 58.865s; **9** Andy Priaulx, GB (BMW 320si), 28m 02.331s; **10** Sergio Hernández, E (BMW 320si), 28m 02.793s.
Fastest race lap: Alain Menu, CH (Chevrolet Cruze), 1m 34.837s, 87.154mph/140.261km/h.
Pole position: Porteiro.

RACE OF MEXICO, Autódromo Miguel E. Abed, Puebla-Amozoc, Mexico, 22 March. 2 x 16 laps of the 2.013-mile/3.240km circuit.
Round 3 (32.212 miles/51.840km).
1 Rickard Rydell, S (SEAT Leon TDI), 26m 40.728s, 72.443mph/116.586km/h; **2** Augusto Farfus Jr., BR (BMW 320si), 26m 42.236s; **3** Andy Priaulx, GB (BMW 320si), 26m 42.714s; **4** Yvan Muller, F (SEAT Leon TDI), 26m 45.348s; **5** Jörg Müller, D (BMW 320si), 26m 46.445s; **6** Gabriele Tarquini, I (SEAT Leon TDI), 26m 50.201s; **7** Jordi Gené, E (SEAT Leon TDI), 27m 00.127s; **8** Nicola Larini, I (Chevrolet Cruze), 27m 03.522s; **9** Sergio Hernández, E (BMW 320si), 27m 05.453s; **10** Felix Porteiro, E (BMW 320si), 27m 06.718s.
Fastest race lap: Priaulx, 1m 38.076s, 73.898mph/118.928km/h.
Pole position: Farfus Jr., 1m 37.682s, 74.196mph/119.407km/h.

Round 4 (32.212 miles/51.840 km).
1 Yvan Muller, F (SEAT Leon TDI), 26m 41.014s, 72.430mph/116.566km/h; **2** Andy Priaulx, GB (BMW 320si), 26m 41.473s; **3** Rickard Rydell, S (SEAT Leon TDI), 26m 42.254s; **4** Augusto Farfus Jr., BR (BMW 320si), 26m 42.987s; **5** Sergio Hernández, E (BMW 320si), 26m 46.833s; **6** Alessandro Zanardi, I (BMW 320si), 26m 47.295s; **7** Jordi Gené, E (SEAT Leon TDI), 26m 52.769s; **8** Gabriele Tarquini, I (SEAT Leon TDI), 26m 53.203s; **9** Felix Porteiro, E (BMW 320si), 26m 56.527s; **10** Nicola Larini, I (Chevrolet Cruze), 26m 57.607s.
Fastest race lap: Müller (Jörg), 1m 38.287s, 73.739mph/118.672km/h.
Pole position: Larini.

RACE OF MOROCCO, Circuit de Marrakech, Morocco, 3 May. 12 and 13 laps of the 2.821-mile/4.540km circuit.
Round 5 (33.852 miles/54.480km).
1 Robert Huff, GB (Chevrolet Cruze), 24m 04.240s, 84.382mph/135.800km/h; **2** Gabriele Tarquini, I (SEAT Leon TDI), 24m 05.969s; **3** Jordi Gené, E (SEAT Leon TDI), 24m 09.823s; **4** Yvan Muller, F (SEAT Leon TDI), 24m 11.284s; **5** Tiago Monteiro, P (SEAT Leon TDI), 24m 11.650s; **6** Nicola Larini, I (Chevrolet Cruze), 24m 12.817s; **7** Alain Menu, CH (Chevrolet Cruze), 24m 13.283s; **8** Jörg Müller, D (BMW 320si), 24m 14.079s; **9** Mehdi Bennani, MA (SEAT Leon), 24m 14.638s; **10** Andy Priaulx, GB (BMW 320si), 24m 15.251s.
Fastest race lap: Huff, 1m 50.833s, 91.630mph/147.465km/h.
Pole position: Huff, 1m 49.789s, 92.501mph/148.867km/h.

Round 6 (36.673 miles/59.020km).
1 Nicola Larini, I (Chevrolet Cruze), 27m 29.960s, 80.016mph/128.774km/h; **2** Yvan Muller, F (SEAT Leon TDI), 27m 31.359s; **3** Robert Huff, GB (Chevrolet Cruze), 27m 31.738s; **4** Jörg Müller, D (BMW 320si), 27m 32.688s; **5** Gabriele Tarquini, I (SEAT Leon TDI), 27m 33.028s; **6** Augusto Farfus Jr., BR (BMW 320si), 27m 33.951s; **7** Franz Engstler, D (BMW 320si), 27m 36.739s; **8** Tom Coronel, NL (SEAT Leon), 27m 41.044s; **9** Mehdi Bennani, MA (SEAT Leon), 27m 45.604s; **10** Felix Porteiro, E (BMW 320si), 28m 01.873s.
Disqualified: Tiago Monteiro, P (SEAT Leon TDI), finished 7th in 27m 34.867s.
Fastest race lap: Menu, 1m 51.017s, 91.478mph/147.220km/h.
Pole position: Müller (Jörg).

RACE OF FRANCE, Circuit de Pau Ville, Pau, France, 17 May. 19 and 18 laps of the 1.715-mile/2.760km circuit.
Round 7 (32.585 miles/52.440km).
1 Robert Huff, GB (Chevrolet Cruze), 27m 10.540s, 71.942mph/115.780km/h; **2** Augusto Farfus Jr., BR (BMW 320si), 27m 10.801s; **3** Jörg Müller, D (BMW 320si), 27m 11.432s; **4** Andy Priaulx, GB (BMW 320si), 27m 11.645s; **5** Sergio Hernández, E (BMW 320si), 27m 12.483s; **6** Franz Engstler, D (BMW 320si), 27m 20.084s; **7** Alain Menu, CH (Chevrolet Cruze), 27m 20.090s; **8** Tom Coronel, NL (SEAT Leon), 27m 21.590s; **9** Tom Boardman, GB (SEAT Leon), 27m 34.523s; **10** Eric Cayrolle, F (SEAT Leon), 27m 42.044s.
Disqualified: Felix Porteiro, E (BMW 320si), finished 6th in 27m 19.781s (caused accident).
Fastest race lap: Hernández, 1m 24.005s, 73.494mph/118.278km/h.
Pole position: Farfus Jr., 1m 22.473s, 74.860mph/120.475km/h.

Round 8 (30.870 miles/49.680km).
1 Alain Menu, CH (Chevrolet Cruze), 52m 22.260s, 35.366mph/56.916km/h; **2** Augusto Farfus Jr., BR (BMW 320si), 52m 22.611s; **3** Robert Huff, GB (Chevrolet Cruze), 52m 25.326s; **4** Andy Priaulx, GB (BMW 320si), 52m 25.585s; **5** Alessandro Zanardi, I (BMW 320si), 52m 38.413s; **6** Gabriele Tarquini, I (SEAT Leon TDI), 52m 39.988s; **7** Yvan Muller, F (SEAT Leon TDI), 52m 41.946s; **8** Eric Cayrolle, F (SEAT Leon), 52m 44.685s; **9** Nicola Larini, I (Chevrolet Cruze), 52m 44.841s; **10** Kristian Poulsen, DK (BMW 320si), 52m 45.557s.
Fastest race lap: Müller (Jörg), 1m 23.488s, 73.950mph/119.011km/h.
Pole position: Menu.

RACE OF SPAIN, Circuit de la Comunitat Valenciana Ricardo Tormo, Cheste, Valencia, Spain, 31 May. 2 x 13 laps of the 2.489-mile/4.005km circuit.
Round 9 (32.352 miles/52.065km).
1 Yvan Muller, F (SEAT Leon TDI), 23m 13.675s, 83.567mph/134.489km/h; **2** Tiago Monteiro, P (SEAT Leon TDI), 23m 15.559s; **3** Gabriele Tarquini, I (SEAT Leon TDI), 23m 17.832s; **4** Augusto Farfus Jr., BR (BMW 320si), 23m 19.039s; **5** Andy Priaulx, GB (BMW 320si), 23m 19.530s; **6** Jörg Müller, D (BMW 320si), 23m 19.618s; **7** Tom Coronel, NL (SEAT Leon), 23m 21.771s; **8** Sergio Hernández, E (BMW 320si), 23m 25.781s; **9** Stefano D'Aste, I (BMW 320si), 23m 26.976s; **10** Felix Porteiro, E (BMW 320si), 23m 29.521s.
Fastest race lap: Muller (Yvan), 1m 45.735s, 84.730mph/136.359km/h.
Pole position: Tarquini, 1m 44.414s, 85.801mph/138.084km/h.

Round 10 (32.352 miles/52.065km).
1 Augusto Farfus Jr., BR (BMW 320si), 23m 16.075s, 83.423mph/134.257km/h; **2** Jörg Müller, D (BMW 320si), 23m 16.615s; **3** Gabriele Tarquini, I (SEAT Leon TDI), 23m 21.501s; **4** Andy Priaulx, GB (BMW 320si), 23m 21.959s; **5** Alessandro Zanardi, I (BMW 320si), 23m 22.751s; **6** Sergio Hernández, E (BMW 320si), 23m 23.253s; **7** Yvan Muller, F (SEAT Leon TDI), 23m 27.244s; **8** Tiago Monteiro, P (SEAT Leon TDI), 23m 27.644s; **9** Stefano D'Aste, I (BMW 320si), 23m 29.127s; **10** Tom Coronel, NL (SEAT Leon), 23m 33.011s.
Fastest race lap: Farfus Jr., 1m 45.974s, 84.538mph/136.052km/h.
Pole position: Hernández.

RACE OF THE CZECH REPUBLIC, Automotodrom Brno Masaryk Circuit, Brno, Czech Republic, 21 June. 12 and 10 laps of the 3.357-mile/5.403km circuit.
Round 11 (40.287 miles/64.836km).
1 Alessandro Zanardi, I (BMW 320si), 29m 26.496s, 82.102mph/132.131km/h; **2** Jörg Müller, D (BMW 320si), 29m 28.344s; **3** Gabriele Tarquini, I (SEAT Leon TDI), 29m 31.327s; **4** Rickard Rydell, S (SEAT Leon TDI), 29m 31.601s; **5** Sergio Hernández, E (BMW 320si), 29m 31.799s; **6** Tiago Monteiro, P (SEAT Leon TDI), 29m 33.746s; **7** Felix Porteiro, E (BMW 320si), 29m 34.343s; **8** Yvan Muller, F (SEAT Leon TDI), 29m 36.411s; **9** Tom Coronel, NL (SEAT Leon), 29m 37.310s; **10** Vito Postiglione, I (BMW 320si), 29m 37.518s.
Fastest race lap: Andy Priaulx, GB (BMW 320si), 2m 10.622s, 92.527mph/148.909km/h.
Pole position: Augusto Farfus Jr., BR (BMW 320si), 2m 09.590s, 93.264mph/150.094km/h.

Round 12 (33.573 miles/54.030km).
1 Sergio Hernández, E (BMW 320si), 22m 13.734s, 90.619mph/145.837km/h; **2** Yvan Muller, F (SEAT Leon TDI), 22m 16.050s; **3** Tiago Monteiro, P (SEAT Leon TDI), 22m 17.848s; **4** Felix Porteiro, E (BMW 320si), 22m 18.014s; **5** Gabriele Tarquini, I (SEAT Leon TDI), 22m 20.966s; **6** Rickard Rydell, S (SEAT Leon TDI), 22m 21.591s; **7** Jörg Müller, D (BMW 320si), 22m 21.826s; **8** Andy Priaulx, GB (BMW 320si), 22m 22.586s; **9** Tom Coronel, NL (SEAT Leon), 22m 24.103s; **10** Vito Postiglione, I (BMW 320si), 22m 24.285s.
Fastest race lap: Hernández, 2m 12.143s, 91.462mph/147.195km/h.
Pole position: Muller (Yvan).

RACE OF PORTUGAL, Circuito da Boavista, Porto, Portugal, 5 July. 12 and 13 laps of the 2.964-mile/4.770km circuit.
Round 13 (35.567 miles/57.240km).
1 Gabriele Tarquini, I (SEAT Leon TDI), 1h 04m 11.274s, 33.246mph/53.505km/h; **2** Robert Huff, GB (Chevrolet Cruze), 1h 04m 14.208s; **3** Yvan Muller, F (SEAT Leon TDI), 1h 04m 19.122s; **4** Tiago Monteiro, P (SEAT Leon TDI), 1h 04m 19.746s; **5** Nicola Larini, I (Chevrolet Cruze), 1h 04m 27.064s; **6** Jordi Gené, E (SEAT Leon TDI), 1h 04m 27.466s; **7** Rickard Rydell, S (SEAT Leon TDI), 1h 04m 27.914s; **8** Augusto Farfus Jr., BR (BMW 320si), 1h 04m 28.249s; **9** Andy Priaulx, GB (BMW 320si), 1h 04m 29.065s; **10** Stefano D'Aste, I (BMW 320si), 1h 04m 29.490s.
Fastest race lap: Tarquini, 2m 11.154s, 81.356mph/130.930km/h.
Pole position: Tarquini, 2m 09.308s, 82.517mph/132.799km/h.

Round 14 (38.531 miles/62.010km).
1 Augusto Farfus Jr., BR (BMW 320si), 47m 48.304s, 48.360mph/77.828km/h; **2** Yvan Muller, F (SEAT Leon TDI), 47m 50.599s; **3** Rickard Rydell, S (SEAT Leon TDI), 47m 51.114s; **4** Jordi Gené, E (SEAT Leon TDI), 47m 51.689s; **5** Tiago Monteiro, P (SEAT Leon TDI), 47m 52.274s; **6** Robert Huff, GB (Chevrolet Cruze), 47m 52.523s; **7** Andy Priaulx, GB (BMW 320si), 47m 52.887s; **8** Jörg Müller, D (BMW 320si), 47m 53.368s; **9** Stefano D'Aste, I (BMW 320si), 47m 54.732s; **10** Alessandro Zanardi, I (BMW 320si), 47m 55.888s.
Fastest race lap: Farfus Jr., 2m 11.045s, 81.423mph/131.038km/h.
Pole position: Farfus Jr.

RACE OF GREAT BRITAIN, Brands Hatch Grand Prix Circuit, West Kingsdown, Dartford, Kent, Great Britain, 19 July. 2 x 16 laps of the 2.301-mile/3.703km circuit.
Round 15 (36.815 miles/59.248km).
1 Alain Menu, CH (Chevrolet Cruze), 28m 25.945s, 77.689mph/125.029km/h; **2** Robert Huff, GB (Chevrolet Cruze), 28m 26.996s; **3** Andy Priaulx, GB (BMW 320si), 28m 27.185s; **4** Gabriele Tarquini, I (SEAT Leon TDI), 28m 27.969s; **5** Rickard Rydell, S (SEAT Leon TDI), 28m 28.365s; **6** Jörg Müller, D (BMW 320si), 28m 31.760s; **7** Tiago Monteiro, P (SEAT Leon TDI), 28m 32.245s; **8** Augusto Farfus Jr., BR (BMW 320si), 28m 34.252s; **9** Stefano D'Aste, I (BMW 320si), 28m 35.170s; **10** Tom Coronel, NL (SEAT Leon), 28m 36.829s.
Fastest race lap: Menu, 1m 34.362s, 87.782mph/141.272km/h.
Pole position: Menu, 1m 33.521s, 88.572mph/142.543km/h.

Round 16 (36.815 miles/59.248km).
1 Augusto Farfus Jr., BR (BMW 320si), 28m 09.979s, 78.423mph/126.210km/h; **2** Jörg Müller, D (BMW 320si), 28m 12.040s; **3** Gabriele Tarquini, I (SEAT Leon TDI), 28m 17.009s; **4** Rickard Rydell, S (SEAT Leon TDI), 28m 17.377s; **5** Andy Priaulx, GB (BMW 320si), 28m 17.728s; **6** Robert Huff, GB (Chevrolet Cruze), 28m 18.406s; **7** Yvan Muller, F (SEAT Leon TDI), 28m 26.630s; **8** Tiago Monteiro, P (SEAT Leon TDI), 28m 27.423s; **9** Sergio Hernández, E (BMW 320si), 28m 28.170s; **10** Tom Boardman, GB (SEAT Leon), 28m 29.502s.
Fastest race lap: Müller (Jörg), 1m 34.488s, 87.665mph/141.084km/h.
Pole position: Farfus Jr.

RACE OF GERMANY, Motorsport Arena Oschersleben, Germany, 6 September. 2 x 14 laps of the 2.297-mile/3.696km circuit.
Round 17 (32.152 miles/51.744km).
1 Andy Priaulx, GB (BMW 320si), 22m 52.547s, 84.330mph/135.717km/h; **2** Gabriele Tarquini, I (SEAT Leon TDI), 22m 56.486s; **3** Rickard Rydell, S (SEAT Leon TDI), 22m 58.897s; **4** Tom Coronel, NL (SEAT Leon), 23m 07.945s; **5** Augusto Farfus Jr., BR (BMW 320si), 23m 15.100s; **6** Stefano D'Aste, I (BMW 320si), 23m 15.296s; **7** Franz Engstler, D (BMW 320si), 23m 15.591s; **8** Sergio Hernández, E (BMW 320si), 23m 15.939s; **9** Tom Boardman, GB (SEAT Leon), 23m 24.526s; **10** Jaap van Lagen, NL (Lada Priora), 23m 24.606s.
Fastest race lap: Priaulx, 1m 36.754s, 85.450mph/137.519km/h.
Pole position: Tarquini, 1m 39.866s, 82.788mph/133.234km/h.

Round 18 (32.152 miles/51.744km).
1 Augusto Farfus Jr., BR (BMW 320si), 22m 58.530s, 83.964mph/135.128km/h; **2** Andy Priaulx, GB (BMW 320si), 22m 59.174s; **3** Gabriele Tarquini, I (SEAT Leon TDI), 23m 03.707s; **4** Jörg Müller, D (BMW 320si), 23m 06.506s; **5** Sergio Hernández, E (BMW 320si), 23m 07.191s; **6** Nicola Larini, I (Chevrolet Cruze), 23m 12.126s; **7** Yvan Muller, F (SEAT Leon TDI), 23m 17.365s; **8** Tom Coronel, NL (SEAT Leon), 23m 17.700s; **9** Robert Huff, GB (Chevrolet Cruze), 23m 23.907s; **10** Alain Menu, CH (Chevrolet Cruze), 23m 24.913s.
Fastest race lap: Priaulx, 1m 37.350s, 84.927mph/136.677km/h.
Pole position: Engstler.

RACE OF ITALY, Autodromo Enzo e Dino Ferrari, Imola, Italy, 20 September. 13 and 11 laps of the 3.050-mile/4.909km circuit.
Round 19 (39.512 miles/63.588km).
1 Gabriele Tarquini, I (SEAT Leon TDI), 29m 31.701s, 80.285mph/129.207km/h; **2** Yvan Muller, F (SEAT Leon TDI), 29m 32.110s; **3** Robert Huff, GB (Chevrolet Cruze), 29m 32.543s; **4** Alessandro Zanardi, I (BMW 320si), 29m 33.158s; **5** Tom Coronel, NL (SEAT Leon), 29m 35.202s; **6** James Thompson, GB (Lada Priora), 29m 37.321s; **7** Sergio Hernández, E (BMW 320si), 29m 37.703s; **8** Alain Menu, CH (Chevrolet Cruze), 29m 38.091s; **9** Felix Porteiro, E (BMW 320si), 29m 41.705s; **10** Tom Boardman, GB (SEAT Leon), 29m 42.047s.
Fastest race lap: Tarquini, 1m 57.580s, 93.392mph/150.301km/h.
Pole position: Tarquini, 1m 55.530s, 95.049mph/152.968km/h.

Round 20 (33.411 miles/53.770km).
1 Yvan Muller, F (SEAT Leon TDI), 21m 51.680s, 91.699mph/147.575km/h; **2** Gabriele Tarquini, I (SEAT Leon TDI), 21m 51.992s; **3** Alain Menu, CH (Chevrolet Cruze), 21m 55.688s; **4** Alessandro Zanardi, I (BMW 320si), 21m 56.147s; **5** Jordi Gené, E (SEAT Leon TDI), 21m 57.312s; **6** James Thompson, GB (Lada Priora), 21m 58.870s; **7** Rickard Rydell, S (SEAT Leon TDI), 21m 59.292s; **8** Augusto Farfus Jr., BR (BMW 320si), 22m 00.007s; **9** Andy Priaulx, GB (BMW 320si), 22m 00.507s; **10** Stefano D'Aste, I (BMW 320si), 22m 01.179s.
Fastest race lap: Rydell, 1m 57.458s, 93.489mph/150.457km/h.
Pole position: Menu.

RACE OF JAPAN, Okayama International Circuit (TI Circuit Aida), Aida Gun, Okayama Prefecture, Japan, 1 November. 16 and 14 laps of the 2.301-mile/3.703km circuit.
Round 21 (36.815 miles/59.248km).
1 Andy Priaulx, GB (BMW 320si), 32m 18.887s, 68.355mph/110.007km/h; **2** Jörg Müller, D (BMW 320si), 32m 19.371s; **3** Robert Huff, GB (Chevrolet Cruze), 32m 21.439s; **4** Yvan Muller, F (SEAT Leon TDI), 32m 30.953s; **5** Gabriele Tarquini, I (SEAT Leon TDI), 32m 34.644s; **6** Jordi Gené, E (SEAT Leon TDI), 32m 36.018s; **7** Tiago Monteiro, P (SEAT Leon TDI), 32m 37.580s; **8** Augusto Farfus Jr., BR (BMW 320si), 32m 44.290s; **9** Alain Menu, CH (Chevrolet Cruze), 32m 47.050s; **10** Tom Coronel, NL (SEAT Leon), 32m 49.020s.
Fastest race lap: Rickard Rydell, S (SEAT Leon TDI), 1m 51.428s, 74.338mph/119.635km/h.
Pole position: Tarquini, 1m 37.666s, 84.813mph/136.493km/h.

Round 22 (32.213 miles/51.842km).
1 Augusto Farfus Jr., BR (BMW 320si), 26m 55.015s, 71.805mph/115.560km/h; **2** Andy Priaulx, GB (BMW 320si), 26m 55.776s; **3** Yvan Muller, F (SEAT Leon TDI), 26m 58.313s; **4** Alain Menu, CH (Chevrolet Cruze), 27m 00.893s; **5** Nicola Larini, I (Chevrolet Cruze), 27m 08.740s; **6** Robert Huff, GB (Chevrolet Cruze), 27m 12.553s; **7** Gabriele Tarquini, I (SEAT Leon TDI), 27m 19.119s; **8** Rickard Rydell, S (SEAT Leon TDI), 27m 21.227s; **9** Jordi Gené, E (SEAT Leon TDI), 27m 22.287s; **10** Stefano D'Aste, I (BMW 320si), 27m 30.634s.
Fastest race lap: Huff, 1m 52.538s, 73.605mph/118.455km/h.
Pole position: Farfus Jr.

Provisional championship points
Drivers
1 Gabriele Tarquini, I, 115; **2** Yvan Muller, F, 113; **3** Augusto Farfus Jr., BR, 102; **4** Andy Priaulx, GB, 84; **5** Robert Huff, GB, 69; **6** Jörg Müller, D, 66; **7** Rickard Rydell, S, 64; **8** Jordi Gené, E, 39; **9** Alain Menu, CH, 36; **10** Sergio Hernández, E, 36; **11** Tiago Monteiro, P, 36; **12** Alessandro Zanardi, I, 31; **13** Nicola Larini, I, 25; **14** Tom Coronel, NL, 15; **15** Felix Porteiro, E, 10; **16** Franz Engstler, D, 7; **17** James Thompson, GB, 6; **18** Stefano D'Aste, I, 3; **19** Eric Cayrolle, F, 1.

Manufacturers
1 SEAT, 289; **2** BMW, 286; **3** Chevrolet, 193; **4** Lada, 81.

Yokohama Independents' Trophy
1 Tom Coronel, NL, 212; **2** Felix Porteiro, E, 182; **3** Stefano D'Aste, I, 137; **4** Franz Engstler, D, 132; **5** Tom Boardman, GB, 87.

Yokohama Teams' Trophy
1 SUNRED Engineering, 266; **2** Scuderia Proteam Motorsport, 185; **3** Liqui Moly Team Engstler, 170; **4** Wiechers-Sport, 135; **5** Colak Racing Team Ingra, 32.

Results of the Macau races will be given in AUTOCOURSE 2010–2011.

GermanTouring Car Championship (DTM)

GERMAN TOURING CAR CHAMPIONSHIP (DTM), Hockenheimring Grand Prix Circuit, Heidelberg, Germany, 17 May. Round 1. 39 laps of the 2.842-mile/4.574km circuit, 110.844 miles/178.386km.
1 Tom Kristensen, DK (Audi A4 DTM 09), 1h 05m 35.819s, 101.386mph/163.165km/h; **2** Timo Scheider, D (Audi A4 DTM 09), 1h 05m 36.172s; **3** Oliver Jarvis, GB (Audi A4 DTM 08), 1h 05m 40.269s; **4** Markus Winkelhock, D (Audi A4 DTM 08), 1h 05m 46.659s; **5** Paul Di Resta, GB (Mercedes C-Klasse 09), 1h 05m 57.651s; **6** Maro Engel, D (Mercedes C-Klasse 08), 1h 06m 00.796s; **7** Mattias Ekström, S (Audi A4 DTM 09), 1h 06m 12.549s; **8** Jamie Green, GB (Mercedes C-Klasse 08), 1h 06m 22.166s; **9** Ralf Schumacher, D (Mercedes C-Klasse 09), 1h 06m 31.518s; **10** Mathias Lauda, A (Mercedes C-Klasse 08), 1h 06m 36.797s.
Fastest race lap: Ekström, 1m 34.640s, 108.112mph/173.990km/h.
Pole position: Ekström, 1m 32.535s, 110.572mph/177.948km/h.

GERMAN TOURING CAR CHAMPIONSHIP (DTM), EuroSpeedway Lausitz, Klettwitz, Dresden, Germany, 31 May. Round 2. 52 laps of the 2.161-mile/3.478km circuit, 112.379 miles/180.856km.
1 Gary Paffett, GB (Mercedes C-Klasse 09), 1h 10m 01.572s, 96.289mph/154.961km/h; **2** Bruno Spengler, CDN (Mercedes C-Klasse 09), 1h 10m 02.687s; **3** Mattias Ekström, S (Audi A4 DTM 09), 1h 10m 15.800s; **4** Paul Di Resta, GB (Mercedes C-Klasse 09), 1h 10m 16.706s; **5** Timo Scheider, D (Audi A4 DTM 09), 1h 10m 17.327s; **6** Jamie Green, GB (Mercedes C-Klasse 08), 1h 10m 17.898s; **7** Mike Rockenfeller, D (Audi A4 DTM 08), 1h 10m 32.744s; **8** Maro Engel, D (Mercedes C-Klasse 08), 1h 10m 43.118s; **9** Mathias Lauda, A (Mercedes C-Klasse 08), 1h 10m 51.540s; **10** Ralf Schumacher, D (Mercedes C-Klasse 09), 1h 10m 52.224s.
Fastest race lap: Green, 1m 19.040s, 98.432mph/158.411km/h.
Pole position: Ekström, 1m 33.205s, 83.473mph/134.336km/h.

GERMAN TOURING CAR CHAMPIONSHIP (DTM), Norisring, Nürnberg (Nuremberg), Germany, 28 June. Round 3. 80 laps of the 1.429-mile/2.300km circuit, 114.332 miles/184.000km.
1 Jamie Green, GB (Mercedes C-Klasse 08), 1h 08m 39.223s, 99.921mph/160.807km/h; **2** Bruno Spengler, CDN (Mercedes C-Klasse 09), 1h 08m 40.580s; **3** Mattias Ekström, S (Audi A4 DTM 09), 1h 08m 40.901s; **4** Timo Scheider, D (Audi A4 DTM 09), 1h 08m 41.849s; **5** Gary Paffett, GB (Mercedes C-Klasse 09), 1h 08m 42.163s; **6** Ralf Schumacher, D (Mercedes C-Klasse 09), 1h 08m 42.473s; **7** Paul Di Resta, GB (Mercedes C-Klasse 09), 1h 08m 43.030s; **8** Tom Kristensen, DK (Audi A4 DTM 09), 1h 08m 48.489s; **9** Mike Rockenfeller, D (Audi A4 DTM 08), 1h 08m 49.010s; **10** Susie Stoddart, GB (Mercedes C-Klasse 08), 1h 08m 53.646s.
Fastest race lap: Katherine Legge, GB (Audi A4 DTM 08), 48.620s, 105.820mph/170.300km/h.
Pole position: Scheider, 49.012s, 104.973mph/168.938km/h.

GERMAN TOURING CAR CHAMPIONSHIP (DTM), Circuit Park Zandvoort, Netherlands, 19 July. Round 4. 41 laps of the 2.676-mile/4.307km circuit, 109.726 miles/176.587km.
1 Gary Paffett, GB (Mercedes C-Klasse 09), 1h 05m 52.688s, 99.936mph/160.831km/h; **2** Oliver Jarvis, GB (Audi A4 DTM 08), 1h 05m 58.923s; **3** Mattias Ekström, S (Audi A4 DTM 09), 1h 05m 59.119s; **4** Martin Tomczyk, D (Audi A4 DTM 09), 1h 06m 03.672s; **5** Bruno Spengler, CDN (Mercedes C-Klasse 09), 1h 06m 06.041s; **6** Paul Di Resta, GB (Mercedes C-Klasse 09), 1h 06m 07.007s; **7** Maro Engel, D (Mercedes C-Klasse 08), 1h 06m 07.343s; **8** Tom Kristensen, DK (Audi A4 DTM 09), 1h 06m 20.297s; **9** Jamie Green, GB (Mercedes C-Klasse 08), 1h 06m 21.466s; **10** Ralf Schumacher, D (Mercedes C-Klasse 09), 1h 06m 33.796s.
Disqualified: Alexandre Prémat, F (Audi A4 DTM 08), finished 4th in 1h 06m 01.658s; Markus Winkelhock, D (Audi A4 DTM 08), finished 6th in 1h 06m 05.538s; Timo Scheider, D (Audi A4 DTM 09), finished 8th in 1h 06m 06.494s.
Fastest race lap: Prémat, 1m 33.890s, 102.615mph/165.142km/h.
Pole position: Jarvis, 1m 31.966s, 104.761mph/168.597km/h.

GERMAN TOURING CAR CHAMPIONSHIP (DTM), Motorsport Arena Oschersleben, Germany, 2 August. Round 5. 48 laps of the 2.297-mile/3.696km circuit, 110.236 miles/177.408km.
1 Timo Scheider, D (Audi A4 DTM 09), 1h 08m 39.064s, 96.345mph/155.052km/h; **2** Mattias Ekström, S (Audi A4 DTM 09), 1h 08m 44.481s; **3** Martin Tomczyk, D (Audi A4 DTM 09), 1h 08m 48.667s; **4** Paul Di Resta, GB (Mercedes C-Klasse 09), 1h 08m 55.932s; **5** Gary Paffett, GB (Mercedes C-Klasse 09), 1h 08m 56.402s; **6** Bruno Spengler, CDN (Mercedes C-Klasse 09), 1h 09m 14.907s; **7** Maro Engel, D (Mercedes C-Klasse 08), 1h 09m 20.060s; **8** Tom Kristensen, DK (Audi A4 DTM 08), 1h 09m 23.079s; **9** Jamie Green, GB (Mercedes C-Klasse 08), 1h 09m 23.700s; **10** Susie Stoddart, GB (Mercedes C-Klasse 08), 1h 09m 29.241s.
Mike Rockenfeller, D (Audi A4 DTM 08), finished 10th in 1h 09m 27.164s, but penalised 30-sec for causing an accident.
Fastest race lap: Scheider, 1m 23.677s, 98.805mph/159.011km/h.
Pole position: Kristensen, 1m 21.352s, 101.629mph/163.556km/h.

GERMAN TOURING CAR CHAMPIONSHIP (DTM), Nürburgring, Nürburg/Eifel, Germany, 16 August. Round 6. 48 laps of the 2.255-mile/3.629km circuit, 108.238 miles/174.192km.
1 Martin Tomczyk, D (Audi A4 DTM 09), 1h 10m 19.195s, 92.353mph/148.628km/h; **2** Timo Scheider, D (Audi A4 DTM 09), 1h 10m 20.400s; **3** Mattias Ekström, S (Audi A4 DTM 09), 1h 10m 22.164s; **4** Markus Winkelhock, D (Audi A4 DTM 08), 1h 10m 35.224s; **5** Jamie Green, GB (Mercedes C-Klasse 08), 1h 10m 42.544s; **6** Bruno Spengler, CDN (Mercedes C-Klasse 09), 1h 10m 46.697s; **7** Ralf Schumacher, D (Mercedes C-Klasse 09), 1h 10m 47.291s; **8** Gary Paffett, GB (Mercedes C-Klasse 09), 1h 10m 54.914s; **9** Mathias Lauda, A (Mercedes C-Klasse 08), 1h 11m 01.343s; **10** Mike Rockenfeller, D (Audi A4 DTM 08), 1h 11m 25.427s.
Fastest race lap: Ekström, 1m 25.118s, 95.372mph/153.486km/h.
Pole position: Tomczyk, 1m 23.489s, 97.232mph/156.480km/h.

GERMAN TOURING CAR CHAMPIONSHIP (DTM), Brands Hatch Indy Circuit, West Kingsdown, Dartford, Kent, Great Britain, 6 September. Round 7. 90 laps of the 1.199-mile/1.929km circuit, 107.876 miles/173.610km.
1 Paul Di Resta, GB (Mercedes C-Klasse 09), 1h 10m 31.345s, 91.780mph/147.706km/h; **2** Timo Scheider, D (Audi A4 DTM 09), 1h 10m 32.241s; **3** Martin Tomczyk, D (Audi A4 DTM 09), 1h 10m 32.767s; **4** Gary Paffett, GB (Mercedes C-Klasse 09), 1h 10m 33.225s; **5** Mattias Ekström, S (Audi A4 DTM 09), 1h 10m 33.609s; **6** Bruno Spengler, CDN (Mercedes C-Klasse 09), 1h 10m 36.393s; **7** Mike Rockenfeller, D (Audi A4 DTM 08), 1h 10m 37.991s; **8** Oliver Jarvis, GB (Audi A4 DTM 08), 1h 10m 38.542s; **9** Ralf Schumacher, D (Mercedes C-Klasse 09), 1h 10m 39.078s; **10** Maro Engel, D (Mercedes C-Klasse 08), 1h 10m 41.967s.
Fastest race lap: Di Resta, 42.387s, 101.801mph/163.833km/h.
Pole position: Di Resta, 41.750s, 103.354mph/166.333km/h.

GERMAN TOURING CAR CHAMPIONSHIP (DTM), Circuit de Catalunya, Montmeló, Barcelona, Spain, 20 September. Round 8. 59 laps of the 1.850-mile/2.977km circuit, 109.140 miles/175.643km.
1 Timo Scheider, D (Audi A4 DTM 09), 1h 08m 38.739s, 95.394mph/153.521km/h; **2** Tom Kristensen, DK (Audi A4 DTM 09), 1h 08m 40.896s; **3** Martin Tomczyk, D (Audi A4 DTM 09), 1h 08m 42.772s; **4** Gary Paffett, GB (Mercedes C-Klasse 09), 1h 09m 02.208s; **5** Bruno Spengler, CDN (Mercedes C-Klasse 09), 1h 09m 02.731s; **6** Mattias Ekström, S (Audi A4 DTM 09), 1h 09m 03.202s; **7** Paul Di Resta, GB (Mercedes C-Klasse 09), 1h 09m 11.982s; **8** Alexandre Prémat, F (Audi A4 DTM 08), 1h 09m 21.068s; **9** Oliver Jarvis, GB (Audi A4 DTM 08), 1h 09m 21.458s; **10** Maro Engel, D (Mercedes C-Klasse 08), 1h 09m 22.087s.
Fastest race lap: Scheider, 1m 08.048s, 97.863mph/157.495km/h.
Pole position: Kristensen, 1m 06.825s, 99.654mph/160.377km/h.

GERMAN TOURING CAR CHAMPIONSHIP (DTM), Circuit de Dijon-Prenois, Fontaine-les-Dijon, France, 11 October. Round 9. 52 laps of the 2.362-mile/3.801km circuit, 122.815 miles/197.652km.
1 Gary Paffett, GB (Mercedes C-Klasse 09), 1h 04m 38.472s, 113.997mph/183.461km/h; **2** Paul Di Resta, GB (Mercedes C-Klasse 09), 1h 04m 39.306s; **3** Bruno Spengler, CDN (Mercedes C-Klasse 09), 1h 04m 39.527s; **4** Jamie Green, GB (Mercedes C-Klasse 08), 1h 04m 39.780s; **5** Ralf Schumacher, D (Mercedes C-Klasse 09), 1h 04m 40.279s; **6** Timo Scheider, D (Audi A4 DTM 09), 1h 04m 40.711s; **7** Martin Tomczyk, D (Audi A4 DTM 09), 1h 04m 41.732s; **8** Mathias Lauda, A (Mercedes C-Klasse 08), 1h 04m 42.493s; **9** Mattias Ekström, S (Audi A4 DTM 09), 1h 04m 43.049s; **10** Markus Winkelhock, D (Audi A4 DTM 08), 1h 04m 43.460s.
Fastest race lap: Di Resta, 1m 11.644s, 118.678mph/190.994km/h.
Pole position: Spengler, 1m 19.914s, 106.397mph/171.229km/h.

GERMAN TOURING CAR CHAMPIONSHIP (DTM), Hockenheimring Grand Prix Circuit, Heidelberg, Germany, 25 October. Round 10. 39 laps of the 2.842-mile/4.574km circuit, 110.844 miles/178.386km.
1 Gary Paffett, GB (Mercedes C-Klasse 09), 1h 06m 01.702s, 100.724mph/162.099km/h; **2** Timo Scheider, D (Audi A4 DTM 09), 1h 06m 02.745s; **3** Paul Di Resta, GB (Mercedes C-Klasse 09), 1h 06m 03.494s; **4** Alexandre Prémat, F (Audi A4 DTM 08), 1h 06m 06.936s; **5** Jamie Green, GB (Mercedes C-Klasse 08), 1h 06m 07.696s; **6** Oliver Jarvis, GB (Audi A4 DTM 08), 1h 06m 09.439s; **7** Bruno Spengler, CDN (Mercedes C-Klasse 09), 1h 06m 10.366s; **8** Markus Winkelhock, D (Audi A4 DTM 08), 1h 06m 11.549s; **9** Mike Rockenfeller, D (Audi A4 DTM 08), 1h 06m 12.057s; **10** Maro Engel, D (Mercedes C-Klasse 08), 1h 06m 12.711s.
Fastest race lap: Paffett, 1m 34.351s, 108.443mph/174.523km/h.
Pole position: Mattias Ekström, S (Audi A4 DTM 09), 1m 32.525s, 110.584mph/177.967km/h.

Final championship points
Drivers
1 Timo Scheider, D, 64; **2** Gary Paffett, GB, 59; **3** Paul Di Resta, GB, 45; **4** Bruno Spengler, CDN, 41; **5** Mattias Ekström, S, 41; **6** Martin Tomczyk, D, 35; **7** Jamie Green, GB, 27; **8** Tom Kristensen, DK, 21; **9** Oliver Jarvis, GB, 18; **10** Markus Winkelhock, D, 11; **11** Ralf Schumacher, D, 9; **12** Maro Engel, D, 8; **13** Alexandre Prémat, F, 6; **14** Mike Rockenfeller, D, 4; **15** Mathias Lauda, A, 1.

Teams
1 Salzgitter / Mercedes-Benz Bank AMG, 100; **2** Audi Sport Team Abt, 85; **3** Audi Sport Team Abt Sportsline, 76; **4** TRILUX AMG Mercedes, 54; **5** TV Spielfim / Junge Sterne AMG Mercedes, 27; **6** Audi Sport Team Phoenix, 24; **7** Audi Sport Team Rosberg, 15; **8** GQ / stern AMG Mercedes, 9.

BritishTouring Car Championship

BRITISH TOURING CAR CHAMPIONSHIP, Brands Hatch Indy Circuit, West Kingsdown, Dartford, Kent, Great Britain, 5 April. 27, 24 and 25 laps of the 1.1986-mile/1.929km circuit.
Round 1 (32.362 miles/52.082km).
1 Matt Neal, GB (Vauxhall Vectra), 24m 37.729s, 78.839mph/126.880km/h; **2** Fabrizio Giovanardi, I (Vauxhall Vectra), 24m 38.129s; **3** Colin Turkington, GB (BMW 320si), 24m 38.624s; **4** Rob Collard, GB (BMW 320si), 24m 41.029s; **5** Adam Jones, GB (SEAT Leon), 24m 43.946s; **6** Jason Plato, GB (Chevrolet Lacetti), 24m 49.033s; **7** Stephen Jelley, GB (BMW 320si), 24m 49.035s; **8** Harry Vaulkhard, GB (Chevrolet Lacetti), 24m 51.706s; **9** Dan Eaves, GB (SEAT Leon), 24m 52.832s; **10** Martyn Bell, GB (Honda Integra), 24m 53.110s.
Fastest race lap: Collard, 49.433s, 87.289mph/140.478km/h.
Pole position: Neal, 48.857s, 88.318mph/142.134km/h.

Round 2 (28.766 miles/46.295km).
1 Rob Collard, GB (BMW 320si), 20m 10.761s, 85.532mph/137.650km/h; **2** Colin Turkington, GB (BMW 320si), 20m 11.787s; **3** Matt Neal, GB (Vauxhall Vectra), 20m 14.019s; **4** Stephen Jelley, GB (BMW 320si), 20m 14.415s; **5** Andrew Jordan, GB (Vauxhall Vectra), 20m 26.225s; **6** Gordon Shedden, GB (Honda Civic), 20m 29.475s; **7** Adam Jones, GB (SEAT Leon), 20m 29.979s; **8** Dan Eaves, GB (SEAT Leon), 20m 30.313s; **9** Jonathan Adam, GB (BMW 320si), 20m 33.783s; **10** Jason Plato, GB (Chevrolet Lacetti), 20m 35.551s.
Fastest race lap: Neal, 49.324s, 87.481mph/140.788km/h.
Pole position: Neal.

Round 3 (29.965 miles/48.224km).
1 Jason Plato, GB (Chevrolet Lacetti), 21m 22.345s, 84.122mph/135.381km/h*; **2** Jonathan Adam, GB (BMW 320si), 21m 22.500s; **3** Matt Neal, GB (Vauxhall Vectra), 21m 22.623s; **4** Colin Turkington, GB (BMW 320si), 21m 22.745s; **5** Gordon Shedden, GB (Honda Civic), 21m 24.615s; **6** Dan Eaves, GB (SEAT Leon), 21m 28.231s; **7** Adam Jones, GB (SEAT Leon), 21m 29.002s; **8** Rob Collard, GB (BMW 320si), 21m 29.099s; **9** Harry Vaulkhard, GB (Chevrolet Lacetti), 21m 29.802s; **10** Martyn Bell, GB (Honda Integra), 21m 39.567s.
* finished 1st in 21m 18.500s, but penalised 4-sec (caused accident).
Fastest race lap: Adam, 49.597s, 87.000mph/140.013km/h.
Pole position: Plato.

BRITISH TOURING CAR CHAMPIONSHIP, Thruxton Circuit, Andover, Hampshire, Great Britain, 26 April. 18, 19 and 19 laps of the 2.356-mile/3.792km circuit.
Round 4 (42.408 miles/68.249km).
1 Fabrizio Giovanardi, I (Vauxhall Vectra), 25m 16.248s, 100.688mph/162.042km/h; **2** Matt Neal, GB (Vauxhall Vectra), 25m 16.652s; **3** Andrew Jordan, GB (Vauxhall Vectra), 25m 17.261s; **4** Colin Turkington, GB (BMW 320si), 25m 17.771s; **5** Paul O'Neill, GB (Honda Integra), 25m 18.868s; **6** Adam Jones, GB (SEAT Leon), 25m 23.089s; **7** Stephen Jelley, GB (BMW 320si), 25m 24.152s; **8** Mat Jackson, GB (Chevrolet Lacetti), 25m 26.705s; **9** Harry Vaulkhard, GB (Chevrolet Lacetti), 25m 27.320s; **10** Jason Plato, GB (Chevrolet Lacetti), 25m 28.571s.
Fastest race lap: Giovanardi, 1m 18.837s, 107.584mph/173.139km/h.
Pole position: Giovanardi, 1m 17.985s, 108.759mph/175.031km/h.

Round 5 (44.764 miles/72.041km).
1 Colin Turkington, GB (BMW 320si), 28m 38.018s, 93.800mph/150.956km/h; **2** Fabrizio Giovanardi, I (Vauxhall Vectra), 28m 38.259s; **3** Matt Neal, GB (Vauxhall Vectra), 28m 38.641s; **4** Stephen Jelley, GB (BMW 320si), 28m 47.128s; **5** Rob Collard, GB (BMW 320si), 28m 49.223s; **6** Jason Plato, GB (Chevrolet Lacetti), 28m 50.135s; **7** James Thompson, GB (Honda Civic), 28m 50.496s; **8** Adam Jones, GB (SEAT Leon), 28m 53.151s; **9** Mat Jackson, GB (Chevrolet Lacetti), 28m 53.327s; **10** Paul O'Neill, GB (Honda Integra), 28m 56.093s.
Fastest race lap: Giovanardi, 1m 18.719s, 107.745mph/173.399km/h.
Pole position: Giovanardi.

Round 6 (44.764 miles/72.041km).
1 Mat Jackson, GB (Chevrolet Lacetti), 28m 44.716s, 93.435mph/150.370km/h; **2** Adam Jones, GB (SEAT Leon), 28m 45.983s; **3** James Thompson, GB (Honda Civic), 28m 48.362s; **4** Jason Plato, GB (Chevrolet Lacetti), 28m 48.724s; **5** Rob Collard, GB (BMW 320si), 28m 49.772s; **6** Stephen Jelley, GB (BMW 320si), 28m 49.876s; **7** Matt Neal, GB (Vauxhall Vectra), 28m 50.136s; **8** Fabrizio Giovanardi, I (Vauxhall Vectra), 28m 50.591s; **9** Colin Turkington, GB (BMW 320si), 28m 50.832s; **10** David Pinkney, GB (Honda Civic), 28m 51.191s.
Fastest race lap: Jackson, 1m 19.284s, 106.977mph/172.163km/h.
Pole position: O'Neill.

BRITISH TOURING CAR CHAMPIONSHIP, Donington Park National Circuit, Castle Donington, Great Britain, 17 May. 17, 19 and 16 laps of the 1.9573-mile/3.150km circuit.
Round 7 (33.274 miles/53.549km).
1 James Thompson, GB (Honda Civic), 24m 05.122s, 82.890mph/133.399km/h; **2** Andrew Jordan, GB (Vauxhall Vectra), 24m 08.129s; **3** Matt Neal, GB (Vauxhall Vectra), 24m 09.318s; **4** Rob Collard, GB (BMW 320si), 24m 11.051s; **5** Harry Vaulkhard, GB (Chevrolet Lacetti), 24m 12.651s; **6** Jonathan Adam, GB (BMW 320si), 24m 17.466s; **7** Jason Plato, GB (Chevrolet Lacetti), 24m 18.545s; **8** Fabrizio Giovanardi, I (Vauxhall Vectra), 24m 18.746s; **9** Adam Jones, GB (SEAT Leon), 24m 19.196s; **10** Mat Jackson, GB (Chevrolet Lacetti), 24m 20.284s.
Fastest race lap: Jackson, 1m 22.520s, 85.389mph/137.420km/h.
Pole position: Jordan, 1m 13.241s, 96.207mph/154.830km/h.

Round 8 (37.189 miles/59.850km).
1 James Thompson, GB (Honda Civic), 24m 43.484s, 90.247mph/145.239km/h; **2** Matt Neal, GB (Vauxhall Vectra), 24m 43.793s; **3** Fabrizio Giovanardi, I (Vauxhall Vectra), 24m 45.553s; **4** Jason Plato, GB (Chevrolet Lacetti), 24m 45.933s; **5** Colin Turkington, GB (BMW 320si), 24m 47.847s; **6** Mat Jackson, GB (Chevrolet Lacetti), 24m 49.893s; **7** Jonathan Adam, GB (BMW 320si), 24m 51.751s; **8** Adam Jones, GB (SEAT Leon), 24m 53.520s; **9** Rob Collard, GB (BMW 320si), 25m 03.797s; **10** Harry Vaulkhard, GB (Chevrolet Lacetti), 25m 04.537s.
Fastest race lap: Giovanardi, 1m 13.549s, 95.804mph/154.181km/h.
Pole position: Thompson.

Round 9 (31.317 miles/50.400km).
1 Rob Collard, GB (BMW 320si), 22m 09.601s, 84.793mph/136.462km/h; **2** Colin Turkington, GB (BMW 320si), 22m 10.802s; **3** Jason Plato, GB (Chevrolet Lacetti), 22m 13.240s; **4** Mat Jackson, GB (Chevrolet Lacetti), 22m 13.395s; **5** Fabrizio Giovanardi, I (Vauxhall Vectra), 22m 17.926s; **6** James Thompson, GB (Honda Civic), 22m 19.922s; **7** Harry Vaulkhard, GB (Chevrolet Lacetti), 22m 19.940s; **8** Matt Neal, GB (Vauxhall Vectra), 22m 23.734s; **9** Tom Chilton, GB (Ford Focus ST), 22m 32.552s; **10** David Pinkney, GB (Honda Civic), 22m 33.049s.
Fastest race lap: O'Neill, 1m 19.375s, 88.772mph/142.865km/h.
Pole position: Vaulkhard.

BRITISH TOURING CAR CHAMPIONSHIP, Oulton Park Circuit, Tarporley, Cheshire, Great Britain, 31 May. 3 x 15 laps of the 2.226-mile/3.582km circuit.
Round 10 (33.390 miles/53.736km).
1 Colin Turkington, GB (BMW 320si), 22m 14.262s, 90.090mph/144.986km/h; **2** Jason Plato, GB (Chevrolet Lacetti), 22m 17.831s; **3** Jonathan Adam, GB (BMW 320si), 22m 23.223s; **4** Fabrizio Giovanardi, I (Vauxhall Vectra), 22m 26.157s; **5** Stephen Jelley, GB (BMW 320si), 22m 26.271s; **6** Adam Jones, GB (SEAT Leon), 22m 29.045s; **7** Matt Neal, GB (Vauxhall Vectra), 22m 30.433s; **8** James Thompson, GB (Honda Civic), 22m 31.032s; **9** Rob Collard, GB (BMW 320si), 22m 34.216s; **10** Andrew Jordan, GB (Vauxhall Vectra), 22m 40.042s.
Fastest race lap: Mat Jackson, GB (Chevrolet Lacetti), 1m 28.106s, 90.954mph/146.376km/h.
Pole position: Plato, 1m 27.186s, 91.913mph/147.920km/h.

Round 11 (33.390 miles/53.736km).
1 Colin Turkington, GB (BMW 320si), 22m 17.878s, 89.846mph/144.594km/h; **2** Fabrizio Giovanardi, I (Vauxhall Vectra), 22m 25.171s; **3** Jason Plato, GB (Chevrolet Lacetti), 22m 33.452s; **4** Matt Neal, GB (Vauxhall Vectra), 22m 33.663s; **5** Jonathan Adam, GB (BMW 320si), 22m 33.685s; **6** Andrew Jordan, GB (Vauxhall Vectra), 22m 35.697s; **7** James Thompson, GB (Honda Civic), 22m 36.172s; **8** Adam Jones, GB (SEAT Leon), 22m 36.577s; **9** Paul O'Neill, GB (Honda Integra), 22m 40.163s; **10** Alan Morrison, GB (Ford Focus ST), 22m 44.838s.
Fastest race lap: Turkington, 1m 28.375s, 90.677mph/145.930km/h.
Pole position: Turkington.

Round 12 (33.390 miles/53.736km).
1 James Thompson, GB (Honda Civic), 22m 24.113s, 89.429mph/143.923km/h; **2** Andrew Jordan, GB (Vauxhall Vectra), 22m 26.397s; **3** Matt Neal, GB (Vauxhall Vectra), 22m 28.227s; **4** Rob Collard, GB (BMW 320si), 22m 28.449s; **5** Jason Plato, GB (Chevrolet Lacetti), 22m 29.040s; **6** Fabrizio Giovanardi, I (Vauxhall Vectra), 22m 31.479s; **7** Adam Jones, GB (SEAT Leon), 22m 34.818s; **8** Mat Jackson, GB (Chevrolet Lacetti), 22m 35.385s; **9** Paul O'Neill, GB (Honda Integra), 22m 37.507s; **10** Alan Morrison, GB (Ford Focus ST), 22m 39.299s.
Fastest race lap: Collard, 1m 28.121s, 90.938mph/146.351km/h.
Pole position: Thompson.

BRITISH TOURING CAR CHAMPIONSHIP, Croft Racing Circuit, Croft-on-Tees, North Yorkshire, Great Britain, 14 June. 13, 15 and 18 laps of the 2.125-mile/3.420km circuit.
Round 13 (27.625 miles/44.458km).
1 Colin Turkington, GB (BMW 320si), 19m 07.119s, 86.695mph/139.522km/h; **2** Stephen Jelley, GB (BMW 320si), 19m 10.618s; **3** Jason Plato, GB (Chevrolet Lacetti), 19m 16.157s; **4** Rob Collard, GB (BMW 320si), 19m 18.602s; **5** Fabrizio Giovanardi, I (Vauxhall Vectra), 19m 20.851s; **6** Matt Neal, GB (Vauxhall Vectra), 19m 23.466s; **7** Jonathan Adam, GB (BMW 320si), 19m 23.802s; **8** Andrew Jordan, GB (Vauxhall Vectra), 19m 26.070s; **9** Paul O'Neill, GB (Honda Integra), 19m 29.700s; **10** David Pinkney, GB (Honda Civic), 19m 45.414s.
Fastest race lap: Turkington, 1m 26.808s, 88.125mph/141.824km/h.
Pole position: Turkington, 1m 26.006s, 88.947mph/143.146km/h.

Round 14 (31.875 miles/51.298 m).
1 Colin Turkington, GB (BMW 320si), 22m 08.861s, 86.352mph/138.970km/h; **2** Stephen Jelley, GB (BMW 320si), 22m 09.194s; **3** Jason Plato, GB (Chevrolet Lacetti), 22m 12.372s; **4** Rob Collard, GB (BMW 320si), 22m 14.266s; **5** Fabrizio Giovanardi, I (Vauxhall Vectra), 22m 15.180s; **6** Matt Neal, GB (Vauxhall Vectra), 22m 15.790s; **7** Andrew Jordan, GB (Vauxhall Vectra), 22m 16.601s; **8** Adam Jones, GB (SEAT Leon), 22m 17.129s; **9** James Thompson, GB (Honda Civic), 22m 25.770s; **10** Paul O'Neill, GB (Honda Integra), 22m 28.172s.
Fastest race lap: Turkington, 1m 26.882s, 88.050mph/141.703km/h.
Pole position: Turkington.

Round 15 (38.250 miles/61.557km).
1 Fabrizio Giovanardi, I (Vauxhall Vectra), 35m 21.211s, 64.915mph/104.471km/h; **2** James Thompson, GB (Honda Civic), 35m 23.355s; **3** Stephen Jelley, GB (BMW 320si), 35m 23.904s; **4** Andrew Jordan, GB (Vauxhall Vectra), 35m 24.573s; **5** Jason Plato, GB (Chevrolet Lacetti), 35m 28.162s; **6** Colin Turkington, GB (BMW 320si), 35m 29.089s; **7** Rob Collard, GB (BMW 320si), 35m 32.929s; **8** Matt Neal, GB (Vauxhall Vectra), 35m 33.843s; **9** Jonathan Adam, GB (BMW 320si), 35m 34.303s; **10** Tom Chilton, GB (Ford Focus ST), 35m 35.080s.
Fastest race lap: Jordan, 1m 38.264s, 77.851mph/125.289km/h.
Pole position: O'Neill.

BRITISH TOURING CAR CHAMPIONSHIP, Snetterton Circuit, Thetford, Norfolk, Great Britain, 2 August. 19, 18 and 21 laps of the 1.952-mile/3.141km circuit.
Round 16 (37.088 miles/59.687km).
1 Fabrizio Giovanardi, I (Vauxhall Vectra), 23m 43.973s, 93.763mph/150.897km/h; **2** Mat Jackson, GB (Chevrolet Lacetti), 23m 46.342s; **3** Paul O'Neill, GB (Honda Integra), 23m 49.589s; **4** Jonathan Adam, GB (BMW 320si), 23m 50.989s; **5** Colin Turkington, GB (BMW 320si), 23m 51.216s; **6** Stephen Jelley, GB (BMW 320si), 23m 51.695s; **7** Adam Jones, GB (SEAT Leon), 23m 53.896s; **8** David Pinkney, GB (Honda Civic), 23m 54.381s; **9** Matt Neal, GB (Vauxhall Vectra), 23m 57.912s; **10** Harry Vaulkhard, GB (Chevrolet Lacetti), 23m 58.357s.
Fastest race lap: Giovanardi, 1m 12.323s, 97.164mph/156.370km/h.
Pole position: Jason Plato, GB (Chevrolet Lacetti), 1m 12.247s, 97.266mph/156.534km/h.

Round 17 (35.136 miles/56.546km).
1 Fabrizio Giovanardi, I (Vauxhall Vectra), 22m 06.906s, 95.326mph/153.413km/h; **2** Colin Turkington, GB (BMW 320si), 22m 09.156s; **3** Jason Plato, GB (Chevrolet Lacetti), 22m 09.834s; **4** James Thompson, GB (Honda Civic), 22m 13.999s; **5** Paul O'Neill, GB (Honda Integra), 22m 14.596s; **6** Jonathan Adam, GB (BMW 320si), 22m 15.183s; **7** Rob Collard, GB (BMW 320si), 22m 16.284s; **8** James Nash, GB (Chevrolet Lacetti), 22m 17.305s; **9** Harry Vaulkhard, GB (Chevrolet Lacetti), 22m 18.679s; **10** Gordon Shedden, GB (SEAT Leon), 22m 21.196s.
Fastest race lap: Plato, 1m 12.553s, 96.856mph/155.874km/h.
Pole position: Giovanardi.

Round 18 (40.992 miles/65.970km).
1 Colin Turkington, GB (BMW 320si), 30m 33.757s, 80.474mph/129.511km/h; **2** Fabrizio Giovanardi, I (Vauxhall Vectra), 30m 33.990s; **3** Matt Neal, GB (Vauxhall Vectra), 30m 34.282s; **4** Andrew Jordan, GB (Vauxhall Vectra), 30m 36.372s; **5** James Thompson, GB (Honda Civic), 30m 39.109s; **6** Paul O'Neill, GB (Honda Integra), 30m 39.339s; **7** Adam Jones, GB (SEAT Leon), 30m 40.448s; **8** Jonathan Adam, GB (BMW 320si), 30m 40.680s; **9** David Pinkney, GB (Honda Civic), 30m 43.342s; **10** Martin Johnson, GB (Vauxhall Astra Coupe), 30m 44.375s.
Disqualified: Nash finished 1st in 30m 33.273s, 80.496mph/129.545km/h (caused accident).
Fastest race lap: Plato, 1m 12.195s, 97.336mph/156.647km/h.
Pole position: Vaulkhard.

BRITISH TOURING CAR CHAMPIONSHIP, Knockhill Racing Circuit, Dunfermline, Fife, Scotland, Great Britain, 16 August. 27, 26 and 27 laps of the 1.2713-mile/2.046km circuit.
Round 19 (34.325 miles/55.241km).
1 Jason Plato, GB (Chevrolet Lacetti), 26m 22.453s, 78.087mph/125.670km/h; **2** Gordon Shedden, GB (SEAT Leon), 26m 24.862s; **3** Mat Jackson, GB (Chevrolet Lacetti), 26m 25.326s; **4** Colin Turkington, GB (BMW 320si), 26m 25.838s; **5** Jonathan Adam, GB (BMW 320si), 26m 26.261s; **6** Fabrizio Giovanardi, I (Vauxhall Vectra), 26m 26.613s; **7** Andrew Jordan, GB (Vauxhall Vectra), 26m 27.651s; **8** Stephen Jelley, GB (BMW 320si), 26m 30.385s; **9** Paul O'Neill, GB (Honda Integra), 26m 30.441s; **10** Harry Vaulkhard, GB (Chevrolet Lacetti), 26m 31.927s.
Fastest race lap: Plato, 53.756s, 85.138mph/137.016km/h.
Pole position: Plato, 53.370s, 85.753mph/138.007km/h.

Round 20 (33.054 miles/53.195km).
1 Fabrizio Giovanardi, I (Vauxhall Vectra), 24m 12.946s, 81.898mph/131.802km/h; **2** Mat Jackson, GB (Chevrolet Lacetti), 24m 14.323s; **3** Colin Turkington, GB (BMW 320si), 24m 15.021s; **4** Matt Neal, GB (Vauxhall Vectra), 24m 20.253s; **5** Paul O'Neill, GB (Honda Integra), 24m 23.262s; **6** James Thompson, GB (Honda Civic), 24m 25.068s; **7** Jonathan Adam, GB (BMW 320si), 24m 25.690s; **8** Stephen Jelley, GB (BMW 320si), 24m 29.513s; **9** Gordon Shedden, GB (SEAT Leon), 24m 31.027s; **10** Andrew Jordan, GB (Vauxhall Vectra), 24m 31.234s.
Fastest race lap: Giovanardi, 53.664s, 85.283mph/137.251km/h.
Pole position: Plato.

Round 21 (34.325 miles/55.241km).
1 Mat Jackson, GB (Chevrolet Lacetti), 25m 56.689s, 79.380mph/127.750km/h; **2** Jason Plato, GB (Chevrolet Lacetti), 25m 59.914s; **3** Fabrizio Giovanardi, I (Vauxhall Vectra), 26m 06.162s; **4** Matt Neal, GB (Vauxhall Vectra), 26m 06.449s; **5** Colin Turkington, GB (BMW 320si), 26m 06.724s; **6** James Thompson, GB (Honda Civic), 26m 07.003s; **7** Andrew Jordan, GB (Vauxhall Vectra), 26m 07.588s; **8** Tom Chilton, GB (Ford Focus ST), 26m 10.084s; **9** Paul O'Neill, GB (Honda Integra), 26m 10.384s; **10** Stephen Jelley, GB (BMW 320si), 26m 10.622s.
Fastest race lap: Plato, 53.513s, 85.524mph/137.638km/h.
Pole position: Thompson.

BRITISH TOURING CAR CHAMPIONSHIP, Silverstone Short Circuit, Towcester, Northamptonshire, Great Britain, 30 August. 25, 22 and 22 laps of the 1.639-mile/2.638km circuit.
Round 22 (40.975 miles/65.943km).
1 Mat Jackson, GB (Chevrolet Lacetti), 29m 26.257s, 83.515mph/134.405km/h; **2** Jason Plato, GB (Chevrolet Lacetti), 29m 27.503s; **3** James Nash, GB (Chevrolet Lacetti), 29m 27.754s; **4** Colin Turkington, GB (BMW 320si), 29m 28.477s; **5** Fabrizio Giovanardi, I (Vauxhall Vectra), 29m 29.324s; **6** Rob Collard, GB (BMW 320si), 29m 31.427s; **7** Stephen Jelley, GB (BMW 320si), 29m 31.543s; **8** Jonathan Adam, GB (BMW 320si), 29m 32.604s; **9** Paul O'Neill, GB (Honda Integra), 29m 32.953s; **10** Matt Neal, GB (Vauxhall Vectra), 29m 33.567s.
Fastest race lap: Nash, 1m 00.941s, 96.821mph/155.819km/h.
Pole position: Jackson, 1m 00.259s, 97.917mph/157.582km/h.

Round 23 (36.058 miles/58.030km).
1 Jason Plato, GB (Chevrolet Lacetti), 24m 00.312s, 90.125mph/145.042km/h; **2** Fabrizio Giovanardi, I (Vauxhall Vectra), 24m 01.083s; **3** Mat Jackson, GB (Chevrolet Lacetti), 24m 03.493s; **4** Colin Turkington, GB (BMW 320si), 24m 13.260s; **5** Tom Chilton, GB (Ford Focus ST), 24m 13.990s; **6** Andrew Jordan, GB (Vauxhall Vectra), 24m 15.711s; **7** Jonathan Adam, GB (BMW 320si), 24m 16.801s; **8** Johnny Herbert, GB (Honda Civic), 24m 18.572s; **9** Rob Collard, GB (BMW 320si), 24m 20.339s; **10** Paul O'Neill, GB (Honda Integra), 24m 20.828s.
Fastest race lap: Plato, 1m 00.997s, 96.732mph/155.676km/h.
Pole position: Jackson.

Round 24 (36.058 miles/58.030km).
1 Mat Jackson, GB (Chevrolet Lacetti), 22m 46.584s, 94.987mph/152.868km/h; **2** Rob Collard, GB (BMW 320si), 22m 46.797s; **3** Colin Turkington, GB (BMW 320si), 22m 52.739s; **4** Stephen Jelley, GB (BMW 320si), 22m 53.200s; **5** Fabrizio Giovanardi, I (Vauxhall Vectra), 22m 54.686s; **6** Jonathan Adam, GB (BMW 320si), 22m 56.432s; **7** Jason Plato, GB (Chevrolet Lacetti), 23m 00.969s; **8** James Nash, GB (Chevrolet Lacetti), 23m 01.428s; **9** Paul O'Neill, GB (Honda Integra), 23m 01.827s; **10** David Pinkney, GB (Honda Civic), 23m 03.492s.
Fastest race lap: Jackson, 1m 01.045s, 96.656mph/155.553km/h.
Pole position: Collard.

BRITISH TOURING CAR CHAMPIONSHIP, Rockingham Motor Speedway, Corby, Northamptonshire, Great Britain, 20 September. 18, 19 and 18 laps of the 1.940-mile/3.122km circuit.
Round 25 (34.920 miles/56.198km).
1 Stephen Jelley, GB (BMW 320si), 26m 26.025s, 79.262mph/127.560km/h; **2** Jason Plato, GB (Chevrolet Lacetti), 26m 29.424s; **3** Mat Jackson, GB (Chevrolet Lacetti), 26m 30.141s; **4** Rob Collard, GB (BMW 320si), 26m 33.014s; **5** Jonathan Adam, GB (BMW 320si), 26m 36.329s; **6** Fabrizio Giovanardi, I (Vauxhall Vectra), 26m 38.601s; **7** Andrew Jordan, GB (Vauxhall Vectra), 26m 41.267s; **8** James Nash, GB (Chevrolet Lacetti), 26m 43.889s; **9** Paul O'Neill, GB (Honda Integra), 26m 45.201s; **10** Colin Turkington, GB (BMW 320si), 26m 48.586s.
Fastest race lap: Plato, 1m 24.668s, 82.486mph/132.749km/h.
Pole position: Plato, 1m 24.087s, 83.056mph/133.667km/h.

Round 26 (36.860 miles/59.320km).
1 Jason Plato, GB (Chevrolet Lacetti), 29m 05.784s, 76.009mph/122.325km/h; **2** Mat Jackson, GB (Chevrolet Lacetti), 29m 06.670s; **3** Fabrizio Giovanardi, I (Vauxhall Vectra), 29m 07.204s; **4** Colin Turkington, GB (BMW 320si), 29m 07.586s; **5** Jonathan Adam, GB (BMW 320si), 29m 09.446s; **6** Stephen Jelley, GB (BMW 320si), 29m 10.010s; **7** James Nash, GB (Chevrolet Lacetti), 29m 11.791s; **8** Andrew Jordan, GB (Vauxhall Vectra), 29m 14.097s; **9** Tom Chilton, GB (Ford Focus ST), 29m 17.700s; **10** Johnny Herbert, GB (Honda Civic), 29m 19.262s.
Fastest race lap: Plato, 1m 25.105s, 82.063mph/132.068km/h.
Pole position: Jelley.

Round 27 (34.920 miles/56.198km).
1 Stephen Jelley, GB (BMW 320si), 26m 47.230s, 78.216mph/125.877km/h; **2** Andrew Jordan, GB (Vauxhall Vectra), 26m 49.287s; **3** Tom Chilton, GB (Ford Focus ST), 26m 54.935s; **4** Colin Turkington, GB (BMW 320si), 26m 55.685s; **5** Mat Jackson, GB (Chevrolet Lacetti), 26m 57.575s; **6** Jonathan Adam, GB (BMW 320si), 26m 59.605s; **7** Johnny Herbert, GB (Honda Civic), 27m 00.853s; **8** Gordon Shedden, GB (SEAT Leon), 27m 05.412s; **9** Tom Onslow-Cole, GB (Ford Focus ST), 27m 11.616s; **10** Martin Johnson, GB (Vauxhall Astra Coupe), 27m 25.138s.
Fastest race lap: Jelley, 1m 24.829s, 82.330mph/132.497km/h.
Pole position: Chilton.

BRITISH TOURING CAR CHAMPIONSHIP, Brands Hatch Grand Prix Circuit, West Kingsdown, Dartford, Kent, Great Britain, 4 October. 18, 18 and 17 laps of the 2.3009-mile/3.703km circuit.
Round 28 (41.416 miles/66.653km).
1 Jason Plato, GB (Chevrolet Lacetti), 31m 03.701s, 80.001mph/128.749km/h; **2** Tom Chilton, GB (Ford Focus ST), 31m 03.716s; **3** Fabrizio Giovanardi, I (Vauxhall Vectra), 31m 05.574s; **4** Andrew Jordan, GB (Vauxhall Vectra), 31m 06.804s; **5** Matt Neal, GB (Vauxhall Vectra), 31m 07.601s; **6** Rob Collard, GB (BMW 320si), 31m 08.159s; **7** Jonathan Adam, GB (BMW 320si), 31m 08.657s; **8** Colin Turkington, GB (BMW 320si), 31m 09.687s; **9** Paul O'Neill, GB (Honda Integra), 31m 10.238s; **10** Anthony Reid, GB (BMW 320si), 31m 10.617s.
Fastest race lap: Plato, 1m 33.983s, 88.135mph/141.840km/h.
Pole position: Chilton, 1m 33.159s, 88.915mph/143.094km/h.

Round 29 (41.416 miles/66.653km).
1 Jason Plato, GB (Chevrolet Lacetti), 30m 24.717s, 81.710mph/131.500km/h; **2** Fabrizio Giovanardi, I (Vauxhall Vectra), 30m 26.034s; **3** Colin Turkington, GB (BMW 320si), 30m 26.203s; **4** Rob Collard, GB (BMW 320si), 30m 26.698s; **5** Jonathan Adam, GB (BMW 320si), 30m 27.055s; **6** Tom Chilton, GB (Ford Focus ST), 30m 29.545s; **7** Paul O'Neill, GB (Honda Integra), 30m 30.233s; **8** Matt Neal, GB (Vauxhall Vectra), 30m 30.721s; **9** Tom Onslow-Cole, GB (Ford Focus ST), 30m 40.022s; **10** Gordon Shedden, GB (SEAT Leon), 30m 40.242s.
Fastest race lap: Neal, 1m 34.029s, 88.092mph/141.770km/h.
Pole position: Plato.

Round 30 (39.115 miles/62.950km).
1 Jason Plato, GB (Chevrolet Lacetti), 28m 48.039s, 81.488mph/131.142km/h; **2** Colin Turkington, GB (BMW 320si), 28m 49.504s; **3** Tom Chilton, GB (Ford Focus ST), 28m 49.778s; **4** Fabrizio Giovanardi, I (Vauxhall Vectra), 28m 51.023s; **5** Matt Neal, GB (Vauxhall Vectra), 28m 51.614s; **6** Stephen Jelley, GB (BMW 320si), 28m 59.141s; **7** Anthony Reid, GB (BMW 320si), 29m 00.573s; **8** Jonathan Adam, GB (BMW 320si), 29m 01.879s; **9** Gordon Shedden, GB (SEAT Leon), 29m 01.983s; **10** David Pinkney, GB (Honda Civic), 29m 02.176s.
Fastest race lap: Shedden, 1m 34.661s, 87.504mph/140.824km/h.
Pole position: Neal.

Final championship points
Drivers
1 Colin Turkington, GB, 275; **2** Jason Plato, GB, 270; **3** Fabrizio Giovanardi, I, 266; **4** Matt Neal, GB, 170; **5** Mat Jackson, GB, 165; **6** Rob Collard, GB, 145; **7** Stephen Jelley, GB, 137; **8** Jonathan Adam, GB, 116; **9** James Thompson, GB, 114; **10** Andrew Jordan, GB, 114; **11** Adam Jones, GB, 62; **12** Paul O'Neill, GB, 60; **13** Tom Chilton, GB, 55; **14** Gordon Shedden, GB, 34; **15** James Nash, GB, 24; **16** Harry Vaulkhard, GB, 22; **17** David Pinkney, GB, 10; **18** Dan Eaves, GB, 10; **19** Johnny Herbert, GB, 8; **20** Anthony Reid, GB, 5; **21** Tom Onslow-Cole, GB, 4; **22** Martyn Bell, GB, 2; **23** Alan Morrison, GB, 2; **24** Martin Johnson, GB, 2.

Teams
1 VX Racing, 466; **2** Team RAC, 404; **3** Racing Silverline, 358; **4** Airwaves BMW, 255; **5** Team Dynamics, 149; **6** Cartridge World Carbon Zero Racing, 93; **7** Sunshine.co.uk with Tech-Speed Motorsport, 70; **8** RML, 66; **9** Team Aon, 62; **10** Tempus Sport, 9; **11** Club SEAT, 7; **12** bamboo engineering, 6; **13** Boulevard Team Racing, 4; **14** TH Motorsport Racing with JAG, 1.

Manufacturers
1 Vauxhall, 658; **2** Honda, 429; **3** Ford, 341.

Independent Drivers
1 Colin Turkington, GB, 313; **2** Jason Plato, GB, 283; **3** Mat Jackson, GB, 183; **4** Rob Collard, GB, 173; **5** Stephen Jelley, 165.

Independent Teams
1 Team RAC, 348; **2** Racing Silverline, 313; **3** Airwaves BMW, 275; **4** Team Dynamics, 220; **5** Sunshine.co.uk., 159.

IndyCar Series

All cars are Dallara IR4-Honda HI8R.

HONDA GRAND PRIX OF ST. PETERSBURG, St. Petersburg Street Circuit, Florida, USA, 5 April. Round 1. 100 laps of the 1.800-mile/2.897km circuit, 180.000 miles/289.682km.
1 Ryan Briscoe, AUS, 2h 12m 26.8387s, 81.542mph/131.229km/h; **2** Ryan Hunter-Reay, USA, 2h 12m 27.3006s; **3** Justin Wilson, GB, 2h 12m 27.7877s; **4** Dario Franchitti, GB, 2h 12m 28.3617s; **5** Tony Kanaan, BR, 2h 12m 29.1601s; **6** Will Power, AUS, 2h 12m 30.3009s; **7** Graham Rahal, USA, 2h 12m 30.9059s; **8** Darren Manning, GB, 2h 12m 31.5670s; **9** Vitor Meira, BR, 2h 12m 32.7946s; **10** Alex Tagliani, CDN, 99 laps; **11** Robert Doornbos, NL, 96; **12** Stanton Barrett, USA, 96; **13** Marco Andretti, USA, 94 (DNF-accident); **14** Dan Wheldon, GB, 86 (DNF-accident); **15** Hideki Mutoh, J, 86 (DNF-accident); **16** Scott Dixon, NZ, 80 (DNF-accident); **17** Ernest Viso, YV, 75 (DNF-suspension); **18** Ed Carpenter, USA, 71 (DNF-accident); **19** Danica Patrick, USA, 31 (DNF-accident); **20** Raphael Matos, BR, 31 (DNF-accident); **21** Mário Moraes, BR, 31 (DNF-accident); **22** Mike Conway, GB, 1 (DNF-accident).
Most laps led: Wilson, 52.
Fastest race lap: Wilson, 1m 03.2440s, 102.460mph/164.894km/h.
Pole position: Rahal, 1m 02.4110s, 103.828mph/167.095km/h.
Championship points – Drivers: 1 Briscoe, 50; **2** Hunter-Reay, 40; **3** Wilson, 37; **4** Franchitti, 32; **5** Kanaan, 30; **6** Power, 28.

TOYOTA GRAND PRIX OF LONG BEACH, Long Beach Street Circuit, California, USA, 19 April. Round 2. 85 laps of the 1.968-mile/3.167km circuit, 167.280 miles/269.211km.
1 Dario Franchitti, GB, 1h 58m 47.4658s, 84.491mph/135.975km/h; **2** Will Power, AUS, 1h 58m 50.7840s; **3** Tony Kanaan, BR, 1h 58m 51.5195s; **4** Danica Patrick, USA, 1h 58m 52.5400s; **5** Dan Wheldon, GB, 1h 58m 54.0313s; **6** Marco Andretti, USA, 1h 58m 55.0558s; **7** Hélio Castroneves, BR, 1h 58m 56.0990s; **8** Raphael Matos, BR, 1h 58m 56.9493s; **9** Robert Doornbos, NL, 1h 58m 57.4241s; **10** Alex Tagliani, CDN, 1h 59m 01.0843s; **11** Ryan Hunter-Reay, USA, 1h 59m 02.6755s; **12** Graham Rahal, USA, 1h 59m 03.3165s; **13** Ryan Briscoe, AUS, 1h 59m 52.5671s; **14** Vitor Meira, BR, 84 laps; **15** Scott Dixon, NZ, 84; **16** Darren Manning, GB, 84; **17** Stanton Barrett, USA, 84; **18** Ed Carpenter, USA, 82; **19** Mário Moraes, BR, 71 (DNF-accident); **20** Hideki Mutoh, J, 60; **21** Mike Conway, GB, 51 (DNF-accident); **22** Justin Wilson, GB, 24 (DNF-accident); **23** Ernest Viso, YV, 16 (DNF-accident).
Most laps led: Franchitti, 51.
Fastest race lap: Briscoe, 1m 11.2582s, 99.424mph/160.008km/h.
Pole position: Power, 1m 09.7107s, 101.631mph/163.560km/h.
Championship points – Drivers: 1 Franchitti, 84; **2** Power, 69; **3** Briscoe, 67; **4** Kanaan, 65; **5** Hunter-Reay, 59; **6** Wilson, 49.

ROAD RUNNER TURBO INDY 300, Kansas Speedway, Kansas City, Kansas, USA, 26 April. Round 3. 200 laps of the 1.520-mile/2.446km circuit, 304.000 miles/489.240km.
1 Scott Dixon, NZ, 1h 43m 21.0035s, 176.488mph/284.029km/h; **2** Hélio Castroneves, BR, 1h 43m 21.7139s; **3** Tony Kanaan, BR, 1h 43m 22.5057s; **4** Ryan Briscoe, AUS, 1h 43m 22.8907s; **5** Danica Patrick, USA, 1h 43m 23.6537s; **6** Marco Andretti, USA, 1h 43m 24.8048s; **7** Graham Rahal, USA, 1h 43m 28.8268s; **8** Hideki Mutoh, J, 1h 43m 29.5465s; **9** Ed Carpenter, USA, 1h 43m 29.9906s; **10** Dan Wheldon, GB, 1h 43m 30.7716s; **11** Mário Moraes, BR, 1h 43m 41.9083s; **12** Robert Doornbos, NL, 199 laps; **13** Sarah Fisher, USA, 199; **14** Justin Wilson, GB, 199; **15** Ryan Hunter-Reay, USA, 196; **16** Milka Duno, YV, 195; **17** Stanton Barrett, USA, 181 (DNF-accident); **18** Dario Franchitti, GB, 151 (DNF-accident); **19** Mike Conway, GB, 109 (DNF-accident); **20** Raphael Matos, BR, 95 (DNF-accident); **21** Ernesto Viso, YV, 37 (DNF-mechanical); **22** Vitor Meira, BR, 14 (DNF-accident).
Most laps led: Dixon, 134.
Fastest race lap: Briscoe, 25.9367s, 210.975mph/339.532km/h.
Pole position: Rahal, 1m 43.5819s, 211.311mph/340.072km/h (over 4 laps).
Championship points – Drivers: 1 Kanaan, 100; **2** Briscoe, 99; **3** Franchitti, 96; **4** Dixon, 81; **5** Hunter-Reay, 74; **6** Patrick, 74.

93rd INDIANAPOLIS 500, Indianapolis Motor Speedway, Speedway, Indiana, USA, 24 May. Round 4. 200 laps of the 2.500-mile/4.023km circuit, 500.000 miles/804.672km.
1 Hélio Castroneves, BR, 3h 19m 34.6427s, 150.318mph/241.913km/h; **2** Dan Wheldon, GB, 3h 19m 36.6246s; **3** Danica Patrick, USA, 3h 19m 36.9777s; **4** Townsend Bell, USA, 3h 19m 37.3470s; **5** Will Power, AUS, 3h 19m 38.2643s; **6** Scott Dixon, NZ, 3h 19m 38.9415s; **7** Dario Franchitti, GB, 3h 19m 39.5586s; **8** Ed Carpenter, USA, 3h 19m 40.1523s; **9** Paul Tracy, CDN, 3h 19m 41.1607s; **10** Hideki Mutoh, J, 3h 19m 41.9739s; **11** Alex Tagliani, CDN, 3h 19m 45.1778s; **12** Tomas Scheckter, ZA, 3h 19m 45.6301s; **13** Alex Lloyd, GB, 3h 19m 45.8371s; **14** Scott Sharp, USA, 3h 19m 46.0686s; **15** Ryan Briscoe, AUS, 3h 19m 47.3122s; **16** A.J. Foyt IV, USA, 3h 19m 50.1294s; **17** Sarah Fisher, USA, 3h 19m 50.6201s; **18** Mike Conway, GB, 3h 19m 50.9915s; **19** John Andretti, USA, 3h 19m 52.7295s; **20** Milka Duno, YV, 199 laps; **21** Vitor Meira, BR, 173 (DNF-accident); **22** Raphael Matos, BR, 173 (DNF-accident); **23** Justin Wilson, GB, 160 (DNF-accident); **24** Ernesto Viso, YV, 139 (DNF-mechanical); **25** Nelson Philippe, F, 130 (DNF-accident damage); **26** Oriol Servià, E, 98 (DNF-fuel pump); **27** Tony Kanaan, BR, 97 (DNF-accident); **28** Robert Doornbos, NL, 85 (DNF-accident); **29** Davey Hamilton, USA, 79 (DNF-accident); **30** Marco Andretti, USA, 56 (DNF-handling); **31** Graham Rahal, USA, 55 (DNF-accident); **32** Ryan Hunter-Reay, USA, 19 (DNF-accident); **33** Mário Moraes, BR, 0 (DNF-accident).
Did not start: Bruno Junqueira, BR (replaced by Tagliani).
Did not qualify: Stanton Barrett, USA; Buddy Lazier, USA.
Most laps led: Dixon, 73.
Fastest race lap: Franchitti, 40.5325s, 222.044mph/357.345km/h.
Pole position: Castroneves, 2m 40.0967s, 224.864mph/361.884km/h (over 4 laps).
Championship points – Drivers: 1 Franchitti, 122; **2** Castroneves, 117; **3** Briscoe, 114; **4** Dixon, 111; **5** Kanaan, 110; **6** Patrick, 109.

ABC SUPPLY/AJ FOYT 225, The Milwaukee Mile, Wisconsin State Fair Park, West Allis, Wisconsin, USA, 31 May. Round 5. 225 laps of the 1.015-mile/1.633km circuit, 228.375 miles/367.534km.
1 Scott Dixon, NZ, 1h 38m 43.9552s, 138.784mph/223.351km/h; **2** Ryan Briscoe, AUS, 1h 38m 46.0809s; **3** Dario Franchitti, GB, 1h 38m 46.2196s; **4** Graham Rahal, USA, 1h 38m 46.6296s; **5** Danica Patrick, USA, 1h 38m 49.9376s; **6** Raphael Matos, BR, 1h 38m 59.8429s; **7** Marco Andretti, USA, 1h 39m 01.9000s; **8** Hideki Mutoh, J, 224 laps; **9** Mário Moraes, BR, 224; **10** Dan Wheldon, GB, 224; **11** Hélio Castroneves, BR, 222; **12** Ryan Hunter-Reay, USA, 222; **13** Tomas Scheckter, ZA, 222; **14** Robert Doornbos, NL, 220; **15** Justin Wilson, GB, 219; **16** Ed Carpenter, USA, 219; **17** Paul Tracy, CDN, 219; **18** Ernesto Viso, YV, 175 (DNF-suspension); **19** Tony Kanaan, BR, 132 (DNF-fire); **20** Mike Conway, GB, 55 (DNF-accident).
Did not start: Stanton Barrett, USA.
Most laps led: Briscoe, 154.
Fastest race lap: Dixon, 22.2788s, 164.012mph/263.952km/h.
Pole position: Briscoe, 1m 26.7966s, 168.394mph/271.003km/h (over 4 laps).
Championship points – Drivers: 1 Dixon, 161; **2** Briscoe, 157; **3** Franchitti, 157; **4** Patrick, 139; **5** Castroneves, 136; **6** Wheldon, 126.

BOMBARDIER LEARJET 550, Texas Motor Speedway, Fort Worth, Texas, USA, 6 June. Round 6. 228 laps of the 1.455-mile/2.342km circuit, 331.740 miles/533.884km.
1 Hélio Castroneves, BR, 1h 55m 16.1670s, 172.677mph/277.897km/h; **2** Ryan Briscoe, AUS, 1h 55m 16.5574s; **3** Scott Dixon, NZ, 1h 55m 18.4131s; **4** Marco Andretti, USA, 1h 55m 20.5415s; **5** Dario Franchitti, GB, 1h 55m 20.9365s; **6** Danica Patrick, USA, 1h 55m 21.4650s; **7** Dan Wheldon, GB, 1h 55m 23.7873s; **8** Tony Kanaan, BR, 1h 55m 24.6679s; **9** Ed Carpenter, USA, 1h 55m 34.8758s; **10** Mário Moraes, BR, 227 laps; **11** Robert Doornbos, NL, 227; **12** Raphael Matos, BR, 226; **13** Tomas Scheckter, ZA, 226; **14** Alex Tagliani, CDN, 225; **15** Justin Wilson, GB, 225; **16** Ryan Hunter-Reay, USA, 225; **17** Sarah Fisher, USA, 222; **18** Jaques Lazier, USA, 210; **19** Mike Conway, GB, 185; **20** A.J. Foyt IV, USA, 170 (DNF-accident); **21** Hideki Mutoh, J, 153 (DNF-electrics); **22** Graham Rahal, USA, 1 (DNF-accident); **23** Milka Duno, YV, 1 (DNF-accident); **24** Ernesto Viso, YV, 1 (DNF-accident).
Most laps led: Briscoe, 160.
Fastest race lap: Briscoe, 24.4870s, 213.909mph/344.254km/h.
Pole position: Franchitti, 1m 37.6725s, 214.513mph/345.225km/h (over 4 laps).
Championship points – Drivers: 1 Briscoe, 199; **2** Dixon, 196; **3** Franchitti, 188; **4** Castroneves, 186; **5** Patrick, 167; **6** Wheldon, 152.

IOWA CORN INDY 250, Iowa Speedway, Newton, Iowa, USA, 21 June. Round 7. 250 laps of the 0.894-mile/1.439km circuit, 223.500 miles/359.688km.
1 Dario Franchitti, GB, 1h 39m 47.9077s, 134.371mph/216.249km/h; **2** Ryan Briscoe, AUS, 1h 39m 52.9209s; **3** Hideki Mutoh, J, 1h 39m 58.8846s; **4** Dan Wheldon, GB, 1h 40m 05.4884s; **5** Scott Dixon, NZ, 249 laps; **6** Tomas Scheckter, ZA, 249; **7** Hélio Castroneves, BR, 249; **8** Mike Conway, GB, 249; **9** Danica Patrick, USA, 249; **10** Ed Carpenter, USA, 248; **11** Graham Rahal, USA, 245; **12** Marco Andretti, USA, 244; **13** Jaques Lazier, USA, 237; **14** Tony Kanaan, BR, 108 (DNF-accident); **15** Robert Doornbos, NL, 58 (DNF-handling); **16** Raphael Matos, BR, 53 (DNF-accident); **17** Mário Moraes, BR, 52 (DNF-accident); **18** Justin Wilson, GB, 33 (DNF-accident); **19** Ryan Hunter-Reay, USA, 2 (DNF-accident); **20** Ernesto Viso, YV, 0 (DNF-accident).
Most laps led: Briscoe, 85.
Fastest race lap: Mutoh, 18.0128s, 178.673mph/287.546km/h.
Pole position: Castroneves (no qualifying due to waterlogged track).
Championship points – Drivers: 1 Briscoe, 241; **2** Franchitti, 238; **3** Dixon, 226; **4** Castroneves, 212; **5** Patrick, 189; **6** Wheldon, 184.

SUN TRUST INDY CHALLENGE, Richmond International Raceway, Virginia, USA, 27 June. Round 8. 300 laps of the 0.750-mile/1.207km circuit, 225.000 miles/362.102km.
1 Scott Dixon, NZ, 1h 48m 02.4703s, 124.952mph/201.091km/h; **2** Dario Franchitti, GB, 1h 48m 02.7812s; **3** Graham Rahal, USA, 1h 48m 04.8788s; **4** Hideki Mutoh, J, 1h 48m 16.0005s; **5** Danica Patrick, USA, 1h 48m 16.5814s; **6** Tony Kanaan, BR, 299 laps; **7** Marco Andretti, USA, 299; **8** Raphael Matos, BR, 299; **9** Robert Doornbos, NL, 299; **10** Dan Wheldon, GB, 299; **11** Tomas Scheckter, ZA, 299; **12** Ernesto Viso, YV, 299; **13** Ed Carpenter, USA, 299; **14** Justin Wilson, GB, 298; **15** Ryan Hunter-Reay, USA, 298; **16** Mário Moraes, BR, 297; **17** Hélio Castroneves, BR, 245 (DNF-accident); **18** Mike Conway, GB, 135 (DNF-accident); **19** Ryan Briscoe, AUS, 26 (DNF-accident); **20** Jaques Lazier, USA, 0 (DNF-accident).
Most laps led: Dixon, 161.
Fastest race lap: Dixon, 16.6070s, 162.582mph/261.650km/h.
Pole position: Franchitti, 1m 04.5488s, 167.315mph/269.268km/h (over 4 laps).
Championship points – Drivers: 1 Franchitti, 279; **2** Dixon, 278; **3** Briscoe, 253; **4** Castroneves, 225; **5** Patrick, 219; **6** Wheldon, 204.

CAMPING WORLD GRAND PRIX AT THE GLEN, Watkins Glen International, Watkins Glen, New York, USA, 5 July. Round 9. 60 laps of the 3.370-mile/5.423km circuit, 202.200 miles/325.409km
1 Justin Wilson, GB, 1h 48m 24.1947s, 111.915mph/180.110km/h; **2** Ryan Briscoe, AUS, 1h 48m 29.1853s; **3** Scott Dixon, NZ, 1h 48m 29.3579s; **4** Hélio Castroneves, BR, 1h 48m 31.2702s; **5** Marco Andretti, USA, 1h 48m 32.7542s; **6** Mike Conway, GB, 1h 48m 33.5593s; **7** Ernesto Viso, YV, 1h 48m 35.5751s; **8** Tony Kanaan, BR, 1h 48m 37.1967s; **9** Robert Doornbos, NL, 1h 48m 37.4580s; **10** Dan Wheldon, GB, 1h 48m 42.2359s; **11** Danica Patrick, USA, 1h 48m 42.7603s; **12** Raphael Matos, BR, 1h 48m 43.1289s; **13** Graham Rahal, USA, 1h 48m 47.2360s; **14** Mário Moraes, BR, 1h 48m 47.5768s; **15** Dario Franchitti, GB, 59 laps; **16** Ed Carpenter, USA, 59; **17** Milka Duno, YV, 58; **18** Hideki Mutoh, J, 51 (DNF-accident); **19** Richard Antinucci, USA, 47; **20** Paul Tracy, CDN, 29 (DNF-accident); **21** Ryan Hunter-Reay, USA, 0 (DNF-accident).
Most laps led: Wilson, 49.
Fastest race lap: Briscoe, 1m 31.1760s, 133.061mph/214.141km/h.
Pole position: Briscoe, 1m 28.5970s, 136.935mph/220.375km/h.
Championship points – Drivers: 1 Dixon, 313; **2** Franchitti, 294; **3** Briscoe, 294; **4** Castroneves, 257; **5** Patrick, 238; **6** Wheldon, 224.

HONDA INDY TORONTO, Toronto Street Circuit, Ontario, Canada, 12 July. Round 10. 85 laps of the 1.755-mile/2.824km circuit, 149.175 miles/240.074km.
1 Dario Franchitti, GB, 1h 43m 47.1408s, 86.240mph/138.790km/h; **2** Ryan Briscoe, AUS, 1h 43m 48.8153s; **3** Will Power, AUS, 1h 43m 49.2763s; **4** Scott Dixon, NZ, 1h 43m 49.6211s; **5** Justin Wilson, GB, 1h 43m 50.0638s; **6** Danica Patrick, USA, 1h 43m 53.5503s; **7** Ryan Hunter-Reay, USA, 1h 43m 54.3245s; **8** Marco Andretti, USA, 1h 43m 55.3960s; **9** Alex Tagliani, CDN, 1h 44m 00.6153s; **10** Raphael Matos, BR, 1h 44m 03.2391s; **11** Mário Moraes, BR, 1h 44m 06.1549s; **12** Hideki Mutoh, J, 84 laps; **13** Ernesto Viso, YV, 84; **14** Dan Wheldon, GB, 84; **15** Ed Carpenter, USA, 82; **16** Tomas Scheckter, ZA, 74 (DNF-accident); **17** Tony Kanaan, BR, 70 (DNF-accident); **18** Hélio Castroneves, BR, 65 (DNF-accident); **19** Paul Tracy, CDN, 65 (DNF-accident); **20** Graham Rahal, USA, 57 (DNF-accident); **21** Richard Antinucci, USA, 41 (DNF-mechanical); **22** Mike Conway, GB, 32 (DNF-accident); **23** Robert Doornbos, NL, 26 (DNF-electrical).
Most laps led: Franchitti, 45.
Fastest race lap: Briscoe, 1m 02.2313s, 101.524mph/163.388km/h.
Pole position: Franchitti, 1m 01.0249s, 103.532mph/166.618km/h.
Championship points – Drivers: 1 Franchitti, 347; **2** Dixon, 345; **3** Briscoe, 334; **4** Castroneves, 269; **5** Patrick, 266; **6** Wheldon, 240.

REXALL EDMONTON INDY, Rexall Speedway, Edmonton City Centre Airport, Alberta, Canada, 26 July. Round 11. 95 laps of the 1.973-mile/3.175km circuit, 187.435 miles/301.647km.
1 Will Power, AUS, 1h 42m 42.3773s, 109.498mph/176.219km/h; **2** Hélio Castroneves, BR, 1h 42m 43.4709s; **3** Scott Dixon, NZ, 1h 42m 43.6986s; **4** Ryan Briscoe, AUS, 1h 42m 44.2039s; **5** Dario Franchitti, GB, 1h 42m 46.8425s; **6** Paul Tracy, CDN, 1h 42m 48.7714s; **7** Graham Rahal, USA, 1h 43m 08.9473s; **8** Justin Wilson, GB, 1h 43m 09.2942s; **9** Robert Doornbos, NL, 94 laps; **10** Marco Andretti, USA, 94; **11** Danica Patrick, USA, 94; **12** Ernesto Viso, YV, 94; **13** Alex Tagliani, CDN, 94; **14** Hideki Mutoh, J, 94; **15** Dan Wheldon, GB, 94; **16** Ed Carpenter, USA, 93; **17** Ryan Hunter-Reay, USA, 87; **18** Raphael Matos, BR, 85; **19** Tomas Scheckter, ZA, 73 (DNF-accident); **20** Mike Conway, GB, 63; **21** Tony Kanaan, BR, 34 (DNF-pit fire); **22** Richard Antinucci, USA, 20 (DNF-mechanical).
Did not start: Mário Moraes, BR, 0.
Most laps led: Power, 90.
Fastest race lap: Conway, 1m 02.4340s, 113.765mph/183.087km/h.
Pole position: Power, 1m 01.0133s, 116.414mph/187.350km/h.
Championship points – Drivers: 1 Dixon, 380; **2** Franchitti, 377; **3** Briscoe, 366; **4** Castroneves, 309; **5** Patrick, 285; **6** Andretti, 259.

MEIJER INDY 300, Kentucky Speedway, Fort Mitchell, Kentucky, USA, 1 August. Round 12. 200 laps of the 1.480-mile/2.382km circuit, 295.999 miles/476.365km.
1 Ryan Briscoe, AUS, 1h 28m 24.3246s, 200.893mph/323.305km/h; **2** Ed Carpenter, USA, 1h 28m 24.3408s; **3** Tony Kanaan, BR, 1h 28m 24.4860s; **4** Hélio Castroneves, BR, 1h 28m 24.5974s; **5** Graham Rahal, USA, 1h 28m 24.9592s; **6** Dario Franchitti, GB, 1h 28m 26.0916s; **7** Scott Dixon, NZ, 1h 28m 27.5758s; **8** Danica Patrick, USA, 1h 28m 29.0477s; **9** Will Power, AUS, 1h 28m 30.4670s; **10** Marco Andretti, USA, 1h 28m 31.3209s; **11** Dan Wheldon, GB, 1h 28m 37.0843s; **12** Sarah Fisher, USA, 1h 28m 40.2978s; **13** Hideki Mutoh, J, 1h 28m 52.2951s; **14** Ryan Hunter-Reay, USA, 197 laps; **15** Ernesto Viso, YV, 197; **16** Raphael Matos, BR, 196; **17** Mike Conway, GB, 192; **18** Mário Moraes, BR, 186; **19** Robert Doornbos, NL, 185; **20** Milka Duno, YV, 165; **21** Justin Wilson, GB, 120 (DNF-wheel bearing); **22** Tomas Scheckter, ZA, 59 (DNF-rollbar); **23** Jaques Lazier, USA, 43 (DNF-mechanical).
Most laps led: Dixon, 95.
Fastest race lap: Carpenter, 24.3847s, 218.498mph/351.638km/h.
Pole position: Dixon (qualifying cancelled due to water on track).
Championship points – Drivers: 1 Briscoe, 416; **2** Dixon, 409; **3** Franchitti, 405; **4** Castroneves, 341; **5** Patrick, 309; **6** Andretti, 279.

HONDA INDY 200 AT MID-OHIO, Mid-Ohio Sports Car Course, Lexington, Ohio, USA, 9 August. Round 13. 85 laps of the 2.258-mile/3.634km circuit, 191.930 miles/308.881km.
1 Scott Dixon, NZ, 1h 46m 05.7985s, 108.541mph/174.679km/h; **2** Ryan Briscoe, AUS, 1h 46m 35.5788s; **3** Dario Franchitti, GB, 1h 46m 35.8536s; **4** Ryan Hunter-Reay, USA, 1h 46m 39.5292s; **5** Hideki Mutoh, J, 1h 46m 39.9824s; **6** Marco Andretti, USA, 1h 46m 52.5654s; **7** Paul Tracy, CDN, 1h 46m 55.5005s; **8** Graham Rahal, USA, 1h 46m 56.2502s; **9** Raphael Matos, BR, 1h 46m 57.0271s; **10** Tony Kanaan, BR, 1h 46m 57.8795s; **11** Oriol Servià, E, 1h 46m 58.4200s; **12** Hélio Castroneves, BR, 1h 46m 59.0347s; **13** Justin Wilson, GB, 1h 46m 59.3753s; **14** Robert Doornbos, NL, 1h 47m 15.8797s; **15** Ernesto Viso, YV, 84 laps; **16** Dan Wheldon, GB, 84; **17** Ed Carpenter, USA, 84; **18** Richard Antinucci, USA, 83; **19** Danica Patrick, USA, 83; **20** Mike Conway, GB, 69 (DNF-suspension); **21** Milka Duno, YV, 56 (DNF-handling).
Most laps led: Dixon, 51.
Fastest race lap: Dixon, 1m 08.5600s, 118.565mph/190.811km/h.
Pole position: Briscoe, 1m 06.6814s, 121.905mph/196.187km/h.
Championship points – Drivers: 1 Dixon, 460; **2** Briscoe, 457; **3** Franchitti, 440; **4** Castroneves, 359; **5** Patrick, 321; **6** Andretti, 307.

INDY GRAND PRIX OF SONOMA, Infineon Raceway, Sears Point, Sonoma, California, USA, 23 August. Round 14. 75 laps of the 2.303-mile/3.706km circuit, 172.725 miles/277.974km.
1 Dario Franchitti, GB, 1h 49m 23.0073s, 94.745mph/152.477km/h; **2** Ryan Briscoe, AUS, 1h 49m 23.2561s; **3** Mike Conway, GB, 1h 49m 23.8366s; **4** Mário Moraes, BR, 1h 49m 26.6244s; **5** Hideki Mutoh, J, 1h 49m 28.4609s; **6** Oriol Servià, E, 1h 49m 29.3874s; **7** Justin Wilson, GB, 1h 49m 29.7070s; **8** Tony Kanaan, BR, 1h 49m 30.1881s; **9** Raphael Matos, BR, 1h 49m 31.6009s; **10** Robert Doornbos, NL, 1h 49m 33.8248s; **11** Ed Carpenter, USA, 1h 49m 34.3761s; **12** Dan Wheldon, GB, 1h 49m 35.4073s; **13** Scott Dixon, NZ, 1h 49m 36.9041s; **14** Marco Andretti, USA, 1h 49m 37.9051s; **15** Richard Antinucci, USA, 1h 49m 42.0723s; **16** Danica Patrick, USA, 74 laps; **17** Milka Duno, YV, 71; **18** Hélio Castroneves, BR, 66 (DNF-accident); **19** Ryan Hunter-Reay, USA, 65 (DNF-electronics); **20** Franck Montagny, F, 57 (DNF-handling); **21** Graham Rahal, USA, 30 (DNF-driveshaft); **22** Ernesto Viso, YV, 0 (DNF-accident).
Did not start: Will Power, AUS (injured); Nelson Philippe, F (injured).
Most laps led: Franchitti, 75.
Fastest race lap: Castroneves, 1m 18.8427s, 105.156mph/169.233km/h.
Pole position: Franchitti, 1m 16.7987s, 107.955mph/173.737km/h.
Championship points – Drivers: 1 Briscoe, 497; **2** Franchitti, 493; **3** Dixon, 477; **4** Castroneves, 371; **5** Patrick, 335; **6** Andretti, 323.

PEAK ANTIFREEZE AND MOTOR OIL INDY 300, Chicagoland Speedway, Chicago, Illinois, USA, 29 August. Round 15. 200 laps of the 1.520-mile/2.446km circuit, 304.000 miles/489.241km.
1 Ryan Briscoe, AUS, 1h 42m 34.3051s, 177.827mph/286.184km/h; **2** Scott Dixon, NZ, 1h 42m 34.3128s; **3** Mário Moraes, BR, 1h 42m 34.3750s; **4** Dario Franchitti, GB, 1h 42m 34.4048s; **5** Graham Rahal, USA, 1h 42m 34.4346s; **6** Ed Carpenter, USA, 1h 42m 34.4719s; **7** Oriol Servià, E, 1h 42m 34.5663s; **8** Tomas Scheckter, ZA, 1h 42m 34.5734s; **9** Raphael Matos, BR, 1h 42m 34.6407s; **10** Justin Wilson, GB, 1h 42m 34.7395s; **11** Marco Andretti, USA, 1h 42m 34.8275s; **12** Danica Patrick, USA, 1h 42m 34.8891s; **13** Tony Kanaan, BR, 1h 42m 35.1320s; **14** Sarah Fisher, USA, 199 laps; **15** Ryan Hunter-Reay, USA, 199; **16** Mike Conway, GB, 199; **17** Ernesto Viso, YV, 198; **18** Robert Doornbos, NL, 197; **19** Jaques Lazier, USA, 195; **20** Hélio Castroneves, BR, 184 (DNF-accident); **21** Milka Duno, YV, 155 (DNF-overheating); **22** Dan Wheldon, GB, 95 (DNF-driveshafts); **23** Hideki Mutoh, J, 90 (DNF-accident).
Most laps led: Briscoe, 71.
Fastest race lap: Scheckter, 25.0567s, 218.385mph/351.456km/h.
Pole position: Briscoe, 1m 41.6327s, 215.364mph/346.594km/h (over 4 laps).
Championship points – Drivers: 1 Briscoe, 550; **2** Franchitti, 525; **3** Dixon, 517; **4** Castroneves, 383; **5** Patrick, 353; **6** Andretti, 342.

INDY JAPAN 300, Twin Ring Motegi, Motegi-machi, Haga-gun, Tochigi Prefecture, Japan, 19 September. Round 16. 200 laps of the 1.520-mile/2.446km circuit, 304.000 miles/489.241km.
1 Scott Dixon, NZ, 1h 51m 37.6411s, 163.401mph/262.968km/h; **2** Dario Franchitti, GB, 1h 51m 39.0886s; **3** Graham Rahal, USA, 1h 51m 40.8413s; **4** Oriol Servià, E, 1h 51m 45.0131s; **5** Mário Moraes, BR, 1h 51m 50.4054s; **6** Danica Patrick, USA, 1h 51m 53.7803s; **7** Marco Andretti, USA, 1h 51m 54.2924s; **8** Dan Wheldon, GB, 1h 51m 54.9057s; **9** Raphael Matos, BR, 1h 51m 55.2201s; **10** Hélio Castroneves, BR, 199 laps; **11** Tony Kanaan, BR, 199; **12** Justin Wilson, GB, 199; **13** Ed Carpenter, USA, 198; **14** Hideki Mutoh, J, 198; **15** Ernesto Viso, YV, 198; **16** Robert Doornbos, NL, 198; **17** Kosuke Matsuura, J, 195; **18** Ryan Briscoe, AUS, 185; **19** Stanton Barrett, USA, 182; **20** Roger Yasukawa, USA, 172; **21** Ryan Hunter-Reay, USA, 157 (DNF-accident); **22** Mike Conway, GB, 103 (DNF-accident); **23** Tomas Scheckter, ZA, 83 (DNF-gearbox).
Most laps led: Dixon, 139.
Fastest race lap: Dixon, 27.6698s, 197.761mph/318.265km/h.
Pole position: Dixon, 1m 48.3400s, 202.031mph/325.137km/h (over 4 laps).
Championship points – Drivers: 1 Dixon, 570; **2** Franchitti, 565; **3** Briscoe, 562; **4** Castroneves, 403; **5** Patrick, 381; **6** Andretti, 368.

FIRESTONE INDY 300, Homestead-Miami Speedway, Florida, USA, 10 October. Round 17. 200 laps of the 1.485-mile/2.390km circuit, 297.000 miles/477.975km.
1 Dario Franchitti, GB, 1h 28m 28.3117s, 201.420mph/324.154km/h; **2** Ryan Briscoe, AUS, 1h 28m 33.1005s; **3** Scott Dixon, NZ, 1h 28m 34.3323s; **4** Tony Kanaan, BR, 199 laps; **5** Hélio Castroneves, BR, 199; **6** Hideki Mutoh, J, 198; **7** Mário Moraes, BR, 198; **8** Alex Lloyd, GB, 198; **9** Tomas Scheckter, ZA, 197; **10** Justin Wilson, GB, 197; **11** Graham Rahal, USA, 197; **12** Ed Carpenter, USA, 197; **13** Ryan Hunter-Reay, USA, 196; **14** Raphael Matos, BR, 196; **15** Mike Conway, GB, 195; **16** Ernesto Viso, YV, 194; **17** Milka Duno, YV, 194; **18** Sarah Fisher, USA, 187; **19** Danica Patrick, USA, 185; **20** Robert Doornbos, NL, 166 (DNF-lost mirror); **21** Dan Wheldon, GB, 150 (DNF-accident damage); **22** Marco Andretti, USA, 58 (DNF-brakes); **23** Jaques Lazier, USA, 23 (DNF-mechanical).
Most laps led: Briscoe, 103.
Fastest race lap: Dixon, 25.4483s, 210.073mph/338.080km/h.
Pole position: Franchitti, 1m 40.5378s, 212.696mph/342.301km/h (over 4 laps).

Final championship points
1 Dario Franchitti, GB, 616; **2** Scott Dixon, NZ, 605; **3** Ryan Briscoe, AUS, 604; **4** Hélio Castroneves, BR, 433; **5** Danica Patrick, USA, 393; **6** Tony Kanaan, BR, 386; **7** Graham Rahal, USA, 385; **8** Marco Andretti, USA, 380; **9** Justin Wilson, GB, 354; **10** Dan Wheldon, GB, 354; **11** Hideki Mutoh, J, 353; **12** Ed Carpenter, USA, 321; **13** Raphael Matos, BR, 312; **14** Mário Moraes, BR, 304; **15** Ryan Hunter-Reay, USA, 298; **16** Robert Doornbos, NL, 283; **17** Mike Conway, GB, 261; **18** Ernesto Viso, YV, 248; **19** Will Power, AUS, 215; **20** Tomas Scheckter, ZA, 195; **21** Oriol Servià, E, 115; **22** Alex Tagliani, CDN, 114; **23** Paul Tracy, CDN, 113; **24** Milka Duno, YV, 113; **25** Sarah Fisher, USA, 89; **26** Jaques Lazier, USA, 77; **27** Richard Antinucci, USA, 63; **28** Vitor Meira, BR, 62; **29** Stanton Barrett, USA, 62; **30** Alex Lloyd, GB, 41; **31** Darren Manning, GB, 38; **32** Townsend Bell, USA, 32; **33** A.J. Foyt IV, USA, 26; **34** Scott Sharp, USA, 16; **35** Nelson Philippe, F, 16; **36** Kosuke Matsuura, J, 13; **37** John Andretti, USA, 12; **38** Franck Montagny, F, 12; **39** Roger Yasukawa, USA, 12; **40** Davey Hamilton, USA, 10.

Rookie of the Year: Raphael Matos.

NASCAR Sprint Cup Series
2008

The following races were run after AUTOCOURSE 2008–2009 went to press.

DICKIES 500, Texas Motor Speedway, Fort Worth, Texas, USA, 2 November. Round 34. 334 laps of the 1,500-mile/2.414km circuit, 501.000 miles/806.281km.
1 Carl Edwards, USA (Ford Fusion), 3h 28m 26.0s, 144.219mph/232.098km/h; **2** Jeff Gordon, USA (Chevrolet Impala SS), 3h 28m 34.310s; **3** Jamie McMurray, USA (Ford Fusion), 334 laps; **4** Clint Bowyer, USA (Chevrolet Impala SS), 334; **5** Greg Biffle, USA (Ford Fusion), 334; **6** Kyle Busch, USA (Toyota Camry), 334; **7** Kevin Harvick, USA (Chevrolet Impala SS), 334; **8** Martin Truex Jr., USA (Chevrolet Impala SS), 334; **9** Matt Kenseth, USA (Ford Fusion), 334; **10** David Reutimann, USA (Toyota Camry), 334.
Pole position: Gordon (Jeff), 28.652s, 188.469mph/303.311km/h.
Championship points – Drivers: 1 Johnson, 6366; **2** Edwards, 6260; **3** Biffle, 6223; **4** Burton, 6154; **5** Gordon, 6111; **6** Bowyer, 6099.

CHECKER O'REILLY AUTO PARTS 500, Phoenix International Raceway, Arizona, USA, 9 November. Round 35. 313 laps of the 1.000-mile/1.609km circuit, 313.000 miles/503.725km.
1 Jimmie Johnson, USA (Chevrolet Impala SS), 3h 12m 01s, 97.804mph/157.400km/h; **2** Kurt Busch, USA (Dodge Charger), 3h 12m 01.295s; **3** Jamie McMurray, USA (Ford Fusion), 313 laps; **4** Carl Edwards, USA (Ford Fusion), 313; **5** Denny Hamlin, USA (Toyota Camry), 313; **6** Dale Earnhardt Jr., USA (Chevrolet Impala SS), 313; **7** Kevin Harvick, USA (Chevrolet Impala SS), 313; **8** Kyle Busch, USA (Toyota Camry), 313; **9** Jeff Burton, USA (Chevrolet Impala SS), 313; **10** David Ragan, USA (Ford Fusion), 313.
Pole position: Johnson, 26.721s, 134.725mph/216.820km/h.
Championship points – Drivers: 1 Johnson, 6561; **2** Edwards, 6420; **3** Biffle, 6358; **4** Burton, 6292; **5** Harvick, 6233; **6** Bowyer, 6226.

FORD 400, Homestead-Miami Speedway, Florida, USA, 16 November. Round 36. 267 laps of the 1.500-mile/2.414km circuit, 400.500 miles/644.542km.
1 Carl Edwards, USA (Ford Fusion), 3h 05m 36s, 129.472mph/208.365km/h; **2** Kevin Harvick, USA (Chevrolet Impala SS), 3h 05m 43.548s; **3** Jamie McMurray, USA (Ford Fusion), 267 laps; **4** Jeff Gordon, USA (Chevrolet Impala SS), 267; **5** Clint Bowyer, USA (Chevrolet Impala SS), 267; **6** Kasey Kahne, USA (Dodge Charger), 267; **7** Travis Kvapil, USA (Ford Fusion), 267; **8** Casey Mears, USA (Chevrolet Impala SS), 267; **9** Tony Stewart, USA (Toyota Camry), 267; **10** Martin Truex Jr., USA (Chevrolet Impala SS), 267.
Pole position: David Reutimann, USA (Toyota Camry), 31.462s, 171.636mph/276.221km/h.

Final championship points
Drivers
1 Jimmie Johnson, USA, 6684; **2** Carl Edwards, USA, 6615; **3** Greg Biffle, USA, 6467; **4** Kevin Harvick, USA, 6408; **5** Clint Bowyer, USA, 6381; **6** Jeff Burton, USA, 6335; **7** Jeff Gordon, USA, 6316; **8** Denny Hamlin, USA, 6214; **9** Tony Stewart, USA, 6202; **10** Kyle Busch, USA, 6186; **11** Matt Kenseth, USA, 6184; **12** Dale Earnhardt Jr., USA, 6127.

Not involved in 'Chase for the Nextel Cup'
13 David Ragan, USA, 4299; **14** Kasey Kahne, USA, 4085; **15** Martin Truex Jr., USA, 3839; **16** Jamie McMurray, USA, 3809; **17** Ryan Newman, USA, 3735; **18** Kurt Busch, USA, 3635; **19** Brian Vickers, USA, 3580; **20** Casey Mears, USA, 3527; **21** Bobby Labonte, USA, 3448; **22** David Reutimann, USA, 3397; **23** Travis Kvapil, USA, 3384; **24** Elliott Sadler, USA, 3364; **25** Juan Pablo Montoya, CO, 3329; **26** Paul Menard, USA, 3151; **27** David Gilliland, USA, 3064; **28** Mark Martin, USA, 3022; **29** Michael Waltrip, USA, 2889; **30** Dave Blaney, USA, 2851.

Raybestos Rookie of the Year: Regan Smith, USA.
Coors Light Pole Award winner: Jimmie Johnson, USA.

Manufacturers
1 Chevrolet, 219; **2** Ford, 215; **3** Toyota, 207; **4** Dodge, 151.

2009

Cars are Chevrolet Impala SS, Ford Fusion and Dodge Charger.

50th DAYTONA 500, Daytona International Speedway, Daytona Beach, Florida, USA, 15 February. Round 1. 152 laps of the 2.500-mile/4.023km circuit, 380.000 miles/611.551km.
Scheduled for 200 laps, but shortened by rain.
1 Matt Kenseth, USA (Ford), 2h 51m 40s, 132.816mph/213.746km/h; **2** Kevin Harvick, USA (Chevrolet), 152 laps; **3** A.J. Allmendinger, USA (Dodge), 152; **4** Clint Bowyer, USA (Chevrolet), 152; **5** Elliott Sadler, USA (Dodge), 152; **6** David Ragan, USA (Ford), 152; **7** Michael Waltrip, USA (Toyota), 152; **8** Tony Stewart, USA (Chevrolet), 152; **9** Reed Sorenson, USA (Dodge), 152; **10** Kurt Busch, USA (Dodge), 152.
Pole position: Martin Truex Jr., USA (Chevrolet Impala), 47.872s, 188.001mph/302.559km/h.
Championship points – Drivers: 1 Kenseth, 190; **2** Harvick, 170; **3** Allmendinger, 165; **4** Bowyer, 160; **5** Sadler, 160; **6** Ragan, 150.

AUTO CLUB 500, Auto Club Speedway, Fontana, California, USA, 22 February. Round 2. 250 laps of the 2.000-mile/3.219km circuit, 500.000 miles/804.672km.
1 Matt Kenseth, USA (Ford), 3h 40m 51s, 135.839mph/218.611km/h; **2** Jeff Gordon, USA (Chevrolet), 3h 40m 52.463s; **3** Kyle Busch, USA (Toyota), 250 laps; **4** Greg Biffle, USA (Ford), 250; **5** Kurt Busch, USA (Dodge), 250; **6** Denny Hamlin, USA (Toyota), 250; **7** Carl Edwards, USA (Ford), 250; **8** Tony Stewart, USA (Chevrolet), 250; **9** Jimmie Johnson, USA (Chevrolet), 250; **10** Brian Vickers, USA (Toyota), 250.
Pole position: Vickers, 39.250s, 183.439mph/295.217km/h.
Championship points – Drivers: 1 Kenseth, 385; **2** Gordon (Jeff), 304; **3** Busch (Kurt), 294; **4** Stewart, 294; **5** Biffle, 268; **6** Bowyer, 266.

SHELBY 427, Las Vegas Motor Speedway, Nevada, USA, 1 March. Round 3. 285 laps of the 1.500-mile/2.414km circuit, 427.500 miles/687.995km.
1 Kyle Busch, USA (Toyota), 3h 34m 37s, 119.515mph/192.341km/h; **2** Clint Bowyer, USA (Chevrolet), 3h 34m 37.411s; **3** Jeff Burton, USA (Chevrolet), 285 laps; **4** David Reutimann, USA (Toyota), 285; **5** Bobby Labonte, USA (Ford), 285; **6** Jeff Gordon, USA (Chevrolet), 285; **7** Greg Biffle, USA (Ford), 285; **8** Brian Vickers, USA (Toyota), 285; **9** Jamie McMurray, USA (Ford), 285; **10** Dale Earnhardt Jr., USA (Chevrolet), 285.
Pole position: Busch (Kyle), 29.033s, 185.995mph/299.330km/h.
Championship points – Drivers: 1 Gordon (Jeff), 459; **2** Bowyer, 441; **3** Kenseth, 419; **4** Biffle, 419; **5** Reutimann, 408; **6** Busch (Kyle), 405.

KOBALT TOOLS 500, Atlanta Motor Speedway, Hampton, Georgia, USA, 8 March. Round 4. 330 laps of the 1.540-mile/2.478km circuit, 508.200 miles/817.869km.
1 Kurt Busch, USA (Dodge), 3h 59m 01s, 127.573mph/205.308km/h; **2** Jeff Gordon, USA (Chevrolet), 3h 59m 01.332s; **3** Carl Edwards, USA (Ford), 330 laps; **4** Kevin Harvick, USA (Chevrolet), 330; **5** Brian Vickers, USA (Toyota), 330; **6** Clint Bowyer, USA (Chevrolet), 330; **7** Kasey Kahne, USA (Dodge), 330; **8** Tony Stewart, USA (Chevrolet), 330; **9** Jimmie Johnson, USA (Chevrolet), 330; **10** Martin Truex Jr., USA (Chevrolet), 330.
Pole position: Mark Martin, USA (Chevrolet), 29.640s, 187.045mph/301.019km/h.
Championship points – Drivers: 1 Gordon (Jeff), 634; **2** Bowyer, 591; **3** Busch (Kurt), 588; **4** Edwards, 547; **5** Kenseth, 546; **6** Stewart, 521.

FOOD CITY 500, Bristol Motor Speedway, Tennessee, USA, 22 March. Round 5. 503 laps of the 0.533-mile/0.858km circuit, 268.099 miles/431.464km.
1 Kyle Busch, USA (Toyota), 2h 54m 35s, 92.139mph/148.283km/h; **2** Denny Hamlin, USA (Toyota), 2h 54m 35.391s; **3** Jimmie Johnson, USA (Chevrolet), 503 laps; **4** Jeff Gordon, USA (Chevrolet), 503; **5** Kasey Kahne, USA (Dodge), 503; **6** Mark Martin, USA (Chevrolet), 503; **7** Ryan Newman, USA (Chevrolet), 503; **8** Jeff Burton, USA (Chevrolet), 503; **9** Juan Pablo Montoya, CO (Chevrolet), 503; **10** Marcos Ambrose, AUS (Toyota), 503.
Pole position: Martin, 15.256s, 125.773mph/202.413km/h.
Championship points – Drivers: 1 Gordon (Jeff), 794; **2** Busch (Kurt), 718; **3** Bowyer, 715; **4** Busch (Kyle), 709; **5** Edwards, 665; **6** Kahne, 639.

GOODY'S FAST PAIN RELIEF 500, Martinsville Speedway, Virginia, USA, 29 March. Round 6. 500 laps of the 0.526-mile/0.847km circuit, 263.000 miles/423.257km.
1 Jimmie Johnson, USA (Chevrolet), 3h 27m 48s, 75.938mph/122.211km/h; **2** Denny Hamlin, USA (Toyota), 3h 27m 48.774s; **3** Tony Stewart, USA (Chevrolet), 500 laps; **4** Jeff Gordon, USA (Chevrolet), 500; **5** Clint Bowyer, USA (Chevrolet), 500; **6** Ryan Newman, USA (Chevrolet), 500; **7** Mark Martin, USA (Chevrolet), 500; **8** Dale Earnhardt Jr., USA (Chevrolet), 500; **9** A.J. Allmendinger, USA (Dodge), 500; **10** Jamie McMurray, USA (Ford), 500.
Pole position: Gordon (no qualifying).
Championship points – Drivers: 1 Gordon (Jeff), 959; **2** Bowyer, 870; **3** Busch (Kurt), 827; **4** Johnson, 817; **5** Hamlin, 811; **6** Busch (Kyle), 800.

SAMSUNG 500, Texas Motor Speedway, Fort Worth, Texas, USA, 5 April. Round 7. 334 laps of the 1.500-mile/2.414km circuit, 501.000 miles/806.281km.
1 Jeff Gordon, USA (Chevrolet), 3h 25m 22s, 146.372mph/235.563km/h; **2** Jimmie Johnson, USA (Chevrolet), 3h 25m 22.378s; **3** Greg Biffle, USA (Ford), 334 laps; **4** Tony Stewart, USA (Chevrolet), 334; **5** Matt Kenseth, USA (Ford), 334; **6** Mark Martin, USA (Chevrolet), 334; **7** Juan Pablo Montoya, CO (Chevrolet), 334; **8** Kurt Busch, USA (Dodge), 334; **9** Jeff Burton, USA (Chevrolet), 334; **10** Carl Edwards, USA (Ford), 334.
Pole position: David Reutimann, USA (Toyota), 28.344s, 190.517mph/306.607km/h.
Championship points – Drivers: 1 Gordon (Jeff), 1154; **2** Johnson, 992; **3** Busch (Kurt), 974; **4** Bowyer, 967; **5** Stewart, 963; **6** Hamlin, 938.

SUBWAY FRESH FIT 500, Phoenix International Raceway, Arizona, USA, 18 April. Round 8. 312 laps of the 1.000-mile/1.609km circuit, 312.000 miles/502.115km.
1 Mark Martin, USA (Chevrolet), 2h 53m 16s, 108.042mph/173.876km/h; **2** Tony Stewart, USA (Chevrolet), 2h 53m 16.734s; **3** Kurt Busch, USA (Dodge), 312 laps; **4** Jimmie Johnson, USA (Chevrolet), 312; **5** Greg Biffle, USA (Ford), 312; **6** Denny Hamlin, USA (Toyota), 312; **7** Martin Truex Jr., USA (Chevrolet), 312; **8** David Reutimann, USA (Toyota), 312; **9** Sam Hornish Jr., USA (Dodge), 312; **10** Carl Edwards, USA (Ford), 312.
Pole position: Martin, 26.903s, 133.814mph/215.353km/h.
Championship points – Drivers: 1 Gordon (Jeff), 1242; **2** Johnson, 1157; **3** Busch (Kurt), 1144; **4** Stewart, 1138; **5** Hamlin, 1088; **6** Bowyer, 1052.

AARON'S 499, Talladega Superspeedway, Alabama, USA, 26 April. Round 9. 188 laps of the 2.660-mile/4.281km circuit, 500.080 miles/804.801km.
1 Brad Keselowski, USA (Chevrolet), 3h 23m 20s, 147.565mph/237.482km/h; **2** Dale Earnhardt Jr., USA (Chevrolet), 3h 23m 20.175s; **3** Ryan Newman, USA (Chevrolet), 188 laps; **4** Marcos Ambrose, AUS (Toyota), 188; **5** Scott Speed, USA (Toyota), 188; **6** Kurt Busch, USA (Dodge), 188; **7** Greg Biffle, USA (Ford), 188; **8** Brian Vickers, USA (Toyota), 188; **9** Joey Logano, USA (Toyota), 188; **10** Jeff Burton, USA (Chevrolet), 188.
Pole position: Juan Pablo Montoya, CO (Chevrolet), 50.890s, 188.171mph/302.831km/h.
Championship points – Drivers: 1 Busch (Kurt), 1299; **2** Gordon (Jeff), 1294; **3** Johnson, 1235; **4** Stewart, 1232; **5** Hamlin, 1190; **6** Busch (Kyle), 1124.

CROWN ROYAL PRESENTS THE RUSS FRIEDMAN 400, Richmond International Raceway, Virginia, USA, 2 May. Round 10. 400 laps of the 0.750-mile/1.207km circuit, 300.000 miles/482.803km.
1 Kyle Busch, USA (Toyota), 3h 18m 37s, 90.627mph/145.850km/h; **2** Tony Stewart, USA (Chevrolet), 3h 18m 39.751s; **3** Jeff Burton, USA (Chevrolet), 400 laps; **4** Ryan Newman, USA (Chevrolet), 400; **5** Mark Martin, USA (Chevrolet), 400; **6** Sam Hornish Jr., USA (Dodge), 400; **7** Jamie McMurray, USA (Ford), 400; **8** Jeff Gordon, USA (Chevrolet), 400; **9** Casey Mears, USA (Chevrolet), 400; **10** Juan Pablo Montoya, CO (Chevrolet), 400.
Pole position: Brian Vickers, USA (Toyota), 21.238s, 127.131mph/204.597km/h.
Championship points – Drivers: 1 Gordon (Jeff), 1441; **2** Busch (Kurt), 1431; **3** Stewart, 1402; **4** Hamlin, 1321; **5** Busch, 1314; **6** Johnson, 1290

SOUTHERN 500, Darlington Raceway, South Carolina, USA, 9 May. Round 11. 367 laps of the 1.366-mile/2.198km circuit, 501.322 miles/806.800km.
1 Mark Martin, USA (Chevrolet), 4h 11m 19s, 119.687mph/192.617km/h; **2** Jimmie Johnson, USA (Chevrolet), 4h 11m 20.531s; **3** Tony Stewart, USA (Chevrolet), 367 laps; **4** Ryan Newman, USA (Chevrolet), 367; **5** Jeff Gordon, USA (Chevrolet), 367; **6** Martin Truex Jr., USA (Chevrolet), 367; **7** Brad Keselowski, USA (Chevrolet), 367; **8** Greg Biffle, USA (Ford), 367; **9** Joey Logano, USA (Toyota), 367; **10** Matt Kenseth, USA (Ford), 367.
Pole position: Kenseth, 27.394s, 179.514mph/288.899km/h.
Championship points – Drivers: 1 Gordon (Jeff), 1601; **2** Stewart, 1572; **3** Busch (Busch), 1546; **4** Johnson, 1465; **5** Hamlin, 1445; **6** Burton, 1384.

COCA-COLA 600, Lowe's Motor Speedway, Concord, Charlotte, North Carolina, USA, 25 May. Round 12. 227 laps of the 1.500-mile/2.414km circuit, 340.500 miles/547.982km.
Scheduled for 400 laps, but delayed due to rain and stopped early.
1 David Reutimann, USA (Toyota), 2h 48m 59s, 120.899mph/194.568km/h; **2** Ryan Newman, USA (Chevrolet), 227 laps; **3** Robby Gordon, USA (Toyota), 227; **4** Carl Edwards, USA (Ford), 227; **5** Brian Vickers, USA (Toyota), 227; **6** Kyle Busch, USA (Toyota), 227; **7** Kasey Kahne, USA (Dodge), 227; **8** Juan Pablo Montoya, CO (Chevrolet), 227; **9** Joey Logano, USA (Toyota), 227; **10** Matt Kenseth, USA (Ford), 227.
Pole position: Newman, 28.651s, 188.475mph/303.321km/h.
Championship points – Drivers: 1 Gordon (Jeff), 1722; **2** Stewart, 1678; **3** Busch, 1607; **4** Johnson, 1594; **5** Hamlin, 1575; **6** Busch, 1540.

AUTISM SPEAKS 400 PRESENTED BY HELUVA GOOD! SOUR CREAM DIPS AND CHEESE, Dover International Speedway, Delaware, USA, 31 May. Round 13. 400 laps of the 1.000-mile/1.609km circuit, 400.000 miles/643.738km.
1 Jimmie Johnson, USA (Chevrolet), 3h 28m 16s, 115.237mph/185.456km/h; **2** Tony Stewart, USA (Chevrolet), 3h 28m 16.861s; **3** Greg Biffle, USA (Ford), 400 laps; **4** Matt Kenseth, USA (Ford), 400; **5** Kurt Busch, USA (Dodge), 400; **6** Kasey Kahne, USA (Dodge), 400; **7** Carl Edwards, USA (Ford), 400; **8** Ryan Newman, USA (Chevrolet), 400; **9** Casey Mears, USA (Chevrolet), 400; **10** Mark Martin, USA (Chevrolet), 400.
Pole position: David Reutimann, USA (Toyota), 22.960s, 156.794mph/252.336km/h.
Championship points – Drivers: 1 Stewart, 1853; **2** Gordon (Jeff), 1807; **3** Johnson, 1789; **4** Busch (Kurt), 1762; **5** Newman, 1680; **6** Busch (Kyle), 1634.

POCONO 500, Pocono Raceway, Long Pond, Pennsylvania, USA, 7 June. Round 14. 200 laps of the 2.500-mile/4.023km circuit, 500.000 miles/804.672km.
1 Tony Stewart, USA (Chevrolet), 3h 36m 35s, 138.515mph/222.918km/h; **2** Carl Edwards, USA (Ford), 3h 36m 37.004s; **3** David Reutimann, USA (Toyota), 200 laps; **4** Jeff Gordon, USA (Chevrolet), 200; **5** Ryan Newman, USA (Chevrolet), 200; **6** Marcos Ambrose, AUS (Toyota), 200; **7** Jimmie Johnson, USA (Chevrolet), 200; **8** Juan Pablo Montoya, CO (Chevrolet), 200; **9** Jeff Burton, USA (Chevrolet), 200; **10** Sam Hornish Jr., USA (Dodge), 200.
Pole position: Stewart (qualifying rained out).
Championship points – Drivers: 1 Stewart, 2043; **2** Gordon, 1972; **3** Johnson, 1940; **4** Newman, 1840; **5** Busch, 1819; **6** Edwards, 1762.

LIFELOCK 400, Michigan International Speedway, Brooklyn, Michigan, USA, 14 June. Round 15. 200 laps of the 2.000-mile/3.219km circuit, 400.000 miles/643.738km.
1 Mark Martin, USA (Chevrolet), 2h 34m 21s, 155.491mph/250.238km/h; **2** Jeff Gordon, USA (Chevrolet), 2h 34m 23.992s; **3** Denny Hamlin, USA (Toyota), 200 laps; **4** Carl Edwards, USA (Ford), 200; **5** Greg Biffle, USA (Ford), 200; **6** Juan Pablo Montoya, CO (Chevrolet), 200; **7** Tony Stewart, USA (Chevrolet), 200; **8** Kurt Busch, USA (Dodge), 200; **9** Brian Vickers, USA (Toyota), 200; **10** Clint Bowyer, USA (Chevrolet), 200.
Pole position: Vickers, 38.073s, 189.110mph/304.344km/h.
Championship points – Drivers: 1 Stewart, 2189; **2** Gordon, 2142; **3** Johnson, 2047; **4** Busch, 1961; **5** Newman, 1934; **6** Edwards, 1927.

TOYOTA/SAVE MART 350, Infineon Raceway, Sears Point, Sonoma, California, USA, 21 June. Round 16. 113 laps of the 1.990-mile/3.203km circuit, 224.870 miles/361.893km.
1 Kasey Kahne, USA (Dodge), 3h 10m 00s, 71.012mph/114.282km/h; **2** Tony Stewart, USA (Chevrolet), 3h 10m 00.748s; **3** Marcos Ambrose, AUS (Toyota), 113 laps; **4** Jimmie Johnson, USA (Chevrolet), 113; **5** Denny Hamlin, USA (Toyota), 113; **6** Juan Pablo Montoya, CO (Chevrolet), 113; **7** A.J. Allmendinger, USA (Dodge), 113; **8** Clint Bowyer, USA (Chevrolet), 113; **9** Jeff Gordon, USA (Chevrolet), 113; **10** Elliott Sadler, USA (Dodge), 113.
Pole position: Brian Vickers, USA (Toyota), 1m 16.475s, 93.678mph/150.760km/h.
Championship points – Drivers: 1 Stewart, 2364; **2** Gordon, 2280; **3** Johnson, 2207; **4** Busch, 2084; **5** Edwards, 2051; **6** Newman, 2046.

LENOX INDUSTRIAL TOOLS 301, New Hampshire International Speedway, Loudon, New Hampshire, USA, 28 June. Round 17. 273 laps of the 1.058-mile/1.703km circuit, 288.834 miles/464.833km.
1 Joey Logano, USA (Toyota), 2h 57m 45s, 97.497mph/156.906km/h; **2** Jeff Gordon, USA (Chevrolet), 273 laps; **3** Kurt Busch, USA (Dodge), 273; **4** David Reutimann, USA (Toyota), 273; **5** Tony Stewart, USA (Chevrolet), 273; **6** Brad Keselowski, USA (Chevrolet), 273; **7** Kyle Busch, USA (Toyota), 273; **8** Sam Hornish Jr., USA (Dodge), 273; **9** Jimmie Johnson, USA (Chevrolet), 273; **10** Kasey Kahne, USA (Dodge), 273.
Pole position: Stewart (no qualifying).
Championship points – Drivers: 1 Stewart, 2524; **2** Gordon, 2455; **3** Johnson, 2355; **4** Busch, 2254; **5** Edwards, 2157; **6** Hamlin, 2132.

COKE ZERO 400 POWERED BY COCA-COLA, Daytona International Speedway, Daytona Beach, Florida, USA, 4 July. Round 18. 160 laps of the 2.500-mile/4.023km circuit, 400.000 miles/643.738km.
1 Tony Stewart, USA (Chevrolet), 2h 48m 28s, 142.461mph/229.269km/h; **2** Jimmie Johnson, USA (Chevrolet), 2h 48m 28.110s; **3** Denny Hamlin, USA (Toyota), 160 laps; **4** Carl Edwards, USA (Ford), 160; **5** Kurt Busch, USA (Dodge), 160; **6** Marcos Ambrose, AUS (Toyota), 160; **7** Brian Vickers, USA (Toyota), 160; **8** Matt Kenseth, USA (Ford), 160; **9** Juan Pablo Montoya, CO (Chevrolet), 160; **10** Elliott Sadler, USA (Dodge), 160.
Pole position: Stewart (no qualifying).
Championship points – Drivers: 1 Stewart, 2719; **2** Gordon, 2539; **3** Johnson, 2525; **4** Busch, 2414; **5** Edwards, 2317; **6** Hamlin, 2302.

LIFELOCK.COM 400, Chicagoland Speedway, Chicago, Illinois, USA, 11 July. Round 19. 267 laps of the 1.500-mile/2.414km circuit, 400.500 miles/644.542km.
1 Mark Martin, USA (Chevrolet), 2h 59m 39s, 133.760mph/215.266km/h; **2** Jeff Gordon, USA (Chevrolet), 2h 59m 39.415s; **3** Kasey Kahne, USA (Dodge), 267 laps; **4** Tony Stewart, USA (Chevrolet), 267; **5** Denny Hamlin, USA (Toyota), 267; **6** Ryan Newman, USA (Chevrolet), 267; **7** Brian Vickers, USA (Toyota), 267; **8** Jimmie Johnson, USA (Chevrolet), 267; **9** Clint Bowyer, USA (Chevrolet), 267; **10** Juan Pablo Montoya, CO (Chevrolet), 267.
Pole position: Vickers, 29.322s, 184.162mph/296.380km/h.
Championship points – Drivers: 1 Stewart, 2884; **2** Gordon, 2709; **3** Johnson, 2672; **4** Busch, 2526; **5** Hamlin, 2457; **6** Edwards, 2438.

ALLSTATE 400 AT THE BRICKYARD, Indianapolis Motor Speedway, Speedway, Indiana, USA, 26 July. Round 20. 160 laps of the 2.500-mile/4.023km circuit, 400.000 miles/643.738km.
1 Jimmie Johnson, USA (Chevrolet), 2h 44m 31s, 145.882mph/234.774km/h; **2** Mark Martin, USA (Chevrolet), 2h 44m 31.400s; **3** Tony Stewart, USA (Chevrolet), 160 laps; **4** Greg Biffle, USA (Ford), 160; **5** Brian Vickers, USA (Toyota), 160; **6** Kevin Harvick, USA (Chevrolet), 160; **7** Kasey Kahne, USA (Dodge), 160; **8** David Reutimann, USA (Toyota), 160; **9** Jeff Gordon, USA (Chevrolet), 160; **10** Matt Kenseth, USA (Ford), 160.
Pole position: Martin, 49.436s, 182.054mph/292.987km/h.
Championship points – Drivers: 1 Stewart, 3054; **2** Johnson, 2862; **3** Gordon, 2847; **4** Busch, 2608; **5** Edwards, 2556; **6** Hamlin, 2518.

SUNOCO RED CROSS PENNSYLVANIA 500, Pocono Raceway, Long Pond, Pennsylvania, USA, 3 August. Round 21. 200 laps of the 2.500-mile/4.023km circuit, 500.000 miles/804.672km.
1 Denny Hamlin, USA (Toyota), 3h 57m 21s, 126.396mph/203.414km/h; **2** Juan Pablo Montoya, CO (Chevrolet), 3h 57m 21.869s; **3** Clint Bowyer, USA (Chevrolet), 200 laps; **4** Sam Hornish Jr., USA (Dodge), 200; **5** Kasey Kahne, USA (Dodge), 200; **6** Brian Vickers, USA (Toyota), 200; **7** Mark Martin, USA (Chevrolet), 200; **8** Jeff Gordon, USA (Chevrolet), 200; **9** Kurt Busch, USA (Dodge), 200;
Pole position: Tony Stewart, USA (Chevrolet) (no qualifying).
Championship points – Drivers: 1 Stewart, 3188; **2** Johnson, 2991; **3** Gordon, 2989; **4** Busch, 2751; **5** Hamlin, 2713; **6** Edwards, 2665.

HELUVA GOOD! SOUR CREAM DIPS AT THE GLEN, Watkins Glen International, New York, USA, 10 August. Round 22. 90 laps of the 2.450-mile/3.943km circuit, 220.500 miles/354.860km.
1 Tony Stewart, USA (Chevrolet), 2h 26m 31s, 90.297mph/145.319km/h; **2** Marcos Ambrose, AUS (Toyota), 2h 26m 33.969s; **3** Carl Edwards, USA (Ford), 90 laps; **4** Kyle Busch, USA (Toyota), 90; **5** Greg Biffle, USA (Ford), 90; **6** Juan Pablo Montoya, CO (Chevrolet), 90; **7** Kurt Busch, USA (Dodge), 90; **8** Massimiliano Papis, I (Toyota), 90; **9** Clint Bowyer, USA (Chevrolet), 90; **10** Denny Hamlin, USA (Toyota), 90.
Pole position: Jimmie Johnson, USA (Chevrolet), 1m 11.340s, 123.633mph/198.969km/h.
Championship points – Drivers: 1 Stewart, 3383; **2** Johnson, 3123; **3** Gordon, 3041; **4** Busch, 2902; **5** Hamlin, 2847; **6** Edwards, 2830.

CARFAX 400, Michigan International Speedway, Brooklyn, Michigan, USA, 16 August. Round 23. 200 laps of the 2.000-mile/3.219km circuit, 400.000 miles/643.738km.
1 Brian Vickers, USA (Toyota), 3h 02m 28s, 131.531mph/211.678km/h; **2** Jeff Gordon, USA (Chevrolet), 3h 02m 29.409s; **3** Dale Earnhardt Jr., USA (Chevrolet), 200 laps; **4** Carl Edwards, USA (Ford), 200; **5** Sam Hornish Jr., USA (Dodge), 200; **6** Casey Mears, USA (Chevrolet), 200; **7** Joey Logano, USA (Toyota), 200; **8** Clint Bowyer, USA (Chevrolet), 200; **9** David Reutimann, USA (Toyota), 200; **10** Denny Hamlin, USA (Toyota), 200.
Pole position: Vickers, 38.453s, 187.242mph/301.336km/h.
Championship points – Drivers: 1 Stewart, 3500; **2** Gordon, 3216; **3** Johnson, 3197; **4** Edwards, 2995; **5** Hamlin, 2986; **6** Busch, 2957.

SHARPIE 500, Bristol Motor Speedway, Tennessee, USA, 22 August. Round 24. 500 laps of the 0.533-mile/0.858km circuit, 266.500 miles/428.890km.
1 Kyle Busch, USA (Toyota), 3h 08m 31s, 84.820mph/136.505km/h; **2** Mark Martin, USA (Chevrolet), 3h 08m 31.098s; **3** Marcos Ambrose, AUS (Toyota), 500 laps; **4** Greg Biffle, USA (Ford), 500; **5** Denny Hamlin, USA (Toyota), 500; **6** Ryan Newman, USA (Chevrolet), 500; **7** Kurt Busch, USA (Dodge), 500; **8** Jimmie Johnson, USA (Chevrolet), 500; **9** Dale Earnhardt Jr., USA (Chevrolet), 500; **10** Matt Kenseth, USA (Ford), 500.
Pole position: Martin, 15.414s, 124.484mph/200.338km/h.
Championship points – Drivers: 1 Stewart, 3564; **2** Johnson, 3344; **3** Gordon, 3310; **4** Hamlin, 3141; **5** Edwards, 3110; **6** Busch, 3103.

PEP BOYS AUTO 500, Atlanta Motor Speedway, Hampton, Georgia, USA, 6 September. Round 25. 325 laps of the 1.540-mile/2.478km circuit, 500.500 miles/805.476km.
1 Kasey Kahne, USA (Dodge), 3h 44m 03s, 134.033mph/215.705km/h; **2** Kevin Harvick, USA (Chevrolet), 3h 44m 04.766s; **3** Juan Pablo Montoya, CO (Chevrolet), 325 laps; **4** David Reutimann, USA (Toyota), 325; **5** Mark Martin, USA (Chevrolet), 325; **6** Denny Hamlin, USA (Toyota), 325; **7** Brian Vickers, USA (Toyota), 325; **8** Jeff Gordon, USA (Chevrolet), 325; **9** Ryan Newman, USA (Chevrolet), 325; **10** Greg Biffle, USA (Ford), 325.
Pole position: Martin Truex Jr., USA (Chevrolet), 30.106s, 184.149mph/296.360km/h.
Championship points – Drivers: 1 Stewart, 3694; **2** Gordon, 3457; **3** Johnson, 3404; **4** Hamlin, 3296; **5** Edwards, 3162; **6** Kahne, 3153.

CHEVY ROCK & ROLL 400, Richmond International Raceway, Virginia, USA, 12 September. Round 26. 400 laps of the 0.750-mile/1.207km circuit, 300.000 miles/482.803km.
1 Denny Hamlin, USA (Toyota), 3h 06m 20s, 96.601mph/155.464km/h; **2** Kurt Busch, USA (Dodge), 3h 06m 20.378s; **3** Jeff Gordon, USA (Chevrolet), 400 laps; **4** Mark Martin, USA (Chevrolet), 400; **5** Kyle Busch, USA (Toyota), 400; **6** Clint Bowyer, USA (Chevrolet), 400; **7** Brian Vickers, USA (Toyota), 400; **8** Sam Hornish Jr., USA (Dodge), 400; **9** Kevin Harvick, USA (Chevrolet), 400; **10** Ryan Newman, USA (Chevrolet), 400.
Pole position: Martin, 21.292s, 126.808mph/204.078km/h.
Championship points – Drivers: 1 Martin, 5040; **2** Stewart, 5030; **3** Johnson, 5030; **4** Hamlin, 5020; **5** Kahne, 5020; **6** Gordon, 5010.

SYLVANIA 300, New Hampshire International Speedway, Loudon, New Hampshire, USA, 20 September. Round 27. 300 laps of the 1.058-mile/1.703km circuit, 317.400 miles/510.806km.
1 Mark Martin, USA (Chevrolet), 3h 09m 01s, 100.753mph/162.146km/h; **2** Denny Hamlin, USA (Toyota), 300 laps; **3** Juan Pablo Montoya, CO (Chevrolet), 300; **4** Jimmie Johnson, USA (Chevrolet), 300; **5** Kyle Busch, USA (Toyota), 300; **6** Kurt Busch, USA (Dodge), 300; **7** Ryan Newman, USA (Chevrolet), 300; **8** Elliott Sadler, USA (Dodge), 300; **9** Greg Biffle, USA (Ford), 300; **10** Clint Bowyer, USA (Chevrolet), 300.
Pole position: Montoya, 28.545s, 133.431mph/214.737km/h.
Championship points – Drivers: 1 Martin, 5230; **2** Johnson, 5195; **3** Hamlin, 5195; **4** Montoya, 5175; **5** Busch, 5165; **6** Stewart, 5156.

AAA 400, Dover International Speedway, Delaware, USA, 27 September. Round 28. 400 laps of the 1.000-mile/1.609km circuit, 400.000 miles/643.738km.
1 Jimmie Johnson, USA (Chevrolet), 3h 22m 11s, 118.704mph/191.036km/h; **2** Mark Martin, USA (Chevrolet), 3h 22m 12.970s; **3** Matt Kenseth, USA (Ford), 400 laps; **4** Juan Pablo Montoya, CO (Chevrolet), 400; **5** Kurt Busch, USA (Dodge), 400; **6** Jeff Gordon, USA (Chevrolet), 400; **7** A.J. Allmendinger, USA (Dodge), 400; **8** Kasey Kahne, USA (Dodge), 400; **9** Tony Stewart, USA (Chevrolet), 400; **10** Ryan Newman, USA (Chevrolet), 400.
Pole position: Johnson, 22.878s, 157.356mph/253.241km/h.
Championship points – Drivers: 1 Martin, 5400; **2** Johnson, 5390; **3** Montoya, 5335; **4** Busch, 5325; **5** Stewart, 5294; **6** Hamlin, 5292.

PRICE CHOPPER 400 PRESENTED BY KRAFT, Kansas Speedway, Kansas City, Kansas, USA, 4 October. Round 29. 267 laps of the 1.500-mile/2.414km circuit, 400.500 miles/644.542km.
1 Tony Stewart, USA (Chevrolet), 2h 55m 13s, 137.144mph/220.713km/h; **2** Jeff Gordon, USA (Chevrolet), 2h 55m 13.894s; **3** Greg Biffle, USA (Ford), 267 laps; **4** Juan Pablo Montoya, CO (Chevrolet), 267; **5** Denny Hamlin, USA (Toyota), 267; **6** Kasey Kahne, USA (Dodge), 267; **7** Mark Martin, USA (Chevrolet), 267; **8** David Reutimann, USA (Toyota), 267; **9** Jimmie Johnson, USA (Chevrolet), 267; **10** Carl Edwards, USA (Ford), 267.
Pole position: Martin, 30.724s, 175.758mph/282.856km/h.
Championship points – Drivers: 1 Martin, 5551; **2** Johnson, 5533; **3** Montoya, 5500; **4** Stewart, 5484; **5** Busch, 5460; **6** Hamlin, 5452.

PEPSI 500, California Speedway, Fontana, California, USA, 11 October. Round 30. 250 laps of the 2.000-mile/3.219km circuit, 500.000 miles/804.672km.
1 Jimmie Johnson, USA (Chevrolet), 3h 28m 28s, 143.908mph/231.597km/h; **2** Jeff Gordon, USA (Chevrolet), 3h 28m 29.603s; **3** Juan Pablo Montoya, CO (Chevrolet), 250 laps; **4** Mark Martin, USA (Chevrolet), 250; **5** Tony Stewart, USA (Chevrolet), 250; **6** Carl Edwards, USA (Ford), 250; **7** David Ragan, USA (Ford), 250; **8** Kurt Busch, USA (Dodge), 250; **9** Clint Bowyer, USA (Chevrolet), 250; **10** Kevin Harvick, USA (Chevrolet), 250.
Pole position: Denny Hamlin, USA (Toyota), 39.158s, 183.870mph/295.911km/h.
Championship points – Drivers: 1 Johnson, 5728; **2** Martin, 5716; **3** Montoya, 5670; **4** Stewart, 5644; **5** Gordon, 5623; **6** Busch, 5607.

BANKING 500 ONLY FROM BANK OF AMERICA, Lowe's Motor Speedway, Concord, Charlotte, North Carolina, USA, 17 October. Round 31. 334 laps of the 1.500-mile/2.414km circuit, 501.000 miles/806.281km.
1 Jimmie Johnson, USA (Chevrolet), 3h 38m 22s, 137.658mph/221.540km/h; **2** Matt Kenseth, USA (Ford), 3h 38m 24.303s; **3** Kasey Kahne, USA (Dodge), 334 laps; **4** Jeff Gordon, USA (Chevrolet), 334; **5** Joey Logano, USA (Toyota), 334; **6** Clint Bowyer, USA (Chevrolet), 334; **7** Casey Mears, USA (Chevrolet), 334; **8** Kyle Busch, USA (Toyota), 334; **9** Martin Truex Jr., USA (Chevrolet), 334; **10** Kurt Busch, USA (Dodge), 334.
Pole position: Johnson, 28.070s, 192.376mph/309.599km/h.
Championship points – Drivers: 1 Johnson, 5923; **2** Martin, 5833; **3** Gordon, 5788; **4** Stewart, 5768; **5** Busch, 5746; **6** Montoya, 5728.

TUMS FAST RELIEF 500, Martinsville Speedway, Virginia, USA, 25 October. Round 32. 501 laps of the 0.526-mile/0.847km circuit, 263.526 miles/424.104km.
1 Denny Hamlin, USA (Toyota), 3h 34m 44s, 73.633mph/118.502km/h; **2** Jimmie Johnson, USA (Chevrolet), 501 laps; **3** Juan Pablo Montoya, CO (Chevrolet), 501; **4** Kyle Busch, USA (Toyota), 501; **5** Jeff Gordon, USA (Chevrolet), 501; **6** Jamie McMurray, USA (Ford), 501; **7** Ryan Newman, USA (Chevrolet), 501; **8** Mark Martin, USA (Chevrolet), 501; **9** Tony Stewart, USA (Chevrolet), 501; **10** Kasey Kahne, USA (Chevrolet), 501.
Pole position: Newman, 19.563s, 96.795mph/155.776km/h.
Championship points – Drivers: 1 Johnson, 6098; **2** Martin, 5980; **3** Gordon, 5948; **4** Stewart, 5906; **5** Montoya, 5898; **6** Busch, 5858.

AMP ENERGY 500, Talladega Superspeedway, Alabama, USA, 1 November. Round 33. 191 laps of the 2.660-mile/4.281km circuit, 508.060 miles/817.643km.
1 Jamie McMurray, USA (Ford), 3h 13m 54s, 157.213mph/253.010km/h; **2** Kasey Kahne, USA (Dodge), 191 laps; **3** Joey Logano, USA (Toyota), 191; **4** Greg Biffle, USA (Ford), 191; **5** Jeff Burton, USA (Chevrolet), 191; **6** Jimmie Johnson, USA (Chevrolet), 191; **7** Michael Waltrip, USA (Toyota), 191; **8** Brad Keselowski, USA (Chevrolet), 191; **9** Elliott Sadler, USA (Ford), 191; **10** Bobby Labonte, USA (Chevrolet), 191.
Pole position: Johnson.
Championship points – Drivers: 1 Johnson, 6248; **2** Martin, 6064; **3** Gordon, 6056; **4** Montoya, 6009; **5** Stewart, 5969; **6** Busch, 5936.

DICKIES 500, Texas Motor Speedway, Fort Worth, Texas, USA, 8 November. Round 34. 334 laps of the 1.500-mile/2.414km circuit, 501.000 miles/806.281km.
1 Kurt Busch, USA (Dodge), 3h 24m 18s, 147.137mph/236.793km/h; **2** Denny Hamlin, USA (Toyota), 3h 24m 43.686s; **3** Matt Kenseth, USA (Ford), 334 laps; **4** Mark Martin, USA (Chevrolet), 334; **5** Kevin Harvick, USA (Chevrolet), 334; **6** Tony Stewart, USA (Chevrolet), 334; **7** Clint Bowyer, USA (Chevrolet), 333; **8** Greg Biffle, USA (Ford), 333; **9** Jeff Burton, USA (Chevrolet), 333; **10** A.J. Allmendinger, USA (Ford), 333.
Pole position: Gordon, 28.255s, 191.117mph/307.572km/h.
Championship points – Drivers: 1 Johnson, 6297; **2** Martin, 6224; **3** Gordon, 6185; **4** Busch, 6126; **5** Stewart, 6119; **6** Montoya, 6061.

XXXXCHECKER O'REILLY AUTO PARTS 500, Phoenix International Raceway, Arizona, USA, 15 November. Round 35. 313 laps of the 1.000-mile/1.609km circuit, 313.000 miles/503.617km.
1 Jamie McMurray, USA (Ford), 3h 13m 54s, 157.213mph/253.010km/h; **2** Kasey Kahne, USA (Dodge), 191 laps; **3** Joey Logano, USA (Toyota), 191; **4** Greg Biffle, USA (Ford), 191; **5** Jeff Burton, USA (Chevrolet), 191; **6** Jimmie Johnson, USA (Chevrolet), 191; **7** Michael Waltrip, USA (Toyota), 191; **8** Brad Keselowski, USA (Chevrolet), 191; **9** Elliott Sadler, USA (Ford), 191; **10** Bobby Labonte, USA (Chevrolet), 191.
Pole position: Johnson.

Provisional championship points
Drivers
1 Jimmie Johnson, USA, 6248; **2** Mark Martin, USA, 6064; **3** Jeff Gordon, USA, 6056; **4** Juan Pablo Montoya, CO, 6009; **5** Tony Stewart, USA, 5969; **6** Kurt Busch, USA, 5936; **7** Greg Biffle, USA, 5908; **8** Ryan Newman, USA, 5846; **9** Kasey Kahne, USA, 5834; **10** Carl Edwards, USA, 5811; **11** Denny Hamlin, USA, 5800; **12** Brian Vickers, USA, 5697.

Not involved in 'Chase for the Nextel Cup'
13 Kyle Busch, USA, 4043; **14** Matt Kenseth, USA, 3986; **15** Clint Bowyer, USA, 3932; **16** David Reutimann, USA, 3854; **17** Jeff Burton, USA, 3539; **18** Marcos Ambrose, AUS, 3519; **19** Joey Logano, USA, 3494; **20** Casey Mears, USA, 3471; **21** Kevin Harvick, USA, 3380; **22** Jamie McMurray, USA, 3286; **23** Dale Earnhardt Jr., USA, 3197; **24** Martin Truex Jr., USA, 3139; **25** Elliott Sadler, USA, 3134; **26** A.J. Allmendinger, USA, 3084; **27** David Ragan, USA, 2985; **28** Reed Sorenson, USA, 2964; **29** Sam Hornish Jr., USA, 2948; **30** Bobby Labonte, USA, 2942.

Raybestos Rookie of the Year: Joey Logano, USA.
Coors Light Pole Award winner: Mark Martin, USA.

Manufacturers
1 Chevrolet, 247; **2** Toyota, 186; **3** Ford, 154; **4** Dodge, 139.

Result of the Homestead race will be given in AUTOCOURSE 2010–2011.

Other NASCAR Races

BUDWEISER SHOOTOUT, Daytona International Speedway, Daytona Beach, Florida, USA, 7 February. 78 laps of the 2.500-mile/4.023km circuit, 195.000 miles/313.822km.
1 Kevin Harvick, USA (Chevrolet), 1h 31m 57s, 127.243mph/204.778km/h; **2** Jamie McMurray, USA (Ford), 78 laps; **3** Tony Stewart, USA (Chevrolet), 78; **4** Jeff Gordon, USA (Chevrolet), 78; **5** AJ Allmendinger, USA (Dodge), 78; **6** Kasey Kahne, USA (Dodge), 78; **7** Carl Edwards, USA (Ford), 78; **8** Matt Kenseth, USA (Ford), 78; **9** Kurt Busch, USA (Dodge), 78; **10** Kyle Busch, USA (Toyota), 78.
Pole position: Paul Menard, USA (Ford).

SPRINT ALL-STAR RACE, Lowe's Motor Speedway, Concord, Charlotte, North Carolina, USA, 16 May. 100 laps of the 1.500-mile/2.414km circuit, 150.000 miles/241.402km.
1 Tony Stewart, USA (Chevrolet), 100 laps; **2** Matt Kenseth, USA (Ford), 100; **3** Kurt Busch, USA (Dodge), 100; **4** Denny Hamlin, USA (Toyota), 100; **5** Carl Edwards, USA (Ford), 100;

6 Mark Martin, USA (Chevrolet), 100; **7** Kyle Busch, USA (Toyota), 100; **8** Joey Logano, USA (Toyota), 100; **9** Jamie McMurray, USA (Ford), 100; **10** Dale Earnhardt Jr., USA (Chevrolet).
Pole position: Jimmie Johnson, USA (Chevrolet), 44.475s, 121.416mph/195.401km/h.

Firestone Indy Lights

All cars are Dallara IPS-Infiniti.

ST. PETE 100, St. Petersburg Street Circuit, Florida, USA, 4/5 April. Round 1. 2 x 40 laps of the 1.800-mile/2.897km circuit.
Race 1 (72.000 miles/115.873km).
1 Junior Strous, NL, 50m 06.5703s, 86.211mph/138.743km/h; **2** Jonathan Summerton, USA, 50m 07.2908s; **3** J.R. Hildebrand, USA, 50m 08.7274s; **4** Ana Beatriz, BR, 50m 09.3071s; **5** Jay Howard, GB, 50m 16.7228s; **6** James Hinchcliffe, CDN, 50m 16.9609s; **7** Daniel Herrington, USA, 50m 20.6065s; **8** James Davison, AUS, 50m 23.0606s; **9** Mario Romancini, BR, 50m 24.5612s; **10** Charlie Kimball, USA, 50m 24.8717s.
Fastest race lap: Hildebrand, 1m 07.7315s, 95.672mph/153.969km/h.
Pole position: Hildebrand, 1m 07.7704s, 95.617mph/153.881km/h.

Race 2 (72.000 miles/115.873km).
1 Junior Strous, NL, 58m 51.1100s, 73.405mph/118.133km/h; **2** Sebastian Saavedra, CO, 58m 51.5528s; **3** James Hinchcliffe, CDN, 58m 52.9216s; **4** Jonathan Summerton, USA, 58m 53.6669s; **5** Daniel Herrington, USA, 58m 54.3094s; **6** Mario Romancini, BR, 58m 56.6815s; **7** Charlie Kimball, USA, 58m 57.2130s; **8** Jay Howard, GB, 58m 58.8389s; **9** Gustavo Yacaman, CO, 58m 59.5135s; **10** Richard Philippe, F, 58m 59.8113s.
Fastest race lap: Saavedra, 1m 07.2141s, 96.408mph/155.154km/h.
Pole position: Saavedra, 1m 07.2171s, 96.404mph/155.147km/h.

LONG BEACH 100, Long Beach Street Circuit, California, USA, 19 April. Round 2. 45 laps of the 1.968-mile/3.167km circuit, 88.560 miles/142.524km.
1 J.R. Hildebrand, USA, 1h 03m 01.5734s, 84.308mph/135.680km/h; **2** Richard Philippe, F, 1h 03m 03.4049s; **3** James Hinchcliffe, CDN, 1h 03m 04.2441s; **4** Jonathan Summerton, USA, 1h 03m 19.9166s; **5** Ana Beatriz, BR, 1h 03m 26.0418s; **6** Alistair Jackson, GB, 1h 03m 29.6887s; **7** James Davison, AUS, 1h 03m 30.3749s; **8** Sebastian Saavedra, CO, 1h 03m 30.7458s; **9** Gustavo Yacaman, CO, 1h 03m 34.2785s; **10** Daniel Herrington, USA, 1h 03m 34.7116s.
Fastest race lap: Hildebrand, 1m 16.0853s, 93.117mph/149.857km/h.
Pole position: Hildebrand, 1m 15.2695s, 94.126mph/151.481km/h.

KANSAS LOTTERY 100, Kansas Speedway, Kansas City, Kansas, USA, 26 April. Round 3. 67 laps of the 1.520-mile/2.446km circuit, 101.840 miles/163.896km.
1 Sebastian Saavedra, CO, 1h 02m 53.5296s, 97.157mph/156.359km/h; **2** Wade Cunningham, NZ, 1h 02m 53.7853s; **3** Mario Romancini, BR, 1h 02m 54.3838s; **4** Ana Beatriz, BR, 1h 02m 54.6750s; **5** Martin Plowman, GB, 1h 02m 55.6251s; **6** Daniel Herrington, USA, 1h 02m 56.1948s; **7** Jonathan Summerton, USA, 1h 02m 57.9189s; **8** James Davison, AUS, 1h 02m 58.7235s; **9** Andrew Prendeville, USA, 1h 03m 00.9582s; **10** Jay Howard, GB, 1h 03m 03.5664s.
Fastest race lap: Charlie Kimball, USA, 29.2836s, 186.862mph/300.726km/h.
Pole position: Cunningham, 58.3812s, 187.458mph/301.684km/h (over **2** laps).

FIRESTONE FREEDOM 100, Indianapolis Motor Speedway, Speedway, Indiana, USA, 22 May. Round 4. 40 laps of the 2.500-mile/4.023km circuit, 100.000 miles/160.934km.
1 Wade Cunningham, NZ, 50m 42.2548s, 118.333mph/190.439km/h; **2** J.R. Hildebrand, USA, 50m 42.3594s; **3** Mario Romancini, BR, 50m 42.5369s; **4** Jay Howard, GB, 50m 44.1632s; **5** Sebastian Saavedra, CO, 50m 45.6741s; **6** James Davison, AUS, 50m 46.3376s; **7** Daniel Herrington, USA, 50m 46.9510s; **8** Jesse Mason, CDN, 50m 53.1448s; **9** Pablo Donoso, RCH, 50m 54.6071s; **10** Junior Strous, NL, 50m 54.6494s.
Fastest race lap: Hildebrand, 47.1775s, 190.769mph/307.013km/h.
Pole position: Cunningham, 1m 34.6485s, 190.177mph/306.061km/h (over **2** laps).

HUSAR'S HOUSE OF FINE DIAMONDS 100, The Milwaukee Mile, Wisconsin State Fair Park, West Allis, Wisconsin, USA, 31 May. Round 5. 100 laps of the 1.015-mile/1.633km circuit, 101.500 miles/163.348km.
1 Mario Romancini, BR, 53m 26.8054s, 113.945mph/183.377km/h; **2** J.R. Hildebrand, USA, 53m 27.8961s; **3** Sebastian Saavedra, CO, 53m 30.8102s; **4** Gustavo Yacaman, CO, 53m 31.9863s; **5** James Davison, AUS, 53m 33.2337s; **6** Wade Cunningham, NZ, 53m 34.0666s; **7** James Hinchcliffe, CDN, 53m 37.5517s; **8** Andrew Prendeville, USA, 53m 37.7479s; **9** Pippa Mann, GB, 98 laps; **10** Charlie Kimball, USA, 97.
Fastest race lap: Romancini, 25.3397s, 144.201mph/232.068km/h.
Pole position: Romancini, 49.4453s, 147.800mph/237.861km/h (over **2** laps).

MILLER LITE 100, Iowa Speedway, Newton, Iowa, USA, 20 June. Round 6. 115 laps of the 0.894-mile/1.439km circuit, 102.810 miles/165.457km.
1 Ana Beatriz, BR, 48m 05.1062s, 128.285mph/206.455km/h; **2** Wade Cunningham, NZ, 48m 11.9016s; **3** James Hinchcliffe, CDN, 48m 12.0051s; **4** Mario Romancini, BR, 48m 13.7682s; **5** Gustavo Yacaman, CO, 48m 37.9486s; **6** J.R. Hildebrand, USA, 48m 43.1036s; **7** Charlie Kimball, USA, 48m 46.3398s; **8** Martin Plowman, GB, 114 laps; **9** Daniel Herrington, USA, 114; **10** James Davison, AUS, 114.
Fastest race lap: Sebastian Saavedra, CO, 20.0883s, 160.213mph/257.837km/h.
Pole position: Hildebrand, 39.9348s, 161.183mph/259.398km/h (over **2** laps).

CORNING 100, Watkins Glen International, New York, USA, 4 July. Round 7. 30 laps of the 3.370-mile/5.423km circuit, 101.100 miles/162.705km.
1 J.R. Hildebrand, USA, 57m 52.6759s, 104.807mph/168.670km/h; **2** James Davison, AUS, 57m 53.2258s; **3** Felipe Guimarães, BR, 57m 53.9048s; **4** Charlie Kimball, USA, 57m 55.5394s; **5** Richard Philippe, F, 57m 56.1385s; **6** Daniel Herrington, USA, 57m 56.4554s; **7** Gustavo Yacaman, CO, 57m 56.7986s; **8** Pablo Donoso, RCH, 57m 57.9577s; **9** Ana Beatriz, BR, 57m 58.0757s; **10** Martin Plowman, GB, 57m 58.8545s.
Fastest race lap: Saavedra, 1m 37.6704s, 124.214mph/199.903km/h.
Pole position: Davison, 1m 37.1780s, 124.843mph/200.915km/h.

GRAND PRIX OF TORONTO, Toronto Street Circuit, Ontario, Canada, 11 July. Round 8. 50 laps of the 1.755-mile/2.824km circuit, 87.750 miles/141.220km.
1 Sebastian Saavedra, CO, 58m 06.7934s, 90.599mph/145.805km/h; **2** J.R. Hildebrand, USA, 58m 12.6564s; **3** James Hinchcliffe, CDN, 58m 28.0902s; **4** Stefan Wilson, GB, 58m 43.9862s; **5** James Davison, AUS, 58m 49.6773s; **6** Mario Romancini, BR, 59m 01.7104s; **7** Wade Cunningham, NZ, 59m 03.9539s; **8** Gustavo Yacaman, CO, 49 laps; **9** Daniel Herrington, USA, 49; **10** Andrew Prendeville, USA, 49.
Fastest race lap: Davison, 1m 05.8907s, 95.886mph/154.314km/h.
Pole position: Saavedra, 1m 04.6068s, 97.792mph/157.380km/h.

GRAND PRIX OF EDMONTON, Rexall Speedway, Edmonton City Centre Airport, Alberta, Canada, 25 July. Round 9. 50 laps of the 1.973-mile/3.175km circuit, 98.650 miles/158.762km.
1 J.R. Hildebrand, USA, 56m 48.5498s, 104.191mph/167.679km/h; **2** Richard Philippe, F, 57m 02.5652s; **3** Sebastian Saavedra, CO, 57m 09.6142s; **4** James Hinchcliffe, CDN, 57m 11.4413s; **5** Charlie Kimball, USA, 57m 32.7467s; **6** Wade Cunningham, NZ, 57m 59.7947s; **7** Andrew Prendeville, USA, 49 laps; **8** Mario Romancini, BR, 49; **9** Daniel Herrington, USA, 49; **10** James Davison, AUS, 49.
Fastest race lap: Hildebrand, 1m 07.4732s, 105.268mph/169.413km/h.
Pole position: Hildebrand, 1m 05.9065s, 107.771mph/173.440km/h.

KENTUCKY 100, Kentucky Speedway, Fort Mitchell, Kentucky, USA, 1 August. Round 10. 67 laps of the 1.480-mile/2.382km circuit, 99.160 miles/159.583km.
1 Wade Cunningham, NZ, 36m 42.1492s, 162.103mph/260.880km/h; **2** Sebastian Saavedra, CO, 36m 42.2719s; **3** Ana Beatriz, BR, 36m 42.3330s; **4** James Davison, AUS, 36m 42.6696s; **5** Andrew Prendeville, USA, 36m 43.1856s; **6** Daniel Herrington, USA, 36m 44.3613s; **7** James Hinchcliffe, CDN, 36m 45.1618s; **8** Mike Potekhen, USA, 36m 45.4985s; **9** Martin Plowman, GB, 36m 46.8318s; **10** Mario Romancini, BR, 36m 50.5064s.
Fastest race lap: Plowman, 27.7277s, 192.154mph/309.243km/h.
Pole position: Hildebrand (qualifying cancelled due to water on track).

MID-OHIO 100, Mid-Ohio Sports Car Course, Lexington, Ohio, USA, 9 August. Round 11. 40 laps of the 2.258-mile/3.634km circuit, 90.320 miles/145.356km.
1 James Davison, AUS, 52m 09.2142s, 103.909mph/167.225km/h; **2** James Hinchcliffe, CDN, 52m 13.2562s; **3** J.R. Hildebrand, USA, 52m 14.9591s; **4** Felipe Guimarães, BR, 52m 26.1878s; **5** Martin Plowman, GB, 52m 26.8020s; **6** Daniel Herrington, USA, 52m 26.9547s; **7** Andrew Prendeville, USA, 52m 32.0417s; **8** Stefan Wilson, GB, 52m 32.5342s; **9** Richard Philippe, F, 52m 33.1894s; **10** Gustavo Yacaman, CO, 52m 38.3117s.
Fastest race lap: Sebastian Saavedra, CO, 1m 14.1005s, 109.700mph/176.544km/h.
Pole position: Davison, 1m 14.8673s, 108.576mph/174.736km/h.

CARNEROS 100, Infineon Raceway, Sears Point, Sonoma, California, USA, 23 August. Round 12. 40 laps of the 2.303-mile/3.706km circuit, 92.120 miles/148.253km.
1 J.R. Hildebrand, USA, 1h 01m 44.4612s, 89.522mph/144.072km/h; **2** Felipe Guimarães, BR, 1h 02m 00.3530s; **3** James Davison, AUS, 1h 02m 08.0015s; **4** Richard Philippe, F, 1h 02m 21.6492s; **5** Ana Beatriz, BR, 1h 02m 24.6410s; **6** James Hinchcliffe, CDN, 1h 02m 25.2112s; **7** Sebastian Saavedra, CO, 1h 02m 25.4650s; **8** Charlie Kimball, USA, 1h 02m 26.3470s; **9** Mario Romancini, BR, 1h 02m 27.6764s; **10** Martin Plowman, GB, 1h 02m 29.3774s.
Fastest race lap: Hildebrand, 1m 23.9479s, 98.761mph/158.941km/h.
Pole position: Hildebrand, 1m 23.0361s, 99.846mph/160.686km/h.

CHICAGOLAND 100, Chicagoland Speedway, Chicago, Illinois, USA, 29 August. Round 13. 67 laps of the 1.520-mile/2.446km circuit, 101.840 miles/163.896km.
1 Daniel Herrington, USA, 44m 07.3016s, 138.490mph/222.878km/h; **2** James Davison, AUS, 44m 07.3629s; **3** Andrew Prendeville, USA, 44m 07.5338s; **4** Wade Cunningham, NZ, 44m 07.5992s; **5** J.R. Hildebrand, USA, 44m 07.7202s; **6** Sebastian Saavedra, CO, 44m 07.7897s; **7** Charlie Kimball, USA, 44m 07.8043s; **8** Martin Plowman, GB, 44m 08.0429s; **9** Pippa Mann, GB, 64 laps; **10** Rodrigo Barbosa, BR, 61.
Fastest race lap: Kimball, 28.5079s, 191.947mph/308.908km/h.
Pole position: Brandon Wagner, USA, 57.6140s, 189.954mph/305.701km/h (over **2** laps).

MIAMI 100, Homestead-Miami Speedway, Florida, USA, 9 October. Round 14. 67 laps of the 1.485-mile/2.390km circuit, 99.495 miles/160.122km.
1 Mario Romancini, BR, 43m 26.4173s, 137.423mph/221.161km/h; **2** J.R. Hildebrand, USA, 43m 26.4230s; **3** Sebastian Saavedra, CO, 43m 26.8207s; **4** Mike Potekhen, USA, 43m 26.9079s; **5** James Davison, AUS, 43m 28.1039s; **6** Wade Cunningham, NZ, 43m 28.6831s; **7** Martin Plowman, GB, 43m 29.5034s; **8** Pippa Mann, GB, 43m 29.5083s; **9** Logan Gomez, USA, 43m 29.7850s; 10 Andrew Prendeville, USA, 43m 29.8750s.
Fastest race lap: Saavedra, 28.6235s, 186.770mph/300.577km/h.
Pole position: Davison, 57.6245s, 185.546mph/298.607km/h (over 2 laps).

Final championship points
1 J.R. Hildebrand, USA, 545; **2** James Davison, AUS, 447; **3** Sebastian Saavedra, CO, 446; **4** Wade Cunningham, NZ, 416; **5** James Hinchcliffe, CDN, 395; **6** Mario Romancini, BR, 392; **7** Daniel Herrington, USA, 383; **8** Ana Beatriz, BR, 320; **9** Andrew Prendeville, USA, 313; **10** Charlie Kimball, USA, 310; **11** Martin Plowman, GB, 298; **12** Gustavo Yacaman, CO, 269; **13** Richard Philippe, F, 254; **14** Pippa Mann, GB, 237; **15** Rodrigo Barbosa, BR, 190; **16** Alistair Jackson, GB, 172; **17** Jonathan Summerton, USA, 162; **18** Mike Potekhen, USA, 157; **19** Pablo Donoso, RCH, 147; **20** Junior Strous, NL, 146; **21** Jay Howard, GB, 123; **22** Stefan Wilson, GB, 112; **23** Felipe Guimarães, BR, 107; **24** Brandon Wagner, USA, 103; **25** Sergey Mokshantsev, RUS, 92; **26** Jesse Mason, CDN, 69; **27** Sean Guthrie, USA, 65; **28** Logan Gomez, USA, 33; **29** Dillon Battistini, GB, 15; **30** Jonathan Bomarito, USA, 12; **31** Juan Pablo García, MEX, 12; **32** Duncan Tappy, GB, 8.

Cooper Tires presents The Atlantic Championship

All cars are Swift 016.a-Mazda Cosworth MZR.

ATLANTIC CHAMPIONSHIP, Sebring International Raceway, Florida, USA, 20 March. Round 1. 19 laps of the 3.700-mile/5.955km circuit, 70.300 miles/113.137km.
1 John Michael Edwards, USA, 45m 00.439s, 93.718mph/150.825km/h; **2** Frédéric Vervisch, B, 45m 05.170s; **3** Jonathan Summerton, USA, 45m 08.398s; **4** Harald Schlegelmilch, LV, 45m 11.594s; **5** Simona de Silvestro, CH/I, 45m 16.626s; **6** Borja García, E, 45m 18.306s; **7** Tonis Kasemets, EST, 45m 20.082s; **8** James Winslow, GB, 45m 28.606s; **9** Matt Lee, USA, 45m 32.934s; **10** Frankie Muniz, USA, 45m 33.212s.
Most laps led: Edwards, 19.
Fastest race lap: Edwards, 1m 55.942s, 114.885mph/184.890km/h.
Pole position: Summerton, 1m 53.571s, 117.283mph/188.749km/h.

ATLANTIC CHAMPIONSHIP, Miller Motorsports Park, Tooele, Utah, USA, 17 May. Round 2. 31 laps of the 3.048-mile/4.905km circuit, 94.488 miles/152.064km.
1 Simona de Silvestro, CH/I, 51m 25.717s, 110.236mph/177.407km/h; **2** John Michael Edwards, USA, 51m 37.417s; **3** Frédéric Vervisch, B, 51m 39.074s; **4** Frankie Muniz, USA, 52m 04.346s; **5** Tonis Kasemets, EST, 52m 05.409s; **6** Jonathan Summerton, USA, 52m 08.206s; **7** Max Lefèvre, F, 52m 52.269s; **8** James Winslow, GB, 52m 52.499s; **9** Markus Niemelä, FIN, 30 laps (DNF); **10** Michael Mallinen, USA, 29.
Disqualified: Borja García, E, finished 9th in 50m 22.619s (caused accident).
Most laps led: de Silvestro, 31.
Fastest race lap: de Silvestro, 1m 38.553s, 111.339mph/179.183km/h.
Pole position: de Silvestro, 1m 36.891s, 113.249mph/182.256km/h.

ATLANTIC CHAMPIONSHIP, New Jersey Motorsports Park, Millville, New Jersey, USA, 13/14 June. 2 x 38 laps of the 2.170-mile/3.492km circuit.
Round 3 (82.460 miles/132.707km).
1 Jonathan Summerton, USA, 45m 54.359s, 107.777mph/173.450km/h; **2** Simona de Silvestro, CH/I, 46m 01.693s; **3** Borja García, E, 46m 33.274s; **4** Markus Niemelä, FIN, 46m 33.976s; **5** John Michael Edwards, USA, 46m 34.431s; **6** Tonis Kasemets, EST, 46m 54.372s; **7** Frédéric Vervisch, B, 46m 57.475s; **8** Frankie Muniz, USA, 47m 49.053s; **9** James Winslow, GB, 47m 27.176s*; **10** David Garza, MEX, 37 laps.
* demoted one place for causing accident.
Most laps led: Summerton, 38.
Fastest race lap: Summerton, 1m 11.418s, 109.384mph/176.037km/h.
Pole position: Summerton, 1m 11.417s, 109.386mph/176.039km/h.

Round 4 (82.460 miles/132.707km).
1 Simona de Silvestro, CH/I, 46m 04.908s, 107.366mph/172.788km/h; **2** Jonathan Summerton, USA, 46m 05.818s; **3** Frédéric Vervisch, B, 46m 07.801s; **4** Markus Niemelä, FIN, 46m 14.794s; **5** Borja García, E, 46m 32.583s; **6** John Michael Edwards, USA, 46m 33.015s; **7** Tonis Kasemets, EST, 46m 47.218s; **8** Frankie Muniz, USA, 46m 51.860s; **9** James Winslow, GB, 46m 54.993s; **10** David Garza, MEX, 47m 10.429s.
Most laps led: de Silvestro, 38.
Fastest race lap: Niemelä, 1m 11.655s, 109.022mph/175.455km/h.
Pole position: de Silvestro, 1m 10.388s, 110.985mph/178.613km/h.

ATLANTIC CHAMPIONSHIP, Lime Rock Park, Lakeville, Connecticut, USA, 18 July. Round 5. 53 laps of the 1.500-mile/2.414km circuit, 79.500 miles/127.943km.
1 Simona de Silvestro, CH/I, 45m 40.416s, 104.437mph/168.075km/h; **2** John Michael Edwards, USA, 45m 50.420s; **3** Borja García, E, 46m 00.794s; **4** Jonathan Summerton, USA, 46m 01.145s; **5** Tonis Kasemets, EST, 46m 03.115s; **6** Frédéric Vervisch, B, 46m 11.259s; **7** James Winslow, GB, 46m 22.158s; **8** Max Lefèvre, F, 52 laps; **9** Markus Niemelä, FIN, 50; **10** Frankie Muniz, USA, 50.
Most laps led: de Silvestro, 53.
Fastest race lap: Edwards, 50.928s, 106.032mph/170.642km/h.
Pole position: de Silvestro, 59.624s, 90.568mph/145.754km/h.

AUTOBAHN GRAND PRIX, Autobahn Country Club, Joliet, Illinois, USA, 25/26 July. 20 and 22 laps of the 3.560-mile/5.729km circuit.
Round 6 (71.200 miles/114.585km).
1 John Michael Edwards, USA, 46m 19.472s, 92.219mph/148.412km/h; **2** Jonathan Summerton, USA, 46m 25.958s; **3** Simona de Silvestro, CH/I, 46m 27.135s; **4** Frédéric Vervisch, B, 46m 30.413s; **5** Tonis Kasemets, EST, 46m 38.722s; **6** Borja García, E, 46m 39.686s; **7** Frankie Muniz, USA, 46m 58.944s; **8** James Winslow, GB, 46m 59.832s; **9** Max Lefèvre, F, 47m 05.021s; **10** Markus Niemelä, FIN, 1 lap (DNF).
Most laps led: Edwards, 20.
Fastest race lap: Summerton, 2m 06.417s, 101.379mph/163.153km/h.
Pole position: Edwards, 2m 04.600s, 102.857mph/165.532km/h.

Round 7 (78.320 miles/126.044km).
1 John Michael Edwards, USA, 46m 31.809s, 100.993mph/162.532km/h; **2** Simona de Silvestro, CH/I, 46m 44.463s; **3** Tonis Kasemets, EST, 46m 53.064s; **4** Frédéric Vervisch, B, 46m 53.625s; **5** Borja García, E, 46m 58.681s; **6** Markus Niemelä, FIN, 46m 59.412s; **7** Frankie Muniz, USA, 47m 12.410s; **8** Max Lefèvre, F, 47m 22.963s; **9** James Winslow, GB, 47m 41.742s; **10** Eric Jensen, CDN, 21 laps.
Most laps led: Edwards, 22.
Fastest race lap: Edwards, 2m 05.542s, 102.085mph/164.290km/h.
Pole position: Edwards, 2m 06.321s, 101.456mph/163.277km/h.

ATLANTIC CHAMPIONSHIP, Mid-Ohio Sports Car Course, Lexington, Ohio, USA, 8 August. Round 8. 38 laps of the 2.258-mile/3.634km circuit, 85.804 miles/138.088km.
1 Jonathan Summerton, USA, 51m 03.940s, 100.816mph/162.248km/h; **2** Simona de Silvestro, CH/I, 51m 05.940s; **3** Borja García, E, 51m 11.944s; **4** Markus Niemelä, FIN, 51m 37.676s; **5** Frédéric Vervisch, B, 51m 47.306s; **6** James Winslow, GB, 51m 51.000s; **7** Max Lefèvre, F, 51m 57.199s; **8** Frankie Muniz, USA, 52m 06.805s; **9** Michael Mallinen, USA, 35 laps; **10** Hans Peter, USA, 26 (DNF).
Most laps led: Summerton, 38.
Fastest race lap: Summerton, 1m 13.812s, 110.128mph/177.235km/h.
Pole position: Summerton, 1m 12.970s, 111.399mph/179.280km/h.

GRAND PRIX DE TROIS-RIVIERES, Circuit Trois-Rivières, Québec, Canada, 16 August. Round 7. 50 laps of the 1.520-mile/2.446km circuit, 76.000 miles/122.310km.
1 Simona de Silvestro, CH, 50m 00.543s, 91.183mph/146.746km/h; **2** John Michael Edwards, USA, 50m 01.429s; **3** Jonathan Summerton, USA, 50m 05.017s; **4** Tonis Kasemets, EST, 50m 27.380s; **5** Markus Niemelä, FIN, 50m 29.247s; **6** Frankie Muniz, USA, 50m 48.191s; **7** James Winslow, GB, 50m 51.571s; **8** Eric Jensen, CDN, 48 laps; **9** Frédéric Vervisch, B, 38 (DNF-mechanical); **10** Max Lefèvre, F, 36 (DNF-mechanical).
Most laps led: de Silvestro, 50.
Fastest race lap: Summerton, 59.022s, 92.711mph/149.204km/h.
Pole position: de Silvestro, 58.662s, 93.280mph/150.120km/h.

ATLANTIC CHAMPIONSHIP, Mosport International Raceway, Bowmanville, Ontario, Canada, 30 August. Round 8. 33 laps of the 2.459-mile/3.957km circuit, 81.147 miles/130.593km.
1 Jonathan Summerton, USA, 45m 30.034s, 107.006mph/172.209km/h; **2** John Michael Edwards, USA, 45m 31.156s; **3** Frédéric Vervisch, B, 45m 31.643s; **4** Robert Wickens, CDN, 45m 32.313s; **5** Markus Niemelä, FIN, 45m 33.005s; **6** Tonis Kasemets, EST, 45m 33.692s; **7** Borja García, E, 45m 34.631s; **8** Max Lefèvre, F, 45m 45.131s; **9** Eric Jensen, CDN, 32 laps; **10** Simona de Silvestro, CH, 27 (DNF).
Most laps led: Summerton, 33.
Fastest race lap: Edwards, 1m 11.541s, 123.739mph/199.138km/h.
Pole position: Summerton, 1m 12.060s, 122.848mph/197.704km/h.

ATLANTIC CHAMPIONSHIP, Road Atlanta Motorsports Center, Braselton, Georgia, USA, 25 September. Round 9. 34 laps of the 2.540-mile/4.088km circuit, 86.360 miles/138.983km.
1 Jonathan Summerton, USA, 45m 52.977s, 112.931mph/181.745km/h; **2** Simona de Silvestro, CH, 45m 57.185s; **3** John Michael Edwards, USA, 45m 57.741s; **4** Jonathan Bomarito, USA, 46m 01.932s; **5** Markus Niemelä, FIN, 46m 06.345s; **6** Frédéric Vervisch, B, 46m 07.281s; **7** James Winslow, GB, 46m 09.080s; **8** Max Lefèvre, F, 46m 21.537s; **9** Tonis Kasemets, EST, 29 laps (DNF); **10** Greg Mansell, GB, 17 (DNF-mechanical).
Most laps led: Summerton, 34.
Fastest race lap: Summerton, 1m 15.563s, 121.012mph/194.749km/h.
Pole position: Summerton, 1m 15.166s, 121.651mph/195.778km/h.

ATLANTIC CHAMPIONSHIP, Mazda Raceway Laguna Seca, Monterey, California, USA, 11 October. Round 10. 36 laps of the 2.238-mile/3.602km circuit, 80.568 miles/129.662km.
1 John Michael Edwards, USA, 50m 07.252s, 96.448mph/155.219km/h; **2** Jonathan Summerton, USA, 50m 08.632s; **3** Frédéric Vervisch, B, 50m 46.419s; **4** Tonis Kasemets, EST, 50m 58.973s; **5** Markus Niemelä, FIN, 52m 09.503s*; **6** Barrett Mertins, USA, 35 laps; **7** James Winslow, GB, 35; **8** Jonathan Bomarito, USA, 22 (DNF); **9** Max Lefèvre, F, 15 (DNF); **10** Simona de Silvestro, CH, 0 (DNF).
* finished 3rd in 50m 23.503s, but penalised for causing accident.
Most laps led: Edwards, 36.
Fastest race lap: Summerton, 1m 16.499s, 105.319mph/169.495km/h.
Pole position: Edwards, 1m 15.444s, 106.792mph/171.865km/h.

Final championship points
1 John Michael Edwards, USA, 182; **2** Jonathan Summerton, USA, 182; **3** Simona de Silvestro, CH, 176; **4** Frédéric Vervisch, B, 131; **5** Tonis Kasemets, EST, 103; **6** Markus Niemelä, FIN, 98; **7** Borja García, E, 88; **8** James Winslow, GB, 72; **9** Frankie Muniz, USA, 62; **10** Max Lefèvre, F, 58; **11** Jonathan Bomarito, USA, 19; **12** Eric Jensen, CDN, 16; **13** Harald Schlegelmilch, LV, 16; **14** Robert Wickens, CDN, 12; **15** Michael Nacol, USA, 11; **16** Barrett Mertins, USA, 8; **17** David Garza, MEX, 8; **18** Richard Zober, USA, 7; **19** Matt Lee, USA, 6; **20** Greg Mansell, GB, 4.

Rookie of the year: Frédéric Vervisch.

A1GP World Cup of Motorsport 2008–2009

All cars are A1GP-Ferrari V8.

A1GP, Circuit Park Zandvoort, Netherlands, 5 October. Round 1. 10 and 36 laps of the 2.875-mile/4.627km circuit.

Sprint race (28.751 miles/46.270km).
1 Malaysia-Fairuz Fauzy, 19m 44.533s, 87.378mph/140.622km/h; **2** New Zealand-Earl Bamber, 19m 48.007s; **3** France-Lôic Duval, 19m 50.803s; **4** Netherlands-Jeroen Bleekemolen, 19m 57.966s; **5** Switzerland-Neel Jani, 20m 01.429s; **6** South Africa-Adrian Zaugg, 20m 05.458s; **7** Italy-Fabio Onidi, 20m 06.747s; **8** USA-Charlie Kimball, 20m 08.683s; **9** Portugal-Filipe Albuquerque, 20m 13.960s; **10** Lebanon-Daniel Morad, 20m 23.462s; **11** Australia-John Martin, 21m 12.004s; **12** China-Ho-Pin Tung, 9 laps (DNF-spin); **13** Brazil-Felipe Guimarães, 9 (DNF-accident); **14** Korea-Jin-Woo Hwang, 3 (DNF-accident); **15** Indonesia-Satrio Hermanto, 2 (DNF-accident); **16** Ireland-Adam Carroll, 2 (DNF-accident); **17** Monaco-Clivio Piccione, 1 (DNF-accident).
Fastest race lap: France, 1m 45.939s, 97.700mph/157.233km/h.
Pole position: Netherlands, 1m 24.213s, 122.906mph/197.798km/h

Feature race (103.503 miles/166.572km).
1 France-Loic Duval, 1h 11m 58.723s, 86.278mph/138.851km/h; **2** Malaysia-Fairuz Fauzy, 1h 12m 01.011s; **3** New Zealand-Earl Bamber, 1h 12m 01.432s; **4** Australia-John Martin, 1h 12m 05.052s; **5** Netherlands-Jeroen Bleekemolen, 1h 12m 06.996s; **6** Monaco-Clivio Piccione, 34 laps; **7** Korea-Jin-Woo Hwang, 33; **8** Lebanon-Daniel Morad, 32 (DNF-accident); **9** China-Ho-Pin Tung, 31 (DNF-accident); **10** USA-Charlie Kimball, 30 (DNF-spin); **11** Portugal-Filipe Albuquerque, 15 (DNF-accident); **12** Indonesia-Satrio Hermanto, 12 (DNF-accident); **13** South Africa-Adrian Zaugg, 5 (DNF-accident); **14** Italy-Fabio Onidi, 5 (DNF-accident); **15** Brazil-Felipe Guimarães, 5; **16** Ireland-Adam Carroll, 4 (DNF-spin); **17** Switzerland-Neel Jani, 4 (DNF-gearbox).
Fastest race lap: USA, 1m 47.115s, 96.627mph/155.507km/h.
Pole position: Malaysia.
Championship points: 1 Malaysia, 22; **2** France, 22; **3** New Zealand, 18; **4** Netherlands, 11; **5** Australia, 8; **6** Monaco, 5.

A1GP, Chengdu International Circuit, Chengdu City, China, 9 November. Round 2. 18 and 51 laps of the 2.070-mile/3.331km circuit.

Sprint race (37.256 miles/59.958km).
1 Ireland-Adam Carroll, 22m 58.470s, 97.297mph/156.585km/h; **2** Netherlands-Robert Doornbos, 23m 00.507s; **3** Great Britain-Danny Watts, 23m 12.831s; **4** Switzerland-Neel Jani, 23m 13.089s; **5** South Africa-Adrian Zaugg, 23m 18.578s; **6** Portugal-Filipe Albuquerque, 23m 18.945s; **7** New Zealand-Chris van der Drift, 23m 25.694s; **8** France-Nicolas Prost, 23m 26.393s; **9** Monaco-Clivio Piccione, 23m 28.848s; **10** India-Narain Karthikeyan, 23m 30.738s; **11** Australia-John Martin, 23m 31.668s; **12** Lebanon-Daniel Morad, 23m 32.763s; **13** Malaysia-Fairuz Fauzy, 23m 33.125s; **14** Italy-Edoardo Piscopo, 23m 35.011s; **15** USA-Marco Andretti, 23m 36.572s; **16** Mexico-David Garza, 23m 40.981s; **17** China-Ho-Pin Tung, 23m 48.081s; **18** Indonesia-Satrio Hermanto, 24m 02.598s; **19** Korea-Jin-Woo Hwang, 24m 04.641s; **20** Brazil-Felipe Guimarães, 14 laps.
Fastest race lap: Ireland, 1m 16.084s, 97.934mph/157.610km/h.
Pole position: Ireland, 1m 15.423s, 98.792mph/158.991km/h.

Feature race (105.559 miles/169.881km).
1 Portugal-Filipe Albuquerque, 1h 11m 23.179s, 88.722mph/142.784km/h; **2** Ireland-Adam Carroll, 1h 11m 23.750s; **3** Great Britain-Danny Watts, 1h 11m 27.981s; **4** Switzerland-Neel Jani, 1h 11m 30.336s; **5** Malaysia-Fairuz Fauzy, 1h 11m 36.481s; **6** Australia-John Martin, 1h 11m 38.723s; **7** Monaco-Clivio Piccione, 1h 11m 39.415s; **8** USA-Marco Andretti, 1h 11m 39.869s; **9** South Africa-Adrian Zaugg, 1h 11m 41.209s; **10** India-Narain Karthikeyan, 1h 11m 41.938s; **11** New Zealand-Chris van der Drift, 1h 11m 42.854s; **12** China-Ho-Pin Tung, 1h 11m 43.305s; **13** Lebanon-Daniel Morad, 1h 11m 45.759s; **14** Indonesia-Satrio Hermanto, 1h 11m 54.464s; **15** Mexico-David Garza, 50 laps; **16** Netherlands-Robert Doornbos, 50; **17** Korea-Jin-Woo Hwang, 50; **18** France-Nicolas Prost, 37; **19** Italy-Edoardo Piscopo, 30; **20** Brazil-Felipe Guimarães, 13.
Fastest race lap: Netherlands, 1m 15.212s, 99.069mph/159.437km/h.
Pole position: Great Britain, 1m 15.325s, 98.921mph/159.198km/h.
Championship points: 1 Malaysia, 28; **2** Ireland, 23; **3** France, 23; **4** New Zealand, 20; **5** Netherlands, 20; **6** Portugal, 18.

A1GP, Sepang International Circuit, Jalan Pekeliling, Kuala Lumpur, Malaysia, 23 November. Round 3. 11 and 34 laps of the 3.444-mile/5.543km circuit

Sprint race (37.887 miles/60.973km).
1 Switzerland-Neel Jani, 22m 41.567s, 100.173mph/161.213km/h; **2** France-Loïc Duval, 22m 51.479s; **3** New Zealand-Earl Bamber, 22m 53.380s; **4** Portugal-Filipe Albuquerque, 22m 54.020s; **5** Ireland-Adam Carroll, 22m 54.772s; **6** Netherlands-Jeroen Bleekemolen, 22m 56.966s; **7** Italy-Edoardo Piscopo, 23m 01.514s; **8** Australia-John Martin, 23m 03.004s; **9** South Africa-Adrian Zaugg, 23m 09.241s; **10** China-Ho-Pin Tung, 23m 11.059s; **11** Lebanon-Daniel Morad, 23m 13.616s; **12** Monaco-Clivio Piccione, 23m 13.973s; **13** Indonesia-Satrio Hermanto, 23m 20.526s; **14** Mexico-David Garza, 23m 36.622s; **15** Malaysia-Fairuz Fauzy, 10 laps; **16** Great Britain-Danny Watts, 4; **17** Brazil-Felipe Guimarães, 0 (DNF-accident); **18** India-Narain Karthikeyan, 0 (DNF-accident); **19** USA-Marco Andretti, 0 (DNF-accident).
Did not start: Korea-Jin-Woo Hwang.
Fastest race lap: Switzerland, 1m 48.550s, 114.226mph/183.830km/h.
Pole position: Switzerland, 1m 47.154s, 115.715mph/186.225km/h.

Feature race (117.105 miles/188.462km).
1 Ireland-Adam Carroll, 1h 05m 52.205s, 106.668mph/171.667km/h; **2** Portugal-Filipe Albuquerque, 1h 06m 08.201s; **3** USA-Marco Andretti, 1h 06m 39.842s; **4** Australia-John Martin, 1h 06m 43.884s; **5** South Africa-Adrian Zaugg, 1h 06m 44.311s; **6** New Zealand-Earl Bamber, 1h 06m 46.559s; **7** Brazil-Felipe Guimarães, 1h 06m 49.574s; **8** Netherlands-Jeroen Bleekemolen, 1h 06m 49.695s; **9** China-Ho-Pin Tung, 1h 06m 51.363s; **10** Malaysia-Fairuz Fauzy, 1h 06m 56.093s; **11** Italy-Edoardo Piscopo, 1h 06m 58.350s; **12** Lebanon-Daniel Morad, 1h 07m 07.195s; **13** Indonesia-Satrio Hermanto, 1h 07m 07.966s; **14** France-Loïc Duval, 1h 07m 08.668s; **15** Mexico-David Garza, 1h 07m 22.206s; **16** Great Britain-Danny Watts, 28 laps; **17** Monaco-Clivio Piccione, **2** (DNF-misfire); **18** India-Narain Karthikeyan, 0 (DNF-accident); **19** Switzerland-Neel Jani, 0 (DNF-spin).
Did not start: Korea-Jin-Woo Hwang.
Fastest race lap: Ireland, 1m 48.563s, 114.213mph/183.808km/h.
Pole position: Ireland, 1m 47.124s, 115.747mph/186.277km/h.
Championship points: 1 Ireland, 43; **2** Portugal, 35; **3** France, 31; **4** New Zealand, 31; **5** Malaysia, 29; **6** Switzerland, 28.

A1GP, Taupo Racetrack, Lake Taupo, New Zealand, 25 January. Round 4. 15 and 50 laps of the 2.064-mile/3.321km circuit.

Sprint race (30.954 miles/49.815km).
1 Ireland-Adam Carroll, 19m 40.271s, 94.413mph/151.943km/h; **2** Switzerland-Neel Jani, 19m 41.759s; **3** Netherlands-Robert Doornbos, 19m 43.830s; **4** France-Loïc Duval, 19m 48.865s; **5** New Zealand-Chris van der Drift, 19m 51.937s; **6** Portugal-Filipe Albuquerque, 19m 52.936s; **7** Italy-Edoardo Piscopo, 19m 55.230s; **8** Malaysia-Fairuz Fauzy, 19m 56.068s; **9** India-Narain Karthikeyan, 20m 01.244s; **10** South Africa-Adrian Zaugg, 20m 02.301s; **11** USA-Marco Andretti, 20m 10.836s; **12** Great Britain-Dan Clarke, 20m 11.276s; **13** Indonesia-Satrio Hermanto, 20m 12.632s; **14** Brazil-Felipe Guimarães, 20m 13.405s; **15** Mexico-Salvador Durán, 20m 20.872s; **16** Monaco-Clivio Piccione, 20m 29.552s*; **17** China-Cong Fu Cheng, 11 laps (DNF-spin); **18** Lebanon-Daniel Morad, 8 (DNF-suspension); **19** Australia-John Martin, 5 (DNF-suspension).
* includes 25-sec penalty for causing accident.
Fastest race lap: Switzerland, 1m 15.021s, 99.023mph/159.363km/h.
Pole position: Ireland, 1m 14.507s, 99.706mph/160.462km/h.

Feature race (103.179 miles/166.050km).
1 Switzerland-Neel Jani, 1h 06m 19.574s, 93.337mph/150.212km/h; **2** Ireland-Adam Carroll, 1h 06m 20.621s; **3** Portugal-Filipe Albuquerque, 1h 06m 21.953s; **4** Australia-John Martin, 1h 06m 30.167s; **5** Netherlands-Robert Doornbos, 1h 06m 33.976s; **6** France-Loïc Duval, 1h 06m 36.997s; **7** India-Narain Karthikeyan, 1h 06m 39.789s; **8** Italy-Edoardo Piscopo, 1h 06m 42.730s; **9** South Africa-Adrian Zaugg, 1h 06m 42.921s; **10** Malaysia-Fairuz Fauzy, 1h 06m 46.406s; **11** USA-Marco Andretti, 1h 07m 05.373s*; **12** Great Britain-Dan Clarke, 49 laps; **13** New Zealand-Chris van der Drift, 49; **14** China-Cong Fu Cheng, 49; **15** Brazil-Felipe Guimarães, 49 **; **16** Mexico-Salvador Durán, 43 (DNF-puncture); **17** Indonesia-Satrio Hermanto, 42 (DNF-spin); **18** Monaco-Clivio Piccione, 33 (DNF-spin); **19** Lebanon-Daniel Morad, 1 (DNF-accident).
* includes 25-sec penalty for crossing line at pit exit.
** includes 25-sec penalty for causing accident.
Fastest race lap: Portugal, 1m 14.898s, 99.186mph/159.625km/h.
Pole position: Ireland, 1m 14.411s, 99.835mph/160.669km/h.
Championship points: 1 Ireland, 65; **2** Switzerland, 52; **3** Portugal, 49; **4** France, 41; **5** Netherlands, 38; **6** New Zealand, 35.

A1GP, Kyalami Grand Prix Circuit, Gauteng, Johannesburg, South Africa, 22 February. Round 5. 14 and 40 laps of the 2.649-mile/4.263km circuit.

Sprint race (37.085 miles/59.682km).
1 Netherlands-Jeroen Bleekemolen, 21m 35.105s, 103.084mph/165.897km/h; **2** Portugal-Filipe Albuquerque, 21m 39.512s; **3** Switzerland-Neel Jani, 21m 45.705s; **4** Ireland-Adam Carroll, 21m 48.030s; **5** Monaco-Clivio Piccione, 21m 49.468s; **6** India-Narain Karthikeyan, 21m 53.579s; **7** South Africa-Adrian Zaugg, 21m 56.283s; **8** New Zealand-Earl Bamber, 22m 01.644s; **9** Malaysia-Fairuz Fauzy, 22m 02.030s; **10** France-Nicolas Prost, 22m 03.206s; **11** Italy-Edoardo Piscopo, 22m 07.186s; **12** Australia-John Martin, 22m 09.579s; **13** China-Ho-Pin Tung, 22m 12.909s; **14** Germany-Michael Ammermüller, 22m 14.173s; **15** Brazil-Felipe Guimarães, 22m 14.822s; **16** Mexico-Salvador Durán, 22m 20.111s; **17** USA-Marco Andretti, 22m 30.741s; **18** Indonesia-Zahir Ali, 22m 52.829s; **19** Great Britain-Danny Watts, 9 laps (DNF-accident); **20** Lebanon-Daniel Morad, 6.
Fastest race lap: Portugal, 1m 29.072s, 107.060mph/172.296km/h.
Pole position: Netherlands, 1m 27.717s, 108.713mph/174.958km/h.

Feature race (105.956 miles/170.520km).
1 Switzerland-Neel Jani, 1h 02m 24.617s, 101.864mph/163.934km/h; **2** Brazil-Felipe Guimarães, 1h 02m 37.793s; **3** Monaco-Clivio Piccione, 1h 02m 38.810s; **4** Netherlands-Jeroen Bleekemolen, 1h 02m 41.641s; **5** Portugal-Filipe Albuquerque, 1h 02m 42.612s; **6** Lebanon-Daniel Morad, 1h 02m 55.827s; **7** Great Britain-Danny Watts, 1h 02m 58.945s; **8** USA-Marco Andretti, 1h 03m 23.617s; **9** Indonesia-Zahir Ali, 1h 03m 28.612s; **10** Italy-Edoardo Piscopo, 1h 03m 29.473s; **11** Germany-Michael Ammermüller, 1h 03m 33.220s; **12** India-Narain Karthikeyan, 1h 03m 33.767s; **13** Australia-John Martin, 1h 03m 45.162s; **14** China-Ho-Pin Tung, 22 laps (DNF-electrics); **15** Malaysia-Fairuz Fauzy, 17 (DNF-withdrew); **16** South Africa-Adrian Zaugg, 15 (DNF-gearbox); **17** New Zealand-Earl Bamber, 3 (DNF-accident); **18** France-Nicolas Prost, 3 (DNF-accident); **19** Mexico-Salvador Durán, 3 (DNF-accident); **20** Ireland-Adam Carroll, 0 (DNF-accident).
Fastest race lap: Malaysia, 1m 28.306s, 107.988mph/173.791km/h.
Pole position: Monaco, 1m 27.269s, 109.272mph/175.856km/h.
Championship points: 1 Switzerland, 73; **2** Ireland, 70; **3** Portugal, 64; **4** Netherlands, 56; **5** France, 41; **6** New Zealand, 36.

A1GP, Autódromo Internacional do Algarve, Portimão, Portugal, 12 April. Round 6. 11 and 42 laps of the 2.912-mile/4.686km circuit.

Sprint race (32.029 miles/51.546km).
1 Netherlands-Robert Doornbos, 19m 33.501s, 98.257mph/158.129km/h; **2** Ireland-Adam Carroll, 19m 37.136s; **3** Portugal-Filipe Albuquerque, 19m 39.229s; **4** Italy-Vitantonio Liuzzi, 19m 42.588s; **5** Monaco-Clivio Piccione, 19m 43.549s; **6** India-Narain Karthikeyan, 19m 46.097s; **7** Brazil-Felipe Guimarães, 19m 46.798s; **8** Malaysia-Fairuz Fauzy, 19m 51.515s; **9** Mexico-Salvador Durán, 19m 54.046s; **10** Australia-John Martin, 19m 56.184s; **11** Great Britain-Dan Clarke, 19m 56.581s; **12** USA-Marco Andretti, 19m 56.655s; **13** France-Nicolas Prost, 19m 57.676s; **14** Indonesia-Zahir Ali, 20m 12.901s; **15** Switzerland-Neel Jani, 20m 17.797s*; **16** China-Ho-Pin Tung, 20m 24.156s; **17** South Africa-Adrian Zaugg, 9 laps; **18** Lebanon-Daniel Morad, 1 (DNF-accident damage); **19** Germany-Andre Lotterer, 0 (DNF-accident); **20** New Zealand-Earl Bamber, 0 (DNF - spin).
* includes 30-sec penalty for pitting outside the window.
Fastest race lap: Ireland, 1m 31.404s, 114.680mph/184.560km/h.
Pole position: Italy, 1m 30.875s, 115.348mph/185.635km/h.

Feature race (122.293 miles/196.812km).
1 Switzerland-Neel Jani, 1h 10m 45.011s, 103.711mph/166.907km/h; **2** Portugal-Filipe Albuquerque, 1h 10m 51.797s; **3** Malaysia-Fairuz Fauzy, 1h 10m 54.716s; **4** Mexico-Salvador Durán, 1h 11m 01.343s; **5** Ireland-Adam Carroll, 1h 11m 10.422s*; **6** France-Nicolas Prost, 1h 11m 12.333s; **7** Great Britain-Dan Clarke, 1h 11m 14.891s; **8** China-Ho-Pin Tung, 1h 11m 19.597s; **9** Germany-André Lotterer, 1h 11m 28.981s; **10** Indonesia-Zahir Ali, 1h 11m 59.004s; **11** India-Narain Karthikeyan, 39 laps (DNF-wheel bearing); **12** Australia-John Martin, 38 (DNF-relay); **13** Italy-Vitantonio Liuzzi, 18 (DNF-accident); **14** USA-Marco Andretti, 18 (DNF-accident); **15** Monaco-Clivio Piccione, 18 (DNF-accident); **16** South Africa-Adrian Zaugg, 15 (DNF-accident); **17** New Zealand-Earl Bamber, 15 (DNF - accident); **18** Lebanon-Daniel Morad, 1 (DNF-puncture); **19** Netherlands-Robert Doornbos, 0 (DNF-fire); **20** Brazil-Felipe Guimarães, 0 (DNF-accident damage).
* includes 25-sec penalty for jumping the start.
Fastest race lap: Ireland, 1m 31.453s, 114.619mph/184.461km/h.
Pole position: Netherlands, 1m 30.415s, 115.935mph/186.579km/h.
Championship points: 1 Switzerland, 88; **2** Ireland, 86; **3** Portugal, 82; **4** Netherlands, 66; **5** France, 46; **6** Malaysia, 43.

A1GP, Brands Hatch Grand Prix Circuit, West Kingsdown, Dartford, Kent, Great Britain, 3 May. Round 7. 18 and 49 laps of the 2.301-mile/3.703km circuit

Sprint race (41.417 miles/66.654km).
1 Ireland-Adam Carroll, 22m 32.704s, 110.224mph/177.388km/h; **2** India-Narain Karthikeyan, 22m 39.934s; **3** Mexico-Salvador Durán, 22m 45.044s; **4** USA-JR Hildebrand Jr., 22m 45.393s; **5** Portugal-Filipe Albuquerque, 22m 45.722s; **6** Netherlands-Jeroen Bleekemolen, 22m 46.487s; **7** Australia-John Martin, 22m 47.912s; **8** Switzerland-Neel Jani, 22m 54.924s; **9** France-Nicolas Prost, 22m 55.649s; **10** Italy-Vitantonio Liuzzi, 22m 59.766s; **11** Germany-Michael Ammermüller, 23m 04.651s; **12** Indonesia-Satrio Hermanto, 23m 05.863s; **13** Great Britain-Dan Clarke, 23m 06.245s; **14** China-Cong Fu Cheng, 23m 07.667s; **15** South Africa-Alan van der Merwe, 23m 13.192s; **16** Malaysia-Aaron Lim, 23m 14.232s; **17** Lebanon-Daniel Morad, 13 laps (DNF-accident); **18** New Zealand-Earl Bamber, 13 (DNF-accident); **19** Monaco-Clivio Piccione, 8 (DNF-fire).
Did not start: Brazil-Felipe Guimarães (accident damage).
Fastest race lap: Ireland, 1m 12.276s, 114.607mph/184.442km/h.
Pole position: Ireland, 1m 11.615s, 115.665mph/186.145km/h

Feature race (112.746 miles/181.447km).
1 Ireland-Adam Carroll, 1h 04m 14.970s, 105.288mph/169.445km/h; **2** Netherlands-Jeroen Bleekemolen, 1h 04m 25.126s; **3** Switzerland-Neel Jani, 1h 04m 28.534s; **4** Monaco-Clivio Piccione, 1h 04m 29.263s; **5** Portugal-Filipe Albuquerque, 1h 04m 31.454s; **6** Mexico-Salvador Durán, 1h 04m 36.780s; **7** Great Britain-Dan Clarke, 1h 04m 38.379s; **8** Australia-John Martin, 1h 04m 39.463s; **9** Italy-Vitantonio Liuzzi, 1h 05m 00.974s; **10** France-Nicolas Prost, 1h 05m 04.064s; **11** South Africa-Alan van der Merwe, 1h 05m 28.875s; **12** Lebanon-Daniel Morad, 1h 05m 31.227s; **13** Indonesia-Satrio Hermanto, 48 laps; **14** USA-JR Hildebrand Jr., 48; **15** Malaysia-Aaron Lim, 27 (DNF-accident); **16** Germany-Michael Ammermüller, 26 (DNF-exhaust); **17** New Zealand-Earl Bamber, 6 (DNF-spin); **18** China-Cong Fu Cheng, 0 (DNF-accident); **19** India-Narain Karthikeyan, 0 (DNF-accident).
Did not start: Brazil-Felipe Guimarães (accident damage).
Fastest race lap: Australia, 1m 12.698s, 113.942mph/183.372km/h.
Pole position: Ireland, 1m 10.902s, 116.828mph/188.017km/h

Final championship points
1 Ireland, 112; **2** Switzerland, 95; **3** Portugal, 92; **4** Netherlands, 75; **5** France, 47; **6** Malaysia, 43; **7** New Zealand, 36; **8** Australia, 36; **9** Monaco, 35; **10** Great Britain, 28; **11** USA, 24; **12** India, 19; **13** Mexico, 19; **14** South Africa, 19; **15** Brazil, 18; **16** Italy, 17; **17** Lebanon, 8; **18** China, 7; **19** Korea, 4; **20** Indonesia, 3; **21** Germany, 2.

Superleague Formula By Sonangol

All cars are developed by Élan Motorsports Technologies and powered by a Menard 4.2-litre V8 engine.

SUPERLEAGUE FORMULA BY SONANGOL, Circuit de Nevers, Magny-Cours, France, 28 June. Round 1. 30, 31 and 8 laps of the 2.741-mile/4.411km circuit.

Race 1 (82.226 miles/132.330km).
1 Liverpool-Adrián Vallés, E, 45m 57.400s, 107.352mph/172.767km/h; **2** Anderlecht-Yelmer Buurman, NL, 46m 03.698s; **3** Tottenham Hotspur-Craig Dolby, GB, 46m 04.637s; **4** Corinthians-Antônio Pizzonia, BR, 46m 14.368s; **5** Galatasaray-Duncan Tappy, GB, 46m 25.201s; **6** Flamengo-Enrique Bernoldi, BR, 46m 35.207s; **7** Sporting Clube de Portugal-Pedro Petiz, P, 46m 41.578s; **8** FC Midtylland-Kasper Andersen, DK, 46m 53.303s; **9** Al Ain-Miguel Molina, E, 47m 00.681s; **10** FC Basel-Maximilian Wissel, D, 47m 01.307s; **11** PSV Eindhoven-Dominick Muermans, NL, 47m 23.955s; **12** AC Milan-Giorgio Pantano, I, 29 laps; **13** Olympique Lyonnais-Nelson Panciatici, F, 29; **14** Atlético de Madrid-Ho-Pin Tung, CN, 29; **15** AS Roma-Jonathan Kennard, GB, 17; **16** FC Porto-Tristan Gommendy, F, 8; **17** Glasgow Rangers-John Martin, AUS, 1; **18** Olympiacos-Davide Rigon, I, 0.
Fastest race lap: Tottenham Hotspur, 1m 27.284s, 113.046mph/181.930km/h.
Pole position: Corinthians, 1m 26.555s, 113.998mph/183.462km/h.

Race 2 (84.967 miles/136.741km).
1 AC Milan-Giorgio Pantano, I, 46m 57.511s, 108.564mph/174.717km/h; **2** Olympiacos-Davide Rigon, I, 46m 59.784s; **3** FC Basel-Maximilian Wissel, D, 47m 08.883s; **4** Al Ain-Miguel Molina, E, 47m 12.966s; **5** Anderlecht-Yelmer Buurman, NL, 47m 15.498s; **6** Liverpool-Adrián Vallés, E, 47m 16.322s; **7** FC Porto-Tristan Gommendy, F, 47m 17.270s; **8** Flamengo-Enrique Bernoldi, BR, 47m 19.251s; **9** Corinthians-Antônio Pizzonia, BR, 47m 19.509s; **10** Tottenham Hotspur-Craig Dolby, GB, 47m 21.105s; **11** Galatasaray-Duncan Tappy, GB, 47m 29.342s; **12** Atlético de Madrid-Ho-Pin Tung, CN, 48m 06.422s; **13** Olympique Lyonnais-Nelson Panciatici, F, 48m 24.422s; **14** AS Roma-Jonathan Kennard, GB, 28 laps; **15** FC Midtylland-Kasper Andersen, DK, 17; **16** Glasgow Rangers-John Martin, AUS, 16; **17** Sporting Clube de Portugal-Pedro Petiz, P, 6; **18** PSV Eindhoven-Dominick Muermans, NL, 0.
Fastest race lap: Corinthians, 1m 28.120s, 111.973mph/180.204km/h.
Pole position: Olympiacos.

Super Final (21.927 miles/35.288km).
1 Liverpool-Adrián Vallés, E, 11m 49.172s, 111.308mph/179.133km/h; **2** AC Milan-Giorgio Pantano, I, 11m 53.985s; **3** Corinthians-Antônio Pizzonia, BR, 11m 55.946s; **4** Anderlecht-Yelmer Buurman, NL, 11m 58.574s; **5** FC Basel-Maximilian Wissel, D, 12m 13.557s; **6** Olympiacos-Davide Rigon, I, 12m 15.418s.
Fastest race lap: Liverpool, 1m 28.245s, 111.815mph/179.949km/h.
Pole position: Liverpool.

SUPERLEAGUE FORMULA BY SONANGOL, Circuit Zolder, Heusden-Zolder, Belgium, 19 July. Round 2. 2 x 29 laps of the 2.492-mile/4.011km circuit.

Race 1 (72.277 miles/116.319km).
1 Tottenham Hotspur-Craig Dolby, GB, 45m 42.338s, 94.881mph/152.697km/h; **2** Glasgow Rangers-John Martin, AUS, 45m 44.413s; **3** Liverpool-Adrián Vallés, E, 45m 45.750s; **4** FC Basel-Maximilian Wissel, D, 45m 46.379s; **5** AC Milan-Giorgio Pantano, I, 45m 47.076s; **6** Al Ain-Esteban Guerrieri, RA, 45m 49.397s; **7** Flamengo-Enrique Bernoldi, BR, 45m 51.913s; **8** Anderlecht-Yelmer Buurman, NL, 45m 53.107s; **9** Galatasaray-Duncan Tappy, GB, 45m 53.399s; **10** Olympiacos-Davide Rigon, I, 45m 54.104s; **11** AS Roma-Jonathan Kennard, GB, 45m 54.988s; **12** FC Porto-Tristan Gommendy, F, 45m 55.528s; **13** FC Midtylland-Kasper Andersen, DK, **19** laps; **14** Olympique Lyonnais-Nelson Panciatici, F, 11; **15** PSV Eindhoven-Dominick Muermans, NL, 6; **16** Sporting Clube de Portugal-Pedro Petiz, P, 0; **17** Corinthians-Antônio Pizzonia, BR, 0; **18** Atlético de Madrid-Ho-Pin Tung, CN, 0.
Fastest race lap: FC Basel, 1m 19.036s, 113.522mph/182.696km/h.
Pole position: FC Midtylland, 1m 19.878s, 112.325mph/180.770km/h.

Race 2 (72.277 miles/116.319km).
1 Al Ain-Esteban Guerrieri, RA, 46m 34.726s, 93.103mph/149.835km/h; **2** Atlético de Madrid-Ho-Pin Tung, CN, 46m 35.520s; **3** Liverpool-Adrián Vallés, E, 46m 43.458s; **4** Olympiacos-Davide Rigon, I, 46m 44.042s; **5** AS Roma-Jonathan Kennard, GB, 46m 53.630s; **6** FC Midtylland-Kasper Andersen, DK, 46m 58.230s; **7** FC Porto-Tristan Gommendy, F, 46m 59.401s; **8** FC Basel-Maximilian Wissel, D, 47m 04.935s; **9** Tottenham Hotspur-Craig Dolby, GB, 47m 11.595s; **10** Olympique Lyonnais-Nelson Panciatici, F, 19 laps; **11** AC Milan-Giorgio Pantano, I, 15; **12** Corinthians-Antônio Pizzonia, BR, 14; **13** Sporting Clube de Portugal-Pedro Petiz, P, 9; **14** Anderlecht-Yelmer Buurman, NL, 6; **15** Glasgow Rangers-John Martin, AUS, 4; **16** Galatasaray-Duncan Tappy, GB, 3; **17** PSV Eindhoven-Dominick Muermans, NL, 2; **18** Flamengo-Enrique Bernoldi, BR, 2.
Fastest race lap: Tottenham Hotspur, 1m 20.655s, 111.243mph/179.029km/h.
Pole position: Corinthians.

SUPERLEAGUE FORMULA BY SONANGOL, Donington Park National Circuit, Castle Donington, Great Britain, 2 August. Round 3. 31, 30 and 5 laps of the 2.500-mile/4.023km circuit.

Race 1 (77.493 miles/124.713km).
1 FC Basel-Maximilian Wissel, D, 45m 15.840s, 102.721mph/165.314km/h; **2** Glasgow Rangers-John Martin, AUS, 45m 18.020s; **3** Corinthians-Antônio Pizzonia, BR, 45m 18.961s; **4** AC Milan-Giorgio Pantano, I, 45m 19.793s; **5** Tottenham Hotspur-Craig Dolby, GB, 45m 27.330s; **6** Liverpool-Adrián Vallés, E, 45m 28.422s; **7** AS Roma-Jonathan Kennard, GB, 45m 32.255s; **8** FC Porto-Tristan Gommendy, F, 45m 32.693s; **9** Atlético de Madrid-Ho-Pin Tung, CN, 45m 39.373s; **10** FC Midtylland-Kasper Andersen, DK, 45m 40.327s; **11** Sevilla FC-Esteban Guerrieri, RA, 45m 41.679s; **12** Sporting Clube de Portugal-Pedro Petiz, P, 46m 21.063s; **13** Galatasaray-Scott Mansell, GB, 30 laps; **14** Olympique Lyonnais-Nelson Panciatici, F, 30; **15** PSV Eindhoven-Dominick Muermans, NL, 30; **16** Anderlecht-Yelmer Buurman, NL, 7; **17** Olympiacos-Davide Rigon, I, 3; **18** Flamengo-Enrique Bernoldi, BR, 0.
Fastest race lap: FC Basel, 1m 19.662s, 112.967mph/181.803km/h.
Pole position: Corinthians, 1m 22.868s, 108.596mph/174.769km/h.

Race 2 (74.993 miles/120.690km).
1 FC Porto-Tristan Gommendy, F, 45m 36.002s, 98.675mph/158.802km/h; **2** Sporting Clube de Portugal-Pedro Petiz, P, 45m 40.693s; **3** FC Basel-Maximilian Wissel, D, 45m 42.625s; **4** Tottenham Hotspur-Craig Dolby, GB, 45m 43.778s; **5** FC Midtylland-Kasper Andersen, DK, 45m 46.189s; **6** Liverpool-Adrián Vallés, E, 45m 47.542s; **7** Atlético de Madrid-Ho-Pin Tung, CN, 45m 53.470s; **8** Corinthians-Antônio Pizzonia, BR, 45m 53.909s; **9** Olympique Lyonnais-Nelson Panciatici, F, 46m

16.364s; **10** AS Roma-Jonathan Kennard, GB, 46m 17.004s; **11** PSV Eindhoven-Dominick Muermans, NL, 46m 30.948s; **12** Galatasaray-Scott Mansell, GB, 46m 32.636s; **13** Sevilla FC-Esteban Guerrieri, RA, 10 laps; **14** Flamengo-Enrique Bernoldi, BR, 9; **15** Olympiacos-Davide Rigon, I, 3; **16** Glasgow Rangers-John Martin, AUS, 1; **17** AC Milan-Giorgio Pantano, I, 0.
Did not start: Anderlecht-Yelmer Buurman, NL.
Fastest race lap: Corinthians, 1m 19.400s, 113.339mph/182.403km/h.
Pole position: Flamengo.

Super Final (12.499 miles/20.115km).
1 Glasgow Rangers-John Martin, AUS, 6m 43.077s, 111.631mph/179.653km/h; **2** Tottenham Hotspur-Craig Dolby, GB, 6m 46.827s; **3** FC Basel-Maximilian Wissel, D, 6m 49.287s; **4** Corinthians-Antônio Pizzonia, BR, 6m 50.920s; **5** Sporting Clube de Portugal-Pedro Petiz, P, 7m 14.710s; **6** FC Porto-Tristan Gommendy, F, 7m 18.086s.
Fastest race lap: FC Porto, 1m 19.194s, 113.634mph/182.877km/h.
Pole position: FC Basel.

SUPERLEAGUE FORMULA BY SONANGOL, Autódromo Fernanda Pires da Silva, Estoril, Portugal, 6 September. Round 4. 30, 30 and 5 laps of the 2.599-mile/4.182km circuit.
Race 1 (77.957 miles/125.460km).
1 Olympiacos-Esteban Guerrieri, RA, 45m 47.271s, 102.154mph/164.401km/h; **2** Liverpool-Adrián Vallés, E, 45m 49.437s; **3** Corinthians-Antônio Pizzonia, BR, 45m 50.281s; **4** Anderlecht-Yelmer Buurman, NL, 46m 01.063s; **5** Glasgow Rangers-John Martin, AUS, 46m 05.471s; **6** AC Milan-Giorgio Pantano, I, 46m 16.058s; **7** AS Roma-Franck Perera, F, 46m 18.429s; **8** Tottenham Hotspur-Craig Dolby, GB, 46m 23.035s; **9** Sporting Clube de Portugal-Pedro Petiz, P, 46m 48.266s; **10** PSV Eindhoven-Carlo van Dam, NL, 47m 08.375s; **11** Sevilla FC-Sébastien Bourdais, F, 47m 09.661s; **12** Olympique Lyonnais-Nelson Panciatici, F, 48m 12.741s; **13** Flamengo-Enrique Bernoldi, BR, 29 laps; **14** Atlético de Madrid-Maria de Villota, E, 29; **15** FC Midtylland-Kasper Andersen, DK, 28; **16** FC Porto-Álvaro Parente, P, 11; **17** Galatasaray-Ho-Pin Tung, CN, 8; **18** FC Basel-Maximilian Wissel, D, 0.
Fastest race lap: Anderlecht, 1m 29.162s, 104.919mph/168.852km/h.
Pole position: Corinthians, 1m 28.447s, 105.768mph/170.217km/h.

Race 2 (77.957 miles/125.460km).
1 FC Porto-Álvaro Parente, P, 46m 07.422s, 101.410mph/163.204km/h; **2** Sevilla FC-Sébastien Bourdais, F, 46m 08.487s; **3** Flamengo-Enrique Bernoldi, BR, 46m 27.314s; **4** Anderlecht-Yelmer Buurman, NL, 46m 27.795s; **5** Corinthians-Antônio Pizzonia, BR, 46m 28.169s; **6** AC Milan-Giorgio Pantano, I, 46m 36.196s; **7** Galatasaray-Ho-Pin Tung, CN, 46m 41.953s; **8** Glasgow Rangers-John Martin, AUS, 46m 42.688s; **9** Liverpool-Adrián Vallés, E, 46m 46.099s; **10** PSV Eindhoven-Carlo van Dam, NL, 46m 52.454s; **11** FC Basel-Maximilian Wissel, D, 47m 08.063s; **12** AS Roma-Franck Perera, F, 47m 43.403s; **13** Atlético de Madrid-Maria de Villota, E, 29 laps; **14** Olympiacos-Esteban Guerrieri, RA, 28; **15** Olympique Lyonnais-Nelson Panciatici, F, 28; **16** FC Midtylland-Kasper Andersen, DK, 6; **17** Sporting Clube de Portugal-Pedro Petiz, P, 3; **18** Tottenham Hotspur-Craig Dolby, GB, 1.
Fastest race lap: FC Basel, 1m 29.190s, 104.886mph/168.799km/h.
Pole position: Galatasaray.

Super Final (12.993 miles/20.910km).
1 Sevilla FC-Sébastien Bourdais, F, 7m 31.629s, 103.568mph/166.676km/h; **2** Olympiacos-Esteban Guerrieri, RA, 7m 37.213s; **3** Liverpool-Adrián Vallés, E, 7m 37.213s; **4** Anderlecht-Yelmer Buurman, NL, 7m 38.240s; **5** Corinthians-Antônio Pizzonia, BR, 4 laps; **6** AC Milan-Giorgio Pantano, I, 2.
Fastest race lap: Sevilla FC, 1m 29.204s, 104.870mph/168.772km/h.
Pole position: Corinthians.

SUPERLEAGUE FORMULA BY SONANGOL, Autodromo Nazionale di Monza, Milan, Italy, 4 October. Round 5. 2 x 25 laps of the 3.600-mile/5.793km circuit.
Race 1 (89.990 miles/144.825km).
1 Sevilla FC-Sébastien Bourdais, F, 41m 26.833s, 130.271mph/209.652km/h; **2** Olympiacos-Esteban Guerrieri, RA, 41m 27.208s; **3** AS Roma-Julien Jousse, F, 41m 41.763s; **4** Liverpool-Adrián Vallés, E, 41m 44.847s; **5** Tottenham Hotspur-Craig Dolby, GB, 41m 48.911s; **6** Anderlecht-Yelmer Buurman, NL, 41m 52.369s; **7** Galatasaray-Ho-Pin Tung, CN, 41m 54.175s; **8** FC Basel-Maximilian Wissel, D, 42m 02.727s; **9** Corinthians-Antônio Pizzonia, BR, 42m 18.567s; **12** FC Midtylland-Kasper Andersen, DK, 42m 22.153s; **13** Olympique Lyonnais-Nelson Panciatici, F, 42m 23.640s; **14** Atlético de Madrid-Maria de Villota, E, 42m 32.494s; **15** AC Milan-Giorgio Pantano, I, 42m 37.678s; **16** PSV Eindhoven-Carlo van Dam, NL, 42m 40.421s; **17** Flamengo-Jonathan Kennard, GB, 43m 01.553s; **18** Sporting Clube de Portugal-Pedro Petiz, P, 10 laps.
Fastest race lap: Corinthians, 1m 36.466s, 134.333mph/216.188km/h.
Pole position: Olympiacos, 1m 37.649s, 132.705mph/213.569km/h.

Race 2 (89.990 miles/144.825km).
1 Sporting Clube de Portugal-Pedro Petiz, P, 41m 51.037s, 129.016mph/207.631km/h; **2** Tottenham Hotspur-Craig Dolby, GB, 41m 57.088s; **3** Sevilla FC-Sébastien Bourdais, F, 42m 02.473s; **4** Olympiacos-Esteban Guerrieri, RA, 42m 03.982s; **5** Liverpool-Adrián Vallés, E, 42m 09.697s; **6** Anderlecht-Yelmer Buurman, NL, 42m 10.144s; **7** Galatasaray-Ho-Pin Tung, CN, 42m 15.976s; **8** PSV Eindhoven-Carlo van Dam, NL, 42m 25.416s; **9** Corinthians-Antônio Pizzonia, BR, 42m 37.895s; **10** Atlético de Madrid-Maria de Villota, E, 42m 45.592s; **11** AC Milan-Giorgio Pantano, I, 42m 58.550s; **12** Glasgow Rangers-John Martin, AUS, 43m 38.584s; **13** FC Porto-Tristan Gommendy, F, 22 laps; **14** FC Basel-Maximilian Wissel, D, 17; **15** Olympique Lyonnais-Nelson Panciatici, F, 15; **16** FC Midtylland-Kasper Andersen, DK, 5; **17** AS Roma-Julien Jousse, F, 3; **18** Flamengo-Jonathan Kennard, GB, 3.
Fastest race lap: Olympiacos, 1m 36.681s, 134.034mph/215.707km/h.
Pole position: Sporting Clube de Portugal.

SUPERLEAGUE FORMULA BY SONANGOL, Circuito Permanente del Jarama, Madrid, Spain, 8 November. Round 6. 34, 31 and 5 laps of the 2.392-mile/3.850km circuit.
Race 1 (81.337 miles/130.900km).
1 Anderlecht-Yelmer Buurman, NL, 46m 32.409s, 104.861mph/168.757km/h; **2** Sevilla FC-Sébastien Bourdais, F, 46m 46.457s; **3** AC Milan-Giorgio Pantano, I, 47m 03.138s; **4** Tottenham Hotspur-Craig Dolby, GB, 47m 08.333s; **5** FC Basel-Maximilian Wissel, D, 47m 11.573s; **6** FC Porto-Tristan Gommendy, F, 47m 25.554s; **7** Liverpool-Adrián Vallés, E, 47m 26.151s; **8** Olympiacos-Esteban Guerrieri, RA, 47m 28.580s; **9** Olympique Lyonnais-Nelson Panciatici, F, 47m 32.671s; **10** Glasgow Rangers-John Martin, AUS, 47m 36.933s; **11** Flamengo-Enrique Bernoldi, BR, 47m 45.652s; **12** PSV Eindhoven-Carlo van Dam, NL, 47m 49.068s; **13** Sporting Clube de Portugal-Pedro Petiz, P, 33 laps; **14** Corinthians-Antônio Pizzonia, BR, 31; **15** AS Roma-Julien Jousse, F, 31; **16** Galatasaray-Ho-Pin Tung, CN, 7; **17** Atlético de Madrid-Maria de Villota, E, 1; **18** FC Midtylland-Kasper Andersen, DK, 0.
Fastest race lap: Anderlecht, 1m 20.011s, 107.637mph/173.226km/h.
Pole position: Sevilla FC, 1m 20.397s, 107.120mph/172.394km/h.

Race 2 (74.161 miles/119.350km).
1 Galatasaray-Ho-Pin Tung, CN, 45m 42.682s, 97.342mph/156.656km/h; **2** Tottenham Hotspur-Craig Dolby, GB, 45m 46.577s; **3** FC Midtylland-Kasper Andersen, DK, 45m 51.579s; **4** Liverpool-Adrián Vallés, E, 45m 52.711s; **5** FC Porto-Tristan Gommendy, F, 46m 02.413s; **6** Sevilla FC-Sébastien Bourdais, F, 46m 02.413s; **7** Atlético de Madrid-Maria de Villota, E, 46m 05.115s; **8** FC Basel-Maximilian Wissel, D, 46m 06.154s; **9** Glasgow Rangers-John Martin, AUS, 46m 07.369s; **10** Olympiacos-Esteban Guerrieri, RA, 46m 11.676s; **11** Olympique Lyonnais-Nelson Panciatici, F, 46m 49.250s; **12** Flamengo-Enrique Bernoldi, BR, 25 laps; **13** Sporting Clube de Portugal-Pedro Petiz, P, 24; **14** AC Milan-Giorgio Pantano, I, 23; **15** Anderlecht-Yelmer Buurman, NL, 9; **16** AS Roma-Julien Jousse, F, 5; **17** PSV Eindhoven-Carlo van Dam, NL, 0; **18** Corinthians-Antônio Pizzonia, BR, 0.
Fastest race lap: FC Porto, 1m 20.650s, 106.784mph/171.853km/h.
Pole position: FC Midtylland.

Super Final (11.961 miles/19.250km).
1 Anderlecht-Yelmer Buurman, NL, 6m 50.779s, 104.827mph/168.703km/h; **2** Sevilla FC-Sébastien Bourdais, F, 6m 52.172s; **3** Liverpool-Adrián Vallés, E, 6m 55.132s; **4** Galatasaray-Ho-Pin Tung, CN, 6m 59.549s; **5** FC Porto-Tristan Gommendy, F, 7m 01.067s; **6** Tottenham Hotspur-Craig Dolby, GB, 7m 19.266s.
Fastest race lap: Anderlecht, 1m 21.476s, 105.702mph/170.111km/h.
Pole position: Tottenham Hotspur.

Final championship points
1 Liverpool, 412; **2** Tottenham Hotspur, 382; **3** FC Basel, 308; **4** Anderlecht, 305; **5** FC Porto, 302; **6** Olympiacos, 300; **7** AC Milan, 286; **8** Corinthians, 264; **9** Sevilla FC, 253; **10** Glasgow Rangers, 241; **11** Galatasaray, 239; **12** Sporting Clube de Portugal, 215; **13** AS Roma, 211; **14** FC Midtylland, 203; **15** Atlético de Madrid, 202; **16** Flamengo, 191; **17** Olympique Lyonnais, 160; **18** PSV Eindhoven, 145; **19** Al Ain, 135.